SAP® Certified Application Associate — ABAP™ with SAP NetWeaver® 7.0

SAP PRESS is a joint initiative of SAP and Galileo Press. The know-how offered by SAP specialists combined with the expertise of the Galileo Press publishing house offers the reader expert books in the field. SAP PRESS features first-hand information and expert advice, and provides useful skills for professional decision-making.

SAP PRESS offers a variety of books on technical and business related topics for the SAP user. For further information, please visit our website: *www.sap-press.com*.

Karl-Heinz Kühnhauser
Discover ABAP
503 pp., 2008, softcover
ISBN 978-1-59229-152-6

Günther Färber, Julia Kirchner
ABAP Basics
476 pp., 2007, hardcover
ISBN 978-1-59229-153-3

Horst Keller, Sascha Krüger
ABAP Objects –
ABAP Programming in SAP NetWeaver
1059 pp., 2nd edition, 2007, hardcover, with DVD
ISBN 978-1-59229-079-6

Bryan Bee
SAP Certified Application Associate –
Supplier Relationship Management with SAP SRM 5.0
563 pp., 2009, softcover
ISBN 978-1-59229-272-1

Puneet Asthana, David Haslam

SAP® Certified Application Associate — ABAP™ with SAP NetWeaver® 7.0

Bonn • Boston

Galileo Press is named after the Italian physicist, mathematician and philosopher Galileo Galilei (1564–1642). He is known as one of the founders of modern science and an advocate of our contemporary, heliocentric worldview. His words Eppur si muove (And yet it moves) have become legendary. The Galileo Press logo depicts Jupiter orbited by the four Galilean moons, which were discovered by Galileo in 1610.

Editor Stefan Proksch
Technical Reviewer Christine Arundell
Copyeditor Ruth Saavedra
Cover Design Nadine Kohl
Photo Credit Masterfile/I Dream Stock
Layout Design Vera Brauner
Production Iris Warkus
Typesetting SatzPro, Krefeld (Germany)
Printed and bound in Canada

ISBN 978-1-59229-270-7

1st Edition 2010

Contents at a Glance

Contents

PART II: Exam Preparation

Acknowledgments

We wrote this book primarily as a way of teaching. We both recognize that whereas your experience grows with every engagement or project, few take the time to revisit subjects they have already mastered. One of us went through his original training with the "brand new" Release 2.1F of SAP R/3 back in the last millennium. We know that learning new techniques and new abilities within a subject can be difficult.

SAP used to offer delta courses to identify the differences, but these appear to have fallen out of favor. Instead, the material is incorporated into the class material, and those who took the class prior to the change are no wiser to the change. The only place for you to obtain this information is the release notes in the documentation or through word of mouth. As the abilities within ABAP continue to expand and more capabilities are added, it is very easy to become accustomed to doing things the same way even if there are better ways of doing it.

Even the terminology changes, sometimes faster than the capabilities. We know this because there were many discussions from our first chapter to our last about the correct phrase or name.

So our goal for this book was twofold. The primary effort was spent on providing you, the developer, with the information we believe is necessary to successfully become an SAP Certified Development Associate — ABAP with SAP NetWeaver 7.0. Our secondary goal was to identify the best techniques or recommendations from SAP. This is not an altogether altruistic motive, because the certification examinations (especially the professional level) becomes more focused on the best way of performing a task.

This book was much more effort than either of us thought it would be. Fortunately, we had help.

We would like to acknowledge Christine Arundell and SAP Education for their invaluable assistance. Her notes regarding the proper way of explaining a technique or acting as a technical advisor were very much appreciated. Thank you for your time and effort.

We would also like to acknowledge Stefan Proksch, our senior editor at SAP PRESS. He led us through this very unfamiliar world of publishing, guiding us through the process. As our guide through this world, he kept us focused on the task at hand. His encouragement and words of praise were much appreciated. As with program development, time spent upfront designing simplifies the end tasks and provides a much needed target. Thank you for your assistance.

Additionally David would like to thank his family for their support and understanding during this endeavor. I would like to thank my grandchildren, Jordan, Alexis, Kyle, Emily, Woo, and Trystin, for their unconditional love and understanding. The words of encouragement and support from one in particular were most appreciated; you and I both know who you are (and I know that you are a very special child). More than any other, I would like to thank my wife, Patti, for understanding my long hours and supporting the project. She is my foundation, the haven in my life. Without her, I would be lost. I am forever grateful for meeting her.

Additionally Puneet would like to express sincere appreciation to the following individuals for their invaluable contribution throughout his journey in writing this book: I would like to thank to my dear wife, Anita, for her unflinching love, support, and inspiration. Though taken to her wits' end with this seemingly never-ending book project, she not only managed our family single-handedly for the past several months, but also, she chose to smile and encouraged me to fulfill my dream of writing this book. Thanks to my lovely children, six-year-old daughter Amishi and three-year-old son Anchit, for being a constant source of unending happiness and joy and for their love and understanding that Daddy couldn't play with them as he had to complete this project. Thanks to my dear parents, who nurtured me and instilled in me a strong sense of values and principles, and who have profoundly influenced who I have become. Thanks to my brothers and sisters for providing me a loving and encouraging environment during my foundational years. Finally, I would like to thank my co-author David Haslam, for the opportunity to work together on this project.

David Haslam
Principal Platinum Development Consultant

Puneet Asthana
Principal Consultant

Preface

The SAP PRESS Certification Series is designed to provide anyone preparing to take an SAP certified exam with all of the review, insight, and practice they need to pass the exam. The series is written in practical, easy-to-follow language that provides targeted content focused just on what you need to know to successfully take your exam.

This book is specifically written for those preparing to take the SAP Certified Development Associate — ABAP with SAP NetWeaver 7.0 exam, so if you've purchased this book, you're obviously interested in learning how to successfully pass the certification exam, and you've come to the right place. This book will help you become an SAP Certified Development Associate in ABAP. It is your first step to propel your career by setting yourself apart from your peers. The certification exam verifies your knowledge of the fundamentals of Release 7.0 of the SAP NetWeaver Application Server ABAP. This includes knowledge obtained from attending SAP training courses in the ABAP curriculum and project experience. To help prepare you to pass the exam, we'll cover the facts and applications of each topic discussed in this book.

You'll find all of the practical, real-world information you need to get a clear understanding of the topics that will be covered on the exam and insightful tips about the types of questions you'll encounter and the strategies to use to answer correctly. The book is closely aligned with the course syllabus and the exam structure, so all of the information provided is relevant and applicable to what you need to know to prepare for the SAP Certified Development Associate — ABAP with SAP NetWeaver 7.0 exam. We explain the SAP products and features using practical examples and straightforward language, so you can prepare for the exam and improve your skills in your day-to-day work as an ABAP developer.

Each book in the series has been structured and designed to highlight what you really need to know. The chapters begin with a clear list of the learning objectives for the chapter such as this example:

What You'll Learn:

- How to prepare for the exam
- Understanding the general exam structure
- Practice questions and preparation

From there, you'll dive into the chapter and get right into the test objective coverage. So let's take a look at how the book is structured.

Structure of This Book

Let's discuss how you can use this book to prepare for the exam. This book is divided into two sections:

- **Part 1** contains the general introduction to this book and the certification examinations. This section will provide you with an overview of the certification process and the benefit to you and to your customer or company. We'll discuss both the purpose of this certification examination and provide information on additional certification examinations that are available beyond this one.
- **Part 2** of this book is a breakdown of the topics covered in the certification examination for C_TAW12_70, the SAP Certified Development Associate – ABAP with SAP NetWeaver 7.0. Each chapter contains a similar structure to assist with understanding that portion of the certification examination.

Part 2 is the core of the book and discusses each exam topic and determines the key concepts. These key concepts are then explained along with important information that will provide the context for understanding. Each chapter is broken down into one or more subtopics according to complexity. Illustrations and diagrams are included throughout to ensure that you understand important concepts.

Throughout the book, we've also provided several elements that will help you access useful information:

- Tips call out useful information about related ideas and provide practical suggestions for how to use a particular function.
- Notes provide other resources to explore or special tools or services from SAP that will help you with the topic under discussion. The following is an example of such a Note box.

Note

The content provided in each chapter and subtopic does not exhaustively cover everything that appears on the exam. In other words, the certification guide does not cover every exam question, but rather it acts as a refresher to highlight the major points for each topic. In addition, it points out areas where further review is needed.

Each chapter that covers an exam topic is organized in a similar fashion so you can become familiar with the structure and easily find the information you need. Here's an example of a typical chapter structure:

- **Introductory bullets**
  The beginning of each chapter discusses the techniques you must master to be considered proficient in the topic for the certification examination.
- **Topic introduction**
  This section provides you with a general idea of the topic at hand to frame future sections. It also includes objectives for the exam topic covered.
- **Real-world scenario**
  This part shows a scenario that provides you with a case where these skills would be beneficial to you or your company.
- **Objectives**
  This section is followed by one, but often more than one, section reviewing the material the authors feel provides you with the necessary information to pass this portion of the test. This section provides the material you must understand to successfully pass the certification examination.
- **Key concept refresher**
  This section is followed by a key concept refresher where the major concepts of the chapter are identified. This section identifies the tasks you will need to be able to perform properly to answer the questions on the certification examination.

Note

You should pay particular attention to the points raised in the key concept refresher section and those from the objectives section.

- **Main part**
  The next section provides the objectives of the this section of the test. This includes identifying major points of this topic that are discussed in the chapter.

  Often we identify a general weighting SAP uses for this topic. To simplify the discussion, we have produced a general group of three categories or ranges (high, average, and low weighting). You should use this information to assist you in determining which chapters you should spend your time studying to maximize your score.

  Those chapters that are designated as low have the fewest number of questions on the certification examination. Those with a designation of average have an average or medium number of questions on the certification examination. The chapters with a high weighting have more questions than the other chapters.

  The chapter with the highest weighting contains significantly more questions on the certification examination than any other. Unsurprisingly, Chapter 9, Basic ABAP Programs and Interface Creation, which discusses general ABAP program design, has the highest weighting of the examination.
- **Important terminology**
  Just prior to the practice examination, we provide a section to review important terminology. This may be followed by definitions of various terms from the chapter.
- **Practice questions**
  The chapter then provides a series of practice questions related to the topic of the chapter. The questions are structured in a similar way to the actual questions on the certification examination (see below).
- **Practice question answers and explanations**
  Following the practice exercise are the solutions to the practice exercise questions. As part of the answer, we discuss why an answer is considered correct or incorrect.

  Whereas some of the questions in the practice reference actual code, you will find that in the actual certification examination there is a slightly higher number of questions related to actual code solving. However, we feel that an understanding of actual processes will allow you to identify and correctly solve these types of questions. As a consequence, we have attempted to explain processes that occur and what we consider the best way of solving issues. These techniques can be useful to you in your normal work in addition to passing the examination.

- **Take away**
  This section provides a take away or review section identifying what areas you should now understand. The refresher section identifies the key concepts in the chapter. We also provide some tips related to the chapter.
- **Summary**
  Finally, we conclude with a summary of the chapter, which again provides a summary of the content covered in the chapter.

Note

You should be aware that the practice exercise questions are for self-evaluation purposes only and do not appear on the actual certification examination. Answering the practice exercise questions correctly is no guarantee that you will pass the certification exam.

Glimpse into the Exam Structure

To understand the structure of this certification success guide, it is important to understand the base structure of the exam. We only touch upon the topic here because Chapter 1, ABAP Development Certification Track — Overview, covers the exam structure in detail.

Two basic elements define the exam structure for the associate and various levels of certification available. These elements are as follows:

- **Competency level**
  Competency is what you are expected to be able to do at a specific level described. In simple terms, if you have reached a competency, then you can do the tasks described by that competency. SAP Education has developed a set of progressive competency levels. As you become more experienced, your competencies move in sequence from level A to D. The competencies include:
  - Accomplish defined tasks (level A)
  - Build proposed solutions (level B)
  - Conceptualize complex processes (level C)
  - Design integrated strategies (level D)

For example, a simple definition of the level A competency is the ability to accomplish defined tasks during system implementation. As an associate, you should be able to carry out defined tasks given to you when little to no ambiguity exists. For level D, you may devise a roadmap and recommendation to a particular solution or issue.

- **Exam topic**
  This element is much more familiar. ABAP is a complex programming language for business applications with many parts. A team of experts devised which topics should be tested in each exam. This allows a target for the test development, but in addition it provides you a list of focus areas to prepare.

Tip

The chapter that follows dives into great detail for each level of the exam, including a topic and competency breakdown. Please reference Chapter 1, ABAP Development Certification Track — Overview, for additional information.

You should understand the concept of competency and exam topics now. It is important to understand that they work together. The competency areas are applied to separate topics in the exam. Likewise, this book is also broken down by these same topics to set the focus and align content for exam preparation.

The exam topics may overlap between the competency areas in terms of a subject such as objects, but they are unique in content according to the competency. For example, activity at level A is considered more of a design element and explores unique construction of objects. Activity at level B examines a more fundamental understanding of classes and methods. Thus, it's possible to discuss operational solutions for objects in one topic, whereas a separate topic covers more strategic problems or concepts. This will become evident in the chapter content and practice questions.

Practice Questions

We want to give you some background on the test questions before you encounter the first few in the chapters. Just like the exam, each question has a basic structure:

- **Question stimulus**
  The question stimulus varies with the different questions, but its intention is to present a situation or scenario as context for the question. The stimulus complexity depends on the competency level.
- **Actual question**
  The question comes next and relates to the stimulus. Read the question carefully and be sure to consider the details from the stimulus because they can impact the question.
- **Question hint**
  This is not a formal term, but we call it a hint because it will tell you how many answers are correct. If only one is correct, normally it will tell you to choose the correct answer. If more than one is correct, like the actual certification examination, it will not indicate the correct number of answers.
- **Answers**
  The answers to select from depend on the question type. The following question types are possible:
  - **Multiple response**
    More than one correct answer is possible.
  - **Multiple choice**
    Only a single answer is correct.
  - **True/false**
    Only a single answer is correct. These should be minimal, especially as you experience the more advanced exams.
  - **Fill in the blank**
    This type is of question is nearly not found on the associate examination, but is found on the professional-level exam. Although capitalization does not matter, only a limited number of answers are considered valid. You should therefore be careful with typing and spelling.
  - **Sequence/ranking**
    This type of question will also have a single correct answer. The answers will provide the same options in different order, and you must select the correct sequence.

Caution

Media can be presented in a test question as part of the stimulus. For example, a diagram or a code block can be given, followed by the question based on this enriched content. If the question does not appear to make sense by itself, you should look for an exhibit button to display the media.

Summary

With this certification success guide you'll learn how to approach the content and key concepts highlighted for each exam topic. In addition, in each chapter you'll have the opportunity to practice with sample test questions. After answering the practice questions, you'll be able to review the explanation of the answer, which dissects the question by explaining why the answers are correct or incorrect. The practice questions give you insight into the types of questions you can expect, what the questions look like, and how the answers can relate to the question. Understanding the composition of the questions and seeing how the questions and answers work together is just as important as understanding the content. This book gives you the tools and understanding you need to be successful. Armed with these skills, you'll be well on your way to becoming an SAP Certified Development Associate in ABAP.

Part I
General Introduction

ABAP Development Certification Track — Overview

1

Techniques You'll Master:

- Understand the different levels of certification
- Identify the scoring in the exams
- Understand the portion of the certification exam associated with your skills
- Learn about further specifics of the ABAP Development Certification Track

Few credentials in the business world carry the value of SAP certification. Those who hold it have honed their skills through rigorous study or direct experience. They have demonstrated their abilities by passing demanding, process-oriented exams. Regardless of whether you're an SAP partner, customer, or user, SAP certification can give you a distinct competitive advantage.

Over the past two years, SAP Global Education portfolio management completed a comprehensive review of SAP's certification strategy and created a roadmap for enhancing the value of the certification program as a key business enabler for SAP going forward. This program focuses on building a value-add certification community for SAP-certified individuals and helping SAP customers and partners leverage certification as a benchmark for engaging, recruiting, or training properly skilled SAP resources. The roadmap outlines the required steps to introduce multitiered career-enabling certification tracks and advanced-level certification to better address the needs of the markets.

Certification Exam Scoring Changes

To publish more job-task oriented certification exams, and to provide certification at the advanced professional level, SAP has made several important changes to the test models. First, the test design blueprint is created on the basis of a job-task analysis that is created and validated with the help of consultants actively involved in relevant projects.

SAP also changed the exam scoring models for all exams published after September 2007 to a dichotomous scoring model. The dichotomous scoring model scores multiple-response questions as either correct or incorrect and does not give partial grades for responses. This better reflects the need for SAP customers and partners to know whether a certified individual can perform a task to the complete satisfaction of all concerned. The consistency in the difficulty level of the exams is reinforced by thorough standard-setting processes, where the test content is rated by a panel of subject matter experts to determine the final cut score.

Every question should be answered. Leaving a question blank is equivalent to a false response. All tests will be migrated over to the new dichotomous scoring model by mid-2009, and the master certification is expected to be released in 2010.

Note

For older exams, which were released prior to September, 2007 and are not entitled, associate, professional, or master, test takers received points for each section of a question answered correctly.

If a question has five parts and the test taker answers three parts correctly, he would get three out of five of the possible credit available for that question.

Certification Levels

You can now obtain certifications at three levels of expertise — associate, professional, and master. These certifications can help you validate your skills and knowledge and gain the expertise and credentials you need to lead your organization's efforts to implement SAP software, mature its technological capabilities, and transform its IT landscape. Figure 1.1 shows the progression of levels with relation to your experience.

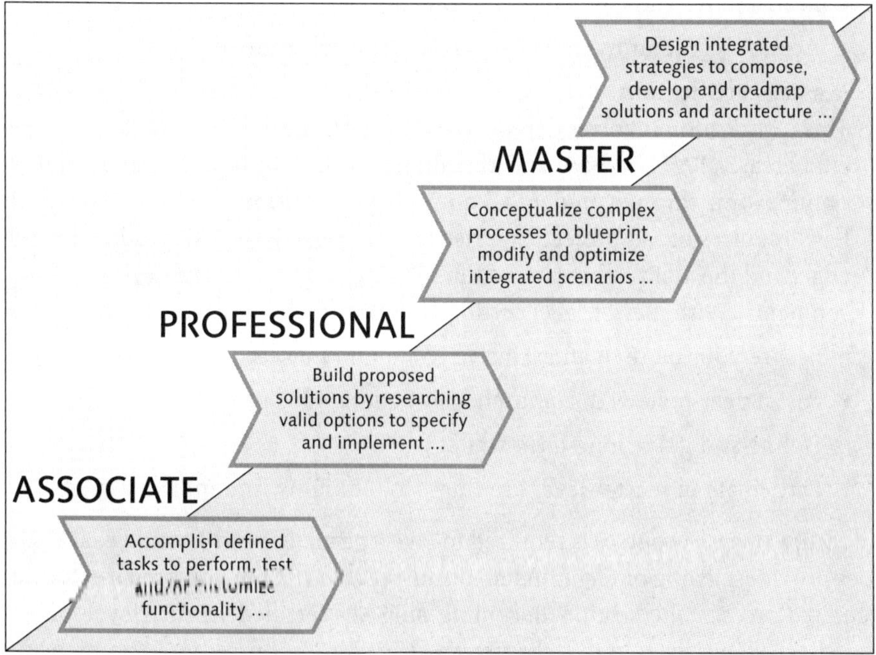

Figure 1.1 Certification Levels

- **Associate certification**
  This certification covers the fundamental knowledge requirements for an SAP consultant, ensuring the successful acquisition of broad SAP solution knowledge and skills. With associate-level certification, you can:
  - Gain an externally recognized mark of excellence that clients seek
  - Differentiate yourself in a crowded marketplace
  - Execute your tasks with confidence and skill
  - Access a community of SAP associate-level certified peers
- **Professional certification**
  This advanced certification requires proven project experience, business process knowledge, and a more detailed understanding of SAP solutions. With professional-level certification, you can:
  - Demonstrate both your experience and your expertise through a rigorous testing process
  - Promote a more globally applicable accreditation with higher billable rates
  - Lead and execute tasks and engagements
  - Access a community of SAP professional-level certified peers
- **Master certification**
  This certification involves demonstrating expert-level understanding of a specific area of SAP software and the ability to drive innovation and solution optimization through in-depth knowledge and vision. Certification at this level requires broad project experience, comprehensive SAP product knowledge, and the ability to create a future IT vision within complex project environments. With master-level certification, you can:
  - Secure your place in an exclusive community of visionary experts
  - Pass a peer-reviewed, comprehensive admissions process
  - Define and guide long-term strategy
  - Participate in master-level briefings, colloquiums, and industry events

No course or set of courses is required to take a particular certification exam. SAP does provide a listing of recommended course work to help you prepare (for this examination, see the section Becoming an SAP Certified ABAP Development Associate — Overview in this chapter and Chapter 2, Courses and Experience).

Tip

It is not necessary for you to have completed a lower-level (associate) exam to take a higher-level (professional) exam; however, many professional-level certification seekers may find it valuable.

Advanced Certification Levels

SAP is moving toward higher-level item writing methods and more advanced assessment techniques to better test understanding, application, and analytical skills rather than knowledge recall. In addition, the tests for the higher levels of certification have been revised to be more clearly job-task aligned and therefore reflective of actual experience.

The new strategy focuses on adding value to the certified individual. Certified consultants will be offered the opportunity to join the new certification community and access a wide range of benefits. The 2006 survey of existing consultants pinpointed the desire for continuous learning, and SAP Education will be outlining clear paths, including fast tracks for existing consultants to move upward or across into further levels. Existing certifications will retain their validity.

You can sit for a particular SAP certification exam a maximum of three times. You must wait 30 days after you have taken an exam before you can sit for it again. This is to give you time for additional preparation in those areas where you were unsuccessful.

Tip

If you are unsuccessful in passing your certification exam after two attempts, and if you have not previously taken SAP training classes, we highly recommend you supplement your current knowledge by completing the training offered by SAP.

The fee for certification retakes is the same as the initial exam. No candidate may sit for the same examination for the same release more than three times. A candidate who has failed an examination three times for a specific release may not attempt that examination again until the next release.

Note

On arriving at the test center, you will be required to present two valid forms of ID, of which one must be a valid photo ID, such as passport, driver's license, or government-sponsored ID card.

Becoming an SAP Certified ABAP Development Associate — Overview

The code used to reference the examination for this book (also known as the *Booking Code*) is C_TAW12_70. The current Certification Test is entitled SAP Certified Development Associate — ABAP with SAP NetWeaver 7.0.

The certification test for SAP Certified Development Associate — ABAP with SAP NetWeaver 7.0 verifies in-depth knowledge in the area of ABAP development. This certificate proves that the candidate has a fundamental understanding within this profile and is able to apply these skills practically under supervision in a project environment.

Associate Examination Specifics

- **Software:** Software components: SAP NetWeaver 7.0
- **Number of questions:** 90
- **Duration:** 180 minutes

Associate certifications are targets for those with between one and three years of knowledge and experience. The primary source of knowledge and skills is based on the corresponding training material.

Note

This certification may have a different passing score from previous or different certification exams (a passing score is calculated by experts in the field and varies between versions of the associate examination for different releases and from the professional examinations).

Remember that for multiple response items, no partial is credit given.

Competency Areas

Table 1.1 and Table 1.2 will help you identify the competency areas covered in this test. The percentage indicates the portion of the test dedicated to a particular competency area. The section WAYS TO ATTAIN identifies standard SAP Education courses that cover the material tested in the certification examination. The primary course focuses specifically on the material in the certification examination, whereas the Alternative and Other columns identify other courses that contain the same material.

Competency	**Importance**		
Build solutions by independently researching valid implementation options. Based on profound understanding and deep application skills, project requirements can be transferred into solid customer solutions in:	40 %		
	Ways to Attain		
Topic	**Primary**	**Alternative**	**Other**
Basic ABAP program and interface creation	TAW10	BC400, BC402	
Class identification analysis and design	TAW12	BC401	
Enhancement and modifications	TAW12	BC425, BC427	
Table relationships	TAW10	BC430	

Table 1.1 Build Proposed Solutions by Independently Researching Valid Implementation Options

Competency	Importance		
Accomplish and identify solutions for defined project tasks. Based on in-depth knowledge and basic understanding, identified tasks can be performed during system implementation, configuration, and testing in the areas of:	60 %		
	Ways to attain		
Topic	**Primary**	**Alternative**	**Other**
SAP NetWeaver Overview	TAW10	NW001	SAPNW
ABAP Workbench usage	TAW10	BC400, BC401	
ABAP Debugger program usage	TAW10	BC400, BC402	
ABAP types and data objects	TAW10	BC400	
Internal table definition and use	TAW10	BC400	
SQL statements including update strategies	TAW10, TAW11	BC400, BC414	
ABAP Dictionary	TAW10	BC430	
Unicode	TAW11	BC402	
Classical screens (Dynpros) and selection screens	TAW10	BC400	
ALV Grid Control	TAW11	BC405	
User interfaces (Web Dynpro)	TAW12	NET310	

Table 1.2 Accomplish Solutions for Defined Project Tasks

To prepare for this exam, remember that the exam covers a broad range of topics and subjects, and it is not therefore possible to ask many questions on any one topic. Certain topics, such as Basic ABAP program and interface creation, class identification analysis and design, enhancements and modifications, ABAP types and data objects, and the ABAP Dictionary receive more emphasis than topics such as ABAP debugger program usage, Unicode, and ALV Grid Control.

Tip

You should use the percentage guides from Table 1.1 and Table 1.2 to guide the allocation of your preparation time.

As you will see in the practice exam questions, a good understanding of various programming techniques and the system architecture is helpful when choosing the best answer from a list of possible approaches. Remember that you must average two minutes per question (there are 90 questions and a time limit of 180 minutes), so arriving at the correct answer quickly is essential to completing the examination.

For these types of questions where multiple answers are correct, it may be helpful to use a selection and elimination strategy. You can possibly eliminate answers that are factually wrong while selecting answers that are clearly correct. This leaves fewer answers you might not be sure of, thus speeding up the selection process. Chapter 2, Courses and Experience, provides several techniques to help you narrow down the options to questions.

For most questions in this examination, the answers can be found in the course material listed for that area (see the ways to attain columns above). Although several answers may be very similar, take sufficient time to clearly understand the meaning of each answer rather than rushing. That will help you distinguish which answers are correct.

Normally, the more ABAP experience you have, the easier you will find the examination. Be conscious that the examination is based on SAP NetWeaver 7.0 and not on previous releases. In places where there are differences between Release 7.0 and previous releases, the examination will normally focus on Release 7.0, although in several cases the way the question is phrased will indicate that it refers to a previous release.

Whereas there are no "trick" questions or answers, you should think through the choices to make sure you understand the exact meaning and impact of each option before making your selection. Some of the programming questions can involve a significant amount of code or provided detail. It can be time-consuming to identify what is actually being asked. It is important to understand the question before attempting to answer it.

All of the questions in this exam provide multiple answers. Some of these require you to select the single correct option, whereas others have multiple correct responses. In the Preface of this book, we discussed the various types of questions you can expect. Remember that there is no partial scoring, and multiple-response questions are scored as either correct or incorrect.

Note

You are not allowed to use any reference materials during the certification test (no access to online documentation or to any SAP system). You will require a Photo ID to be allowed to take the test.

As the certification process is ever evolving, you should always check the certification site for changes to the above information. The certification site can be found on the SAP web site at *http://www.sap.com*. From there, go to SAP Ecosystem and Partners • Services • Education • Certification. Then use the certification finder for SAP NetWeaver • Development • Developer/Development Consultant.

Becoming an SAP Certified ABAP Development Professional — Overview

The professional-level exam provides two different tests: P_ABAP_SI_70 and P_ABAP_GUI70. There is an overlap of the knowledge of P_ABAP_GUI70 and P_ABAP_SI_70. You will find all the topics of P_ABAP_GUI70 in P_ABAP_SI_70, but some topics in P_ABAP_SI_70 will not be found in P_ABAP_GUI70.

SAP Certified Development Professional — ABAP System Integration — SAP NetWeaver 7.0

The booking code for this examination is P_ABAP_SI_70. The current certification test is entitled SAP Certified Development Professional — ABAP System Integration — SAP NetWeaver 7.0.

The certification test for SAP Certified Development Professional — ABAP System Integration — SAP NetWeaver 7.0 verifies in-depth knowledge in the area of ABAP system interfaces. The difference between the associate and the Professional is that more skills are included. Whereas a certified associate is expected to complete tasks, a certified professional is more self-sufficient and deals with more uncertainty and design decisions. This certificate proves that the candidate has an advanced understanding within this profile and is able to apply these skills practically and provide guidance in project implementation.

Professional Examination Specifics

- **Software**
  Software components: SAP NetWeaver 7.0
- **Number of questions**
  90
- **Duration**
  180 minutes

Professional certifications are targeting profiles with a minimum of four to seven years of experience. Besides the recommended education courses, practical job experience is also required and tested.

Competency Areas

Table 1.3, Table 1.4, and Table 1.5 will help you to identify the competency areas covered in this test. The percentage indicates the portion of the test dedicated to a particular competency area. The section WAYS TO ATTAIN identifies standard SAP Education courses that cover the material being tested in the certification examination. The primary course focuses specifically on the material in the certification examination, and the Alternative and Other columns identify other courses that contain the same material.

Competency	Importance
Conceptualize complex processes into customer-prominent solutions. Based on professional application and advanced analysis qualification, customer business requirements can be recognized and transferred into concepts and blueprints of prominent customer solutions in:	40 %

Table 1.3 Conceptualize Complex Processes into Customer-Prominent Solutions

	Ways to Attain		
Topic	**Primary**	**Alternative**	**Other**
Web services	BC416		
Data Transfer Workbench and Legacy System Migration Workbench	BC420		
Enhancement framework (BAdIs, user exits)	BC425, BC427		
Communication interfaces (ALE, IDoc, RFC, etc.)	BC415		
Creating and customizing BAPIs for interfaces	BC417		
Leveraging ALE technology	BIT300	BIT350	

Table 1.3 Conceptualize Complex Processes into Customer-Prominent Solutions (cont.)

Competency	Importance		
Build solutions by independently researching valid implementation options. Based on profound understanding and deep application skills, project requirements can be transferred into solid customer solutions in:	40 %		
	Ways to Attain		
Topic	**Primary**	**Alternative**	**Other**
ABAP Objects	BC401		
Advanced programming	BC402		
SQL/database	BC400, BC430		

Table 1.4 Build Proposed Solutions by Independently Researching Valid Implementation Options

Performance analysis of programs	BC490
Change and transport system (Workbench/Customizing, transport tools, TMS)	ADM325
SAP Notes Assistant	BC425
Internet Control Framework	NET900

Table 1.4 Build Proposed Solutions by Independently Researching Valid Implementation Options (cont.)

Competency	**Importance**		
Accomplish and identify solutions for defined project tasks. Based on profound knowledge and basic understanding, identified tasks can be performed during system implementation, configuration, and testing in the areas of:	20 %		
	Ways to Attain		
Topic	**Primary**	**Alternative**	**Other**
Components of SAP NetWeaver (PI, Portal, MDM, etc.)	SAPTEC	NW001, SAPNW	
SOA basic knowledge	SOA100		
Composite Application Framework, Composite Applications			
SAP Solution Manager	SM001		

Table 1.5 Accomplish Solutions for Defined Project Tasks

SAP Certified Development Professional — ABAP User Interfaces — SAP NetWeaver 7.0

The booking code for this examination is P_ABAP_GUI70. The current certification test is entitled SAP Certified Development Professional — ABAP User Interfaces — SAP NetWeaver 7.0.

The certification test for SAP Certified Development Professional — ABAP User Interfaces — SAP NetWeaver 7.0 verifies in-depth knowledge in the area of ABAP user interfaces. This certificate proves that the candidate has an advanced understanding within this profile and is able to apply these skills practically and provide guidance in project implementation.

Professional Examination Specifics

- **Software**
  Software components: SAP NetWeaver 7.0
- **Number of questions**
  90
- **Duration**
  180 minutes

Professional certifications are targeting profiles with a minimum of four to seven years of experience. Besides the recommended education courses, practical job experience is also required and tested.

Competency Areas

Table 1.6, Table 1.7, and Table 1.8 will help you to identify the competency areas covered in this test. The percentage indicates the portion of the test dedicated to a particular competency area. The section Ways to Attain identifies standard SAP Education courses that cover the material being tested in the certification examination. The primary course focuses specifically on the material in the certification examination, and the Alternative and Other columns identify other courses that contain the same material.

Competency	**Importance**		
Conceptualize complex processes into customer-prominent solutions. Based on professional application and advanced analysis qualification, customer business requirements can be recognized and transferred into concepts and blueprints of prominent customer solutions in:	40 %		
	Ways to Attain		
Topic	**Primary**	**Alternative**	**Other**
Classic Dynpros	BC410		
Web Dynpro ABAP	NET310		
Controls	BC412		
Customer enhancements	BC425 and BC427		

Table 1.6 Conceptualize Complex Processes into Customer-Prominent Solutions

Competency	**Importance**		
Build solutions by independently researching valid implementation options. Based on in-depth understanding and deep application skills, project requirements can be transferred into solid customer solutions in:	40 %		
	Ways to Attain		
Topic	**Primary**	**Alternative**	**Other**
ABAP Objects	BC401		
Advanced programming	BC402		

Table 1.7 Build Proposed Solutions by Independently Researching Valid Implementation Options

Topic	Primary	Alternative	Other
SQL/database	BC400, BC430		
Performance analysis of programs	BC490		
Change and Transport System (Workbench/ Customizing, transport tools, TMS)	ADM325		
SAP Notes Assistant	BC425		
Business Server Pages	NET200		
SAP Interactive Forms by Adobe	BC481		

Table 1.7 Build Proposed Solutions by Independently Researching Valid Implementation Options (cont.)

Competency	Importance		
Accomplish and identify solutions for defined project tasks. Based on profound knowledge and basic understanding, identified tasks can be performed during system implementation, configuration, and testing in the areas of:	20%		
	Ways to Attain		
Topic	**Primary**	**Alternative**	**Other**
SOA basic knowledge	SOA100		
Composite Application Framework			
SAP Solution Manager	SM001		
SAP NetWeaver Visual Composer	ANA10, NWC110		
Components of SAP NetWeaver (PI, Portal, MDM, etc.)	SAPTEC	NW001, SAPNW	

Table 1.8 Accomplish Solutions for Defined Project Tasks

As the certification process is ever evolving, you should always check the certification site for changes to the above information. The certification site can be found on the SAP web site at *http://www.sap.com*. From there, go to SAP ECOSYSTEM AND PARTNERS • SERVICES • EDUCATION • CERTIFICATION. Then use the certification finder for SAP NETWEAVER • DEVELOPMENT • DEVELOPER/DEVELOPMENT CONSULTANT.

Summary

You now have an understanding of the differences between the various certification examinations for ABAP. This knowledge will allow you to identify which certification examination is most appropriate for your knowledge level and will allow you to focus your study on areas where your knowledge may need some assistance. Your understanding of where you need to study will make the use of your time more productive.

Courses and Experience

2

Techniques You'll Master:

- Learn about additional sources of information
- Structure your understanding and thinking
- Explore the SAP test design
- Access and use general test taking help

This book is not a substitute for SAP courses or experience. Whereas we would like to provide all of the information you need, it is simply not practical. As a result, we will identify which training provided by SAP Education is necessary and provide generally available information. SAP provides access to the documentation, and we find the information in the SAP Developer Network (SDN) to be extremely beneficial.

Training Courses for ABAP

The courses available for ABAP are divided into two curriculum tracks: one focused on the certification examination (see Table 2.1) and one organized by topic (see Table 2.2).

Course	Description	Length
TAW10	ABAP basics	10 days
TAW11	ABAP details	eLearning (~20 hours)
TAW12	ABAP Objects and how to use it	10 days

Table 2.1 Minimum Certification Training

Course	Description	Length
BC400	ABAP Workbench foundations	5 days
BC401	ABAP Objects	5 days
BC402	Advanced ABAP	5 days
BC405	Programming ABAP reports	5 days
BC414	Programming database changes	2 days
BC425	Enhancements and modifications	3 days
BC427	Enhancement Framework	2 days
BC430	ABAP Dictionary	3 days

Table 2.2 Topic Courses for Certification Training

Course	Description	Length
NET310	Fundamentals of Web Dynpro ABAP	5 days
NW001	Technology solutions powered by SAP NetWeaver	eLearning (~8 hours)

Table 2.2 Topic Courses for Certification Training (cont.)

Sources of Information

In addition to the course material, you may find additional information on the SAP Developer Network (SDN) at *http://sdn.sap.com.* Select the path SAP NETWEAVER CAPABILITIES • DEVELOPMENT AND COMPOSITION • ABAP to find a very useful site containing information in the form of whitepapers, articles, blogs, wikis, and eLearning material.

One area within SDN that is often overlooked and that we have found to be very useful for preparation is trial versions. On *http://sdn.sap.com*, navigate to DOWNLOADS • SAP NETWEAVER MAIN RELEASES, which contains trial versions of SAP NetWeaver that you can install and explore for both Windows and Linux. Several of the screen shots in this book were taken from these trial versions. If your company or customer is not yet running SAP NetWeaver 7.0, this mini version will allow you to explore the new features of the release including the ABAP Debugger and Web Dynpro ABAP.

The mini version, although not a complete copy of an SAP Enterprise Core Components (ECC) system, does provide a functional system. Also included are all of the examples from the standard programming book by Horst Keller: *ABAP Objects — ABAP Programming in SAP NetWeaver* (SAP PRESS 2007).

Note

If you have questions about the installation process, a search on SDN for "How to install SAP NetWeaver" will provide blogs, forums, PDFs, and even eLearning to be successful.

Another often overlooked area is the SAP Help Portal (*http://help.sap.com*). If you go to SAP NETWEAVER • SAP NETWEAVER 7.0 (2004S), you will find a number of useful areas that document changes and functionality of ABAP:

- **Release Overview**
  Find out what's new and what's changed since the previous release.
- **What's New — Release Notes**
  A starting point to use SAP software and changes to SAP NetWeaver 7.0.
- **SAP NetWeaver at a Glance**
  An overview of available IT scenarios.
- **System Administration**
  An overview of how SAP NetWeaver is maintained and configured.
- **Installation, Configuration, Upgrade**
  Information related to planning, installing, upgrading, and maintaining IT scenarios.
- **Development**
  Developers guides, presentations, and forums of information about different technologies including ABAP, Java, and .NET.
- **Power User Information**
  Instructions on specialized functions for advanced users.
- **Functional View**
  The documentation for SAP NetWeaver 7.0.
- **Supplementary Information**
  How-to guides, SAP notes, learning maps, and best practices.

Another useful web site is the SAP PRESS web site: *http://www.sap-press.com*. There you can find a number of other books that can be extremely useful.

Tip

A name we especially look for regarding books is Horst Keller — always timely information with the latest capabilities of ABAP.

Strategic Understanding

Structuring your thinking is one of the main ways to build an effective memory. Those with a perfect memory can simply review the material and pass the test, but for the rest of us, our success is linked to our understanding. As you go through this book, try to keep the following thoughts in mind. Remember that in many cases an understanding of why something occurs will provide you the correct answer even if you do not know the answer. The following is the wisdom gleaned from many sources.

- **Monitor your comprehension**
  You can only remember and fully use ideas that you understand. Find ways to monitor your comprehension. Get in the habit of saying to yourself, "Do I understand this?"
- **Always check the logic behind the ideas**
  For example, do things happen in a way that you would predict? If you can see the logic in something, you are much more likely to be able to reconstruct that idea even if you cannot immediately recall it.
- **Watch out for anything that seems counterintuitive**
  You are less likely to remember something that does not seem logical or that you do not agree with.
- **Test your own understanding**
  You can do this by discussing your thoughts about a topic with colleagues to see if they see things the same way as you. Listen to their input and evaluate your comprehension.
- **Generate your own examples**
  Use your general knowledge and experience to relate ideas to what you already know. Then, bring your examples into a context you are already familiar with.
- **Think in pictures, shapes, and colors**
  Concrete images are easier to remember than abstract ideas.
  - While studying, consider making notes with pictures, shapes, and colors, and then review your notes often to solidify the images in your memory.
  - Use shapes such as flow charts, triangles, boxes, and circles to organize ideas.
  - Build a picture or play (set of actions) around an idea and rerun it in your head.
- **Use mnemonics for important ideas**
  Mnemonics are memory-training devices or ways of making associations to aid in recall. There are several kinds you may be familiar with already:
  - Rhymes
  - Acronyms to collapse the beginning letters of a set of information into one or a few words to help you remember all of the components

  - Building the beginning letters of a set of information into a sentence, which usually results in a somewhat whimsical sentence that is easily remembered

- **Repetition**
  The more times you review something, the better you will be able to recall that information. To enhance this effect, whenever you go through something, try to find a different angle so that you are not just repeating exactly the same activity. By varying your approach, you will create more connections in long-term memory.

SAP Examination Strategies

As the scheduled date of your examination comes closer, the following points should be reviewed. Whereas these points will not help with your understanding, they may assist you if you become stuck while taking the examination. The points you should keep in mind while preparing to take the examination are:

- SAP exams are given online. This is an advantage because you can mark questions you are unsure of and return to them if you have time remaining.
- The questions are grouped in sections by topic. Therefore, Section 2 of this book covers a chapter to each of these topics.
- The exam has several exam versions. This means that you may not receive the same questions on a retry.
- No exam questions concern menu paths or transaction codes.
- Concentrate on the concepts and reasoning used within a topic.
- Learn the methodology behind a topic. You will be asked the "why of doing something." For example, "Why doesn't this line of code work as expected?"
- Think of scanning the exam first to get a feel for the types of questions and consider doing the easy ones first to boost self-confidence.
- Answer all of the questions (unanswered questions are worth zero). If you do not know the answer and cannot reason it out, at least guess. You may not get it right, but if you skip it you are guaranteed to get it wrong.
- If you get stuck on a question, mark it and move on. All questions marked can be returned to before completing the examination.

- Stay "within the box." Consider the topic section in which you are currently working. An answer unrelated to this topic is probably incorrect.
- Read you're the questions slowly and do not make assumptions.
- When reviewing SAP material, be aware of certain words and phrases. Conditional words such as *or* or *can* in relation to SAP are more likely to be true than "hard" words such as *cannot*.
- Although the exam is aimed at understanding rather than memory, *memorization* is not a dirty word. Frequent, thorough review will result in memorizing many facts and will help tremendously in eliminating some incorrect responses immediately.
- Think and use terms the way SAP uses them. It will help in the exam environment.
- Be reasonable. Recognize common sense versus nonsense. If an answer seems strange, it likely is.
- The questions will be based on an understanding when SAP NetWeaver 7.0 was originally released. Changes to functionality based on back ports from future releases will not be on the examination. An example is that the types `decfloat16` and `decfloat34` will eventually be part of SAP NetWeaver 7.0 through support packages, but there will not be questions related to them on this exam.
- Rest is important. Try to get a good night's sleep. Studies indicate that lack of sleep affects concentration, a major ingredient in a multiple-choice exam.

Note

You may or may not get your results immediately after the exam is completed.

- If you do receive your results right away:

  You will not get specific details on what questions were correct or incorrect and why.

  You will receive the percentage of correct answers you achieved for each topic section presented.
- If you do not receive your results right away:

  Your results will be mailed to you.

General Examination Strategies

This examination is multiple choice and multiple response. We provide some guidelines that will help you correctly answer multiple-choice questions on exams:

- **Notice important words in the item**
  This will help you focus on the information most needed to identify the correct answer choice.
- **Read all of the answer choices before selecting one**
  The last answer choice could be just as correct as the first.
- **Eliminate answer choices you are certain are not correct**
  This will help you narrow down the correct answer choice and focus more accurately.
- **Are there two answer choices that are opposites**
  One of these two answer choices is likely to be correct.
- **Look for hints about the correct answer choice in other questions on the test**
  The correct answer choice may be part of another question somewhere else on the test.
- **Look for answer choices that contain language and terminology used by your instructor or found in this book**
  An answer choice that contains such language is usually correct.
- **Stick with your initial answer unless you are sure another answer choice is correct**
  Most often, your first choice is correct.

Knowing how multiple-choice items are constructed and using these guidelines will help you improve your score on a multiple-choice test.

Summary

You now have additional sources of information that can be useful for the certification examination. You can now structure your thinking, and this will increase both your understanding of the subject and provide you with mechanisms to work through questions on the examination. Your understanding of how SAP designs the test will allow you to eliminate incorrect answers.

Part II
Exam Preparation

SAP NetWeaver — Overview

Techniques You'll Master:

- Explain the difference between the classic SAP Application Server and the SAP NetWeaver Application Server
- Understand the SAP Business Suite
- Describe the purpose of kernel and administration services
- Recognize the structure of an ABAP application server
- Determine the structure of a work process

The SAP NetWeaver Application Server is the current technical platform on which ABAP runs. It can be used for a number of business applications. In this chapter you will be provided with a basic understanding of how an ABAP application server functions. We will discuss the evolution of the classic SAP Application Server into the SAP NetWeaver Application Server, and you will learn about the components running on SAP NetWeaver and how it can be configured. We will also delve into the structure and use of work processes on an ABAP application server.

Real-World Scenario

You have been asked to lead a new project installing a new implementation of an SAP system. It is your responsibility to put together a presentation explaining to management the basics of how an SAP NetWeaver Application Server works and provides scalability, data integrity, and hardware and database independence.

Objectives of this Portion of the Test

The purpose of this portion of the certification examination is to verify that you have general knowledge of the SAP NetWeaver Application Server ABAP (AS ABAP) and how the different processes work together. This portion of the examination will test your knowledge of a narrow range of topics. The points you will need to understand from this section include:

- What components are a part of the SAP NetWeaver Application Server
- What components are a part of the SAP NetWeaver Application Server ABAP
- The use of a dialog step in a work process
- How parts of the kernel and administration services make the SAP NetWeaver Application Server both database and platform independent

Key Concepts Refresher

If you are new to ABAP development, you may want to return to this chapter after you read Chapter 8, SQL Statements Including Update Strategies, including update strategies. In many ways these two chapters are closely related. You will find the technical reasons here in this chapter for logical units of work and the SAP lock objects.

SAP Products in a Nutshell

SAP offers a number of products for companies of all sizes. The products are scalable, to ensure that they can be adjusted to any size organization, and are adaptable to a company's constantly changing processes.

- *SAP Business One* is designed for small companies with fewer than 100 employees and 30 users, and it covers their core processes (such as finance, sales, customer service, and operations).
- *SAP Business ByDesign* is designed for small and midsize companies with between 100 and 500 employees that want to use an on-demand solution to improve their core processes.
- *SAP Business All-in-One* is designed for small and midsize companies with very industry-specific requirements that have several divisions and a mature IT infrastructure.
- *SAP Business Suite* is an extended family of business applications that enables companies to manage their entire business.

The SAP Business Suite consists of a number of modular enterprise software products that support end-to-end company processes. The SAP Business Suite is part of the Business Process Platform. The Business Process Platform (BPP) is a prerequisite for the deployment of a service-oriented architecture (SOA) for business applications. It is composed of the following parts:

- The SAP Business Suite, which provides ready-to-execute software for business processes.
- Reusable enterprise services for use in composite applications.
- SAP NetWeaver, which is an open integration and application platform for all SAP applications and certain SAP partner applications. It supports open standards. SAP NetWeaver is interoperable with the most important technology standards such as Java 2 Platform, Java Enterprise Edition (Java EE) and Microsoft .NET.

Some of the applications included in the SAP Business Suite are:

- SAP Enterprise Resource Planning (SAP ERP)
- SAP ERP Human Capital Management (SAP ERP HCM)
- SAP ERP Financials
- SAP ERP Operations
- SAP Customer Relationship Management (SAP CRM)
- SAP Supplier Relationship Management (SAP SRM)
- SAP Supply Chain Management (SAP SCM)
- SAP Product Lifecycle Management (SAP PLM)
- SAP ERP Corporate Services

Product Evolution

Through the 1990s, SAP provided two basic products: SAP R/2 (mainframe based) and SAP R/3 (which is client/server based). They provided similar functionality, and R/3 is often referred to as a successor to R/2. The development of the underlying technical platform was closely linked to the application development. For example, the release names of the SAP technical platform corresponded to the versions of the application themselves. They were therefore referred to as, for example, SAP Basis 4.0B (the technical platform) and SAP R/3 4.0B (the application). Most just used the term 4.0B to refer to both.

In the late 1990s, the number of SAP products grew significantly, and new products required frequent changes and enhancements to the SAP technical platform more than to SAP R/3. This shift in development began the transition of the technical platform from the classical SAP Basis to SAP Web Application Server (SAP Web AS), primarily to allow direct access to HTTP requests.

This transition also produced a naming change to the products. Table 3.1 shows the evolution of the names and the gradual separation of the Basis and the application. As shown in Table 3.1, the technical basis and application development were linked, up to and including SAP R/3 4.6C. The concept of SAP R/3 Enterprise Extensions was introduced starting with SAP R/3 Enterprise (4.7), which is based on SAP Web Application Server 6.20 (the technical platform after evolving into a web server). The introduction of Enterprise Extensions allowed the core application to remain stable and provided new business functionality.

Part of SAP NetWeaver	Basis Functionality	Business Functionality	Business Extension Set	Part of SAP ERP
	3.1I	3.1I		
	4.0B	4.0B		
	4.5B	4.5B		
	4.6B	4.6B		
	4.6C	4.6C		
	4.6D	–		
	6.10	–		
	6.20	4.7	1.10	(2003)
(2003)	6.30	4.7	2.00	(2003)
2004 ('04)	6.40	5.0	5.00	2004
7.0 (2004s)	7.00	6.0	6.00	6.0 (2005)
7.1	7.10	–	–	–

Table 3.1 Evolution from SAP R/3 to SAP ECC

A central application of the SAP Business Suite is SAP ERP (Enterprise Resource Planning). The central software component of SAP ERP is SAP ERP Central Component (SAP ECC). SAP ECC 5.0 can thus be considered the successor of SAP R/3 Enterprise and operates on the basis of SAP NetWeaver Application Server 6.40. At the time of this writing, the current version is SAP ERP 6.0 (previously SAP ERP 2005), which includes SAP ECC 6.0 and other components and operates on the basis of SAP NetWeaver AS 7.00.

The technical platform during this same timeframe also went through several name changes as the platform evolved. Up through Release 4.6, the technical platform was referred to as *SAP Basis*. With the introduction of Internet capability in Release 6.20, the technical platform was referred to as *SAP Web Application Server,* and with the ability to include both the ABAP database and the Java database in one system with Release 6.40, the name became *SAP NetWeaver Application Server*.

The ABAP Release is currently still linked to the technical platform functionality release and is the reason this certification examination specifies SAP NetWeaver 7.0.

Note

SAP NetWeaver AS 7.10 (or SAP NetWeaver 7.1) is not currently used as the technical basis for an SAP ECC system. However, other SAP NetWeaver components, such as SAP NetWeaver Process Integration (PI) and SAP NetWeaver Composition Environment (CE), already require this SAP NetWeaver release level.

With SAP Web AS 6.10, new technologies based on highly scalable infrastructure were implemented to process HTTP requests *directly* from the Internet or to send them as HTTP client requests to the Internet. Before this an *Internet Transaction Server* was required to deal with these requests. The SAP kernel was enhanced to include a process known as the Internet Communication Manager (ICM) to achieve this functionality. The kernel uses the ICM to directly handle HTTP requests, allowing for new web-based applications, for example, Business Server Pages (BSPs). Incoming web requests are received by the ICM, which uses the URL to decide where to forward the request.

Figure 3.1 shows the basic architecture of an SAP NetWeaver server. An SAP NetWeaver server is a further evolution of the technical platform. This platform allows both ABAP and Java to exist and function within the same system. You will notice similar functions on both the ABAP and Java stacks in the figure. Similar functions are performed by the dispatcher and the Java dispatcher to connect a work process to a consumer or user of the process. The ABAP Work Processes and the Java Server Work Processes perform processing and database access. On the ABAP side, the gateway communicates with external servers, and as mentioned above, the ICM processes all HTTP requests. The SDM (Software Deployment Manager) is a standard tool used to install J2EE components on the Java application server.

These web technologies were first used with Business Server Pages (BSP) in SAP Web Application Server 6.20. BSP applications are self-contained applications similar to an SAP transaction. Unlike an SAP transaction, the presentation layer is not the SAP GUI, but a web browser. The BSP dynamically generates HTML pages to provide the presentation. It defines the elements for user interaction, in other words, input fields and pushbuttons. These are created using server-side scripting in ABAP. The application logic is provided through the event handling of a Business Server Page. Beginning with SAP NetWeaver 7.0, Web Dynpro ABAP is also possible — it has been possible to create Web Dynpro Java applications since SAP NetWeaver AS 6.40 (see Chapter 16, User Interfaces (Web Dynpro), for details on Web Dynpro).

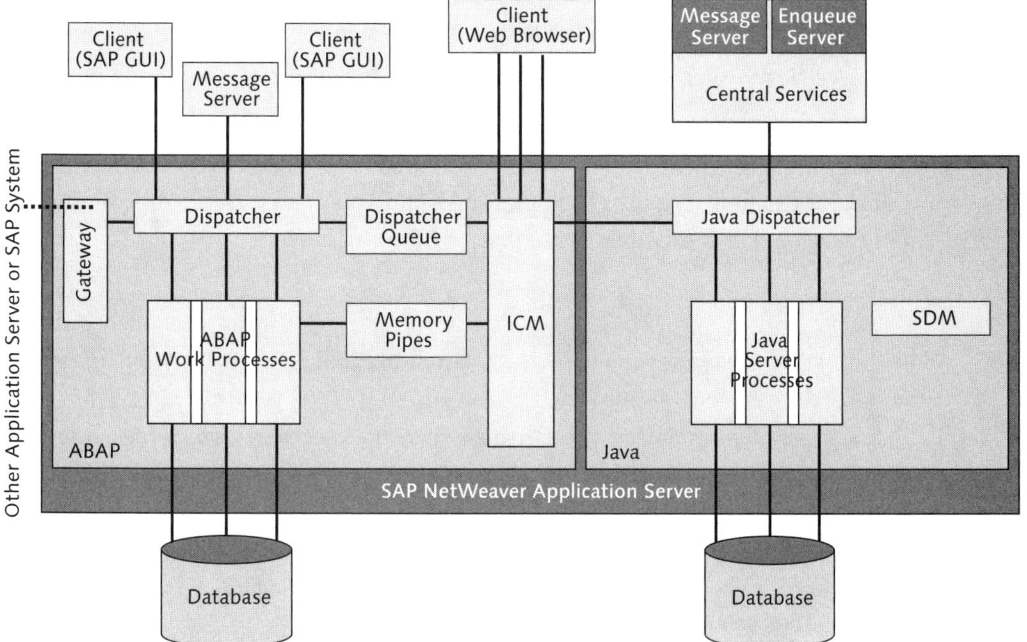

Figure 3.1 Components of SAP NetWeaver Application Server with the ABAP and Java Stacks

SAP Web Application Server 6.20 also provided a Java and an ABAP stack. SAP NetWeaver Application Server Java features the Java dispatcher and Java server process components, which perform tasks similar to the ABAP dispatchers and work processes. Release 6.40 provided the database with two schemas: one for the ABAP data and one for the Java data, in other words, one set of ABAP tables and one set of Java tables depending on the SAP products you use. This was the first release that permitted both ABAP and Java to run together on the same server, or you could have just one or the other. As the data in the database is separated, access of data from one stack to the other is accomplished through the Java Connector (JCo).

SAP NetWeaver Architecture

This evolution of the technical platform into SAP NetWeaver provides us with several different ways to install and use the SAP NetWeaver platform. The installation options for SAP NetWeaver Application Server are as follows:

- SAP NetWeaver Application Server ABAP System
- SAP NetWeaver Application Server Java System
- SAP NetWeaver Application Server ABAP+Java System

Different SAP NetWeaver components require the SAP NetWeaver Application Server to be run with certain stacks configured. SAP NetWeaver Process Integration, for example, requires both the ABAP and Java stacks. Depending on the use of the server, it is possible to use just ABAP or just Java.

Note

When talking about an SAP NetWeaver Application Server, the term *instance* is often used. An instance:

- Always has exactly one dispatcher (see the User View section below for its use).
- Starts when the dispatcher starts.
- Requires at least two dialog work processes (see the Structure of a Work Process section below for details), but has at least a minimum number of work processes defined by the system.
- Is also called the *application server* in the software-oriented view of the client-server model (the next note discusses the differences between the software-oriented and hardware-oriented views). From a software-oriented view, the collection of services shown in Figure 3.1 is an application server, but from a platform-oriented view it's an instance.

An instance is an administrative unit that combines SAP system components that provide one or more services. The services provided by an instance are started or stopped together. Each instance has its own memory buffer areas. An instance runs on one physical server, but there can be multiple instances on one physical server. An instance is identified by the system ID (SID) and the instance number.

When you install an SAP system, you have the option of separating the processes at the application level from those at the database level. This means that the database for an SAP system can be installed and operated on a separate physical server from the instances of the SAP system, and in fact this is usually the case. There is exactly one database for each SAP system.

The central instance of the SAP system is distinguished by the fact that it offers services that no other instance of the system offers. For the AS ABAP, these are the message server and the enqueue work process. The other instances of the system are typically called dialog instances.

Note

Before we discuss various client-server configurations in the context of SAP systems, we need to define the concepts of client and server. There are basically two ways to do this:

- In the hardware-oriented view, the term *server* means the central server in a network that provides data, memory, and resources for the workstations or clients.
- The other way is a software-oriented view. A service that is provided is called a server, and a service that consumes or uses that service is called a client. At the same time, clients can also be servers for other specific services (as you will see below).

Because this book is about programming certification, the rest of the chapter will use terminology from this software perspective. It is important to understand that our use of the term *system* relates to the whole technical platform and *application server* or *server* refers to a server running in a system, not the actual physical hardware. It is possible to implement an entire application on a single hardware system (for example, the trial version mentioned in Chapter 2, Courses and Experience, allows you to have a working system on your own PC). In most customer situations the development and sandbox (if one exists) are typically a single physical system running a single server. A single physical system can also support multiple servers or you can have multiple physical systems each running as a single server.

Kernel and Administration Services

The kernel and administration services component is a runtime environment for all ABAP applications that is hardware independent, operating system independent, and database independent. The kernel and administrative services are another way of looking at the SAP NetWeaver system. The tasks of the kernel and administration services component are:

- **Running applications**
  All ABAP applications run on software processes (virtual machines) within this component.
- **User and process administration**
  The component is responsible for the tasks that usually belong to an operating system. Users log onto the SAP NetWeaver Application Server and run ABAP applications within it. They do not have direct contact with the actual operating system of the host. AS ABAP is the only user of the host operating system.
- **Database access**
  Each AS ABAP is linked to a database system, consisting of a database management system (DBMS) and the database itself. The ABAP applications do not communicate directly with the database. Instead, they use administration services.

  These services handle, as we will discuss shortly, the SAP table buffering on the application server, the translation from Open SQL to Native SQL for the database, and the handling of SAP-specific concepts, for example, the client number or the structure of a cluster table.
- **Communication**
  ABAP applications can communicate both with other SAP systems and with external systems. It is also possible to access ABAP applications from external systems using a Business Application Programming Interface (BAPI) or just a Remote Function Call (RFC). The services required for communication are all part of the kernel and administration services component.
- **Control and administration of AS ABAP**
  This component contains programs that allow you to monitor and control the SAP NetWeaver Application Server while it is running and to change its runtime parameters.

Software-Oriented View

Figure 3.2 represents the software-oriented view of an SAP system. In an ABAP-based SAP system, the AS ABAP consists of all SAP GUI (graphical user interface) components and the ABAP application servers. In this simplified version, be aware that the SAP GUI can be replaced by a web browser in the presentation layer (see below); in other words, users can access the SAP system through a web browser instead of the traditional SAP GUI (this is shown only once, but is not restricted to the single occurrence).

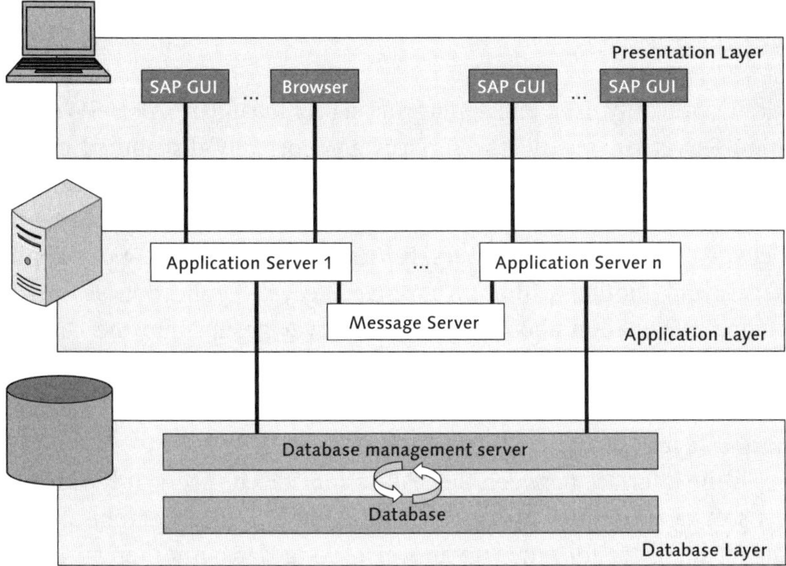

Figure 3.2 Components of SAP NetWeaver Application Server

An SAP system is a multitier client-server system. The individual software components are arranged in tiers and function, depending on their position, as clients for the components below them or servers for the components above them. The classic configuration of an SAP system contains the following three software layers:

- **Database layer**
  The database layer, which is accessed by the SAP NetWeaver Application Server, consists of a central database system. This central database system is made up of the database management system (DBMS) and the database itself.

  The database contains the master data and transaction data for your ABAP application programs. It also contains the control and customizing data for the application and the SAP NetWeaver Application Server and the ABAP application programs themselves. The development objects (programs, screen definitions, menus, function modules, and so on) are all stored in a special part of the database known as the Repository. These objects are therefore also referred to as *Repository objects*. The ABAP Workbench allows you to work with these objects.

- **Application layer**
  The software components of the application layer of AS ABAP consist of one or more ABAP application servers and a message server. Each application server contains a set of services used to run the SAP NetWeaver Application Server.

  Theoretically, you only need one application server to run an SAP NetWeaver Application Server. In reality, the services are normally distributed across more than one application server. This means that not all application servers provide the full range of services. The message server provides for communication between the application servers. It passes requests between one application server and another within an SAP NetWeaver Application Server. It also contains information about application server groups and the current load balancing within them. When a user logs onto the system, this information is used to choose an appropriate server.
- **Presentation layer**
  This layer is the interface between the SAP system and its users. It is possible to use its software components referred to as the SAP GUI (graphical user interface) in this layer for entering and displaying data. Another option is through a web browser that also can be used in the presentation layer. The presentation layer sends the user's input to the application server, and receives data for display from it. While a SAP GUI component is running, it remains linked to a user's terminal session in the AS ABAP.

There are a number of benefits to the distribution of the SAP system over three layers. It distributes the system load, leading to better system performance. It provides high scalability because the software components can be distributed among different hardware virtually without restriction. In the application layer, you can meet increasing demand by installing additional ABAP application servers.

User-Oriented View

From a user's perspective, the SAP system is not seen as systems or servers, but as components that appear as a window on a screen (on either a PC, a web browser, or other device). The presentation layer of the AS ABAP creates these windows.

To connect or log on to the SAP system, a user must start an SAP GUI utility called *SAP Logon*. The user chooses one of the available SAP systems listed in SAP

Logon, and the program connects to the message server of the AS ABAP in the selected SAP system. The message server obtains the address of a suitable (one with the most unused capability) ABAP application server. SAP Logon starts an SAP GUI connected to that application server, and then SAP Logon is then no longer required for this connection. The SAP GUI initially displays the logon screen. The process is similar for Web Dynpro, but instead of starting a preinstalled application, you use a web browser and begin with a URL that launches a logon screen if you are not already logged on.

After the user successfully logs on, the SAP GUI displays the initial screen of the SAP system in a window on the screen. Each window within the SAP GUI represents a session. After you log on, you can open additional sessions (the exact number is determined by a system parameter, though the default is six sessions) within the single SAP GUI. These windows, or sessions, behave almost like independent SAP applications. They allow you to run different applications independently of one another from different sessions.

As you run applications in a session, they may call or trigger more windows (such as dialog boxes and graphic windows). These additional windows are not independent; they belong to the session from which they were called. These windows can be either *modal* (the original window is not ready for input) or *amodal* (both windows are ready for input and interact with each other).

You can open other SAP GUIs, by using SAP Logon. To log onto another SAP system, each SAP GUI is totally independent from others. This means that you can have SAP GUIs representing the presentation layers of several SAP systems open simultaneously on your personal computer.

All ABAP programs run on the ABAP application servers of AS ABAP, in other words, in the instance of the AS ABAP stack. The application layer of the multitier architecture of an ABAP-based SAP system is made up of all of the ABAP application servers. These application servers execute ABAP applications and communicate with the presentation components, the database, and each other through the message server.

Figure 3.3 shows the structure of an ABAP application server: The number of work processes and their types are determined at the startup of the AS ABAP; each ABAP application server also contains a dispatcher, a gateway, and shared memory. The tasks of these components are briefly described below.

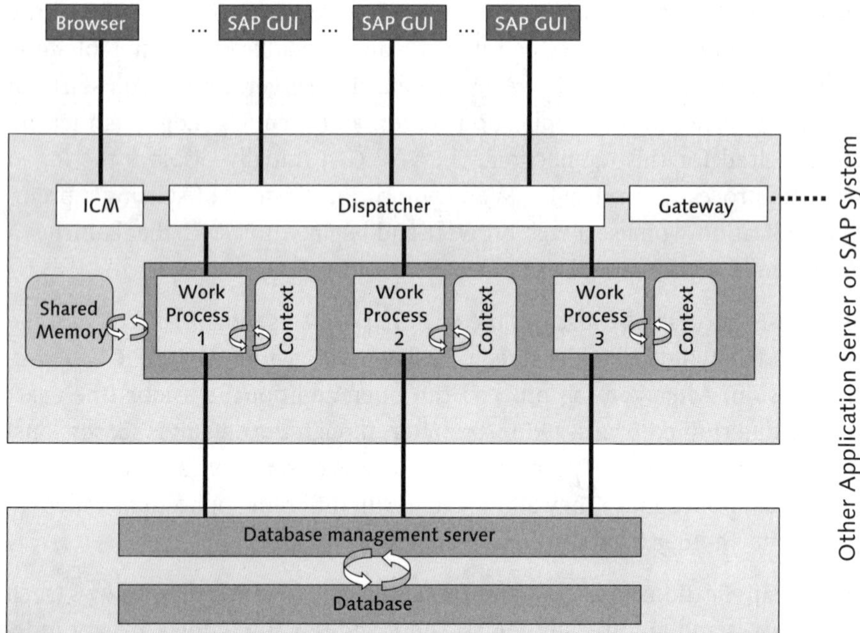

Figure 3.3 ABAP Application Server

- **Work process**
  Work processes are components that execute an application. For a dialog work process, each executes one dialog step (for the definition of a dialog step see the Definitions to Remember section below). Each work process is linked to a memory area that contains the context of the executing application. This context contains the data for the application. After the work process completes the dialog step, the link to the user and the program context is removed, which frees it for another user.

- **Dispatcher**
  The dispatcher provides the link between the work process and the user logged onto the application server (or more accurately, the user's SAP GUIs or web browser). It receives requests from an SAP GUI or web browser and directs the request to a free work process. Once the work process completes the dialog step, the resulting screen output is returned to the appropriate user before the link is released.

- **Gateway**
  The gateway is the interface for the communication protocols of AS ABAP (RFC and CPI/C). Its purpose is to communicate with other ABAP application

servers within this system (internally), externally with other SAP systems, or externally with non-SAP systems.

In an ABAP application server all work processes use a common main memory area called *shared memory* to save contexts or to locally buffer constant data. Resources that work processes share or use, for example, programs and buffered table contents, are placed in shared memory.

Local buffering of data in the shared memory of the ABAP application server reduces the number of database reads required (see Chapter 8, SQL Statements Including Update Strategies, for details), considerably reducing the access times for ABAP application programs.

When you start an AS ABAP, each ABAP application server registers its work processes with the database layer and receives a single dedicated channel (sometimes referred to as a database work process) for each work process. While the SAP NetWeaver Application Server is running, each work process is a user (acting as a client) of the database system (acting as a server). It is not possible to change the work process registration while the system is running or to reassign a database channel from one work process to another. Therefore, a work process can only make database changes within a single database logical unit of work (LUW). For more on a database logical unit of work see Chapter 8, SQL Statements Including Update Strategies.

Structure of a Work Process

There is a difference between user interaction and processing logic in ABAP programming. This separation is discussed in more detail in Chapter 12, Classical Screens, and Chapter 16, User Interfaces (Web Dynpro). From a programming perspective, user interaction is controlled by screens (at least for applications in the SAP GUI). A screen consists of two parts: the actual input mask and the flow logic, which controls a large part of the user interaction. The AS ABAP contains a special language for programming screen flow logic. Within a work process (Figure 3.4 shows the components of a work process), the *screen processor* executes the screen flow logic. Through the dispatcher, it takes over the responsibility for communication between the work process and the SAP GUI, calls modules in the flow logic, and ensures that the field contents are transferred from the screen to the flow logic (see Chapter 12, Classical Screens, for details).

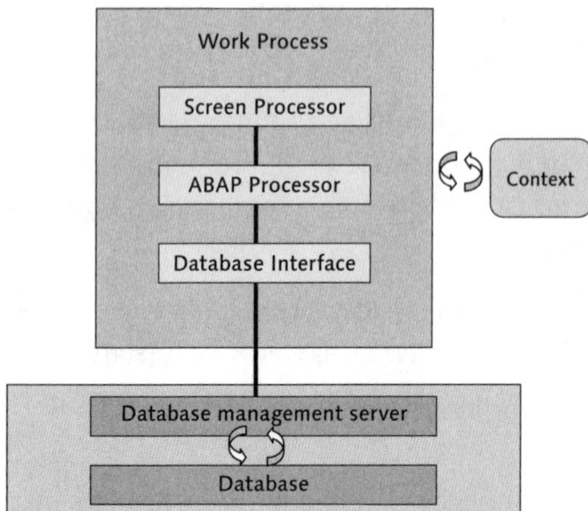

Figure 3.4 Components of a Work Process

The actual processing logic of an application program is written in ABAP. The *ABAP processor* within the work process executes the processing logic of the application program and communicates with the database interface. The screen processor tells the ABAP processor which module of the screen flow logic should be processed next.

The following services are provided by the database interface:

- Establishing and terminating connections between the work process and the database
- Access to the database tables
- Access to Repository objects
- Access to catalog information (ABAP Dictionary)
- Controlling transactions (commit and rollback handling)
- Table buffer administration on the ABAP application server

Figure 3.5 shows that there are two different ways of accessing SAP database tables: Native SQL and Open SQL using ABAP. Open SQL statements are a subset of standard SQL that is fully integrated in ABAP. These statements allow you to access data irrespective of the database system. Open SQL consists of the Data Manipulation Language (DML) part of standard SQL. It therefore allows you to read (`SELECT`) and change (`INSERT`, `MODIFY`, `UPDATE`, and `DELETE`) data. The tasks of the Data Definition Language (DDL) and Data Control Language (DCL) parts of standard SQL are performed in the AS ABAP by the ABAP Dictionary and the authorization system. These provide a unified range of functions, regardless of database, and contain functions beyond those offered by the various database systems.

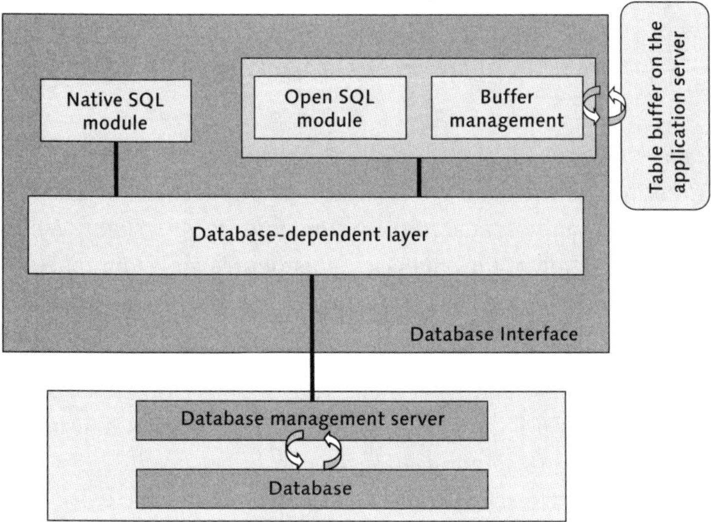

Figure 3.5 Components of the Database Interface

Open SQL goes beyond standard SQL to provide statements that in conjunction with other ABAP constructions can simplify or speed up database access. It allows you to buffer certain tables on the ABAP application server, saving excessive database access. The database interface is responsible for managing the buffer with the database. Database table buffers are partly stored in the working memory of the current work process and partly in the shared memory for all work processes on an ABAP application server. In cases where the AS ABAP is distributed across more than one ABAP application server, the data in the various buffers is synchronized at set intervals by the buffer management. When you buffer a database table, you must remember that the data in the buffer may not always be up to date. As a result, you should only use the buffer for data that does not change often or where the data does not need to be current.

Native SQL is only loosely integrated into ABAP and allows access to all of the functions contained in the programming interface of the respective database system. In Native SQL, you can primarily use the database-specific SQL statements. The Native SQL interface sends them as is to the database system where they are executed. You can use the full SQL language scope of the respective database, which makes all programs using Native SQL specific for the database system installed. A small set of SAP-specific Native SQL statements are handled in a special way by the Native SQL interface. SAP recommends that ABAP applications should contain as little Native SQL as possible, because it reduces the portability and maintainability of your code. Only a few SAP standard components actually contain Native SQL, for example, to create or change table definitions in the ABAP Dictionary.

The *database-dependent layer* in Figure 3.5 hides the differences between database systems from the rest of the database interface. Owing to the standardization of SQL, the differences in the syntax of the statements are very slight. When you use Native SQL, the function of the database-dependent layer is minimal (see Chapter 8, SQL Statements Including Update Strategies, for additional details).

Before you start the AS ABAP, you determine how many work processes each ABAP application server will have and what their types will be. Because all work processes have the same structure, the type of work process does not determine the technical attributes of the ABAP application server, but instead determines the type of tasks that can be performed on it. The dispatcher starts the work processes and only assigns them tasks that correspond to their type. This allows you to distribute work process types to optimize the use of resources on your ABAP application server.

Figure 3.6 again shows the structure of an ABAP application server, but this time includes various possible work process types: Dialog work processes process requests from an active user to execute dialog steps. Update work processes execute database update requests. Update requests are part of an SAP LUW that bundle the database operations resulting from the dialog in a database LUW for processing in the background. Background work processes run programs that can be executed without user interaction (background jobs).

The enqueue work process administers a logical lock table in the shared memory area. This single lock table contains all of the logical database locks for an AS ABAP and is an important part of the SAP LUW process. There is therefore only one ABAP application server with enqueue work processes. It is normally sufficient for a single enqueue work process to perform the required tasks.

The spool work process passes sequential datasets to a printer or to optical archiving. Each ABAP application server may contain only one spool work process. The last two types of processes are the message server and the gateway: The message server routes messages between application servers, and the gateway routes messages in and out of the system to external systems.

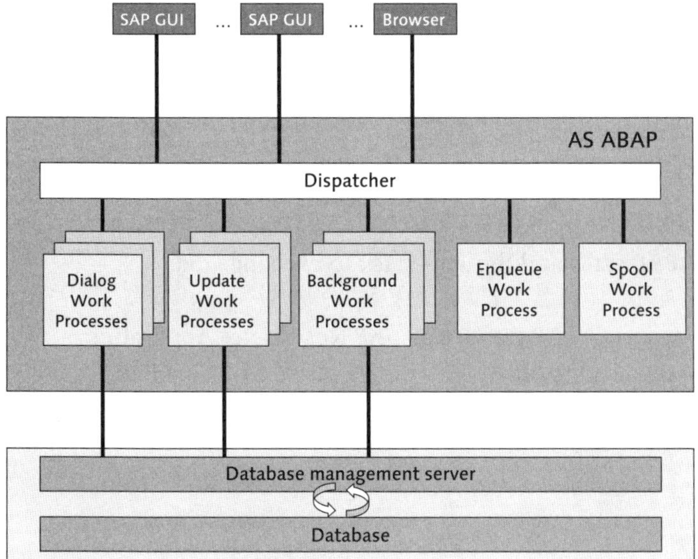

Figure 3.6 ABAP Application Server

Important Terminology

A dialog step is the program processing that occurs after a screen is released by a user or, put another way, the processing that occurs during a screen change (even if the same screen is being redisplayed). After the completion of a dialog step, the work process is released while the next screen is processed by the user on the presentation server.

A Repository object is one of the components (program, screen definitions, menus, function modules, and so on) stored in a special part of the database known as the Repository.

Practice Questions

The practice questions below will help you evaluate your understanding of the topic. The questions shown are similar in nature to those found on the certification examination. Whereas none of these questions will be found on the exam itself, they allow you to review your knowledge of the subject. Select the correct answers and then check the completeness of your answers in the following solu-

tion section. Remember that you must select all correct answers and only correct answers to receive credit for the question.

1. The Internet Communication Manager (ICM):

- ☐ **A.** Replaced SAP ITS
- ☐ **B.** Allows SAP NetWeaver Application Server to process HTTP requests
- ☐ **C.** Allows the ABAP stack and the Java stack to exchange data

2. The Java stack and the ABAP stack of an SAP NetWeaver Application Server must always be installed together.

- ☐ **A.** True
- ☐ **B.** False

3. A work process:

- ☐ **A.** Stays linked to a screen through the dispatcher
- ☐ **B.** Becomes inactive while waiting for a user
- ☐ **C.** Uses a common memory area called shared memory

4. Each work process:

- ☐ **A.** Is independent of other work processes
- ☐ **B.** Uses a pool of database connections established when the SAP NetWeaver Application Server ABAP started
- ☐ **C.** Uses a database work process established when the SAP NetWeaver Application Server ABAP started
- ☐ **D.** Can only make database changes within a single database LUW
- ☐ **E.** Can make database changes spanning multiple database LUW

5. Each work process is assigned a type of task that can be performed. Which statements are true related to this?

- ☐ **A.** To switch a work process type requires a restart of the SAP NetWeaver Application Server ABAP.
- ☐ **B.** All work processes have the same structure.
- ☐ **C.** All work processes communicate with the database.

- [x] **D.** All work processes communicate with the dispatcher.
- [ ] **E.** A work process can communicate directly with an external system through a Remote Function Call.
- [ ] **F.** It is possible to have multiple enqueue work processes on an SAP NetWeaver Application Server.
- [ ] **G.** It is possible to have multiple spool work processes on an ABAP application server.

Practice Question Answers and Explanations

1. Correct answer: **B**

   Beginning with SAP NetWeaver 6.10, new technologies based on highly scalable infrastructure were implemented to process HTTP requests directly from the Internet or to send them as HTTP client requests to the Internet. The SAP kernel was enhanced to include a process known as the Internet Communication Manager (ICM) to achieve this functionality.

2. Correct answer: **B**

   Different SAP NetWeaver components require the SAP NetWeaver Application Server to be run with certain stacks configured. It is possible to install both the ABAP and Java stacks, but depending on the use of the server, it is possible to use just ABAP or just Java.

3. Correct answer: **C**

   All of the work processes of an ABAP application server use a common main memory area called shared memory to save contexts or to buffer constant data locally. The resources that all work processes use, for example programs and table contents, are contained in shared memory. Memory management in the AS ABAP ensures that the work processes always address the correct context.

4. Correct answers: **A**, **D**

   Each individual work process works independently, which makes them suitable for a multiprocessor architecture.

   When you start up an AS ABAP, each ABAP application server registers its work processes with the database layer and receives a single dedicated channel for each. While the SAP NetWeaver Application Server is running, each work process is a user (acting as a client) of the database system (acting as a server). You cannot change the work process registration while the system is running. It is also not possible to reassign a database channel from one work process to another. For this reason, a work process can only make database changes within a single database logical unit of work (LUW). A work process must open a separate database LUW for each dialog step. The work process sends a commit command (database commit) to the database at the end of each dialog step in which it makes database changes. These commit commands are called implicit database commits, because they are not explicitly written into the application program.

5. Correct answers: **B, D, F**

   You can use the system administration functions to switch a work process while the system is running. Because each work process has the same structure, they are interchangeable. All work processes must communicate with the dispatcher (which assigns the user to a work process), but enqueue work processes and spool work processes do not communicate with the database. All communication for a work process occurs with either the dispatcher or the database.

   Whereas it is normal to only have one enqueue work process (a single enqueue work process is normally sufficient to perform the required tasks), it is possible to have multiple enqueue work processes running. In SAP NetWeaver Application Server you can only have one lock table, but multiple enqueue work processes, running. Each ABAP application server can contain only one spool work process.

Take Away

Now that you have learned how an ABAP application server operates, you can take away the differences between an SAP NetWeaver Application Server and a classic SAP Application Server. You have also learned the components of a work process and how they work with other components of an ABAP application server or other layers, for example, the presentation server and the database server.

Refresher

You must understand the purpose of the different layers or tiers of an SAP NetWeaver Application Server. It is important to understand the architecture and why it is both efficient and scalable. You must understand how this system design handles both the database (SAP LUW) and execution of programs (dialog steps).

Table 3.2 shows the key concepts for the SAP NetWeaver Overview.

Key Concept	Definition
SAP NetWeaver Application Server	The application platform of SAP NetWeaver.
SAP NetWeaver Application Server ABAP	The stack within SAP NetWeaver Application Server used to execute ABAP applications
ABAP application server	A software component of the SAP NetWeaver Application Server ABAP that runs all ABAP programs. This is the application layer of the multi-tier architecture of an ABAP-based SAP system.
Work process	A component that is able to execute an application. It executes a single dialog step.
Dispatcher	Establishes the link between the user logged on and a work process.
Gateway	The interface for communication between the SAP NetWeaver Application Server ABAP and another system (either another ABAP Application Server, another SAP NetWeaver Application Server, or an external non-SAP system.)
Screen Processor	A component of a work process that executes the screen flow logic
ABAP Processor	A component of a work process that executes the processing logic of the application program and communicates with the database interface
Database Interface	A component of a work process establishes a connection between the work process and the database, provides access to the database tables and Repository objects, controls transaction processing (commit and rollback), and provides table buffering on the ABAP application server

Table 3.2 Key Concepts Refresher

Tips

An understanding of the underlying architecture of the system and servers will make you a better developer and help you understand the reasoning for selecting better or more efficient techniques. This topic, however, is one most developers do not understand, and they are therefore unable to take advantage of the strengths of SAP NetWeaver.

Summary

You should now have a basic understanding of how an ABAP application server operates. You should know why an SAP NetWeaver Application Server is different than a classic SAP Application Server. You should understand which components run on SAP NetWeaver and what general configuration is possible for an SAP NetWeaver Application Server. You should also know the components of a work process and how they work with other components of the ABAP application server or other layers (presentation server and database server). An understanding of the SAP NetWeaver architecture will give you a solid foundation, and you will be successful in this and other sections of the exam.

ABAP Workbench Usage

4

Techniques You'll Master:

- Describe the features and capabilities of the ABAP Workbench
- Explain the structure of the Object Navigator
- Use the Repository Browser to edit repository objects
- Access the Repository Information System to search for repository objects
- Understand the Enhancement Information System and its use
- Work with the ABAP Workbench tools
- Identify the new Front-End Editor and the various settings to improve productivity
- Determine the concept of the Development Package and the Transport Organizer

The ABAP Workbench is the development environment for the SAP NetWeaver Application Server ABAP and is available in every ABAP-based SAP system. The ABAP Workbench provides the development tool needed for application development. The Object Navigator, the central entry point into the ABAP Workbench, contains the most commonly used development tools and is the recommended development environment.

In this chapter we will cover in detail the ABAP Workbench tool and the Object Navigator. We will cover features and capabilities of the ABAP Workbench, discuss the structure of the Object Navigator, and discuss in detail the various browsers available in the Object Navigator. We will cover in detail the new Front-End Editor, the Repository Information System, and the Enhancement Information System. We will also cover ABAP Workbench tools such as the ABAP Editor, Screen Painter, Menu Painter, ABAP Dictionary, Class Builder, Function Builder, and Web Application Builder. Finally, we will discuss packages and their attributes and the Transport Organizer.

Real-World Scenario

You have started on a customer project as an SAP development lead and have been asked to explain to the project team about the ABAP Workbench. You have to explain to the project team about the SAP development tools and the various features of the ABAP Workbench and the Transport Organizer.

As a development lead, you have to organize the technical development for the project. Your job is to define the development standard and the tools to be used for the various developments. You also have to define the development project, package, system landscape, and transport strategy for all of the developments in the project.

Objectives of this Portion of the Test

One of the objectives of the ABAP certification examination is to verify your knowledge of the ABAP Workbench and the various tools associated with it. You need to understand the following to be a successful ABAP developer:

- ABAP Workbench and development tools
- ABAP Workbench settings
- The use of various browsers in the ABAP Workbench
- The new Front-End Editor and the settings to improve productivity
- Development Packages and Transport Organizer

Key Concepts Refresher

The ABAP Workbench is the integrated development environment for the application developer. The Workbench has most of the tools a developer needs to develop an application. Some of the most commonly used workbench tools are:

- ABAP Editor
- Screen Painter
- Menu Painter
- ABAP Dictionary
- Web Dynpro development tools
- Package Builder and Transport Organizer
- Repository Browser
- Repository Information System
- Enhancement Information System

ABAP Workbench

ABAP stands for *Advanced Business Application Programming* and is the language in which most of the SAP business applications are written. The ABAP Workbench is the development environment for the ABAP developer. The ABAP Workbench consists of the development tools required for creating repository objects. The ABAP Workbench can be started via Transaction SE80. The Object Navigator can be accessed from the menu path Overview Object Navigator and is the main entry point to ABAP Workbench.

The main screen of the ABAP Workbench is divided into the navigation area and the tool area (see Figure 4.1). The navigation area displays the object list as a hierarchy tree. The object list consists of all of the objects within an application area, package, program, global class, module pool, function group, and so on. The benefit of editing or displaying the object within the Object Navigator is that you can view all of the related objects for the program, class, module pool, or package as a tree structure and can access them from the navigation area by just double-clicking on the object. If you work with the repository object with the individual tool, then you only have the option to work with one type of object at a time with one tool.

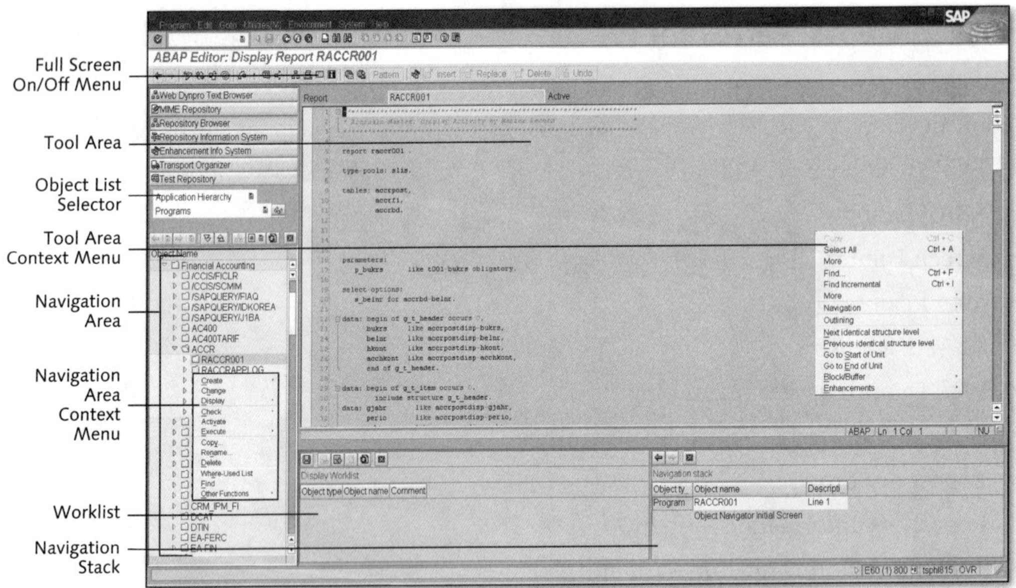

Figure 4.1 ABAP Workbench Screen

The tool area is used to display or edit the repository object using the relevant tool editor. The navigation area or the tool area can be resized. You can hide the navigation area by clicking on the FULL SCREEN ON/OFF icon () on the application toolbar. The object navigation history with the ABAP workbench is stored in the navigation stack. The Object Navigator has a menu option to display the navigation history. You can display the navigation window from the menu option UTILITIES • DISPLAY NAVIGATION WINDOW, and an additional window for the navigation stack will be displayed under the tool area of the workbench. You can also display the navigation window by clicking on the DISPLAY NAVIGATION WINDOW icon () on the application toolbar. You can scroll back through the navigation stack by clicking on the blue left arrow or forward by clicking on the right arrow icon in the navigation stack window. This tool helps you scroll through the objects you have viewed during the logon session.

You can create your own worklist within the ABAP Workbench. A worklist is useful to help you manage the development objects on which you need to work. To create your worklist you need to display or edit the repository object first in the tool area of the ABAP Workbench and then from the menu option select UTILITIES • WORKLIST • INSERT CURRENT OBJECT. This inserts the object in the worklist. You can display the worklist via the menu path UTILITIES • WORKLIST • DISPLAY, and an additional window for the worklist will be displayed under the tool area of the ABAP workbench.

You can access the Reuse Library from the Workbench menu path ENVIRONMENT • REUSE LIBRARY. The Reuse Library provides you with a set of reusable objects with example code and documentation. You can execute the code to display the result and copy the reusable code for your application development. The Reuse Library is displayed in the browser, and you can display the individual development objects within the Reuse Library by double-clicking on the product and reading the example code. You can also access the Reuse Library via Transaction SE83.

Similar to the Reuse Library, you can access the ABAP examples via the menu path ENVIRONMENT • EXAMPLE • ABAP EXAMPLE. The ABAP example programs are displayed in the browser, and you can display individual programs by double-clicking on the example program in the navigation area. The actual program is displayed in the tool area of the Object Navigator. ABAP examples provide examples of most of the keywords and syntax based on the ABAP documentation. You can also access the ABAP documentation from the ABAP examples screen. ABAP examples can also be displayed by executing Transaction ABAPDOCU.

You can display the context menu for an object within both the navigation area and the tool area by right-clicking on the object. The context menu offers only the functions that are relevant for the selected repository objects. You have the option to add your development objects to your favorites list within the Object Navigator by clicking on the FAVORITES icon ( ) in the navigation window.

You can access the individual tools to create the repository objects using individual transaction codes or access the most commonly used tools from the Object Navigator. The initial screen of the Object Navigator displays the Browser list on the top-left section of the screen. The Object Navigator has several browsers that you can use for various development needs. You have the option to navigate to the relevant tool based on the selected browser from the browser list (see Figure 4.2). You can add or remove browsers from the list via the menu path UTILITIES • SETTINGS.

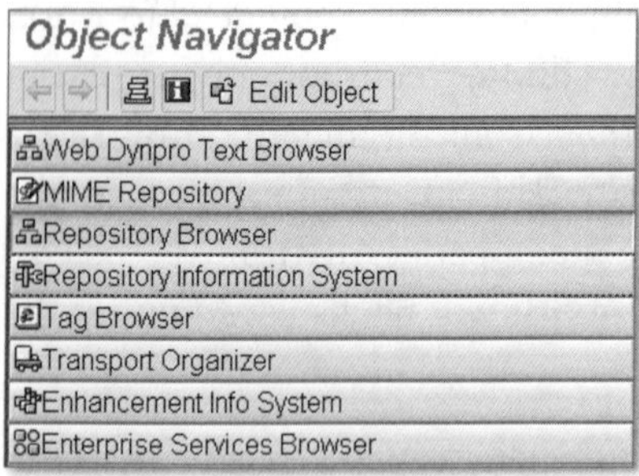

Figure 4.2 Object Navigator

The Object Navigator list has the following browser selection options in the object navigation:

- **Web Dynpro Text Browser**
  You use the Web Dynpro Text Browser to edit the text of the Web Dynpro UI elements that are created or managed in the Online Text Repository (OTR). This tool allows you to change the only texts for the Web Dynpro views that have been stored in the OTR or inserted from the OTR in the Web Dynpro application.
- **MIME Repository Browser**
  You use the MIME Repository Browser (Multipurpose Internet Mail Extensions) to browse or import MIME objects such as style sheets, icons, graphics, and so on from the ABAP Workbench. The MIME Repository stores these MIME objects in the SAP system. The MIME Repository Browser automatically creates a folder for Business Server Pages (BSP) applications. You can import MIME objects from the Repository Browser or view the MIME objects by double-clicking on them.
- **Tag Browser**
  The Tag Browser provides the documentation of the user interface elements that can be used for web page development for BSP applications and Internet Transaction Server (ITS) templates. You have the option to filter the tags for the BSP application or the tags for the ITS templates. The Tag Browser provides documentation for HTMLB, BSP extension, BSP Directives, HTML, WML, and XHTML.

- **Test Repository Browser**
  You use the Test Repository Browser to manage test cases. You can display eCATT test scripts, manual test cases, and external test cases. You also have the option to create test cases within the Test Repository Browser. It's a good tool for you to manage the test cases within the Test Repository.

Other browsers such as the Repository Browser, the Repository Information System, the Enhancement Information System, and the Transport Organizer are discussed in detail in the following.

Repository Browser

The Repository Browser is one of the menu options in the Object Navigator and is started by default when you execute the Object Navigator (Transaction SE80). You can create and edit repository objects in the Repository Browser. The Repository Browser is the central tool for managing your development objects within the Object Navigator and is the most commonly used tool.

When we talk about repository objects, we mean all of the SAP-delivered objects and customer-developed objects. These repository objects consist of programs, classes, ABAP Dictionary objects, functions modules, screens, menus, and so on.

The object list displayed in the Repository Browser is a hierarchical tree structure. You can navigate to a repository object by the application hierarchy, whereby you can list the objects within each of the SAP application components. The objects can also be listed in a hierarchical tree structure within a package, program, class or interface, BSP application, Web Dynpro application, local object, and so on.

You can display the object from the navigation area by double-clicking on it. The object will be displayed in the tool area of the object browser in the editor that has been used to create the object. The ABAP development objects are displayed in the ABAP Editor, whereas the Dictionary objects are displayed in the ABAP Dictionary tool. Similarly, you display the screens and the menus in the tool area in the Screen Painter or Menu Painter by double-clicking on the screen or menu in the navigation area. You can use the context menus in the navigation area to create or edit the object in the application area or package (see Figure 4.3).

You can create or edit repository objects only if you have the appropriate developer authorization and your user ID has been registered in the SAP Service Marketplace as a developer. You need to provide the developer access key for the first time you create any repository object. You only have to provide the access key once because the system stores it for you in the table DEVACCESS.

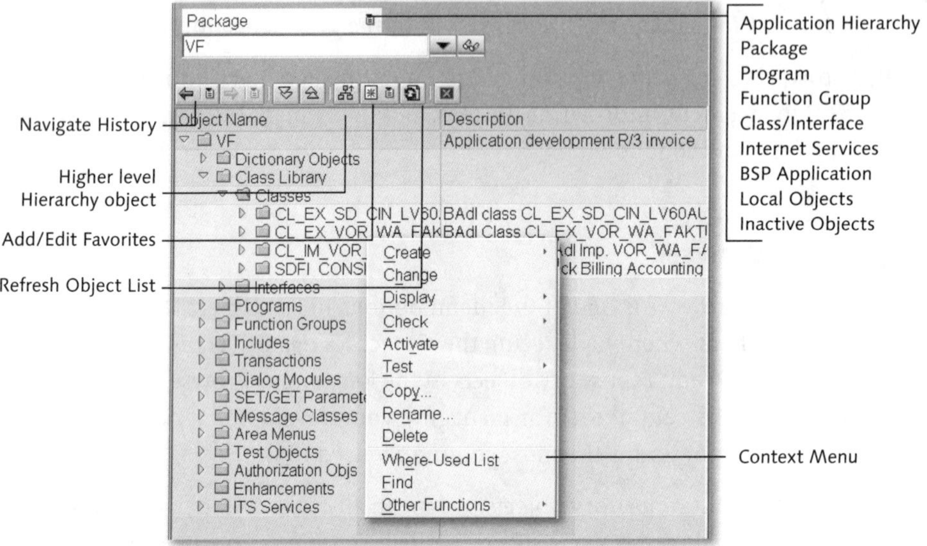

Figure 4.3 Repository Browser Navigation Area

Some of the common context menu functions for repository objects are to check repository objects, activate an object, copy or rename objects, and change the package assignment of an object or write the object to the change request. You also have the where-used list function of the object from the context menu.

Repository Information System

The Repository Information System Browser is used to search for repository objects in the SAP system. The initial screen of the Repository Information System displays a hierarchical list of the categories of repository objects in the SAP System (see Figure 4.4).

The Repository Information System has a selection screen to provide the search criteria for the repository objects. You can search for repository objects within a package or search for ABAP Dictionary objects or programs by specifying the search criteria on the selection screen. Figure 4.5 displays the Repository selection screen for database tables within ABAP Dictionary objects.

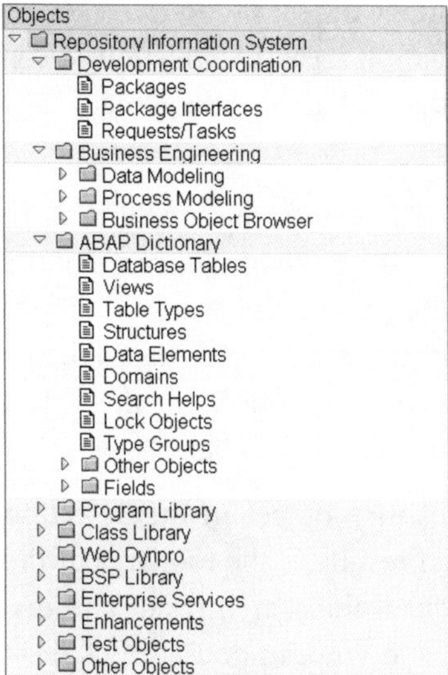

Figure 4.4 Repository Information System

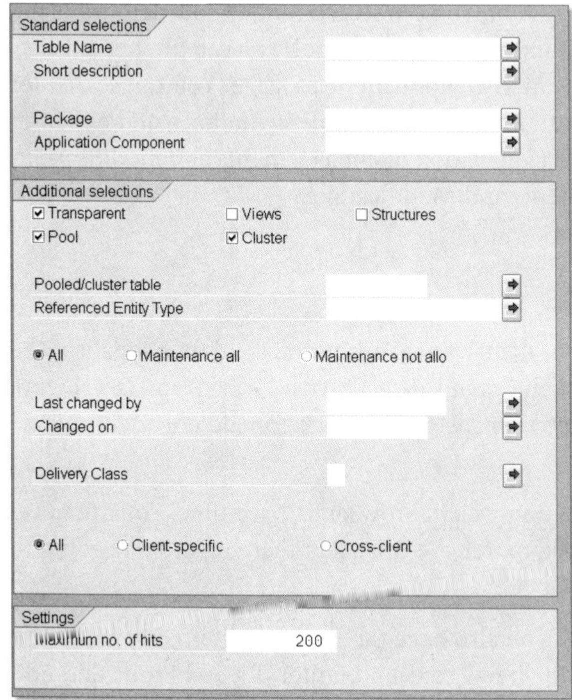

Figure 4.5 Repository Selection Screen for ABAP Dictionary Objects

You can access the selection screen for the repository object by double-clicking on the type of repository object in the object navigation area; the selection screen relevant for the object will then be displayed in the tool area of the Object Navigator.

You can customize the selection screen of the Repository Information System. To customize the selection screen select EDIT • SETTINGS from the initial screen of the Repository Information System browser. You can specify in the customization if you want to see the default selection screen or the screen with all of the available selection criteria. You can also display all of the selection criteria for the object by clicking on the appropriate icon ( ) on the application toolbar.

You can specify the search criteria for the repository object in the selection screen and execute. The system displays the search results in the tool area of the Object Navigator. You can also select the object from the search result and display the where-used list of the object if required, and you can double-click on it to look at the object itself in the appropriate tool.

The Repository Information System is a useful tool to display the available enhancements within the SAP system. You can search for both the definition and the implementations of the enhancement with this tool. You can filter your selection of enhancements by application component or package. You can search for Business Add-Ins, customer exits, enhancement implementations, and enhancement definitions. For a detailed explanation of enhancements and modifications refer to Chapter 18, Enhancements and Modifications.

Workbench Settings

You can configure the ABAP Workbench to change its look and functionality. The workbench is configured from the menu path UTILITIES • SETTINGS (see Figure 4.6). The Workbench settings are user specific and therefore do not affect anyone else in the system.

The Object Navigator can display only eight browser lists at a time. You can unselect the browser selection checkbox for the browsers that you are not going to use very often.

Within the Workbench settings you also have the option to configure the ABAP Editor settings. You can select the new Front-End Editor, the old Front-End Editor, or the standard Back-End Editor and customize its settings. You have the option to set your default ABAP Debugger to either the classic or new ABAP Debugger. You can change your Pretty Printer settings, Split Screen settings, and the Pattern settings. You can maintain the settings for the Class Builder, Screen Painter, Menu Painter, Function Builder, Repository Information System, Data Browser, Internet Transaction Server, Business Server Pages, Web Dynpro, Transport Organizer, SAPscript, eCATT, and proxy generation from the Workbench settings as well.

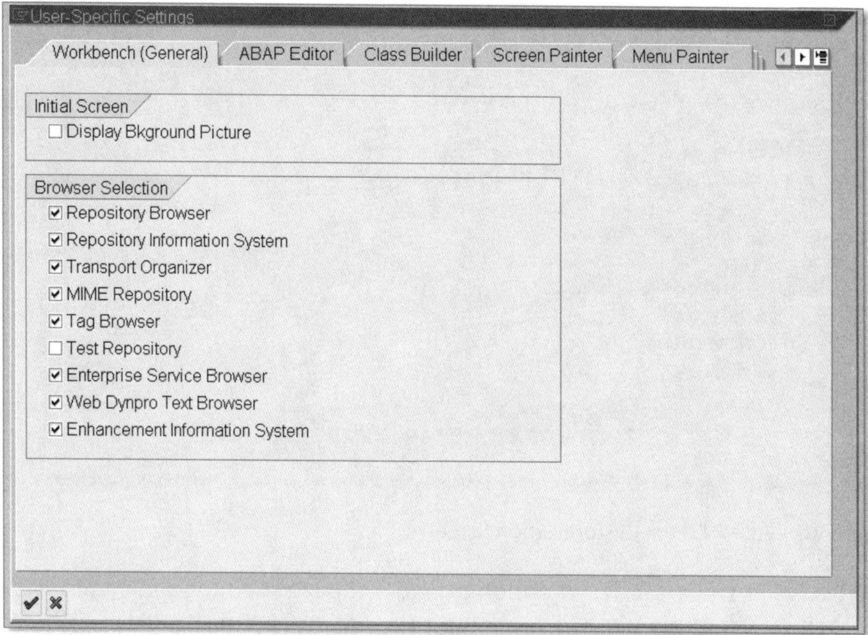

Figure 4.6 ABAP Workbench Customization Screen

New ABAP Editor and Workbench Settings

There are three different modes for the ABAP Editor:

- Front-End Editor (source code mode — new)
- Front-End Editor (plain text mode — old)
- Back-End Editor (line-based mode)

The three editors are fully compatible and interchangeable. The source code created in one editor can be viewed by all other modes.

The choice of the editor is based on the user-specific settings made in the ABAP Workbench. The editor can be configured within the ABAP Editor via the menu path UTILITIES • SETTINGS • ABAP EDITOR (see Figure 4.7).

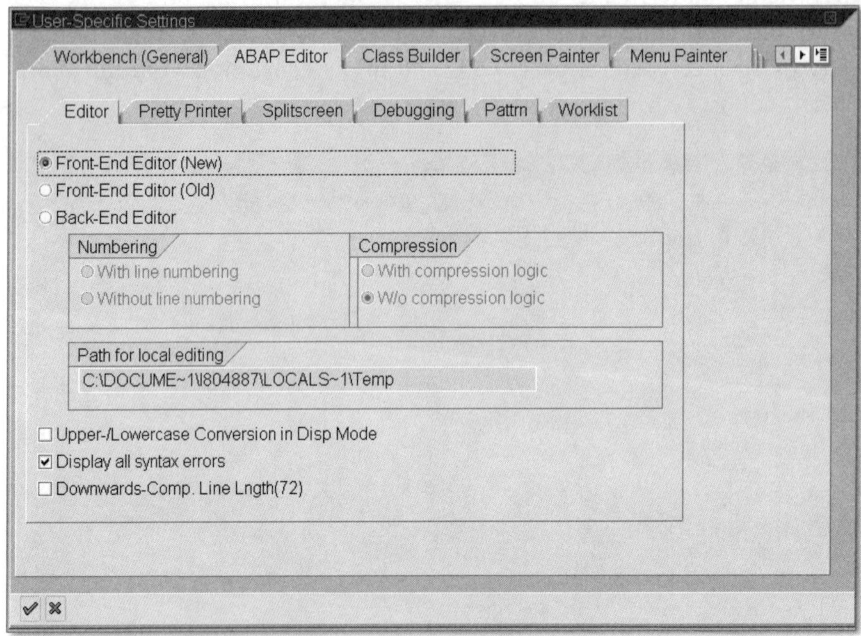

Figure 4.7 ABAP Editor Customization Screen

The FRONT-END EDITOR (NEW) option provides the latest editor and comes with SAP GUI for Windows 7.0. The new editor is an ActiveX control and is fully integrated into the SAP NetWeaver 7.0 environment.

The new editor has all of the modern code editing features:

- The left margin of the main screen of the editor displays any bookmarks and breakpoints. Breakpoints are displayed with a red stop sign, and bookmarks are displayed as a blue flag in the editor margin. You can set up to nine bookmarks and an unlimited number of bookmarks that are not numbered on the editor for fast navigation within the code.
- The editor has a line number margin next to the editor margin, where the line number is displayed.
- The code changes are marked with a red triangle against the line number.
- The status bar displays the current status of the code.

- The vertical scroll tip provides information about the current scroll position within the code, current function, class, or method.
- You can split the code editor screen horizontally by double-clicking on the splitter line on the vertical scroll bar. You can also just drag the splitter line to split the editor screen horizontally.
- You can collapse or expand blocks of code such as `IF-ENDIF` or `CASE-ENDCASE`.
- The status bar of the editor displays the current status of the Caps Lock and Num Lock, and the line number of the cursor position. The Caps Lock and the Num Lock can be changed by double-clicking on them. Double-clicking on the line number displays the Go to Line dialog.
- The Front-End Editor has two types of context menu; the context menu options depend on the area selected for the context. The margin context menu is displayed by right-clicking on the left margin and has the option to set breakpoints, delete breakpoints, set bookmarks, clear bookmarks, or navigate to a bookmark (see Figure 4.8).

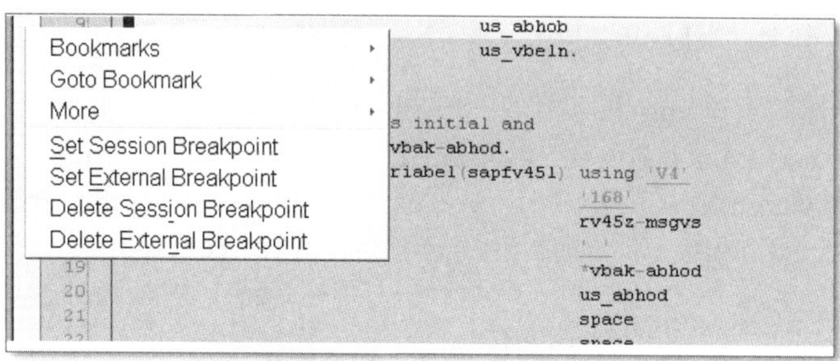

Figure 4.8 Margin Context Menu

The context menu in the editing area displays the menu options for the ABAP code. The editing area context menu has various formatting, editing, and navigation options (see Figure 4.9).

- The editor provides code hints at runtime as you type by suggesting keyword hints, block templates, and so on. You can accept the code hint by pressing the [Tab] key or insert a block template by selecting [Ctrl]+[Enter]. Furthermore, the editor supports WYSIWYG export functionality. It supports export to HTML, PDF, and RTF formats.
- The new ABAP Editor is a fully integrated development environment (IDE) for ABAP programming. It supports syntax highlighting, outlining language structures, real-time code hints, and auto completion of language structures.

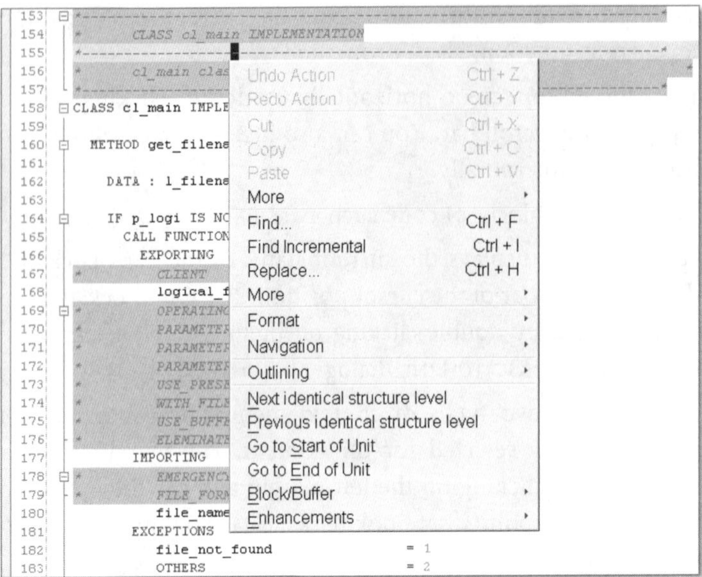

Figure 4.9 Context Menu for Text Formatting

- With the new code editor you can customize the highlighting for the keyword, strings, and comments. You can customize the font, color, and size for ABAP keywords and comments. Similarly, you can customize font, color, and size for strings, breakpoints, and other display items in the code editor (see Figure 4.10).

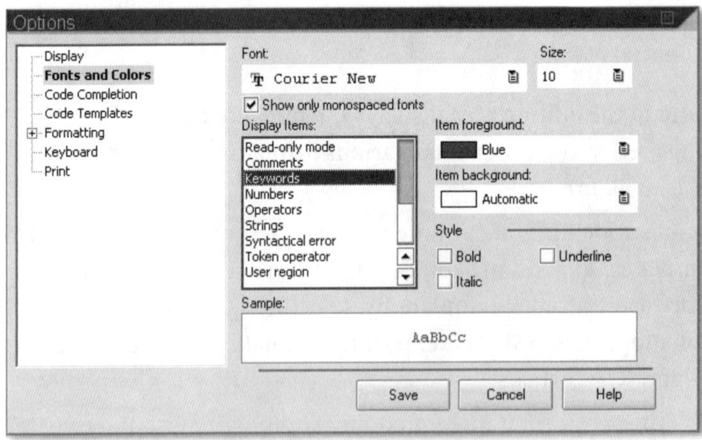

Figure 4.10 Code Editor Customization for Color Schemas

- You can customize the display settings of your editor. Figure 4.11 shows the display customization screen. The display and the word wrap options can be switched on or off according to you preference.

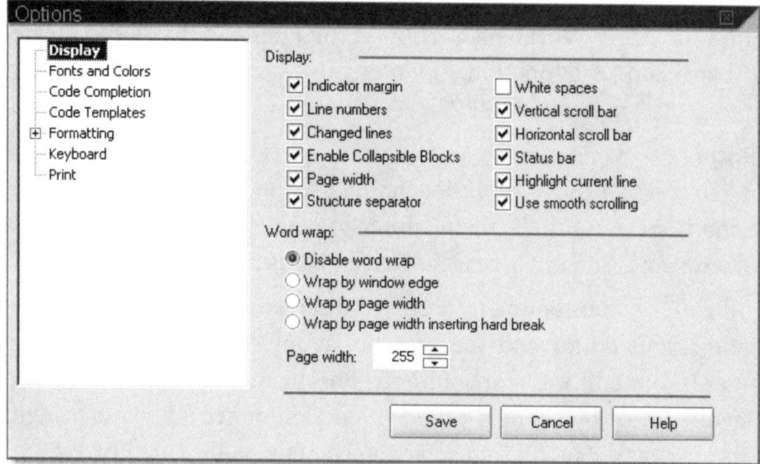

Figure 4.11 Display Customization for the Editor

- Lastly, you can customize the code completion options for the editor. This option allows you to complete the available keyword from the dictionary or complete the class, method, or variable name within the scope of the visibility.

ABAP Workbench Tools in Detail

With the Object Navigator you work directly with the repository object. The relevant tool for the repository object is automatically selected when you double-click on the repository object. The SAPscript Editor, Smart Forms Editor, and Customer Enhancement Projects are some of the development tools that are not available within the Object Navigator. Following are the most commonly used ABAP Workbench development tools.

- **ABAP Editor**
  The ABAP Editor is used to develop programs and can be executed via Transaction SE38. You use the editor to write ABAP programs.
- **Class Builder**
  The Class Builder allows you to create ABAP classes within the ABAP Workbench. You can create ABAP classes and interfaces, implement inheritance rela-

tionships, and create attributes, methods, and events for the global classes and interfaces that you build. You can access the Class Builder via Transaction SE24.

- **Function Builder**
  You use the Function Builder to write function modules and define function groups within the ABAP Workbench. You use the Function Builder to create, change, display, and test function modules. You can access the Function Builder directly via Transaction SE37.

- **Screen Painter**
  The Screen Painter is an ABAP Workbench tool used to create screens for SAP GUI transactions. You use the Screen Painter to create screens and write the flow logic for screens. You can access the Screen Painter via Transaction SE51.

  The Screen Painter layout editor to design the screen has two versions: the alphanumeric layout editor and the graphic layout editor. By default, the Screen Painter layout editor is alphanumeric, but the mode can be changed to graphical layout editor by changing the Screen Painter setting via the menu path UTILITIES • SCREEN PAINTER and selecting GRAPHICAL LAYOUT EDITOR.

  You define the screen attributes and the screen field attributes for the screen fields and the flow logic using the Screen Painter. You can create Tab Strips, Table Controls, Subscreens, and Custom Containers using the Screen Painter, among other screen elements.

- **Menu Painter**
  The Menu Painter is an ABAP Workbench tool to create the user interface for your program or transaction. This consists of the Menu Bar, Standard toolbar, application toolbar, and GUI Title using the Menu Painter. You also assign the function keys to the functions you create in the Menu Painter. You can execute the Menu Painter outside the ABAP Workbench via Transaction SE41.

- **ABAP Dictionary**
  The ABAP Dictionary tool is an integral part of the ABAP Workbench. The ABAP Dictionary is used to create, change, and display transparent tables, pooled and cluster tables, views, types, domains, data elements, structures, table types, search helps, and lock objects. The database utility is also an integral part of the ABAP Dictionary tool. You can directly access the ABAP Dictionary tool outside the ABAP Workbench via Transaction SE11.

- **Web Application Builder**
  You can build Web Applications within the ABAP Workbench. The ABAP Workbench delivers the tool to develop ITS web applications or BSP applications.

- ITS was the first approach by SAP to extend business applications to web browsers by converting the SAP Dynpro screen into HTML format, making it possible to access SAP transactions via web browsers. For ITS applications you can create Internet services for existing SAP transactions, HTML templates for the transaction screens, and MIME objects to add icons and graphics to the web screen layout.
- You can also develop Business Server Pages (BSP) applications with the Web Application Builder. You can design your web page for the BSP application using HTML and ABAP or Java Scripting language. You can define the page flow and implement the event handler with ABAP with the Web Application Builder for BSP. The Web Application Builder also allows you to define the theme for your layout and integrate the MIME objects into the web application.

- **Web Dynpro Explorer**
  The Workbench has a tool for development of Web Dynpro ABAP applications (as of SAP NetWeaver 7.0). The tool consists of the runtime environment and the graphical tool to design the Web Dynpro views within the ABAP development environment.

Enhancement Information System

The Enhancement Information System provides an overview of the defined enhancements and the enhancement implementations within the Enhancement Framework. The Enhancement Framework is the technical basis for SAP's new enhancement concept; for detailed information refer to Chapter 18, Enhancements and Modifications. It enables you to see the enhancement definitions and implementations in the system.

The Enhancement Information System is a tree display structure for enhancement definitions and enhancement implementations. The enhancement element definition is displayed under the enhancement spot definition, which in turn is displayed under the composite enhancement spot. Similarly, the enhancement element implementation is displayed under the simple enhancement implementation, which in turn is displayed under the composite enhancement implementation. The enhancement implementation node is not displayed if the enhancement has not been implemented. Also, it is not necessary that all enhancement spot definitions or implementations are assigned to a composite enhancement definition. Enhancement definitions and implementations are discussed in detail in Chapter 18, Enhancements and Modifications.

You can filter the display of the enhancements within the Enhancement Information System. You have the option to display the composite enhancement, or enhancement spot, enhancement implementation, or composite enhancement implementation within the Enhancement Information System (see Figure 4.12).

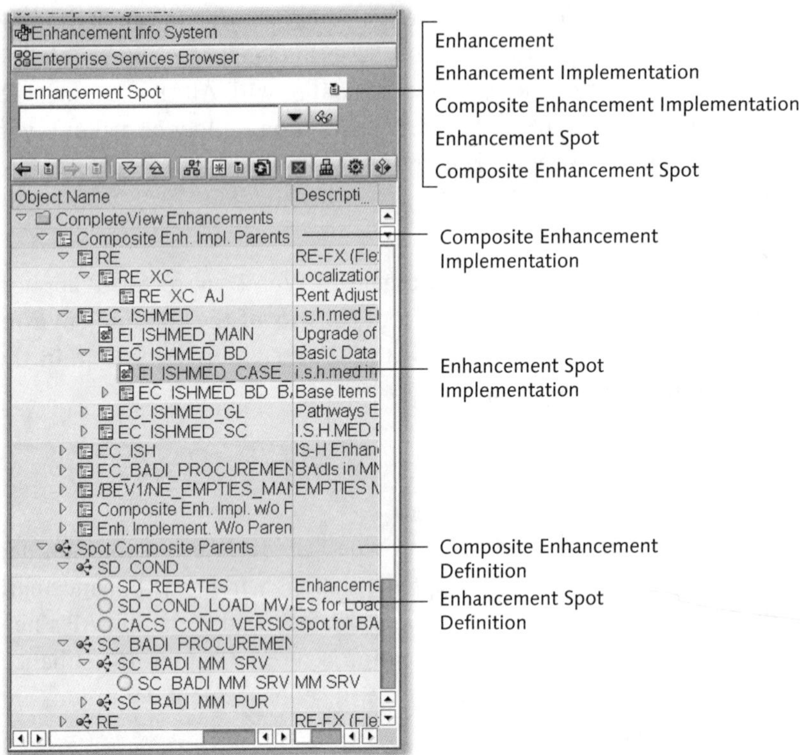

Figure 4.12 Enhancement Information System Navigation Screen

The enhancement spot definition can be displayed in the ABAP Workbench tool area by double-clicking on the enhancement spot definition in the navigation area. Figure 4.13 displays the Enhancement Spot definition screen in the tool area. Similarly, you can display the Enhancement Implementation screen in the tool area of the ABAP Workbench by double-clicking on the enhancement spot implementation (see Figure 4.14).

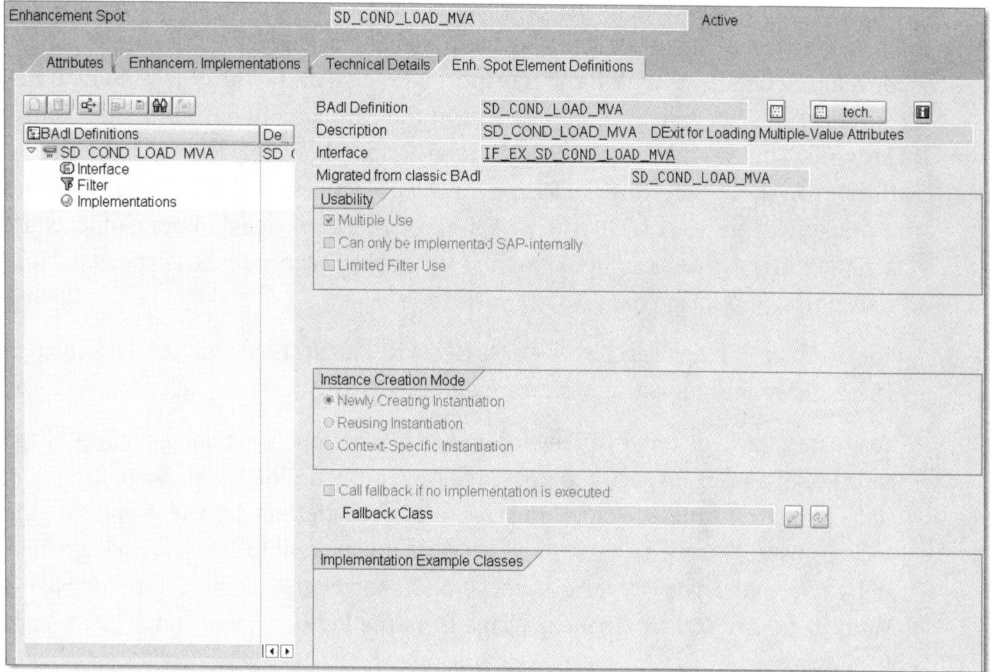

Figure 4.13 Enhancement Spot Definition Screen

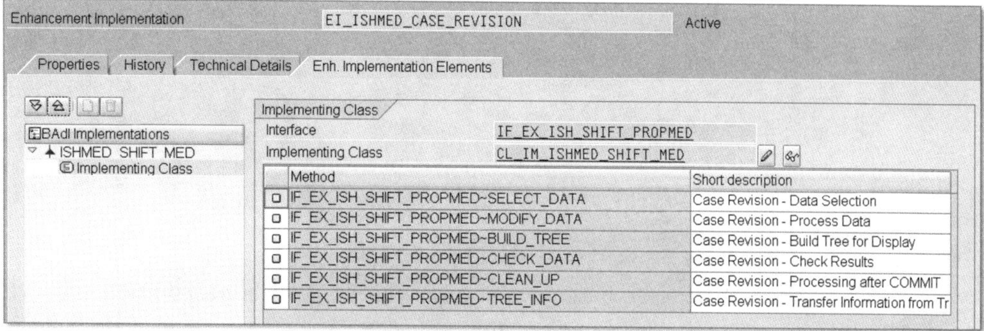

Figure 4.14 Enhancement Spot implementation Screen

Packages and their Attributes

Prior to Release 4.6C all ABAP development objects were assigned to development classes that were used to group related development objects. Packages were assigned to the application components. There can be multiple packages for an application component. As of Release 4.6C and beyond, all ABAP development objects are to be assigned to the package. Packages are containers for the development objects within the transport layer that allow the objects to be transported. You can create or edit packages in the Package Builder in the Repository Browser. You can display all of the objects assigned to the package in the Repository Browser by selecting a package for the object list type. The SAP system has a predefined package, `$TMP`, to which all of the local development objects are assigned. Local objects assigned to the `$TMP` package cannot be transported. Nontransportable package names start with `$`.

The Package Builder can also be accessed via Transaction SE21 or SPACKAGE. The Package Builder is used to create and assign attributes to packages.

To create a package for your development project, you can create a main package and the subpackage, specify the package hierarchy, define the package interface, add elements to the package interface, and then define the use access for the package user. You create main packages only if you want to create a package hierarchy. Normally you create a package and specify the package type as NOT A MAIN PACKAGE. You create the package from the Repository Browser (see Figure 4.15).

Package Builder: Create Package

Package	ZSD001
Short Description	Custom SD Application Development Pagkage
Applic. Component	SD
Software Component	HOME
Transport Layer	ZFLC
Package Type	Not a Main Package

Figure 4.15 Create Package Screen

You specify the package name, short description, application component, software component, transport layer, and package type and then click on the CREATE PACKAGE icon. Customer package names should start with the letter `Z` or `Y`. The software component for a customer package is always `HOME`. The transport layer determines if the object assigned to the package is local or transportable. Normally you carry out all of your development activity in the development system and then move your objects to the quality assurance system and the production system. Your system administration team will set up a transport layer for your development system for which the transport route is defined to move the object from one system to another. Based on the transport layer, the objects assigned to the package are moved to the different systems defined in the transport route for the transport layer.

You can specify the package properties, use access, interface, and package hierarchy in the Package Builder screen in change mode. However, you are not required to specify the package interface or use access unless you want to protect the object assigned to the package from being used arbitrarily by other packages. Figure 4.16 displays the Package Builder screen where you can specify the package attributes.

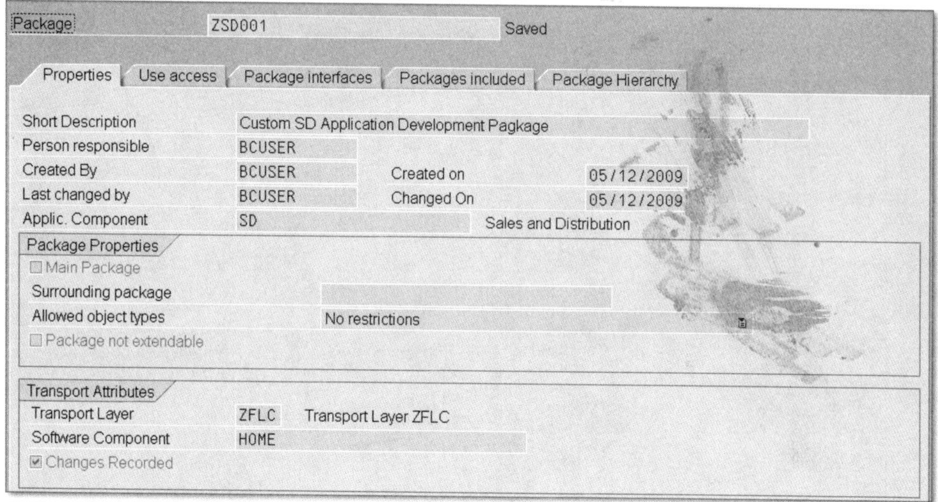

Figure 4.16 Package Builder Screen for Package Attributes

Packages have attributes such as nesting, package interfaces, visibility, and use access.

- Nesting allows you to embed packages in other packages, thus allowing you to split larger units of repository objects and structure them in a hierarchy.
- Visibility is a property of the package element. Elements within the package are visible to all other elements within the same package and are always invisible to the elements outside of the subpackage.
- Elements within a package can be made visible outside the package by defining a package interface.
- Use access is the right of one package to use the visible elements of the other package interface.

Packages use interfaces and visibility to make their elements visible to other packages. All visible elements of a package can be used by the other package. Use access restricts the use of the visible elements of the package. The visible elements of the provider package can only be used by the package if the use access of the interface has been created in the package (see Figure 4.17).

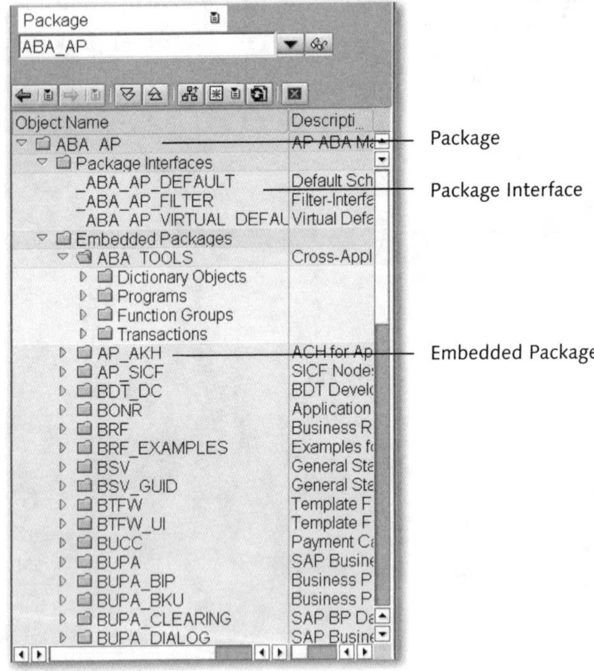

Figure 4.17 Package Structure in Object Navigator of ABAP Workbench

Package interface and visibility are useful if you want to make an element of your subpackage visible to the higher-level package or main package.

The system checks that your package complies to the above rules based on the entry in the table `PAKPARAM`. The package check is switched off by default in the customer system. The entry `GLOBAL_SWITCH` for the key field `NAME` in the table `PAKPARAM` controls the behavior of the package check. By default, the `GLOBAL_SWITCH` key is set to `OFF` in the table `PARPARAM`. To switch on package check, set the `GLOBAL_SWITCH` key to `RESTRICTED` or `R3ENTERPRISE`.

Table 4.1 displays the values for `GLOBAL_SWITCH` and their effects on package check.

Value	Behavior
RESTRICTED	The package check is only performed if you have selected the PACKAGE CHECK as client or PACKAGE CHECK as SERVER ATTRIBUTE in the package.
R3ENTERPRISE	The same checks that are performed for entry RESTRICTED are performed here. With objects belonging to structure packages, an additional check is performed to determine whether use access has been defined between them. Note that in this case an additional entry has to be made in the table PAKPARAM with the key field NAME equal to SAP_DEV_SYSTEM and VALUE set to X.
OFF	Switches off package check.

Table 4.1 Valid Values for Package Check

Transport Organizer

The Change and Transport System (CTS) provides you with a tool to organize your ABAP Workbench, cross-client customization, and customization work and then transport the changes through your system landscape. The CTS records all of the changes in the change request. The change request is also referred to as the transport request. You can release your task and the change request once you have completed and tested your development. You have to ensure that your development object is syntactically correct and active before you release the change request. The change request is then used to transport the changes to other systems or clients based on the transport route.

Repository objects and cross-client customizations are assigned to a workbench request, whereas the client-specific customization objects are assigned to a Customizing request. Each change request can have one or multiple tasks, and the repository objects or the customization objects are assigned to one of these tasks. The task is assigned to a user, and only the owner of the task can record his changes to the task.

There are two types of workbench tasks: development/correction and repair tasks. The repository object changes are recorded in the development/correction task if the current system is the original system of the object. The object is recorded in the repair task if the current system is not the original system of the object. All SAP standard object modifications are recorded in the repair task of the workbench request. Figure 4.18 displays the change request structure. The top level is the change request, and the lower-level number is the task of the change request.

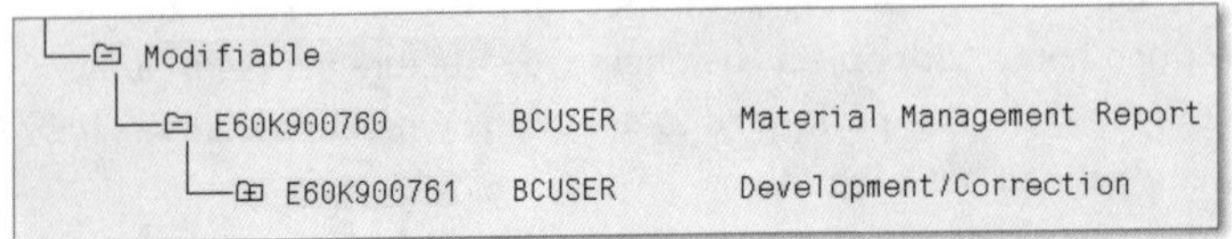

Figure 4.18 Transport Request Structure

Each repository object is assigned to a package, and the package is assigned to the transport layer. If the route for the transport layer is defined in the Transport Management System, then the object recorded in the transport task is transportable; otherwise, the task belongs to the local change request.

The system administration team creates the transport layer in the Transport Management System (TMS) to transport the objects in your system landscape. The transport layer is assigned to the development system. The admin team needs to set up a transport route after creating the transport layer.

There are two types of transport routes: Your admin team will set up the consolidation route for each transport layer and then the delivery route. The development system is the source system for the consolidation route and the quality assurance system is the target system. You define the delivery route to transport the objects from the quality system to the other target system, which can be production and other training systems. So once the object is imported to the quality system you, need delivery routes to transport the objects from the quality system to other systems.

The Transport Organizer is integrated with the Object Navigator or can be accessed via Transaction SE10. You can display the transport request and the associated tasks of the request from the workbench by double-clicking the request in the navigation area of the workbench. The request will be displayed in the tool area, whereby you can display the properties, objects, and documentation of the request. The request editor displays all of the recorded changes within the request (see Figure 4.19).

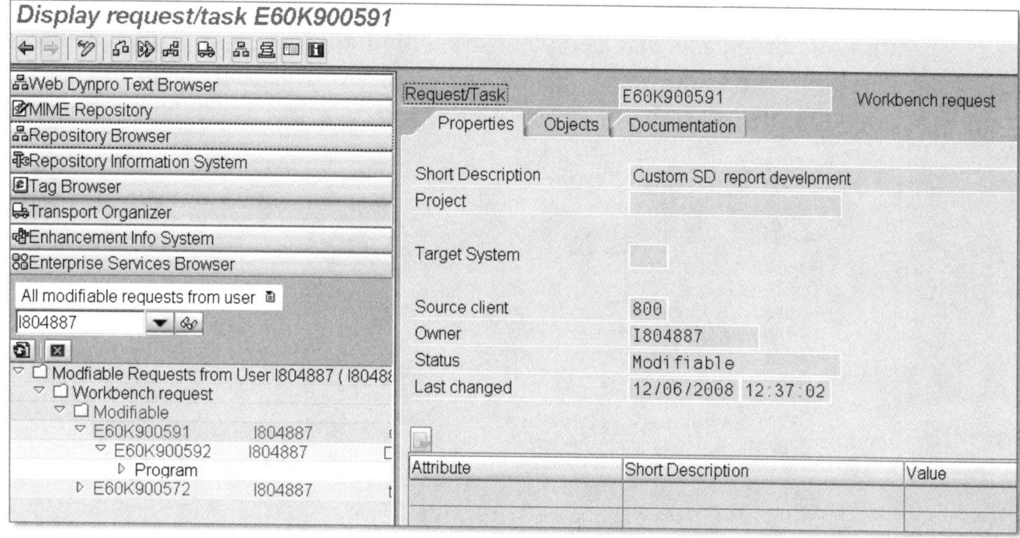

Figure 4.19 Request Editor in ABAP Workbench

You can create change requests by creating the repository object. A dialog window appears when you are creating the repository object to allow you to create a new request or assign the object to an existing request. The transport attributes are populated automatically based on the attributes of the repository object. Figure 4.20 displays the initial transport request screen.

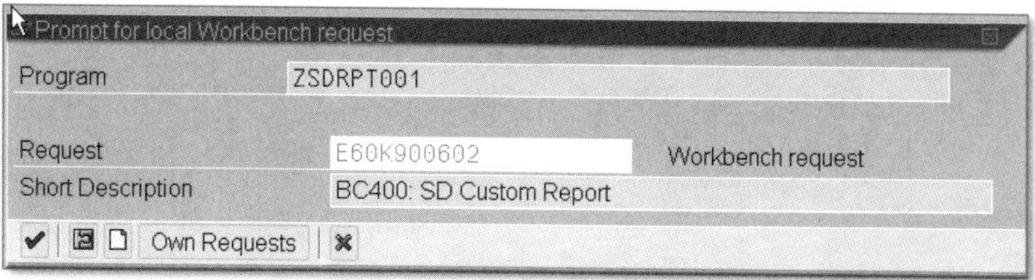

Figure 4.20 Transport Request Screen

You can also create the transport request from the transport organizer, but you have to populate the transport attributes on your own. You release all of the tasks within the change request and then the change request itself to transport the objects through your system landscape. The system administrator imports the objects to the target system. You can display the transport log by selecting the transport log menu option.

The Transport Organizer tools are integrated with the Transport Organizer. They are a set of programs that help you work with the Transport Organizer. You can start the tool from the initial screen of the Transport Organizer via the menu path GOTO • TRANSPORT ORGANIZER TOOLS (see Figure 4.21).

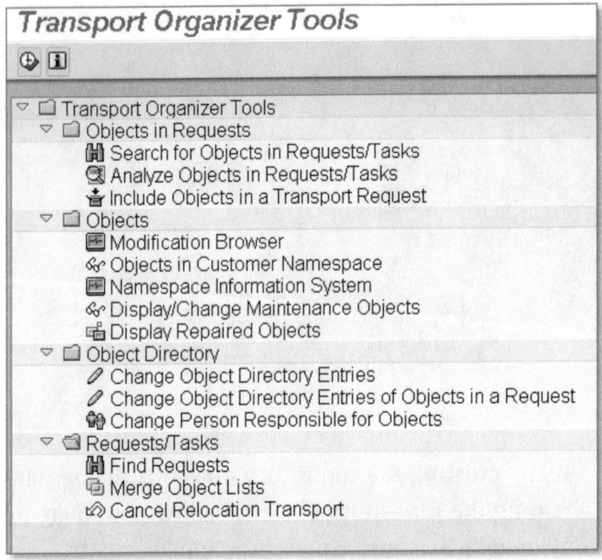

Figure 4.21 Transport Organizer Tools

The tools can be used to search for objects in transport requests or include objects in the transport requests. You can search the request or task based on different search criteria. Similarly, you can display all of the modifications in the customer system using the modification browser.

Practice Questions

The practice questions below will help you evaluate your understanding of the topic. The questions shown are similar in nature to those found on the certification examination, but whereas none of these questions will be found on the exam itself, they allow you to review your knowledge of the subject. Select the correct answers and then check the completeness of your answers in the following solution section. Remember that you must select all correct answers and only correct answers to receive credit for the question.

1. The Object Navigator incorporates a total of 10 browsers.

- [ ] **A.** True
- [ ] **B.** False

2. The Repository Browser is started by default when you execute Transaction SE80 for the Object Navigator.

- [ ] **A.** True
- [ ] **B.** False

3. You can list a maximum of six browsers in the Object Navigator.

- [ ] **A.** True
- [ ] **B.** False

4. You can maintain SAPscript forms and SAP Smart Forms within the ABAP Workbench.

- [ ] **A.** True
- [ ] **B.** False

5. Which of the following about the Object Navigator are true statements?

- [ ] **A.** ABAP programs can be displayed and edited in the Object Navigator.
- [ ] **B.** Screens can be displayed and edited in the Object Navigator.
- [ ] **C.** Menus can be displayed and edited in the Object Navigator.
- [ ] **D.** You can create BAdI implementations in the Object Navigator.
- [ ] **E.** You can create customer projects (Transaction CMOD) in the Object Navigator.
- [ ] **F.** The ABAP Dictionary can be maintained in the Object Navigator.

6. The Repository Information System is a useful tool to search for customer exits/function exits and BAdIs in the SAP system.

- [ ] **A.** True
- [ ] **B.** False

7. Enhancement definitions and implementations can be displayed in the Enhancement Information System.

☐ **A.** True

☐ **B.** False

8. Which of the following is a true statement? There can be more than one correct answer.

☐ **A.** All customer repository objects have to be assigned to a package.

☐ **B.** Packages use interfaces and visibility to make their elements visible to other packages.

☐ **C.** The transport layer is a mandatory input field for the package.

☐ **D.** A package can be nested.

9. The software component for a customer package can be ____

☐ **A.** `HOME`

☐ **B.** Any SAP software component (i.e., `SAP_APPL`, `SAP_BASIS`, `SAP_HR`, etc.).

10. Which of the following is a true statement? There can be more than one correct answer.

☐ **A.** All transportable objects have to be assigned to a package.

☐ **B.** Local repository objects can be transported.

☐ **C.** Repository objects and cross-client customization objects are assigned to the workbench request.

☐ **D.** Client-specific customization objects are assigned to the customizing request.

☐ **E.** Inactive objects can be transported.

11. Which of the following is true? There can be more than one correct answer.

☐ **A.** The repository objects and cross-client customization objects are recorded in a task belonging to a local change request if there is no consolidation route leading from the current system defined in the Transport Management System for the transport layer.

- [ ] **B.** The repository objects and the cross-client customization are recorded in a task belonging to the transportable request if the consolidation route is defined in the Transport Management System.

12. There are ____ versions of the ABAP Editor.

- [ ] **A.** 3
- [ ] **B.** 4
- [x] **C.** 2

Practice Question Answers and Explanations

1. Correct answer: **B**

   The Object Navigator has a total of nine browsers, and in earlier releases it was less than nine. The following are the object browsers available in the ABAP Workbench:

   - Repository Browser
   - Repository Information System
   - Transport Organizer
   - MIME Repository
   - Tag Browser
   - Test Repository
   - Enterprise Service Browser
   - Web Dynpro Text Browser
   - Enhancement Information System

2. Correct answer: **A**

   The Repository Browser is the default browser for the ABAP Workbench.

3. Correct answer: **B**

   You can display up to eight browsers in the ABAP workbench

4. Correct answer: **B**

   You cannot maintain SAPscript forms or SAP Smart Forms in the ABAP Workbench.

5. Correct answer: **A**

   You can search for enhancements including Business Add-Ins and customer exits with the Repository Information System.

6. Correct answers: **A, B, C, F**

   You can edit or display ABAP programs in the ABAP Workbench in the ABAP Editor. You can display or edit screens within the ABAP workbench in the screen painter. You can display and edit menus within the ABAP workbench in the Menu Painter. The BAdI implementation tool is not integrated within the Object Navigator, so it's not possible to create BAdI implementations in the Object Navigator. The customer project (CMOD) is not integrated within the ABAP Workbench, so it's not possible to create customer projects with the ABAP Workbench. The ABAP Dictionary is integrated within the ABAP Workbench, so it can be maintained in ABAP Workbench.

7. Correct answer: **A**

   Enhancement definitions and implementations can be displayed in the Enhancement Information System.

8. Correct answers: **B, D**

   You can create a local object, but you have to assign the object to a package if you want to transport the object from one system to other. A package has to define a package interface and visibility to make its elements visible to other packages. The transport layer is not a mandatory input field for the package. The transport layer is assigned to the package if it is defined for the system. A package can be nested.

9. Correct answer: **A**

   The software component of the customer package should always be `HOME`.

10. Correct answers: **A, C, D**

    The repository object has to be assigned to the package to transport the object to another system within the system landscape. You cannot transport a local repository object. Repository objects and cross-client customization objects are assigned to a workbench request. Client-specific customization objects are assigned to the customization request and are not assigned to the package. Inactive objects can be transported.

11. Correct answers: **A, B**

    A local change request is created if the consolidation route is not defined; otherwise, a transportable change request is created if the consolidation route for the transport layer is defined.

12. Correct answer: **C**

    There are three modes of ABAP Editor: the new Front-End Editor, the old Front-End Editor, and the Back-End Editor.

Take Away

You should now understand the ABAP Workbench features and be able to navigate within it. You should be able to use the available browsers within the ABAP Workbench and complete your development in an efficient manner. You should know how to configure the ABAP workbench and the various development tools.

To be a successful developer you should know about all the available development tools and their uses. It is important to understand the features of the new ABAP Editor because it will be very helpful for your application development and will increase the productivity of your development team.

Finally, you should understand the package concept and the use of the Transport Organizer. You should understand the concept of the transport request and the different types of transport request and its use for the migration of development objects from the development environment to the production environment.

Refresher

Table 4.2 shows key concepts about the ABAP Workbench.

Key Concept	Definition
ABAP Workbench	The ABAP Workbench is an integrated development environment for the ABAP developer.
Repository Browser	The Repository Browser is a tool within the Object Navigator and is used by the developer to access the repository objects and workbench tools to create repository objects.
Repository Information System	The Repository Information System Browser is a search tool to search for repository objects.

Table 4.2 Key Concept Refresher

Key Concept	Definition
Enhancement Information System	The Enhancement Information System is a tool to search for Enhancement definitions and implementations in the SAP system.
Transport Organizer	The Transport Organizer is a tool to work with the change request and the objects within the change request. Using this tool, you can view the objects assigned to the change request and the transport log of the request.

Table 4.2 Key Concept Refresher (cont.)

Summary

In this chapter we have covered the ABAP Workbench and its use in detail. We have covered some of the most commonly used browsers such as the Repository Browser, Repository Information System, Enhancement Information System, and Transport Organizer. Furthermore, we have covered in detail the ABAP Workbench, the new ABAP Editor, and the concepts of package and transport request. This knowledge will allow you to easily pass this topic on the certification examination.

ABAP Debugger Program Usage

Techniques You'll Master:

- Examine the runtime behavior of ABAP programs using the ABAP Debugger
- Use the ABAP Debugger to systematically test ABAP programs
- Plan correctness of your ABAP programs
- Use watchpoints, breakpoints, assertions, and checkpoint groups effectively
- Understand the design differences between the two versions of the Debugger

A debugger is typically a major component of every development environment. During the development of applications, either simple or complex, the Debugger is a valuable tool in detecting and analyzing error situations. You need to be familiar with the functional scope of the ABAP Debugger, and this chapter covers the most important concepts of this very useful tool. It is a tool used during development, during testing, and when attempting to analyze problems in the production system.

We will cover the primary differences between the old "classic" Debugger that has existed since SAP R/3 and the new Debugger, first available in a limited form in version 6.40 and then completely in SAP NetWeaver 7.0. We will also cover a number of the tools available in the new Debugger and the user interface. Also covered will be customizing the Debugger to meet your needs and preferences, assertions, watchpoints, and breakpoints. Each of these topics will be covered separately and will be followed by the practice exercise and the solution to the exercise.

Real-World Scenario

A report currently in use in production does not produce correct results. This program was developed by a programmer who is no longer with the company, and there is no documentation.

Sometimes an error message is produced in production that cannot be reproduced in any of the other systems in the landscape, and no one is sure what is causing the message. You have been told to identify why the message is being produced and to correct the report.

After examining the program in the ABAP Editor, you are still unable to determine the cause of the problem. The report does a number of dynamic calls based on values read from database tables and performs some routines based on the user's authorization checks.

The solution to quickly identify what the program is doing is to use the ABAP Debugger in the production system. To identify where the error message is being produced, you create breakpoints on the statement `MESSAGE`. Once the message statement that is producing the unknown error is identified, the cause of the error can be easily deduced. It is also possible to examine variables to determine the actual flow of the program and then identify why the results are incorrect.

Objectives of this Portion of the Test

The purpose of this portion of the certification examination is to verify that you have detailed knowledge of the ABAP Debugger, which is a major component of the environment. By verifying that you have the appropriate knowledge to use the Debugger efficiently, you will become a more effective and efficient programmer.

This portion of the examination will test your knowledge of the Debugger. The points that you need to understand from this section include:

- Various ways to start the Debugger
- Breakpoints
- Watchpoints
- Assertions
- Viewing and modifying data objects
- Understanding the architecture of the Debugger

Key Concepts Refresher

The ABAP Debugger is part of the ABAP Workbench that you use either as an integrated testing tool or to identify issues with code execution. The Debugger allows you to execute ABAP programs, by line or by section. With this tool, you can display data objects and check the flow logic of programs. The running program is interrupted after each step, allowing you to check its processing logic and the results of individual statements.

You typically use the Debugger as a way of identifying errors in ABAP programs. It contains the following functions:

- Different ways of starting the Debugger
- Different views of contents of data objects
- Different execution options
- Displaying source code in the Debugger
- Setting and deleting breakpoints
- Setting and deleting watchpoints
- Setting and deleting database locks
- Stopping code execution at a particular statement or event

- Displaying and changing field contents at runtime
- Displaying objects and references
- Displaying and positioning strings
- Opening the code in the ABAP Editor or Object Navigator

New and Classic Debugger

Currently, you have access to two versions of the ABAP Debugger. The older version (commonly called the classic Debugger), which has existed since the beginning of SAP R/3, has always had the majority of the functions listed above. As the language has evolved, the Debugger has also evolved, for example, the inclusion of objects in both ABAP and the Debugger. Figure 5.1 shows the flow control area, and Figure 5.2 shows the variable display area of the classic Debugger.

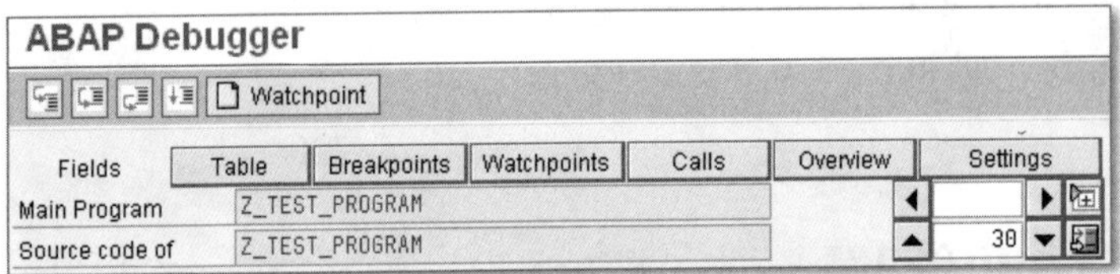

Figure 5.1 Standard Flow Control of the Classic Debugger

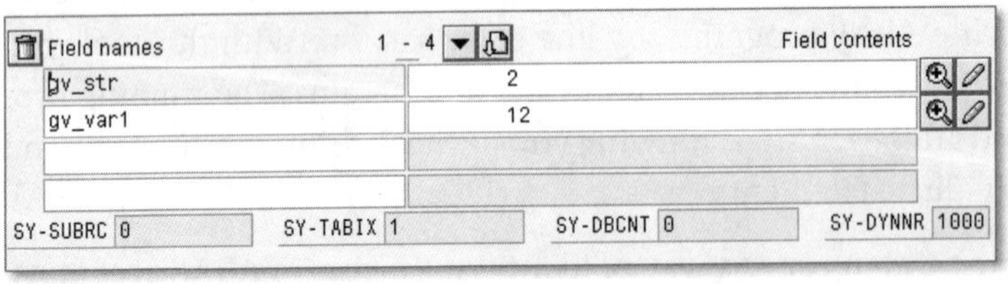

Figure 5.2 Variable Display of the Classic Debugger

The original Debugger has always had certain limitations: The layout is mostly fixed, and there were restrictions on the amount of data that could be displayed at one time. For example, a maximum of eight data objects could be displayed, and of those, only four at a time. Only one internal table could be displayed, and table scrolling, especially horizontally, was often tedious. Whereas it is possible to reorder columns, knowledge of the fields of the internal table was necessary to complete it. Other areas also required detailed knowledge of the executing code. There is no way, from within the Debugger, to look up within the repository a function module, method, or subroutine name to set a breakpoint.

This Debugger shared the same external mode roll area of the code being debugged. This external mode corresponds to the session window in which you are running the code. This restricted the amount of interaction the Debugger had with the repository or the system as a whole without impacting the code being debugged. Each of the Debugger's actions could influence the program flow of the application and was limited as a result.

Also with the classic Debugger, it is generally not possible to analyze programs in debugging mode that run in an ABAP processor unit and are called recursively from a subordinate unit. For example, a conversion exit cannot be analyzed using this Debugger if it runs within a `WRITE` statement. A conversion exit executes whenever is sent to the presentation or retrieved from the presentation layer. If called from a `WRITE` statement, the Debugger is called recursively from within itself.

Starting with SAP NetWeaver 6.40, SAP released a new version of the Debugger. The Debugger available in Release 6.40 was not considered complete (and was not the default debugger as a result); it did eliminate the above restrictions.

The reason for this is that the new Debugger executes in its own external mode. This allows the code to be analyzed to run with virtually no impact from the Debugger. This separation of functionality allows for much greater interaction with the system, allowing search help use, the display of more than one internal table simultaneously, and an unlimited number of data objects.

The Debugger specified as the default starts when needed. You can change the default, in either the ABAP Editor (Transaction SE38) or the Object Navigator (Transaction SE80), by following the menu path Utilities • Settings • ABAP Editor • Debugging. Figure 5.3 and Figure 5.4 show the menu and resulting dialog box. Both Debuggers are started in exactly the same way.

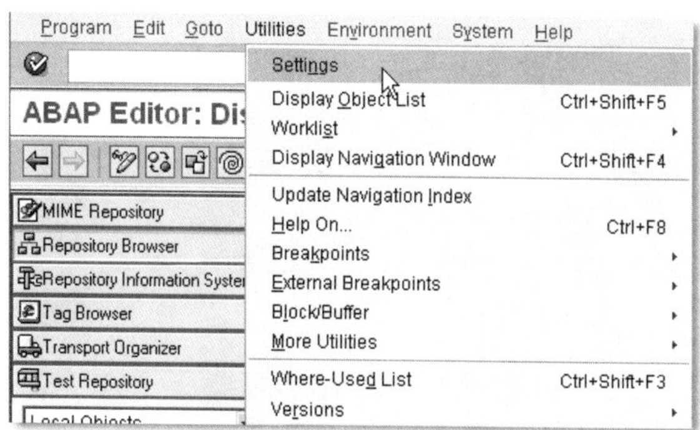

Figure 5.3 Menu Path To Set the Default Debugger

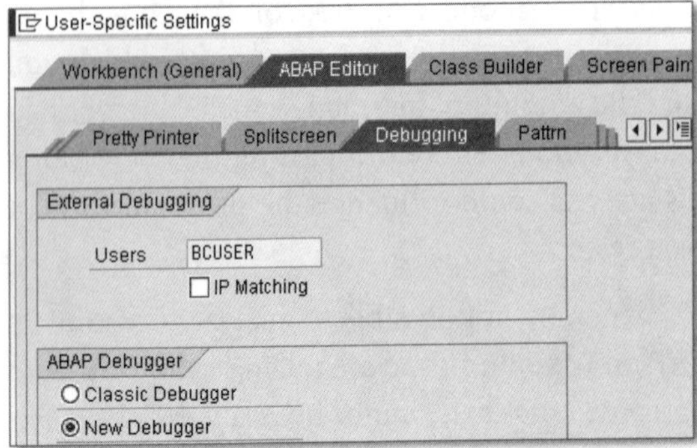

Figure 5.4 Dialog to Set the Default Debugger

Note

Primary methods of starting the Debugger:

1. In the navigation area, select the menu path Execute N Debugging for the selected program. This is shown in Figure 5.5.
2. In the editing area, select the desired program line and select Set/Delete Breakpoint. Then start the program by selecting (Execute) Direct Processing or [F8].
3. Select System • Utilities • Debug ABAP or System • Utilities • Debug Screen.
4. Enter "/h" in the command field in the standard toolbar and press [↵] or use a shortcut to provide the command to the session.

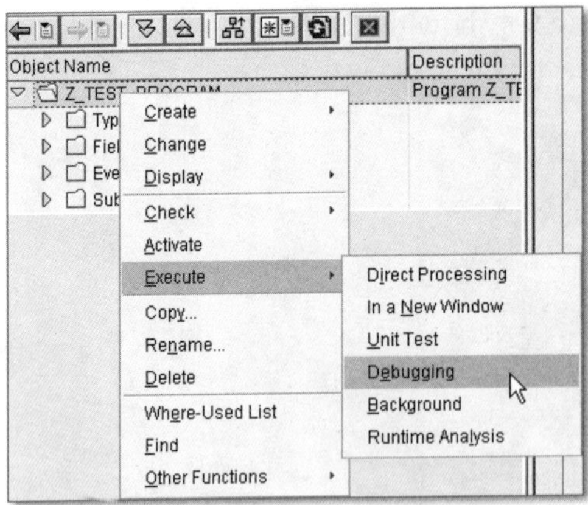

Figure 5.5 Navigation Start of the Debugger

However, each time the new Debugger is started, a new mode is started automatically. You have a maximum of six external modes available as a default, though your system may be configured differently. If no further external mode is available when the new Debugger is started, the message "No additional external mode for new ABAP debugger available" is displayed, the new Debugger start is cancelled, and the classic Debugger is started in its place. In this case, you should close modes that are no longer required.

In the new Debugger, control can be passed from the application to the new Debugger at any time using the function code /h, even if the Debugger was already started.

You can exit the new Debugger with one of several methods:

- If the Debugger is ready for input (active) and the application is waiting, you can select DEBUGGER • EXIT DEBUGGER, which closes just the Debugger, and the application continues to run.
- You can select DEBUGGER • EXIT APPLICATION AND DEBUGGER, which closes both the Debugger and the application.
- The third option is if the application is ready for input and the Debugger is waiting, in which case you can enter "/hx" in the command field and press [↵], which closes just the Debugger and allows the application to continue to run.

It is possible to switch between the classic Debugger and the new Debugger by selecting DEBUGGER • SWITCH TO NEW ABAP DEBUGGER or DEBUGGER • SWITCH TO CLASSIC ABAP DEBUGGER. You must be aware, however, if you switch from the new Debugger to the classic Debugger when the ABAP code is called from the kernel of the application server (primarily conversion and field exits), that the runtime error `RPERF_ILLEGAL_STATEMENT` will be triggered as a result of the recursive call.

You will find the functions for analyzing source code similar between versions of the Debugger. It is possible to navigate from the variable overview to the detailed view of the data object simply by double-clicking. The difference with the new Debugger is simply that you can process an unlimited number of data objects simultaneously, and the number visible at a single time depends on the size of the window and the font size. You also need to double-click on the CHANGE icon (the pencil icon) to open up the data object for change and then press [↵] to confirm the change, unlike the classic Debugger, where the field was always open and you needed to click on the CHANGE icon to accept the change.

New Debugger Tools and UI

As soon as you start the new Debugger, using one of the methods shown in the previous note (from a menu, with a breakpoint, or the command "/h"), you will see the message "Session "x" connected to Debugger" in the status line of the application. "x" is the number of the current external mode. When the Debugger starts, you will see the window title (x) – ABAP DEBUGGER CONTROLS SESSION X (EXCLUSIVE), where again "x" is the external mode of the application. This provides a visible link between application and Debugger mode at all times. If it is not possible to achieve an exclusive mode, the title will be (x) – ABAP DEBUGGER CONTROLS SESSION X (NOT EXCLUSIVE).

If the Debugger obtains an exclusive mode, it means that the application to be analyzed exclusively occupies a work process of the application server during debugging. If all exclusive debug work processes are occupied, the Debugger is switched to non-exclusive mode. In this state, you can attempt to occupy a work process exclusively by selecting DEBUGGER • EXCLUSIVE DEBUGGING MODE ON (shown in Figure 5.6). However, this is only possible if another exclusive debug work process has become available in the meantime.

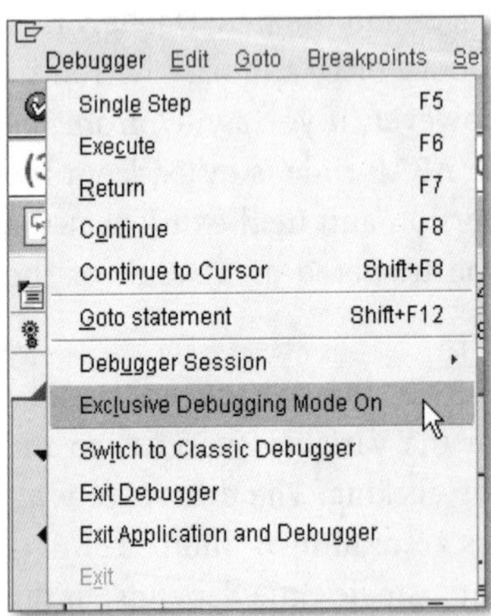

Figure 5.6 Menu to Turn Exclusive Mode On

Tip

The difference between exclusive and non-exclusive modes is that you will find the Debugger function limited in non-exclusive mode. The limitations are mostly due to the fact that a roll-out is forced in the application after each Debugger view while in non-exclusive mode. Therefore, a database commit must be executed. This has the following consequences:

- It is not possible for you to debug between the statements `SELECT` and `ENDSELECT` because the database cursor needs to be closed using a commit. In this case, program execution is terminated.
- Debugging mode is not possible for conversion or field exits.
- Owing to the commit, inconsistent datasets can occur in the database.

Because inconsistent datasets in the database are possible, the non-exclusive mode is impossible in productive systems. If the number of exclusive debugging work processes is occupied, the runtime error `DEBUGGING_NOT_POSSIBLE` is triggered whenever you attempt to start another Debugger.

The number of work processes that are available exclusively for debugging is defined by the profile parameter `rdisp/wpdbug_max_no`. In development systems, this should be approximately half the number of dialog work processes.

The special requirements demanded of debugging in a production client are the same for the new and the classic Debugger. Therefore, they are processed exactly the same as in the classic Debugger.

You will find 11 work areas or desktops when the new Debugger starts. This is an increase from the previous version in SAP NetWeaver 6.40 because not all of the tools were complete. You can customize the first three desktops so that they will start with the Debugger to satisfy your own preferences and eight "predefined" desktops. You can modify each of these desktops at any time.

Each desktop can hold from one to four tools. The tools displayed on a desktop can be the same or different based on your needs at the time. You can change the size or location of any of these tools while in the Debugger. For example, for tools placed horizontally, the right or left tool can be either made wider or narrower. You can make tools with a vertical alignment longer or shorter. Tools can be swapped vertically, horizontally, or diagonally. You can replace any tool with any other by simply clicking on the REPLACE button. An individual tool can be maximized to fill the entire desktop. You can undo any layout change with the BACK button (or F3).

At this time you can create 15 tools. The tools are grouped into three categories: STANDARD TOOLS, DATA OBJECTS, and SPECIAL TOOLS (see Figure 5.7).

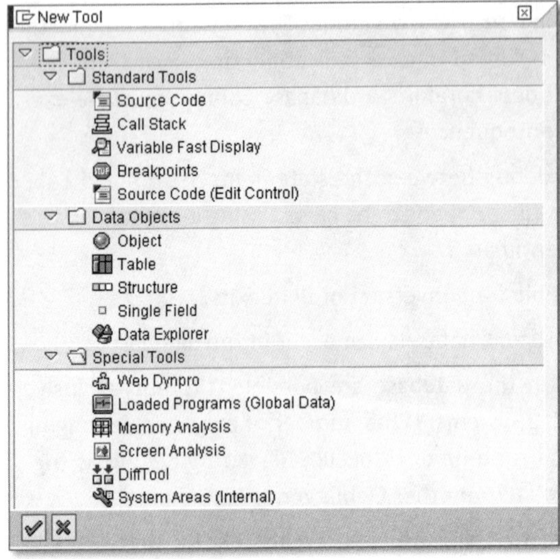

Figure 5.7 New Tool Dialog

You will see differences between the two source code displays. The SOURCE CODE shows the code as with the "old front-end editor." The SOURCE CODE (EDIT CONTROL) uses the "new front-end editor," which displays additional formatting and provides information regarding data objects when you hover over the name with the mouse.

Table 5.1 shows where the tools can be found in the new Debugger when started before modification; Figure 5.8 and Figure 5.9 show the desktops.

Tool	Initially Found on Desktop
Source Code	(Not initially found on a desktop)
Call Stack	Desktop 2 and Standard
Variable Fast Display	Desktop 1 and Standard
Breakpoints	Break./Watchpoints
Source Code (Edit Control)	Desktop 1, Desktop 2, Desktop 3, and Standard

Table 5.1 Debugger Tools

Tool	Initially Found on Desktop
Object	Objects
Table	Tables
Structure	Structures
Single Field	Detail Displs
Data Explorer	Data Explorer
Web Dynpro	Desktop 3
Loaded Programs (Global Data)	(Not initially found on a desktop)
Memory Analysis	(Not initially found on a desktop)
Screen Analysis	(Not initially found on a desktop)
Diff Tool	Diff
System Areas (Internal)	(Not initially found on a desktop)

Table 5.1 Debugger Tools (cont.)

Figure 5.8 First Six Desktops

Figure 5.9 Last Five Desktops

Most of the tools also provide additional services. You will always be able to access the tool services by clicking on the SERVICES OF THE TOOL button as shown in the Figure 5.10 or through the context menu of the tool.

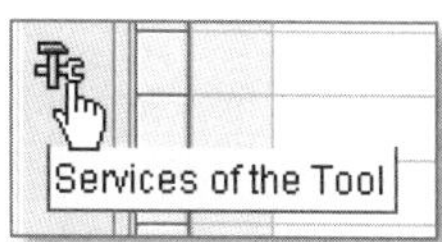

Figure 5.10 Services of the Tool

The services provided vary depending on the tool. For example, the SOURCE CODE tool only allows you to navigate to the currently executing line or to open the editor. Most provide the ability to save the contents of the tool to a local file or to search. The Variable Fast Display provides options for sorting the local or global data objects or saving the data as test data in Transaction SE37, whereas the internal table services provide the ability to append, insert, or delete rows in the table. You have the option to change the sequence of the fields through the service or just drag them as you would in an ALV (the ABAP List Viewer or, as it has been renamed, the SAP List Viewer is discussed in Chapter 15, ALV Grid Control) or table control.

All of the tools except the standard tools provide a history of all objects displayed in the tool, and any prior one can be retrieved simply by selecting it from the list.

The table tool has many more capabilities than the classic Debugger provided. Whereas you could handle standard internal tables through the use of the CHANGE, INSERT, APPEND, and DELETE buttons below the table display, keyed tables (sorted or hashed) were more restricted. With those you only had access to the CHANGE and DELETE buttons to modify the contents of non-key fields or to remove the record. The new Debugger offers many more options (see Figure 5.11 and Figure 5.12).

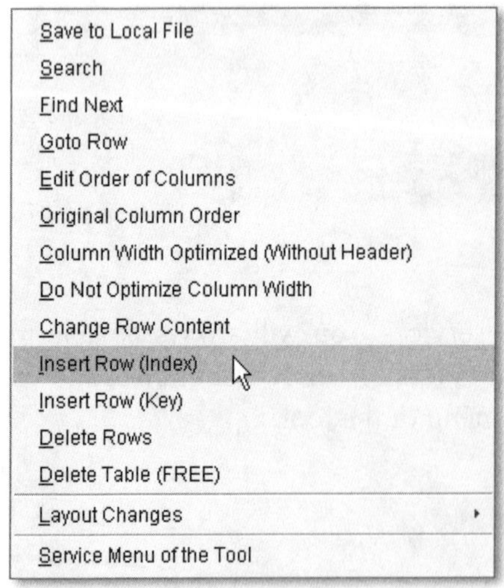

Figure 5.11 Context Menu of the Table Tool

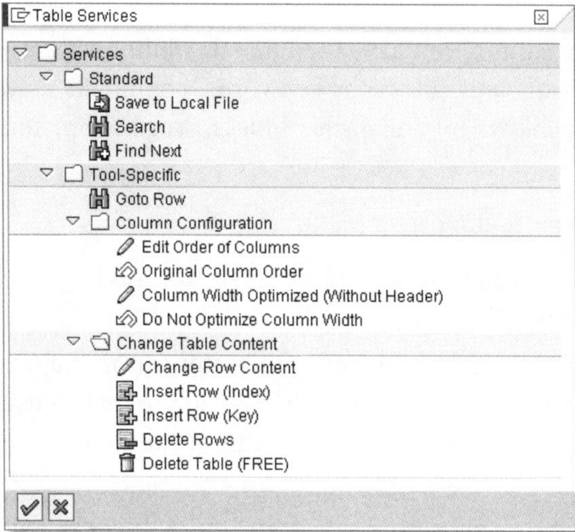

Figure 5.12 Table Service Menu

You have multiple ways of modifying the internal table through either the context menu (right mouse-click while over a row containing data) or the service menu of the tool. The same options exist for a standard internal table, whereas a hashed internal table does not allow you to insert using an index. If you use the INSERT ROW (KEY) option, regardless of where you attempt to insert the record for sorted or hashed internal tables, the row will be inserted in the correct location.

The dialog presented (shown in Figure 5.13) allows you to copy the contents of an existing row to use a template. The new row is indicated without a numerical line number (there is an icon in its place) until you press the [↵] key to accept the row into the internal table.

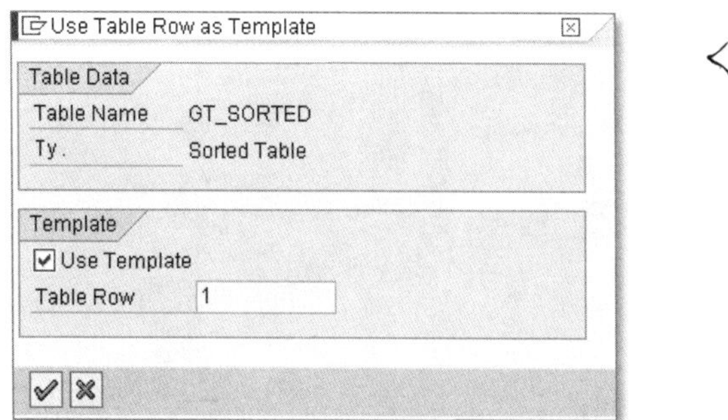

Figure 5.13 Insert Using Key

Using SOURCE CODE (EDIT CONTROL) provides several advantages over the older SOURCE CODE. First, as in the new editor, you have the same flexibility with settings. You can define different fonts and colors for keywords, comments, and other types of items. The display allows for collapsible blocks, word wrap, and other visual feedback.

Figure 5.14 shows several of the more important features:

- The arrow heads in the top-left corner, as with all tools, allows you to resize the tool to different widths or heights.
- On the right side of the tool, the third, fourth, and fifth buttons from the top allow you to maximize the tool to fill the desktop, maximize the tool to use the entire height of the desktop, and maximize the width of the tool to the entire desktop.
- The status bar at the bottom of the tool shows the scope of the line selected, in this case within a function and within an `IF`.
- The closest scope to the cursor, in this case, the `IF` keywords, are also made bold.
- The status bar also shows the line and column of the cursor, and double-clicking on this box produces the go to line dialog box.
- The line to be executed is indicated with a yellow arrow, and hovering over variables with the mouse produces quick information (tooltip) showing the variable name, value, and type.

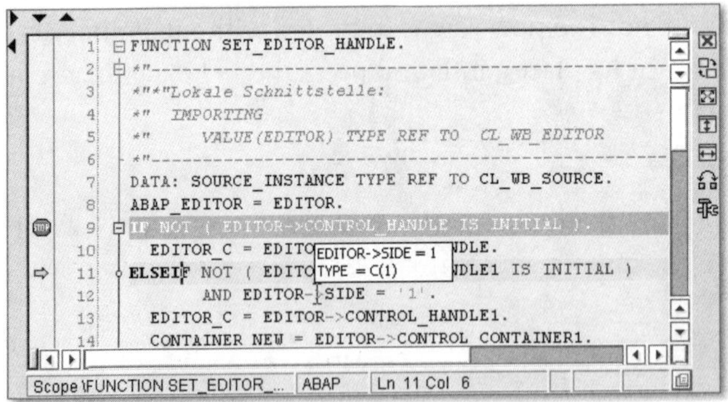

Figure 5.14 Source Code (Edit Control) Tool

You can now instruct a breakpoint to skip a number of occurrences before stopping. You simply enter the number of skips in the skip column (any positive number between 0 and 4,294,967,296 [2^{32}] can be used) to prevent the breakpoint from stopping. You can change a breakpoint to active or inactive or delete the breakpoint. In addition, you can edit conditional and unconditional checkpoints using the Breakpoint tool. You first set conditional checkpoints in the source code using the `ASSERT` statement; unconditional checkpoints are set using the `BREAK-POINT` statement. These have the effect that programs will be continued only if a preset condition is fulfilled. These checkpoints can be searched for, activated, or deactivated.

As with a breakpoint, watchpoints are places in the program that instruct the ABAP runtime processor to interrupt the program execution at a particular point. In contrast to breakpoints, however, watchpoints do not activate debugging mode until the contents of a specified field change. You can define watchpoints only within the Debugger (shown in Figure 5.15).

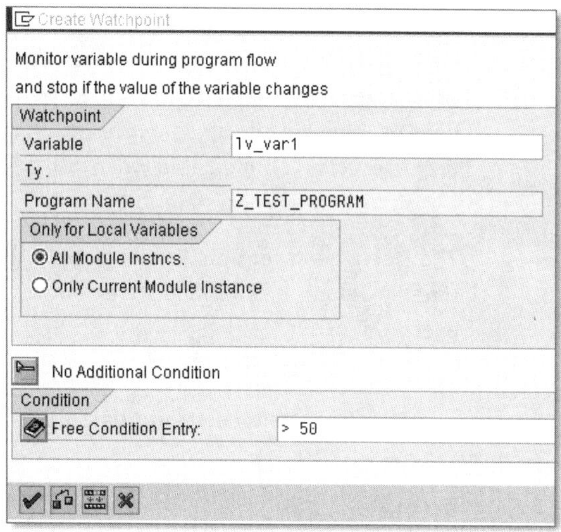

Figure 5.15 Creating a Conditional Watchpoint

Watchpoints, like breakpoints, are user specific and do not affect other users running the same program. Unlike the classic Debugger, which has a limit of 10 watchpoints, there is no limit on the number of watchpoints at one time in the new Debugger. If you set a watchpoint for a field without specifying a relational operator or comparison value, program execution continues until the contents of the field change. If you specify a relational operator and comparison value when you define a watchpoint, program execution continues until the specified condition is met. You can use watchpoints to display changes to references of strings, data, or objects, as well as internal tables.

The ABAP Debugger differentiates between the breakpoint variants shown in Table 5.2.

Type of Breakpoint	Behavior
Static breakpoints	Keyword `BREAK-POINT` inserts a user-independent breakpoint as an ABAP statement in the source text. Related is the statement `BREAK <user_name>`, which sets a user-dependent breakpoint in the source text.
Directly set dynamic breakpoints	These are set in the ABAP Editor or the Debugger (by either double-clicking before the line number if you are using the older source code display or single-clicking before the line number if you are using the newer source code with edit control). Dynamic breakpoints are always user specific and are deleted when you log off from the SAP system.
Breakpoints for statements, subroutines, function modules, or methods	The Debugger interrupts the program directly before the specified statement is executed.
Breakpoints for exceptions and system exceptions	The Debugger interrupts the program directly after a runtime error is raised.

Table 5.2 Types of Breakpoints

Assertions and Breakpoints

Checkpoints define places in a program where the program state can be tested during execution. A `BREAK-POINT` statement represents an unconditional checkpoint. In this case, the program execution is unconditionally interrupted at this point in the program, and the Debugger is started.

Assertions are another form of checkpoint, which you use to implement conditional checkpoints within your program. An assertion checks whether a defined condition is satisfied. An assertion is defined by an `ASSERT` statement as a conditional checkpoint.

Assertions and `BREAK-POINT` statements are either always active or can be activated by assigning them to a checkpoint group (shown in Figure 5.16).

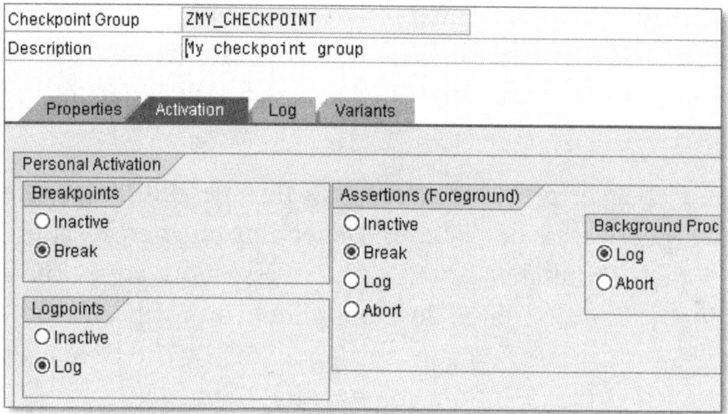

Figure 5.16 Checkpoint Group

When the program reaches an active assertion, it evaluates the corresponding condition or logical expression. If no checkpoint group is assigned to a failed assertion, the default behavior is for a runtime error to be produced. If the condition is violated, the program terminates with a runtime error, accesses the ABAP Debugger, or creates a log entry; otherwise, the program continues with the next statement. If you assign the assertion to a checkpoint group, the program behavior is controlled by the corresponding activation settings of the checkpoint group.

You can also edit the conditional and unconditional checkpoints using the Breakpoint tool in the Debugger as shown in Figure 5.17.

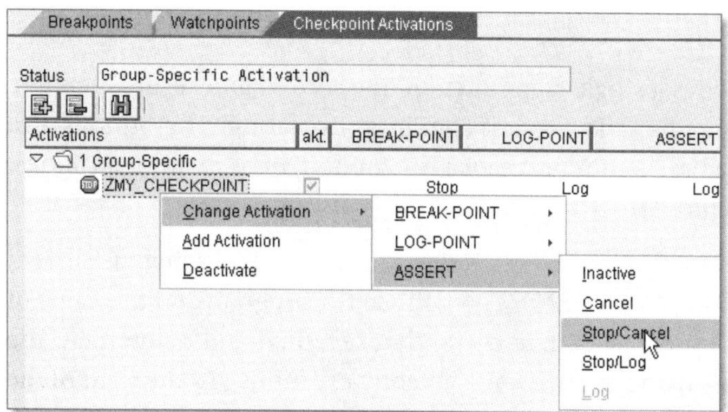

Figure 5.17 Changing the Activation in the Debugger

New Debugger Customization and Settings

One of the main benefits of the Debugger interface redesign is to have the option of making it configurable for your use. This provides you with the option of being able to set the views and their sizes as required. You also have the ability to group certain views together and have them available at each restart of the new Debugger.

In its current form, the Debugger provides you with a flexible and designable interface with a total of 11 work areas or desktops. Depending on your selection, you can have up to four tools simultaneously in each of these work areas. Their sizes can be set individually. The first three desktops allow you to specify individual settings using the SAVE LAYOUT function (see Figure 5.18). The Debugger will use your last saved settings the next time you start the Debugger.

Figure 5.18 Save Layout Button

When you start the Debugger, below the title bar in the application tool bar you will find the standard flow control buttons (see Figure 5.19). These flow control buttons remain unchanged from the classic version of the Debugger.

Figure 5.19 Flow buttons

The first button provides a single-step function, the second an execute function, the third a return function, and the last continues execution. The buttons also provide a way to set a breakpoint or create a watchpoint, or as mentioned above, save the layout configuration.

Below the application toolbar you will find the information regarding the current code being executed (see Figure 5.20). You will see the program and the name of the Include or program of the source currently executing, and below that, the program event and the name of the event currently executing. To the right of the Include or program name is the current line that will execute. The button directly below this line number positions the screen to show this line in the source code tool. The blue I button displays the program attributes of the source code. The buttons displayed before the program name or event, if clicked, open a new window with the source code displayed. The same button is available when viewing the ABAP call stack tool for each call. Again, clicking on the button opens the source code at that point in the program.

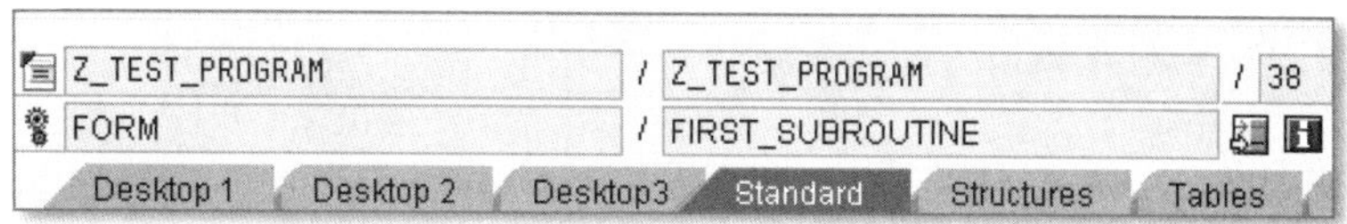

Figure 5.20 Program Information

To the right of the program information you will find two system variables and their contents displayed. The default is `SY-SUBRC` (the system variable containing the statement return code) and `SY-TABIX` (the system variable containing the internal table row last accessed), but you can override either or both simply by typing over their names.

Most of the screen is used to display the desktops or tool area. Unlike the classic Debugger, the larger your screen or the higher your screen resolution, the more data can be displayed.

The Variable Fast Display tool currently has four tabs (see Figure 5.21). The first two are provided empty, and you can either type or double click a name in the source code to add it to the list. The third tab (LOCALS) shows all local variables for the current program modularization unit, and the fourth (GLOBALS) shows all global variables in the current program.

Variables 1 | Variables 2 | Locals | Globals

St...	Variable	Va...	Val.
	GT_STANDARD		Standard Table[5x3(36)
	GT_SORTED		Sorted Table[5x3(36)]
	GT_HASHED		Hashed Table[6x3(36)]

Figure 5.21 Variable Fast Display

The Variable Fast Display on the first two tabs also provides a button to select two objects displayed and do a comparison. Alternatively, you can navigate to the DIFFERENCE tab and specify the variables directly (see Figure 5.22 for the Diff tool).

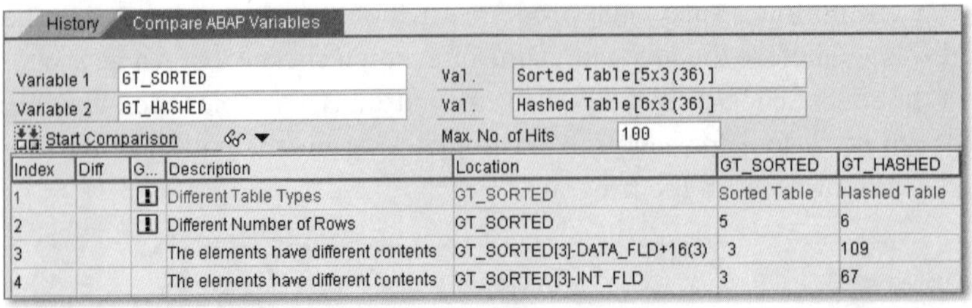

History | Compare ABAP Variables

Variable 1 GT_SORTED Val. Sorted Table[5x3(36)]
Variable 2 GT_HASHED Val. Hashed Table[6x3(36)]
Start Comparison Max. No. of Hits 100

Index	Diff	G...	Description	Location	GT_SORTED	GT_HASHED
1		!	Different Table Types	GT_SORTED	Sorted Table	Hashed Table
2		!	Different Number of Rows	GT_SORTED	5	6
3			The elements have different contents	GT_SORTED[3]-DATA_FLD+16(3)	3	109
4			The elements have different contents	GT_SORTED[3]-INT_FLD	3	67

Figure 5.22 Diff Tool

Finally, it is possible to change how secondary tools, for example, the editor, are opened: either in a new parallel window or in the current window. It is also possible to customize the behavior of the navigation to Detail Views and where the variable will be displayed when clicked on from the source code tool.

Important Terminology

You will need to understand the difference between a breakpoint and a watchpoint for effective use of the Debugger. Remember that a breakpoint relates to the actual code, either a statement or point within the code, whereas a watchpoint is related to the value of a data object. It is also important to understand how checkpoint groups can modify the behavior of breakpoints.

Another possible cause of confusion is the difference between an external mode and an exclusive mode. Remember that an external mode describes the number of sessions opened within a login session, whereas an exclusive mode is what keeps the Debugger in one work process within the server. Remember that a non-exclusive mode will be rolled out between steps in the Debugger and may switch work processes.

Practice Questions

The practice questions below will help you evaluate your understanding of the topic. The questions shown are similar in nature to those found on the certification examination, but although none of these questions will be on the exam itself, they allow you to review your knowledge of the subject. Select the correct answers and then check the completeness of your answers in the following solu-

tion section. Remember that you must select all correct answers and only correct answers to receive credit for the question.

1. The Debugger displays a maximum of eight data objects at one time.

☑ **A.** True

☐ **B.** False

2. A watchpoint stops program execution every time the condition specified is met.

☐ **A.** True

☑ **B.** False

3. Both the classical Debugger and the new Debugger can be used on all ABAP code without restriction.

☐ **A.** True

☑ **B.** False

4. Under which circumstances will the classical Debugger start as the Debugger? (Select all that apply.)

☐ **A.** None. The new Debugger will always start as the Debugger.

☑ **B.** When five modes already exist for this logon session.

☐ **C.** When the number of debugging sessions exceeds half the number of dialog sessions.

☑ **D.** When you specify the default as the classical Debugger in the settings of the Object Navigator.

☐ **E.** If you manually switched to the classical Debugger during your last session.

5. A non-exclusive debugging mode means? (Select all that apply.)

☑ **A.** A roll-out is forced in the application after each Debugger view.

☐ **B.** Someone else is debugging the same source code.

☑ **C.** Debugging is not possible between the statements `SELECT` and `ENDSELECT` because the database cursor needs to be closed using a `COMMIT`.

- [x] **D.** Debugging is not possible for conversion or field exits.
- [x] **E.** Owing to the commit, inconsistent datasets can occur in the database.
- [ ] **F.** It may be used anywhere in the landscape.

6. What is the maximum number of watchpoints that can exist at one time?

- [ ] **A.** 8
- [x] **B.** 10
- [ ] **C.** 16
- [ ] **D.** No limit

7. Setting breakpoints for a method or function module within the Debugger allows the use of F4 (value help) to find the correct name.

- [ ] **A.** True
- [ ] **B.** False

8. All breakpoints are valid for the entire Debugger session, and all can be changed by the Debugger.

- [x] **A.** True
- [ ] **B.** False

9. It is possible to make multiple changes to data objects at the same time in the Debugger.

- [x] **A.** True
- [ ] **B.** False

10. When starting the Debugger, what circumstance causes the runtime error `DEBUGGING_NOT_POSSIBLE`?

- [ ] **A.** Starting a non-exclusive mode in a productive system.
- [ ] **B.** When more than five sessions are already associated with this login user.
- [ ] **C.** When the number of debugging sessions on the server exceeds the value defined by the profile parameter `rdisp/wpdbug_max_no`.

11. There are ___ work areas available in the Debugger.

- ☐ **A.** 7
- ☐ **B.** 9
- ☐ **C.** 11
- ☐ **D.** 15

12. What button undoes layout changes to the Debugger? (Fill in the blank.)

____

Practice Question Answers and Explanations

1. Correct answer: **A**

   The classic Debugger only allowed a maximum of eight data objects. The new Debugger allows an unlimited number (restricted only by font and window size) to be displayed at the same time.

   If you encounter a question discussing an ability or limitation of the classic Debugger, you should assume that the question refers to the classic Debugger and answer accordingly. If the question references the new Debugger, the answer would be false.

2. Correct answer: **B**

   Whereas it is true that if a condition is specified, the watchpoint will not stop until the condition is true, the watchpoint will not be triggered until the variable contents change. Therefore if you set a watchpoint that is already true, the watchpoint will not be triggered.

3. Correct answer: **B**

   The classic Debugger cannot analyze conversion exits or field exits. It also has side effects with search help (F1), value help (F4), and list output.

4. Correct answers: **B, D**

   When you already have five external modes in use (or more accurately when you only have one external mode remaining), the classic Debugger is automatically started when starting another external mode would prevent further sessions from being created. If you have the default Debugger specified as the classic, it will always start with this version.

5. Correct answers: **A, C, D, E**

   A non-exclusive mode means the session is not locked into a work process and will be rolled out and rolled in between steps. The roll-out forces a COMMIT WORK between steps, which means the database cursor will be lost, causing a short dump if it occurs between a SELECT and ENDSELECT. Because database commits occur without regard to logical units of work, the database may become inconsistent. The Debugger prevents this inconsistency in a production environment.

6. Correct answer: **B**

   Only 10 watchpoints can exist at one time with the classic Debugger. The new Debugger has no limit.

   If you encounter a question discussing an ability or limitation of the classic Debugger, you should assume that the question refers to the classic Debugger and answer accordingly. If the question references the new Debugger the answer would be option D.

7. Correct answer: **A**

   With the new Debugger executing in a separate mode, it has access to search helps that may be used for setting breakpoints.

   If you encounter a question discussing the absence of an ability of the classic Debugger, you should assume that the question refers to the new Debugger and answer accordingly.

8. Correct answer: **A**

   Breakpoints set in the editor can be changed in the Debugger. Local breakpoints can be converted to either session or external breakpoints.

9. Correct answer: **A**

   If you open up multiple data objects for change, the [↵] key will accept all changes to all objects.

10. Correct answer: **A**

    If you attempt to start the Debugger on a production system and an exclusive mode is not available, the system will produce the runtime error DEBUGGING_NOT_POSSIBLE. On a non-productive system you would receive the indication of a non-exclusive mode in the title, but owing to the potential for inconsistent data, this mode is not allowed on production systems.

11. Correct answer: **C**

    There are 11 desktop areas currently available for use.

12. Correct answer: **Back**

    The BACK button undoes the layout changes you have made to each desktop. Using the BACK button multiple times will undo each layout change.

Take Away

You should now be able to examine the runtime behavior of ABAP programs using the ABAP Debugger. By examining data objects within the Debugger, it is possible to determine why a program behaves correctly or incorrectly. If you determine the cause of a problem in the program, it is easier to provide a correction or a solution to the issue.

If you design programs with an eye to identifying issues during testing through the use of assertions and checkpoint groups, your programs will be easier to maintain and produce fewer issues once they are in production.

Refresher

You must understand watchpoints and breakpoints — both their use and how to define them. You need to understand how to define and use assertions and checkpoint groups in your program.

The final thing you should take away from this unit is the differences between the classical Debugger and the new Debugger. You should understand the architecture of each, what limitations exist, and why the limitations exist. It is also important to understand the tools and what options exist within the different tools.

Table 5.3 shows the key concepts of the Debugger.

Key Concept	Definition
Architecture of the Debugger	The classic Debugger shared the same external mode roll area as the executing program, whereas the new Debugger runs in its own external mode.
Desktops and their tools	The desktops in the Debugger and how the various tools function in the Debugger.

Table 5.3 Key Concepts Refresher

Key Concept	Definition
Checkpoint groups	Used to define and use assertions and checkpoint groups and their behavior during program execution.
Breakpoints	Used to define various types of breakpoints.
Watchpoints	Used to define a watchpoint.

Table 5.3 Key Concepts Refresher (cont.)

Tips

As you take the examination, read the questions carefully. If a question or answers are valid for only one of the two Debuggers, you should answer the question assuming that the question refers to that Debugger. The majority of the questions can be answered for either Debugger because both contain very similar functionality. If the question specifies a specific Debugger, answer the question as it pertains to that specific Debugger.

As with the majority of the subjects in the certification examination, it is important to have as much practical experience with the subject as possible. Unlike the majority of subjects in the certification examination, you typically will learn more using the Debugger than just reading about it.

Summary

You should now be able to examine the runtime behavior of an ABAP program using the ABAP Debugger to identify issues with the program and to systematically test the program. You should be able to identify and create watchpoints and breakpoints and know the various types of breakpoints. Lastly, you should understand the differences between the two versions of the Debugger. These abilities will enable you to pass this section in the certification exam easily.

ABAP Types and Data Objects

Techniques You'll Master:

- Describe ABAP data types and data objects
- Define data objects using predefined and generic data types
- Understand the local data types
- Understand the global data types
- Understand the visibility of data objects
- Understand flat structures and deep structures and differentiate between the two

Data types are required to define the technical attribute of a data object. Depending on the data type, you might have to define the length and number of decimal places to fully define a data object in the program. You can use predefined or ABAP Dictionary data types to define a data object. You can also define local data types with the program and use them to define data objects in the program. Data objects are temporary storage in the program and occupy memory; they exist for the duration of the program.

In this chapter you will learn about data types and data objects and the difference between them. You will learn about elementary data types, local data types, and global data types. You will learn how to define data types and data objects and use them in the program. Finally, you will learn about the visibility of the data objects within ABAP programs.

Real-World Scenario

You have started on a new project and have to develop an application for the project. To develop an application you have to understand the data types and data objects available within the ABAP programming language and which ones to use in the application because to process data such as reading from a database table or sequential file and displaying them on the screen, you must read and store the data temporarily in a data object.

Data objects contain data with which programs work at runtime, and they exist for the duration of the program. To define a data object you require a data type, which can be a local or global data type. So to write any application in a system, you need the definition of a data type and object to read and process the data in the application.

You need to know the predefined and generic data types you can use and the valid operations on the various data types, as well as the difference between local and global data types. You also need to know the syntax for data declarations and their usage in the program in order to write robust applications.

Objectives of this Portion of the Test

The objective of this portion of the ABAP certification is to test your knowledge about the basic understanding of the ABAP data types and data objects in the ABAP programming language. The certification exam expects a good understanding of the following from the application developer:

- Concept of data types and data objects
- Predefined and generic data types
- Valid operations on the various data objects and their usage in programs
- Concept of local data types and the global data types
- Structure declarations and the differences between flat, nested, and deep structures

Key Concepts Refresher

Programming languages require variables or fields to store data locally in the program. A data object is also referred to as variable and is the temporary internal storage within the application. The type of operation that can be performed on the variable or data object depends on its data type. The ABAP language has predefined and generic data types, and the syntax for the data declaration for the data objects is dependent on the data types you use.

Like any programming language the data declarations within the ABAP program can be local or global. The scope and the validity of the data object depend on the definition of the data object within the program. Therefore, you should have a good understanding of the following to write a robust business application:

- Differentiate between the predefined and generic data types and their usage within the program
- Syntax of the data declaration
- Describe the valid operations of the data objects

ABAP Types and Data Objects

Programs in any programming language work with local data, and this data is stored in the program variables. Variables have names and type attributes, which can be numeric, character, or string depending on the data type supported by the language.

In the ABAP language the variable is called a *data object* and it is defined concretely by a data type. Data objects are always defined with the `DATA` keyword. You can use ABAP type, local type, and global type to type data objects.

Data Types

The data type is just a description and does not occupy memory; it can be defined in the program independently. You can define your own data type based on the predefined data types or global data types. Local data types are defined in the program, whereas global data types are defined in the ABAP Dictionary. Local data types are defined using the `TYPES` statement, whereas global data types are defined in the ABAP Dictionary using data elements, type pools or type groups, table types, structures, and tables. ABAP Dictionary objects such as tables and structures and their components can also be used to define data types. Local data types are available to the program in which they are declared, whereas the global data types are available to all programs in the SAP system.

- Data types are used for the definition of data objects. They define the technical attributes of the data objects, how the data object is stored in memory, and what operations are possible on the data object based on the data type.
- Data types are also used for the definition of interface parameters. The type of the interface parameter determines the type of the actual parameters or values that are transferred when a modular unit is called. The modular unit can be a subroutine, function module, or method.
- They can also be used for the definition of the input/output fields in the ABAP program. They are used to declare `PARAMETERS` and `SELECT-OPTIONS` for program selection screens and dynpro screen fields created in the Screen Painter. For details regarding `PARAMETERS` and `SELECT-OPTIONS` refer to Chapter 13, Selection Screens, and for dynpro screen refer to Chapter 12, Classical Screens.

The ABAP data types can be classified into predefined or standard ABAP types and local and global data types (see Figure 6.1). These data types are discussed in detail in the subsequent sections.

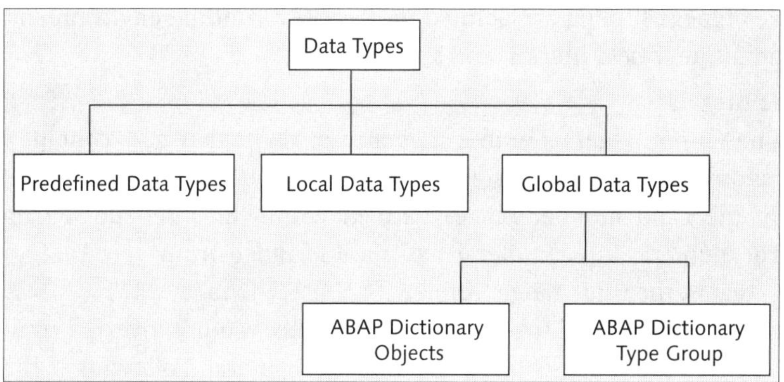

Figure 6.1 ABAP Data Types

Data Objects

Data objects are temporary storage in the program and occupy memory to store data. Data objects contain data for the program, and they exist for the duration of the program. The technical attributes of a data object are its length, number of decimal places, and the data type, if it is defined using the elementary data type. For the data objects defined with reference to the ABAP Dictionary object, the technical attributes such as length, number of decimals, and data type are derived from the ABAP Dictionary object.

ABAP programs work with the contents of the data objects and interpret them according to their data type. You declare the data objects statically in the ABAP program or dynamically at runtime. You can create the data object dynamically when you call the procedure with a parameter, such as when you call from routine with parameters in the program. The program treats literals like data objects, but literals are data objects with a fixed value.

Data objects can be declared with the predefined data types, local data types, or global data types. Data objects are defined in the program by using the `DATA` statement and can be assigned a starting value with the `VALUE` statement. ABAP contains the following types of data objects:

- **Literals**
  Literals are unnamed data objects with fixed values and are created in the source code of the program. The literal value cannot be changed, and they have fixed attributes such the data type and length and number of decimal

places. Three types of literal are defined in the ABAP runtime environment: numeric literals, text field literals, and string literals.

- **Numeric literals**

  You define numeric literals with a sequence of digits that may contain a plus or minus sign; that is, the sign is not mandatory. The numeric literals represent the valid number ranges defined within the predefined data types. The numeric integer literal has a value range from `-2**31+1` to `2**31-1`, that is, the value range from `-2,147,483,648` to `+2,147,483,647`. To assign a numeric literal to a variable, you do not require inverted commas (single quotation marks) around the numeric literal. Following is the syntax from the numeric literal definition:

  ```
  DATA: var1 TYPE I VALUE 12345.
  ```

- **Text field literals**

  The text field literals are defined in the program with a sequence of characters within single inverted commas ('). The text literal can be from 1 to 255 characters in length and is of data type `c`. Trailing spaces in the text field literal are ignored. Following is the syntax for text literal definition:

  ```
  DATA: c_var1(3) TYPE C VALUE 'abc'.
  ```

- **String literals**

  The string literal is defined as a sequence of characters enclosed with back quotes (`). The length of the string literal can be up to 255 characters and is of data type `STRING`. Trailing blanks in the string literal are not ignored, unlike with the text literals. Following is the syntax to define a `STRING` data object:

  ```
  DATA: str_var TYPE STRING VALUE `TEXT`.
  ```

- **Constants**

  Constants are named data objects that have fixed values and are defined statically using a declarative statement. You define constants with the `CONSTANTS` keyword and assign the value to the data object with the `VALUE` statement addition. The value of constants cannot be changed during the execution of the program. If you try to change the value of the constant, a runtime error occurs.

  It is recommended that you use constants instead of literals in the program. You declare constants using the following syntax:

```
CONSTANTS:  c_nump TYPE P DECIMALS 3 VALUE '123.657',
            c_city TYPE C LENGTH 10 VALUE 'BERLIN'.
```

- **Text symbols**

  Text symbols are another kind of named data object and belong to a specific program. Text symbols are generated from the text pool in the ABAP program when you start the program. Program titles, such as headings and the selection texts, are text elements of the program. The text elements of the program are stored as text symbol data objects.

  Text symbols are stored outside the source code in the text pool repository object for the program. Text symbols can be translated in different languages and stored in the text pool with the language indicator. The program or selection screen uses the text symbol to display the text, and text can be displayed in the logon language automatically if the text symbol is maintained for the logon language. Text symbols are of data type `C` and are accessed by a three-character alphanumeric ID.

  To access the text symbol in the program you need to address it as `TEXT-XXX`, where `XXX` is the text ID for the text symbol maintained in the text pool repository for the program. You maintain the text symbol from the ABAP Editor from the menu path GOTO • TEXT ELEMENTS • TEXT SYMBOLS. You can also access the text symbol from the ABAP program by double-clicking on the text symbol in the program, as shown in the following statement:

  ```
  WRITE text-001.
  WRITE 'THIS is an English text' (002).
  ```

- **Predefined data objects**

  Predefined data objects are the ones that are always available during the runtime of the program and are not required to be declared in the program. Predefined data objects are also called *system variables*. The system fields `SY` is a structure with the ABAP Dictionary data type `SYST`. The system fields `SY` are automatically filled and updated by the runtime environment. System fields are variables and can be changed during the execution of the program, but this is not recommended. Figure 6.2 displays the structure of the ABAP Dictionary `SYST`.

- **Variables**

  Variables are called data objects, and are either declared statically in the program or created dynamically during the execution of the program. Variables allow you to store data locally for the program in memory, and their value can be changed during the execution of the program. You can statically declare variables with the following declarative statements:

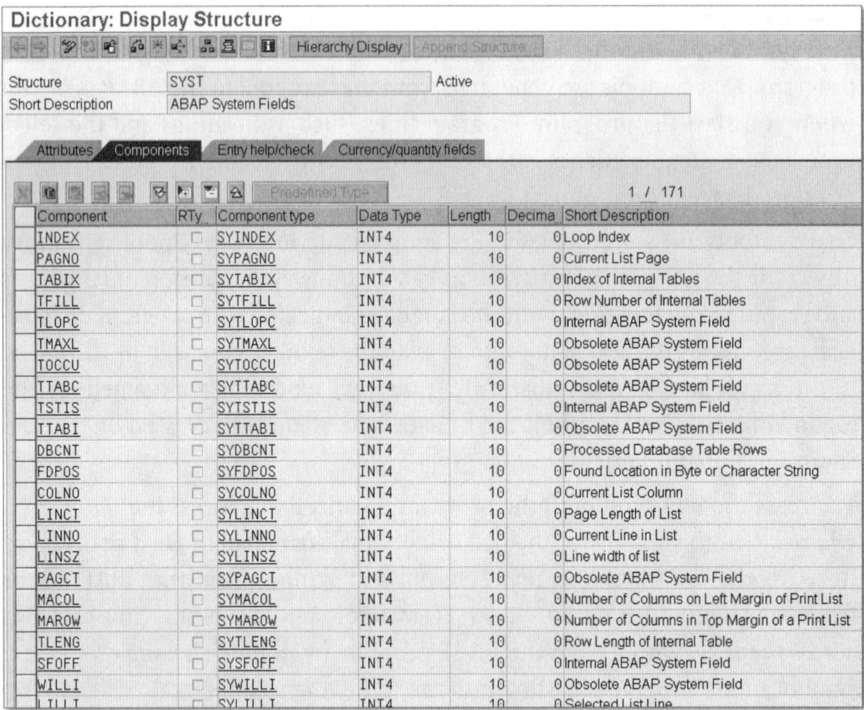
Dictionary: Display Structure

Hierarchy Display | Append Structure

Structure: SYST — Active

Short Description: ABAP System Fields

Attributes | Components | Entry help/check | Currency/quantity fields

Predefined Type — 1 / 171

Component	RTy	Component type	Data Type	Length	Decima	Short Description
INDEX	☐	SYINDEX	INT4	10	0	Loop Index
PAGNO	☐	SYPAGNO	INT4	10	0	Current List Page
TABIX	☐	SYTABIX	INT4	10	0	Index of Internal Tables
TFILL	☐	SYTFILL	INT4	10	0	Row Number of Internal Tables
TLOPC	☐	SYTLOPC	INT4	10	0	Internal ABAP System Field
TMAXL	☐	SYTMAXL	INT4	10	0	Obsolete ABAP System Field
TOCCU	☐	SYTOCCU	INT4	10	0	Obsolete ABAP System Field
TTABC	☐	SYTTABC	INT4	10	0	Obsolete ABAP System Field
TSTIS	☐	SYTSTIS	INT4	10	0	Internal ABAP System Field
TTABI	☐	SYTTABI	INT4	10	0	Obsolete ABAP System Field
DBCNT	☐	SYDBCNT	INT4	10	0	Processed Database Table Rows
FDPOS	☐	SYFDPOS	INT4	10	0	Found Location in Byte or Character String
COLNO	☐	SYCOLNO	INT4	10	0	Current List Column
LINCT	☐	SYLINCT	INT4	10	0	Page Length of List
LINNO	☐	SYLINNO	INT4	10	0	Current Line in List
LINSZ	☐	SYLINSZ	INT4	10	0	Line width of list
PAGCT	☐	SYPAGCT	INT4	10	0	Obsolete ABAP System Field
MACOL	☐	SYMACOL	INT4	10	0	Number of Columns on Left Margin of Print List
MAROW	☐	SYMAROW	INT4	10	0	Number of Columns in Top Margin of a Print List
TLENG	☐	SYTLENG	INT4	10	0	Row Length of Internal Table
SFOFF	☐	SYSFOFF	INT4	10	0	Internal ABAP System Field
WILLI	☐	SYWILLI	INT4	10	0	Obsolete ABAP System Field
LILLI	☐	SYLILLI	INT4	10	0	Selected List Line

Figure 6.2 ABAP Dictionary Structure SYST

- The DATA keyword is used to declare the data in the program whose lifetime and visibility are dependent on the context of the declaration. If the variable is defined in a subroutine, then it is valid for the lifetime of the subroutine and only in the subroutine. Otherwise, if it is defined at the top of the program, it is globally available in the program. You provide the initial value to the data object using the VALUE keyword:

```
DATA: count TYPE I,
      count2 TYPE I value 10.
```

- The STATICS keyword is used to declare the data with the static validity within the procedure. Variables declared with the DATA statement exist as long as the context in which they are defined. Variables defined in the ABAP main program exist until the runtime of the program and the local variables defined in procedure are only available inside the procedure as long as the procedure is running. You can declare a variable using the STATICS keyword to retain a local variable (defined inside the procedure) beyond the runtime of the procedure. The declared variable within the procedure will exist for the lifetime of the main program but is available within the procedure. Hence, if you want to keep the value of the local data object beyond the runtime of the subroutine, then you should use the `STATICS` keyword to declare the variable. The following example displays the use of the `STATIC` keyword:

```
REPORT DEMO_STATIC_DATA_OBJECT.
DO 5 TIMES.
PERFORM dataobject_example.
ENDDO.
FORM dataobject_example.
DATA        count1  TYPE I.
   STATICS  count2  TYPE I.
count1 = count1 + 1.
count2 = count2 + 1.
WRITE: / 'Count1: ', count1, 'Count2: ', count2.
ENDFORM.
```

When you execute the program, the following is displayed:

```
Count1: 1 Count2: 1
Count1: 1 Count2: 2
Count1: 1 Count2: 3
Count1: 1 Count2: 4
Count1: 1 Count2: 5
```

In the above example the variable `count1` does not retain the value because it is declared with the `DATA` keyword, whereas the variable `count2`, declared with the `STATICS` keyword, retains the value for the runtime of the program. The variable `count1` is initialized again when the subroutine is called the next time, whereas the variable `count2` is initialized only during the first call and keeps incrementing the value during the subsequent call.

- `CLASS-DATA`

  The `CLASS-DATA` keyword is used to declare a static attribute for the class and is valid for all of the instances of the class within the program.

- `PARAMETERS`

  The `PARAMETERS` keyword is used to declare an elementary data object that is also displayed as an input field on the selection screen.

- `SELECT-OPTIONS`

  The `SELECT-OPTIONS` keyword is used to declare an internal table that is also displayed as an input field on the selection screen.

You declare variables with the `DATA` keyword with the following syntax:

```
DATA: var1 TYPE I.
DATA: var2 LIKE var1.
DATA: var3 TYPE STRING VALUE 'Hello'.
```

The variable name <VAR1> can be up to 30 characters long. You define the technical attributes of the data object during the declaration. You define the data type, length, and number of decimal places, although for some types the length and number of decimal places are fixed (for example, type d, type t, etc.) or come from the Dictionary. The variable is declared using the ABAP Dictionary type.

If you are using the TYPE keyword to declare the data, then the <type> could be a predefined ABAP data type, existing local data type within the program, or ABAP Dictionary data type. If you are using the LIKE keyword to declare the data object, then the <obj> must be an existing data object in the program that has already been declared, or it can be a database table, view, or structure or a component of the table or structure.

The VALUE keyword is used to define a starting <val> value for the variable. The LIKE statement is allowed in ABAP objects only to declare local data objects or SY fields such as SY-UNAME, SY-DATUM, and so on.

ABAP Data Types

ABAP data types are the predefined data types provided by the ABAP runtime environment. The predefined data types can be used in all ABAP programs. You use predefined data types to define local data types and data objects in your program.

ABAP data types can be used to describe a single variable and elementary data objects. They can be used to describe the components of the structured data objects as well. One way of classifying the predefined elementary data types is fixed length versus variable length.

There are a total of 10 predefined elementary data types. There are eight fixed-length predefined elementary data types and two variable-length data types. Following are the eight predefined fixed-length data types.

- The four *character types* are numeric text (N), character text (C), date type (D), and time type (T). Fields of these types are known as character fields. Each position in these fields takes enough space for the code of the one character. With the adoption of Unicode, each character occupies two to four bytes.

- The three *numeric types* are integer (i), floating point number (f), and packed number (p), which are used in ABAP to display and calculate numbers. The numeric data types (i, f, and p) differ in the inner representation of values, value ranges, and the arithmetic used in the calculation.
- The integer type represents a whole number. The value range for a type I number is -2,147,483,648 to +2,147,483,647. Non-integer results of arithmetic operation are rounded, not truncated. The following example displays the result of integer operation:

  ```
  DATA: num1 TYPE I VALUE 5,
        num2 TYPE I VALUE 2,
        Result TYPE I.
        Result = num1 / num2.
  ```

  The result here would be 3.

The value range of type F numbers is 1*10**-307 to 1*10**308 for positive and negative numbers including zero; that is, valid values of type F numbers are -1,7976931348623157EE+308 to -2,2250738585072014EE-308 for the negative area, the value zero (0) , and +2,2250738585072014EE-308 to +1,7976931348623157EE+308 for the positive area. The accuracy range is approximately 15 decimals. You should not use floating point numbers if high accuracy is required; otherwise, use type P data.

Data objects of type P can have decimal values. The number of decimal places can be specified in the definition of the data object. The value range of type P data depends on its length and the number of digits after the decimal point. The valid length can be from 1 to 16 bytes. Data objects of type P can have a maximum of 14 decimal places. The initial value of type P data is zero. When working with type P data, it is important to set the program attribute to FIXED POINT ARITHMETIC; otherwise, type numbers are treated as integers. The data objects of type P are also called packed data objects. Following is the syntax for the data object of type P:

```
DATA: pack_num1 TYPE P LENGTH 8 DECIMALS 2,
      pack_num2 TYPE P LENGTH 8 DECIMALS 2  VALUE  '2.55'.
```

The length of 8 bytes in the above data object definition corresponds to 2*8-1 numbers including the decimals places.

The hexadecimal type, type X, is a data type used to define a byte in memory. One byte is represented by two-digit hexadecimal display. The syntax to declare a data object of type X is as follows:

```
DATA: hex(1) TYPE X VALUE '09'.
```

The two elementary data types of variable length are STRING and XSTRING:

- The STRING data type is a variable-length character string. A string can contain any number of alphanumeric characters. No memory is allocated to the string until a value is assigned to it, because we wouldn't know how much memory to allocate. The memory is assigned dynamically when we know what the value will be. There is technically no maximum length for the string data type. The maximum amount of memory that can be assigned to the string is dependent on the profile parameter ztta/max_memreq_MB.
- The type XSTRING is a variable-length hexadecimal byte sequence. It can contain any number of bytes. The length of the byte string is the same as the number of bytes. Similar to the type STRING, the memory is allocated dynamically at runtime when a value is assigned to a data object of this type.

The predefine data types can be further categorized as complete data types and incomplete data types. For the complete data types, we don't specify the length, either because they have a fixed length such as data type D (we wouldn't ever need a different length other than 8 characters for a date) or because it is a variable-length string and therefore we don't specify the length because the memory is allocated dynamically at runtime when we assign a value to it. Hence, the data object definition does not require an additional length specification when using complete data types.

Table 6.1 specifies the predefined elementary data types that do not require a length specification for the definition when defining data objects.

Data Type	Length	Initial Value	Meaning
I	4	0	Integer data type
F	8	0	Floating point number
D	8	'00000000'	Date field in the format 'YYYYMMDD'
T	6	'000000'	Time field in the format 'HHMMSS'
STRING	Dynamic		Dynamic-length character string
XSTRING	Dynamic		Dynamic-length byte sequence (hexadecimal string)

Table 6.1 Standard Fixed-Length Data Types

Data types that require the length specification to define the data object are called the incomplete data types. If you do not specify the length, then the default length for the data type will be used. Table 6.2 lists the incomplete data types.

Data Type	Default Length	Initial Value	Meaning
C	1	' '	Text field, alpha numeric characters
N	1	'0..0'	Numeric text field
P	8	0	Packed number
X	1	'X0...0'	Hexadecimal byte sequence

Table 6.2 Incomplete ABAP Data Types

Following is the syntax to declare incomplete data types:

```
DATA var1 TYPE C.   "character variable of length 1
DATA: var2(3) TYPE C.   "character variable of length 3
DATA: var3 TYPE C LENGTH 3. "character variable of length 3
```

The complete data types D, F, I, and T define the data object fully. The data types C, N, P, and X are generic and require a length specification to define the data object fully. Following is the syntax for the data type and data objects:

```
TYPES: v_char1(2) TYPE C.
Types: v_char2 TYPE C LENGTH 10.
TYPES: num1 TYPE P DECIMALS 2.
Data: name(20) TYPE C.
DATA: price TYPE P DECIMALS 2.
```

Local Data Types

Local data types are defined inside the ABAP program and are visible to that program only. You can use predefined, local, or global types to define them within the program. You define local data types using the TYPES statement:

```
TYPES: <type_name> ... [TYPE <ABAP-Type> | LIKE <obj>] .
```

The type name can be up to 30 characters and can use letters, digits, and underscores. <ABAP-Type> could be a predefined elementary data type, another local data type defined in the program, or a Dictionary type. You can use the LIKE statement to refer to a database table or ABAP Dictionary structure, but it is recommended that you use TYPE as ABAP object-oriented programming; you can use the LIKE statement only of local attributes or SY fields.

The local data types are declared using the TYPES keyword:

```
TYPES:  char1 TYPE C LENGTH 8,
        num1  TYPE N LENGTH 6,
        pack1 TYPE P LENGTH 3 DECIMALS 2.
```

The complex types consist of a sequence of elementary data types, complex data types, or reference types. You can also use ABAP Dictionary objects such as data elements, structures, tables, and components of structures or tables to define the individual component of the complex type.

Complex data types consist of structure types and table types. Structure data types can be made up of components of any data types. The components of the structure data type can be a sequence of related elementary data types, complex data types, or reference data types. Depending on the type of component, the structure type can be a flat structure, nested structure, or deep nested structure.

A flat structure type contains fixed-length components, whereas a nested structure type contains a substructure within the structure type; that is, components which are not elementary. A flat structure can also be nested. A structure type is called deep when it contains an internal table or variable-length component. The individual components of the structure are accessed within the program by using a hyphen between the structure name and the component.

Following is the syntax to define the structure data type in an ABAP program:

```
TYPES: BEGIN OF address_ty,
         firstname TYPE C LENGTH 20,
         lastname  TYPE C LENGTH 20,
         street    TYPE C LENGTH 30,
         city      TYPE C LENGTH 20,
       END OF address_ty.
```

You can use the above TYPES definition to declare the data object and then access the individual component in the program to assign value. The following example code displays the syntax to access individual components of the structure data type in the program:

```
DATA: addrs TYPE address_ty.
      addrs-firstname = 'Bob',
      addrs-lastname  = 'Johnson'
```

```
addrs-street    = '123 Adam Lane'.
WRITE: addrs-firstname, addrs-lastname, addrs-street.
```

Following is an example code to define a nested structure type locally in an ABAP program:

```
TYPES: BEGIN OF stru1,
         fld1 TYPE I,
         BEGIN OF stru2,
           fld2 TYPE C,
           fld3  TYPE I,
         END OF stru2,
       END of stru1.
TYPES: BEGIN of addr1,
         street_no  TYPE C LENGTH 30,
         city       TYPE C LENGTH 20,
         state      TYPE C LENGTH 30,
         country    TYPE C LENGTH 20,
       END of addr1.
TYPES: BEGIN OF contact_det,
         firstname TYPE C LENGTH 20,
         lastname  TYPE C LENGTH 20,
         address   TYPE addr1,
         phoneno   TYPE C length 15,
       END OF contact_det.
```

Table types consist of any number of lines of the same data type, and are used to describe internal tables. This topic is discussed in more detail in Chapter 7, Internal Table Definition and Use. The table line can have an elementary data type or a complex data type. The local table for the ABAP program is called an internal table. We use the following syntax to create a table type:

```
TYPES:  <Table_type>
        TYPE  <tablekind> OF <linetype> [WITH <key>].
```

The `TYPES` statement can define a table type with access type `<tablekind>`, line type `<linetype>`, and key `<key>`. The `<linetype>` is a known data type in the program. The following is an example code for table type definition:

```
TYPES:  BEGIN of flightinfo,
          carrid    TYPE s_carr_id,
          carrname  TYPE s_carrname,
          connid    TYPE s_conn_id,
          fldate    TYPE sy-datum,
          fltime    TYPE s_fltime,
```

```
        END OF flightinfo.
TYPES: itab TYPE SORTED TABLE OF flightinfo
            WITH UNIQUE KEY carrid.
```

The above program statements define the table type `itab` with a line type of structure `flightinfo` and unique key of structure component `NAME`. Please refer to Chapter 7, Internal Table Definition and Use, for detailed information about internal tables and their use in ABAP programs.

Global Data Types

Data types defined in the ABAP Dictionary are called global data types and are available system-wide. Global data types consist of data elements, structures, and table types:

- Data elements refer to the predefined Dictionary types which largely correspond to the predefined ABAP types.
- Structures consist of sequences of data elements or even another structure data type as one of the components.
- Table types are internal tables defined in the ABAP Dictionary.

You can use existing ABAP Dictionary data types or create new data types in the ABAP Dictionary. The following ABAP Dictionary objects are used to define the global data types:

- Database tables or views are used to define a flat structure data type. The individual fields of the database table are the components of the flat structure data type. You can also define a type using the individual components or fields of the database table or view. The syntax for the type declaration with the database table is:

  ```
  TYPES: <db_type> TYPE <dbtab>.
  TYPES: mara_ty TYPE mara.
  TYPES: <t> TYPE <bdtab>-<c>.
  TYPES: matnr_ty TYPE mara-matnr.
  ```

  You can also use the database table to define data objects or a work area with your program. The syntax to define the data object with reference to a database table is:

  ```
  DATA : mara_ls TYPE mara.
  ```

- You can define elementary types, reference types, and complex types in the ABAP Dictionary. Data elements, table types, and structures are the ABAP

Dictionary global data types. You can refer to these data types in the program to define a local data type or data object. The data element defines an individual field in the ABAP Dictionary or an elementary data object or variable in your program.

Data elements allow you to define elementary types, reference types, and complex type Dictionary objects. Data elements allow you to define complex types if they are used to type on one of the components of the complex type. On their own they are elementary types that are visible globally. You can define data types locally by referring to a data element in the ABAP program as follows:

```
TYPES: <t> TYPE <data element>.
TYPES: site_ty TYPE werks_d.
DATA : wa_site TYPE site_ty.
```

- You can define structure types in the ABAP Dictionary. The structure type can be a flat structure, deep structure, or nested structure. You can refer to the ABAP Dictionary structure to declare a local structure data type. A local complex data type with reference to the global structure is declared as follows:

```
TYPES: <t> TYPE <structure>.
TYPES: marc_ty TYPE dmarc.
DATA: wa_marc TYPE marc_ty.
```

  You can also define a local structure or a work area directly using the following syntax:

```
DATA: wa_marc TYPE dmarc
```

- Table types is are an internal table template stored in the ABAP Dictionary. You specify the line type, access type, and key during the creation of the table type in the ABAP Dictionary. For more about the table type refer to Chapter 7, Internal Table Definition and Use. The syntax to define an internal table locally in the ABAP program with reference to the table type is as follows:

```
DATA: MARM_lt TYPE marm_ty.
```

- Type groups are ABAP Dictionary types whereby you can store any type definition globally in the ABAP Dictionary and use them in your program locally. You have to declare the type group in the program before you can refer to the data types in the type group. The syntax to declare type groups in ABAP program is as follows:

```
TYPE-POOlS: <type pools>.
```

The following example displays the syntax to use the data type `slis_t_fieldcat_alv` defined in a type group. To define a data object that refers to a data type defined in the type group `SLIS`, you have to declare the type group in ABAP program with the syntax `TYPE-POOLS: SLIS` and then define the data object with reference to the data type defined in the type group.

```
TYPE-POOLS: SLIS.
DATA: fieldcat TYPE slis_t_fieldcat_alv.
```

The type `slis_t_fieldcat_alv` is a defined as a global data type in the `TYPE GROUP SLIS`.

Data Object Visibility

The visibility of the data object is dependent on the context of the variable. The following rules apply for data objects declared locally within the program:

- If the variable is defined with a `DATA` statement within a subroutine between `FORM` and `ENDFORM`, then it's a local data for the subroutine. Hence, the data is not visible and is not accessible outside the subroutine.
- If the data object is declared within a function module, then it is a local data object for the function module. The function group itself may have variables, and these will be in the Top Include of the function group and will be accessible to all function modules within the group.
- Data objects declared at the start of the program with the `DATA`, `PARAMETERS`, or `SELECT-OPTIONS` keywords are visible to the entire program and are global data objects.
- If the data object is declared between the `MODULE` and `ENDMODULE` of a PAI or PBO module for a screen, then it is visible to the entire program. Similarly, any data objects declared in an ABAP event block, for example `START-OF-SELECTION`, are visible to the entire program.
- Data objects defined with the `TABLES` statement are visible to the entire program even if the `TABLES` statement is declared in an ABAP subroutine.

Caution

Be aware of the visibility declared locally within the program:

- Data objects declared between `MODULE` and `ENDMODULE` are visible to the entire program.
- Data objects declared in an ABAP event block are visible to the entire program.
- Data objects declared with the `TABLES` statement are visible to the entire program even if the `TABLES` statement appears in a subroutine within the `FORM` and `ENDFORM`.

Important Terminology

You should now understand the difference between the data type and data object and their use in ABAP programs.

Data types are used for the definition of data objects. They define the technical attributes of the data object, how the data object is stored in memory, and what operations are possible on the data object based on the data type. You can use both predefined data types and global data types to define technical attributes of the data object. Depending on the data type, you might have to define the length and the number of decimal places to fully define the technical attribute of the data object. For a data object defined with reference to the ABAP Dictionary object, the technical attributes such as length, number of decimal places, and the data type are derived from ABAP Dictionary objects.

Data objects are temporary storage in the program and occupy memory to store the data. Data objects contain data for the program, and they exist for the duration of the program.

Practice Questions

The practice questions below will help you evaluate your understanding of the topic. The questions shown are similar in nature to those found on the certification examination, but whereas none of these questions will be found on the exam itself, they allow you to review your knowledge of the subject. Select the correct answers and then check the completeness of your answers in the following solution section. Remember that you must select all correct answers and only correct answers to receive credit for the question.

1. Data types store data and occupy memory.

☐ **A.** True

☐ **B.** False

2. A data object is concretely defined by means of data type and occupies memory. It contains data with which ABAP programs work at runtime.

☐ **A.** True

☐ **B.** False

3. The predefined data types are defined locally in the ABAP program.

☐ **A.** True

☐ **B.** False

4. The default length of the type `C` data type is:

☐ **A.** 1

☐ **B.** 10

☐ **C.** 1-65535

5. If data objects of type `I` are being used to store the result of a calculation, the decimals will be truncated.

☐ **A.** True

☐ **B.** False

6. The default length of the type `P` data type is:

☐ **A.** 8

☐ **B.** 1

☐ **C.** 1-16

7. A variable-length structure is called:

☐ **A.** Nested structure

☐ **B.** Deep structure

☐ **C.** Flat structure

8. Local data objects can be defined using ABAP Dictionary types.

- [x] **A.** True
- [ ] **B.** False

9. Global data types defined in SAP systems are:

- [x] **A.** Data defined in the program that is visible to the all the routines/statements within the ABAP program
- [x] **B.** ABAP Dictionary types
- [ ] **C.** Date types defined in the program using ABAP Dictionary types

10. Which of the following are incorrect statements:

- [ ] **A.** `TYPES: carrid_ty LIKE spfli-s-carr_id.`
- [x] **B.** `TYPES: werks TYPE C LENGTH 4.`
- [ ] **C.** `TYPES: date_ty TYPE D LENGTH 10.` ✓
- [ ] **D.** `TYPES: Str TYPE STRING LENGTH 20.` ✓

11. What is the result of the following arithmetic operation.

```
DATA: int TYPE I.
int = 5 * ( 3 / 10 ).
```

- [ ] **A.** 1
- [x] **B.** 2
- [ ] **C.** 1.5
- [ ] **D.** 0

12. What is the result of the following arithmetic operation:

```
DATA : int TYPE I
int =  5 / 10.
```

- [x] **A.** 1
- [ ] **B.** .5
- [ ] **C.** 0

Practice Question Answers and Explanations

1. Correct answer: **B**

   A data type is just the description and does not occupy memory.

2. Correct answer: **A**

   A data object is an instance of the data type and does occupy memory. Data types define the technical attributes of the data object.

3. Correct answer: **B**

   Predefined data types are provided by the ABAP runtime environment and are available system-wide.

4. Correct answer: **A**

   The default length of the character data type `C` is one. If you want the data object to be more then one character, then you have to specify the length.

```
TYPES: var1 TYPE C.            "is a character data type
                               "of length 1.
TYPES: var2(10) TYPE C.        "is a character data type
                               "of length 10.
TYPES: var2 TYPE C LENGTH 15.  "is a character data type
                               "of length 15.
```

5. Correct answer: **B**

   The type `I` data objects round the value and do not truncate.

```
DATA:  int1  TYPE I,
       int2  TYPE I,
       int3  TYPE I.
int1 = 4/10.  "value of int1 = 0
int2 = 5/10   "value of int2 = 1
int3 = 16/10. "value on int3 = 2
```

6. Correct answer: **A**

   The default length of the type `P` data type is eight. If you want to have more or less than eight, then you can specify the length with the length keyword or in parentheses after the name of the data object or data type.

7. Correct answer: **B**

   The variable-length structure is called a deep structure. Any structure that has a variable-length component is called a deep structure. For example, a structure with an internal table as one of its components is a deep structure, as is a structure with a component of type `STRING`.

8. Correct answer: **A**

   Local data objects can be defined using ABAP Dictionary objects.

9. Correct answer: **B**

   Global data types are ABAP Dictionary objects, like data elements, Dictionary structures, tables, table types, and type pools.

10. Correct answers: **C, D**

    Data type `D` is a fixed-length predefined data type and does not require a length specification. The data type `STRING` is a dynamic-length data type and does not require a length specification.

11. Correct answer: **D**

    The correct answer is 0:

    ```
    int1 = 5 * ( 3/10).
    int1 = 5 * ( 0 ) "because 3/10 = 0, due to integer rounding
    int1 = 0.
    ```

12. Correct answer: **A**

    The correct answer is 1 because the integer data type `I` rounds the number during the arithmetic operation.

Take Away

You should understand the ABAP data types and data objects. You should understand the meaning of ABAP predefined standard data types, local data types, and global data types. It is important that you know the differences between local data types and global data types, and between flat structures, nested structures, and deep structures. All this will help you write more efficient code. Finally, you should understand the scope and validity of the data objects within the ABAP program.

Refresher

Table 6.3 repeats the key concepts of this chapter in short form.

Key Concept	Definition
ABAP data types	Predefined elementary data types provided by the ABAP runtime environment are also called ABAP data types.
Data type	A data type is a description and is not allocated any memory. Data types are used to define data objects.
Data objects	Data objects are instances of the data types and occupy memory. They store data temporarily that is used in the program.
Local data type	Local data types are defined using the `TYPES` statement in the ABAP program. They can refer to predefined data types or global data types from the ABAP Dictionary.
Global data types	Global data types are defined in the ABAP Dictionary.
Flat structures, nested structures, and deep structures	Flat structures contain fixed-length components. A structure is nested if it contains another structure as its component. A structure is called a deep structure if it contains an internal table or a variable-length component.

Table 6.3 Key Concept Refresher

Summary

In this chapter you have learned about ABAP data types and data objects, including local data types, predefined data type, global data types, and their uses in programs. You have also learned the syntax to define data objects using the ABAP Dictionary data type and local and predefined data types. This knowledge will allow you to easily pass this topic on the certification examination.

Internal Table Definition and Use

Techniques You'll Master:

- Define internal tables
- Categorize different types of internal tables and their uses
- Define internal table type and internal table data object in the program
- Understand operations on internal tables
- Define ABAP Dictionary table types and the syntax to use them in programs

Internal tables are program variables and store multiple identical structured data records in the ABAP runtime memory. They are used to process large data sets in a structured manner. They are beneficial for improving data processing in the program if used correctly.

In this chapter you will learn about the various elements of internal tables. You will learn about various kind of internal tables and the syntax to create and use them in programs. You will learn to define internal tables, access internal table records, modify, delete, and perform various other operations on the internal table records in programs.

Real-World Scenario

Imagine you have to write an application that reads data from a number of SAP database tables and performs some comparisons and calculations and displays the result. For example, you have to display the details of the open purchase order in the SAP system along with the material details such as description and material type and vendor details.

To write such an application, it would be a good idea to read all open purchase orders from the database and store the purchase order details in an internal table and then loop through the internal table, read the material and vendor information for each purchase order, and display the result on the screen. You may also want to store the material and vendor details in an internal table so that you don't have to read the details from the database table again if the same material and vendor exists in more than one purchase order.

To write this application, you need to understand the concept of internal tables, including how to store and access the data from the internal table. You also need to understand the various types of internal tables in order to write an efficient program.

Objectives of this Portion of the Test

The objective of this portion of the certification exam is to verify your knowledge about the concept of internal tables and their use in ABAP programs or applications. You are expected to understand how to define the internal table, access the internal table, and know about the various types of internal table.

The exam will test your knowledge about the benefit of using different types of internal tables in an application and about the syntax used to define the internal table, create the internal table, and access different types of the internal table.

Key Concepts Refresher

An internal table is a program variable used to store multiple identically structured records in the memory of an application. This chapter provides a complete description of how to work with internal tables. It describes the use of internal tables, definition of internal tables, various operations on them, and different kinds of tables. After completing this chapter you should be able to do the following:

- Define different types of internal tables
- Populate an internal table
- Access the data in an internal table
- Understand the performance considerations during table definition and processing

Internal Table Definition and Use

Internal tables are structured data objects and are defined in the ABAP program locally. They allow you to store variable amounts of structured data records in memory. They store any number of identical structured records within the ABAP memory. An internal table is like an array found in other programming languages. Internal tables are dynamic data objects and save the programmer the task of dynamic memory management. The ABAP runtime system dynamically manages the size of an internal table. The maximum number of data records in an internal table is restricted upon installation of the hardware and the operating system. ABAP runtime dynamically manages the size of the internal table. As a developer you do not have to do any work concerning memory management.

Following are some of the features of an internal table:

- It is used for processing large data sets in a structured manner. Typical use of internal tables could be to read and store data from database tables or a sequential file and then formatting the data to be displayed on screen or report output. You can also store data in an internal table to pass it to a function module, method, or subroutine for further processing.

- Processing a large volume of data in an internal table is beneficial for performance improvement, if used correctly in the program, compared to accessing the data sequentially from the database table. Processing an internal table is fast because the data is stored in the memory.
- Internal tables are defined when you start the program, and data is populated, modified, or processed while you are processing the program. The data definition and the content exist only for the runtime of the program. You lose the table content once the program ends.
- Internal tables can contain components, columns, and fields derived from different database tables, or you can define an internal table based on local variables or structure definitions in your program. You can include fields from several database tables as fields in your internal tables if you plan on working with data from multiple database tables, for example, if you want to display the content of those tables in reports.
- An internal table has a table body, and the table body contains the identical structured data records. Individual data records in an internal table are called a *table row* or *table entry*. Individual components of a table row are called the *columns* or *fields*. The row type of an internal table is specified through any data type and describes the row structure of the table entries. Each table row has the same structure.

Figure 7.1 displays the individual components of an internal table.

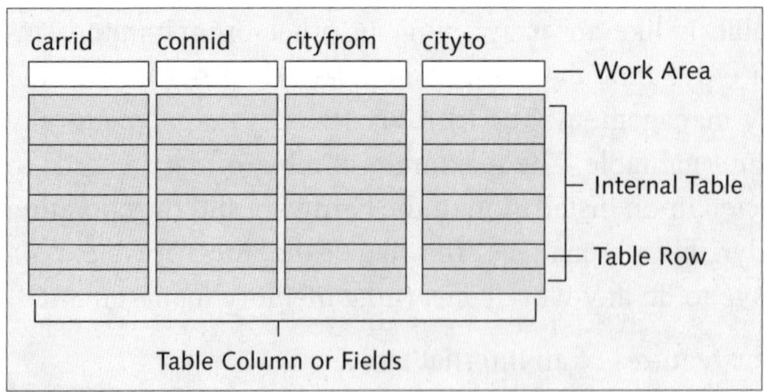

Figure 7.1 Individual Elements of an Internal Table

Listing 7.1 displays the internal table definition in an ABAP program. The sample code refers to the ABAP Dictionary data type used in flight table SPFLI to define the structure data type (line type). The local data type is used to define an internal table data object. The internal table data object and the work area are defined using the DATA statement.

```
TYPES: BEGIN OF line_type,
         airline_code      TYPE s_carr_id,
         connection_no     TYPE s_conn_id,
         from_city         TYPE s_from_cit,
         to_city           TYPE s_to_city,
       END OF line_type
DATA: itab TYPE STANDARD TABLE OF line_type.
DATA: wa TYPE line_type.
```

Listing 7.1 Internal Table Definition in an ABAP Program

The data type of an internal table is specified by the following attributes:

- **Line type**
  The line type describes the row structure of the table entries, and defines the attributes of the individual components of the table row. The line type is generally defined as structure type, but almost any data type can be used for the line type definition.
- **Table key**
  The table key consists of key fields and their order, identifying a table row similar to the key of the database table. An internal table can have a unique key or a non-unique key. An internal table with unique key cannot contain duplicate entries. Entries in the table must differ by at least one key field. The non-unique key means the table can have duplicate entries, and this is perfectly legitimate because this is an internal table, rather than a database table.

Furthermore, the table can have a standard key and user-defined key. If the line type of an internal table is a structure, then the default standard key consists of all non-numeric fields of the structure. A user-defined key is any subset of the structure fields that are not references or themselves an internal table.

You can define an internal table with a header line or without a header line. Header lines are the old way of defining internal tables and are still valid, although if you are defining an internal table, it is recommended that you define one with a separate work area. The work area is a new standard of defining the work area of the internal table and is explicitly defined in the program. The header line for an internal table is the same name as the internal table, whereas the work area has different name. Internal tables with header line definitions are not supported in object-oriented ABAP programming.

The header line or the work area is used to transfer data records from the table for further processing. You populate the header line or the work area with the data and then transfer the record to create the table entry. Similarly, you read the data from an internal table into the header line or work area for processing an existing table row. An internal table definition with a separate work area can have a line type that is itself a deep structure, whereas an internal table with a header line can only have a line type that is a flat structure.

Internal tables can be of different types depending on the way they access the individual entries in the table. There are three types of internal tables:

- **Standard tables**
  With standard tables, row numbering (index) is maintained internally, and they can be accessed using the key or an index. This type of table cannot have a unique key and can therefore have duplicate entries. The response time of a standard table is better if accessed with index. Key access for the standard table is not optimized because sequential search across all rows is carried out.

  A standard table is declared using the `STANDARD TABLE` addition. The table indexing is managed internally. When a record is deleted or inserted the indexing is reorganized. You can add a new record to a standard table by using the `APPEND` statement.
- **Sorted tables**
  Sorted tables are defined using the `SORTED TABLE` addition. Table records are stored in sorted order according to the table keys, and the table is sorted in ascending order by default. The index of the sorted internal table is maintained internally.

  A sorted table can have a unique or non-unique key. You simply state this when defining the internal table. The sorted internal table can be accessed with the table key or index. The system always uses the binary search algorithm for the sorted table when you access it using the table key (or part of the key from left to right). You fill a sorted table using the `INSERT` statement. The table entries are inserted according to the defined sort sequence. Both sorted and standard tables are also called *index tables* because they can be accessed using an index.
- **Hashed tables**
  Hashed tables are defined using the `HASHED TABLE` addition. They do not have

indexes, and hence they cannot be accessed using an index; only key access can be used. The sequence of the entries is managed by hash algorithm. A hash table must have a unique key because it can only be accessed using the key.

Hashed internal tables are ideal for storing large numbers of entries, where you need to read those entries using the key, because the response time is not dependent upon the number of entries. The hash algorithm is used to find the appropriate record. Standard tables and sorted tables can be accessed with the index or key, but hashed tables can only be accessed with a unique key. Key access with the standard table is a linear search; for the sorted table key access is a binary search, and for the hashed table the key access uses the hash algorithm.

As already stated, standard tables and sorted tables can be accessed using the index or using the key, but hashed tables can only be accessed with the key. Key access to a standard table results in a sequential search; for a sorted table key access results in a binary search, and for a hashed table key access uses the hash algorithm to find the appropriate record.

Table 7.1 displays the possible table access and the characteristics for the different kinds of table.

	Index Tables		Hashed Table
Table Kind	**Standard Table**	**Sorted Table**	**Hashed Table**
Index access	Index possible	Index possible	Not possible
Key access	Can be accessed	Can be accessed	Can be accessed
Uniqueness of key	Non-unique	Unique and non-unique	Unique
Access	Primarily using index	Should be primarily accessed using key, not index	Only using key

Table 7.1 Access Options for Different Kinds of Table

Defining ABAP Internal tables

Internal tables are data objects and are defined using the `DATA` statement. To fully define an internal table, you must define the line type, key, and table type. Line types can be defined locally in the program or globally as a data type in the ABAP

Dictionary. You can define internal tables locally or define them in the ABAP Dictionary as table type.

You can define global table type in the ABAP Dictionary or use the existing one (predefined by SAP) in your program. Global table types are valid system-wide and can be used in any program in the system. Table type describes the structure and the attribute of an internal table.

You can reference a table type defined in the ABAP Dictionary in your program using the following syntax:

```
DATA mara_lt TYPE mara_tab.
```

This syntax creates an internal table `mara_lt` with the structure and attribute defined for table type `mara_tab` in the ABAP Dictionary.

The table type is an ABAP Dictionary data type and is defined by specifying the line type, access, and key of the internal table. The line type defines the structure of an internal table. Line type can be a flat structure, deep structure, or nested structure. Line type defines the row, and the individual component of the line type defines the column of the internal table.

Figure 7.2 displays the line type for the ABAP Dictionary table type. In Figure 7.2, ABAP Dictionary table `MARM` is used to define the line type for the table type `marm_tab`. You can use an ABAP Dictionary table or structure to define line type.

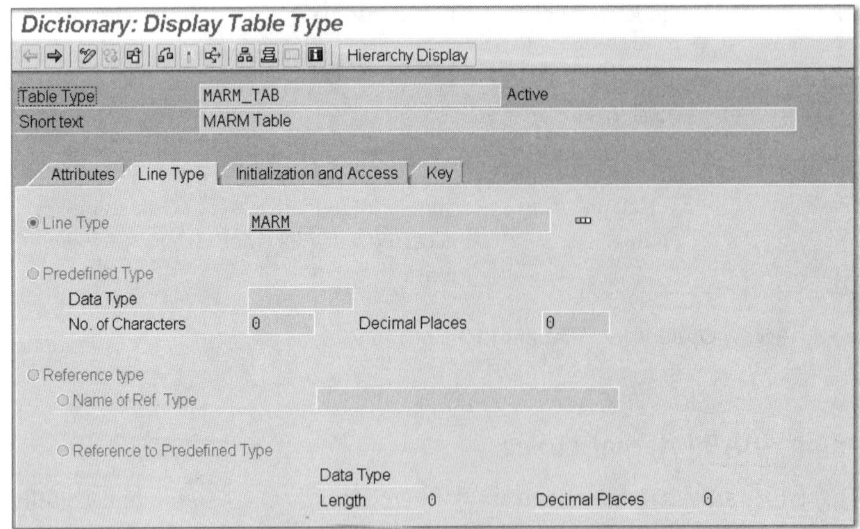

Figure 7.2 Line Type Definition in ABAP Dictionary Table Type

You can specify the access mode for the table type. Access mode defines how to access the data in the internal table when performing key operations on the internal table such as `READ TABLE`, `INSERT TABLE`, `MODIFY TABLE`, and so on. Figure 7.3 displays the possible access mode for the table type.

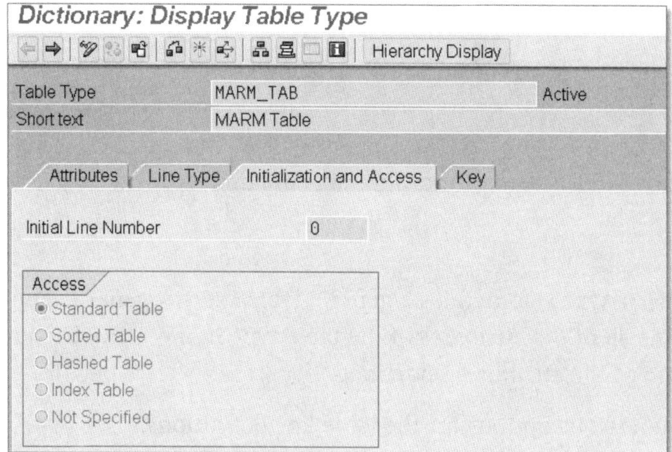

Figure 7.3 Table Access Definition in ABAP Dictionary Table Type

You can have following access modes for the table type:

- STANDARD TABLE
  The key access for the standard table uses a sequential search, and performance depends on the number of entries in the table.
- SORTED TABLE
  The internal table is stored internally sorted by key. You should always access the sorted internal table by key. The key access for a sorted internal table uses binary search to access table records.
- HASHED TABLE
  The table is internally managed using hash procedures. All entries in the table should have a unique key.
- INDEX TABLE
  The table can be a standard or sorted table. Index access is allowed for index tables.
- NOT SPECIFIED
  The table can be a standard table, a sorted table, or a hash table. The valid operations on such a table are the intersection of the valid operations on stan-

dard, sorted, and hash tables. You cannot access tables of this type with index operations.

You can specify the table key and define the key category for table type. You have three options to specify the key category:

- UNIQUE
  With the UNIQUE key category, the table can contain records with unique keys.
- NON-UNIQUE
  With the NON-UNIQUE key category, the table can contain records with duplicate keys.
- NOT SPECIFIED
  The key category NOT SPECIFIED defines a generic table type. A generic table type does not define all of the attributes of the table type in the ABAP Dictionary; it leaves some of the attributes undefined.

Figure 7.4 displays the various options for the table key definitions.

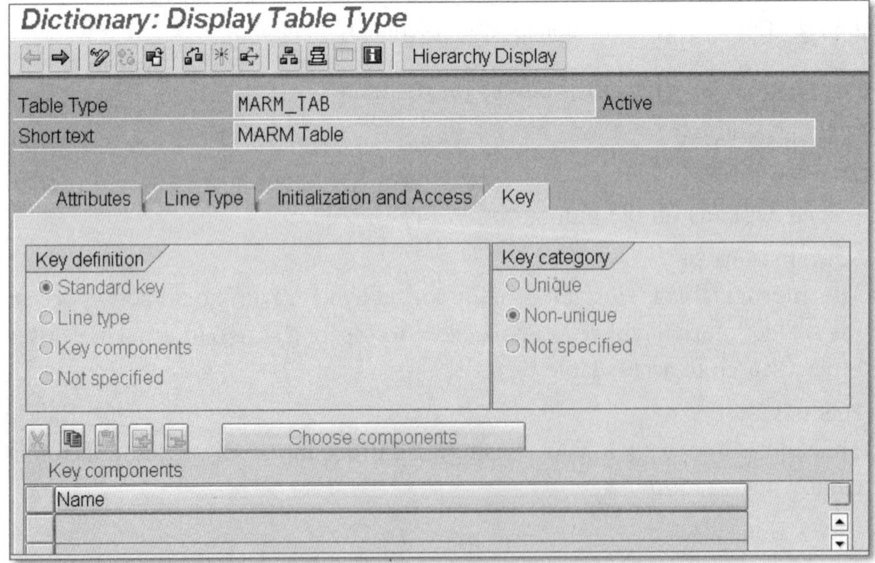

Figure 7.4 Table Key Definition in ABAP Dictionary Table Type Definition

You can define an internal table locally if you do not use the table type defined in the ABAP Dictionary or if the one defined in the ABAP Dictionary does not satisfy you development requirement. You can use the `TYPES` and `DATA` statements to declare an internal table. The line type for the internal table is defined using the TYPES statement, and the internal table data object is defined using the DATA statement.

Listing 7.2, Listing 7.3, and Listing 7.4 show the syntax to define an internal table in the program. The example uses ABAP Dictionary data types such as matnr and werks to define the line type for the internal table structure. The first statement in Listing 7.4 uses the table type itab_type defined in the program to define the internal table itab_lt, and in the second statement the internal table is defined with reference to the line type defined in the program.

```
TYPES: BEGIN OF mat_type,
         material TYPE matnr,
         plant TYPE werks_d,
         qty TYPE P DECIMALS 2.
       END OF mat_type.
```

Listing 7.2 Line Type Definition for Internal Table

```
TYPES: itab_type TYPE STANDARD TABLE OF mat_type
                 WITH NON-UNIQUE KEY material.
```

Listing 7.3 Standard Table Type Definition with Reference to Line Type Defined Above

```
DATA: itab_lt TYPE itab_type.
```

or

```
DATA: itab_lt TYPE STANDARD TABLE OF mat_type.
```

Listing 7.4 Standard Internal Table Definition with Reference to Local Table Type Defined Above

The line type can be a local type declaration or a global type from the ABAP Dictionary, such as a structure, a database table, or data elements. Local types are defined in the ABAP program, and the declaration is valid for that specific program. For the local type, the table structure is defined using the TYPES statement. In a local type definition, you can define an individual component of the table record structure or include the ABAP Dictionary structure along with your local field declaration. An ABAP Dictionary structure is included in the type definition by using the INCLUDE statement.

Listing 7.5 displays the syntax to declare an internal table line type using the ABAP Dictionary structure.

```
TYPES: BEGIN OF mat_ty.
         INCLUDE STRUCTURE mara.
       END OF mat_ty.
```

Listing 7.5 Line Type Definition with Reference to ABAP Dictionary Structure

An internal table line type can be a flat structure, deep structure, or nested structure. You must define a separate work area to work with the internal table. Listing 7.6 displays the syntax to define an internal table with reference to the ABAP Dictionary table. The line type of the internal table in this example corresponds to the MARA structure, where MARA is an ABAP Dictionary table.

```
DATA: itab_lt TYPE STANDARD TABLE OF mara
              WITH NON-UNIQUE KEY matnr.
DATA: itab_wa LIKE LINE OF itab_lt.
```

Listing 7.6 Internal Table Definition with Reference to ABAP Dictionary Table

Tip

The line type for an internal table with a header line must be a flat structure, whereas the line type for an internal table without a header line can be flat structure, deep structure, or nested structure.

The STANDARD addition is optional for the declaration of the standard table. If you do not provide the table type, the default table type is a standard internal table. For a standard table, if you do not specify a key, the system automatically adopts a default key as the table key. The default key for a standard table consists of all of the non-numeric fields, in the sequence in which they appear in the line type.

Following is the syntax to define a standard table with a default key:

```
DATA: itab TYPE TABLE OF mara.
```

The additions INITIAL SIZE and WITH HEADER LINE are also possible for the data type or data object declaration. The INITIAL SIZE <n> addition enables the system to reserve the first block of memory for the internal table; any subsequent memory requirement is managed by the system dynamically.

The syntax to define an internal table with initial size is as follows:

```
DATA: itab TYPE TABLE OF mara INITIAL SIZE 4.
```

ABAP runtime dynamically manages the memory if the initial size for the internal table is not specified during the internal table definition. When the initial size is full, the system makes twice as much extra space available up to a limit of 8KB, and thereafter each subsequent addition is created with 12KB. It makes sense to specify the initial size only if you are sure about the number of lines in the internal table. Otherwise, it is recommended that you leave out this addition and let the system manage the memory for internal tables.

Listing 7.7 shows the syntax to define a sorted and a hashed internal table. In this example we have defined the line type for the internal table, table type, and sorted and hashed internal table data object.

```
TYPES: BEGIN OF line_type,
         material TYPE matnr,
         plant TYPE werks_d,
         po_numb TYPE ebeln,
       END OF line_type.
TYPES: itab01 TYPE SORTED TABLE OF line_type
              WITH UNIQUE KEY material plant.
TYPES: itab02 TYPE HASHED TABLE OF line_type
              WITH UNIQUE KEY material plant.
```

Listing 7.7 Syntax for Sorted and Hashed Table Types

Listing 7.8 shows two possibilities to create a sorted internal table. You can also use the ABAP Dictionary structure or table to define an internal table, as shown in Listing 7.9.

```
DATA: itab01_lt TYPE itab01.
```

or

```
DATA: itab01_lt TYPE SORTED TABLE OF line_type
                WITH UNIQUE KEY material plant.
```

Listing 7.8 Sorted Internal Table Data Objects

```
DATA: itab TYPE SORTED TABLE OF marc
           WITH UNIQUE KEY matnr werks.
```

Listing 7.9 Define Internal Table

Finally, Listing 7.10 shows the possible syntax to define a hashed internal table. A unique key attribute is required for the hashed table and should be specified during the definition of the table. The sorted table can have a unique or a non-unique key; the data is inserted in a sorted order in the sorted table according to its key.

```
DATA: itab02_lt TYPE itab02.
```

or

```
DATA: itab02_lt TYPE HASHED TABLE OF line_type
                WITH UNIQUE KEY material plant.
DATA: itab03 TYPE HASHED TABLE OF marc
             WITH UNIQUE KEY matnr werks.
```

Listing 7.10 Hashed Internal Table Data Objects

Internal Table with Header Line

You could declare an internal table with a header line using the DATA statement with the addition of OCCURS followed by the declaration of a flat structure. Object-oriented programming does not support internal tables with header lines, so you shouldn't use this syntax anymore with object-oriented programming. Also, the line type for the internal table with a header line supports only a flat structure. The line type of an internal table with a header line cannot be a nested structure or deep structure.

Listing 7.11 displays an example code to define an internal table with a header line.

```
DATA: BEGIN OF itab_lt OCCURS 0,
        material LIKE mard-matnr,
        plant    LIKE mard-werks
        mat_desc LIKE makt-maktx,
        stock    LIKE mard-labst,
      END OF itab_lt.
```

or

```
DATA: BEGIN OF itab_lt OCCURS 0,
        material TYPE matnr,
        plant    TYPE werks_d
        mat_desc TYPE maktx,
        stock    TYPE labst,
      END OF itab_lt.
```

Listing 7.11 Definition of Internal Table with Header Line

You define the internal table structure within the `DATA: BEGIN OF <internal table name>` and `END OF <internal table name>` statement. You can use the `LIKE` statement or `TYPE` statement to define the individual component of the structure as shown in the example above. The `OCCURS` addition defines the expected number of lines for an internal table. If you do not specify the `OCCURS` addition, then the data object definition is simply a structure or a work area. So without the addition `OCCURS` in the above example, the data object is not an internal table. With the addition `OCCURS` the system creates a standard internal table with a header line.

You specify the initial size of the internal table with `OCCURS <no of line>`, and the system reserves the memory for the internal table. The ABAP runtime dynamically manages the size of the internal table, so unless you know the number of rows of the internal table, it does not make sense to specify the number of lines. You can simply specify `OCCURS 0` and let the system manage the memory for an internal table. As mentioned earlier, `OCCURS` additions were used in old releases, and it not recommended that you use internal tables with `OCCURS` clauses in new releases; this is not supported in object-oriented programming.

Listing 7.12 displays another example code to define an internal table with a header line.

```
TYPES: BEGIN OF itab_ty,
         matnr TYPE matnr,
         werks TYPE werks,
         maktx TYPE maktx,
         labst TYPE labst,
       END OF itab_ty.
DATA: itab_lt TYPE itab_ty OCCURS 0 WITH HEADER LINE.
```

Listing 7.12 Definition of Internal Table with Header Line

The optional addition `HEADER LINE` creates an addition data object with the same name and the line type of an internal table. The header line is not an internal table, but it's a structure that can hold a single table record.

Caution

Internal tables with header lines are not supported in object-oriented programming.

Using ABAP Internal Tables

In the previous section we discussed the syntax for defining internal tables. In this section we will discuss how to populate an internal table and how to access an internal table, including sorting and the various other internal table operations. We will assume in this section that the internal table does not have a header line, and a table-line-compatible work area is defined for the various operations because in newer release it is not recommended that you define internal tables with a header line.

Appending Lines to Internal Tables

As a developer, your first task in the program is to fill the internal table once you have defined it. To add new records to an internal table you use the APPEND or INSERT statement. You can also use the SELECT statement to populate them from the database table (see Chapter 9, Basic ABAP Programs and Interface Creation, for syntax and detail).

Following is the syntax to populate an internal table with a select clause:

```
DATA: mara_lt TYPE STANDARD TABLE OF mara.
SELECT * FROM mara INTO TABLE mara_lt.
```

Here MARA is a database table in SAP system, and mara_lt is an internal table. The SELECT statement populates the content of the MARA table into the internal table mara_lt.

The APPEND statement is normally used only for the standard internal table. However, it can also be used to append to a sorted table if the line to be appended maintains the sort order, but because it would be difficult to know if this would be the case, it is recommended that you do not use APPEND with the sorted internal table. The APPEND statement can be used to append either one or several table lines to standard internal tables. You populate the work area and then transfer the work area content to the standard internal table.

The syntax to append internal tables is as follows:

```
DATA: itab_wa TYPE mara.
DATA: itab_lt TYPE STANDARD TABLE OF mara.
APPEND itab_wa TO itab_lt.
```

itab_wa is the work area of the table, and itab_lt is the internal table itself. You would have to populate the work area in the program and then use the above

APPEND statement to append a single line into the internal table. The APPEND statement appends the line as the last line in the internal table. You could use the following syntax to append multiple lines to an internal table.

```
APPEND lines OF itab1 TO itab2.
APPEND lines OF itab1 FROM 1 TO 50 TO itab2.
```

The above APPEND statement appends the lines of internal table itab1 to internal table itab2. If the addition FROM <idx1> TO <idx2> is specified in the APPEND statement, then only the rows from <idx1> to <idx2> will be transferred from itab1 to itab2.

Inserting Lines in an Internal Table

The INSERT statement is also used to insert lines into an internal table and is generally used to fill sorted and hashed tables. Unlike the APPEND statement, which only appends lines at the end of the internal table, you can insert lines anywhere in the internal table using INSERT. For sorted internal tables the new line is inserted according to the sort sequence as specified by the table key definition of the internal table; duplicate lines are inserted above the existing line with the same key. Duplicated records can be inserted for sorted internal tables with non-unique keys, but they cannot be inserted for an internal table with a unique key. With a hashed internal table the lines are inserted in the hash management table according to its table key.

Listing 7.13 displays the syntax for the INSERT statement.

```
TYPES: BEGIN OF line,
         material  TYPE matnr,
         plant     TYPE werks_d,
         quantity  TYPE menge,
       END OF line.
DATA: itab01 TYPE SORTED TABLE OF line
             WITH UNIQUE KEY material.
DATA: itab_wa TYPE line.
itab_wa-material = 'M2'.
itab_wa-plant = '1000'.
itab_wa-quantity = 100.
INSERT itab_wa INTO TABLE itab01.

itab_wa-material = 'M1'.
itab_wa-plant = '1000'.
```

```
itab_wa-quantity = 200.
INSERT itab_wa INTO TABLE itab01.

itab_wa-material = 'M3'.
itab_wa-plant = '1000'.
itab_wa-quantity = 100.
INSERT itab_wa INTO TABLE itab01.
```

Listing 7.13 Code for the INSERT Statement

The above statement inserts the content of the work area itab_wa into an internal table itab1 in the sort sequence as specified by the key definition. The work area has to be populated in the program before transferring the lines into the internal table.

Following is the syntax to insert multiple lines into an internal table from another internal table:

```
INSERT LINES OF itab1 [FROM <idx1>] [TO <idx2>]
       INTO TABLE itab2.
```

The above statement inserts lines from internal table itab1 into table itab2. It inserts the lines from <idx1> to <idx2> of table itab1 into table itab2 if the FROM <idx1> and TO <idx2> addition is specified in the INSERT statement; otherwise, *all* records are transferred. The multiple lines insert statement follows the rules of inserting the single table lines for the various kinds of internal table; for example, for a sorted internal table the sort order will be maintained.

Appending Summarized Lines into an Internal Table

The COLLECT statement can also be used to insert lines into an internal table. The COLLECT statement works only with internal tables that have a flat structure and is used to sum or add up the numeric table fields. For a standard internal table the COLLECT statement sums the numeric field values if a line with the key values already exists; otherwise, it appends the line to the end of the internal table. Similarly, for sorted and hashed tables the COLLECT statement sums up the numeric field values if a line with the same key value already exists; otherwise, it inserts the line into the internal table. The system field sy-tabix contains the index of the line inserted or modified in the collect statement.

Listing 7.14 displays the syntax and usage of the COLLECT statement. The example code uses the COLLECT statement to populate an internal table. COLLECT sums up the numeric value if the line already exists in the internal table. In this example it will sum up the quantity if the table record for material already exists.

```
TYPES: BEGIN OF line,
         matnr TYPE matnr,
         qty1 TYPE i,
       END OF line.
DATA: itab_wa TYPE line.
DATA: itab01 TYPE STANDARD TABLE OF TYPE line.
  itab_wa-matnr = 'M1'.
  itab_wa-qty1  = 10.
COLLECT itab_wa INTO itab01.
  WRITE: /'Index of inserted/modified line'
  WRITE sy-tabix.
    itab_wa-matnr = 'M2'.
    itab_wa-qty1  = 20.
COLLECT itab_wa INTO itab01.
  WRITE: / sy-tabix.
    itab_wa-matnr = 'M1'.
    itab_wa-qty1  = 10.
COLLECT itab_wa INTO itab01.
  WRITE: / sy-tabix.
    itab_wa-matnr = 'M2'.
    itab_wa-qty1  = 40.
COLLECT itab_wa INTO itab01.
  WRITE: / sy-tabix.
Clear itab_wa.
LOOP AT itab01 into itab_wa.
  WRITE: / itab_wa-matnr, itab_wa-qty.
ENDLOOP.
```

Listing 7.14 Syntax of COLLECT Statement for Internal Table

The output of Listing 7.14 is:

```
Index of inserted/modified line: 1 2 1 2
M1, 20
M2, 60
```

Reading Internal Table Lines

You use the `READ TABLE` statement to read individual lines from the internal table. To use the read statement you have to provide either the key or the index of the internal table line you want to read. The `READ TABLE` statement processes one record at a time, but you should use the LOOP statement if you want to process multiple lines from the internal table. The LOOP statement is discussed in detail later in this chapter.

The simplest syntax to read based on the table index is as follows:

```
DATA:   itab_wa TYPE marc,
        itab_lt TYPE STANDARD TABLE OF marc.
FIELD-SYMBOLS: <fs> TYPE marc
READ TABLE itab INDEX 10 INTO itab_wa
```

This READ TABLE statement reads the internal table line with the INDEX 10 and transfers the content to the work area itab_wa. The result of the READ statement is transferred to itab_wa only if the READ statement successfully finds a line with the INDEX 10 in the internal table itab. SY-SUBRC is set to 4 if no record corresponding to the above READ statement is found in the internal table; otherwise, it is set to 0.

This following statement reads the table line and assigns it the field symbol. The result of the READ TABLE statement is transferred to the work area or field symbol only if the READ TABLE statement successfully finds a line corresponding to conditions specified for the READ statement. SY-SUBRC is set to 4 if no record is found for the READ statement; otherwise, it is set to 0.

```
READ TABLE itab WITH KEY matnr = 'M1' ASSIGNING <fs>.
READ TABLE itab INDEX 10 ASSIGNING <FS>.
```

The data type of the work area should be compatible with the line type of the internal table. An easy way to define a work area for the internal table is as follows:

```
DATA: wa LIKE LINE OF itab.
```

You can use the TRANSPORTING addition after the INTO wa statement. With this option you can select the components or fields that you want to be transferred to the work area:

```
DATA: idx TYPE syindex.
idx = 10.
READ TABLE itab INDEX idx INTO wa
                TRANSPORTING comp1 comp3.
```

This statement reads the internal table itab with the INDEX idx and copies the content of the components or fields comp1 and comp3 from the table line to the work area wa.

If you specify the `ASSIGNING <fs>` addition, then the table line with the index `idx` is assigned to the field symbol `<fs>`. This addition is helpful if you want to modify the selected line after the `READ` statement. You can modify the table line directly by using the field symbol; otherwise, you have to use the `MODIFY` statement to modify the table line.

Note

It is important to note that the field symbol points to the table line in the memory, so you can modify the table line directly via the field symbol, and therefore performance is better.

Listing 7.15 displays the example code to modify a table record.

```
TYPES: BEGIN OF line,
         matnr TYPE matnr,
         qty1 TYPE I,
       END OF line.
DATA: itab_wa TYPE line.
DATA: itab_lt TYPE STANDARD TABLE OF TYPE line.
  itab_wa-matnr = 'M1'.
  itab_wa-qty1  = 10.
APPEND itab_wa to itab_lt.
  itab_wa-matnr = 'M2'.
  itab_wa-qty1  = 20.
APPEND itab_wa to itab_lt.
  itab_wa-matnr = 'M3'.
  itab_wa-qty1  = 30.
APPEND itab_wa to itab_lt.
LOOP AT itab_lt WHERE matnr = 'M1' INTO itab_wa.
  itab_wa-qty1 = 100.
  MODIFY itab_lt FROM itab_wa TRANSPORTING qty1.
ENDLOOP.
```

Listing 7.15 Code to APPEND and MODIFY an Internal Table

However, with the `READ TABLE` statement the above code could also be implemented as follows:

```
READ TABLE itab_lt key matnr = 'M1' ASSIGNING <fs>.
<fs>-qty1 = 100.
```

You can also read the internal table record based on any field in the table record. Following is the example code for the `READ` statement with the `WITH KEY` addition:

```
TYPES: BEGIN OF  line,
         kunnr  TYPE kunnr,     "Customer no.
         land   TYPE land1_gp,  "Country
         name1  TYPE name1_gp,  "Name
         ort01  TYPE ort01_gp,  "City
         pstlz  TYPE pstlz,     "ZIP code
       END OF line.
DATA: itab02 TYPE STANDARD TABLE of line.
DATA: wa LIKE LINE OF itab02.
SELECT * from KNA1 INTO CORRESPONDING FIELDS OF TABLE itab02.
SORT itab02 by kunnr.
READ TABLE itab02 WITH KEY kunnr = '12345'
  INTO wa BINARY SEARCH.
```

With the above `READ` statement you specify the search key to read the line from the internal table. You could use any component or field of the table line to search the table. The content of the first found line of the internal table that matches the search key is transferred to the work area. The above `READ` statement provides you with only one record even if more than one record matches the search key. You have to use the `LOOP` statement if you want all of the records matching the search key.

Standard internal tables are subject to sequential search with the above `READ` statement. With the addition `BINARY SEARCH` the search is binary instead of sequential, which considerably improves search performance at runtime. For binary search the standard internal table must be sorted by the search key in ascending order; otherwise, the search result will not find the correct row or record. The search algorithm depends on the table type if you do not specify the `BINARY SEARCH` addition.

- For sorted internal tables the search is always binary, and the addition `BINARY SEARCH` has no effect.
- For a hashed internal table the hash algorithm is used to search if the specified key is the internal table key; otherwise, the search is sequential. The addition `BINARY SEARCH` is not permitted for hashed internal tables.

Tips

The BINARY SEARCH addition is valid for standard internal tables only. The standard internal table should be sorted to use the BINARY SEARCH addition:

- The addition BINARY SEARCH does not have any effect on the READ statement for sorted internal tables.
- The BINARY SEARCH addition is not permitted with the READ statement for hashed internal tables.

The other variants of the READ statements are:

```
READ TABLE itab02 FROM wa ASSIGNING <fs>
```

and

```
READ TABLE itab02 WITH TABLE KEY
  kunnr = '12345' pstlz = '95118'.
```

For the first variant the work area must be a data object that is compatible with the line type of the internal table. The search is performed based on the content of the work area wa. The result of the READ TABLE statement for which the values in the columns of the table matches the values of the corresponding components of the work area is assigned to the field symbol.

For the second READ statement variant you have to specify the *full* table key to read the line of the internal table. If you cannot provide the full key, then you should use WITH KEY and not WITH TABLE KEY. Standard tables are read using a sequential search, sorted internal tables are searched using the binary search, and for hashed internal tables the hash algorithm is used to search for the table line.

Processing Multiple Lines of an Internal Table

You process internal table lines sequentially by using the LOOP and ENDLOOP statements. This allows you to process multiple lines in the internal table sequentially one after the other. Listing 7.16 is an example code for the LOOP statement:

```
TYPES: BEGIN OF itab_ty,
         matnr TYPE matnr,
         werks TYPE werks_d,
       END OF itab_ty.
DATA: itab_lt TYPE STANDARD TABLE OF itab_ty.
DATA: wa LIKE LINE OF itab_lt.
```

```
SELECT matnr werks FROM marc INTO TABLE itab_lt.
LOOP at itab_lt into wa.
  WRITE: / wa-matnr, wa-werks.
ENDLOOP.
```

Listing 7.16 Syntax for the LOOP Statement

The above `LOOP` statement reads each line one at a time and transfers that table line to the work area. The work area `wa` data object should be compatible with the line type of the internal table. You can use the addition `TRANSPORTING` to specify the fields to be transferred to the work area. The internal table lines are available within the `LOOP` block, and you can perform operations on the individual lines within the loop statement.

Other variants of the `LOOP` statement are:

```
LOOP AT itab_lt  WHERE matnr = '12345' INTO wa.
  WRITE: / wa-matnr, wa-werks.
ENDLOOP.
```

and

```
LOOP AT itab_lt FROM 1 TO 10 INTO wa.
  WRITE: / wa-matnr, wa-werks.
ENDLOOP
```

In the first syntax variant you have the option to specify the conditional selection of the table lines from the internal table by specifying the `WHERE` condition for the `LOOP` statement. This statement sequentially searches each line of the table for the condition specified with the `WHERE` condition. With the second variant of the `LOOP` statement mentioned above, you can limit the number of table lines to be processed by specifying the `FROM idx1` or `TO idx2` for the `LOOP` statement.

You can also perform control-level processing within the statement block of the `loop` statement. The control statements for the control-level processing are within the `AT` and `ENDAT` statements. The statement block within the `AT` and `ENDAT` statements is executed at the control break. The control break happens when the control structure for the internal table changes.

The syntax below displays control break statements when looping through the internal table.

```
LOOP at itab INTO wa.
  AT FIRST.
  ...
```

```
  ENDAT.
  AT NEW comp1.
    ...
  ENDAT.
  AT END of comp1.
    ...
  ENDAT.
  AT LAST.
    ...
  ENDAT.
ENDLOOP.
```

For control-level processing to work properly, the following rules must be followed:

- The internal table should be sorted in the sequence of the component of the line type.
- The internal table cannot be modified within the LOOP statement.
- The conditional selection of the internal table lines should not be specified for the LOOP statement; that is, you cannot use the WHERE addition to the LOOP statement.

Modifying the Internal Table Lines

You use the MODIFY statement to change the content of the lines of the internal table. You can also modify the internal table line by modifying the field symbol <fs> or reference variable <dref>, which is linked to the line of the internal table as a result of the READ statement.

The syntax to modify the internal table using the MODIFY statement is:

```
TYPES: BEGIN OF line,
         material TYPE matnr,
         plant TYPE werks_d
         fld1 TYPE I,
         fld2 TYPE I,
       END OF line.
DATA: itab TYPE STANDARD TABLE OF line.
DATA: wa TYPE line.
MODIFY TABLE itab FROM wa.
MODIFY TABLE itab FROM wa TRANSPORTING fld1 fld2.
```

This code searches for the internal table line whose key components match the key values of the work area and then modifies the selected internal table line. With the addition `TRANSPORTING`, only the fields specified after the `TRANSPORTING` statement are modified.

You can modify multiple lines of the internal table with the following syntax:

```
MODIFY itab FROM wa TRANSPORTING flds1 fld2
            WHERE material = '12345'.
```

This modifies all of the table lines that satisfy the logical `WHERE` condition. With the `TRANSPORTING` addition only the components or fields specified after the `TRANSPORTING` statement are modified.

The following `MODIFY` statement modifies the internal table line with the `INDEX idx` using the contents of the work area `wa`. The work area `wa` should be compatible with the line type of the internal table.

```
MODIFY itab FROM wa INDEX idx.
```

Listing 7.17 displays the use of the `MODIFY` statement within the `LOOP` block. The `MODIFY` statement modifies the current internal table line within the `LOOP` statement with the contents of the work area `wa`.

```
TYPES: BEGIN OF line,
         material TYPE matnr,
         plant TYPE werks_d
         fld1 TYPE I,
         fld2 TYPE I,
       END OF line.
DATA: itab TYPE STANDARD TABLE OF line.
DATA: wa TYPE line.
LOOP AT itab INTO wa.
  wa-fld1 = 100.
  wa-fld2 = 200.
  MODIFY itab FROM wa.
ENDLOOP.
```

or

```
LOOP AT itab INTO wa.
  wa-fld1 = 100.
  wa-fld2 = 200.
```

```
  MODIFY itab FROM wa TRANSPORTING fld1 fld2.
ENDLOOP.
```

Listing 7.17 Use of Modify Statement within the LOOP Statement

Deleting Internal Table Lines

You use the DELETE statement to delete lines from an internal table. Following is the syntax of the delete statement:

```
DELETE itab INDEX idx.
```

This statement deletes the table line with the INDEX idx.

The following syntax deletes multiple lines of the internal table specified by the index range or the logical expression specified by the WHERE addition:

```
DELETE itab FROM idx1 TO idx2.
```

or

```
DELETE itab FROM WHERE material = '12345'.
```

The following statement deletes multiple lines from the internal table that is sorted. This statement compares the table components and deletes the adjacent duplicates. It makes sense to use the following statement as long as the contents of the internal table are sorted:

```
DELETE ADJACENT DUPLICATES FROM TABLE itab
                COMPARING material plant.
```

or

```
DELETE ADJACENT DUPLICATES FROM TABLE itab.
```

The following delete syntax deletes the internal table lines based on the table key:

```
DELETE TABLE itab WITH TABLE KEY
                  material = '12345' plant = 'abcd'.
```

Sorting Internal Tables

You use the SORT statement to sort the internal table. You can only sort a standard or a hashed table using the SORT statement. You cannot use the SORT statement for a sorted internal table because, by definition, it is already sorted.

Following is the syntax for the SORT statement:

```
SORT itab.
SORT itab ASCENDING.
SORT itab DESCENDING.
```

The above statement sorts the internal table in ascending order by its key. By default, the system sorts the internal table in ASCENDING order if you do not specify the addition ASCENDING or DESCENDING. Other variants of SORT statement are:

```
SORT TABLE itab BY material plant DESCENDING.
SORT TABLE itab AS TEXT.
```

The first statement sorts the internal table by the field's material and plant in descending order. The second SORT statement with the addition AS TEXT sorts the character type components according to the current text environment setting specified in the user master record. Without the AS TEXT addition the internal table is sorted according to the encoding specified by the hardware platform.

Emptying the Internal Table

Depending on the table definition, you can empty the internal table by using the CLEAR or REFRESH statement. You can clear an internal table with a header line with the following statement:

```
CLEAR itab[].
```

or

```
REFRESH itab.
```

The above CLEAR and REFRESH statements delete the table body lines only, but you can use the following syntax to clear the header line and the body of the internal table:

```
CLEAR: itab, itab[].
```

or

```
CLEAR: itab.
REFRESH itab.
```

The CLEAR statement with square brackets around itab[] or REFRESH itab deletes or initializes the internal table body lines, whereas the CLEAR itab statement clears the header line.

You can use the CLEAR statement to delete or initialize the body lines of the internal table without a header line. The following statement deletes or initializes the body lines of the internal table without header lines:

```
CLEAR itab.
```

The FREE statement works like the REFRESH statement, but in addition it releases the memory area of the internal table. With the FREE statement the table body is deleted and the memory area reserved for the internal table is released. The syntax for the FREE statement as follows:

```
FREE itab.
```

Important Terminology

You should know how to define internal tables in the program and be aware of different kinds of internal table such as standard, sorted, and hashed internal tables.

- The APPEND and INSERT statements are used to populate the internal table.
- You use the READ TABLE statement to read individual records of an internal table. You can also use the addition INDEX or KEY with the READ TABLE statement to read individual records from the internal table.
- The LOOP statement is used to process individual internal table lines. This statement loops through the internal table and places the individual table records in the work area of the internal table.
- The MODIFY statement is used to modify existing records of the internal table. If the MODIFY command is used in a LOOP statement to modify the internal table, then the current line of the internal table is changed.
- The DELETE statement is used to delete a record of an internal table. You can also use the DELETE statement with the addition WITH TABLE KEY to delete records from the internal table for the specified key in the DELETE statement.
- The SORT statement is used to sort the internal table.

Practice Questions

The practice questions below will help you evaluate your understanding of the topic. The questions shown are similar in nature to those found on the certification examination, but whereas none of these questions will be found on the exam itself, they allow you to review your knowledge of the subject. Select the correct answers and then check the completeness of your answers in the following solution section. Remember that you must select all correct answers and only correct answers to receive credit for the question.

1. How many kinds of internal table are supported in the ABAP language?

☐ **A.** 2

☑ **B.** 3

☐ **C.** 1

2. Which of the following statements are true? There can be more than one true statement.

☑ **A.** Standard tables can be accessed by index.

☐ **B.** Standard tables cannot be accessed by index.

☐ **C.** A sorted table is always accessed by a unique key.

☑ **D.** Hashed tables are always accessed by index.

☑ **E.** Hashed tables are accessed by a unique key.

3. The `OCCURS` statement is required to define an internal table with a header line.

☑ **A.** True

☐ **B.** False

4. You can use the `APPEND` statement to fill a sorted internal table.

☐ **A.** True

☑ **B.** False

5. You cannot use the `INSERT` statement to insert lines into a standard internal table.

☐ **A.** True

☑ **B.** False

6. You can use a table with a header line for object-oriented programming.

☐ **A.** True

☑ **B.** False

7. An internal table line type with a deep or nested structure can be defined for internal tables with a header line.

☐ **A.** True

☑ **B.** False

8. Internal tables cannot have a deep or nested structure in their line type.

☑ **A.** True

☑ **B.** False

9. The `READ` statement with the addition `BINARY SEARCH` for a sorted internal table is better for performance.

☐ **A.** True

☑ **B.** False

10. The `READ` statement with the `BINARY SEARCH` addition cannot be used for a sorted internal table.

☐ **A.** True

☑ **B.** False

11. The `BINARY SEARCH` addition cannot be used with the `READ` statement for the `HASHED` table.

☑ **A.** True

☐ **B.** False

12. Which of the following is a true statement:

☑ **A.** A sorted table can have a unique or a non-unique key.

☐ **B.** A standard table should always have a unique key.

☑ **C.** A hashed table should always have a unique table key.

13. You can empty the body of the internal table `itab` with a header line using the `CLEAR itab` statement.

☐ **A.** True

☑ **B.** False

14. You can modify an internal table by using the `UPDATE` statement.

☐ **A.** True

☑ **B.** False

15. Internal tables can also be modified after executing the `READ` statement with the addition `ASSIGNING`.

☐ **A.** True

☑ **B.** False

16. You cannot use a `SORT` statement for a sorted internal table.

☑ **A.** True

☐ **B.** False

Practice Question Answers and Explanations

1. Correct answer: **B**

   There are three types of internal tables: standard, sorted, and hashed.

2. Correct answers: **A, E**

   A standard table can be accessed by the index or the key. A hashed table is accessed by the unique key, and it used to hash algorithms to access the table record. A sorted table can be accessed by the index or the key. A sorted table can have a unique or a non-unique key.

3. Correct answer: **B**

   You require an `OCCURS` addition to declare a internal table with a header line, but you can define an internal table with header line using the `WITH HEADER LINE` addition.

4. Correct answer: **B**

   Sorted tables should not be filled using the `APPEND` statement. Instead, they should be filled with the `INSERT` statement. You cannot use the `APPEND` statement because the table is stored in a sorted order. `APPEND` always adds the record as the last entry in the table, so sorted tables use the `INSERT` statement to insert table records in the internal table.

5. Correct answer: **B**

   You can use the `INSERT` statement to insert records in a standard internal table, the record will be added to the end of the table.

6. Correct answer: **B**

   You cannot use an internal table with a header line in object-oriented programming.

7. Correct answer: **B**

   You cannot define an internal table with a header line that has a deep or nested structure.

8. Correct answer: **B**

   You can define internal tables with deep or nested structure line types, but the internal table must be one without a header line.

9. Correct answer: **B**

   `BINARY SEARCH` does not have any effect on the sorted internal table. Sorted internal tables always use a binary search to read the table records with the `READ` statement.

10. Correct answer: **B**

    You can use the `BINARY SEARCH` with the `READ` statement for sorted tables, but it does not have any effect.

11. Correct answer: **A**

    You cannot use `BINARY SEARCH` with the `READ` statement to read hashed internal tables. Hashed internal tables require a unique key to read the internal table record, and they use a hash algorithm to find the table record.

12. Correct answers: **A, C**

    The standard internal table can have a non-unique key, and the hashed internal table must always have a unique key.

    The sorted table can have a unique or a non-unique key.

13. Correct answer: **B**

    You cannot clear an internal table with a header line with the `CLEAR itab` statement. To empty the table body you have to use the `CLEAR itab[]` statement.

14. Correct answer: **B**

    The `UPDATE` statement cannot be used to modify the internal table. You use the `MODIFY` statement to modify the internal table.

15. Correct answer: **A**

    You can modify internal tables using the `ASSIGINING` statement because the `ASSIGINING` points to the memory address of the table record or field.

16. Correct answer: **A**

    A sorted internal table is sorted by default, and hence you cannot use the `SORT` statement to sort a sorted internal table.

Take Away

You need to understand the syntax to create internal tables, be able to define a data type, and use it to define an internal table in the program. You need to understand the difference between internal tables with header lines and without header lines, and you should know how to define such a table in the program. You also must be aware that the internal table with header line is not supported in ABAP Objects programming. You should be able to differentiate between the different kinds of internal table such as standard, sorted, and hashed and be able to use them in a program. You should also be able to populate internal tables with the `APPEND` and `INSERT` statements and be able to perform various operations on the internal table. You should know the syntax to update, modify, delete, and read individual records from the internal table.

Refresher

You should now be able to describe internal tables and their use in the ABAP programming language. You should know the keywords and the syntax to define and access the internal table. You should be able to use internal tables in a program to store data temporarily and be able to process the data in the table.

Table 7.2 repeats the key concepts of this chapter in short form.

Key Concept	Definition
Internal table	An internal table is a local program variable-data object and is used to store multiple structured data records temporarily in memory.
Kinds of internal table	There are three kinds of internal tables: standard table, sorted table, and hashed table.
Standard internal table	Standard tables can have a unique or a non-unique key and can be accessed with the key or an index. They can be filled with the `APPEND` or `INSERT` statement, or you can use the select statement to populate them from the database (see Chapter 9, Basic ABAP Programs and Interface Creation)
Sorted internal table	Sorted tables can have a unique or a non-unique key. The table records are stored in a sorted order, and by default are sorted in ascending order. You fill the sorted internal table with the `INSERT` statement.
Hashed internal table	Hashed internal tables must have a unique key that you must use to access the table record. A hash algorithm is used to read the hashed internal table.

Table 7.2 Key Concept Refresher

Summary

You have learned in detail the concepts of internal tables, the different kinds of internal table, and the valid operations on each kind of internal table. You should know the syntax to define internal tables, access internal tables and process the table records in the internal table. This knowledge will allow you to easily pass this topic on the certification examination.

SQL Statements Including Update Strategies

8

Techniques You'll Master:

- Understand the purpose and benefits of using a data model in application development
- Access specific columns and rows within a particular database table or tables
- Explain the terms database LUW and SAP LUW and the differences between them
- Bundle changes to database tables in the client-server architecture of an SAP system
- Understand the role of lock objects and how to set and release SAP locks
- Perform database changes using various update techniques

The three-tier architecture used by SAP provides for the user who interacts with the presentation layer. This in turn controls the business logic running on an application server, which may retrieve and store data in the database server. The system is designed as database neutral, meaning that it works with a number of databases. Normally from your perspective, the underlying database is not a prime concern.

In this chapter, we will touch briefly on data modeling, or table design. We follow this with methods of retrieving data from the database and efficient use of the database (using SQL). Lastly, the chapter covers logical units of work (LUW), lock objects, and update tasks.

Each of these topics is covered separately and is followed by the practice exercise and the solution to the exercise.

Real-World Scenario

Imagine you want to develop a new transaction that uses database tables provided by SAP and new database tables unique to your process. This new transaction will access data from standard SAP database tables and update the new database tables based on user interaction through multiple dialog steps. The transaction will be used by multiple users simultaneously and needs to provide a consistent state when committing changes to the database.

The transaction will provide access to the records being updated for a single user, but the database tables not being updated will allow multiple users to see the data simultaneously. Owing to the complexity of the process, it requires multiple dialog screens to gather the data for eventual update across multiple database tables.

The number of records that actually are updated or posted during the process may vary anywhere from zero to several thousand at a time. You were tasked with providing a quickly responding transaction for the user and maintaining a consistent database state. This means that if any update fails, you are able to return to the last consistent state before any change was made.

Objectives of this Portion of the Test

The purpose of this portion of the certification examination is to verify that you have detailed knowledge of how to retrieve data from the database and how to make changes to database tables in a manner in which the data remains consistent while allowing the user to continue to work as efficiently as possible.

This portion of the examination will test your knowledge of Open SQL and different mechanisms for making changes. The points that you will need to understand from this section include:

- Data selection techniques from the database
- Update strategies for the database
- Bundling changes to the database

Key Concepts Refresher

Typically, you need to access and change data within the database. As a consequence, you need to understand and be able to perform the following types of tasks when developing ABAP programs, so you should be able to do the following functions or processes:

- Design tables for efficient use
- Read data from a single or multiple database tables
- Create and using lock objects
- Select the most appropriate type of update
- Describe a logical unit of work from both a database and application perspective

Data Modeling

When you develop business applications, parts of the real world must be represented as data. A business unit represents an entity, and these entities exist in relationship with each other andare fixed in the underlying data model. This is referred to as an *entity relationship model* (ERM).

You use this data model to implement appropriate table definitions including their relationships with each other in the ABAP Dictionary. Activating the table definitions in the ABAP Dictionary, automatically creates the corresponding database tables in the database.

Note

SAP uses the so-called flight model throughout its training materials, online documentation, and ABAP keyword documentation. We use the same model during our explanation in this section because it is well known and easy to understand from both a business perspective and a user perspective.

Imagine a simple example from the SAP flight model: If customers of a travel agency want to travel from one place to another, they require the travel agency to find out:

- Which connection offers the flight that is most direct?
- On the day of travel which flights provide acceptable flight times?
- Dependent on individual's needs, which is the cheapest flight, the fastest connection, or a connection with a particular arrival time?

This perspective differs from that of a travel agency. The data is stored according to technical criteria in a central database within the data model that manages this required data. The amount of data stored far exceeds the requirements of a specific customer. The travel agency needs to be able to access the data to meet the individual requirements of the customer using application programs.

The flight data model contains entities for all business information that is logically connected, such as cities, airports, airlines, flight routes, flights, and so on. These entities all relate to each other in certain ways:

- Each flight schedule contains exactly one airline, one departure airport, and one destination airport.
- Each bookable flight always belongs to exactly one existing flight schedule.

You manage the data, without redundancies, using these relationships. The travel agency can provide any data requested by the customer.

For each entity in the data model, the developer creates a transparent table in the ABAP Dictionary. The ABAP Dictionary is a platform-independent description of a database table, not actually the database table itself. However, when a transparent table is activated in the ABAP Dictionary, a table of the same name is automatically created within the database.

A transparent table contains fields that allow you to store data records in a structured way. You declare some of the table fields as key fields when they are to be used for the unique identification of data records within the database table. The field or fields used for this unique identification are also called the primary key. You cannot have data records in the same table with the same primary key; they each must have a unique primary key.

In the ABAP Dictionary, a transparent table is an implemented description of the corresponding database table that contains the actual application data. The fields of the transparent table form the identically named columns of the corresponding database table. Data elements are normally used to describe the individual fields. The data elements themselves define keywords and headers and refer to domains for their technical properties, thus providing the link between the data object and the domain.

Within the ABAP Dictionary, a transparent table is a description of the corresponding database table that contains the actual data. The fields of the transparent table in the ABAP Dictionary match the identically named columns of the corresponding database table. Data elements are normally used to describe the individual fields. The data elements themselves define the semantic use and refer to domains for their technical attributes, providing the link between the data object and the domain. Programmatically, you address data elements in ABAP programs with the `TYPE` statement. This allows you to define elementary types that have the type attributes of a particular data element. These type attributes include one of the recognized ABAP Dictionary data types, the field length, and, where appropriate, the number of decimal places. More information regarding the ABAP Dictionary can be found in Chapter 10.

As well as the list of fields, the transparent tables contain other attributes that are required to create a table of the same name in the database and describe its properties in full:

- The primary key for the database table (key fields)
- The technical properties required by the database to create the database table (the expected size and expected frequency of access)
- Settings for technologies that can improve performance when accessing the database table (this includes secondary indexes and types of buffering)

The definition of a transparent table appears to be very similar to the definition of a global structure type. Transparent tables can be used in programming in the same way as structure types. For example, they can be used to define a structured data object or a structure variable, to type an interface parameter, or as a line type of a global or local table type. When used this way only the list of fields is important. The other properties of the transparent table are irrelevant when using it as a data type.

One other difference between using a transparent table and structure type is that a transparent table only contains a list of elementary fields, but the components of a structure type can themselves be structured again, producing nested structures. A component of a structure can even be typed with a table type, producing a deep structure.

Tip

In older versions of code (prior to Release 4.0), transparent tables were often used as data types. It is currently recommended that they only be used directly in connection with access to the database. It is not recommended that transparent tables be used in defining user interfaces.

The problem is in the unwanted dependency between the definition of database objects or interfaces and the user interface.

You can call up detailed information on the SAP data model (graphical display, data records, and fields) within the SAP development environment using the SAP Transaction SD11.

Data Retrieval

Every relational database system has its own native SQL. This native SQL is unfortunately database specific. Therefore, if you write an ABAP program using native SQL, you lose much of the standard functionality of an SAP system, for example, access to data being buffered on application servers, the use of the database interface, syntax checking, and a number of the performance tools.

SAP, to overcome this restriction provides Open SQL, which is an SAP-defined database-independent SQL standard for ABAP. The Open SQL statements are dynamically converted to the corresponding native SQL statements of the current database system and are therefore independent of the database. They allow you uniform access to the data, regardless of the database system installed.

Before programming direct access to database tables, you should look for reuse components that provide a read process. Four types of reuse components encapsulate database access:

- Logical databases
- Function modules
- BAPIs
- Methods of global classes

If no reuse are components available or usable for your data selection, you have to implement the read process yourself. It is recommended that you encapsulate the access in a reuse component, that is, create a function module or method within a global class.

You use the Open SQL statement `SELECT` to read records from the database. The `SELECT` statement contains a series of clauses, each of which has a different task (an example of the clauses is shown in Listing 8.1):

- The `SELECT` clause describes which fields or columns of the database table you want to retrieve.
- The `FROM` clause identifies the source, either a database table or view, from which the data is selected.
- The `INTO` clause determines the target into which the selected data is placed.
- The `WHERE` clause specifies the condition that identifies which record or records you will retreve.

```
SELECT fldate planetype seatsocc seatsmax
       FROM sflight
       INTO (fldate,planetype,seatsocc,seatsmax)
       WHERE carrid = flight-carrid
       AND   connid = flight-connid.
ENDSELECT.
```

Listing 8.1 SELECT Example

A `SELECT` statement is a loop. However, there are two variations that do not behave as a loop: a `SELECT SINGLE` and an array fetch (using either the additions `INTO TABLE` or `APPENDING TABLE`).

You use the first variation, the `SELECT SINGLE` statement, to read a single record. Correct usage requires you to provide a unique access to the record; unique access requires you to specify all key fields in the `WHERE` clause. The exception to this is the client field, which you do not normally specify because the database interpreter automatically supplies your current client.

Caution

It is important to remember that you cannot specify a client in the `WHERE` clause unless you provide the clause `CLIENT SPECIFIED`.

You specify a field list of an asterisk (*) to indicate that all fields of the table row should be read. If you only want specific columns, you list the required fields for the field list. You use the `INTO` clause to identify the target data object where the read data is placed. The data object you specify in the `INTO` clause should have the same structure as the field list. As an alternative to specifying a single data object as the target, you can also specify a list of target fields with the `INTO` clause.

Note

Only the field types have to match the target. The names of the target structure are not taken into account. If you want to use a structure variable as a target that has the same names as the target list, but has a different structure (additional fields or a different order of fields), you would use the addition `CORRESPONDING FIELDS OF`. This only fills the fields of the same name in the target area. Again the corresponding field types must be the same; otherwise, a conversion takes place, and it is possible that incomplete data can be transported to the target field.

The advantages of this variation are:

- The target structure does not have to be left-justified or in the same order as the field list.
- It is easy to maintain, because extending the field list or target structure does not require any other changes to be made to the program, as long as there is a field in the structure that has the same name (and preferably the same type).

The disadvantage of this variation is that it requires more work from the system, and it therefore does not perform as quickly.

You use a `SELECT` loop to read several rows of a database table into the program. You use the `WHERE` clause to determine which rows are read into the target structure and processed using the statement block within the loop body. You can also connect multiple logical conditions within the `WHERE` clause through the use of `AND` or `OR`.

The database provides the data to the database interface of the application server in blocks called packages. The data is then copied into the target area row by row for processing.

You use the `INTO TABLE` addition to copy the data into an internal table directly instead of row by row. Performance on this is faster than processing row by row because the internal table is filled in blocks, not by rows. Also, because this Array Fetch fills the entire internal table in one pass, the `SELECT` is no longer a loop (the second variation that is not a loop) and does not require an `ENDSELECT`. Finally, the Array Fetch replaces the contents of the internal table. If you want to append rows instead, you use the `APPENDING TABLE` addition.

Performance of Database Access

In many cases, the database accesses occupy the majority of runtime of an ABAP application. To not overload the system and to keep the wait time for a user to a minimum, you should pay special attention to runtime requirements with database access in particular. A number of technologies are available in Open SQL that enable you to optimize the runtime.

Each database manages data records within a database table based on the contents of key fields. If your access to the database table is restricted to all or at least the first few key fields through the use of the `WHERE` clause, the database can retrieve the required data very quickly and efficiently. However, should you try to access data in a table with fields that are not part of the table key (non-key fields), the database cannot use its indexing of the records for rapid access. In the worse case, the entire database table has to be searched for the required entries. This is referred to as a sequential search. This can produce very long wait times for the database access.

If you access the same non-key field search often, you can create a secondary index defining the fields contained in this non-key field search improve performance. If the database optimizer finds a more efficient way of obtaining the requested data through a different index that more closely matches the `WHERE` clause, it will use this secondary index to retrieve the data.

A secondary index is an index created in addition to the primary index of a database table. It can be created or examined by using the INDEXES... button on the application toolbar when displaying a table in either Transaction SE11 or SE80.

Whether an existing secondary index is used in a database, access depends on a function in the database system known as the Database Optimizer. In Open SQL, it is not possible or necessary to explicitly specify the use of a secondary index in the `SELECT` statement.

Tip

With selections from client-specified database tables, the client is always transmitted to the database. It therefore makes sense to include the client field as the first field when you define an index for such tables.

With data retrieval, a major proportion of the runtime is needed to transfer the data from the database server to the application server. If the data is read frequently and seldom changed, you can reduce the runtime by buffering the data on the application server. The decision to buffer data must be made separately for each database table. Because a limited amount of buffer space is available on the application server, the ideal database table is small, read frequently, rarely changed, and normally accessed directly with its key fields. The buffer settings are defined in the transparent tables in the ABAP Dictionary with use of the TECHNICAL SETTINGS button.

Caution

The decision to buffer a database table is not a simple one and should be made by an experienced ABAP developer in consultation with the system administrator. Each application server contains its own SAP table buffer. If a system is composed of several application servers, a special synchronization mechanism ensures that database changes will invalidate the corresponding buffer contents. However, this means that time lags in the synchronization process will, for a short period of time, allow the buffer to be out-of-date or that invalid data could be read from the buffer. You must take this into account when making a decision about buffering.

If an ABAP program requests data from a buffered table, the database interface first tries to retrieve the data from the SAP table buffer. If it is successful, this speeds up your access between 10 and 100 times in contrast to actually retrieving it from the database.

There are also additions for the `SELECT` statement that always cause data to be read directly from the database regardless of the buffer settings. You should be aware of the possible performance problems that can result using this type of access on buffered tables. If you find it is necessary to use a statement that bypasses the buffer, you should try to minimize the number of times the statement is used.

Often you are required to read data from multiple database tables. The use of a table join usually provides the best performance. You must specify three things when defining a table join:

- Join tables describe what database tables should be accessed.
- A join condition describes how the records of the two tables are connected.
- Join columns describe which columns from the join tables should be retrieved.

There are two options for implementing a table join:

- You create a database view in the ABAP Dictionary that corresponds to a table join and select from it in your program.
- You can implement a join yourself using the `SELECT` statement in your program (ABAP join) (an example is shown in Listing 8.2). At runtime, the system dynamically generates an appropriate database query in the database interface.

Tip

A database view is a view of the relevant database tables and does not contain data redundantly.

```
SELECT *
       FROM  sflight
         LEFT JOIN scarr
         ON sflight~carrid = scarr~carrid
       INTO CORRESPONDING FIELDS OF TABLE gt_sflight
       WHERE  sflight~carrid IN s_carrid
       AND    sflight~connid IN s_connid
       AND    sflight~fldate IN s_fldate.
```

Listing 8.2 An ABAP Join into a Table

In addition to the `SELECT` statement, Open SQL also contains `INSERT`, `DELETE`, `UPDATE`, and `MODIFY` statements. You should only use these latter statements with an understanding of the SAP transaction concept as discussed below; otherwise, you may cause data inconsistencies.

One or more rows can be processed using an SQL command. Commands that process several rows usually provide better performance than the corresponding single set version. The exception is mass data change using `MODIFY`.

All Open SQL commands update the system return code. The return value (`SY-SUBRC`) will be 0 (zero) if the command was successfully executed, and the system field `SY-DBCNT` will return the number of rows for which the command was carried out. Any return code other than zero indicates that the command was unsuccessful; the exact meaning depends on the actual command.

Caution

Open SQL commands do not perform any authorization checks automatically. You must execute these explicitly in your program.

If an Open SQL statement that executes a change to the database returns a return code other than zero, you should make sure the database is returned to its original consistent state before you attempt to make another database change. To achieve this you perform a database rollback that reverses all changes in the current database LUW.

There are two ways of causing a database rollback:

- Sending a termination dialog message (a message with type `A` [termination type])
- Using the ABAP statement `ROLLBACK WORK`

The transmission of an `A` type message causes a database rollback and terminates the program. All other message types (`E` [error type], `W` [warning type], and `I` [information type]) also involve a dialog, but do not trigger a database rollback.

The ABAP statement `ROLLBACK WORK` causes a database rollback, but does not terminate the program.

Logical Units of Work

An SAP LUW (logical unit of work) is a group of changes that belong together in the SAP system from a logical point of view. These changes are either carried out made together or they are not made at all.

In general you will not normally find that a business transaction is processed by a single SAP LUW. The entire process is split up into individual, logical parts. Each of these parts corresponds to an SAP LUW. The definition of SAP LUWs depends on the entire process and its modeling.

A database LUW consists of changes that are executed until the database status is "sealed," also known as the data being committed to the database (shown in Figure 8.1). Within a database LUW, it is possible to discard all of the changes that have taken place up to that point through the use of a database rollback. A database rollback resets the database to the status it had before the current database LUW. You would use this database rollback function to restore the previous consistent database status if an error has occurred.

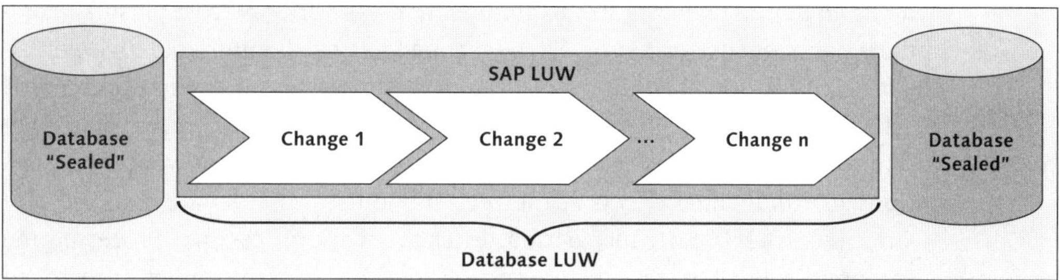

Figure 8.1 SAP LUW within a Database LUW

When you use the ABAP statements `ROLLBACK WORK` and `COMMIT WORK`, you explicitly implement a database rollback or database commit. There are also instances when a database commit is triggered implicitly. Implicit database commits are always initiated whenever the program has to wait (as part of the release of the work process), such as in the following cases:

- When the system sends an SAP screen to the presentation layer
- When the system sends a dialog message to the presentation layer
- Whenever there are synchronous and asynchronous RFC calls (Remote Function Call)
- Statements `CALL TRANSACTION <tcode>` or `SUBMIT <program>`

If you encounter an error during the processing of an SAP LUW, it should be possible to return to a consistent database status that existed before the beginning of the SAP LUW. For this to be possible, the SAP LUW must be placed within a database LUW.

Caution

With the above implicit database commits, you cannot place changes that belong to an SAP LUW in different dialog steps (a dialog step is the program processing after a screen). This would place these steps in a separate database LUW, violating the SAP LUW.

This is not a trivial matter. Usually the SAP transaction has several screens or a single screen with multiple subscreens in the form of a tab strip, and whenever there is a screen change (a full screen or subscreen), an implicit database commit is triggered. You must be able to bundle the entries from the user that form the SAP LUW from different screens and make these changes within the database LUW.

The three-tier architecture means that many users with low-cost personal computers (with low performance) can be mapped to a small number of high-performance and considerably more expensive work processes on application servers. Each work process on an application server is assigned a work process on a high-performance database server. Distributing user requests to work processes means that individual clients at the presentation server level are assigned to a work process for a particular period. After the work process has processed the user input in a dialog step, the user along with the program context is removed from the work process, thus freeing it for another user.

With the three-tier architecture, the number of database users is considerably lower than the number of active users in the system. This has a positive effect on the behavior of the database. Releasing the work process before each user dialog ensures that the user actions, normally longer lasting than the actual system processing, do not block any work processes on the application server and particularly on the database server. This produces a smaller load on database resources. Only when the user has completed processing the screen, requiring the program processing to continue, is the program context rolled back in.

Enqueue and Dequeue

If several users are competing for access to the same table or tables, you need to find a way of synchronizing access to protect the consistency of the data. Locks are a way of coordinating competing access to a resource. Each user requests a lock before accessing critical data to prevent other users from modifying it before this use is complete. It is important to obtain the lock as late as possible and release it as quickly as possible so as to not create a bottleneck for other users unnecessarily.

The *Database Management System* (DBMS) physically locks the table lines that are read with the intent of being changed (`SELECT SINGLE <f> FROM <dbtab> FOR UPDATE`). This is a database lock. Other users who want to access the locked record or records must wait until after the physical lock is released. The lock remains until the end of a database LUW, triggered by the database commit, when the Database Management System releases all locks that were set during the database LUW.

Within the SAP system, this means each database lock is released whenever a screen is displayed because the screen change triggers an implicit database commit. Database locks are not sufficient if data is collected throughout several screens and are required to remain locked.

To keep a lock through a series of screens, the SAP system has a global lock table on one application server that is used to set logical locks for table entries (see Figure 8.2). The lock table and the enqueue work process that manages the lock table is on a uniquely defined application server of the SAP system. The server containing this enqueue work process is known as the *central instance*. All of the logical lock requirements of the SAP system, regardless of which application server requested the lock, run on this system-wide, unique work process.

It is also possible to use logical locks to "lock" table entries that do not yet exist within the database. This is useful when you create new table rows, and is not possible with database locks.

You set a logical lock by calling the lock module. This special, table-related function module is created automatically when you activate a table-related lock object. When you call the lock module, logical locks are set for the entries in the respective tables.

You maintain lock objects in the ABAP Dictionary. The customer namespace for lock objects is either `EY` or `EZ`. When you create a lock object, you specify the table whose entries will be locked later. This is known as the *primary* or *basis table*. However, you can specify other tables that have a foreign key relationship to the primary table, which are known as *secondary tables*.

The lock module created by the system automatically contains input parameters for the lock parameters. The lock parameters are used to communicate with the lock module which records are to be logically locked and consist of the key fields of the primary table. When the lock object is successfully activated, the system generates one function module for creating or enqueuing a lock and one function module for releasing or dequeuing a lock. The function modules are named `ENQUEUE_<lock_object_name>` and `DEQUEUE_<lock_object_name>`. A logical lock is set when you call the enqueue function module, but you can only create a lock if no other lock entry conflicts with it. The lock module produces an exception if the lock cannot be obtained.

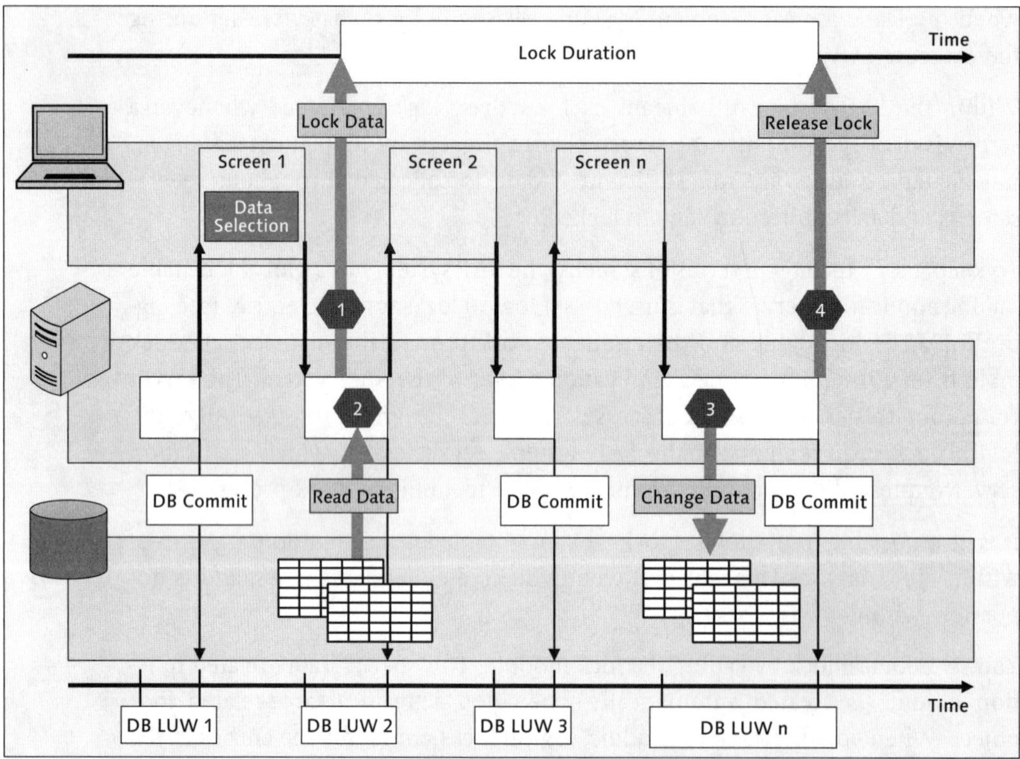

Figure 8.2 Locking Data through Database LUWs

Depending on the bundle technique used for database updates, an application program may need to delete the lock entries it created (for an inline update) or have them deleted automatically (during the update task). If a program that created lock entries is terminated, the locks are automatically released (implicitly). A program termination occurs with the production of a message of either type `A` or `X`, with the execution of the statements `LEAVE PROGRAM` and `LEAVE TO TRANSACTION`, or if the user enters "/n" in the command field.

At the end of the dialog program or when proceeding to another record, you call the DEQUEUE function module to release the lock entries in the lock table. Unlike the ENQUEUE function module, the DEQUEUE function modules do not trigger any exceptions. If you want to release all locks, you can use the function module DEQUEUE_ALL.

If you call a lock module with a lock parameter set to its initial value or not specified, the system will interpret this as a generic value and lock all table lines based on the parameter values you did supply. The client parameter is an exception to this rule. If the client is not provided when the ENQUEUE function is called, the lock only applies to the current execution client. If the client is specified, the lock only applies to that client. If the client is specified as a space, the lock applies to all clients.

You can override the default lock mode of the lock module specified in the lock object by using the parameter override MODE_<tablename>. The parameter X_<lock_parameter> allows you to lock table records that contain an initial value in the corresponding lock parameter.

- The parameter _SCOPE defines the validity area of the lock. The values and their meanings are shown in Table 8.1.

Value	Meaning
1	The lock remains in the program that set it and is deleted again by the program. This is for use with inline updates.
2	The lock is passed to the update program or called programs (this is the default). This is for updates through an update program.
3	Two locks are set. One stays with the program and must be deleted within the program. The other is passed to the update program. This is required whenever the update task is triggered for a partial update, but the record should remain locked in the program for further updates.

Table 8.1 Scope Parameters

- The _WAIT parameter defines whether a lock request should be repeated if the first lock attempt fails.
- You use the _COLLECT parameter to store the lock request in a local lock container until the lock container is collected and passed on as a unit to the enqueue server.

Requesting any lock from a program is a communication step with lock administration. If you set a lock for several objects, this communication occurs for each lock. If you use the local lock container, you can reduce the technical effort for this step. You set the parameter _COLLECT = 'X' whenever you call the lock module. This collects the lock requests in the local lock container for processing together. You send the contents of the lock container with the function module FLUSH_ENQUEUE.

If you are able to successfully obtain all lock requests, the system deletes the entire contents of the local lock container. If one of the locks in the container is not successful and cannot be set, the function module triggers the exception FOREIGN_LOCK. When this happens, none of the locks registered in the container are set, and the contents of the container will remain intact for further dispatch attempts. If you need to delete the contents of the local lock container, you call the function module RESET_ENQUEUE.

Table 8.2 shows the effect of the MODE_<tablename> parameter.

Lock Mode	Meaning
E	Extensible — lock for data change (accumulative exclusive lock)
X	Exclusive — lock for data change (exclusive write lock)
S	Shared — lock for protected data display (shared lock)

Table 8.2 Lock Modes

The only difference between modes E and X is that E allows accumulation of locks and X does not allow accumulation of locks. You implement the mode S if you wish to ensure that the data displayed in your program cannot be changed by other users while it is displayed. This is a case where you are not attempting to change the data, but do not want any one else changing the data while you are using it.

Existing exclusive locks (E or X) always reject every lock attempt of another user, regardless of the mode used by the other user. An existing shared lock (S), allows other shared locks for protected display.

Caution

If you want to ensure that you are using up-to-date data in your program with the intention of changing the data and then saving it to the database, you must perform the following steps in this order (the later on following Figure 8.3 shows these four points with the corresponding numbers):

- Set locks for the data to be processed.
- If the lock is successfully set, read the current data from the database table.
- Change the program data and update the changes to the database.
- Release the locks you set.

This order ensures that you only read data that has been changed consistently by other programs and that your changes run completely under the protection of locks. This assumes that all application programs use the SAP lock concept and adhere to the given step sequence.

If you do not adhere to the sequence, there is the danger that your program will read data from the database that is currently locked by another program. In this case, even if the lock is successfully set after the read action, the data read by your program and displayed is already out of date.

Listing 8.3 shows a call to a lock object with a `MODE_<tablename>` parameter, a `_SCOPE` parameter, and a `_WAIT` parameter specified. You should note the parameter named `x_name`. This parameter, if supplied with an `'X'`, prevents the parameter `name` from behaving in a generic manner and instead locks a blank value.

```
CALL FUNCTION 'ENQUEUE_ESRDIRE'
  EXPORTING
    mode_trdir     = l_enq_mode
    name           = incl2
    x_name         = ' '
    _scope         = '2'
    _wait          = ' '
  EXCEPTIONS
    foreign_lock   = 01
    system_failure = 02.
IF sy-subrc NE 0 AND rs38l-extern = space.
  MESSAGE ID     sy-msgid
          TYPE   'E'
          NUMBER sy-msgno
          WITH   sy-msgv1 sy-msgv2 sy-msgv3 sy-msgv4.
ENDIF.
```

Listing 8.3 Call to a Lock Object

Inline Updates

If your transaction makes database updates from within your dialog program (inline updates), you must bundle all of the database changes into a single dialog step, normally the last. This is the only way to ensure that all of your database changes are processed as a single unit. To accomplish this within your dialog program, the changes are stored within the global data of the program until the point where the changes will be made to the database.

If you update the database directly from within your program, you must set and release the SAP locks. Use the steps in the previous caution box and shown in the later on following Figure 8.3 to ensure access to consistent data.

Tip

Remember that in this case your program must delete the lock entries. To release the lock entry you execute either the unlock function module `DEQUEUE_<lock_object>`, which belongs to the lock object, or the general unlock function module `DEQUEUE_ALL`, which releases all lock entries.

Perform on Commit

You can bundle database updates from a dialog program for execution by using the special subroutine technique `PERFORM <subroutine> ON COMMIT`. This registers the specified subroutine for execution, but the subroutine will not be executed until the system reaches the next `COMMIT WORK` statement. If you encapsulate the database updates in the subroutines, they can be separated from the program logic and processed at the end of the LUW.

A subroutine registered with `PERFORM ON COMMIT` can be registered multiple times, but only executes once per LUW in the order it was first registered. If you nest `PERFORM ON COMMIT` calls after Release 4.6 a runtime error, will be triggered. The `COMMIT WORK` statement carries out all subroutines registered to be executed, in the registration order one after the other, and then triggers a database commit after processing all registered subroutines. If you encounter an error during the processing of a registered subroutine, you can terminate processing from within the subroutine with a type `A` message, and the previous consistent database status will be restored.

The subroutines called with `PERFORM ON COMMIT` cannot have an interface. They must work with global data and will use the values the data objects contain at the point when the subroutine is actually run.

Update Modules

Update techniques allow you to separate the user dialog program used to accept user entries and the program that updates the data in the database. Figure 8.3 shows the steps that occur when a program uses an update request:

1. The dialog program receives the data changed by the user and writes it to a special log table using an entry called a request. Later the update program writes the data contained within the log tables to the database. The dialog program may write several entries to the log table. The entries in the log table represent the LUW.
2. The dialog program closes the data packet (LUW) and informs the Basis system that a packet exists for update by creating a header for the request records.
3. A Basis program reads the data associated with the LUW from the log table and supplies it to the update program.
4. The update program accepts the transferred data and updates the database with the entries in the request.
5. If the update is successful, a Basis program deletes all entries for this LUW from the log table. If an error occurs, the entries remain in the log table, although they are flagged as incorrect. The user who triggered the update is normally (the behavior is controlled by certain system parameters) informed by express mail about the error.

You implement the update program as a special function module known as an update module. Update modules only have an interface for transferring data through the `IMPORTING` and `TABLES` parameters. These must be typed using reference fields or structures.

You create update requests by calling the respective update function module in a dialog program using the `IN UPDATE TASK` addition. This addition writes the function module and the input data as an exception request and does not execute the function module immediately.

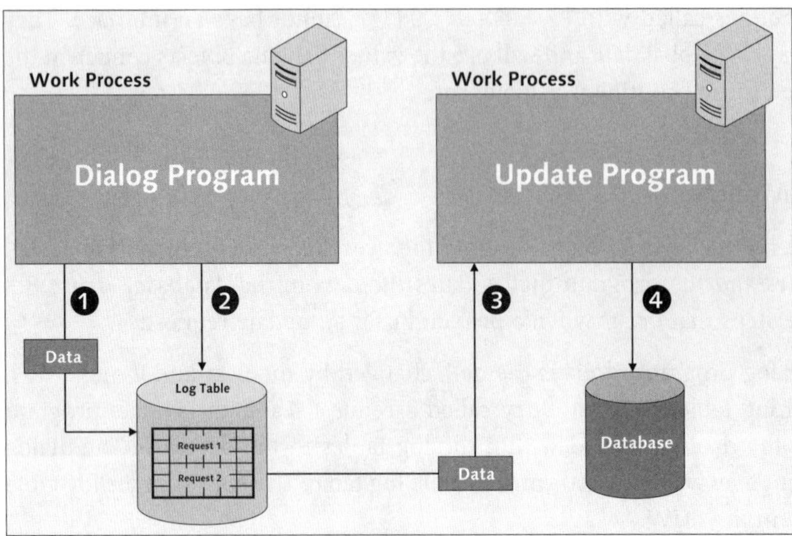

Figure 8.3 Process Flow of an Update

The same update key is used to store all of the update flags for an SAP LUW. When the system executes a `COMMIT WORK` statement, it creates a header entry for the request entries, and then the unit is closed. The log header contains information about the dialog program that wrote the log entries and the update modules to be executed. Once the log header is created, the system informs the dispatcher process that an update package is available for processing.

You may need to discard all change requests that were written for the current SAP LUW. To discard the current SAP LUW during the generation phase, which is before the commit work occurs, as you do with an inline update, you use the ABAP statement `ROLLBACK WORK` or produce a type `A` message.

Both methods delete all previous update flags, delete all previously set locks, discard all updates executed in the current database LUW, and discard all form routines registered using `PERFORM ON COMMIT`.

If you need to trigger a database rollback within the update module, you issue a type `A` message. The processing of the current SAP LUW will be terminated, and the log entry belonging to the SAP LUW is flagged as containing an error. The termination message is also entered in the log.

Listing 12.4 shows a call to a module from an SAP NetWeaver 7.0 system. Note the `IN UPDATE TASK` following the function module name.

```
CALL FUNCTION 'WFRULES_WRITE_DOCUMENT' IN UPDATE TASK
  EXPORTING
    objectid              = objectid
    tcode                 = tcode
    utime                 = utime
    udate                 = udate
    username              = username
    planned_change_number = planned_change_number
    upd_twfns             = upd_twfns
    upd_twfsa             = upd_twfsa
  TABLES
    xtwfns                = xtwfns
    ytwfns                = ytwfns
    xtwfsa                = xtwfsa
    ytwfsa                = ytwfsa.
```

Listing 8.4 Call to an Update Module

Figure 8.4 shows the attributes of the called update module. Note the first three options below the UPDATE MODULE radio button. The first two, which cause an immediate start of the update module, cause the update module to run as a V1 (a primary or time-critical update), whereas the third causes the update module to run as a V2 (a secondary or non-time-critical update).

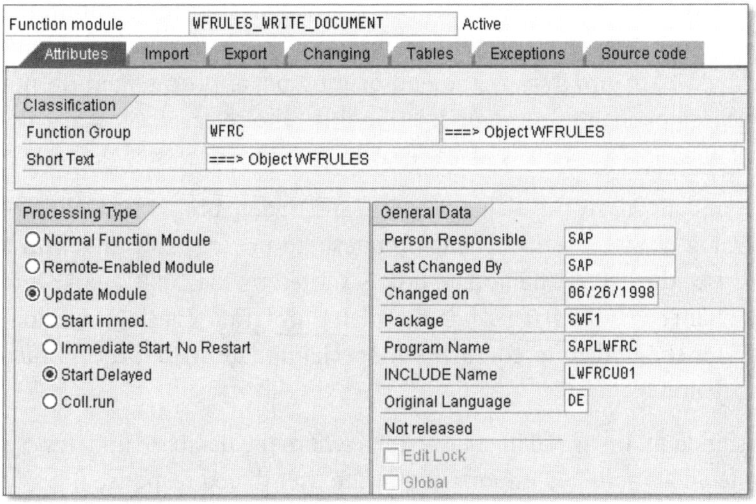

Figure 8.4 Attributes of the Update Module

Listing 8.5 shows the beginning of the update module code. Note that when an error condition is found, a type A message is used to abort the process, log the cause of the error, and abort the update. You cannot use the explicit ABAP statements COMMIT WORK or ROLLBACK WORK in an update module.

```
FUNCTION wfrules_write_document           .

  CALL FUNCTION 'CHANGEDOCUMENT_OPEN'
    EXPORTING
      objectclass             = 'WFRULES          '
      objectid                = objectid
      planned_change_number   = planned_change_number
      planned_or_real_changes = planned_or_real_changes
    EXCEPTIONS
      sequence_invalid        = 1
      OTHERS                  = 2.
  CASE sy-subrc.
    WHEN 1. MESSAGE a600 WITH 'SEQUENCE INVALID'.
    WHEN 2. MESSAGE a600 WITH 'OPEN ERROR'.
  ENDCASE.
```

Listing 8.5 Code of an Update Module

If you set locks in the dialog program with the update technique with _scope = 2, these are passed on to the update task at COMMIT WORK. After the commit, the locks are no longer accessible by the dialog program. These locks are automatically released by a Basis program at the end of the update process and do not need to be released explicitly in the update module. The release of locks at the end of the update task always takes place regardless of the success of the task.

Asynchronous updates allow the dialog program and update program to run separately. The dialog program writes change requests to the log table and with a COMMIT WORK closes the LUW. The update task is started by the COMMIT WORK and processes the change requests. This lets the dialog program continue without having to wait for the update to complete. A special update work process runs the update program.

Asynchronous updates are useful in transactions where the database updates can take a long time and where it is important that the user dialog response time, in other words, the perceived performance, is important. You will find that asynchronous updating is the standard technique used in dialog programming.

A synchronous update is triggered by the statement `COMMIT WORK AND WAIT`. In this case, the dialog program waits for the update to end before the program processing continues. You would use a synchronous update mode if the result of the update is necessary for further processing or a dialog program termination. You determine the processing success of a synchronous update by examining the system field `SY-SUBRC` when using `COMMIT WORK AND WAIT`. While waiting for the synchronous update to complete, the dialog program is in a rolled-out state. This means the dialog work process is released for further use. When the update completes, the system assigns the dialog program to a free dialog work process to continue processing.

With local updates, everything runs in a single work process. The update functions are run in the same dialog process used by the dialog program. Processing of the dialog program continues after the update is complete. This is another form of synchronous update. To have the update modules executed locally, you must use the statement `SET UPDATE TASK LOCAL` before you write the requests. When the requests are closed with the `COMMIT WORK`, these updates are processed in the same dialog work process. After the local update is successfully processed, a database commit is initiated explicitly, and the dialog program continues.

If an error occurs, and one of the update modules produces a termination message, the system executes an automatic database rollback to discard the changes in the current LUW, and the dialog program is terminated with the display of the termination message.

When you are in the local update mode, changes are not written to the database table `VBLOG`, but instead are kept in memory. This makes this update quicker than either synchronous or asynchronous updates; however, because this has an exclusive use of a work process, it is only appropriate in batch mode. The `SET UPDATE TASK LOCAL` is only possible if you have not created any requests for the current LUW and is only in effect until the next `COMMIT WORK`.

There are two types of update modules: V1 and V2. The type of update module determines its processing mode. All V1 requests in the dialog program are executed as independent database LUWs. Only if they are executed successfully are the V2 requests processed. These are also executed as independent database LUWs.

- V2 update modules are used for database changes that are linked to the V1 change, but that are not necessary to have completed with the main change, for eample, the updating of statistics.

- V1 modules can be either restartable or non-restartable. If there is an update error, you can manually restart requests that were created by restartable update modules using Transaction SM13. You can always restart V2 update modules if there is an error.

Tip

Each time a data change is made to the database, the database physically locks the record to the end of the current database LUW, either the database commit or database rollback. The same is true if you are reading with `SELECT ... FOR UPDATE`. However, read accesses to a record are not allowed for the duration of the physical lock, and many programs execute read access without locks. You should attempt to keep these database locks as short as possible for performance reasons.

You should adhere to the following rules when programming inline changes and update modules:

- Create new table entries first. Their database locks produce the least impact on other users.
- You should perform table updates that are not critical to performance. Generally, these tables are accessed simultaneously by relatively few users.
- You should change central resources in the system late, if possible, within an LUW so that the database locks only impact others for as short a time as possible.

During the update, the goal is to execute changes to central tables (those tables that are performance critical and often accessed simultaneously by several users) as late as possible in the LUW. One method to accomplish this is to use the `PERFORM ON COMMIT` technique within the update. If you encapsulate changes to central tables as form routines within the appropriate function group of the update module and then call the routines from within the update module using the `PERFORM ON COMMIT`, the form routines are then not executed until the last update module is processed. Remember that you must use global data within these form routines of the function group.

Practice Questions

The practice questions below will help you evaluate your understanding of the topic. The questions shown are similar in nature to those found on the certification examination. Whereas none of these questions will be found on the exam itself, they allow you to review your knowledge of the subject. Select the correct answers and then check the completeness of your answers in the following solution section. Remember that you must select all correct answers and only correct answers to receive credit for the question.

1. Update tasks are the only method of making changes to the database.

☐ **A.** True

☐ **B.** False

2. Which statement is true?

☐ **A.** A database LUW must be placed within an SAP LUW.

☐ **B.** An SAP LUW must be placed within a database LUW.

3. Which actions release a database lock?

☐ **A.** `COMMIT WORK`

☐ **B.** `ROLLBACK WORK`

☐ **C.** The display of an SAP screen

☐ **D.** The display of a dialog message type `E`

☐ **E.** The display of a dialog message type `A`

☐ **F.** `ENQUEUE_<lock_object>`

☐ **G.** `DEQUEUE_<lock_object>`

☐ **H.** A call to a function module

☐ **I.** A `CALL TRANSACTION`

☐ **J.** A `SUBMIT`

☐ **K.** An "/n" in the command field

4. Which actions release a lock object (with a default value for `_SCOPE`)?

☐ **A.** `COMMIT WORK`

☐ **B.** `ROLLBACK WORK`

☐ **C.** The display of an SAP screen

☐ **D.** The display of a dialog message type `E`

☐ **E.** The display of a dialog message type `A`

☐ **F.** ENQUEUE_<lock_object>

☐ **G.** DEQUEUE_<lock_object>

☐ **H.** A call to a function module

☐ **I.** A CALL TRANSACTION

☐ **J.** A SUBMIT

☐ **K.** An "/n" in the command field

5. How can you implement a table join other than the using the JOIN statement? (Fill in the blank.)

   ____

6. The data buffered on each application server is:

☐ **A.** Always the same

☐ **B.** Never the same

☐ **C.** Depends on the users

7. The target structure of a SELECT statement requires the field names to match the columns selected and to be in the same left-justified order.

☐ **A.** True

☐ **B.** False

8. When is an ENDSELECT not required for a select?

☐ **A.** When the FROM is a view

☐ **B.** When you specify a join of tables

☐ **C.** When you do a SELECT SINGLE

☐ **D.** When you specify into a table

☐ **E.** When you specify appending a table

9. The database always uses the primary key when the WHERE clause contains any of the key fields.

☐ **A.** True

☐ **B.** False

10. Open SQL does not allow you to specify a secondary index during a `SELECT`.

☐ **A.** True

☐ **B.** False

11. You should always buffer database tables that contain fewer than 100 records.

☐ **A.** True

☐ **B.** False

12. Buffering data can speed up access to data up to 100 times when compared to reading it from the database.

☐ **A.** True

☐ **B.** False

13. All Open SQL commands allow processing on multiple rows.

☐ **A.** True

☐ **B.** False

14. The `_WAIT` parameter of a lock object waits for the lock to be successful.

☐ **A.** True

☐ **B.** False

15. It is recommended to place the `COMMIT WORK` in the update task.

☐ **A.** True

☐ **B.** False

16. It is possible to `PERFORM <subroutine> ON COMMIT` in an update task.

☐ **A.** True

☐ **B.** False

17. The correct order for using a lock object is:

☐ **A.** Read the data, set the lock, change the data, release the lock

☐ **B.** Set the lock, read the data, change the data, release the lock

☐ **C.** Set the lock, read the data, release the lock, change the data

18. Local update tasks are quicker because they stay within the same work process.

- [ ] **A.** True
- [x] **B.** False

19. V1 update tasks are always non-restartable, whereas V2 update tasks are always restartable.

- [ ] **A.** True
- [x] **B.** False

Practice Question Answers and Explanations

1. Correct answer: **B**

   In addition to the various types of update tasks, it is also possible to use inline updates to make changes to the database.

2. Correct answer: **B**

   If you encounter an error during the processing of an SAP LUW, it should be possible to return to the consistent database status that existed prior to beginning the SAP LUW. This is only possible is if the SAP LUW is placed within a database LUW.

3. Correct answers: **A, B, C, D, E, I, J, K**

   A database lock is released when the database performs a rollback or database commit. When you execute the ABAP statements `ROLLBACK WORK` and `COMMIT WORK`, you explicitly implement a database rollback or database commit. There are also instances when a database commit is triggered implicitly. Implicit database commits are always initiated whenever the program has to wait, such as when the system sends an SAP screen, when the system sends a dialog message, whenever there are synchronous and asynchronous RFC calls (the question referenced a normal function call, not a Remote Function Call), or when you use the statements `CALL TRANSACTION <tcode>` or `SUBMIT <program>`.

4. Correct answers: **A, B, E, G, K**

   If a lock is enqueued with a `_scope` of 2 (the default), the lock is released after you execute the ABAP statements `ROLLBACK WORK` and `COMMIT WORK`, or after a program termination. A program termination is produced after a message with the type of either A or X, with the execution of the statements LEAVE PROGRAM and LEAVE TO TRANSACTION, or if the user enters "/n" in the command field. The lock can also be released by calling the DEQUEUE function module or the function module DEQUEUE_ALL.

5. Correct answer: **A database view**

   There are two ways to implement a table join. One is to create a database view in the ABAP Dictionary that corresponds to the table join and use this view. The other is to define the join directly in your program as an ABAP join.

6. Correct answer: **C**

   SAP table buffers exist separately for each application server, and there is a limited amount of buffer space on each. As data is accessed by users, the data that is contained within the table buffers changes as more recent data replaces older data. This means that it is normally a very rare occurance that the contents of the buffers across application servers match.

7. Correct answer: **B**

   It is not necessary for the field names to match the columns selected. What is necessary is for the size and type of the fields to match.

8. Correct answer: **C, D, E**

   An ENDSELECT is not required because these SELECT statements do not loop. A SELECT SINGLE statement only returns one record, and both the INTO TABLE and APPENDING TABLE fill the destination in a block mode. Because none of these statements is a SELECT loop, the ENDSELECT is not necessary.

9. Correct answer: **B**

   The database optimizer determines which index to use. Under most circumstances, it is based on the fields provided in the WHERE clause, and which indexes exist for the database table.

10. Correct answer: **A**

    This is correct. Open SQL does not allow you to provide any direction directly to the underlying database.

11. Correct answer: **B**

    The decision to buffer database tables is more complex than a simple determination based on the expected size of the table. Again the ideal table is small, read frequently, rarely changed, and normally accessed directly with its key fields. However, the decision to buffer a database table should be made by experienced ABAP developers in consultation with the system administrator.

12. Correct answer: **A**

    A table that is buffered can speed up your access between 10 and 100 times compared to reading it from the database. The caveat for the speed, however, is that for the buffer to be used, it must be a `SELECT` statement that specifies the full buffered key with equalities only.

13. Correct answer: **A**

    All Open SQL commands allow processing on multiple rows.

14. Correct answer: **B**

    The `_WAIT` parameter defines whether a lock request should be repeated if the first lock attempt fails. It does not wait for the lock to become available.

15. Correct answer: **B**

    You must not use the explicit ABAP statements `COMMIT WORK` or `ROLLBACK WORK` in the update module.

16. Correct answer: **A**

    The goal in the update task is to execute changes to central tables as late as possible in the LUW. To achieve this, you can use the `PERFORM ON COMMIT` technique in the update. If you encapsulate changes to central tables as form routines within the appropriate function group of the update module and then call the routines from within the update module using the `PERFORM ON COMMIT`, the form routines will not be executed until the last update module is processed.

17. Correct answer: **B**

    This order should be natural. Obtain the lock so that you know the data is not being modified elsewhere and is therefore consistent, read the data to begin with the current consistent state, make your change, and finally release the lock to make the data available for others who may be waiting for the data.

18. Correct answer: **B**

    Local updates are quicker because they do not provide updates to the log table. Because there is less database activity, the process runs quicker. However, if there is a problem, there is no way of knowing what data was lost because there are no requests in the log table.

19. Correct answer: **B**

    V1 modules can either be restartable or non-restartable. V2 tasks are always restartable.

Take Away

You should now be able access fields from a database table or tables efficiently. You should also be able to describe the difference between an SAP LUW and a database LUW. You should also understand why update tasks need to be bundled. You must understand the different types of Open SQL `SELECT` statements and what improves or decreases access performance.

Refresher

You will need a thorough understanding of the different types of update, commit, and rollback strategies. You must also understand efficient data access. You must understand when to choose a type of update strategy and why it is the best solution. You must understand the concept of logical units of work and how SAP LUWs and database LUWs work together. Table 8.3 shows the key concepts for the SQL statements and update strategies.

Key Concept	Definition
`SELECT`	Defines how to retrieve data from a single database table or multiple database tables efficiently
Bundling updates	Defines what types of asynchronous and synchronous update tasks may be performed
Commit and rollback	Defines how the commit and rollback provides a consistent database
Locks	Defines how locks should be used to synchronize users' access to data

Table 8.3 Key Concepts Refresher

Tips

As a percentage of the certification test, this subject is one of the top three with the most questions. An understanding of how to optimize data access and an understanding of update tasks for dialog programming is required for the portion of the test covered in this chapter.

The more practical experience you have with this subject, the simpler you will find the questions in this portion of the certification examination. However, inefficient programming techniques inevitably lead to incorrect answers in this portion of the test. You must understand why one technique should be used in place of another.

Summary

You should have mastered the various types of Open SQL statements and their different variations. You should understand update tasks, record locks, and logical units of work and how they interact with the user, application server, and database. You should understand how to keep data in a constant state within the database. Your knowledge of these topics will allow you to successfully complete this portion of the certification exam.

9

Basic ABAP Programs and Interface Creation

Techniques You'll Master:

- Organize development objects
- Identify different types of programs
- Determine program event blocks
- Use dynpros, selection screens, and modal dialog boxes
- Use authorization checks
- Explain the different types of modularization units
- Identify the effect of messages on program execution

This chapter provides you with a basic understanding of how development objects are organized. We will discuss how these objects are grouped into change requests (commonly called transports) and moved throughout the system landscape. We will cover the different types of programs, identifying their similarities and differences. We will discuss the majority of the event blocks and the basics of Dynpros (often just referred to as screens), selection screens, and modal dialog boxes (see Chapter 12, Classical Screens, and Chapter 13, Selection Screens, as well). We will cover the use of authorization checks and the different types of modularization units, again identifying both their similarities and differences. Lastly, we will cover the use of the `MESSAGE` statement on program execution.

Each of these topics is covered separately, and they are followed by the practice exercise and the solution to the exercise.

Real-World Scenario

You have been asked to lead a new project implementing a new group of application programs for use in your company's SAP system. It is your responsibility to put together a development team and produce the subsystem.

In examining the requirements of the subsystem, you see that there are a number of dialog transactions and several report transactions. Some of the data is sensitive, so both the dialog transactions and report transactions will require separate authorization checks to determine if the user is allowed to view the data. The dialog programs will also need to check for authorization to create or change the data. If the user is not authorized to perform the operation, a message must be displayed.

Once you have your development team in place, you will be required to organize the development so that it all reaches production at the same time for go-live. Owing to the complexity of accessing the data and the numerous types of authorization checks, a decision was made to encapsulate the tables' access into global reuse components. This will also provide the option of buffering retrieved data during dialog transactions.

Objectives of this Portion of the Test

The purpose of this portion of the certification examination is to verify that you have detailed knowledge of the ABAP development environment and the capabilities of different types of programs. This portion of the examination will test your knowledge of a wide range of topics. The points you will need to understand from this section include:

- What types of programs exist
- Event blocks
- Dynpros, selection screens, modal dialog boxes
- Different methods of executing programs
- Authorization checks
- Modularization units
- The effect of messages in a program

Because this is an ABAP certification examination, assessing your general knowledge of ABAP and its environment is the most important objective of the test. The certification examination will give more weight to the material in this chapter than all of the other topics in the examination. This means there will be a higher percentage of questions related to this chapter than any other chapter.

Key Concepts Refresher

Unsurprisingly, you typically need to develop ABAP programs as an ABAP developer. You therefore need to understand and be able to perform the following types of tasks when developing ABAP programs:

- Create various types of programs
- Test various types of development
- Move development objects from your development environment to your test and production systems
- Encapsulate data and processing
- Interact with users
- Verify that the user is authorized to perform a specific function
- Inform users about errors and program status

Organizing Development

Development projects start out in a development system. The development objects edited or created in a project must then be transported to subsequent systems when the project is complete.

At the start of a development project, normally, the project manager creates a change request, in which he identifies who will be working on the project, in either the Transport Organizer or directly in the ABAP Workbench. Then he creates a task for each project employee or developer within the change request. In some cases, where the development is limited, there may be only a single task in a single change request.

As a development object is edited or created, for example, a program or data element, you assign this object to the change request. The object is thus entered into your task. All repository objects that you work on during a development project are collected within your task. When you complete your development tasks, you perform syntax checking, activation, and testing before you release the task in the change request. Once the project development is complete and all tasks are released, the change request itself is released, but it cannot be released until all of its tasks are released (see Figure 9.1).

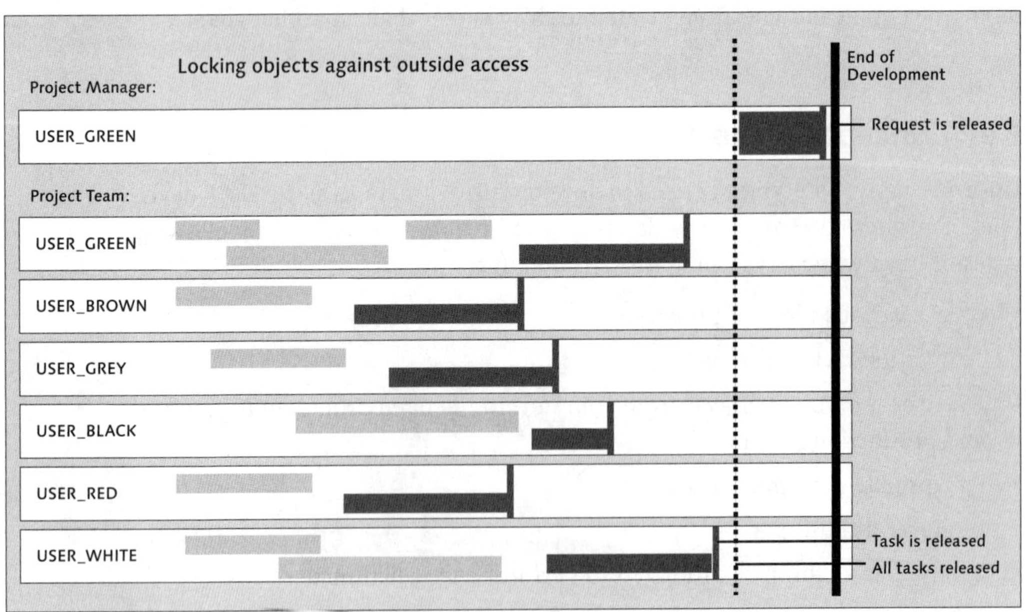

Figure 9.1 Project Timeline of a Change Request

Organizing a development project using a change request offers the following advantages:

- Each developer can track and check his project-specific activities.
- The development objects can be processed by all developers involved in the project. For developers who do not belong to the project team, the repository objects remain locked until the project is completed and the change request is released.
- The joint transport of the development objects processed in the project at the time of project completion is automatically ensured by assigning the objects to the change request. The transport route of the involved packages specifies to which subsequent system they are transported.

Unlike packages that distinguish between Repository objects in a logical and functional way, change requests are project-related and therefore delimit the objects over a period of time. Therefore, although a program always belongs to only one package, it can, at different times, belong to different projects or change requests. It is possible for a single change request (actually, it is very likely unless the change request contains all new development for a specific purpose) to contain multiple development packages.

ABAP Programming Overview

ABAP is a programming language developed by SAP for programming business applications within the SAP environment. As discussed in Chapter 3, SAP NetWeaver – Overview, and Chapter 8, SQL Statements Including Update Strategies, the three-tier architecture used by SAP provides for the user who interacts with the presentation layer, which controls the business logic running on an application server, which retrieves and stores data in the database server. ABAP is the language that controls the business logic running on the application server. ABAP programs are executed in the ABAP runtime environment. The main role of the ABAP program in the application layer is the processing and formatting of data from the database layer and its interaction with the user input from the presentation layer.

ABAP provides integrated database access to multiple database systems through the use of Open SQL. It optimizes database access through the use of SAP buffering and provides internal tables for processing tabular data within the program. It uses the concept of online transaction processing (OLTP) integrated into the ABAP runtime environment, enabling multiple users to access the database at the same time using the SAP LUW. It provides outside access to other programming environments with the Remote Function Call (RFC). Also, ABAP has an integrated interface to XML.

ABAP supports both procedural and object-oriented programming models based on subroutines, function modules, and methods of classes. As appropriate for a language designed around international business, the textual language is handled independently of the programming language. ABAP provides for the separation of language-specific program components from the source code, and they are loaded during program execution based on the user's logon language. ABAP supports code pages, single-byte, double-byte, and after Release 6.10, even Unicode.

Each ABAP program starts with an introductory statement. The functions of an ABAP program are implemented in processing blocks. The processing blocks are defined using modularization statements. The order of the processing blocks is irrelevant for program execution. Following the introductory statement, every program contains a global declaration section where you implement definitions of data objects (for example, variables, structures, and internal tables) and data declarations that are visible in the entire program. Whereas the order of individual definitions and declarations does not matter generally, you must take into account that an ABAP statement can only refer to existing definitions and declarations. Therefore, they must be defined before they can be declared and declared before they can be used. For example, a definition of a local type must occur prior to its first use in the program, normally either as a data declaration or as part of an interface to a modularization unit.

Because ABAP is a language that has evolved over time, it contains several obsolete statements or forms of statements that were replaced with improved language constructs, but were not eliminated, to ensure downward code compatibility. ABAP Objects prevent the use of almost all of these obsolete additions. In general, you should no longer use these additions in new programs, but you may encounter them in older programs.

The introductory statement must be the first statement in the program after the include programs are expanded during program generation. It can only appear once in the program.

Introductory program statements include:

- Executable programs (REPORT)
- Module pools (PROGRAM)
- Function groups (FUNCTION-POOL)
- Class pools (CLASS-POOL)
- Interface pools (INTERFACE-POOL)
- Subroutine pools (PROGRAM), which are now considered obsolete
- Type groups (TYPE-POOL)

All of these are stand-alone compilation units or program types. Include programs are only used in the context of superior programs. Type groups, also known as type pools (program type T), are stand-alone programs from a logical point of view. However, they do not contain executable code but only type definitions and constant definitions. Therefore, type groups have their own introductory program statement, the TYPE-POOL.

When you create a program, the ABAP Workbench automatically generates the introductory statement from the program type. If changes are necessary, only the introductory statement's additions should be edited. An example of a new report and some possible additions are shown in Listing 9.1 and Listing 9.2.

```
*&---------------------------------------------------------------------
*& Report  Z_NEW_REPORT
*&
*&---------------------------------------------------------------------
*&
*&
*&---------------------------------------------------------------------

REPORT  z_new_report.
```

Listing 9.1 A New Introductory Statement for a Report

```
*&---------------------------------------------------------------------
*& Report  Z_NEW_REPORT
*&
*&---------------------------------------------------------------------
*&
*&
*&---------------------------------------------------------------------
REPORT  z_new_report
```

```
LINE-SIZE 250
NO STANDARD PAGE HEADING
MESSAGE-ID z_message_class.
```

Listing 9.2 A Modified Report Introductory Statement

In particular, the keywords FUNCTION-POOL, CLASS-POOL, INTERFACE-POOL, and TYPE-POOL should only be generated by the corresponding tools of the ABAP Workbench. The creation of a function group also automatically generates the main program including the top include containing the FUNCTION-POOL statement. The complete name of the program for a function group in the Repository consists of the prefix SAPL and the name of the function pool (function group). All statements following the introductory program statement or those that are included as include programs are treated as a single unit by the ABAP compiler.

Each ABAP program is divided into processing blocks. Each accessible statement of an ABAP program that does not belong in the global declaration section belongs to a processing block.

The possible processing blocks are:

- **Procedures**
  - Methods
  - Function modules
  - Subroutines
- **Dialog modules** (exclusively for Dynpros)
- **Event blocks**

Function modules are always defined globally, whereas methods can be defined either globally or locally within the program, and subroutines should only ever be defined locally (subroutine pools now being considered obsolete). The flow logic of Dynpro calls dialog modules to perform their processing. Event blocks are triggered by events in the ABAP runtime environment.

The parameter interface of a procedure consists of formal parameters and specifies the possible exceptions of the procedure. The formal parameters are input, output, input/output parameters and return values. There are also the obsolete table parameters. Subroutines do not provide input or output parameters directly because both USING and CHANGING are treated as a type of changing parameter; they do not provide for returning values. Function modules do not provide returning values. Formal parameters are either generic or completely typed. You can specify either pass by reference or pass by value for most formal parameters, although for some formal parameters, pass by value is mandatory.

The differences and similarities are discussed in detail below in the sections ABAP Subroutine, ABAP Function Module, and ABAP Classes and Methods.

Class-based exceptions can be declared using `RAISING` for all procedures (methods, function modules, and subroutines) and can then be propagated from the procedure. Also, `EXCEPTIONS` can be used in methods and function modules to define non-class-based exceptions, which can then be triggered in the procedure using either `RAISE` or `MESSAGE ... RAISING`.

Listing 9.3 shows the older exceptions that were `MESSAGE` based and could only exist in function modules or methods. Listing 9.4 shows an example of a class-based exception. A single procedure can only use one type — not both.

```
MESSAGE e008(38) WITH 'FOOBAR'
  RAISING table_cannot_be_loaded.
```

Listing 9.3 Example of a MESSAGE-Based Exception

```
RAISE EXCEPTION TYPE cx_sy_dynamic_osql_semantics
  EXPORTING textid =
    cx_sy_dynamic_osql_semantics=>unknown_table_name
            token  = 'FOOBAR'.
```

Listing 9.4 Example of a Class-Based Exception

When you decide whether to use pass by reference or pass by value for a formal parameter, you must compare the relative performance and robustness for each type of transfe:.

- A pass by reference parameter provides a pointer to the original data object in memory, and the procedure operates directly on the original object.
- A pass by value parameter copies the value to a new data object, or in the case of a changing parameter copies it once when called and once again upon completion.

In ABAP, pass by reference is always quicker because no local object is created and no data transport is necessary when calling the procedure. Simply for performance reasons, pass by reference is usually preferred unless there is an explicit or implicit write to an input parameter within the procedure or you want to ensure that an input/output (changing) or output parameter is only returned if the procedure ends without error. In such cases pass by value is mandatory, so that the assigned parameter is not simultaneously modified in the calling code when there is a write access to a formal parameter.

The following example shows a very simple example of the behavior difference of call by reference versus call by value. Notice that the code (shown in Listing 9.5) provides four variables to the formal parameters of the subroutine. Two are passed by value and two are passed by reference; one of each pair is passed as a `USING` parameter, and one of each pair is passed as a `CHANGING` parameter. At the point in the program when the call is made (`PERFORM pass_by_example`), the values of the variables in the calling routine are all zero (see Figure 9.2). At the point of the `BREAK-POINT` statement (see Figure 9.3), all of the formal parameters have a value of one. However, if the debugger point of view is changed to the calling routine, the original variables passed by reference have changed, whereas the variables passed by value have not (see Figure 9.4).

```
FORM pass_by.
  DATA:
    lv_num1               TYPE i,
    lv_num2               TYPE i,
    lv_num3               TYPE i,
    lv_num4               TYPE i.
  PERFORM pass_by_example
        USING lv_num1 lv_num2
        CHANGING lv_num3 lv_num4.
ENDFORM.                          "pass_by

FORM pass_by_example USING value(p_by_value1) TYPE i
                           p_by_ref1     TYPE i
                  CHANGING value(p_by_value2) TYPE i
                           p_by_ref2     TYPE i.
  ADD 1 TO: p_by_value1, p_by_ref1, p_by_value2, p_by_ref2.
  BREAK-POINT.
ENDFORM.                          "pass_by_example
```

Listing 9.5 Example Code

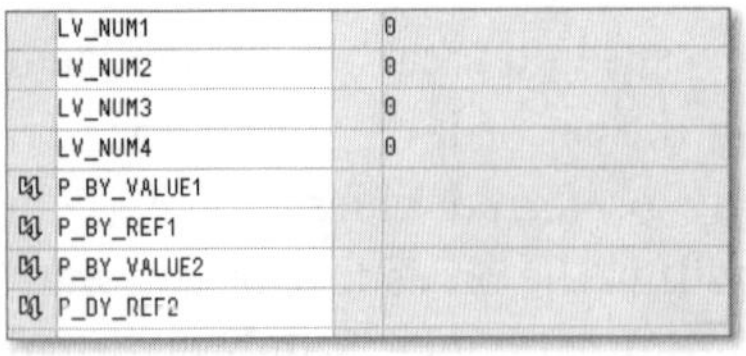

Variable	Value
LV_NUM1	0
LV_NUM2	0
LV_NUM3	0
LV_NUM4	0
P_BY_VALUE1	
P_BY_REF1	
P_BY_VALUE2	
P_BY_REF2	

Figure 9.2 At the Point of the Point of the Call

LV_NUM1	
LV_NUM2	
LV_NUM3	
LV_NUM4	
P_BY_VALUE1	1
P_BY_REF1	1
P_BY_VALUE2	1
P_BY_REF2	1

Figure 9.3 At the BREAK-POINT Statement

LV_NUM1	0
LV_NUM2	1
LV_NUM3	0
LV_NUM4	1
P_BY_VALUE1	
P_BY_REF1	
P_BY_VALUE2	
P_BY_REF2	

Figure 9.4 At the BREAK-POINT Statement in the Calling Routine

You should note the following behavior when using pass by reference:

- In subroutines, write access can occur to an input parameter defined with `USING` without the occurrence of syntax errors. This is not the case with methods or function modules defined with `IMPORTING`.
- An output parameter that is passed by reference acts like an input/output (changing) parameter. If there is a read access to an output parameter in the procedure before the value of the parameter is changed, this value is not initial, unlike with pass by value, but is the same as the current value of the actual parameter from the calling code. This also means that if the called procedure does not change an output parameter, the actual parameter in the calling code remains unchanged.
- If a procedure is stopped because of an error, in other words stopped for a reason other than that it has reached its last statement or a `RETURN`, all parameters retain the values they contained when the procedure was stopped.

To summarize, pass by reference is always preferable when performance is an issue, whereas pass by value is more suitable for situations where robustness and data consistency are important.

Only pass by reference can be specified for the obsolete table parameters in either subroutines or function modules. As mentioned above, pass by value is mandatory for the return value of functional methods, the output parameters of events in ABAP Objects, and all formal parameters of function modules that are either RFC enabled or are update modules.

ABAP Event Blocks

Event blocks are units of code that are executed in a sequence determined by external events: often the runtime environment for ABAP, occasionally by a user's actions. The sequence in which the processing blocks occur in the program is irrelevant. However, to make your programs easier to understand, you should include the event blocks in your program in approximately the same order in which they will be called by the system and prior to subroutines or local class implementations.

Event blocks are started using an event keyword and ended by the next processing block: either another event block or other type of procedural block. Within an event block, you cannot declare local data types or data objects. All declarative statements in event blocks belong to the ABAP program and are visible globally (in all subsequent processing blocks). There are two exceptions: The event blocks `AT SELECTION-SCREEN` and `GET` are implemented internally as procedures and can contain local data.

Event blocks can be grouped by type. Table 9.1 shows the event types that exist.

Type of Event	Event Occurs in Program Types
Program constructor event	All program types
Reporting event	Only in executable programs
Selection screen event	Only during selection screen processing
List event	Only during list processing

Table 9.1 Types of Events

With the exception of `AT SELECTION-SCREEN` and `GET`, event blocks can be listed multiple times in a program, but normally you will not see this (the valid case where this would be used is extremely convoluted, involving sharing code between multiple programs or include programs or when the code is inadvertently included multiple times). Event block `START-OF-SELECTION` can also be implicitly listed multiple times. Whenever an event occurs, all associated event blocks are executed in the order of their occurrence. Again, the event blocks are triggered by events in the ABAP runtime environment.

In the following list, we list the event blocks and when or how they are triggered.

- `LOAD-OF-PROGRAM`
  This event keyword is triggered when the program is initially loaded into memory. This program constructor event is triggered for all program types. This can be useful to initialize or instantiate a data object when the program begins only once or to indicate to an external process that the program has started. The event is only triggered once, before any other event of a program.
- `INITIALIZATION`
  This reporting event keyword is triggered by the actual start of the program and before the selection screen processing of any existing standard selection screen (the only event that can occur before this is `LOAD-OF-PROGRAM`).

  When an executable program defines that a standard selection screen is called again by the ABAP runtime environment after an execution, the `INITIALIZATION` event is triggered again. An example of this is a report in which after displaying the report, the user clicks on the BACK button or presses F3 and returns to the selection screen to rerun the report. In this case, initializing parameters or selection criteria of the selection screen has no effect because they are automatically supplied with the preceding user inputs from the selection screen during the selection screen event `AT SELECTION-SCREEN OUTPUT`.
- `START-OF-SELECTION`
  In an executable program, all statements that are not declarations and are listed before the first explicit processing block, or if the program does not contain any explicit processing blocks, then all functional statements of the program are assigned to an implicit event block `START-OF-SELECTION`, which is inserted before any `START-OF-SELECTION` event blocks. This event keyword is triggered when the program has completed all selection screen events.

  If the program is linked to a logical database, preparatory tasks can be performed at `START-OF-SELECTION` before the logical database imports the data. If the program is not linked to a logical database, this event block becomes a type of "main program" from which procedures or screens are called. See Listing 9.6 for an example of an explicit example and Listing 9.7 for an implicit example.

```
* PAI
AT SELECTION-SCREEN.
  PERFORM pai_of_selection_screen.
START-OF-SELECTION.
  PERFORM selection.
END-OF-SELECTION.
  PERFORM e05_layout_build USING gs_layout.   "wg. Parameters
* Call ABAP/4 List Viewer
  CALL FUNCTION 'REUSE_ALV_HIERSEQ_LIST_DISPLAY'
       EXPORTING
            i_callback_program       = g_repid
*           I_CALLBACK_PF_STATUS_SET = ' '
*           I_CALLBACK_USER_COMMAND  = ' '
            is_layout                = gs_layout
            it_fieldcat              = gt_fieldcat[]
*           IT_EXCLUDING             =
            it_special_groups        = gt_sp_group[]
*           IT_SORT                  =
*           IT_FILTER                =
*           IS_SEL_HIDE              =
*           I_SCREEN_START_COLUMN    = 0
*           I_SCREEN_START_LINE      = 0
*           I_SCREEN_END_COLUMN      = 0
*           I_SCREEN_END_LINE        = 0
*           i_default                = g_default
            i_save                   = g_save
            is_variant               = g_variant
            it_events                = gt_events[]
*           IT_EVENT_EXIT            =
            i_tabname_header         = g_tabname_header
            i_tabname_item           = g_tabname_item
            is_keyinfo               = gs_keyinfo
*           IS_PRINT                 =
*      IMPORTING
*           E_EXIT_CAUSED_BY_CALLER  =
       TABLES
            t_outtab_header          = gt_scarr
            t_outtab_item            = gt_spfli.
```

Listing 9.6 Example of Several Event Blocks

```
*&---------------------------------------------------------
*& Report  Z_HELLO_WORLD_SIMPLE
*&
*&---------------------------------------------------------
```

```
*&
*&
*&---------------------------------------------------------------
report  z_hello_world_simple.
write / 'Hello World'.
```

Listing 9.7 Example of an Implicit START-OF-SELECTION

- `GET node`

  The reporting `GET` event defines an event block whose result is triggered by the ABAP runtime environment, if the logical database to which the program is linked provides data in the work area `node`. `GET node` also controls the behavior of the logical database. The event blocks after `GET` are implemented internally as procedures. Declarative statements in `GET` event blocks create local data. `GET` event blocks follow the `START-OF-SELECTION` event and are followed by the event block `END-OF-SELECTION`.

- `END-OF-SELECTION`

  In this report event block, all data read by the logical database can be processed. In an executable program without a logical data base, there is no need to implement the event block `END-OF-SELECTION`.

- `AT SELECTION-SCREEN`

  This statement defines event blocks that are triggered by the ABAP runtime environment during selection screen processing. The event `AT SELECTION-SCREEN` is the basic form of a whole series of events that occur while the selection screen is being processed. The standard selection screen in an executable program or in the logical database linked to it is automatically called between the `INITIALIZATION` and `START-OF-SELECTION` events. You can define event blocks for these events in your program to change the selection screen or process user input.

  Selection screen events occur immediately before sending a selection screen, during the PBO of the selection screen (`AT SELECTION-SCREEN OUTPUT`), after certain user actions on a displayed selection screen, for example, `ON VALUE REQUEST` or `ON HELP REQUEST`, or prior to proceeding to the `START-OF-SELECTION` event during execution. They assist in selection screen processing in the ABAP program or provide validations for the selection screen.

- `TOP-OF-PAGE`

  This list creation event is triggered by the ABAP runtime environment during the creation of a list. This occurs when a new page is started, that is, immediately before the first line in a new page is to be output. All list outputs that take place in the event block are placed below the standard page header of the list. You cannot output more lines than are available in the page within the event block, and the `NEW-PAGE` statement is ignored within this event block.

- `END-OF-PAGE`
  This list creation event is triggered by the ABAP runtime environment during the creation of a basic list, if there is a line reservation in the addition `LINE-COUNT` of the initiating statement for a page footer. A list output that takes place in the event block is placed in this area. Output statements that exceed the reserved area will be ignored.
- `AT LINE-SELECTION`
  This display of a screen list event is triggered by the ABAP runtime environment, provided the screen cursor is on a list line and you select a function using the function code `Pick` (or press F2 or double-click on a list line). This was often used to provide drill-down capability or to provide additional detail. During the line selection process any fields output or placed on the line with the `Hide` command are returned to their respective global data objects.
- `AT USER-COMMAND`
  This display of a screen list event is triggered by the ABAP runtime environment if, during the display of a screen list, a function with a self-defined function code was chosen.

Basic ABAP Statements

The ABAP syntax is platform independent. This means that it always has the same meaning or function, irrespective of the relational database system and operating system for the application and presentation server. Applications implemented in ABAP will also be able to run in future releases owing to the upward compatibility of the language. The only type of upward compatibility issue would be related to changing from a non-Unicode system to a Unicode system. For more information on this topic, please see Chapter 11, Unicode.

For the ABAP syntax, the general rules apply:

- ABAP programs consist of individual sentences (statements).
- The first word in a statement is called the *ABAP keyword*, although the keyword may be optional — `COMPUTE`, for example.

- Each statement ends with a period.
- Words must always be separated by at least one space.
- Statements can be indented.
- ABAP keywords, additions, and operands can be either upper- or lowercase (the ABAP runtime system does not differentiate).
- Statements can extend beyond one line.
- You can place several statements on a single line (though this is not generally recommended).
- Lines beginning with an asterisk (*) in the first column are recognized as comment lines and ignored.
- Double quote marks (") indicate that the remainder of the line is a comment.

Note

Although the ABAP runtime system does not differentiate between upper- and lowercase, it has become customary to write keywords and their additions in uppercase letters and operands in lowercase. This form of representation is also be used throughout the book. It can be achieved in your own program by using the PRETTY PRINTER button and setting the appropriate option in the settings (UTILITIES • SETTINGS • ABAP EDITOR • PRETTY PRINTER).

You can combine consecutive statements with an identical beginning into a chained statement:

- Write the identical beginning part of the statement followed by a colon.
- After the colon, list the end parts of the statements (separated by commas).

Note

This short form merely represents a simplified form of syntax and does not offer an improvement in performance. The ABAP runtime system processes each of the individual statements. The short form makes the most sense with certain statements, for example, `TYPES`, `DATA`, `SELECT-OPTIONS`, `PARAMETERS`, `CLEAR`, `MOVE`, `ADD`, or `WRITE`.

Normally, a program is not made up of a single block, but of several units. Many of these modularization units can be used in more than one program. A good program should have at least the database access encapsulated (known also as a reuse component). This creates a division between the design of the program and the database accesses. It is then possible for you to use the same database accesses for different user dialogs or programs.

As an additional benefit of such an encapsulation, often it is possible to buffer the data within the encapsulation, meaning that it only needs to be retrieved from the database once. As an example, a number of standard function modules retrieve data from various tables and store it within the function group. Later attempts to retrieve the same data retrieve it from the internal tables within the function group rather than retrieve it again from the database tables. A common example of this type of buffering within a database encapsulation is the retrieval of address data. As a result, any address retrieval for a customer, vendor, or partner benefits from this optimization. An example of this can be seen in Figure 9.5.

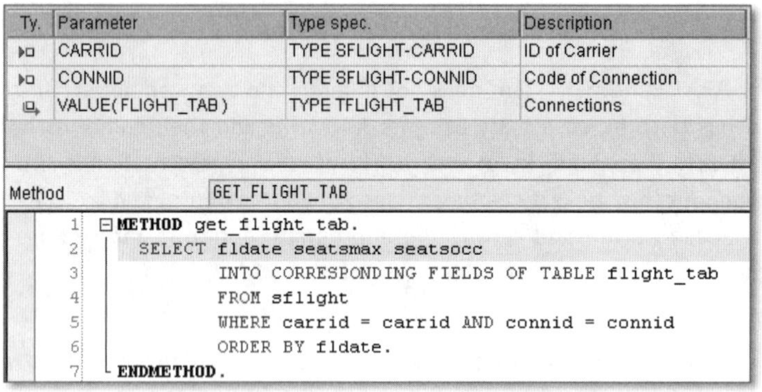

Ty.	Parameter	Type spec.	Description
	CARRID	TYPE SFLIGHT-CARRID	ID of Carrier
	CONNID	TYPE SFLIGHT-CONNID	Code of Connection
	VALUE(FLIGHT_TAB)	TYPE TFLIGHT_TAB	Connections

Method GET_FLIGHT_TAB

```
METHOD get_flight_tab.
  SELECT fldate seatsmax seatsocc
         INTO CORRESPONDING FIELDS OF TABLE flight_tab
         FROM sflight
         WHERE carrid = carrid AND connid = connid
         ORDER BY fldate.
ENDMETHOD.
```

Figure 9.5 Example of Database Encapsulation

A modularization unit is a part of a program where a particular function is encapsulated. You place part of the source code in a "module" to improve the transparency of the program and to use the corresponding function in the program several times (or indeed in other programs if the modularization is global) without having to implement the entire source code again on each occasion. The improvement in transparency results from the program becoming more function oriented. It divides the overall task into subfunctions, which are the responsibility of the corresponding modularization unit.

Modularization also simplifies both program maintenance and future design changes. It simplifies maintenance because you only need to make changes to the function or corrections to the modularization unit once and not throughout the programs. If the requirements change, often it is possible to switch out the one modularization call for another. You can also process a call as a unit in the Debugger when executing your program.

It is possible to provide modularization either *locally* or *globally*. You have two techniques for local program modularization: subroutines (form routines) and methods within local classes. Local modularization units, by definition, are only available in the program in which they are implemented. No other program must be loaded to the user context at runtime when you use a local modularization unit.

Caution

For historical reasons, it is technically possible to call a subroutine from another program. You should not use this option, however, because this technique contradicts the principle of encapsulation of data and functions.

As with local program modularization, there are two techniques for global modularization: function modules and methods within global classes. Global modularization units can be used by any number of programs at the same time. The globally defined modularization units are stored in the ABAP Repository and only loaded when requested by the calling program.

Ideally, the modularization units that are called do not use the data objects of the calling program directly. Nor should the calling program change the data objects of the modularization unit directly. This principle is known as *data encapsulation*. This is an important technique in developing transparent, maintainable source code.

Parameters are used to exchange data between the calling code and the modularization unit. The total number of parameters in a modularization unit is called the interface or signature. Parameters are differentiated on whether they are used to pass data into the modularization unit (importing parameters) or return data from the modularization unit (exporting parameters) or to pass data into and return from the modularization unit (changing parameters).

ABAP Subroutine

A subroutine is:

- Introduced with the `FORM` statement.
- You specify the name of the subroutine and the interface after `FORM`.

- The statements of the subroutine follow the FORM statement.
- The ENDFORM statement concludes the subroutine.

In the interface definition, you list the formal parameters of the subroutine and type them. A formal parameter is how you address the data object provided in the calling code within the subroutine. You must specify the pass type for each parameter.

- Call by value: USING VALUE
- Call by value and result: CHANGING VALUE
- Call by reference: CHANGING or USING (although CHANGING is recommended if the contents are changed).

You must specify the additions TABLES, USING, CHANGING, and RAISING, in this order (see Listing 9.8 and Listing 9.9 for an example of multiple types). Specifying TABLES after USING or CHANGING creates a formal parameter called TABLES. Likewise, specifying USING after CHANGING creates a formal parameter called USING.

```
IF cursor_field = 'SOURCE_ID' AND cursor_value NE space.
  PERFORM create_request
    USING cursor_value
          abap_pgeditor->abap_editor->context->context_type
    CHANGING l_wb_request.
ELSE.
```

Listing 9.8 Call to a Subroutine with both USING and CHANGING

```
FORM create_request USING    p_name TYPE progname
                             p_type
                    CHANGING p_l_wb_request.
  DATA: l_scope_objects  TYPE rinfoobj,
        l_scope_objtypes TYPE rseutypes,
        l_object_type    TYPE seu_objtype,
        l_object_name    TYPE rsfind.
  l_object_type = p_type.
  l_object_name = p_name.
  CALL METHOD
    cl_wb_infosystem=>create_where_used_list_request
    EXPORTING
      p_object_type        = p_object_type
      p_object_name        = l_object_name
```

```
      p_scope_objects      = l_scope_objects
      p_scope_object_types = l_scope_objtypes
    IMPORTING
      p_wb_request         = p_l_wb_request
    EXCEPTIONS
      execute_in_batch     = 1
      action_cancelled     = 2
      error_occured        = 3
      OTHERS               = 4.
ENDFORM.                    "create_request
```

Listing 9.9 The Subroutine (FORM Routine)

With the addition of RAISING, class-based exceptions can be passed, which are triggered in the subroutine or propagated to the subroutine by the ABAP runtime environment or by using the statement RAISE EXCEPTION, but are not handled in a TRY block.

Internal tables should be passed with either USING or CHANGING. The other advantage of using one of these is that you can pass internal tables other than standard tables, for example sorted or hashed. It is recommended that all parameters for any type of modularization unit be typed. Typing provides additional syntax checking during activation and provides faster execution during runtime.

ABAP Function Module

A function module is a routine or reuse component that is stored centrally in the Function Library of an SAP system. Each function module has an interface with parameters for importing or exporting data. The main purpose of a function module is its reusability. It therefore belongs to the reuse components. Function modules can also be accessed from outside the system by external systems or processes if they are a remote-enabled module.

Function modules are assigned to a function group. Each function group is a collection of function modules that have similar functions or process the same data. A function group can contain the same components as an executable program (from a system perspective, they are a type of program, but are not executable directly). Table 9.2 shows the types of components that can be placed in a function group.

Component	Purpose
Data Object	These are global in relation to the function group, that is, they are visible to and can be changed by all function modules within the group.
Subroutine	These can be called from all function modules in the group.
Screens	These also can be called from all function modules within the group.

Table 9.2 Function Module Elements

As for subroutines, a function module can contain its own local types and data object definitions. These can only be seen within the function module. The interface of a function module can contain the elements shown in Table 9.3. Figure 9.6 shows a function module with all elements. You should type interface parameters with types from the ABAP Dictionary.

Element	Purpose
Import parameter	Values or variables of the calling program can be transferred to them when calling the function module. The optional parameters do not need to be supplied during the call.
Export parameter	The calling program accepts the output of the function module by assigning a receiving variable to an export parameter. Export parameters are always optional.
Changing parameter	You can transfer variables from the calling program to the function module, where they are changed and returned to the calling program.
Tables parameter (obsolete)	This parameter is similar to the changing parameter in that the table provided can be changed. However, it can only be used for standard tables. The formal parameter specified by this parameter within the function module will always have a header line. Internal tables should be passed with Import, Export, or Changing parameters. The other advantage of using one of these (as with subroutines) is that you can pass internal tables other than standard tables, for example, sorted or hashed tables.

Table 9.3 Function Module Elements

Element	Purpose
Exceptions	These can be raised by the function module in error situations and provide information regarding the processing error. Exceptions should always be caught and handled by the calling program.

Table 9.3 Function Module Elements (cont.)

```
FUNCTION bp_job_select.
*"----------------------------------------------------------------------
*"*"Global Interface:
*"  IMPORTING
*"     VALUE(JOBSELECT_DIALOG) LIKE  BTCH0000-CHAR1
*"     VALUE(JOBSEL_PARAM_IN) LIKE  BTCSELECT STRUCTURE  BTCSELECT
*"       DEFAULT SPACE
*"     VALUE(ENDDATE) LIKE  TBTCO-ENDDATE DEFAULT '        '
*"     VALUE(ENDTIME) LIKE  TBTCO-ENDTIME DEFAULT '      '
*"     VALUE(SELECTION) TYPE  CHAR2 DEFAULT 'AL'
*"  EXPORTING
*"     VALUE(JOBSEL_PARAM_OUT) LIKE  BTCSELECT STRUCTURE  BTCSELECT
*"  TABLES
*"      JOBSELECT_JOBLIST STRUCTURE  TBTCJOB
*"      JOBNAME_EXT_SEL STRUCTURE  NJRANGE OPTIONAL
*"      USERNAME_EXT_SEL STRUCTURE  UNRANGE OPTIONAL
*"  CHANGING
*"     REFERENCE(ERROR_CODE) TYPE  I OPTIONAL
*"  EXCEPTIONS
*"      INVALID_DIALOG_TYPE
*"      JOBNAME_MISSING
*"      NO_JOBS_FOUND
*"      SELECTION_CANCELED
*"      USERNAME_MISSING
*"----------------------------------------------------------------------
```

Figure 9.6 A Function Module Interface is Documented as Comments

You can use the logical expression IS SUPPLIED within a function module to see if an actual parameter was set for a formal parameter during a call. The older logical expression IS REQUESTED should no longer be used. The older logical expression IS REQUESTED checked only the output parameter, whereas the logical expression IS SUPPLIED can be used with all optional parameters. The expression IS INITIAL should not be used because it does not take into account that a default value was used.

If a program calls a function module, the entire corresponding function group is loaded into the same internal session as the calling program, and the function module is executed. The function group remains loaded in memory until the calling program is closed. When you call another function module of this group, it is processed without needing to be reloaded, and the same global data exists. Therefore, if you call a function module that stores values in a global data object of the function group, other function modules in the same group can access this data when they are called during the same program.

You should note in Figure 9.7 the OPTIONAL and PASS VALUE checkboxes (which in the example are shortened to OPT... and PA...), which control if the parameter is required and if it is copied (pass by value). In Figure 9.8, you should note that the Optional checkbox does not exist because all export parameters are optional. Figure 9.9 shows the changing parameters. Figure 9.10 shows the table parameters. Note that the pass by value option does not exist. Finally, Figure 9.11 shows the exceptions for this function module.

Function module: BP_JOB_SELECT — Active

Attributes | Import | Export | Changing | Tables | Exceptions | Source code

Parameter Name	Type...	Associated Type	Default value	Opt...	Pa...	Short text
JOBSELECT_DIALOG	LIKE	BTCH0000-CHAR1		☐	☑	Dialog Box Yes(Y) / No(N)
JOBSEL_PARAM_IN	LIKE	BTCSELECT	SPACE	☑	☑	Selection Parameters (Input)
ENDDATE	LIKE	TBTCO-ENDDATE	' '	☑	☑	
ENDTIME	LIKE	TBTCO-ENDTIME	' '	☑	☑	
SELECTION	TYPE	CHAR2	'AL'	☑	☑	Single-Character Flag

Figure 9.7 Function Module Input Parameters

Function module: BP_JOB_SELECT — Active

Attributes | Import | Export | Changing | Tables | Exceptions | Source code

Parameter Name	Type spec.	Associated Type	Pass Val...	Short text
JOBSEL_PARAM_OUT	LIKE	BTCSELECT	☑	Selection Parameters (Output)

Figure 9.8 Function Module Export Parameters

Function module: BP_JOB_SELECT — Active

Attributes | Import | Export | Changing | Tables | Exceptions | Source code

Parameter Name	Type spec.	Associated Type	Default value	Optional	Pass Val...	Short text
ERROR_CODE	TYPE	I		☑	☐	Special Additional Error Code

Figure 9.9 Function Module Changing Parameters

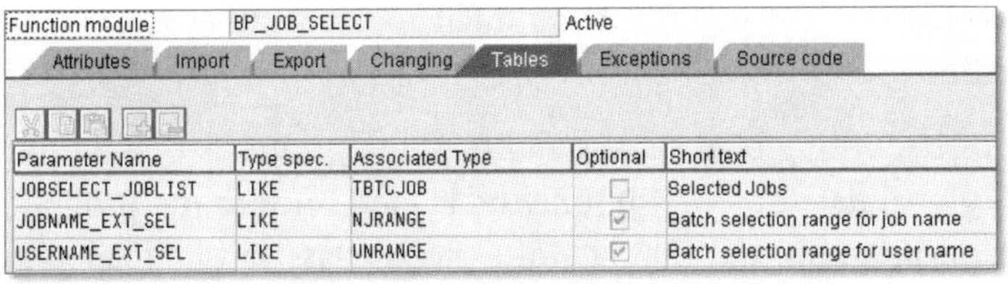

Function module: BP_JOB_SELECT Active

Attributes | Import | Export | Changing | Tables | Exceptions | Source code

Parameter Name	Type spec.	Associated Type	Optional	Short text
JOBSELECT_JOBLIST	LIKE	TBTCJOB	☐	Selected Jobs
JOBNAME_EXT_SEL	LIKE	NJRANGE	☑	Batch selection range for job name
USERNAME_EXT_SEL	LIKE	UNRANGE	☑	Batch selection range for user name

Figure 9.10 Function Module Tables Parameters

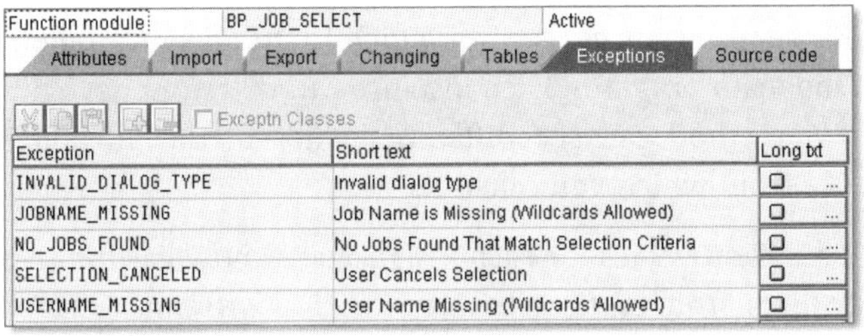

Function module: BP_JOB_SELECT Active

Attributes | Import | Export | Changing | Tables | Exceptions | Source code

☐ Exceptn Classes

Exception	Short text	Long txt
INVALID_DIALOG_TYPE	Invalid dialog type	☐ ...
JOBNAME_MISSING	Job Name is Missing (Wildcards Allowed)	☐ ...
NO_JOBS_FOUND	No Jobs Found That Match Selection Criteria	☐ ...
SELECTION_CANCELED	User Cancels Selection	☐ ...
USERNAME_MISSING	User Name Missing (Wildcards Allowed)	☐ ...

Figure 9.11 Function Module Exceptions

ABAP Classes and Methods

In the course of extending the ABAP language to include object-oriented concepts, global classes were introduced that use methods to provide functions. Like function modules, methods also have an interface, known as a signature, which consists of importing, exporting, changing, and returning parameters and exceptions.

In addition to methods, classes have other components. They contain global data objects known as *attributes*. In the same way that global data objects of a function group can be accessed by all the function modules in the group, all methods can access the attributes of their classes.

With function groups, the global data objects are not visible outside the function group. This is the encapsulation of data in a function group. Attributes are also normally encapsulated within the class and can therefore only be read or changed using methods of the same class. However, in contrast to function modules, classes also allow you to make specific attributes visible to the users of the class. A distinction is therefore made between public and private attributes.

This distinction is applied not only to attributes, but also to methods. Whereas all function modules can be called from outside the function group, only public methods are available outside the class. Private methods can only be called by other methods of the same class and are thus similar to subroutines (form routines) within a function group.

The major difference between global classes and function groups is that a function group with its global data objects can only be loaded once to the program context for each main program, but the data of a global class can be loaded as many times as you like. This is known as *multiple instantiation* of the class. In practice, it means the global data object values are the same for all function module calls, because we have only one copy of each of the data objects of a function group. A class can have several instances, each of which is stored separately in the program context of the main program. Each instance can therefore have different attribute values. A method can see different values in the attributes depending on the instance from which you called it.

Attributes that can have different values for each instance are known as *instance attributes* to distinguish them from *static attributes* (or *class attributes*). Static attributes exist only once for each program context regardless of how many class instances are generated. If instance methods access a static attribute, all instances see the same value.

Note the PASS VALUE and OPTIONAL checkboxes (which in the example are shortened to P... and O...), which control if the parameter is copied (pass by value) and is required.

Figure 9.12 shows the attributes of a method. Figure 9.13 shows the parameters for the method. Figure 9.14 shows the exceptions for the method. The beginning of the method is shown in Listing 9.10.

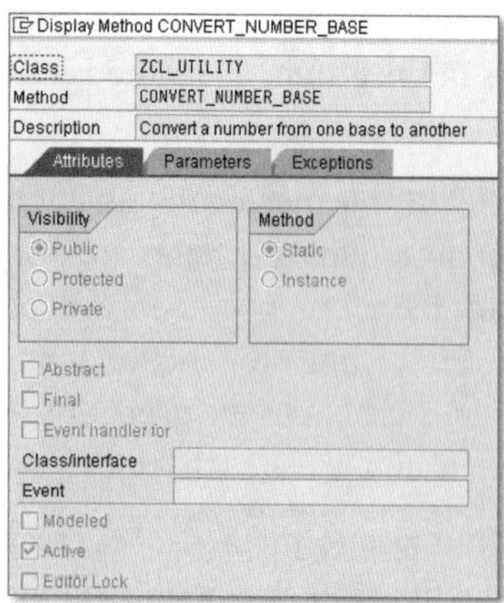

Figure 9.12 Method Attributes

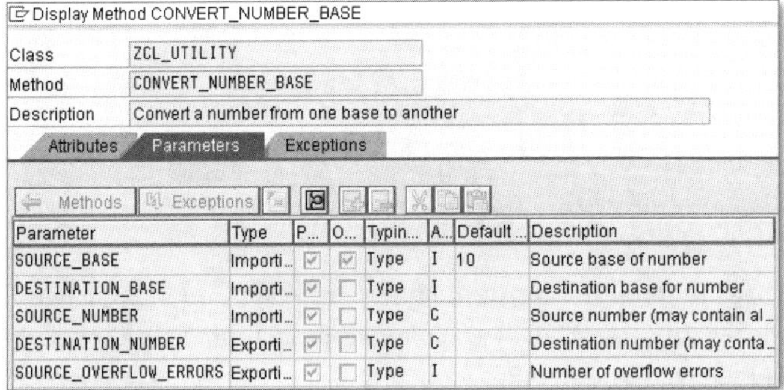

Figure 9.13 Method Parameters

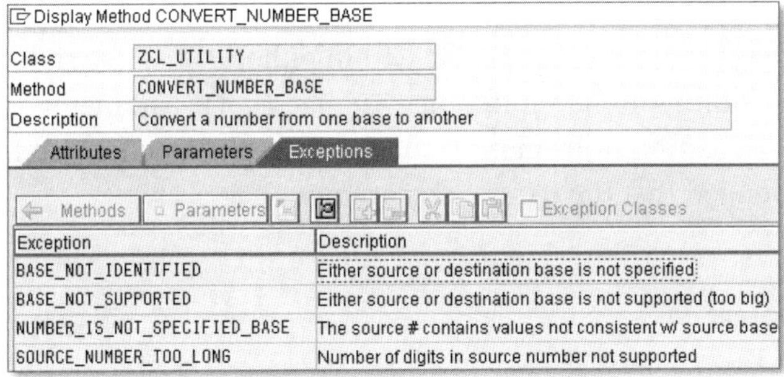

Figure 9.14 Method Exceptions

```
method convert_number_base.
  data:
    lv_factor           type p length 10,
    lv_converted_number type p length 10,
    lv_src_nbr          type c length 99,
    lv_iterations       type i,
    lv_position         type i,
    lv_max_value        type i,
    lv_digit            type i,
    lv_exponent         type i.
  field-symbols:
    <digit>             type c.
  constants:
    lc_starting_factor  type i value '19',
    lc_number_base      type c length 36
               value '0123456789ABCDEFGHIJKLMNOPQRSTUVWXYZ'.
  if source_base is initial or
     destination_base is initial.
```

```
    raise base_not_identified.
  endif.
  lv_iterations = strlen( lc_number_base ).
```

Listing 9.10 Method Coding

Note

You should note that the terms *instance* and *object* are often used interchangeably. Further details regarding ABAP Object-Oriented programming is discussed in Chapter 14, ABAP Object-Oriented Programming.

As with function modules and subroutines, you have the capability to import, export, change, and produce exceptions. Methods also provide the ability to return a value, which allows the call to be placed within either a `COMPUTE` statement or a logical expression. Another difference is that every parameter is required to be typed. This is different from both subroutines and function modules, where it is recommended that the parameters are typed.

ABAP Selection Screen

In general, selection screens are used for entering selection criteria for data selection. From a technical perspective, selection screens are Dynpros. However, they are not designed by the developer directly, but generated in accordance with declarative statements in the source code.

The selection screen has the following standard functions:

- Text on the selection screen can be maintained in several languages. At runtime the text is automatically displayed in the user's logon language.
- The system checks types automatically.
- In addition to single value entries (`PARAMETERS`), you can also implement complex selections (`SELECT-OPTIONS`) on the selection screen. With a complex selection (`SELECT-OPTIONS`), the user can enter multiple values, intervals, comparative conditions, or even patterns as restrictions.
- If the input field is defined using an ABAP Dictionary element, the field documentation can be displayed on the input field using the F1 function key. The value help attached to the Dictionary type displaying possible inputs can

be called up using the F4 function key. It is also possible for the label (selection text) to use the long text of the data element.

- You can easily save the values (or calculation in the case of a dynamic date or time calculation) of complicated selection screens as selection screen variants for reuse or use in background processing.

Listing 9.11 shows the coding for a selection screen, and Figure 9.15 shows the resulting generated selection screen.

```
***-------------------------------- Parameters/Select-options
selection-screen begin of block c01
  with frame title text-c01.
parameters:
  p_custzg as checkbox default 'X',
  p_wrkbch as checkbox default 'X',
  p_repair as checkbox default 'X',
  p_others as checkbox default 'X'.
selection-screen end   of block c01.
selection-screen begin of block c02
  with frame title text-c02.
parameters:
  p_r_po  radiobutton group sort,
  p_e_s_r radiobutton group sort,
  p_r_s_d radiobutton group sort,
  p_d_s_r radiobutton group sort,
  p_r_d_s radiobutton group sort.
selection-screen end   of block c02.
selection-screen begin of block c03
  with frame title text-c03.
select-options:
  s_trkorr for gs_outtab-trkorr.
selection-screen end   of block c03.
selection-screen begin of block c04
  with frame title text-c04.
select-options:
  s_user   for gs_outtab-as4user modif id c04.
selection-screen end   of block c04.

parameters:
  p_relsed as checkbox default 'X',
  p_byuser as checkbox user-command activate,
  p_missng as checkbox,
  p_apprvl as checkbox,
```

```
p_apmiss as checkbox,
p_sumrze as checkbox default 'X'.
```

Listing 9.11 Coding for a Selection Screen

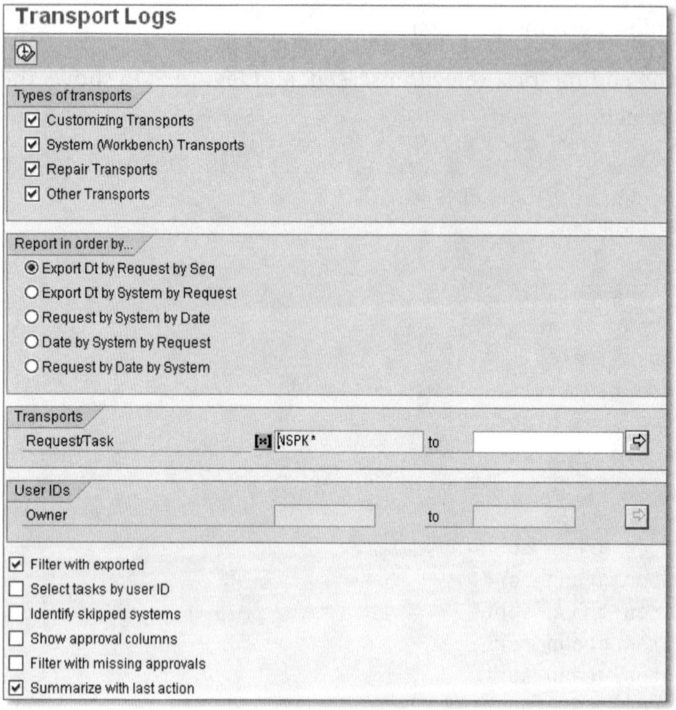

Transport Logs

Types of transports
- [x] Customizing Transports
- [x] System (Workbench) Transports
- [x] Repair Transports
- [x] Other Transports

Report in order by...
- (•) Export Dt by Request by Seq
- ( ) Export Dt by System by Request
- ( ) Request by System by Date
- ( ) Date by System by Request
- ( ) Request by Date by System

Transports
Request/Task NSPK* to

User IDs
Owner to

- [x] Filter with exported
- [ ] Select tasks by user ID
- [ ] Identify skipped systems
- [ ] Show approval columns
- [ ] Filter with missing approvals
- [x] Summarize with last action

Figure 9.15 Generated Selection Screen

Further details regarding selection screens are discussed in Chapter 13, Selection Screens.

Authorization Checks

Critical data and parts of the functional scope of the SAP system must be protected from unauthorized access. You have to implement authorization checks in your program so that the user can only access areas for which they are authorized. To code an authorization check you use the `AUTHORITY-CHECK` statement to check whether the current user has the authorization required for executing the function in his master record. Depending on the check result returned in the `SY-SUBRC`, you can continue accordingly. If the return code equals 0 (zero), the user has the required authorization. Authorization objects can also be defined in report transaction codes to provide additional restriction other than simply by transaction code.

Under normal circumstances, the definition of authorization objects is part of data modeling and the creation of database tables. Implementing the authorization check is one of the tasks of the developer who programs access to the database tables. The subsequent steps, such as defining the authorizations and user profiles and assigning them to the user master records, are the tasks of the administrator or security team.

Before you can implement the required authorization check in your program, you must first determine the structure (the fields) of the corresponding authorization object. An object usually consists of the `ACTVT` (activity) field and one or several other fields, which specifies the data type to be protected, for example, material number, organization unit, account number, and so on.

Tip

If you do not want to carry out a check for a field, either do not enter it in the `AUTHORITY-CHECK` statement or enter `DUMMY` as the field value. `DUMMY` is a predefined description entered without quotation marks.

Example of a suppressed field check: When a change transaction is called, the system should always check immediately whether the user has any change authorization. If the check fails, an appropriate message is to be output to the user immediately (see the first `AUTHORITY-CHECK` in Listing 9.12 for an example of the syntax; the authorization object can be seen in Figure 9.16).

```
if p_s_develop-devclass =  space.
  authority-check object 'S_DEVELOP'
    id 'DEVCLASS' dummy
    id 'OBJTYPE'  field p_s_develop-objtype
    id 'OBJNAME'  field p_s_develop-objname
    id 'P_GROUP'  dummy
    id 'ACTVT'    field l_develop_actvt.
else.
  authority-check object 'S_DEVELOP'
    id 'DEVCLASS' field p_s_develop-devclass
    id 'OBJTYPE'  field p_s_develop-objtype
    id 'OBJNAME'  field p_s_develop-objname
    id 'P_GROUP'  dummy
```

```
    id 'ACTVT'    field l_develop_actvt.
endif.
```

Listing 9.12 Call to an Authorization Check

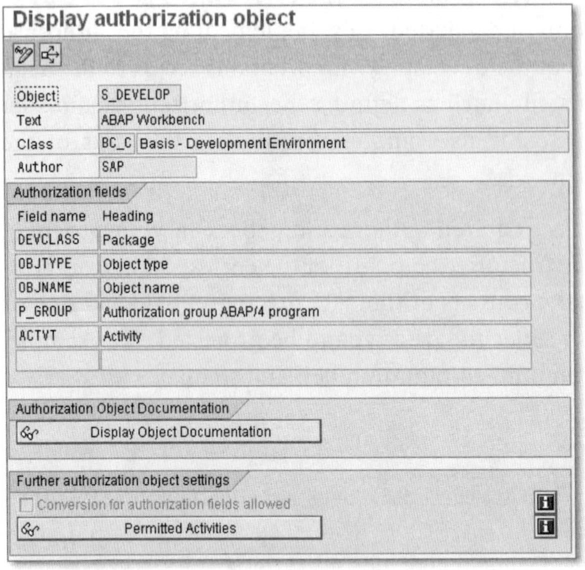

Figure 9.16 Authorization Object

Again to avoid spelling errors in object and field names, you can use the PATTERN button to generate the appropriate `AUTHORITY-CHECK` statement.

ABAP Dynpros

As mentioned earlier, standard screens or Dynpros are designed by the developer directly through the use of the Screen Painter. A screen consists not only of its layout with input and output fields, buttons, and other screen elements, but also a processing logic known as *flow logic*. The fact that the ABAP Dictionary is integrated into the system provides automatic consistency checks for screen input fields. These checks include type checks, foreign key checks, and fixed value checks.

The above checks can be complemented with other program checks. Techniques are available for screens that allow you to control the order in which checks are performed. If an error occurs, the appropriate fields are made input ready again.

The layout can be designed very flexibly, with input fields, output fields, radio buttons, check fields, and buttons with which corresponding functions of the program can be executed.

Further, screens have the same formatting options as lists and selection screens: Fixed point numbers and dates are formatted according to the settings in the user master record, times are formatted as `HH:MM:SS`, currency amounts are formatted according to the currency, and physical measurements (lengths, weights, quantities, etc.) are formatted according to their unit fields.

In theory, there are two options for starting a screen sequence:

- By calling the first screen (using the `CALL SCREEN` statement) from a processing block in your program
- By creating a dialog transaction that references the program and the first screen

After a screen is processed, the statically or dynamically defined screen sequence is processed. A formal next screen of 0 (zero) returns processing to the point where the screen was called or ends the dialog transaction.

Screens can appear in executable programs, function groups, or module pools:

- **Executable program**
  Executable programs (reports) use screens to display data in addition to the list output, or to replace the list output display completely, and sometimes for the display of an ALV grid. You can also use screens to enter and change data in the list. For the purpose of reusability and data encapsulation, you should no longer create screens directly in reports, but use screens in function groups instead.
- **Function group**
  Function groups often use screens to encapsulate a screen or screen sequence for reuse. SAP provides a vast number of such encapsulated screens or screen sequences. Various SAP standard function modules can be found in the Repository Information System simply by looking for "popup" as part of the function module name. These encapsulated screens exist for displaying messages, accepting values, and selecting between options.
- **Module pool**
  Module pools can only be started with a transaction code; they cannot be tested as other types of executable programs directly in the ABAP Workbench (Transaction SE80) or ABAP Editor (Transaction SE38). In contrast to screens

in function groups, you cannot encapsulate module pools or provide an external interface.

When a screen is displayed for a user, the presentation server performs all interactions until a function is selected. A function corresponds to either a button on the application toolbar, a menu, one of the function keys (F1 through F12), or the ↵ key. Each of these actions by a user assigns the function code defined by the programmer to a special field associated with every screen. This field is normally referred to as the `OK_CODE`. You normally name this field and provide a global field with the same name to receive the value in your program. The field should be defined to use the type `SYUCOMM`. This transport to this variable is automatic. During the PAI (process after input) you can determine what action the user performed through the contents of this variable.

The statement `CALL SCREEN` accesses the Dynpros of the relevant main program of the current program group, and these use the global data and dialog modules of the main program. If the specified Dynpro does not exist in the main program of the program group, an untreatable exception occurs.

You use the addition `STARTING AT` to open a new popup level and to display all screens of the called Dynpro sequence in a modal dialog box rather than as a full screen. The upper-left corner of the dialog window is determined by the values following the addition `STARTING AT` for the column and line. The values refer to the window with popup level 0. The lower-right corner is set automatically from the size of the window, or you can specify it after `ENDING AT`. For column and line number (for either the top-left or bottom-right corner), data objects of type `i` are expected. The values of the top-left corner should be smaller than those of the bottom-right corner; otherwise, the behavior is undefined. The maximum popup level is 9.

If during the processing of a modal dialog box a new Dynpro sequence is called, it must be started in another popup level. You cannot use the statement `CALL SCREEN` without adding `STARTING AT` in this case. When calling a Dynpro in a dialog window, specify the window as a modal dialog window in its properties and set an appropriate GUI status beforehand. It is recommended that a Dynpro sequence in a modal dialog window consist of only one Dynpro.

Further details regarding Dynpro screens are discussed in Chapter 12, Classical Screens.

Dialog Messages

You use the MESSAGE statement to send dialog messages to the users of your program. When you do this with an actual message defined from a message class, you must specify at least a three-digit message number, the message class, and the type of the message. It is also possible to provide the text of the message or just the type of the message.

Message number and message class clearly identify the message to be displayed. You use the message type (either A, E, I, S, W, or X; see Table 9.4) to define how the ABAP runtime should process the message.

Type	Function	General Program Behavior
A	Termination	The message appears in a dialog box, and the program terminates. When the user has confirmed the message, control returns to the next-highest area menu.
E	Error	Depending on the program context, an error dialog appears or the program terminates.
I	Information	The message appears in a dialog box. Once the user has confirmed the message, the program continues immediately after the MESSAGE statement.
S	Status	The program continues normally after the MESSAGE statement, and the message is displayed in the status bar of the next screen
W	Warning	Depending on the program context, a warning dialog appears or the program terminates.
X	Exit	No message is displayed, and the program terminates with a short dump. Program terminations with a short dump normally only occur when a runtime error occurs. Message type X allows you to force a program termination. The short dump contains the message ID.

Table 9.4 Message Types and their Behavior

If the specified message contains placeholders (specified as either an & or &#, where the # is 1, 2, 3, or 4), you can supply them with values from your program by using the WITH addition. Instead of the placeholders, the transferred values then appear in the displayed message text. There can only be up to four placeholders, and if a number is part of the placeholder, it specifies the order in which the placeholders are filled. This allows for text translation that may require the placeholders in a different order (see Listing 9.13 for an example). Messages can either be displayed in modal dialog boxes or in the status bar of the screen based on the user's settings. How a message is processed depends on its type and on the context in which it is sent.

If the introductory statement of a program contains the addition `MESSAGE-ID id` and your message to be displayed is of the same class, you can use the short form of the message statement without specifying the class. Listing 9.14 contains two examples of messages using this form, and Listing 9.15 shows the introductory statement.

```
call function 'ENQUEUE_ESRDIRE'
  exporting
    mode_trdir     = l_enq_mode
    name           = incl2
    x_name         = ' '
    _scope         = '2'
    _wait          = ' '
  exceptions
    foreign_lock   = 01
    system_failure = 02.
if sy-subrc ne 0 and rs38l-extern = space.
  message id     sy-msgid
          type   'E'
          number sy-msgno
          with   sy-msgv1 sy-msgv2 sy-msgv3 sy-msgv4.
endif.
```

Listing 9.13 Message Specifying All Options

```
call function 'CHANGEDOCUMENT_OPEN'
  exporting objectclass = 'WFRULES          '
            objectid    = objectid
            planned_change_number = planned_change_number
            planned_or_real_changes = planned_or_real_changes
  exceptions sequence_invalid = 1
             others           = 2.
case sy-subrc.
  when 1. message a600 with 'SEQUENCE INVALID'.
  when 2. message a600 with 'OPEN ERROR'.
endcase.
```

Listing 9.14 Two Messages in the Shortened Form

```
function-pool wfrc
  message-id cd                    .
```

Listing 9.15 Introductory Statement Specifying the Message Class

This general behavior is ultimately driven by the context of where the call to the message statement occurs. One unique context is when you have no screen. This includes the following processing blocks; all other processing blocks are associated with screen processing and are reacting to user input:

- The program constructor `LOAD-OF-PROGRAM`
- PBO modules (PBO of screens)
- The selection screen event `AT SELECTION-SCREEN OUTPUT` (PBO of a selection screen)
- The reporting events `INITIALIZATION`, `START-OF-SELECTION`, `GET`, and `END-OF-SELECTION`
- The list events `TOP-OF-PAGE` and `END-OF-PAGE`

To make Table 9.5 more concise, the above-mentioned processing blocks are structured into two groups:

- Group 1
  `LOAD-OF-PROGRAM`, PBO module of screens, `AT SELECTION-SCREEN OUTPUT`
- Group 2
  Reporting and list events (`INITIALIZATION`, `START-OF-SELECTION`, `GET`, `END-OF-SELECTION`, `TOP-OF-PAGE` and `END-OF-PAGE`)

Type	Display	Processing
A	Dialog box	Program terminates, and control returns to last area menu.
E	Group 1: Dialog box Group 2: Status line of current window	Group 1: Behaves as type A. Group 2: Program termination and display of an empty screen with empty GUI status. After the user action: Return to the calling position of the program.

Table 9.5 General Message Type Behavior

Type	Display	Processing
I	Group 1: Status line of the next screen Group 2: Dialog box	Program continues processing after the MESSAGE statement.
S	Status line of next screen	Program continues processing after the MESSAGE statement.
W	Group 1: Status line of the next screen Group 2: Status line of the current window	Group 1: Behaves as type S. Group 2: Program termination and display of an empty screen with empty GUI status. After the user action: Return to the calling position of the program.
X	None	Triggers a runtime error with short dump

Table 9.5 General Message Type Behavior (cont.)

Another unique context includes all situations where a screen is being processed, that is, the program is reacting to user input. In ABAP programs, this means all PAI (process after input) modules. Table 9.6 shows the message behavior during PAI.

Type	Display	Processing
A	Dialog box	Program terminates, and control returns to last area menu
E	Status line	PAI processing is terminated, and control returns to the current screen. All of the screen fields for which there is a FIELD or CHAIN statement are ready for input. The user must enter a new value. The system then restarts PAI processing for the screen using the new values. Error messages are not possible in POH (process on help-request) or POV (process on value-request) processing. Instead, a runtime error occurs.
I	Dialog box	Program continues processing after the MESSAGE statement

Table 9.6 Message Behavior During PAI

Type	Display	Processing
S	Status line	Program continues processing after the MESSAGE statement
W	Status line	Like type E, but the user can confirm the message by pressing [↵] without having to enter new values. The system then resumes PAI processing directly after the MESSAGE statement. Warning messages are not possible in POH or POV processing. Instead, a runtime error occurs.
X	None	Triggers a runtime error with short dump

Table 9.6 Message Behavior During PAI (cont.)

A unique context includes all situations where a selection screen is being processed, that is, the program is reacting to user input. In ABAP programs, this corresponds to the AT SELECTION-SCREEN processing blocks, except those with the OUTPUT addition. This is shown in Table 9.7.

Type	Display	Processing
A	Dialog box	Program terminates, and control returns to last area menu.
E	Status line	Selection screen processing terminates, and the selection screen is redisplayed. The screen fields specified through the additions to the AT SELECTION-SCREEN statement are ready for input. If there are no additions to the statement, then all screen fields are ready for input. The user must enter a new value. The system then restarts the selection screen processing using the new values. You cannot use error messages with the ON HELP-REQUEST, ON VALUE-REQUEST, and ON EXIT additions. Instead, a runtime error occurs.
I	Dialog box	Program continues processing after the MESSAGE statement.
S	Status line	Program continues processing after the MESSAGE statement.

Table 9.7 Messages During a Selection Screen

Type	Display	Processing
W	Status line	Like type E, but the user can confirm the message by pressing [↵] without having to enter new values. The system then resumes selection screen processing directly after the MESSAGE statement. You cannot use warnings with the ON HELP-REQUEST, ON VALUE-REQUEST, and ON EXIT additions. Instead, a runtime error occurs.
X	None	Triggers a runtime error with short dump.

Table 9.7 Messages During a Selection Screen (cont.)

A unique context includes all situations where a list is being processed, that is, the program is reacting to user interaction with lists. In ABAP programs, this includes the following processing blocks:

- AT LINE-SELECTION
- AT USER-COMMAND
- AT PFnn
- TOP-OF-PAGE DURING LINE-SELECTION

Table 9.8 shows the behavior during list processing.

Type	Display	Processing
A	Dialog box	Program terminates, and control returns to last area menu.
E	Status line	Processing block terminates. Previous list levels remain displayed.
I	Dialog box	Program continues processing after the MESSAGE statement.
S	Status line	Program continues processing after the MESSAGE statement.
W	Status line	Like type E.
X	None	Triggers a runtime error with short dump.

Table 9.8 Messages During List Processing

The last unique context is in function modules and methods. Messages have two different functions in function modules and methods:

- Normal message
- Triggering an exception

If you use messages in function modules and methods without the `RAISING` addition in the `MESSAGE` statement, the message is handled normally according to the context in which it is called within the function module or method. In other words, if it is not caught, it behaves as it would from one of the other contexts depending on where the call for the function module or method occurs.

If you use messages in function modules and methods with the addition `RAISING exc` in the `MESSAGE` statement, the way in which the message is handled depends on whether the calling program catches the exception `exc` or not.

- If the calling program does not catch the exception, the message is displayed and handled according to the context in which it occurs in the function module or method from which it was called. This again is as if the error occurred where the call to the function module or method was made.
- If the calling program catches the exception, the message is not displayed. Instead, the procedure is interrupted in accordance with the message type, and processing returns to the calling program. The contents of the message are placed in the system fields `SY-MSGID`, `SY-MDGTY`, `SY-MSGNO`, and `SY-MSGV1` through `SY-MSGV4`.

Important Terminology

For the certification, you should know that Repository objects are development objects such as programs or classes in the ABAP Workbench. Each Repository object is assigned to a package. A change request contains at least one task for each developer working on the change. A change request records and manages all changes made to Repository objects and Customizing settings during a development project. A task is the information carrier for entering and managing all changes to Repository objects and Customizing settings performed by developers within a development project. Simply put, development is assigned to a task that is part of a change request.

You should understand that global declarations appear in a section after the introductory program statement of an ABAP program in which the data types, classes, and data objects that are visible in the whole program can be declared.

A modularization unit of an ABAP program is something that cannot be separated or nested. Processing blocks are procedures, dialog modules, and event blocks. They contain statements that are structured using control structures in statement blocks. Every non-declarative statement of an ABAP program is part of a processing block. A procedure interface consists of formal parameters and states the possible exceptions of the procedure.

With pass by reference, you pass only the address of the actual parameter to the formal parameter. Formal parameters do not occupy their own memory space. Within the subroutine, you work only with the field from the calling program. If you change the formal parameter, the field contents in the calling program change too.

In pass by value, a local data object is created as a copy of the actual parameter, and when the procedure is called, the value of the actual parameter is passed to it. Changed formal parameters are only passed to the actual parameter if the procedure ends without errors.

The term *event* can mean either a component of a class or interface declared using `(CLASS-)EVENTS` or an event of the ABAP runtime environment. We discussed the latter in this chapter. More details of the former can be found in Chapter 14, ABAP Object-Oriented Programming. Events in classes trigger event handlers, and events of the ABAP runtime environment trigger event blocks. An event block is a processing block without a local data area that can be defined in every ABAP program — except for subroutine pools, class pools, and interface pools — and is processed when a specific event of the ABAP runtime environment occurs. It begins with an event keyword and ends with the start of the next modularization.

Practice Questions

The practice questions below will help you evaluate your understanding of the topic. The questions shown are similar in nature to those found on the certification examination. Whereas none of these questions will be found on the exam itself, they allow you to review your knowledge of the subject. Select the correct answers and then check the completeness of your answers in the following solu-

tion section. Remember that you must select all correct answers and only correct answers to receive credit for the question.

1. ABAP is a programming language that:

- ☐ **A.** Executes on all three levels of the three-tier architecture
- ☐ **B.** Controls the business logic
- ☐ **C.** Processes and formats data
- ☐ **D.** Interacts with the user
- ☐ **E.** Separates program code from language text

2. Which events can exist in all types of programs that actually contain executable statements?

- ☐ **A.** `LOAD-OF-PROGRAM`
- ☐ **B.** `INITIALIZATION`
- ☐ **C.** `START-OF-SELECTION`
- ☐ **D.** `AT LINE-SELECTION`
- ☐ **E.** `AT USER-COMMAND`
- ☐ **F.** `AT PF##`

3. Dynpros can be placed in which program types?

- ☐ **A.** Executables
- ☐ **B.** Module pools
- ☐ **C.** Function groups
- ☐ **D.** Class pools

4. A change request is part of a task?

- ☐ **A.** True
- ☐ **B.** False

5. Which statements about ABAP are true?

- ☐ **A.** Each statement must begin with a keyword.
- ☐ **B.** Each statement must end with a period.
- ☐ **C.** ABAP keywords and additions must be in uppercase.

6. A development object can be assigned to only one package.

- ☐ **A.** True
- ☐ **B.** False

7. A development object can be assigned to only one change request.

- ☐ **A.** True
- ☐ **B.** False

8. Each ABAP program:

- ☐ **A.** Is divided into processing blocks
- ☐ **B.** Assigns every executable statement to a processing block regardless of it being in a processing block
- ☐ **C.** Only assigns executable statements in a processing block to a processing block
- ☐ **D.** Uses event blocks to trigger events in ABAP
- ☐ **E.** Has declarative statements outside of processing blocks which are considered local
- ☐ **F.** has declarative statements inside of processing blocks which are considered local
- ☐ **G.** Can be tested from the ABAP Workbench by pressing [F8]

9. Which modularization units can raise an exception?

- ☐ **A.** Function modules
- ☐ **B.** Methods
- ☐ **C.** Subroutines (`FORM` routines)

10. Which types of programs or parts of programs can be tested directly from the ABAP Workbench or ABAP Editor?

- ☐ **A.** `REPORT`
- ☐ **B.** `PROGRAM`
- ☐ **C.** `FUNCTION-POOL`
- ☐ **D.** `FUNCTION MODULE`
- ☐ **E.** `CLASS-POOL`

☐ **F.** `METHOD`

☐ **G.** `INTERFACE-POOL`

☐ **H.** `TYPE-POOL`

☐ **I.** `INCLUDE`

11. Which method of passing parameters is preferred for its performance?

☐ **A.** Pass by reference

☐ **B.** Pass by value

12. Which modularizations units are global?

☐ **A.** Function modules

☐ **B.** Subroutines (`FORM` routines)

☐ **C.** Methods within a local class in the program

☐ **D.** Methods within class pools

13. `FORM` routines (subroutines) can be used in which type of program:

☐ **A.** Executables

☐ **B.** Module pools

☐ **C.** Function groups

☐ **D.** Class pools

☐ **E.** Interface pools

☐ **F.** Subroutine pools

☐ **G.** Type groups

14. You can use the logical expression `IS SUPPLIED` for any formal parameter passed to which modularization unit?

☐ **A.** Subroutine (`FORM` routine)

☐ **B.** Function module

☐ **C.** Static method

☐ **D.** Instance method

15. A selection screen can only be defined in an executable program.

☐ **A.** True

☐ **B.** False

16. Subroutines provide which types of parameters?

☐ **A.** Input

☐ **B.** Output

☐ **C.** Input/output (changing)

☐ **D.** Return values

☐ **E.** Exceptions

17. Function modules provide which types of parameters?

☐ **A.** Input

☐ **B.** Output

☐ **C.** Input/output (changing)

☐ **D.** Return values

☐ **E.** Exceptions

18. Methods provide which types of parameters?

☐ **A.** Input

☐ **B.** Output

☐ **C.** Input/output (changing)

☐ **D.** Return values

☐ **E.** Exceptions

19. It is not possible to test a function module if another function module of the same function group contains a syntax error.

☐ **A.** True

☐ **B.** False

20. Each button on a Dynpro (screen) requires the assignment of a function code. This function code:

☐ **A.** Is used to define global variables that receive a value when the button is clicked

☐ **B.** Can be used to identify when the button is clicked by looking for the function code in the screen's `OK_CODE` field

☐ **C.** Prevent the function code from be assigned to a menu item

21. Which message types behave the same regardless of the context in which they are called?

☐ **A.** `A`

☐ **B.** `E`

☐ **C.** `I`

☐ **D.** `S`

☐ **E.** `W`

☐ **F.** `X`

Practice Question Answers and Explanations

1. Correct answers: **B, C, D, E**

   ABAP does not, however, execute on the database server. Although it can be considered to interact with the database through the database interface, it does not execute on the database level. Nor does it actually execute on the presentation server. It interacts with the presentation server normally through the SAP GUI, but the only execution occurs on the application servers.

2. Correct answer: **A**

   The only event common to all executable programs is `LOAD-OF-PROGRAM`.

3. Correct answers: **A, B, C**

   Dynpros are not possible in methods or classes.

4. Correct answer: **B**

   A change request holds a task.

5. Correct answer: **B**

   All ABAP statements must end with a period. Whereas it is certainly true that ABAP requires the statement to begin with a keyword, there are cases where the keyword is optional. The most obvious is the `COMPUTE` keyword, which we have never seen coded in a program (though it certainly helps to know the keyword exists when you are trying to find help on an arithmetic function while in the editor). ABAP does not care if the case of the statements is upper, lower, or mixed.

6. Correct answer: **A**

   A development object can only be assigned to a single package. It can be reassigned to a different package, but it is only ever assigned to one package at a time.

7. Correct answer: **B**

   A development object can only be assigned to multiple projects or change requests. Only one project or change request can be active at a time, but over time, it is common for development objects to be assigned to different projects and change requests, and they are changed.

8. Correct answers: **A, B, F**

   A program is divided into processing blocks, and every executable statement is assigned to a processing block either explicitly or implicitly. Any statement not explicitly included in a processing block is implicitly included in `START-OF-SELECTION`. Declarative statements inside a modularization unit are considered local, whereas those outside the modularization units are considered global. Event blocks are called when the ABAP runtime triggers them.

   Whereas almost every ABAP program can be tested simply by pressing [F8] while in the editor, one type (a module pool) cannot be started from the editor or ABAP Workbench directly. Module pools (dialog programs) must start with a particular screen, and the only way is to run the transaction code that associates the first screen to process. To be able to test in the ABAP Workbench, you must first navigate to the transaction code, which you can then execute by pressing [F8].

9. Correct answers: **All options**

   It is currently possible to raise a class-based exception from all three of these modularization units.

10. Correct answers: **A, D, E, F**

    Reports, function modules, classes, and methods can all be executed and tested directly. Programs (module pools) can be indirectly tested by testing their corresponding transaction code. Function groups, interface pools, type pools, and includes cannot be tested independently.

11. Correct answer: **A**

    Pass by reference is always preferable when performance is an issue, whereas pass by value is more suitable for situations where robustness and data consistency are important.

12. Correct answers: **A, D**

    Any modularization that can be reused is considered global. A method defined within a program cannot be reused, nor should a subroutine (form routine). Both function modules and methods defined in a class pool are considered global.

13. Correct answers: **A, B, C, F**

    Subroutines cannot be used in classes. Interface pools and type pools cannot have any executable code.

14. Correct answers: **B, C, D**

    Subroutines do not have optional parameters, and therefore the logical expression `IS SUPPLIED` cannot be used.

15. Correct answer: **B**

    Selection screens can be defined in any program that allows screens. Originally, only one selection screen was allowed in an executable program (screen 1000), but with later releases it is now possible to define as many as you want. This capability is why it is possible to place selection screens in programs other than just executable programs.

16. Correct answers: **C, E**

    Subroutines technically only provide input/output (changing) types of parameters (through `USING` and `CHANGING`) and exceptions.

17. Correct answers: **A, B, C, E**

    Function modules provide input (`IMPORTING`), output (`EXPORTING`), and input/output (`CHANGING`) types of parameters and exceptions (`EXCEPTIONS`).

18. Correct answers: **All options**

    Methods provide input (IMPORTING), output (EXPORTING), input/output (CHANGING), and return value (RETURNING) types of parameters and exceptions (EXCEPTIONS).

19. Correct answer: **A**

    ABAP looks at the whole program during both generation and execution. A syntax error in any part will prevent it from executing.

20. Correct answer: **B**

    The function code of any menu, button, or Function key is always placed into the OK_CODE field associated with the screen. It can also be found in the system variable SY-UCOMM.

21. Correct answers: **A, F**

    The abort or terminate message type always causes a program termination, and control returns to last area menu. The exit message type always triggers a runtime error with short dump.

Take Away

You will need to understand how transports are organized. Remember that a change request is commonly called a transport and contains tasks assigned to specific developers. It is also important to recognize the various types of programs: Executable programs, also known as reports, module pools, also known as dialog programs, function groups, which contain function modules, and class pools, which contain methods, are the primary program types you need to understand. Within each of these, you need to understand the types of modularization and how events are triggered.

You also need to be able to distinguish which types of screens, when displayed, use the SAP GUI versus a Web browser. Classical screens, or Dynpros, and selection screens use the SAP GUI, whereas Web Dynpro and Business Server Pages, for example, use a Web browser. Web Dynpro is discussed in detail in Chapter 20, User Interfaces (Web Dynpro). You are expected to be able to identify how a classic screen (Dynpro) handles fields and buttons and their use in function modules. Included with this classic screen handling are both selection screens and modal dialog boxes.

You will need to understand the use of authorization checks and modularization units. This includes how to call them and options for providing data.

Last is how messages work in different contexts. You will need to understand where messages are displayed and the behavior of the program following the message production.

Refresher

You must understand various types of modularization blocks. Events, subroutines, methods, function modules, and dialog modules will all play a part in the certification examination. You must know how they are defined, how they are called including their interface or signature, and how they behave with the production of a dialog message. You must have a thorough understanding of the techniques of both pass by value and pass by reference.

Classical screen (Dynpro) handling is also essential knowledge. You must understand how screens are called, what distinguishes a screen from a modal dialog box and from a selection screen. You should understand how to define all three and in which types of programs they can be produced.

Table 9.9 shows the key concepts of basic ABAP programs and interfaces creation.

Key Concept	Definition
Modularization units	The procedural modularization units of an ABAP program are its processing blocks.
Dynamic program (Dynpro)	A dynamic program consists of a screen image or layout and its underlying flow logic. The main components of a screen are: ▸ Attributes: such as screen number and next screen ▸ Layout: the arrangement of texts, fields, and other elements ▸ Element attributes: definitions of the properties of individual elements ▸ Flow logic: calls of the relevant ABAP modules

Table 9.9 Key Concepts Refresher

Key Concept	Definition
Authorization check	Check to determine whether the current program user has a certain authorization. For each authorization field of an authorization object, a value to be checked is compared with the corresponding entry in the user master record. The corresponding ABAP statement is `AUTHORITY-CHECK`.

Table 9.9 Key Concepts Refresher (cont.)

Tips

As with the majority of the subjects covered in the certification examination, it is important to have as much practical experience with the subject as possible. Unlike the majority of subjects found in the certification examination, this is an area where if you have been programming in ABAP, you will already have sufficient experience.

Whereas the vast majority of the concepts presented in this chapter should be second nature, it is important that you understand the behavior differences of interfaces (or signatures) and of message production.

Summary

You should now be able to create various types of ABAP programs. You should also have an understanding of the different types of encapsulation that a program can use and the interaction between a user and the program through the use of screens and messages. These skills will allow you to successfully complete this portion of the certification exam.

10 ABAP Dictionary

Techniques You'll Master:

- Describe the functions of the ABAP Dictionary in the SAP system
- Define data types in the ABAP Dictionary
- Understand database objects and their use in the ABAP Dictionary
- Define and create domains, data elements, and tables in the ABAP Dictionary
- Explain tables types in the ABAP Dictionary
- Define the technical attributes of tables in the ABAP Dictionary
- Determine database views, maintenance views, project views, and help views in the ABAP Dictionary
- Understand search helps and lock objects

The ABAP Dictionary centrally manages all of the global data definition in the SAP system. The ABAP Dictionary helps you define user-defined data types, that is, data elements, structures, and table types. You can define the structure of database objects such as tables and views and the index for the database objects. An ABAP Dictionary table defined in the ABAP Dictionary automatically creates a database in the underlying database. Search helps are an ABAP Dictionary service used to display a list of possible values for screen fields. Lock objects are another ABAP Dictionary service, which is used to control the access of the same data, by a program or user, using the logical lock mechanism.

In this chapter we will cover the ABAP Dictionary in detail. We will discuss the technical details of the ABAP Dictionary domain, data elements, structure and table types, tables, joins, and database tables. We will also cover various types of ABAP Dictionary views and their use in SAP systems. Finally, we will discuss ABAP Dictionary services such as search help and lock objects, their use, and the steps to create custom search help and lock objects.

Real-World Scenario

Imagine you have to develop various custom applications on your customer project implementation.

You would need a custom table to store the application data and would require a number of structures to design the screen. You have to design and create transparent tables, data elements, domains, search helps, and lock objects. To create transparent tables you need to create domains and data elements. You also have to create search helps and lock objects for your application that would be used in the SAP screen design and development.

As a development lead, you need to have a thorough understanding of the ABAP Dictionary objects and be able to explain ABAP Dictionary concepts to your development team.

Objectives of this Portion of the Test

The objective of this portion of the test is judge your understanding of the ABAP Dictionary objects because the ABAP Dictionary is one of the key components of the SAP system and is required in almost any application development. It is expected that you have a thorough understanding of ABAP Dictionary objects such as domains, data elements, structures, and type groups. You should be able to differentiate between the different types of tables, that is, transparent tables, pools and clusters, in the SAP system.

The certification exam will test your knowledge regarding the steps required to create tables. You will be expected to describe the features of lock objects, search help, and database views.

Key Concepts Refresher

The ABAP Dictionary is a key component of any application developed in an SAP system. You need to understand the various ABAP Dictionary objects and their uses in SAP application development. Without knowledge of the ABAP Dictionary, it would be almost impossible for you to develop your custom application.

You need to know the following about the ABAP Dictionary objects:

- Basic data types and complex data types found in the ABAP Dictionary
- ABAP Dictionary objects such as domains and data elements that can be used to create transparent tables
- How to create tables with the correct attributes based on you application requirements
- How to perform the tuning of the ABAP Dictionary table to improve performance without modifying the application program
- Database views and maintenance views
- The use of lock objects and search helps

Overview

The ABAP Dictionary is the tool used to manage all Dictionary objects centrally in the SAP system. You create ABAP Dictionary data types such as data elements, structures, and table types centrally within the ABAP Dictionary tool. Any change to a data type definition is automatically propagated to all of the system components using the data type. The data types can be used in your custom programs and applications or other Dictionary objects that you might create. ABAP Dictionary data types are also referred to as global data types and are available to all of the Repository objects within the system.

There are three categories of ABAP Dictionary types:

- **Data elements**
  This is an elementary ABAP Dictionary type and can therefore be used to describe a single field or data element. It describes the type, length, and possibly the number of decimal places. You also define the field labels, output characteristics, and documentation for the data elements.
- **Structures**
  This is a complex data type that consists of multiple components. Structures can be used for ABAP Dictionary table definitions, function module parameters, object method parameters, and for the design and definition of ABAP screens. Any changes in the structure or its component are automatically propagated to the repository objects wherever the specific structure is being used.
- **Table types**
  This is a complete description of an internal table. It gives us the line type (which columns internal table will have), the access type (whether it will be a standard, sorted, or hashed internal table), and the information about the key.

Database objects such as tables, indexes, databases views, and maintenance views are defined in the ABAP Dictionary. An ABAP Dictionary table defined in the ABAP Dictionary automatically creates a database table in the underlying database using the structure defined in the ABAP Dictionary when the table definition is activated. Changes in the definition of the table, view, or index are automatically made to the underlying database. Indexes are defined to speed up database access to the table. An index created in a Dictionary table also creates an index for the underlying database table.

The ABAP Dictionary provides a number of services for application development. You can create lock objects in the ABAP Dictionary; the function modules to set and release locks are automatically generated in the system upon activation of the lock object. You use the function modules to lock the table or the table records, if the user intends to change a record and does not want anyone to change it at the same time. You can also use lock objects to apply the read lock, where you are just reading the data but want to ensure that no one else changes the data while you are using it. Similarly, the Dictionary provides you with the option to create search helps that can be linked to the screen fields to help the user search for application data in the SAP system. The Dictionary also provides you with services for input checks against the user input. The valid values for the table field are defined via the check table or the value range for the domain of the data element. Refer to Chapter 19, Table Relationships, for more detail on this topic. Figure 10.1 displays the initial screen of the ABAP Dictionary tool, which is used to create the Dictionary objects.

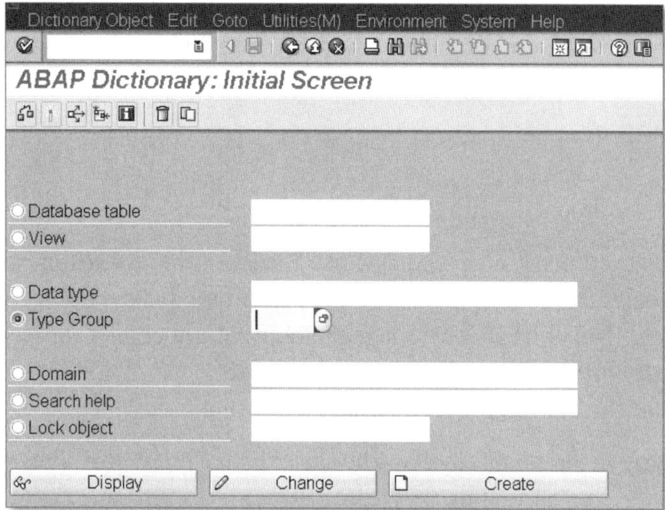

Figure 10.1 ABAP Dictionary Tool

In summary, you could create or update the definition of SAP tables; views; data types including data elements, structures, and table types; domains; search helps; lock objects; and type groups with the ABAP Dictionary tool. We will discuss each of these Dictionary objects and services in detail in the following sections.

Basic and Complex Data Types

Global data types are defined in the ABAP Dictionary. Data types defined in the ABAP Dictionary can be referenced in an ABAP program with the `TYPE` addition for the corresponding data object definition. You can also refer to the data types defined in the ABAP Dictionary for the parameters of function modules or the methods interface (see also Chapter 6, ABAP Types and Data Objects).

Data types created in the ABAP Dictionary can be used by more than one ABAP Dictionary object such as a table, structure, or table type, as well as in ABAP programs, screens, function module interfaces, and so on. Data types can be maintained centrally, and accordingly, all of the programs or the relevant objects using the data type are adjusted during runtime if you make any changes in the data type in the Dictionary. You can enter semantic information such as the field labels and documentation detail for the type in the data type definition in the ABAP Dictionary.

There are three basic data types in the ABAP Dictionary, that is, data elements, structure and table types, briefly mentioned earlier. We will discuss these types in detail in this section, but first, we need to discuss and understand the concept of a domain.

Domains

A domain is an ABAP Dictionary object that is used to describe the technical attributes of a data element. Domains cannot be used as a type for data objects in the program directly. Domains can be assigned to any number of data elements, and any changes in the technical attributes of the domain will automatically be applied to all of the data elements in which it is being used.

A domain can be used by several data elements because the technical attribute of the data element can be the same, but they can have different meanings. An example for a field with the same domain would be the data elements S_FROM_CIT and S_TO_CITY in the table SPFLI. Both of the data elements use the domain S_CITY because at they are both city codes, but they have different meanings and hence the two data elements. Thus, we define the domain and can use it for multiple data element definitions instead of assigning a type and length directly to the data element. Figure 10.2 and Figure 10.3 display the use of domains for the definition of data elements. Both of the data elements use the same domain for the reason explained above.

Domains have the following technical attributes:

- Domain formats
- Domain output properties

With the *domain format* you define the format for the domain. The input for the format specification is the data type, the number of characters, which is dependent upon the data type, and the number of decimal places if the data type is a numeric data type. You can only use predefined ABAP Dictionary data types for a domain definition.

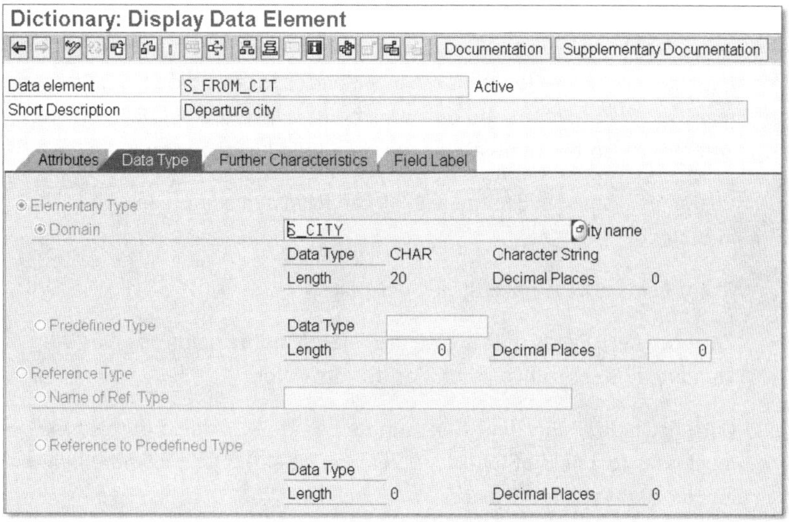

Figure 10.2 Data Element Definition Departure City

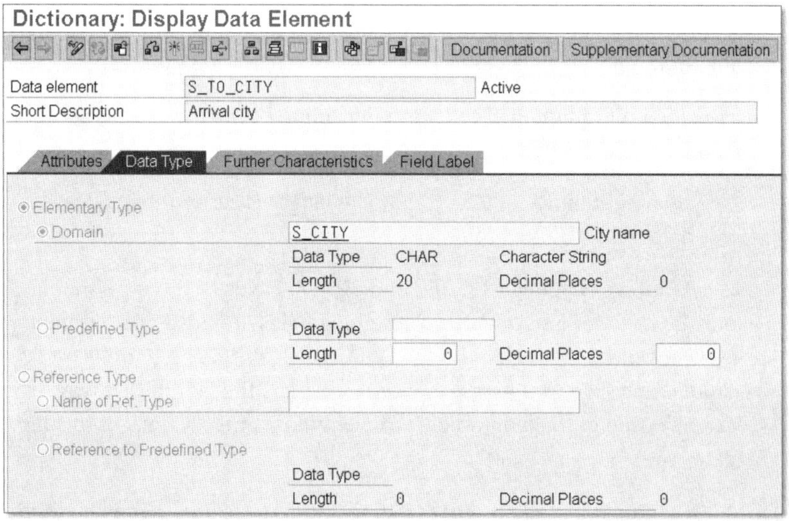

Figure 10.3 Data Element Definition for Arrival City

The ABAP Dictionary has 24 predefined data types. ABAP Dictionary data types are mapped to the ABAP runtime data types that you can use to define your data objects, such as type `I`, type `C`, and so on. Table 10.1 lists the valid ABAP Dictionary data types, and Table 10.2 shows the mapping of the ABAP Dictionary data types and the ABAP runtime data types.

Data Type	Description
ACCP	Posting period. The length is set to six places for this data type. The format is YYYYMM. In input and output, a point is inserted between the year and month, so the template of this data type has the form YYYY.MM.
CHAR	Character string. Fields of type CHAR can have a maximum length of 255 in tables.
CLNT	Client fields always have three CHAR places.
CUKY	Currency key. Fields of this type are referenced by fields of type CURR. The length is set to five places for this data type.
CURR	Currency field. Equivalent to an amount field DEC. A field of this type must refer to a field of type CUKY (reference field). The maximum length for this data type is 31 places.
DATS	Date. The length is set to 8 places for this data type. The output template can be defined with the user profile.
DEC	Counter or amount field with decimal point, sign, and commas separating thousands. A DEC field has a maximum length of 31 places.
FLTP	Floating point number. The length (including decimal places) is set to 16 places for this data type.
INT1	1-byte integer between 0 and 255. The length is set to three places for this data type.
INT2	2-byte integer between –32767 and 32767. Fields of this type should only be used for length fields. These long fields are positioned immediately in front of a long field (type LCHR, LRAW). With INSERT or UPDATE on the long field, the database interface enters the length that was actually used in the length field. The length is set to five places for this data type.
INT4	4-byte integer between –2147483647 and 2147483647. The length is set to 10 places for this data type.

Table 10.1 ABAP Dictionary Predefined Data Types

Data Type	Description
LANG	Language key. Has its own field format for special functions. This data type always has length of one. The language key is displayed at the user interface with two places, but is stored with only one place in the database. The conversion exit ISOLA converts the display at the user interface for the database and vice versa. This conversion exit is automatically allocated to a domain with data type LANG at activation.
LCHR	Character string of any length, but it has to be declared with a minimum of 256 characters. Fields of this type must be located at the end of transparent tables (in each table there can be only one such field) and must be preceded by a length field of type INT2. If there is an INSERT or UPDATE in ABAP programs, this length field must be filled with the length actually required. If the length field is not filled correctly, this may lead to a data loss in the LCHR field. A field of this type cannot be used in the WHERE condition of a SELECT statement.
LRAW	Uninterpreted byte string of any length, but it has to be declared with a minimum length of 256. Fields of this type must be located at the end of transparent tables (in each table there can be only one such field) and must be preceded by a length field of type INT2. If there is an INSERT or UPDATE in ABAP programs, this length field must be filled with the length actually required. If the length field is not filled correctly, this may lead to a data loss in the LRAW field. A field of this type cannot be used in the WHERE condition of a SELECT statement.
NUMC	Long character field in which only numbers can be entered. The length of this field is limited to a maximum of 255 places.
PREC	Accuracy of a QUAN field. The length is set to two places for this data type.
QUAN	Quantity. Equivalent to an amount field DEC. A field of this type must always refer to a units field with UNIT format (reference field). The maximum length for this data type is 31 places.
RAW	Uninterpreted byte string. Fields of type RAW can have only a maximum length of 255 in tables. If longer raw fields are required in tables, you should select data type LRAW.

Table 10.1 ABAP Dictionary Predefined Data Types (cont.)

Data Type	Description
RAWSTRING	Uninterpreted byte string of variable length. In the Dictionary a length can be specified for this type (at least 256 characters). This data type can only be used in types (data elements, structures, table types) and domains. You can store binary data of type RAWSTRING in the database. However, there are restrictions; for a description of them, refer to the documentation of the ABAP statement STRING. In ABAP, this type is implemented as a reference to a storage area of variable size. As default for the output length, 132 characters are proposed. You cannot attach search helps to components of this type.
STRING	Character string with variable length. This data type can only be used in types (data elements, structures, table types) and domains. In the Dictionary a length can be specified for this type (at least 256 characters). It can be used in database tables, but only with restrictions. For a description of these refer to the documentation of the ABAP statement STRING. In ABAP, this type is implemented as a reference to a storage area of variable size. As default for the output length, 132 characters are proposed. You cannot attach search helps to components of this type.
SSTRING	Short character string with variable length. In the Dictionary the number of characters can be specified for this type (1-255). This data type can only be used in types (data elements, structures, table types) and domains. It can be used in database tables; however, to do so refer to the documentation of the ABAP statement STRING. In ABAP, this type is implemented as a reference to a storage area of variable size. String fields of this type can be used in indexes and in the WHERE condition of a SELECT statement. You cannot use them in table keys.
TIMS	Time. The length is set to six places for this data type. The format is HHMMSS. The template for input and output has the form HH.MM.SS.
UNIT	Unit. Fields of this type are referenced by fields of type QUAN. The length of this data type is set to two or three places.
VARC	Character field of variable length. Creation of new fields of this data type is not supported as of Release 3.0. However, existing fields with this data type can still be used. A field of this type cannot be used in the WHERE condition of a SELECT statement.

Table 10.1 ABAP Dictionary Predefined Data Types (cont.)

ABAP Dictionary Type	ABAP Type
ACCP	N(6)
CHAR n	C(n)
CLNT	C(3)
CUKY	C(5)
CURR n,m	P((n+1)/2) DECIMAL m
DEC n,m	P((n+1)/2) DECIMAL m
DATS	D(8)
FLTP	F(8)
INT1	X(1)
INT2	X(2)
INT4	X(4)
LANG	C(1)
NUMC n	N(n)
PREC	X(2)
QUAN n,m	P((n+1)/2) DECIMAL m
RAW n	X(n)
TIMS	T(6)
UNIT	C(n)
VARC n	C(n)
LRAW	X(n)
LCHR	C(n)
STRING	STRING
RAWSTRING	XSTRING

Table 10.2 Mapping of ABAP Dictionary and ABAP Runtime Data Types

In the *domain output properties* you specify the maximum field length, which includes the editing characters such as commas and periods for inputting and outputting values. The output length is populated automatically once you enter the data type and the number of characters and decimal places has been specified, but it can be overwritten. The output format has an effect on the screen and selection screen. The specification from this area is used when the data element linked to this domain is used to describe the screen field, but the output characteristic can be modified in the Screen Painter.

You can also specify a conversion routine for the domain. The conversion routine is used to convert the contents of a screen field from the display format to SAP internal format for data storage and vice-versa. The conversion routine for the domain is identified as a five-character name, and it generates two function modules for the conversion routine. The following function modules would be generated for the conversion routine `XXXXX`:

- The `CONVERSION_EXIT_XXXXX_INPUT` converts the display format to the SAP internal format.
- The `CONVERSION_EXIT_XXXXX_OUTPUT` converts the SAP internal format to the display format.

For the numeric data types such as `DEC`, `FLTP`, `QUAN`, and `CURR` the checkbox for the +/- sign is ready for input. If the checkbox is selected, then the first character of the field is reserved for the +/– sign, and the output length should be increased by one. For the character data type you have the option to select the lowercase checkbox to allow the storage and display of lowercase characters. If this checkbox is not checked, the data is always stored and displayed as uppercase. Figure 10.4 displays the technical attributes for the domain definition.

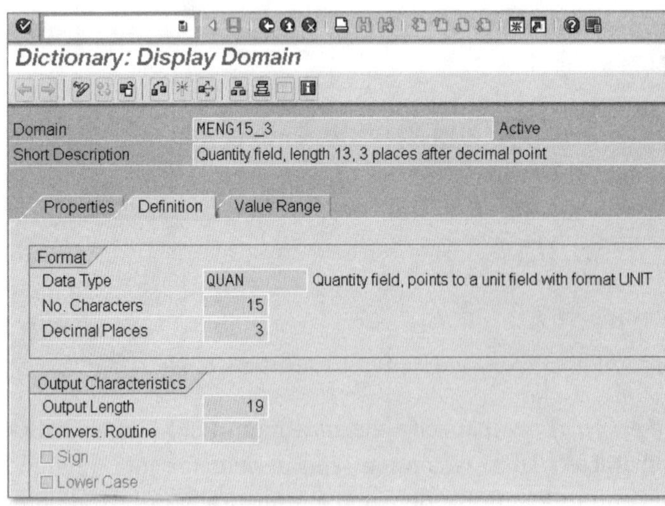

Figure 10.4 Domain Definition

In addition to the above attributes, you can also define the valid values for the domain. Although the type of the domain will dictate which values are valid, you can restrict this further on the VALUE RANGE tab for the domain. The domain can have a single fixed value, value ranges, or a value table (see Chapter 19, Table Relationships, for more detail on this topic). Domains are assigned to the data element, and the data element is assigned to fields of a table, structure, or view. Any table or structure field that uses this data element can have the valid value defined for the domain. The value range definition is not mandatory and hence can be left blank (see Figure 10.5).

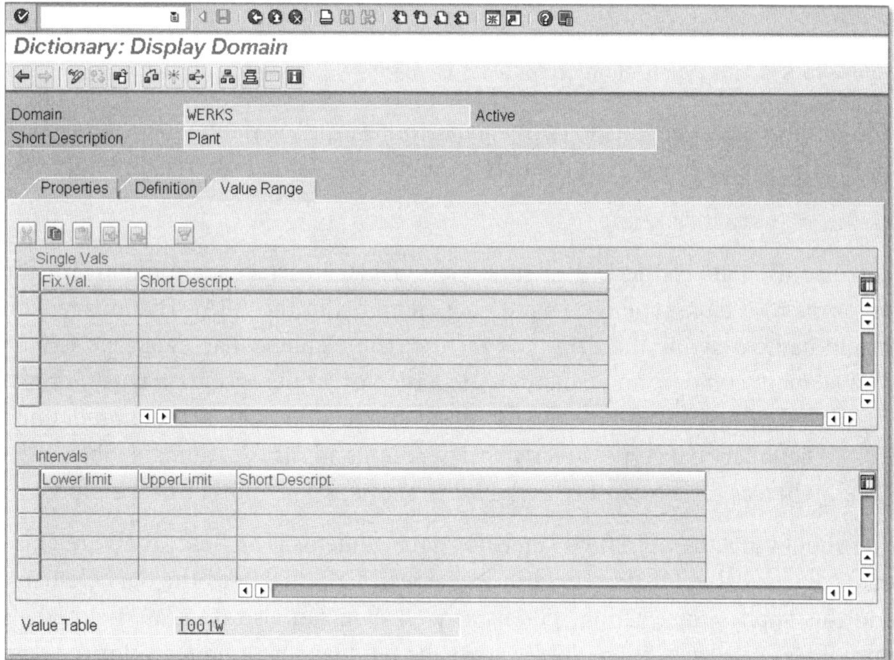

Figure 10.5 Value Range Definition for Domain

Data Elements

Data elements provide a complete description of a field with both semantic and technical information. Data elements can be used in ABAP programs to define data objects by using the `TYPE` addition for the data object declaration (see Figure 10.6 for the data element `MATNR` definition).

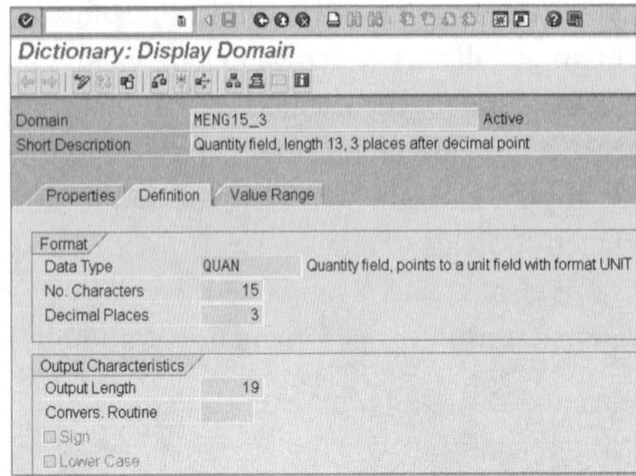

Figure 10.6 Data Type Definition for Data Element

You can use data elements to define a data object (i.e., variable) in an ABAP program. The syntax to define a data object in an ABAP program is as follows:

```
DATA : wa_matnr TYPE matnr.
```

You also use data elements to define view fields, structure components, or the row type of a table type. To create data elements in the ABAP Dictionary, you would have to define the data type for the data element. The data type for the data element could be an elementary data type or a reference data type. For elementary data types you have the option to assign a domain or use a predefined ABAP Dictionary data type directly (SAP recommends using a domain where possible), whereas for a reference data type you can assign another data element.

You should maintain the field labels for data elements. The field labels are automatically available for display with any screen field that uses the data element, and this applies to selection screens as well. You can also translate field labels into other languages. Figure 10.7 shows the field label maintenance for the data element.

Data element: MATNR — Active
Short Description: Material Number

Attributes | Data Type | Further Characteristics | Field Label

	Length	Field Label
Short	10	Material
Medium	15	Material
Long	20	Material
Heading	18	Material

Figure 10.7 Field Label Description for Data Element

You can define additional characteristics for the data element such as search helps, parameter IDs, and the English default name for the data element. The additional characteristic can be maintained on the FURTHER CHARACTERISTICS tab of the data element maintenance screen (see Figure 10.8).

- The SEARCH HELP (F4 value help) can be used to provide input help for a screen field based on the data element (see Chapter 19, Table Relationships, for more detail on this topic).
- The PARAMETER ID is used to store (SET) the screen field value in memory if the parameter ID is defined for the screen field. Similarly, the parameter ID is used to get the input field value from memory by using the GET parameter statement. You can also set the screen field attribute in Screen Painter to automatically read the value from memory without using the GET parameter statement. The parameter ID value is only available if it has been set in an application and is available in the memory. The parameter ID holds the value per session and per user and is not available once you have logged off.
- The DEFAULT COMPONENT NAME is used if this data element is used to describe fields in a BAPI structure for a BAPI definition.

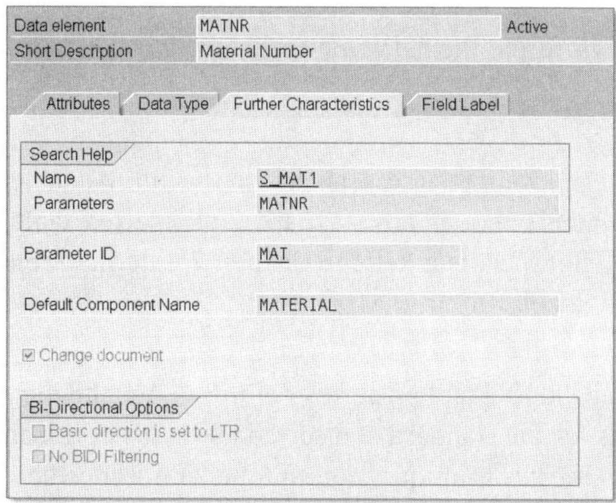

Figure 10.8 Additional Characteristic for the Data Element Definition

Structures

Structures consist of sequences of components. The components of the structure can be a sequence of elementary fields, other structures, or table types. Hence, you can define a flat, nested, or deep structure in the ABAP Dictionary. The components of the structure can have data elements assigned to them or defined using the predefined ABAP Dictionary data types directly. Structures can also be used in table definitions or table type definitions or for screen design. You can only use flat structures inside ABAP Dictionary table definitions. Data elements, structures, and table types belong to the same namespace, and hence a data element, structure, or table type cannot have same name even though they are essentially different things.

Table Types

Table types define the structure and the technical attributes of an internal table. You can refer to the ABAP Dictionary table types in an ABAP program to define an internal table with the following statement (here for the `mara_tab` table type definition):

```
DATA: itab TYPE mara_tab.
```

You define the line type, access mode, and key for the table type in the ABAP Dictionary.

- **Line type**
  The line type defines the structure and the data type of the internal table, that is, columns.
- **Access mode**
  The access mode defines how you want to access the data in the internal table. The possible values for the access modes are standard table, sorted table, hashed table, index table, and not specified. Refer to Chapter 7, Internal Table Definition and Use, for more details on internal tables.
- **Key**
  You can specify the key for the internal table. The key definition is mandatory for the hashed table, whereas for the standard and sorted tables it's optional. The category defines whether the key is unique, non-unique, or not specified. The key category for hashed tables must be unique.

Figure 10.9, Figure 10.10, and Figure 10.11 display the screens for table type definitions.

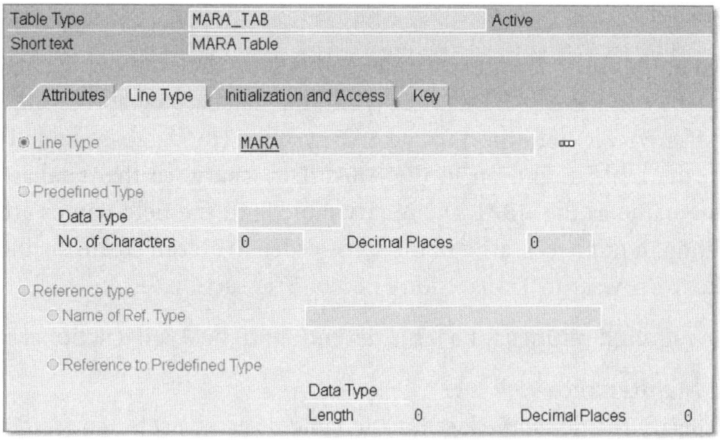

Table Type MARA_TAB Active
Short text MARA Table
Attributes | Line Type | Initialization and Access | Key
Line Type MARA
Predefined Type
Data Type
No. of Characters 0 Decimal Places 0
Reference type
Name of Ref. Type
Reference to Predefined Type
Data Type
Length 0 Decimal Places 0

Figure 10.9 Line Type Definition for Table Type

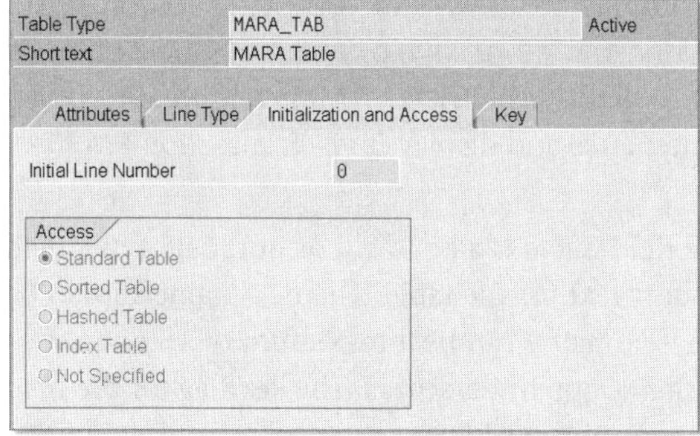

Figure 10.10 Access Mode for Table Type Definition

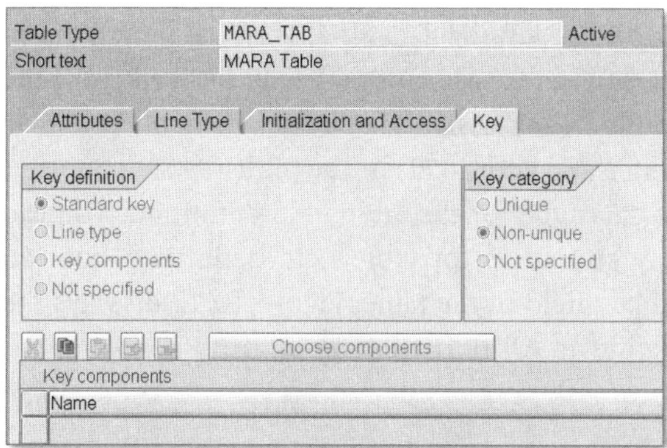

Figure 10.11 Key Definition for Table Type

Transparent Tables

Tables are defined in the ABAP Dictionary independently of the underlying database. You define tables in the ABAP Dictionary, and the database table is created upon activation of the table definition in the SAP system. The database table is created based on the table definition in the ABAP Dictionary, so the database table has the same name as the ABAP Dictionary table, and the field names are also the same (although not necessarily in the same order). You can create a table from the Repository Browser in Transaction SE80 or Transaction SE11.

Following are the required settings for a table definition in the ABAP Dictionary:

- **Delivery and Maintenance**
  You need to specify the delivery class for the table. It can be selected from a drop-down box. You also need to specify the DATA BROWSER/TABLE VIEW MAINTENANCE for the table. The valid values can be selected from a drop-down list as well. For the options DISPLAY/MAINTENANCE ALLOWED WITH RESTRICTION and DISPLAY/MAINTENANCE ALLOWED you have the option to generate the table maintenance dialog. The DISPLAY/MAINTENANCE ALLOWED option also allows table maintenance and display it via Transaction SM30.
- **Table Fields**
  You must define whether the field name is a key field or not, field type, field length, decimal places, and short text for the table. The field name should be unique within the table. The field name can be a maximum of 16 characters long and can contain letters, digits, and underscores. The key flag for the field defines whether the field belongs to the table key.

  The table can have one or more key fields. The key fields should be unique and identify the record in the table. The fields of the table are either assigned to a data element or mapped to a predefined data type. The field length, number of decimal places, and the field text are automatically derived from the data element/domain if the table field is assigned to a data element. You have to define the technical attributes and short text for the table field if you use a predefined ABAP Dictionary data type for the table field definition. You can also include ABAP Dictionary structures for table field definition, but you have to define the individual key field of the table. Figure 10.12 displays the use of include structure to define an ABAP Dictionary table.

Dictionary: Display Table

Technical Settings | Indexes... | Append Structure...

Transp. Table: MARA — Active
Short Description: General Material Data

Attributes | Delivery and Maintenance | Fields | Entry help/check | Currency/Quantity Fields

Srch Help | Predefined Type — 1 / 243

Field	Key	Initial	Data element	Data Type	Length	Decima	Short Description
MANDT	☑	☑	MANDT	CLNT	3	0	Client
MATNR	☑	☑	MATNR	CHAR	18	0	Material Number
.INCLUDE	☐	☐	EMARA	STRU	0	0	Data Division MARA
ERSDA	☐	☐	ERSDA	DATS	8	0	Created On
ERNAM	☐	☐	ERNAM	CHAR	12	0	Name of Person who Created the Object
LAEDA	☐	☐	LAEDA	DATS	8	0	Date of Last Change
AENAM	☐	☐	AENAM	CHAR	12	0	Name of Person Who Changed Object
VPSTA	☐	☐	VPSTA	CHAR	15	0	Maintenance status of complete material
PSTAT	☐	☐	PSTAT_D	CHAR	15	0	Maintenance status
LVORM	☐	☐	LVOMA	CHAR	1	0	Flag Material for Deletion at Client Level
MTART	☐	☐	MTART	CHAR	4	0	Material Type
MBRSH	☐	☐	MBRSH	CHAR	1	0	Industry sector
MATKL	☐	☐	MATKL	CHAR	9	0	Material Group
BISMT	☐	☐	BISMT	CHAR	18	0	Old material number
MEINS	☐	☐	MEINS	UNIT	3	0	Base Unit of Measure
BSTME	☐	☐	BSTME	UNIT	3	0	Purchase Order Unit of Measure
ZEINR	☐	☐	DZEINR	CHAR	22	0	Document number (without document management system)
ZEIAR	☐	☐	DZEIAR	CHAR	3	0	Document type (without Document Management system)
ZEIVR	☐	☐	DZEIVR	CHAR	2	0	Document version (without Document Management system)
ZEIFO	☐	☐	DZEIFO	CHAR	4	0	Page format of document (without Document Management system)
AESZN	☐	☐	AESZN	CHAR	6	0	Document change number (without document management system)
BLATT	☐	☐	BLATT	CHAR	3	0	Page number of document (without Document Management system)
BLANZ	☐	☐	BLANZ	NUMC	3	0	Number of sheets (without Document Management system)

Figure 10.12 Table Definition with Include Structure

Attaching a search help to the table field itself is only possible if the table field is assigned to a data element. Otherwise, if you are using a predefined ABAP Dictionary type, search help definition for the table field is not possible. Reference type specification for the CURR and QUAN data type fields is required. You must specify the reference table for the CURR and QUAN data type field. A reference table should have the CUKY (currency key) data type field for CURR data type and UNIT (unit of measure) data type field for QUAN data type field. A currency key is required because a price of 100 means nothing until we know whether it is \$100 or £100. Figure 10.13 displays the reference type definition for a CURR data type field.

- **Foreign Key**

  You define the foreign key relationship between the tables in the ABAP Dictionary. Using the foreign key you can create a value check for the table field. You can define the foreign key for the table by selecting the foreign keys icon (🔑; see Figure 10.14). Refer to Chapter 19, Table Relationships, for details on this topic.

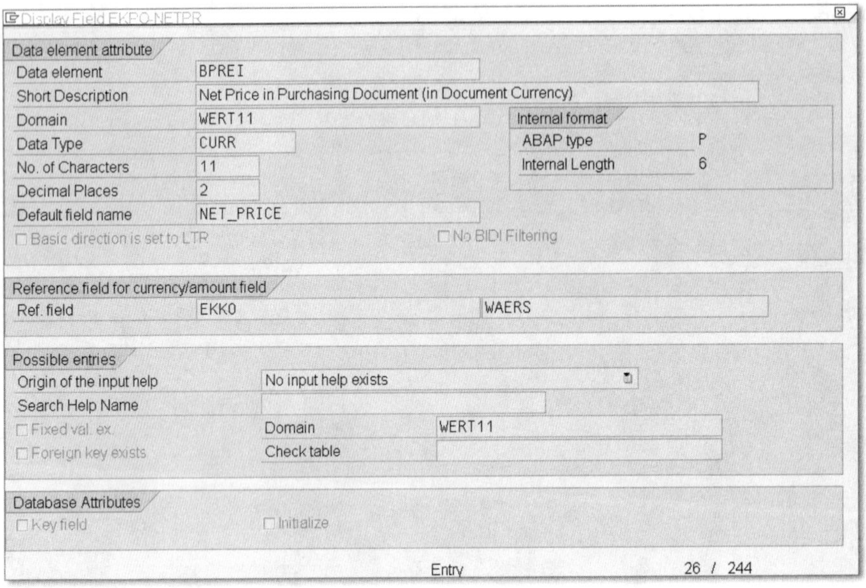

Display Field EKPO-NETPR

Data element attribute

Data element	BPREI
Short Description	Net Price in Purchasing Document (in Document Currency)
Domain	WERT11
Data Type	CURR
No. of Characters	11
Decimal Places	2
Default field name	NET_PRICE

Internal format: ABAP type P; Internal Length 6

☐ Basic direction is set to LTR ☐ No BIDI Filtering

Reference field for currency/amount field

Ref. field EKKO WAERS

Possible entries

Origin of the input help: No input help exists

Search Help Name

☐ Fixed val. ex. Domain WERT11

☐ Foreign key exists Check table

Database Attributes

☐ Key field ☐ Initialize

Entry 26 / 244

Figure 10.13 Reference Table and Field Assignment for Net Price Field

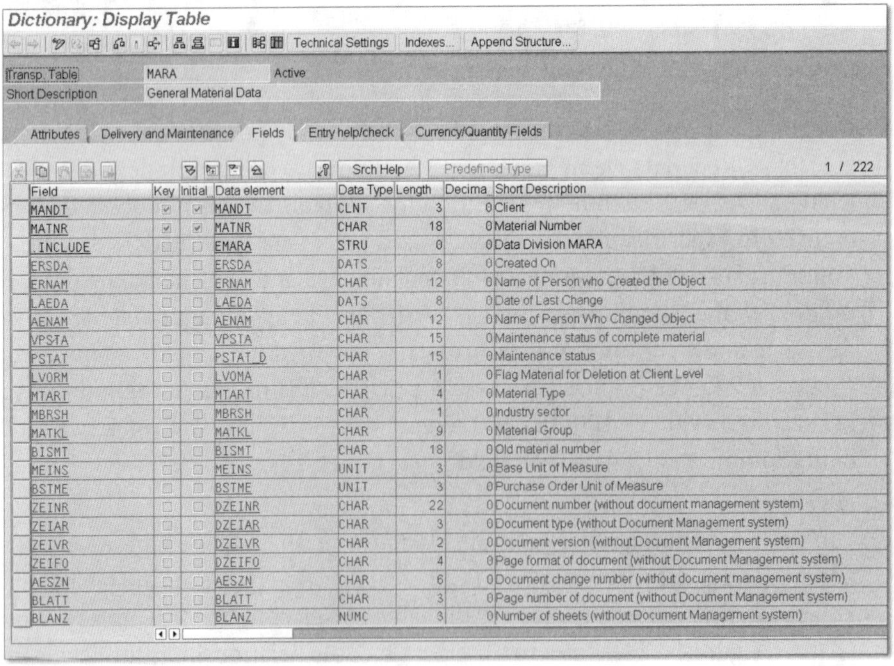

Dictionary: Display Table

Technical Settings Indexes... Append Structure...

Transp. Table MARA Active

Short Description General Material Data

Attributes | Delivery and Maintenance | Fields | Entry help/check | Currency/Quantity Fields

Srch Help Predefined Type 1 / 222

Field	Key	Initial	Data element	Data Type	Length	Decima	Short Description
MANDT	☑	☑	MANDT	CLNT	3	0	Client
MATNR	☑	☑	MATNR	CHAR	18	0	Material Number
.INCLUDE	☐	☐	EMARA	STRU	0	0	Data Division MARA
ERSDA	☐	☐	ERSDA	DATS	8	0	Created On
ERNAM	☐	☐	ERNAM	CHAR	12	0	Name of Person who Created the Object
LAEDA	☐	☐	LAEDA	DATS	8	0	Date of Last Change
AENAM	☐	☐	AENAM	CHAR	12	0	Name of Person Who Changed Object
VPSTA	☐	☐	VPSTA	CHAR	15	0	Maintenance status of complete material
PSTAT	☐	☐	PSTAT_D	CHAR	15	0	Maintenance status
LVORM	☐	☐	LVOMA	CHAR	1	0	Flag Material for Deletion at Client Level
MTART	☐	☐	MTART	CHAR	4	0	Material Type
MBRSH	☐	☐	MBRSH	CHAR	1	0	Industry sector
MATKL	☐	☐	MATKL	CHAR	9	0	Material Group
BISMT	☐	☐	BISMT	CHAR	18	0	Old material number
MEINS	☐	☐	MEINS	UNIT	3	0	Base Unit of Measure
BSTME	☐	☐	BSTME	UNIT	3	0	Purchase Order Unit of Measure
ZEINR	☐	☐	DZEINR	CHAR	22	0	Document number (without document management system)
ZEIAR	☐	☐	DZEIAR	CHAR	3	0	Document type (without Document Management system)
ZEIVR	☐	☐	DZEIVR	CHAR	2	0	Document version (without Document Management system)
ZEIFO	☐	☐	DZEIFO	CHAR	4	0	Page format of document (without Document Management system)
AESZN	☐	☐	AESZN	CHAR	6	0	Document change number (without document management system)
BLATT	☐	☐	BLATT	CHAR	3	0	Page number of document (without Document Management system)
BLANZ	☐	☐	BLANZ	NUMC	3	0	Number of sheets (without Document Management system)

Figure 10.14 Table Field Definition

- **Technical Settings**

  You must maintain the technical settings when you create an ABAP Dictionary table. Some of the technical settings are mandatory. The technical settings are used to optimize the data storage and access for the table. You need to define the data class, size category, and setting regarding buffering.

  - The data class defines the physical area of the database (tablespace) in which the table should be created. The most important data classes defined in the ABAP Dictionary are `APPL0`, for master data that is not frequently modified compared to the transaction data, `APPL1` for transaction data, and `APPL3` for the organization data. The other two data classes, `USR` and `USR1`, are provide for customers and should be used by the customer. A special storage area must be allocated for the customer-specific data classes.
  - The size category defines the size of the extents created for the table. The size category defines the expected space for the database. You can choose the size for 0 to 4, and each category is assigned a fixed memory size in the database. When you create a table, initial space is saved for it in the database. If more space is required later as a result of data that has been entered, the storage is increased in accordance with the size category selected.
  - Buffering settings define how the table should be buffered. Table buffering improves the performance of the database access. The contents of table are buffered on the application server and can be accessed from the application server instead of the database server. The buffered table is invalidated if the entries in the database table change.

    You can select the BUFFERING NOT PERMITTED option, in case the application data is being changed too frequently. In this case the most recent data is available for the application, and it will always be fetched from the database.

    You can select the BUFFERING ACTIVATED option if the data is not being changed frequently. You have to specify the buffering type if you select the buffering activated option.

    You also have the option to specify BUFFERING PERMITTED BUT NOT ACTIVATED. In this case buffering is allowed technically but has been deactivated because performance behavior is not known in the customer system.
  - The Buffering type determines which records are to be buffered on the application server. FULL BUFFERING loads all of the records of the table into

the buffer even if only one record of the table is accessed. The SINGLE-RECORD BUFFER loads only the record being accessed into the buffer. GENERIC BUFFERING loads the left-justified generic key record into the buffer.

- You also have the option to specify whether any changes to the table entries should be logged. If LOG DATA CHANGES is selected, then any changes in the table record will be logged in the log table `DBTABPRT`, or it can be viewed via Transaction SCU3. Switching this may slow down any update to the table because the updates need to be logged as well.

See Figure 10.15 for technical settings for the table.

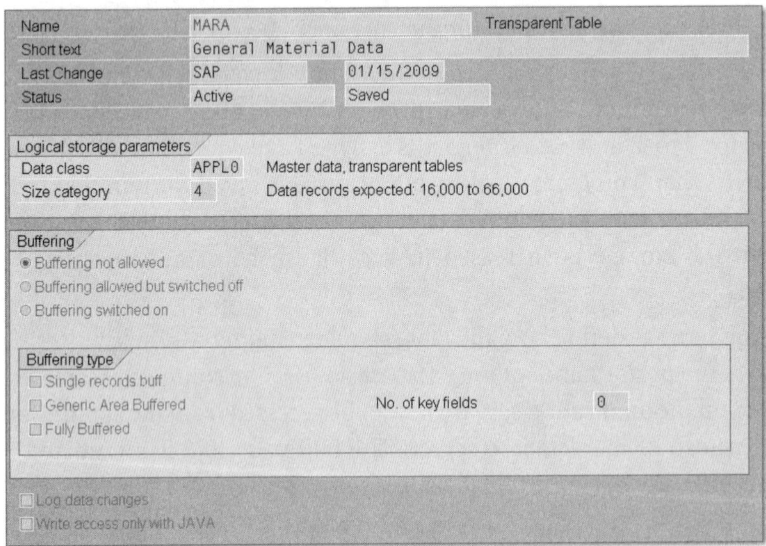

Figure 10.15 Technical Setting for the ABAP Dictionary Table

- **Index**

  The primary index of the table is automatically created based on the table key. An index can be considered a copy of the database that has been reduced to certain fields. The copy is always in sorted order and provides faster access to the data record in the table. The index also contains a pointer to the corresponding record in the actual database table. You can also create multiple secondary indexes for the table. A secondary index may be necessary if the table is frequently accessed in a way that does not take advantage of the primary index access. In such a case you can create a secondary index with the fields other that the key field of the table.

You should not create too many indexes for the table because it may slow down the database update. Each index has to be readjusted any time the database content changes, so creating too many indexes is not recommended. Figure 10.16 displays the multiple secondary index for the table MARA.

Indices for Table MARA

Ind	Ext.	Short text	Status	Unique	Last Changed By	Date
A	☐	Old Material Number	Active	☐	SAP	04/07/2009
BMA	☐	Number of Internal Material Master Record	Active	☐	SAP	04/07/2009
L	☐	Material Group	Active	☐	SAP	04/07/2009
M01	☑		New	☐	SAP	06/22/2005
M02	☑		New	☐	SAP	06/22/2005
M03	☑		New	☐	SAP	12/27/2005
MPN	☐	Manufacturer Part Number / Number of a Ma	Active	☐	SAP	04/07/2009
O	☐	Configurable Material	Active	☐	SAP	04/07/2009
PMA	☐	Pricing Reference Material	Active	☐	SAP	04/07/2009

Figure 10.16 Multiple Secondary Index for the Table MARA

Tip

You should not create too many indexes for the table because it may slow down the database update. For any changes in the database content, each of the indexes has to be readjusted, which may affect the performance adversely.

Search Helps

Search helps are an ABAP Dictionary service used to display a list of possible values for screen fields. The value selected by the user from the selection list is copied to the screen field. Search helps are one form of value help (F4 help) for the screen fields.

Not all screen fields have input help. Fields that do can be recognized by the Input help key on the right of the screen field. The Input help key appears on the screen as soon as you position the cursor on the screen field. Search helps for a screen field can be started by pressing the F4 function key or by selecting the input help key on next to the screen field.

Normally, search helps are assigned to a data element, and the search help is available to any field that refers to the data element. The search help can also be attached directly to a field of a table or a structure, and to a check table. The definition of the attachment is similar to the foreign key. You can also assign search helps directly to a screen field as one of the field attributes in the Screen Painter, although this is not recommended.

The following types of search helps can be defined and are created with the ABAP Dictionary tool:

- Elementary search helps
- Collective search helps
- Append search helps

Elementary Search Helps

Elementary search helps are basic search helps, and define the search path for a field. They must define from where the data for the search help would be read. This is determined by the SELECTION METHOD input field.

The selection method can be a transparent table, database view, projection view, or help view. If the table entered for the selection method has a text table, then the text table is automatically populated to the corresponding field, and its fields are also available for the input help and SEARCH HELP PARAMETER selection, so users can use the field value description when searching. The possible values for the hit list are determined at runtime by the database selection. If the data for the hit list comes from more than one table, then you must define a database view for the table and enter the view for the SELECTION METHOD (see Figure 10.17).

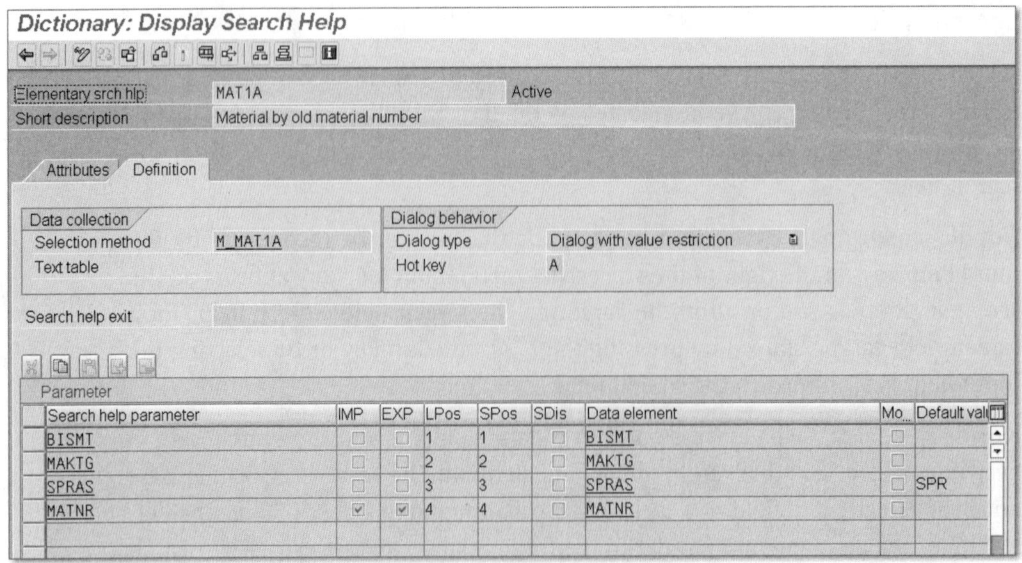

Figure 10.17 Elementary Search Help Definition

You must specify search help parameters for a search help. The parameters are used for the value selection and for the hit list display. The parameters for the search help correspond to the fields of the table or the view entered for the SELECTION METHOD.

- The interface of the search help is defined by means of importing (IMP) and exporting (EXP) parameters. You must specify the interface for the search help in order for it to exchange the data from the screen template to the selection method and from the selection method to the screen field. The importing parameters are required to pass the values to the selection method, and the exporting parameters are required to return the values to the input screen fields. You select the IMP flag if the parameter is the importing parameter, and EXP flag if the parameter is an exporting parameter. Search help parameters can be importing as well as exporting.
- The dialog for the input help is defined with the fields LPOS, SPOS, and SDIS. The parameter position in the hit list is defined by LPOS, and the parameter position on the dialog screen is defined by SPOS. The parameter is not displayed if the value of LPOS or SPOS is initial or 0. You set the SDIS flag for the parameter if the search help parameter is for the value selection only.
- The dialog type defines whether the dialog box for value selection is to be displayed or not. You select SELECT VALUES IMMEDIATELY for the DIALOG TYPE if you do not want a dialog screen for restricting the search value. This option is meaningful if the list contains only few entries. You can select the option DIALOG DEPENDING ON NUMBER OF VALUES. The search result in this case will be displayed immediately if the number of entries is less than 100; otherwise, a dialog screen will be displayed to restrict the number search result. You also have the option to select COMPLEX DIALOG WITH VALUE RESTRICTION for the DIALOG TYPE. In this case the dialog screen for value restriction will be displayed for search list display.

Collective Search Helps

A collective search help combines several elementary search helps. Collective search helps provide several alternative search paths for possible entries. The collective search help exchanges data with the screen with the EXPORT and IMPORT interface parameter. Collective search helps can be attached to fields, check tables, or data elements just like the elementary search help. Only one search help can be attached to a field, table, or data element, but several search paths are available with collective search help. Each elementary search help is represented to the user by a separate tab page.

To define the collective search help you include all of the elementary search helps and define the search help parameters for the collective search help and thereafter assign the elementary search help parameter to the collective search help parameters (see Figure 10.18 and Figure 10.19).

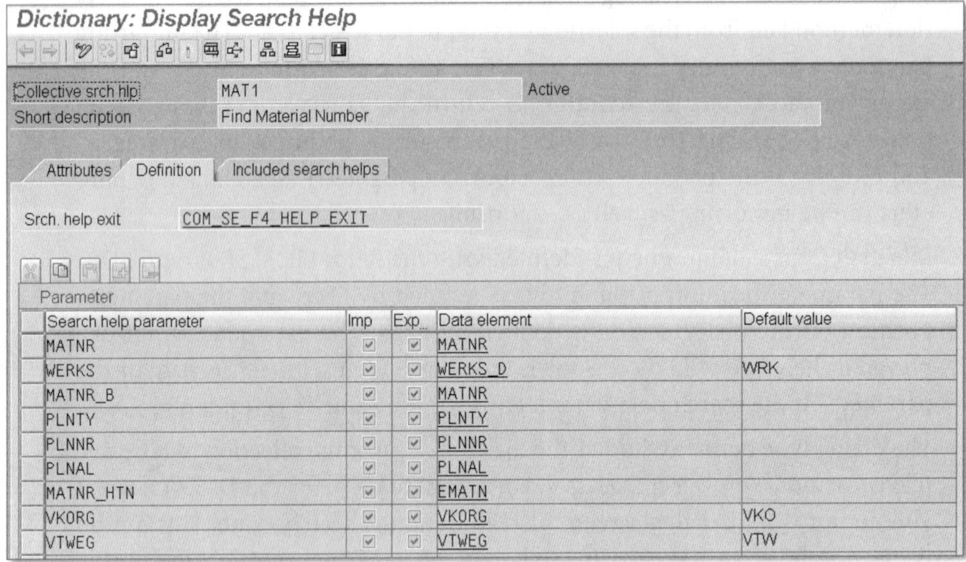

Search help parameter	Imp	Exp	Data element	Default value
MATNR	☑	☑	MATNR	
WERKS	☑	☑	WERKS_D	WRK
MATNR_B	☑	☑	MATNR	
PLNTY	☑	☑	PLNTY	
PLNNR	☑	☑	PLNNR	
PLNAL	☑	☑	PLNAL	
MATNR_HTN	☑	☑	EMATN	
VKORG	☑	☑	VKORG	VKO
VTWEG	☑	☑	VTWEG	VTW

Figure 10.18 Collective Search Help Parameter Definition

Dictionary: Display Search Help

Collective srch hlp MAT1
Short description Find Material Number

Attributes Definition Included search helps

Param. assignment

Search Help	Hid	Short t
MAT1_A	☐	Find M
MAT1_MPN	☐	Searcr
MAT1_TREX	☐	Collect
EANE_RFQ_QUOTE_HELP	☐	Materi
/BEV2/ED_MAT_NUMBER	☐	Excise

Dictionary: Display Search Help

Parameter Assignment for Search Help MAT1_A

Reference parameter	Type	Collective search help params
MATNR	C	MATNR
WERKS	C	WERKS
		MATNR_B
PLNTY	C	PLNTY
PLNNR	C	PLNNR
PLNAL	C	PLNAL
		MATNR_HTN
		VKORG
		VTWEG

Figure 10.19 Collective Search Help Parameter Assignment

Append Search Helps

Append search helps can be used to enhance collective search helps delivered by SAP for customer-specific requirements without modification. You have to define your own custom elementary search help and then attach it to the append search help. You can append a search help via the menu path GOTO • APPEND SEARCH HELP.

Lock Objects

Lock objects are required to protect the consistency of the data if several users or programs try to modify or access the same data at the same time. Within the SAP system you can control the access to the same data using the logical lock mechanism. A typical example would be that two users are trying to update the material master at same time and you want to ensure that the data is consistent. In the SAP system you lock the material master record so that no other user can change the data while you are working on the data. You release the lock once you are done with your changes.

You set and release locks by calling function modules for lock objects in your program. The lock objects created in the ABAP Dictionary are not the database lock. Instead it's a logical lock table that the SAP application uses. To lock records in your application you have to create a lock object (for example, if you are updating a table) or use an existing SAP lock object. The name of the lock object must start with `EZ` or `EY` if you are creating your own. The function modules for the lock object are automatically generated when you create and activate the lock object in the ABAP Dictionary.

The two function modules generated during the activation of the lock object are `ENQUEUE_<lock_object>` and `DEQUEUE_<lock_object>`. The generated function modules are automatically assigned to a function group. You should never change the function module or the function group assignment. The function group or the module for the lock object should never be transported on their own. Instead you transport the lock object, and the function modules are generated in the target system during the activation of the lock objects. You call the `ENQUEUE_<lock_object>` function module to lock the table record or table. The key of the record you want to lock has to be passed to the function module to lock the record. You call the `DEQUEUE_<lock_object>` to release the lock on the table record. The lock mode used to lock the record can also be passed to the function module, although all lock objects have a default lock mode.

The lock objects are defined for the tables in which data records should be locked in the application. Lock objects can be defined for a single table or for a set of logically related tables. Here, you have to define a primary table and any number of secondary tables using foreign key relationships. The argument of the lock object consists of the key fields of the table. The lock argument fields become some of the input parameters for the lock object function modules to lock or unlock the table records. The lock argument defines the key for the table row to be locked. Lock objects can also lock a logical object, which can consist of a header record and the related detail of the header record in the secondary table. Figure 10.20 and Figure 10.21 show the screens for the lock object definition. To define a lock object you have to define the lock table, the lock mode as displayed in Figure 10.20, and the lock parameters as displayed in Figure 10.21.

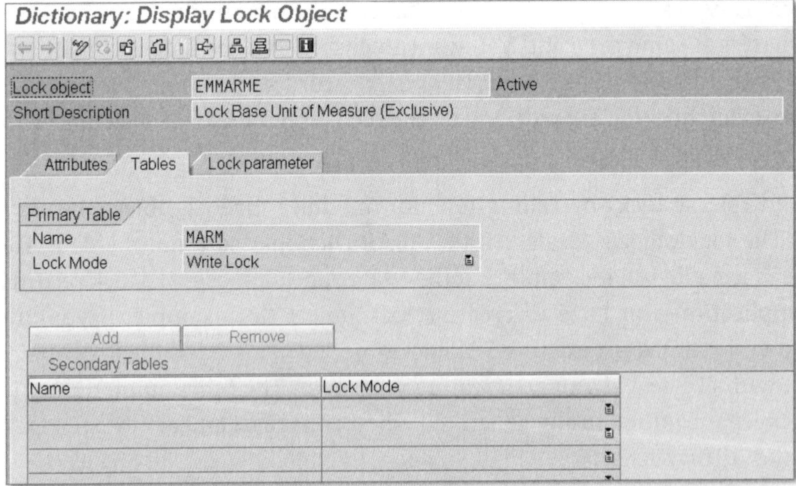

Figure 10.20 Table Assignment for the Lock Object

Dictionary: Display Lock Object

Lock object: EMMARME — Active

Short Description: Lock Base Unit of Measure (Exclusive)

Attributes | Tables | Lock parameter

W	Lock parameter	Table	Field
☑	MANDT	MARM	MANDT
☑	MATNR	MARM	MATNR
☑	MEINH	MARM	MEINH

Figure 10.21 Lock Parameter Assignment for the Lock Object

The lock mode is also an input parameter for the function modules of the lock object, and it defines how other users or applications can access the locked record. You can assign separate lock modes for individual tables in the lock object. Table 10.3 displays the lock modes and their meanings.

Type of Lock	Lock Mode	Meaning
Shared lock/read lock	S (shared)	More than one application can set a shared lock on the same record. An exclusive lock cannot be set for a record with an existing shared lock.
Exclusive lock/write lock	E (exclusive)	Exclusive locks protect the lock object against all types of locks from any application. Only the application that locked the object can reset the lock. Locked data can be edited or displayed by a single user.
Exclusive and non-cumulative	X (exclusive non-cumulative)	Exclusive locks can be requested several times within the same application and are processed successfully. In contrast, exclusive but non-cumulative locks can be applied only once within an application; all other lock requests are rejected.

Table 10.3 Lock Modes for Lock Objects

Locked records can be viewed via Transaction SM12. You can also manually delete the locked record from this transaction if the SAP dispatcher or network connection fails and the dispatcher is unable to delete the lock entries (see Chapter 8, SQL Statements Including Update Strategies, for detail regarding the update strategies).

View Types and Maintenance

Application data is usually stored across several database tables. By defining a view you can provide the means to access those tables as if they were one table. A database view is derived by combining (JOIN) the data from one or more tables and is based on an inner join. You can use a database view in an ABAP program for data retrieval, that is, when you use the SELECT statement. You can mask one or more fields from the base table to create a view or include only some entries from the database tables that satisfy certain conditions.

Following are the steps to define a view:

1. Select the base tables for the view.
2. Define the join conditions to link the base tables of the view.
3. Select the fields of the base table to be used in the view.
4. You can also define a selection condition to restrict record selection in the view, although we do not use this option often.

The join conditions for the view define how the records of the different tables are related, that is, how you know which records in one table correspond to a record in another table. The selection of the records from the view tables is restricted by the join condition.

You can define a selection condition to filter the table records for the view. You can define several selection conditions by using the logical operators `AND` and `O`. Be aware that this will restrict how many applications can use the view. This is similar to the `WHERE` clause used in the `SELECT` statement to filter the record retrieval from the table.

You pick fields from each of the tables that you want to include in the view. The set of fields selected for the view is the called the projection. The data to be selected for the view is dependent on whether the view is implemented as an *inner join* or an *outer join*. With the inner join you get all of the records for which there is an entry for the join condition in all tables included for the view. With the outer join, records are also selected for which there is no entry in some of the tables included in the view.

See Figure 10.22 and Figure 10.23 for inner and outer joins, respectively. The inner join view as shown in Figure 10.22, contains all records from tables `TAB1` and `TAB2`, which satisfies the join condition, that is, `TAB1-FIELD1 = TAB2-FIELD3`. Similarly, the outer join view as specified in Figure 10.23 contains all of the records from `TAB1` and the records from `TAB2` that satisfy the join condition, that is, `TAB1-FIELD1 = TAB2-FIELD3`. All records in the left-hand or first table will be included in the result set, regardless of whether the other tables have a corresponding entry.

TAB1

Field1	Field2
490001	2009
490002	2009
490003	2009

TAB2

Field3	Field4	Field5
490001	10	MAT1
490001	20	MAT2
490002	10	MAT3
490002	20	MAT3

Join Condition: TAB1-FIELD1 = TAB2-FIELD3

Field1	Field2	Field3	Field4	Field5
490001	2009	49001	10	MAT1
490001	2009	49001	20	MAT2
490002	2009	49002	10	MAT3
490002	2009	49002	20	MAT3

Figure 10.22 Inner Join View

TAB1

Field1	Field2
49001	2009
49002	2009
49003	2009

TAB2

Field3	Field4	Field5
490001	10	MAT1
490001	20	MAT2
490002	10	MAT3
490002	20	MAT4

Outer Join Condition: TAB1-FIELD1 = TAB2-FIELD3

Field1	Field2	Field3	Field4	Field5
49001	2009	49001	10	MAT1
49001	2009	49001	20	MAT2
49002	2009	49002	10	MAT3
49002	2009	49002	20	MAT4
49003	2009			

Figure 10.23 Outer Join View

Database views implement an inner join and hence select records for which there are entries in all of the tables included in the view. Help views and maintenance views implement outer joins. You cannot select data from the maintenance view. If you want to use an outer join in your application, you have to program it yourself.

The maintenance status of the view controls whether data records in the table can be inserted or changed through the view. You have the option to specify READ ONLY maintenance status for the view. With this option you can only read data from the view. If you select the READ AND CHANGE status, you can update or change the table records through the view. Database views permit read-only access.

The following types of view are possible in the ABAP Dictionary:

- **Database view**
  Database views are automatically created in the underlying database when they are activated. A database view should be created if you want to access logically connected records from different tables simultaneously. Selection from the database view is generally faster than selection from the individual tables using a nested select. Database views can only contain transparent tables.
- **Projection view**
  Projection views are used to mask the fields of a table. A projection view contains exactly one table, and you cannot define the selection condition for the projection view. A projection view does not create a corresponding object in the underlying database like a database view. Data selection from the projection view should be fast owing to a smaller number of fields in the projection view. Projection views can be created for pooled or cluster tables also because the projection view is mapped to the corresponding database tables of the table included in the view.
- **Maintenance view**
  A maintenance view is implemented as an outer join, and all the tables included in the maintenance view must be linked with a foreign key. The join conditions of the maintenance view are always derived from the foreign keys. You cannot enter the join condition for the maintenance view manually as you can for the database view. Maintenance views allow an easy way to maintain complex application objects.

Maintenance views, as their name suggests, allow you to maintain the data for the application object together, and the data is automatically distributed to all of the underlying database tables. The maintenance status determines whether a change to the database tables is allowed through the maintenance view. The maintenance view is a left outer join, so the first table included in the join is important. All of the records of the first table are included in the maintenance view.

- **Help view**
  Help views can be used as a selection method for a search help. Help views are implemented as an outer join, and all tables included in the help view should be connected by foreign keys.

Generally, the selection method for the search help is a database view or table. However, you have to use a help view as a selection method for a search help if a view with an outer join is required for data selection.

Important Terminology

You should now know about various ABAP Dictionary objects and their functions. You should also have a good understanding of search help and lock objects.

Search helps are ABAP Dictionary services used to display a list of possible values (value help) for screen help and are generally associated with the data elements. They can also be assigned to dialog screen, in which case you would not have to program value help for the screen field in the screen flow logic. Otherwise, you would have to program for value help for the screen field, if input help for the field is required.

Similarly, lock objects are required to protect the consistency of the data if several users or programs try to access and modify the same data at same time. You can control the access of the same data by two or more users by using the logical lock mechanism. Two function modules, `ENQUEUE_<lock_object>` and `DEQUEUE_<lock_object>`, are generated for each ABAP Dictionary lock object. You call the `ENQUEUE_<lock_object>` function module to lock a table or a table record and `DEQUEUE_<lock_object>` function module to unlock a table or a table record.

Practice Questions

The practice questions below will help you evaluate your understanding of the topic. The questions shown are similar in nature to those found on the certification examination, but whereas none of these questions will be found on the exam itself, they allow you to review your knowledge of the subject. Select the correct answers and then check the completeness of your answers in the following solution section. Remember that you must select all correct answers and only correct answers to receive credit for the question.

1. A Transparent table can include a deep structure.

☐ **A.** True

☐ **B.** False

2. ABAP data types can be used for a domain definition.

☐ **A.** True

☐ **B.** False

3. Which of the following statements are true?

☐ **A.** A conversion routine can be assigned to a domain.

☐ **B.** A conversion routine can be assigned to a data element.

☐ **C.** You define the value range in the data element.

☐ **D.** You can enter documentation for the data element in the ABAP Dictionary.

4. F1 Help on the screen field displays the data element documentation.

☐ **A.** True

☐ **B.** False

5. Which of the following are true statements?

☐ **A.** The technical attributes of the data element can be defined by a domain, that is, the data type, the field length, and the number of decimal places.

☐ **B.** You can also select predefined data types to define the data type of the data element.

☐ **C.** Reference data types can be used to define the data type of the data element.

☐ **D.** Field labels are defined for the domain.

6. You can define search helps and parameter IDs for a data element.

☐ **A.** True

☐ **B.** False

7. The line type for a table type can contain a flat, nested, or deep structure.

☐ **A.** True

☐ **B.** False

8. Which of the following are true statements?

☐ **A.** Table fields can be assigned to a data element.

☐ **B.** Table fields can be assigned to an ABAP Dictionary data type directly.

☐ **C.** Search helps can be defined for a table field that is assigned to a predefined data type.

☐ **D.** A reference table and field are required for fields with the data types `QUAN` and `CURR`.

9. Which of the following is a true statement regarding search helps?

☐ **A.** You can use a maintenance view for the search help selection method.

☐ **B.** You can use a database view for the search help selection method.

☐ **C.** Help views can also be used for the selection method for search help.

☐ **D.** You can use transparent tables for the search help selection method.

10. Which of the following regarding search helps is a true statement?

☐ **A.** The interface for the search help is defined by the IMP (import) and EXP (export) flag of the search help parameter.

☐ **B.** The LPos parameter defines the position of the search help parameter in the search hit list.

☐ **C.** The SPos parameter defines the position of the input field on the dialog screen.

- ☑ **D.** The text table for the selection method is automatically populated if the text table is attached to the database table being used as the selection method.

11. Which of the following are true statements?

- ☑ **A.** A database view is implemented as an inner join.
- ☑ **B.** A maintenance view is implemented as an outer join.
- ☐ **C.** A database view is implemented as an outer join.
- ☐ **D.** A maintenance view is implemented as an inner join.

12. Which of the following are true statements?

- ☑ **A.** The tables included in the maintenance view should have foreign key relationships.
- ☐ **B.** The tables included in the help view should have a foreign key relationship.
- ☑ **C.** Projection views can have more than one table included for the view definition.
- ☐ **D.** You cannot use a pooled or cluster table for database view.

13. You can create projection views for pooled or cluster tables.

- ☐ **A.** True
- ☑ **B.** False

Practice Question Answers and Explanations

1. Correct answer: **B**

   Transparent tables can include flat structures only. A deep structure is not allowed.

2. Correct answer: **B**

   You can use ABAP Dictionary data types for domain definition. ABAP data types cannot be used for the domain definition.

3. Correct answers: **A, D**

   A conversion routine can be assigned to the domain and cannot be assigned to a data element. The value range is assigned to the domain during its definition and not to the data element. However, the data element inherits the value range if it's assigned to a domain with a value range definition. You provide the documentation for the data element during the definition.

4. Correct answer: **A**

   F1 help displays the data element documentation.

5. Correct answers: **A, B, C**

   The technical attributes of the data element are defined by the domain if the domain is used for the data type definition for the data element. The data type for the data element can be a predefined ABAP Dictionary type or domain or a reference data type. Field labels are defined for the data element only and not for domain.

6. Correct answer: **A**

   You can define a search help and parameter ID for the data element.

7. Correct answer: **A**

   The line type for the ABAP Dictionary table type can be a complex structure. It can be a flat, deep, or nested structure.

8. Correct answers: **A, B, D**

   Table fields can be assigned to the data element or the predefined type directly. Search helps cannot be defined for a table field assigned to the predefined data types. Search helps can be defined for fields assigned to the data element. The reference table and field are required for the table field assigned to data types `QUAN` and `CURR`. The reference type field should be `UNIT` and `CUKY`.

9. Correct answers: **B, C, D**

   The selection method for the search help can be a transparent table, database view, or help view. You cannot have a maintenance view as a selection method for the search help.

10. Correct answers: **A, B, C, D**

    The interface for the search help is defined by the import and export parameter of the search help parameter. LPos defines the position of the parameter on the hit list, whereas SPos defines the position of the parameter on the input screen. The text table is automatically assigned to the selection method if it is assigned to the selected transparent table of the selection method.

11. Correct answers: **A, B**

    A database view is implemented as an inner join, whereas a maintenance view is implemented as an outer join.

12. Correct answers: **A, B, D**

    Tables included in a maintenance view and help view should have a foreign key relationship. You cannot use pooled and cluster tables for the database view. Projection views can include only one table for the view definition and can include pooled or cluster tables for the view definition.

13. Correct answer: **A**

    A projection view can include pooled or cluster tables for view definition.

Take Away

You should now understand the various ABAP Dictionary objects and services. You should be able to explain the concept of domains, data elements, table types, structures, tables, indexes, and views. You should be able to distinguish between different types of view supported by the SAP system and their uses.

You must also understand the lock object concept and its definition and the use of search helps. It is important to know which type of object can be used for the selection method of the search helps. You should also know the difference between the elementary search help and collective search help and the steps to create the search help.

Lock objects are important for any application development, and you should be able to create lock objects and use them in your application.

Refresher

You must understand ABAP Dictionary objects and the supported services, that is, lock objects and search helps. You should be able to define domains, data elements, structures, table types, and transparent tables. You should know the supported data types for domain and data element definition and the concept of a value table and value range and its use in the domain definitions. It is important to understand which Dictionary objects can be used in the ABAP program and their scopes.

You also must understand the difference between outer join and inner join and which type of join is implemented in different types of view.

Table 10.4 shows the key concepts of the ABAP Dictionary.

Key Concept	Definition
Domain	Domains are used to manage technical properties of the data object centrally and cannot be used in the program directly. A domain can use an ABAP Dictionary data type only for its definition.
Data elements	A data element is a complete description of a field. Data elements provide F1 help for the screen field and field label for the screen.
ABAP Dictionary table	Tables are defined in the ABAP Dictionary independently of the underlying database. A physical table definition is created in the database upon activation of the ABAP Dictionary table.

Table 10.4 Key Concepts Refresher

Summary

You should now be able to define ABAP Dictionary objects and use them in your program or application. You should also know how to lock tables or the table record within an application. Lastly, you should be able to define elementary search helps and collective search helps and know how to enhance a standard search help. The knowledge of the ABAP Dictionary and its function will easily allow you to pass this topic on the certification examination.

11 Unicode

Techniques You'll Master:

- Enforce Unicode checks (on a non-Unicode system)
- Explore the difference between byte-type and character-type data objects
- Determine the fragment view of structures in Unicode
- Understand new additions to statements
- Learn about new relational operators

In this chapter you will be provided with the knowledge of how to make your ABAP programs Unicode compliant. Unicode is intended to be a universal character set supporting every written script used on Earth. Unicode attempts to connect a rune or glyph (a character's visual representation) with a character — a unit of phonetic or semantic meaning. Thus, a single character that has different appearances has multiple runes; for example, Arabic characters change appearance dependent on the position in a word.

We will cover how to enforce the Unicode checks even in a non-Unicode system. We will discuss the differences in the majority of the statement changes regarding the Unicode checks. Lastly, we will explain the Unicode fragment view and provide a brief explanation of how it works.

Each of these topics will be covered separately and will be followed by the practice exercise and the solution to the exercise.

Real-World Scenario

Your company had put off switching from multiple code pages when it last upgraded from SAP R/3 4.6C to SAP NetWeaver 6.40. Now it is forced to do so by SAP (a system with either blended code pages or more than one code page beginning with SAP NetWeaver 7.0 is no longer supported and requires a conversion to Unicode). You have been asked to identify issues of upgrading your company's SAP system from SAP NetWeaver 6.40 to SAP NetWeaver 7.0 and switching to Unicode (in other words, changing all character-based data stored in the database from one code page to Unicode) as part of the upgrade process.

It is your responsibility to identify which custom programs have issues that need correcting prior to performing the upgrade. Once you have a list of programs and their problems, you must make changes to correct the issues.

To speed up the correction process owing to the expected number of programs that may be affected, you have also been asked to explain the process and the types of program changes necessary to the entire development team so all members can make changes and learn the rules so that new development is also Unicode compliant.

Objectives of this Portion of the Test

The purpose of this portion of the certification examination is to verify that you know how to make programs Unicode compliant but also to understand, from a programming perspective, the advantages of having a Unicode-compliant program. This portion of the examination will test your knowledge of a number of topics. The points you will need to understand from this section include:

- How to enforce Unicode checks prior to the actual switch to Unicode
- How to identify programs with issues that need correcting, in other words, which programs will produce errors as a result of the stricter enforcement of syntax checking of a Unicode system
- Which ABAP statements behave differently as a result of byte-type versus character-type validations
- How the Unicode fragment view is used for assignment and conditional statements
- New additions to existing statements to differentiate between byte-type and character-type data
- New relational operations for byte-type objects

The certification examination will give minimal weight to this chapter compared to all of the other topics in the examination. Therefore, this chapter is among those where the percentage of questions related to the topic is smaller than most other chapters. We suspect the reasoning for a minimal weighting is that the causes of errors produced during code activation related to Unicode are situation specific. You must solve the issue before you can proceed with activation. From a practical test design, there are also only so many ways to ask about the difference between a character and a byte, and it is still possible to have a single-byte code page system. Therefore, although this information is important (and will help you produce more robust programming), it is not mandatory in all environments — yet.

Key Concepts Refresher

If you have developed on SAP Releases 6.20 or later, much of this chapter is probably already known to you. Eventually, the expectation is that all SAP implementations will be running Unicode-compliant systems.

As with many new abilities, SAP provides the tools (specifically, Transaction UCCHECK and the program attribute for Unicode enforcement) and encourages you to use them. Early acceptance of the tools and enforcement of the compliance rules will make the eventual conversion run smoothly because you will be able to focus on the data conversion knowing that the programs' behavior is already correct and properly tested. You need to understand the following to make your ABAP programs Unicode compliant:

- Byte-type data objects versus character-type data objects
- The fragment view of a structure
- File handling
- New additions to the ABAP language
- How to scan programs for errors

Unicode Compliance

Prior to Release 6.10, SAP supported different codes for representing characters of different fonts, for example, ASCII, EBCDIC, and single-byte code pages or double-byte code pages:

- ASCII (American Standard Code for Information Interchange) encodes every character with one byte. This means that a maximum of 256 characters can be represented (strictly speaking, standard ASCII only encodes one character using 7 bits and can therefore only represent 128 characters). The extension to 8 bits was introduced with ISO-8859).
- EBCDIC (Extended Binary Coded Decimal Interchange) also encodes each character using one byte, and can therefore also represent 256 characters.
- Double byte code pages require between 1 and 2 bytes per character. This enables the representation of 65,536 characters, of which only 10,000 to 15,000 characters are normally used. For example, the code page SJIS is used for Japanese, and BIG5 is used for traditional Chinese fonts.

Using these character sets, all languages can be handled individually in one ABAP-based SAP system. Difficulties arise if texts from different incompatible character sets are mixed in one central system. The difficulty is due to an 8-bit representation of a byte being interpreted differently based on the code page to show the data. The exchange of data between systems with incompatible charac ter sets can also lead to problems.

The solution to this problem is the use of a character set that includes all characters at once. Unicode provides this ability. A variety of Unicode character representations are possible for the Unicode character set, for example, UTF, in which a character can occupy between 1 and 4 bytes.

From Release 6.10 on, the SAP NetWeaver Application Server supports both Unicode and non-Unicode systems. Non-Unicode systems are conventional ABAP systems, in which one character is usually represented by one byte. Unicode systems are ABAP systems that are based on a Unicode character set and that have a corresponding underlying operating system and database. To determine if your system is a Unicode system, select System • Status and look at the SAP data in the center of the dialog box (see Figure 11.1).

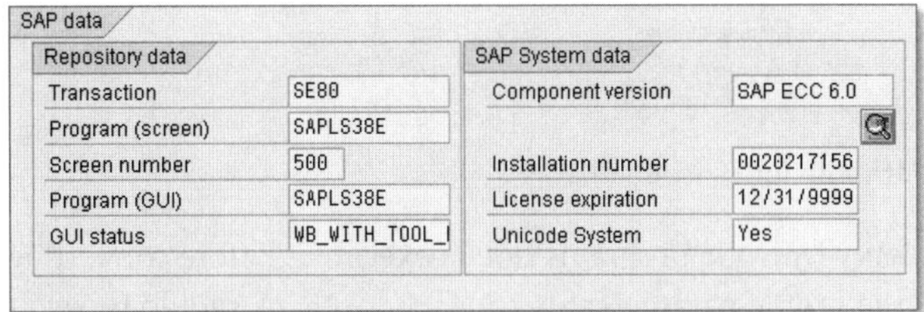

Figure 11.1 SAP Data from the Status Dialog

Before Release 6.10, many ABAP programming methods were based on the fact that one character corresponded to one byte. Before a system is converted to Unicode, ABAP programs must therefore be modified at all points where an explicit or implicit assumption is made about the internal length of a character.

Unicode Tools

ABAP supports this conversion using new syntax rules and new language constructs, by placing an emphasis on retaining as much of the existing source code as possible. To simplify preparation for the conversion to Unicode, the Unicode checks active checkbox can be selected in the program attributes (see the example in Figure 11.2) starting from Release 6.10. Program attributes are displayed via Goto • Attributes in the ABAP editor.

Transaction UCCHECK supports the activation of this check for existing programs. If this property is set, the program is identified as a Unicode program. For a Unicode program, a stricter syntax check is performed than is for non-Unicode programs. In some cases, statements must also be enhanced by using new additions. A syntactically correct Unicode program will normally run with the same semantics and the same results in Unicode and non-Unicode systems. (Exceptions to this rule are low-level programs that query and evaluate the number of bytes per character.) Programs that are required to run in both systems should therefore also be tested on both platforms.

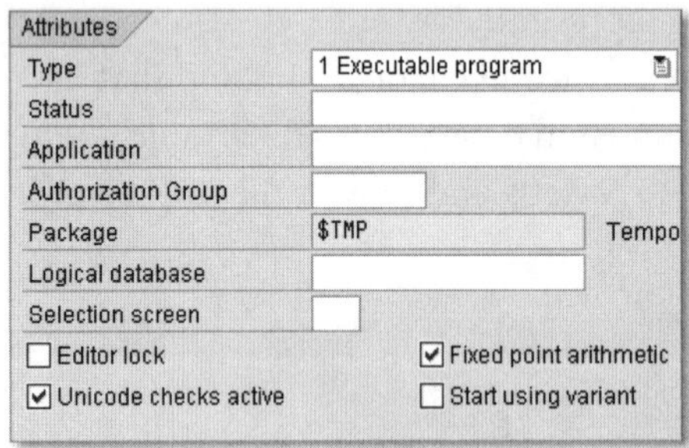

Figure 11.2 Program Attribute for Unicode Checks

In a Unicode system, only Unicode programs can be executed. Before converting to a Unicode system, the profile parameter `abap/unicode_check` should be set as on. This parameter is available starting with Release 6.10. It can be used to enforce the enhanced syntax check for all objects in non-Unicode systems. When you set this parameter, only Unicode-enabled objects (objects with the Unicode flag) are executable. This parameter should be set as on only if all customer programs have been enabled according to Transaction UCCHECK. Non-Unicode programs can only be executed in non-Unicode systems. All language constructs that have been introduced for Unicode programs can, however, also be used in non-Unicode programs.

To run Transaction UCCHECK, you enter the programs you want to check: all objects in the customer namespace, all objects of type `FUGS` (function group with customer include), and any SAP programs you modified. The initial selection screen is shown in Figure 11.3, and an example of a detected problem is shown in Figure 11.4.

Because existing programs that were programmed without errors mostly fulfill the new Unicode rules, they require little modification. Conversely, most programs that require significant changes are due to an error-prone programming style. Unicode programs are preferable because they are more easily maintained and less prone to errors. Just as outdated and dangerous language constructs are declared obsolete and are no longer permitted for use in ABAP Objects, the rules for Unicode programs also offer increased security when programming. This applies particularly for the storage of external data, in other words, in files. When creating a new program, the recommendation is for you to always identify the program as a Unicode program, and older programs can be converted in stages.

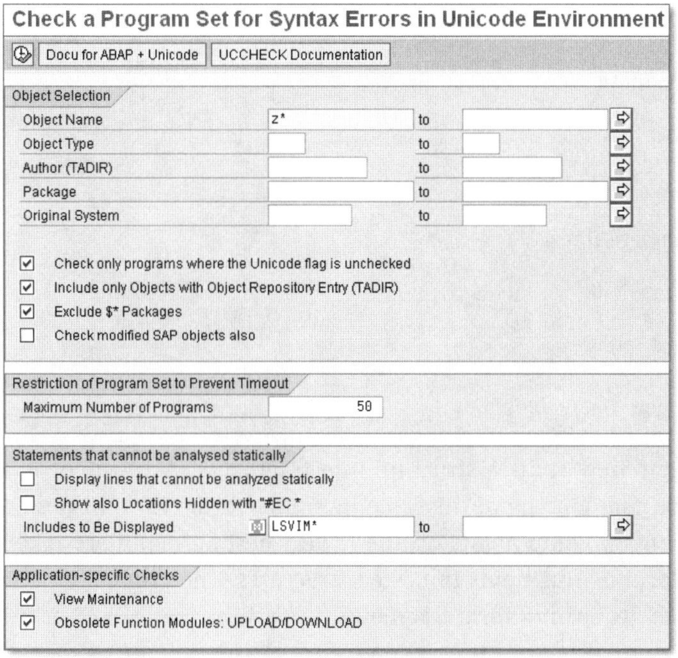

Check a Program Set for Syntax Errors in Unicode Environment

Docu for ABAP + Unicode | UCCHECK Documentation

Object Selection

Object Name	z*	to	
Object Type		to	
Author (TADIR)		to	
Package		to	
Original System		to	

- [x] Check only programs where the Unicode flag is unchecked
- [x] Include only Objects with Object Repository Entry (TADIR)
- [x] Exclude $* Packages
- [ ] Check modified SAP objects also

Restriction of Program Set to Prevent Timeout

Maximum Number of Programs 50

Statements that cannot be analysed statically

- [ ] Display lines that cannot be analyzed statically
- [ ] Show also Locations Hidden with "#EC *

Includes to Be Displayed LSVIM* to

Application-specific Checks

- [x] View Maintenance
- [x] Obsolete Function Modules: UPLOAD/DOWNLOAD

Figure 11.3 Selection Screen of Transaction UCCHECK

SAP

Editor | Conversion Error | Set Unicode Attribute

Result of Unicode Syntax Check

Exception	UC	Org.	Program	Include	Row	Error Code	Message
		NSP	Z_NEW_REPORT	Z_NEW_REPORT	83	MESSAGEG-H	The offset declaration "57" exceeds the length of the characte
		NSP	Z_NEW_REPORT	Z_NEW_REPORT	83	MESSAGEG-H	(=21) of the structure. This is not allowed in Unicode progran

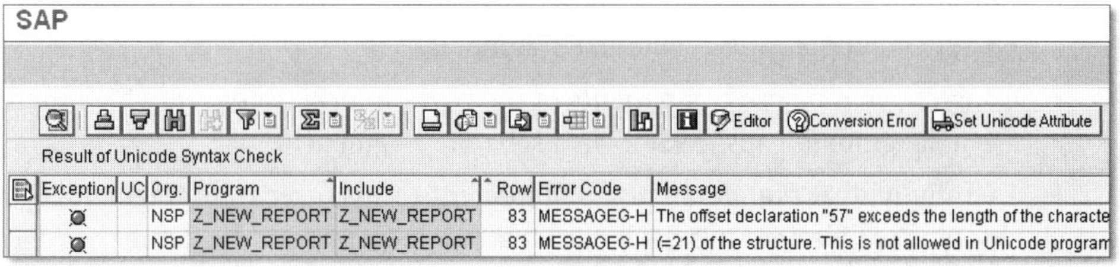

Figure 11.4 Detected Errors of Transaction UCCHECK

One of the most important differences between a Unicode and non-Unicode program is the clear distinction between byte-type and character-type data objects and the restriction of data types whose objects can be viewed as character type. This has an influence on all statements in which character-type operands are expected and in particular on byte and character string processing.

In Unicode programs, only the elementary data objects shown in Table 11.1 are now character type. Structures are character-type data objects if they contain only flat character-type components (only components from the Table 11.1 excluding text strings).

Data type	Meaning
c	Text field
d	Date field
n	Numerical text
t	Time field
string	Text string

Table 11.1 Character-Type Data Objects

The Unicode fragment view splits a structure into fragments. A fragment is a grouping of structure components of the same or similar data types. In nested structures, the elementary components on the lowest nesting depth are taken into account when forming fragments in nested structures. The following parts of a structure are each grouped to form fragments:

- Consecutive flat character-like components of the types c, n, d, and t, between which there are no alignment gaps, form character-like fragments.
- Consecutive flat byte-like components of the type x, between which there are no alignment gaps, form byte-like fragments.
- Consecutive numeric components of the types i and f, between which there are no alignment gaps, each form a separate fragment.
- Each individual numeric type p component forms a separate fragment. For this type of fragment it is the length that is important, not the number of decimal places.
- In deep structures, each deep component (reference) forms a separate fragment.
- Each alignment gap is regarded as a fragment.

In Unicode programs, a structure can now essentially only be used at an operand position that expects a single field if the structure is character type. An example of this is shown in Figure 11.5. The statement that produces the error with Unicode checking shows a simple assignment, but the structure is not considered a character type because it contains a hexadecimal and a numeric field. The statement above it references a structure that is considered to be a character type. It is then handled in the same way as a data object of type `c` without error. In non-Unicode programs, all flat structures and byte-type data objects are also still handled as character-type data objects (implicit casting).

```
DATA:
  BEGIN OF struc1,
    a(2) TYPE c,
    n(6) TYPE n,
    d    TYPE d,
    t    TYPE t,
  END OF struc1,
  BEGIN OF struc2,
    a(2) TYPE c,
    b(2) TYPE c,
    x(1) TYPE x,
    i    TYPE i,
  END OF struc2,
  lv_string  TYPE string.

lv_string = struc1.
lv_string = struc2.
```

Scope \FORM unicode2

Syntax error

	Description	Row	Type
	Program Z_NEW_REPORT	110	
	"LV_STRING" and "STRUC2" are not mutually convertible in a Unicode		

Figure 11.5 A Non-Flat Structure

Note

The incorrect use of a structure at operand positions is greatly restricted in Unicode programs. For example, a structure that contains a numeric component can no longer be used at a numeric operand position.

In Unicode programs, elementary data objects of types `x` and `xstring` are byte type. In non-Unicode programs, data objects of this type are generally handled as character type.

Some data types, such as numeric data types, other than p, and the deep data types have specific alignment requirements that depend on the hardware platform. Fields in the memory that have one of these types must begin at addresses that can be divided by 4, 8, or 16. In Unicode systems, in addition to the alignment requirements for numeric data objects of types i and f and of all deep data objects, data objects of character-like data types must also be located in storage addresses that can be divided by 2 or 4, depending on the Unicode character representation. As a consequence, in structures with components of different data types, the alignment gaps in Unicode systems may be different than those in non-Unicode systems. Alignment gaps can also occur at the end of structures because the overall length of the structure is determined by the component with the largest alignment requirement.

Caution

In Unicode programs, the storage of byte strings in character-type containers causes problems because the byte order of character-type data objects in Unicode systems is platform dependent. In non-Unicode systems, this only applies for data objects of numeric data types. The content of the data object is interpreted incorrectly if a container of this type is stored and then imported into an application server with a different byte sequence.

Offset and length are specified by appending `[+off][(len)]` to the name of a data object in the operand position, and the specifications are used to access subareas of a data object. This type of programming is no longer completely possible in Unicode systems because it is not possible to define whether offset and length should be specified in characters or bytes. Also, restrictions have been introduced that forbid access to memory areas outside of flat data objects.

Offset and/or length specifications are permitted for character-type and byte-type data objects. The specification of offset and length is interpreted as either a number of characters or as a number of bytes. The rules that determine which data objects in Unicode programs count as character-type or byte-type objects do not allow for offset and length specifications for data objects of numeric data types.

Note

The method of using data objects of type `c` as containers for storing structures of different types, which often are not known until runtime, where components are accessed using offset and length is no longer possible in Unicode programs. Instead of these containers, the statement `CREATE DATA` can be used to generate data objects of any structure. To access existing containers, these can be assigned to a field symbol using the `CASTING` addition of the `ASSIGN` statement.

In Unicode, an offset and/or length specification for a structure is only permitted if the structure is:

- A character type (it only contains flat character-type components)
- Flat (it has a character-type initial fragment according to the Unicode fragment view, and the offset and/or length specification accesses this initial fragment)

In both cases the specification of offset and/or length is interpreted as a number of characters. Figure 11.6 shows a structure with both character-type and non-character-type components. The Unicode fragment view splits the structure into five areas as shown in Figure 11.7.

```
DATA:
  BEGIN OF struc,
    a TYPE c LENGTH 3,      "Length 3 characters
    b TYPE n LENGTH 4,      "Length 4 characters
    c TYPE d,               "Length 8 characters
    d TYPE t,               "Length 6 characters
    e TYPE f,               "Length 8 bytes
    f TYPE c LENGTH 28,     "Length28 characters
    g TYPE x LENGTH 2,      "Length 2 bytes
  END OF struc.

struc(21) = 'a'.
struc+7(14) = '12345678901234'.
struc+57(2) = 'xy'.
```

Syntax error

Description	Row	Type
Program Z_NEW_REPORT	80	
The offset declaration "57" exceeds the length of the character-type start (=21) of the structure. This is not allowed in Unicode programs.		

Figure 11.6 Invalid Offset in Unicode

```
[ aaa | bbbb | cccccccc | ddd | AAA | eeee | ffffffffffff | gg ]
[            F1                | F2  | F3   |      F4      | F5 ]
```

Figure 11.7 Fragment View of a Structure

Offset and/or length access is only possible for the character-type initial fragment F1. Specifications such as struc(21) or struc+7(14) are accepted and are handled as a single field of type c. An access such as struc+57(2), however, as shown in Figure 11.6 produces an error in a Unicode program.

In Unicode programs for actual parameters specified in a PERFORM statement, it is not possible to specify a memory area outside of the actual parameter using offset and/or length specifications. It is no longer possible to specify an offset without a length because this would implicitly set the length of the actual parameter.

Tip

Previously, cross-field offset and/or length accesses could be usefully implemented in the ASSIGN statement for processing repeating groups in structures. To enable this in a Unicode program, the ASSIGN statement has been enhanced with the additions RANGE and INCREMENT.

The most important differences between the behavior of a Unicode program and a non-Unicode program are the changed conversion rules for structures, for assignments, and for comparisons.

Note

Two structures in Unicode programs are only compatible when all alignment gaps are identical on all platforms. This applies in particular for alignment gaps that are created by included structures.

In non-Unicode programs, incompatible flat structures are treated as data objects of the type c, but in Unicode programs, conversion rules apply that assign the Unicode fragment view of the structures. In non-Unicode programs, flat structures are treated as data objects of the type c for an assignment to or from an elementary data object. However, again in Unicode programs, a conversion rule applies according to which the structure must be character type either completely or at least for the initial fragment.

As with the assignment, comparison of structures is not treated as c fields, but according to their Unicode fragment view (see Figure 11.5 for an example). The same is true when comparing a structure to an elementary data object. The system again checks whether the structure is character type either completely or at least for the initial fragment.

Since Release 3.0, the ABAP Dictionary structures and database tables that are delivered by SAP can be enhanced with customer includes or append structures. Such changes cause problems in Unicode programs if the enhancement changes the Unicode fragment view. Therefore, the option to classify structures and database tables was introduced in Release 6.20, which makes it possible to recognize and handle problems related to structure enhancements. This classification is used during the program check to create a warning at all points where it works with structures, and where later structure enhancements can cause syntax errors or changes in program behavior. When you define a structure or a database table in the ABAP Dictionary, you can specify the enhancement categories.

The dialog shown in Figure 11.8 is found in the menu EXTRAS • ENHANCEMENT CATEGORY... when editing a table, view, or structure. The meanings of the different settings are shown in Table 11.2.

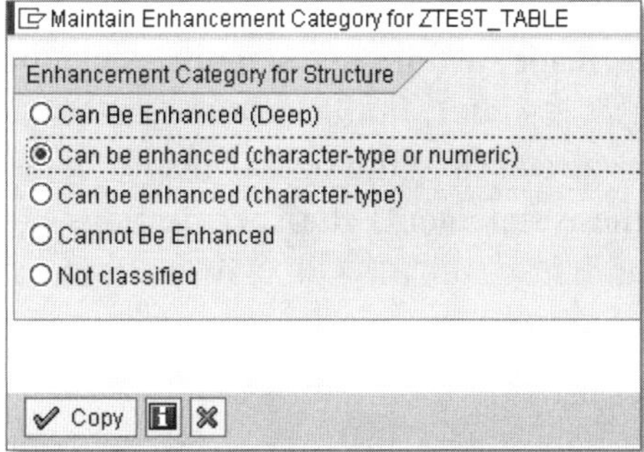

Figure 11.8 Assigning an Enhancement Category

Level	Category Meaning
Not classified	The structure does not have an enhancement category.
Cannot be enhanced	The structure cannot be enhanced.

Table 11.2 Enhancement Category Meanings

Level	Category Meaning
Can be enhanced and character-type	All structure components and their enhancements have to be character-type and flat.
Can be enhanced and character-type or numeric	All structure components and their enhancements have to be flat.
Any enhancements	All structure components and their enhancements can have any data type; for example, you could include a table type component.

Table 11.2 Enhancement Category Meanings (cont.)

In Unicode programs, byte and character string processing are strictly separated. The operands of byte string processing must be byte-type data objects, and operands in character string processing must be character-type data objects. In non-Unicode programs, byte strings are normally handled in the same way as character strings.

In Unicode programs, statements that can be used for byte and character string processing require that a distinction be made within the statement by the optional addition `IN BYTE MODE` or `IN CHARACTER MODE`. In this case `IN CHARACTER MODE` is the default. The same additions are also used in the statements for determining length and offset (although in these statements the specifications are mandatory): `DESCRIBE FIELD ... LENGTH` and `DESCRIBE DISTANCE`. An example of both modes is shown in Listing 11.1.

```
DATA:
  lv_text  TYPE c LENGTH 1,
  lv_hex   TYPE x LENGTH 1,
  lv_blen  TYPE i,
  lv_clen  TYPE i,
  lv_bytes TYPE i.

DESCRIBE FIELD lv_text: LENGTH lv_blen IN BYTE MODE,
                        LENGTH lv_clen IN CHARACTER MODE.
lv_bytes = lv_blen / lv_clen.
```

Listing 11.1 Calculating Bytes per Character

There are relational operators for byte strings and for character strings. In Unicode programs, the latter (for example, CO, CA, CS) can no longer be used for byte strings. For byte strings, there are new relational operators (for example, BYTE-CO, BYTE-CA, BYTE-CS). So you would use

```
IF lv_hex1 BYTE-CO lv_hex2
```

instead of

```
IF lv_hex1 CO lv_hex2.
```

Likewise, the description functions are divided into description functions for byte strings and description function for character strings. In particular, in a Unicode program, STRLEN can now only be used for character-type arguments, whereas XSTRLEN is available for byte-type arguments. So you would do

```
lv_clen = STRLEN( lv_text )
```

for a character field and

```
lv_blen = XSTRLEN( lv_hex )
```

for a byte string.

When structured data objects are used in Open SQL statements, in a non-Unicode program, their structure is not taken into account; only the length and the alignment are checked. In a Unicode program, for structured work areas, the Unicode fragment view must be correct, and elementary work areas must be character type.

Because the content of files frequently reflects the structure of data in the working memory, the file interface in a Unicode program must fulfill the following requirements:

- It must be possible to exchange data between Unicode and non-Unicode systems.
- It must be possible to exchange data between different Unicode systems.
- It must be possible to exchange data between different non-Unicode systems that use different code pages.

Therefore, in Unicode programs, you must always define the code page used to encode the character-type data that is written in text files or that is read from text files.

You must also consider that a Unicode program must be executable in a non-Unicode system as well as a Unicode system. Some of the syntax rules for the file interface have therefore been modified so that programming data access in Unicode programs is less prone to errors than in non-Unicode programs.

Before every read or write access, a file must be opened explicitly using `OPEN DATASET`. If a file is already open, it cannot be opened again. In a non-Unicode program, the first time a file is accessed it is implicitly opened using the standard settings. The statement for opening a file can be applied to an open file in non-Unicode programs, although a file can only be opened once within a program. When opening the file, the access type and the type of file storage must be specified explicitly using the additions `INPUT|OUTPUT|APPENDING|UPDATE` and `[LEGACY] BINARY|TEXT MODE`.

When opening a file in `TEXT MODE`, the `ENCODING` addition must be used to specify the character representation. When opening a file in `LEGACY MODE`, the byte order (endian) and a non-Unicode code page must be specified. In non-Unicode programs, if nothing is entered, a file is opened with implicit standard settings. An example using the encoding statement is:

```
OPEN DATASET gv_filelist
  FOR INPUT IN TEXT MODE ENCODING DEFAULT.
```

- If a file is opened for reading, the context can only be read. In non-Unicode programs, it is also possible to gain write access to these files.
- If a file is opened as a text file, only the contents of character-type data objects can be read or written. In non-Unicode programs, byte-type and numeric data objects are also allowed.

The issue with ABAP lists is correct column alignment of East Asian characters: In Unicode systems, the number of memory cells does not match the number of screen columns if the texts contain East Asian characters (full-width characters). The memory cells used for these characters (fields of type `c` with length 1) are 8 bits long in non-Unicode systems and 16 bits long in Unicode systems. In Unicode systems, almost all characters (including East Asian characters) fit in one memory cell. However, East Asian full-width characters take up two screen columns in ABAP lists, whereas European characters take up only one screen column.

Important Terminology

Elementary data objects of types `x` and `xstring` are byte type, and the following elementary data objects are considered character type: `c`, `d`, `n`, `t`, `string`. Structures in Unicode are grouped by components of the same or similar data types, which produces a fragment view. Fragments can also be based on alignment gaps.

Practice Questions

The practice questions below will help you evaluate your understanding of the topic. The questions shown are similar in nature to those found on the certification examination, but whereas none of these questions will be found on the exam itself, they allow you to review your knowledge of the subject. Select the correct answers and then check the completeness of your answers in the following solution section. Remember that you must select all correct answers and only correct answers to receive credit for the question.

1. Unicode checks can be made:

☐ **A.** In any system (after Release 6.10) by specifying the program has Unicode checks active

☐ **B.** By running Transaction UCCHECK

☐ **C.** Only in a Unicode system or as part of a conversion to a Unicode system

☐ **D.** Cannot be enforced

2. Memory requirements are identical in a non-Unicode system and in a Unicode system.

☐ **A.** True

☐ **B.** False

3. A difference between a Unicode and non-Unicode program is:

☐ **A.** Byte-type data objects cannot be assigned to character-type data objects.

☐ **B.** Byte-type data objects cannot be compared to character-type data objects.

- ☐ **C.** Offset positioning in a Unicode structure is restricted to character data objects.
- ☐ **D.** Offset positioning in a Unicode structure is restricted to flat data objects.

4. Two structures in Unicode programs are only compatible if all alignment gaps are identical on all platforms.

- ☐ **A.** True
- ☐ **B.** False

5. The enhancement category for a database table or structure:

- ☐ **A.** Makes a table Unicode compliant
- ☐ **B.** Specifies the types of changes that can be made to the structure
- ☐ **C.** Can produce warnings at incompatible points for the structure
- ☐ **D.** Can identify where program behavior may change

6. In a Unicode system when opening a file in `TEXT MODE`, you must specify:

- ☐ **A.** The `ENCODING` addition
- ☐ **B.** The byte order
- ☐ **C.** The code page

7. In a non-Unicode system when opening a file in `TEXT MODE`, you should specify:

- ☐ **A.** The `ENCODING` addition
- ☐ **B.** The byte order
- ☐ **C.** The code page

Practice Question Answers and Explanations

1. Correct answers: **A, B**

   SAP provides the tools to perform or enforce the Unicode checks prior to your actual conversion. The ability to enforce Unicode checks exists in any release after Release 6.10 (when Unicode was supported) without the need to actually convert to Unicode. The recommendation is to turn the check on as soon as possible to minimize the amount of changes to developed programs. It is better to develop new programs correctly rather than possibly introduce an issue when going back to make a change to the program later.

2. Correct answer: **B**

   No, memory requirements will always be larger on a Unicode system owing to the increased size of the characters. Depending on the method of encoding, the increase may be slight, but it will be larger.

3. Correct answers: **All options**

   Owing to the enforcement of byte-type and character-type rules, on a Unicode system only byte-type fields may be assigned or compared to other byte-type fields. The same is true for character-type fields. Offset positioning is restricted to flat data objects or a character data objects.

4. Correct answer: **A**

   Two structures in Unicode programs are only compatible when all alignment gaps are identical on all platforms. This applies in particular for alignment gaps that are created by included structures.

5. Correct answers: **B, C, D**

   The enhancement category makes it possible to recognize and handle problems related to structure enhancements. This classification is used during the program check to create a warning at all points where it works with structures, and where later structure enhancements can cause syntax errors or changes in program behavior.

6. Correct answer: **A**

   In a Unicode system you must specify the `ENCODING` addition when opening a file (dataset).

7. Correct answers: **B, C**

   In a non-Unicode system you must specify both the byte order and the code page when opening a file (dataset).

Take Away

You will need to understand what Unicode is and why it is necessary in a global environment. You should have knowledge of differences between data objects in a non-Unicode system and data objects in a Unicode system. You should have an understanding of what additions to statements exist and what changes to syntax validation are enforced in Unicode.

Refresher

You need to understand the different data object types that produce either a byte-type data object or a character-type data object or a structure and how the fragment view restricts certain assignments or comparisons. You will also need to understand what restrictions for file processing exist with Unicode.

Table 11.3 lists the key concepts of Unicode.

Key Concept	Definition
Byte type	Elementary data objects of types `x` and `xstring` are byte type.
Character type	The following elementary data objects are now character type: `c`, `d`, `n`, `t`, `string`.
Fragment view	A fragment is a grouping of structure components of the same or similar data types.

Table 11.3 Key Concepts Refresher

Tips

Whereas the vast majority of the concepts presented in this chapter should be second nature, especially if you have programmed on SAP Release 6.20 or later, it is important that you understand the behavior differences of assignments, comparisons, and file processing.

Summary

You should now be able to make an ABAP program Unicode compliant. You should have an understanding of the potential issues related to data objects and file processing. This knowledge will enable you to successfully pass this portion of the certification examination.

Classical Screens

12

Techniques You'll Master:

- Design screens with the Screen Painter
- Design a GUI status and GUI title using the Menu Painter
- Set the GUI status and process function codes in the Process After Input (PAI) flow logic screen
- Understand screen events such as `PROCESS BEFORE OUTPUT`, `PROCESS AFTER INPUT`, `PROCESS ON HELP-REQUEST`, and `PROCESS ON VALUE-REQUEST`
- Write dialog programs

A dialog-driven program consists of screens, the GUI status, a GUI title, and an ABAP program.

- Each dialog in the system is controlled by one or more screens. The screens have a layout that determines the position of input/output fields and other graphical elements such as checkboxes and radio buttons. You design a screen layout using the Screen Painter in the ABAP Workbench. Each screen has flow logic that influences the program flow. The flow logic consists of Process Before Output (PBO) and Process After Input (PAI) logic, and optionally, Process on Help-Request (POH) and Process on Value-Request (POV) for any actions required.
- Each screen has a GUI status, which controls the menu bars, standard toolbars, and application toolbars with which the user chooses the function in the application.
- The GUI title is used to define the title for a screen. This is especially important if there is more than one screen in a sequence of screens within a GUI dialog.
- An ABAP program contains the dialog module that is called by the screen flow logic and processes the user input from the GUI status. Type `M` programs are the containers of dialog modules and therefore are known as module pools and can only be started using transaction codes.

In this chapter we will cover module pool programming and the various program objects required to create a module pool program. We will cover screen design using the Screen Painter, screen events, and screen flow logic. We will cover GUI status and GUI title design and its use in dialog programming. Finally, we will cover screen processing, dynamically modifying screens, and screen design using table controls.

Real-World Scenario

You have to write a custom dialog program for your customer to allow them to maintain employee master data and payroll information because the SAP standard application does not satisfy their business requirement.

The application should have two screens: In the first screen you will enter the employee personal information, and in the second one you will enter the payroll-related data. The dialog program should allow the user to enter data on the screen and save the data in the database when the user clicks on the Save button on the screen. The dialog program should also have the option to edit and display the saved data. The transaction should be user friendly and should validate user input and display F1 Help for the screen fields and value help (via the [F4] key) wherever possible.

Objectives of this Portion of the Test

The objective of this portion of the exam is to verify your knowledge regarding the dialog programs. You are expected to be able to write a dialog program. You should be able to design screens using the Screen Painter, design a GUI status using the Menu Painter, and create GUI titles for a screen. You are also expected to be aware of possible screen events such as PBO (PROCESS BEFORE OUTPUT), PAI (PROCESS AFTER INPUT), POH (PROCESS ON HELP-REQUEST), and POV (PROCESS ON VALUE-REQUEST). You should be able to handle the transaction flow based on user actions.

The certification examination will give minimal weight to this chapter compared to all of the other topics in the examination. This means that this chapter is among those where the percentage of questions related to the topic is smaller than most other chapters. The reason it is given average weight is that there is less of a chance that you would have to write custom Dialog program in a project.

Key Concepts Refresher

You need to understand the dialog programming concept to create a dialog transaction. Dialog programming consists of screen, GUI status, GUI title, module pool program, and transaction. You have to create a module pool program, screen, GUI status, GUI title, and transaction code to execute a dialog program.

To develop a dialog transaction you have to use the Screen Painter to design the screens and populate the screen attributes. You also have to write the screen flow logic to control the data transfer from the screen area to the ABAP program and vice versa.

In screen flow logic you have to write code for PROCESS BEFORE OUTPUT, PROCESS AFTER INPUT, PROCESS ON HELP-REQUEST, and PROCESS ON VALUE-REQUEST. The PBO event is triggered before the screen is displayed, so generally you populate screen fields with default values, and set the GUI status and screen title in the

PBO event block. The PAI event is triggered when the user performs some action on the screen such clicking on a button, selecting a menu entry, pressing enter, or selecting a function on the screen. You write code for the PAI event block to interpret the user action, validate user entries, and control the flow of the transaction accordingly. Similarly, POH and POV are the events that are triggered when the user selects F1 help for a screen element or requests value help via F4 for a screen field.

Note

You can write code to provide your own F1 help and F4 help in the POH and POV event block, but remember that the F1 help usually comes from a data element and that F4 input can be provided by search helps.

Also, to write a dialog program you have to design the GUI status, which consists of menus, toolbars, and function codes, and the GUI title and be able to assign these to the screen in the screen flow logic.

Screen Design

ABAP programs or dialog transactions use screens to interact with the user. The screens for dialog programming are created with the Screen Painter. Selection screens are created for an executable ABAP program with ABAP declarative statements (i.e., `PARAMETERS` and `SELECT-OPTIONS`) to obtain user input for the program. You do not have to define the screen flow logic for selection screens, whereas for dialog screens you do. Screens in module pools can only be addressed using dialog transactions.

Selection Screen

The standard selection screen for executable ABAP programs is called and controlled by the ABAP runtime environment; selection screens are discussed in detail in Chapter 13, Selection Screens. In this chapter we will be discussing dialog screens, which are created with the Screen Painter. You can create screens to be used in any program of type `1` (executable program), `M` (module pools), and `F` (function groups).

A program can consist of a single screen or a sequence of screens. You can start a single screen or start a sequence of screens from an ABAP program by using the

`CALL SCREEN` statement. For screens in a module pool program of type `M`, the start screen is specified in the transaction code you assign to the module pool. A default next screen is defined in the Screen Painter for all dialog screens, but this can be overridden dynamically within the program, specifically in the PAI flow logic for the screen.

A screen is a form of dialog between the user and the program. A screen can contain various elements for allowing the user to interact with the program or for displaying the field content. A typical dialog screen consists of screen elements such as input/output fields, buttons, radio buttons, checkboxes, and screen flow logic. The screen flow logic consists of PBO (`Process Before Output`), PAI (`Process After Input`), POH (`Process on Help-Request`), and POV (`Process on Value-Request`) event blocks.

The screen flow logic must contain at least PBO and PAI event blocks. Each screen has its own flow logic that calls dialog modules in the ABAP program to prepare the data for display on the screen or to process the user's entries. Generally, you prepare data or modify the screen display in the PBO event block and react to the user action in the PAI event block. You can define the F1 help for the screen field in the POH event and value help in the POV event, but it is recommended that you use the F1 help and value help (possible entries) from the ABAP Dictionary. You can write your own F1 help and F4 input help only if you want to override the ABAP Dictionary help. Hence, POH and POV event blocks are optional.

Screen Painter

Each screen has a GUI status, containing the menu bar, the standard toolbar, and optionally, an application toolbar. The GUI status also contains the function codes for each of the functions in the menus and toolbars. You should create a GUI title for each screen. This helps the user, especially if you have a sequence of several screens. You can also create a GUI title for the screen dynamically within the program. The GUI status and title are discussed in detail later in this chapter.

You design the screen layout with the Screen Painter. The Screen Painter has a layout editor that has a graphical mode and an alphanumeric mode. Both editors offer the same functionality but with different interfaces. The graphical mode is easy to use and uses a drag-and-drop interface, whereas with the alphanumeric editor you use menus and the keyboard to design the screen. You can switch between the two modes via the menu path UTILITIES • SETTINGS • GRAPHICAL LAYOUT EDITOR. The Screen Painter can be accessed from the ABAP Workbench or via Transaction SE51.

You define the screen attributes, screen layout, and the flow logic in the Screen Painter. The screen attributes describe the properties of the screen as a whole and its runtime behavior. Figure 12.1 displays the screen attribute in the Screen Painter.

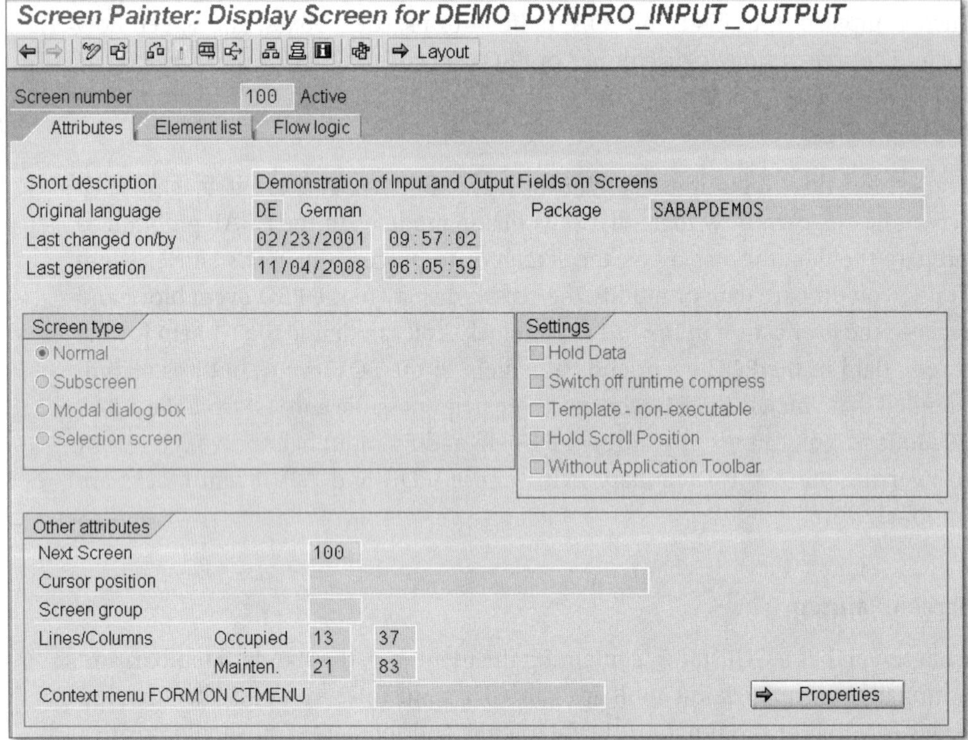

Figure 12.1 Screen Painter — Screen Attribute Definition

The general screen attributes are specified on the ATTRIBUTES tab. Following are some of the screen attributes required to create a screen:

- PROGRAM
  Each screen is associated with an ABAP program. The program type can be `1`, `M`, or `F`. If you create the screen from the program itself, this will be populated automatically. The name of the program appears as the screen title (see Figure 12.1).

- SHORT TEXT
  A short meaningful text for the screen.
- SCREEN NUMBER
  The screen number can be up to four digits long, and must be a unique number within the container program.

Caution

Selection screen numbers and Screen Painter screen numbers belong to the same namespace, so your dialog screen number cannot be 1000 if your program has a selection screen as well.

- SCREEN TYPE
  The screen type can be a normal screen, subscreen, or dialog box. A normal screen occupies the whole GUI window, whereas the dialog box occupies only part of the GUI window. Subscreens are displayed in a subscreen area of another screen.
- NEXT SCREEN
  This defines the default next screen in the screen sequence. The screen will call itself if the next screen number is the same as the current screen number. You define the current screen as the last screen in the chain by leaving the next screen field blank or setting it to 0 (zero). The next screen number can be dynamically changed within the program to override the statically defined screen number. At runtime the screen number is stored in the system variable. The next screen number can be changed dynamically in the PAI flow logic by the ABAP statement `SET SCREEN <screen_no>`.
- CURSOR POSITION
  This defines the cursor position when the screen is displayed. By default, the cursor is positioned on the first input field on the screen. You can also dynamically specify the cursor position within the program.

Screen Layout

The next step when creating the screen is to define the screen layout. You can place input/output fields, texts, buttons, checkboxes, radio buttons, table controls, tabstrip controls, and so on on the screen. Screen elements can be defined by adopting the attributes of fields from the ABAP Dictionary, or you can use a data object defined in your program. Generally, you create the screen elements from the ABAP Dictionary, because this way you get access to the field labels, input help, documentation, and so on. The screen layout can be designed in the Graphical Screen Painter. Figure 12.2 displays the screen layout in the Screen Painter.

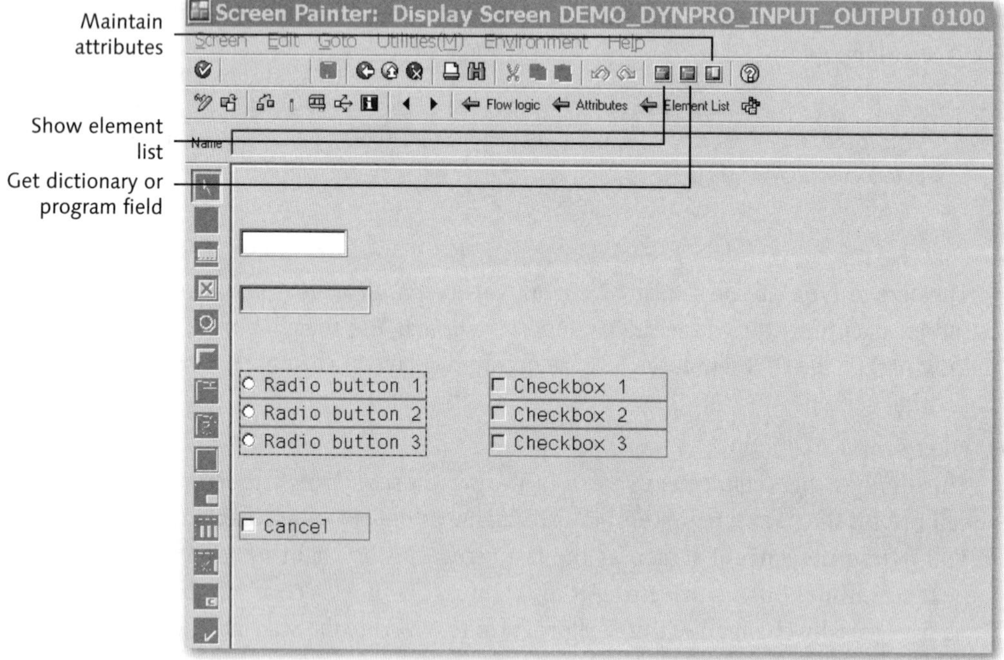

Figure 12.2 Create Screen Layout

The graphical layout editor has three buttons, as depicted in Figure 12.2:

- Maintain element attributes

  The Maintain element attributes button opens a new window for you to maintain the screen element attributes. These differ depending on the type of element you have chosen, for example, an input field or button. Figure 12.3 displays screen element attribute maintenance screen.

  You can define general attributes such as screen group, function code, function type, search help, parameter ID, and so on. You can also specify the Dictionary attributes, program attributes, and display attributes for the screen elements.

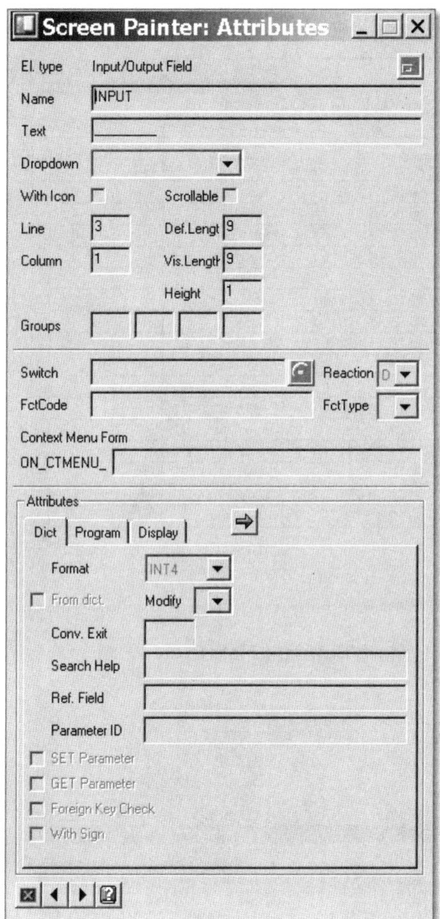

Figure 12.3 Screen Element Attribute

- GET DICTIONARY/PROGRAM FIELDS

  The GET DICTIONARY/PROGRAM FIELDS button opens a new window to create the screen elements and input/output fields with reference to Dictionary and program fields (see Figure 12.4).

- SHOW ELEMENT LIST

  The SHOW ELEMENT LIST button opens a new window to show all available screen elements belonging to the screen, including their attributes for maintenance. Figure 12.5 displays the screen element list screen.

Screen Painter: Dict./Program Fields

Table/Field Name: SPFLI — [Get from Dictionary] [Get from Program]

Switch: — Reaction — RFC Destination

Table Name	Field Name	Description	I/O Field		None	Short	Medium	Long	Header	Text	Copy as Text	ChkB	RadB
SPFLI	MANDT		CLNT	3	○	○ 10	◉ 15	○ 20	○ 3	Client	◉	○	○
SPFLI	CARRID		CHAR	3	○	○ 7	◉ 16	○ 16	○ 2	Airline	◉	○	○
SPFLI	CONNID		NUMC	4	○	○ 10	◉ 15	○ 20	○ 3	Flight Number	◉	○	○
SPFLI	COUNTRYFR		CHAR	3	○	○ 10	◉ 12	○ 20	○ 3	Country	◉	○	○
SPFLI	CITYFROM		CHAR	20	○	○ 10	◉ 11	○ 14	○ 12	Depart.city	◉	○	○
SPFLI	AIRPFROM		CHAR	3	○	○ 10	◉ 15	○ 20	○ 9	Dep. airport	◉	○	○
SPFLI	COUNTRYTO		CHAR	3	○	○ 10	◉ 12	○ 20	○ 3	Country	◉	○	○
SPFLI	CITYTO		CHAR	20	○	○ 10	◉ 17	○ 20	○ 20	Arrival city	◉	○	○
SPFLI	AIRPTO		CHAR	3	○	○ 10	◉ 15	○ 20	○ 3	Dest. airport	◉	○	○
SPFLI	FLTIME		INT4	6	○	○ 10	◉ 15	○ 20	○ 9	Flight time	◉	○	○
SPFLI	DEPTIME		TIMS	8	○	○ 10	◉ 15	○ 20	○ 8	Departure	◉	○	○
SPFLI	ARRTIME		TIMS	8	○	○ 10	◉ 15	○ 20	○ 8	Arrival Time	◉	○	○
SPFLI	DISTANCE		QUAN	11	○	○ 7	◉ 10	○ 14	○ 5	Distance	◉	○	○
SPFLI	DISTID		UNIT	3	○	○ 4	◉ 13	○ 13	○ 3	Distance in	◉	○	○
SPFLI	FLTYPE		CHAR	1	○	○ 7	◉ 7	○ 11	○ 7	Charter	◉	○	○
SPFLI	PERIOD		INT1	3	○	○ 10	◉ 15	○ 25	○ 25	n day(s) later	◉	○	○

Figure 12.4 Select Screen Element — Get Dictionary/Program Fields

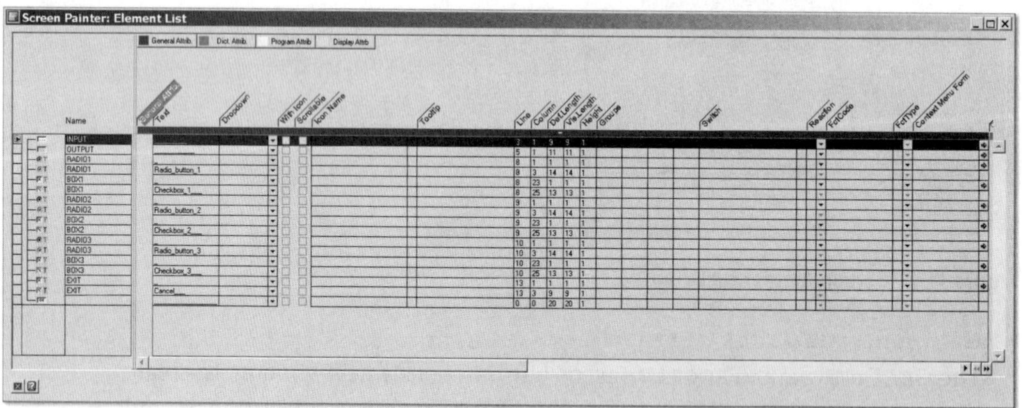

Figure 12.5 Screen Element List

Every screen has the 20-character OK field, which is not displayed on the screen and which you must name. The name we usually give it is OK_CODE. The OK field is also referred to as the *function code*. You need to assign a name to the OK field to use it in the program. You also need to declare a data variable with exactly the same name, of type SY-UCOMM. This way the contents are automatically transported from the screen to the ABAP program. A user action triggers the PAI event, and the function code chosen by the user is stored in this field and is passed to the ABAP program. Based on the function code (or `OK`), you control the program flow and dictate what happens next.

Tip

The following are recommendations for screen layout design:

- It is recommended that you use ABAP Dictionary tables or structures to define screen layout. This way the screen field can adopt the Dictionary attributes such as field label, value help, and F1 help. You do not have to write POH or POV functions unless you want to override ABAP Dictionary F1/F4 functions.
- If you use the ABAP Dictionary, the system provides you with the automatic consistency check for the input fields. These checks include type check, foreign key check, and fixed value check. All of these checks are automatically supplied with the information in the ABAP Dictionary.
- You should also declare a Dictionary structure as the work area using the `TABLES` statement in the ABAP program. This way the screen field contents are automatically copied in the ABAP program with the matching field name.

Screen Flow Logic

The screen flow logic is created after the screen attributes and the layout of the screen have been defined. Screen flow logic is created in the flow logic editor of the Screen Painter, and you cannot use ABAP statements directly here. Screens have their own set of keywords for use in the PBO, PAI, POH, and POV event blocks. The allowed keywords for the screen flow logic are mentioned later in this section.

You create special module calls in screen flow logic, and it is these modules that contain the ABAP statements. Modules are like subroutines for the screens. They can be created by double-clicking on the module name in the flow logic editor or by right-clicking on the program name in Transaction SE80. Modules that are called in the PBO processing block must be defined using the `MODULE <name> OUTPUT` statement and `ENDMODULE` at the end. The modules that are called in the PAI processing block must be defined using `MODULE <name> INPUT` in the ABAP program.

If you create the module using forward navigation, then it will be created with the above-mentioned syntax. Listing 12.1 displays the screen flow logic, and Listing 12.2 displays the module definition for the ones defined in the screen flow logic.

```
PROCESS BEFORE OUTPUT.
  MODULE init_screen_100.
PROCESS AFTER INPUT.
  MODULE user_command_100.
```

Listing 12.1 Screen Flow Logic

```
*&---------------------------------------------*
*&      Module  INIT_SCREEN_100  OUTPUT
*&---------------------------------------------*
MODULE init_screen_100 OUTPUT.
  CLEAR input.
  SET PF-STATUS 'STATUS_100'.
  radio1 = 'X'.
  CLEAR: radio2, radio3.
ENDMODULE.          "INIT_SCREEN_100  OUTPUT

*&---------------------------------------------*
*&      Module  USER_COMMAND_100  INPUT
*&---------------------------------------------*
MODULE user_command_100 INPUT.
  output = input.
  box1 = radio1.
  box2 = radio2.
  box3 = radio3.
  IF exit NE space.
    LEAVE PROGRAM.
  ENDIF.
ENDMODULE.              "USER_COMMAND_100  INPUT
```

Listing 12.2 PBO and PAI Module Definition

The screen flow logic must contain at least the two statements PROCESS BEFORE OUTPUT and PROCESS AFTER OUTPUT, and these are created automatically when you create the screen itself. Table 12.1 displays the keywords you can use in these event blocks.

Keyword	Function
MODULE	Calls a dialog module in ABAP programs
FIELD	Specifies the point at which the contents of the screen field must be transported
ON	Used in conjunction with FIELD
VALUES	Used in conjunction with FIELD
CHAIN	Starts a processing chain
ENDCHAIN	Ends a processing chain
CALL	Calls a subscreen
LOOP	Starts processing a screen table
ENDLOOP	Stops processing a screen table

Table 12.1 Keywords for Screen Flow Logic

Screen Processing

The ABAP processor controls the program flow within a module, and the dynpro/screen processor controls the flow logic and prepares data to be displayed on the screen. For a screen and its ABAP program to be able to communicate, the screen and the ABAP program field names should be identical. When this is the case, the contents of the screen fields are transported to the ABAP program fields with the same name, and vice versa. You should use Dictionary structures or program fields to define the screen elements and input/output fields and declare the Dictionary structure as a work area in the program by using the TABLES statement. This ensures that screen field content is copied automatically from the screen to the ABAP data object with the matching name and vice versa.

The contents of the ABAP work area are copied to their corresponding screen fields after all of the modules defined in the PBO processing block have been executed. Similarly, the system copies the contents of the screen fields to the corresponding fields in the ABAP work area before the first module in the PAI processing block is executed, unless this transport has been delayed by the use of the FIELD statement.

When a screen is processed, the PROCESS BEFORE OUTPUT event is triggered, the corresponding event block in the screen flow logic is executed, and then the screen is displayed. The PROCESS AFTER INPUT event is triggered and the corresponding event block is executed when the user selects a function code on the screen, for example, clicking on button, selecting a menu entry, pressing a function key on the keyboard, or just pressing [↵]. If the user requests field help by pressing [F1] or value help by pressing [F4], it triggers the PROCESS ON HELP-REQUEST and PROCESS ON VALUE-REQUEST event.

PBO is about preparing the screen, perhaps providing default values for the screen fields that may or may not come from the database, and setting up the GUI status and GUI title. The PAI event is triggered when the user interacts with the screen, perhaps by clicking on a button on the screen; selecting a function from the menu, standard toolbar, or application toolbar; pressing a function key on the keyboard, and so on. The function code is passed to the OK_CODE screen field from the element list and is passed to the identically named field in the ABAP program.

We have already discussed that you can call the ABAP dialog modules from the screen flow logic by using the MODULE statement. You can also call ABAP dialog modules in a controlled manner by using the FIELD statement in the screen flow logic (see Listing 12.3).

```
PROCESS BEFORE OUTPUT.
  MODULE init_screen_100.
PROCESS AFTER INPUT.
  MODULE user_command_0100.
  MODULE module_1.
  FIELD box2.
  MODULE module_2.
  FIELD: box1, box3.
  MODULE module_3.
```

Listing 12.3 Controlled ABAP Dialog

- FIELD
  The FIELD statement is used in PAI, POH, and POV event blocks. It does not have any effect on the PBO event block and hence should not be used in PBO event blocks. It can be used with PAI modules for input checks on the screen field. The input field against the FIELD keyword will be ready for re-input if the module defined for the FIELD statement issues an error or warning mes-

sage. You can also call the ABAP dialog modules conditionally by using the addition `ON INPUT` or `ON REQUEST` with the `FIELD` statement.

- `CHAIN...ENDCHAIN`

  The `CHAIN` and `ENDCHAIN` statements can be used to validate user input on a set of fields on a dialog screen. You can send an error or warning message from the module that is call using the `FIELD` statement. All of the fields that belong to the processing chain within the `CHAIN` and `ENDCHAIN` statement are ready for input if an error or a warning message is sent from the module. For the warning message, all of the fields within the chain block will be ready for input, but you can continue with the transaction by pressing the [↵] key. However, for an error message you have to resolve the error, and then you can proceed with the transaction.

  If you use the `FIELD` statement outside a `CHAIN` statement, only single field is made ready for input when a warning or error message is displayed, whereas with the `CHAIN` and `ENDCHAIN` statements, the set of fields with the statement block is made ready for input if an error or warning is displayed. Listing 12.4 displays the screen flow logic for an input check with the `CHAIN` and `ENDCHAIN` statements, and Listing 12.5 displays the module for an input check.

```
PROCESS BEFORE OUTPUT.
  MODULE init_screen_9001.
PROCESS AFTER INPUT.
  MODULE cancel AT EXIT-COMMAND.
  FIELD input1 MODULE module_1.
  FIELD input2 MODULE module_2.
  FIELD input3 MODULE module_3.
  CHAIN.
    FIELD input4.
    MODULE chain_module_1.
    FIELD input5.
    FIELD input6 MODULE chain_module_2.
  ENDCHAIN.
  MODULE execution.
```

Listing 12.4 Input Check with CHAIN and ENDCHAIN Statements

```
*---------------------------------------------*
*  MODULE chain_module_1 INPUT
*---------------------------------------------*
MODULE chain_module_1 INPUT.
  IF input4 < 10.
```

```
    MESSAGE w000(fb) WITH text-003 '10' text-002.
  ENDIF.
ENDMODULE                  " CHAIN_MODULE_1  INPUT
*-------------------------------------------*
*  MODULE chain_module_2 INPUT
*-------------------------------------------*
MODULE chain_module_2 INPUT.
  CLEAR sum.
  sum = input4 + input5 + input6.
  IF sum <= 100.
    MESSAGE e000(fb) WITH text-004 '100' text-002.
  ENDIF.
ENDMODULE.              " CHAIN_MODULE_2  INPUT
```

Listing 12.5 Input Check Module

- `ON INPUT`

  The `ON INPUT` addition for the `FIELD` statement calls the ABAP dialog when the screen field contains a value other than the initial value for that screen field. The initial value for the screen field is determined by the data type of the screen field. The initial value is space ( ) for character fields and 0 (zero) for numeric fields.

- `ON REQUEST`

  The `ON REQUEST` addition for the `FIELD` statement calls the ABAP dialog module only if the user has entered something in the screen field. The module is executed even if the user enters the initial value for the data type of the screen field or overwrites an existing value with the same value.

- `ON CHAIN-INPUT` and `ON-CHAIN REQUEST`

  The `ON CHAIN-INPUT` and `ON-CHAIN REQUEST` additions work the same way as `ON INPUT` and `ON REQUEST` except that the ABAP dialog module is called if *at least* one field listed in the `FIELD` statement within the `CHAIN` statement meets the condition. Listing 12.6 displays the conditional processing of an ABAP dialog.

```
PROCESS BEFORE OUTPUT.
  MODULE init_screen_9002.
PROCESS AFTER INPUT.
  MODULE cancel AT EXIT-COMMAND.
  CHAIN.
    FIELD: input1, input2.
    MODULE chain_module_1 ON CHAIN-INPUT.
```

```
    FIELD  input3
    MODULE chain_module_2 ON CHAIN-REQUEST.
  ENDCHAIN.
```

Listing 12.6 Conditional ABAP Dialog

- AT CURSOR-SELECTION
  The AT CURSOR-SELECTION addition calls the ABAP dialog module if the cursor is positioned on a particular screen element.

Automatic input checks are performed in the PAI event before the data is transferred to the ABAP program. The automatic checks are performed based on the screen element attributes. If a screen field is mandatory, then the user must enter data before the PAI event block can start. If the screen input field refers to an ABAP Dictionary field, then the field-level validation defined in the ABAP Dictionary such as checks against the check tale or domain fixed values is performed before the PAI processing can start.

The user input for the field should match the format defined for the field in the Screen Painter; otherwise, the user gets an error message before the PAI processing can start. In such a case you can exit the screen only by entering a valid value or selecting the menu item of function type E. For the menu item of function type E you have to code the exit logic within the dialog module defined with the addition AT EXIT-COMMAND in PAI. Listing 12.6 displays the usage of AT EXIT-COMMAND in screen flow logic, and Listing 12.7 displays the code in the module for AT EXIT-COMMAND.

```
*&---------------------------------------------*
*&      Module  CANCEL  INPUT
*&---------------------------------------------*
MODULE cancel INPUT.
  CASE ok_code.
    WHEN 'BACK'.
      LEAVE.
      SET SCREEN 0.
      LEAVE SCREEN.
    WHEN 'EXIT'.
      LEAVE.
      SET SCREEN 0.
      LEAVE SCREEN.
    WHEN 'CANCEL'.
      SET SCREEN 0.
      LEAVE SCREEN.
```

```
  ENDCASE.
  LEAVE PROGRAM.
ENDMODULE.                      " CANCEL  INPUT
```

Listing 12.7 Module for AT EXIT-COMMAND

You can validate the user input with the screen flow logic by the addition VALUES with the FIELD statement or by checking against a database table. Listing 12.8 displays the use of the FIELD and VALUE keyword to validate the user input.

```
PROCESS BEFORE OUTPUT.
  MODULE init_screen_0100.
PROCESS AFTER INPUT.
  MODULE cancel AT EXIT-COMMAND.
  FIELD carrier VALUES (not 'AA', 'LH', between 'QF' and 'UA').
  MODULE module_1.
  FIELD connect SELECT  *
                FROM  spfli
                WHERE carrid = carrier AND connid = connect
                WHENEVER NOT FOUND SEND ERRORMESSAGE 107
                                   WITH carrier connect.
  MODULE module_2.
```

Listing 12.8 Input Check in Screen Flow Logic

If you call a module using a FIELD statement, when issuing an error or warning message after doing the checks in the module, only the input fields mentioned against the FIELD keyword will be available for re-input. The user should be allowed to correct incorrect entry. This can be done by sending an error message or a warning message (see Listing 12.9 and Listing 12.10). With a warning message the user will be given an option to re-input a valid value but can proceed without entering the value by pressing the [↵] key.

```
PROCESS BEFORE OUTPUT.
  MODULE init_screen_9001.
PROCESS AFTER INPUT.
  MODULE cancel AT EXIT-COMMAND.
  FIELD input1 MODULE module_1.
  FIELD input2 MODULE module_2.
  FIELD input3 MODULE module_3.
  CHAIN.
    FIELD input4.
    MODULE chain_module_1.
    FIELD input5.
```

```
    FIELD input6 MODULE chain_module_2.
  ENDCHAIN.
  MODULE execution.
```

Listing 12.9 Input Check in ABAP Dialog

```
*&---------------------------------------------*
*&      Module  MODULE_1  INPUT
*&---------------------------------------------*
MODULE module_1 INPUT.
  IF input1 < 50.
    MESSAGE e000(fb) WITH text-001 '50' text-002.
  ENDIF.
ENDMODULE.                    " MODULE_1  INPUT

*---------------------------------------------*
*  MODULE module_2 INPUT
*---------------------------------------------*
MODULE module_2 INPUT.
  IF input2 < 100.
    MESSAGE e000(fb) WITH text-001 '100' text-002.
  ENDIF.
ENDMODULE.                    " MODULE_2  INPUT
*--------------------------------------------*
*  MODULE module_3 INPUT
*---------------------------------------------*
MODULE module_3 INPUT.
  IF input3 < 150.
    MESSAGE w000(fb) WITH text-001 '150' text-002.
  ENDIF.
ENDMODULE.                    " MODULE_3  INPUT

*--------------------------------------------*
*  MODULE chain_module_1 INPUT
*---------------------------------------------*
MODULE chain_module_1 INPUT.
  IF input4 < 10.
    MESSAGE w000(fb) WITH text-003 '10' text-002.
  ENDIF.
ENDMODULE.                 " CHAIN_MODULE_1  INPUT

*---------------------------------------------*
*  MODULE chain_module_2 INPUT
*--------------------------------------------*
```

```
MODULE chain_module_2 INPUT.
  CLEAR sum.
  sum = input4 + input5 + input6.
  IF sum <= 100.
    MESSAGE e000(fb) WITH text-004 '100' text-002.
  ENDIF.
ENDMODULE.                 " CHAIN_MODULE_2  INPUT
```

Listing 12.10 ABAP Dialog for Input Check

In the flow logic MODULE_1 is called using the FIELD statement for the field input1. If an error message is triggered from module_1, then the field input1 will be ready for input again, allowing the user to enter a new value.

Similarly, if an error or warning message is sent from the module using the FIELD statement within CHAIN and ENDCHAIN, then all fields within the CHAIN and END-CHAIN statements are ready for input. In Listing 12.11 if the module CHAIN_MODULE_2 sends an error message, then all of the fields within the CHAIN and END-CHAIN are ready for input again.

```
CHAIN.
  FIELD input4.
  MODULE chain_module_1.
  FIELD input5.
  FIELD input6 module chain_module_2.
ENDCHAIN.
```

Listing 12.11 Input Field Check in ABAP Dialog

Lastly, you can code your own F1 field help and value help functions for screen fields, but you should only do this if the Dictionary fields that your screen fields are based upon do not have F1/F4 help or if you want to override it. There are three ways to provide F1 field help for the user.

- You can use ABAP Dictionary fields for the screen element definition, in which case F1 help automatically displays the data element documentation.
- You can display data element supplementary documentation for F1 help if the data element documentation is not sufficient for your application. You can display or maintain the data element supplementary documentation via the menu path Goto • Documentation • Supplementary Documentation. Data element supplementary documentation is program and screen specific, and the link is maintained in table THLPF. Figure 12.6 displays the data element

supplement link for the ABAP Dictionary data element MATNR, along with the program and the screens for which this extra documentation has been created.

Program	Screen number	Field name	Help status	DE Supplement
MMRE0001	1000	MARA-MATNR		0040
RMMMMPOI	1000	MARA-MATNR		0070
RWRPLVFB	0001	MARA-MATNR		0810
SAPLCV00	0201	MARA-MATNR		0090
SAPLCV00	0231	MARA-MATNR		0090
SAPLCV00	0232	MARA-MATNR		0090
SAPLCV00	0801	MARA-MATNR		0090

Figure 12.6 Table Entry for Data Element Supplement Help

The syntax to display the data element supplementary documentation for F1 help is as follows:

```
PROCESS ON HELP-REQUEST.
  FIELD mara-matnr MODULE f1_help_matnr WITH var.
```

You can populate the var in the module f1_help_matnr or use the literal instead of variable:

```
PROCESS ON HELP-REQUEST.
  FIELD mara-matnr WITH 0090.
```

The above syntax is only valid if the program, screen number, field name, and supplement documentation number are maintained in the table THLPF.

- If the above two methods for the display of help are not sufficient for your application, then you can display F1 help from the dialog modules by writing your own code. Generally, you can use the function module HELP_OBJECT_SHOW_FOR_FIELD or HELP_OBJECT_SHOW to display help instead of creating your own screen from scratch for your application to display help. Listing 12.12 displays the screen flow logic for F1 help, and Listing 12.13 displays the F1 help implementation for a dialog module.

```
PROCESS BEFORE OUTPUT.
PROCESS AFTER INPUT.
  MODULE cancel AT EXIT-COMMAND.
PROCESS ON HELP-REQUEST.
  FIELD demof1help-field2 MODULE f1_help_field2 WITH var.
  FIELD field3 MODULE f1_help_field3.
  FIELD field4 MODULE f1_help_field4.
```

Listing 12.12 Screen Flow Logic for F1 Help with Dialog Module

```
*---------------------------------------------*
*  MODULE f1_help_field2 INPUT
*--------------------------------------------*
MODULE f1_help_field2 INPUT.
  int = int + 1.
  CASE int.
    WHEN 1.
      var = '0100'.
    WHEN 2.
      var = '0200'.
      int = 0.
  ENDCASE.
ENDMODULE.                       "f1_help_field2 INPUT

*---------------------------------------------*
*  MODULE f1_help_field3 INPUT
*---------------------------------------------*
MODULE f1_help_field3 INPUT.
  CALL FUNCTION 'HELP_OBJECT_SHOW_FOR_FIELD'
    EXPORTING
      doklangu         = sy-langu
      doktitle         = text-002
      called_for_tab   = 'DEMOF1HELP'
      called_for_field = 'FIELD1'.
ENDMODULE.                       "f1_help_field3 INPUT

*---------------------------------------------*
*  MODULE f1_help_field4 INPUT
*---------------------------------------------*
MODULE f1_help_field4 INPUT.
  CALL FUNCTION 'HELP_OBJECT_SHOW'
    EXPORTING
      dokclass = 'TX'
      doklangu = sy-langu
      dokname  = 'DEMO_FOR_F1_HELP'
      doktitle = text-003
    TABLES
      links    = links.
ENDMODULE.                       "f1_help_field4 INPUT
```

Listing 12.13 F1 Help Implementation for Dialog Module

Similar to F1 help, you can display F4 input help based on ABAP Dictionary fields, based on the screen field attributes where you can attach a search help for the input field, or by writing your own dialog module. You use the syntax in Listing 12.14 for value help if you are going to program it yourself in the screen flow logic:

```
PROCESS ON VALUE-REQUEST.
  FIELD carrier MODULE value_carrier.
  FIELD connection MODULE value_connection.
```

Listing 12.14 Screen Flow Logic for Value Help

Coding for the F4 help is in the modules `value_carrier` and `value_connection`. Listing 12.15 displays this value help code within the module.

```
MODULE value_carrier INPUT.
  CALL FUNCTION 'F4IF_FIELD_VALUE_REQUEST'
       EXPORTING
            tabname     = 'DEMOF4HELP'
            fieldname   = 'CARRIER1'
            dynpprog    = sy-repid
            dynpnr      = sy-dynnr
            dynprofield = 'CARRIER'.
ENDMODULE.

MODULE value_connection INPUT.
  CALL FUNCTION 'DYNP_VALUES_READ'
       EXPORTING
            dyname             = sy-repid
            dynumb             = sy-dynnr
            translate_to_upper = 'X'
       TABLES
            dynpfields         = dynpro_values.
  READ TABLE dynpro_values INDEX 1 INTO field_value.
  SELECT  carrid connid
    FROM  spfli
    INTO  CORRESPONDING FIELDS OF TABLE values_tab
    WHERE carrid = field_value-fieldvalue.
  CALL FUNCTION 'F4IF_INT_TABLE_VALUE_REQUEST'
       EXPORTING
            retfield    = 'CONNID'
            dynpprog    = sy-repid
            dynpnr      = sy-dynnr
            dynprofield = 'CONNECTION'
            value_org   = 'S'
       TABLES
```

```
              value_tab    = values_tab.
ENDMODULE.
```

Listing 12.15 F4 Input Help Implementation

However, it is recommended that you use the input help from the ABAP Dictionary. You can also attach a search help in the screen field attributes. Hence, it is recommended that you program the input help if you want to override the ABAP Dictionary input help.

GUI Status and Title Design

The GUI status and GUI title together make up the user interface for the screen. The GUI status for a screen consists of the menu bar, a standard toolbar, the application toolbar, and the function key settings, and is designed using the Menu Painter tool. The GUI title is used to define the title for the screen. Each screen should have a GUI status and GUI title (see Figure 12.7). The GUI status consists of a menu bar, standard toolbar and application toolbar. You can also assign function keys to the menu items.

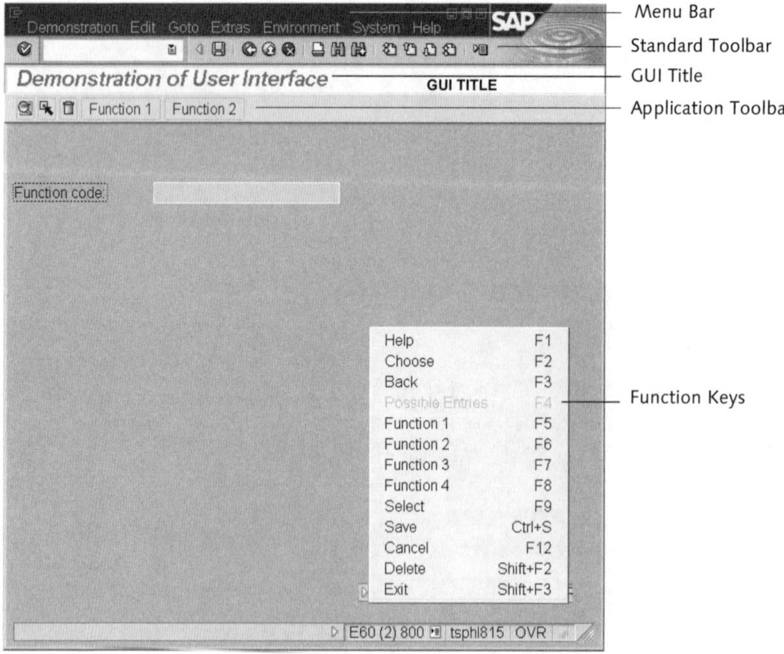

Figure 12.7 SAP User Interface

Menus are an element that provides the user with a range of functions that are relevant to the screen or application. A menu bar is made up of individual menus and can have up to eight menus including the SYSTEM and HELP menus. The entries under the menu can be functions, separators, or submenus. To create a GUI status in the Menu Painter, create the status, create the menu bar, create the menu entries, define the function key settings, define the standard toolbar and application bar, and as a final step activate the status.

Note

The SYSTEM and HELP menus are always present for every screen and have identical functions that cannot be modified.

Once you have created the GUI status, you need to create the menu bar and then create the individual menu functions and entries. To create a menu bar click on the EXPAND icon (⊞) of the menu bar text field and then enter the menu title (or use the predefined standard), and replace the first menu title.

Each menu can have up 15 entries or functions. To add functions to a menu double-click on the menu bar and then add the function code and function text in the CODE and TEXT columns, respectively. To add submenus enter just the text in the TEXT column, double-click, and then enter the code and text in the cascading menu. The function within the menu can be active or inactive. You can activate or deactivate menu items via the menu path EXTRAS • FUNCTION ACTIVE<->INACTIVE. You can also activate or deactivate the menu item dynamically with the PBO event block. Activation and deactivation of menu items is useful when the same GUI status is being used for a number of screens within the transaction. When you have a screen sequence in a transaction, some menu options will be relevant for some screens and not for the others, but to maintain consistency, the same GUI status can be used for each screen, with menu functions switched off when they are not relevant.

Functions within the menu or toolbars are identified by function codes. It doesn't matter where the function appears or is triggered from (i.e., menu, toolbar or function key), but the function type is relevant. The attribute FUNCTION TYPE determines the intended purpose of the function. The function type is also sometimes referred to as a *functional type*. The function type can tell when and how to carry out the processing of the function. Table 12.2 displays the valid function types for the functions belonging to SAP screens.

Type	Meaning
Blank	Normal function code processing in PAI module. For normal function code you can leave the function type blank; that is, blank means normal function code.
E	Triggers an AT EXIT-COMMAND module in the PAI processing block.
T	Call another transaction.
S	Triggers a system function and is used internally in standard SAP application. You shouldn't use this in your own applications.
P	Triggers a function defined locally at the GUI. This function does not trigger the PAI event; instead, it is processed at the presentation server level. As good example of this function type is function codes attached to tabstrips, where the user can switch between tabs without any logic happening in the screen flow logic.

Table 12.2 Function Types in SAP Systems

For functions with function type E, the system executes the dialog module that is called with the addition AT EXIT-COMMAND, if one has been defined in the PAI event block. The syntax for AT EXIT-COMMAND and the example code was discussed earlier in the Screen Processing section of this chapter. The system executes the MODULE XXX AT EXIT-COMMAND *before* the automatic input checks and before any other modules in the PAI event block. When a function of type T is triggered, the system leaves the calling program and calls the transaction that is to be found in the function code. This has the same effect as the LEAVE TO TRANSACTION statement. Most of the function code will have the functional type blank (' '). Figure 12.8 displays the function code attribute screen.

A function can be created with static texts or dynamic texts. A static text is one that is specified when you design the function, whereas with dynamic text, a placeholder is used that will be populated at runtime. For dynamic texts you have to assign a field to the function, and the contents of the field are displayed as the menu text at runtime. You can assign an icon (Icon Name attribute) to the function if a function has a static text. An icon is displayed instead of function text if the function is assigned to the button. The Function Text is displayed as quick info text for the icon or button. The contents of the Info Text attribute are displayed on the status bar of the screen when the user selects the function for which this attribute is populated. The button displays the icon and the content of the Icon Text if the Icon Text attribute is populated. The Fast Path attribute can be populated by specifying a single letter, which is used to select a menu function without using the mouse.

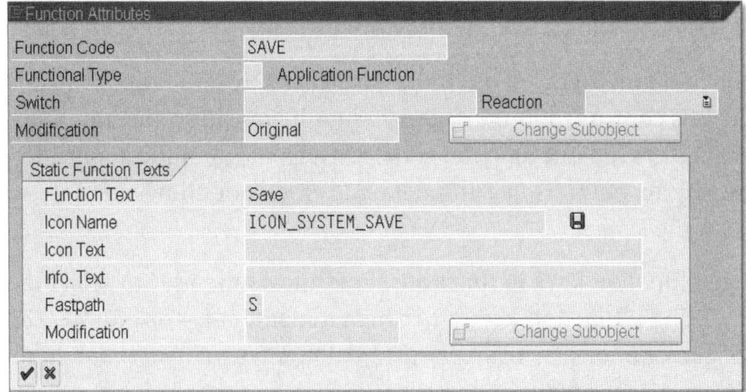

Figure 12.8 Function Code Attribute Screen

Figure 12.9 displays the function setting for the menu item in the GUI status along with the Fast Path attribute.

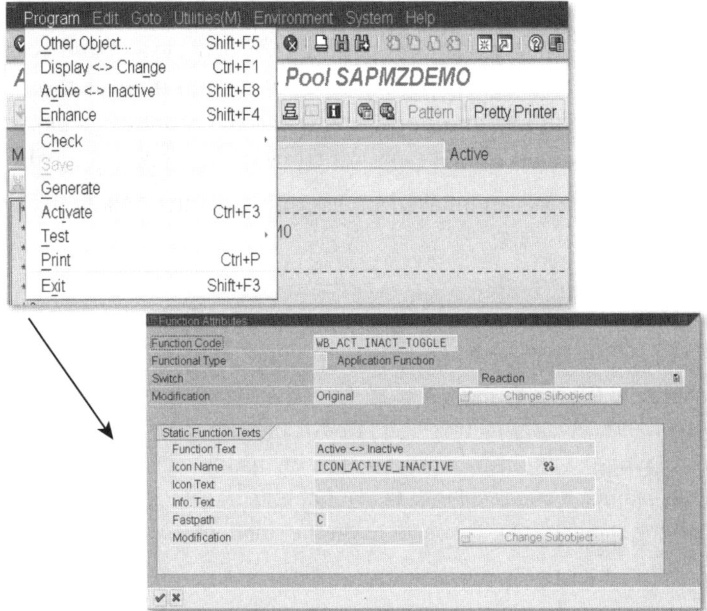

Figure 12.9 GUI Status with Function Code Attribute

The application toolbar contains buttons for the most frequently used functions specific to the application. The application toolbar can contain up to 35 buttons, or separators. The standard toolbar is the same for every screen in the SAP system. It contains a set of buttons with a fixed assignment of a function key, such as the SAVE and PRINT functions.

The button or the function is grayed out if the particular function is not available for the screen. This is controlled in the Menu Painter by making a function inactive. An example of a grayed out function is the SAVE icon (💾) if the application has the functionality to only display the data and does not allow the user to change the data on the screen.

You can also assign function keys to functions. This allows the user to select the function code by using a function key rather than a menu entry or button. The function key assignment consists of *reserved* function keys, *recommended* function keys, and *freely assigned* function keys.

- Reserved function keys are the ones whose assigned value cannot be changed and are assigned to functions on the standard toolbar. You can activate or deactivate their functions, even though you cannot change the function key assignment. These functions appear on the standard toolbar on screens and lists.
- Recommended function keys are just a proposal by the SAP system and comply with the SAP system ergonomic standards; that is, the same function is represented by this function key in other screens, and therefore users expect this function to be represented by the same function key in your screen also.
- Freely assigned function keys can be used for assigning a function key to any other function code.

Tip

You should always define function code type E for your dialog screen and code for those functions in the dialog module that called the PAI event block with the addition AT EXIT-COMMAND. This allows users to exit the screen by selecting the function code of type E, without entering the value on mandatory input fields on the screen. These function codes are the standard one such as BACK, CANCEL, and EXIT in most of the standard SAP transactions on the standard toolbar.

Creating a GUI Status and GUI Title

You create the GUI status and GUI title in the Menu Painter or with the Repository Browser. The Menu Painter can be accessed directly from ABAP Workbench or via Transaction SE41. The GUI status and title are always program specific, so the program name is required to define the GUI status. You need to specify the program name, and the GUI status name can be up to 20 characters long.

Figure 12.10 displays the Menu Painter initial screen from the ABAP Workbench. The first screen shows the menu path from the ABAP Workbench to start the Menu Painter, and the second screen is the initial screen of the Menu Painter. Figure 12.11 displays the Menu Painter interface.

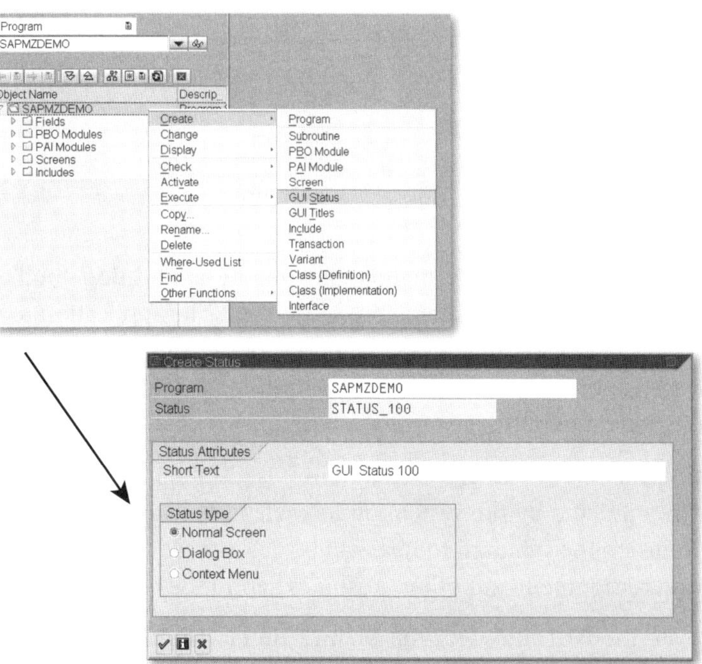

Figure 12.10 Create GUI Status from ABAP Workbench

You create menus bar by clicking on the EXPAND icon (icon) of the menu bar text field. You create functions for the menu by double-clicking on the menu header. For each menu you specify the functions, which consist of a function code and text and optionally submenus and separators. The submenus can be up to three levels deep. You can also define a fast path for each menu item. A menu can have up to 15 entries.

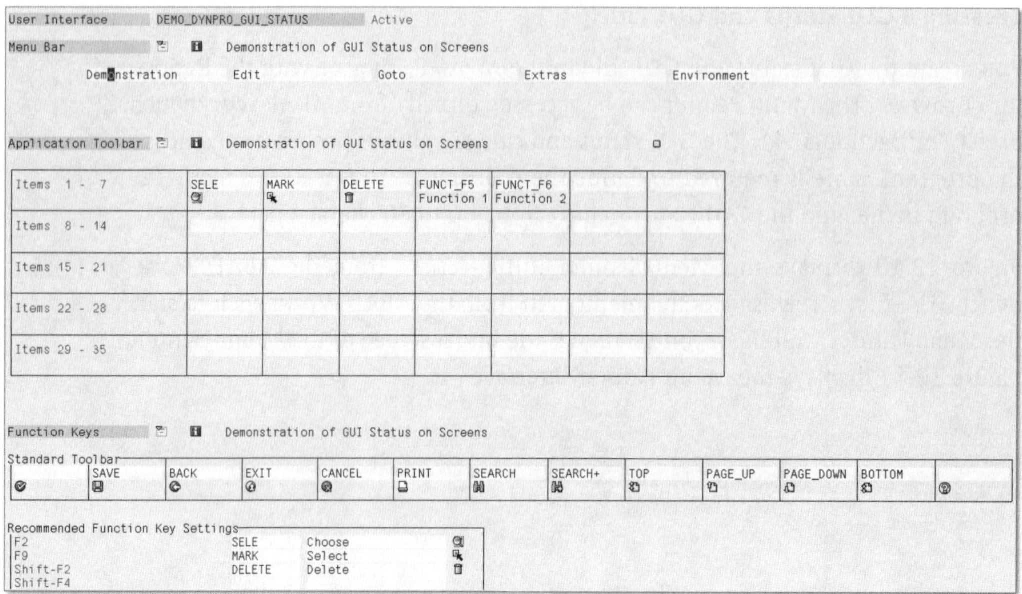

Figure 12.11 Menu Painter Interface

Most functions should appear in the menus and on the application toolbar, because some users prefer menus and some prefer buttons. The application toolbar can be created by clicking on the EXPAND icon (icon) of the application toolbar text. Each application toolbar item can be assigned an icon, info text, and fast path, or you can include separators instead of a function.

You must assign a function key to most commonly used menu functions. The standard toolbar is generated by the system on its own and always includes the same functions. Items on the standard toolbar can be deactivated if not required, but the function key assignment and other attributes cannot be changed.

Similarly, you create the GUI title with the Menu Painter. The GUI title is also program specific and is represented by a code that can be up to 20 characters long. The title text itself can be up to 60 alphanumeric characters long. The title appears as the screen heading and can have up to nine variables that can be dynamically populated in the program. The GUI title can be translated. Figure 12.12 displays the interface for the GUI title definition.

Note

At runtime the value of the screen title is stored in the system variable SYST-TITLE.

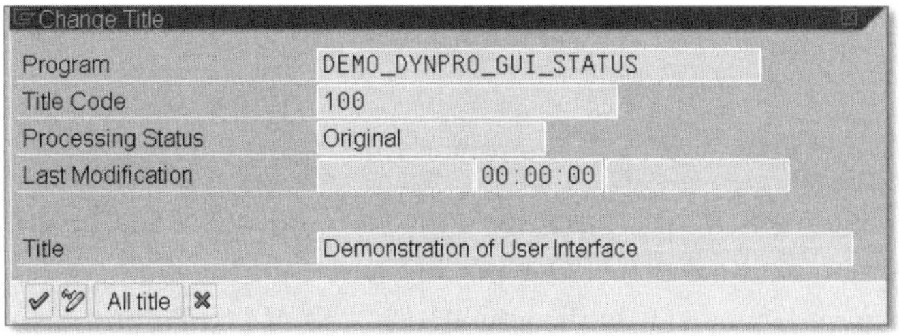

Figure 12.12 GUI Title Definition

Setting the GUI Status and the GUI Title

The GUI status and GUI title are assigned to the screen inside a dialog module called in the PBO event block. It is recommended that you define the GUI status and GUI title for each screen. If you have not assigned the GUI status and GUI title for the screen, then it inherits them from the previous screen of the transaction.

A screen can have more than one GUI status. For example, the GUI status for display mode might be different than the GUI status for edit or change mode. Therefore, the GUI status can be assigned dynamically to the screen. The GUI status and GUI title are set in the PBO event block by using the statements `SET PF-STATUS` and `SET TITLEBAR`, respectively, inside the dialog module with the PBO event block. You can also define buttons in your screen and assign the function code and use it instead of function codes or menu items defined via the GUI status.

The syntax to assign the GUI status and GUI title for the screen is shown in Listing 12.16.

```
MODULE init_screen_0100 output.
 IF SY-TCODE-TCODE = 'ZCHANGE'
  SET PF-STATUS 'STATUS_100'.
  SET TITLEBAR '100'.
 ELSEIF SY-TCODE = 'ZDISPLAY'.
  SET PF-STATUS 'STATUS_200'.
  SET TITLEBAR '200'.
 ENDIF.
ENDMODULE.
```

Listing 12.16 Assignment of GUI Status and GUI Title in PBO Module

The syntax to set a title that contains variables is as follows:

```
SET TITLEBAR XXX WITH <&1> ... <&9>
```

where XXX is the title name and <&1> to <&9> are variables from 1 to 9.

The GUI status might have many menu items and functions, but these can be disabled or deactivated dynamically in the PBO event block within the dialog module, or as we have discussed, they can be deactivated in the Menu Painter also. The functions can be deactivated by using the EXCLUDING <fcode> addition with the statement SET PF-STATUS. <fcode> can be hard-coded, a variable, or an internal table containing many function codes. The internal table should have all of the functions that have to be deactivated. The syntax to deactivate the function codes of the GUI status is shown in Listing 12.17.

```
MODULE status_0100 output.
  APPEND 'CHANGE' TO fcode.
  APPEND 'CHANGE' TO fcode.
  SET PF-STATUS 'STATUS_100' EXCLUDING fcode.
ENDMODULE.
```

Listing 12.17 Example Code to Deactivate Function Code

You then have to define the internal table fcode in the main program. The syntax of the internal table should be as follows:

```
DATA fcode TYPE TABLE OF sy-ucomm.
```

The selection of the function code on the screen triggers the PAI event, and based on the function code you can control the flow of the program. The function code is placed in the system variable SY-UCOMM and in the OK_CODE field of the screen, in the PAI event. If you have defined a variable with the same name as the OK type screen field, the function code will automatically be copied and can therefore be evaluated in the ABAP code. Listing 12.18 shows an example code for processing the function code in the PAI event block.

```
PROCESS AFTER INPUT
  ...
  MODULE USER_COMMAND_9001.
MODULE user_command_9001 INPUT.
  save_ok = ok_code.
  CLEAR ok_code.
   CASE save_ok.
    WHEN 'BACK'
     SET SCREEN 9000.
```

```
    WHEN 'EXIT'  or 'CANCEL'.
       LEAVE PROGRAM.
     WHEN OTHERS.
       output = save_ok.
  ENDCASE.
ENDMODULE.
```

Listing 12.18 Code to Control Program Flow for Individual Function Code

Table Control Programming

A table control is an area on the screen that is used to display or enter data in a tabular form. A table control has a table header, column headers, and columns. At runtime, a table control provides the functionality of vertical and horizontal scrolling, column width adjustment, row and column selection, and the ability to change the positions of columns. Figure 12.13 displays the various table control components.

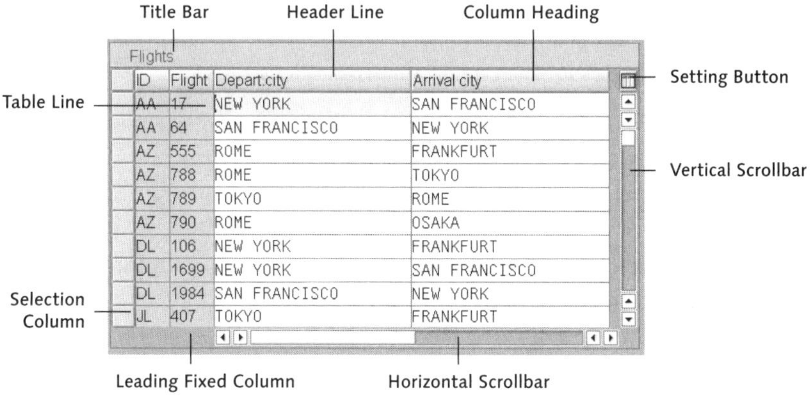

Figure 12.13 Components of Table Control

To define a table control you have to define the table control area, the table control elements, and the table title for the table control. All this is defined within the Screen Painter. You also need to declare the table control in the program. The Table Control icon is selected from the element pallet of the Screen Painter to create the table control area. Table columns for the control can be created from ABAP Dictionary fields or program fields. Column headings can be the ABAP Dictionary text associated with the field or can be custom text defined with a text field on the screen. The attributes of the table control and the table columns also have to be maintained, as do any other elements on the screen.

You can use the Table Control Wizard to create a table control quickly. This allows you to automatically create the table control, assign ABAP Dictionary or program fields for the columns, assign the attributes for the table columns, create some of the screen flow logic, generate the relevant PBO and PAI modules for the table maintenance, and generate the data definitions for the table control in the ABAP program. Table 12.3 displays the table control attributes you will specify on the Screen Painter during screen design.

Attribute	Description and Use
Tab Title	Indicates whether table control should have title or not.
w/ColHeads	Allows you to create column headings for the table control.
Configbl	Allows the user to save the table control settings at runtime.
Resizing	Indicates that the table supports vertical and horizontal sizing. You set this attribute if you want the table size to change with the GUI window size.
Separators	You can specify whether you want to have vertical and horizontal separators for the table columns and lines.
Line Sel.	Allows the user to select lines. You have the option of `NONE`, `SINGLE`, and `MULTIPLE` line selection for this attribute.
Column	Allows column selection. Choose `NONE`, `SINGLE`, or `MULTIPLE`.
w/sel. Column	Specifies whether a line selection column should appear for the table control. You have to specify the name of this column if you want to have the line selection column.
Fixed Column	Excludes one or more columns from horizontal scrolling.

Table 12.3 Table Control Attributes

The syntax for the table control in the program is as follows:

```
CONTROLS flights TYPE TABLEVIEW USING SCREEN 100
```

The table control name is `flights`, and it is created on screen number `100`. The table control name in an ABAP program should be identical to the table control created on the screen.

Screen Flow Logic for Table Control

When you process table controls, you must use the LOOP...ENDLOOP statement in the PBO and PAI event blocks in the screen flow logic. This statement is required for each table control on your screen. It is required to copy the data back and forth from the ABAP program to the table control fields and vice-versa.

The LOOP is required because the table control consists of several rows. You can also use the LOOP AT <INTERNAL_Table>... ENDLOOP statement in the screen flow logic. This form of the LOOP statement loops through the screen table and the internal table in parallel. Using this form of the loop statement, the system transfers the internal table rows to the screen fields and vice versa. Figure 12.14 displays the screen flow logic without an internal table, and Figure 12.15 displays screen flow logic with an internal table.

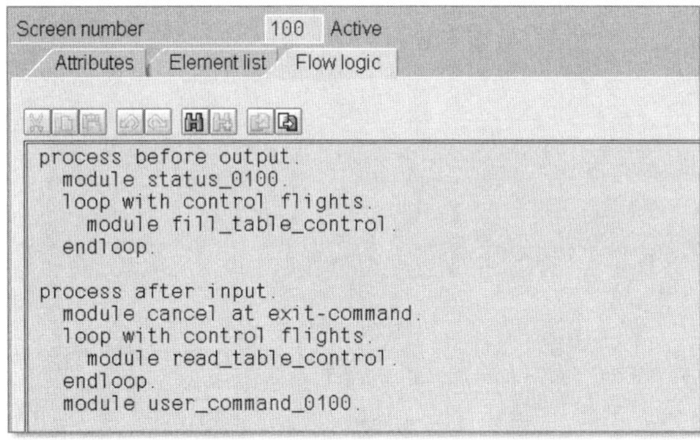

Figure 12.14 Flow Logic without Internal Table

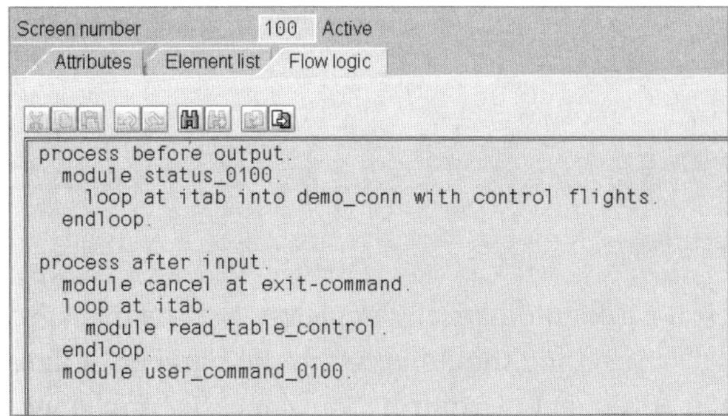

Figure 12.15 Flow Logic with Internal Table

The table control must be declared in the ABAP program for each table control defined on the screen. The control `flights` is the name of the table control on the screen. This statement declares a deep structure for the table control `flights` and is used to read the table attributes in the ABAP program. The data type of the deep structure corresponds to the type `CXTAB_CONTROL` defined in the ABAP Dictionary type group `CXTAB`.

The structure `CXTAB_CONTROL` is type `SCXTAB_CONTROL` and contains components that represent the attributes of the table control. The component `CXTAB_COLUMN` is a table of type `SCXTAB_COLUMN` and contains the attributes of the columns of the table control. Internal table `CXTAB_COLUMN` is a component of the structure `CXTAB_CONTROL`.

Figure 12.16 displays the structure `CXTAB_CONTROL`, and Figure 12.17 displays the structure `CXTAB_COLUMN`.

Structure: SCXTAB_CONTROL — Active
Short Description: TPDA: Table Control Settings = CXTAB_CONTROL

Attributes | Components | Entry help/check | Currency/quantity fields

Predefined Type — 1 / 13

Component	RTy...	Component type	Data Type	Length	Decima...	Short Description
FIXED_COLS			INT4	10	0	Number of Fixed Columns
LINES			INT4	10	0	Number of Lines to Be Displayed
TOP_LINE			INT4	10	0	Top Line for Next Picture Output PBO
CURRENT_LINE			INT4	10	0	Current Line in LOOP Processing
LEFT_COL			INT4	10	0	First Scrollable Column After the Fixed Area
LINE_SEL_MODE			INT4	10	0	Line Selection None(0), Single(1)
COL_SEL_MODE			INT4	10	0	Column Selection Multiple(2)
LINE_SELECTOR			CHAR	1	0	Indicator 'with Line Selection Col'
V_SCROLL			CHAR	1	0	not used
H_GRID			CHAR	1	0	Indicator 'Horizontal Grid Lines'
V_GRID			CHAR	1	0	Indicator 'Vertival Grid Lines'
COLS		SCXTAB_COLUMN_IT		0	0	TableControl Column Table
INVISIBLE			CHAR	1	0	

Figure 12.16 Table Control Structure

The ability to scroll using a scroll bar is automatically implemented and managed by the system. The control `flights-lines` should be set to the number of lines in the internal table before you edit the table control. You can easily implement the coding for scrolling the table control such as page up, page down, or goto page no. by using the table control attributes.

Structure SCXTAB_COLUMN Active
Short Description TableControl Column Settings

Attributes | Components | Entry help/check | Currency/quantity fields

Predefined Type 1 / 5

Component	RTy..	Component type	Data Type	Length	Decima..	Short Description
SCREEN		SCREEN		0	0	Structure Description for the System Data Object SCREEN
INDEX			INT4	10	0	Position of Column Within Table Control
SELECTED			CHAR	1	0	'Column Selected' Indicator
VISLENGTH		ICONLENGTH	INT1	3	0	Icon: Output length
INVISIBLE			CHAR	1	0	

Figure 12.17 Structure of the Table Control Column

Figure 12.18 displays the use of the table control attribute to implement page up and page down functionality for scrolling the table control.

```
module read_table_control input.
  lines = sy-loopc.
  modify itab from demo_conn index flights-current_line.
endmodule.

module user_command_0100 input.
  save_ok = ok_code.
  clear ok_code.
  case save_ok.
    when 'NEXT_LINE'.
      flights-top_line = flights-top_line + 1.
      limit = fill - lines + 1.
      if flights-top_line > limit.
        flights-top_line = limit.
      endif.
    when 'PREV_LINE'.
      flights-top_line = flights-top_line - 1.
      if flights-top_line < 0.
        flights-top_line = 0.
      endif.
    when 'NEXT_PAGE'.
      flights-top_line = flights-top_line + lines.
      limit = fill - lines + 1.
      if flights-top_line > limit.
        flights-top_line = limit.
      endif.
    when 'PREV_PAGE'.
      flights-top_line = flights-top_line - lines.
      if flights-top_line < 0.
        flights-top_line = 0.
      endif.
    when 'LAST_PAGE'.
      flights-top_line =  fill - lines + 1.
    when 'FIRST_PAGE'.
      flights-top_line = 0.
  endcase.
endmodule.
```

Figure 12.18 Implement Scroll Functionality with Table Control Attribute

Tip

See the demo programs `demo_dynpro_tabcont_loop` and `demo_dynpro_tabcont_loop_at` in the SAP system for the implementation of table control.

Modifying Screens Dynamically

You normally set the attribute of the screen element in the Screen Painter, but it is also possible to override the screen attribute in the ABAP program with the system table `SCREEN`. `SCREEN` is an internal table with the header line, and you do not need to declare this in the program. You cannot see this table in the Debugger, and you can only access it through its header line. Table 12.4 displays the structure of the `SCREEN` table.

Component	Length	Type	Meaning
NAME	132	C	Name of the screen field
GROUP1	3	C	Modification group 1
GROUP2	3	C	Modification group 2
GROUP3	3	C	Modification group 3
GROUP4	3	C	Modification group 4
REQUIRED	1	C	Field input is mandatory
INPUT	1	C	Field is ready for input
OUTPUT	1	C	Field is ready for output
INTENSIFIED	1	C	Field is highlighted
INVISIBLE	1	C	Field is suppressed
LENGTH	1	X	Field length
ACTIVE	1	C	Field is active
DISPLAY_3D	1	C	Three-dimensional box
VALUE_HELP	1	C	Input help button display
REQUEST	1	C	Input exists

Table 12.4 Screen Table Structure

You can modify the attribute of the screen element in an ABAP program during the PBO event block. You have an entry for each screen element in the system internal table SCREEN. You override the static screen attribute by modifying the screen attribute in the PBO event block. Listing 12.19 shows the example code to modify the screen attribute in the ABAP program.

```
PROCESS BEFORE OUTPUT.
MODULE modify_status_9001.
MODULE modify_status_9001 OUTPUT.
LOOP AT SCREEN.
  IF SCREEN-GROUP1 = 'GR1'
    SCREEN-INPUT = '0'.
  ELSEIF SCREEN-GROUP1 = 'GR2'.
    SCREEN-REQUIRED = '1'.
  ELSEIF SCREEN-GROUP1 = 'GR3'.
    SCREEN-ACTIVE = '0'.
  ENDIF.
ENDLOOP.
ENDMODULE.
```

Listing 12.19 Example Code to Modify Screen Attribute Dynamically in Program

Creating a Module Pool Program

Screens can be created for an executable programs, function groups, and module pools. You can start a screen in an executable program and function group using the CALL SCREEN statement, but screens in module pools can only be addressed using dialog transactions. In this section we will discuss the steps to create a module pool program, as follows:

1. Create a module pool program in the ABAP Workbench.
2. Create screens for the module pool program.
3. Create the flow for the screen in the PBO and PAI event blocks and optionally in the POH or POV event blocks if required.
4. Create PBO and PAI modules as processing blocks for the corresponding event.
5. Create the GUI status to evaluate user actions.
6. Create the GUI title.
7. Create the dialog transaction.

The program name for the module pool program should start with SAPMZ and then any meaningful name. For our example we will use the name SAPMZDEMO. You create the module pool program in the ABAP Workbench, and it proposes the top include module. You should select the proposal and continue. The top include module name for the above module pool program proposed by system is MZDEMOTOP.

After creating the module pool program, you can create new program objects such as screens, GUI status, and GUI titles for your program from the context menu in the object navigation area. Figure 12.19 displays the context menu (CREATE • PROGRAM) used to create the program objects from the object navigation area.

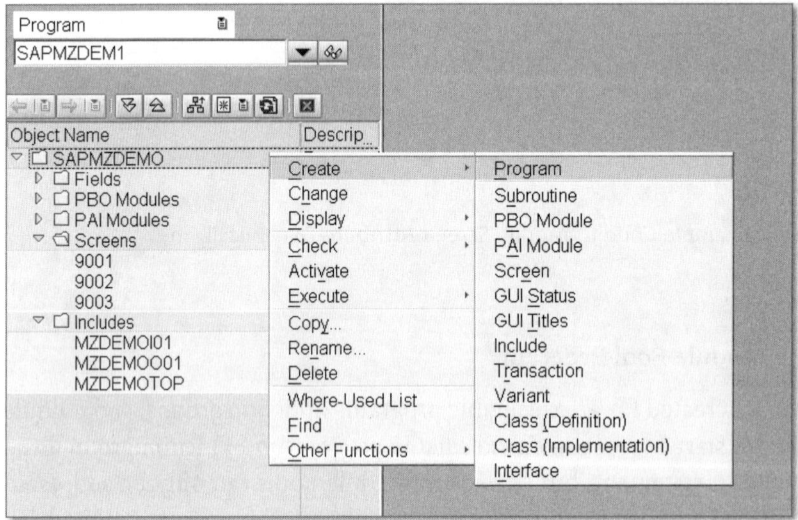

Figure 12.19 Context Menu to Create Program Objects

You then create the screen, screen flow logic, GUI status, and GUI title for the program, followed by the dialog module in the ABAP program. You can create the dialog module by forward navigation from the screen flow logic. The system will propose the include name for the PBO and PAI event modules. The standard name proposed by the system for the above program would be MZDEMOO01 for PBO modules and MZDEMOI01 for PAI modules, but you can create your own name and create a separate include for each module if you want (however, it's not recommended).

The forward navigation (by double-clicking on the module name in the screen flow logic) creates an empty module in the include program for each module defined in the flow logic. It is your task to write the code within the empty modules using ABAP language statements. You also need to declare the global variable in the top include program, `ZDEMOTOP`. This includes the declaration of the table structure used to create the screen fields or the user-defined screen element used to create the screen fields. Doing this ensures that the screen content is copied to the ABAP area with the matching field names.

Finally, you create the dialog transaction for the module pool program, whereby, at the most, you have to specify the module pool program, transaction text, and start screen for the transaction.

Important Terminology

You will need to understand the difference between the dialog screen and the selection screen. The selection screen for the executable program is called and controlled by the ABAP runtime. With the dialog screen you can control the screen flow, and you have to write the screen flow logic.

You cannot use the ABAP statement in the screen flow logic. In the screen flow logic you call the dialog module, and within the dialog module you can use ABAP statements.

There are four event blocks in the dialog screen: PBO, PAI, POV, and POH. The code within the PBO event block is executed before the screen is displayed, and the code within the PAI block is triggered when the user performs an action on the screen such as selecting the menu item, clicking on the button on the screen, pressing [↵], or selecting a function on a screen.

The GUI status is used to set the status of the screen that is used to display the menu bar, menu item, toolbar, and application bar. The GUI title is used to assign the heading to the screen. Finally, it is important to remember that the module pool program can only be accessed by the transaction code.

Practice Questions

The practice questions below will help you evaluate your understanding of the topic. The questions shown are similar in nature to those found on the certification examination, but whereas none of these questions will be found on the exam itself, they allow you to review your knowledge of the subject. Select the correct answers and then check the completeness of your answers in the following solution section. Remember that you must select all correct answers and only correct answers to receive credit for the question.

1. Which of the following is correct:

☐ **A.** The screen attributes can be modified in the `PROCESS AFTER INPUT` event block.

☑ **B.** The screen attributes can be modified in the `PROCESS BEFORE OUTPUT` event block.

☐ **C.** The screen attributes can be modified in the `PROCESS BEFORE OUTPUT` and `PROCESS AFTER INPUT` event blocks.

☐ **D.** None of the above

2. The static sequence of the default next screen can be established by the value in the screen attribute "next screen."

☐ **A.** True

☑ **B.** False

3. If you enter the value "0" or blank (" ") as the next screen, then the system resumes processing from the point at which the screen was initiated, assuming the next screen attribute is overridden dynamically in the program.

☑ **A.** True

☐ **B.** False

4. The next screen attribute can be temporarily overwritten by the set screen statement, that is, `SET SCREEN 200`.

☑ **A.** True

☐ **B.** False

5. The `FIELD` statement does not have any effect in the PBO event block, and it should not be used in the PBO event block.

☑ **A.** True

☐ **B.** False

6. The `FIELD` statement with the `ON INPUT` addition is used to conditionally call the ABAP dialog module. The ABAP dialog module is called if the value of the screen field is other than the initial value.

☐ **A.** True

☐ **B.** False

7. The `FIELD` statement with the `ON REQUEST` addition calls the ABAP dialog module if any value is entered in the screen field.

☐ **A.** True

☐ **B.** False

8. You can call a module for the `FIELD` statement to validate user entry on the input field. You can validate the entry on the input field and send an error or a warning message from an ABAP dialog module.

☐ **A.** True

☐ **B.** False

9. If an error or warning message is sent from the ABAP dialog module for the `FIELD` statement within the `CHAIN` and `ENDCHAIN` statements, then all of the fields within `CHAIN` and `ENDCHAIN` are ready for user input again.

☐ **A.** True

☐ **B.** False

10. The user interface consists of the GUI status and GUI title.

☐ **A.** True

☐ **B.** False

11. A menu bar can have at most 10 menus.

☐ **A.** True

☐ **B.** False

12. The application toolbar can have up to __ buttons on the screen.

☐ **A.** 20

☐ **B.** 30

- ☐ C. 10
- ☑ D. 35
- ☐ E. None of the above

13. A menu can have up to __ menu items on the screen including functions, separators, and submenus.

- ☑ A. 15
- ☐ B. 10
- ☐ C. 15
- ☐ D. None of the above

Practice Question Answers and Explanations

1. Correct answer: **B**

   The screen attributes can be modified in the `PROCESS BEFORE OUTPUT` event block.

2. Correct answer: **A**

   The screen sequence can be determined from the content of the next screen attribute field, but it can be overridden.

3. Correct answer: **A**

   If the next screen attribute is not specified, then the system will resume processing from the point at which the screen was initiated. Basically, a next screen of `0/space` terminates the screen sequence. This may result in the user exiting the application.

4. Correct answer: **A**

   The next screen attribute can be overwritten temporarily by using the `SET SCREEN` statement.

5. Correct answer: **A**

   The `FIELD` statement is used in conjunction with the module statement in the PAI event block to validate user input or to delay the transport of a field value from the screen to the ABAP program. The ABAP dialog module is called only if the value of the field is changed depending on whether the addition `ON INPUT` or `ON REQUEST` is used.

6. Correct answer: **A**

   The FIELD statement used in conjunction with the module statement with the ON INPUT addition is used to conditionally execute the ABAP dialog module if the input value of the field is other than the initial value according to the data TYPE of the input field.

7. Correct answer: **A**

   The ON REQUEST addition for the FIELD statement calls the ABAP dialog module only if a value is entered in the screen field.

8. Correct answer: **A**

   You call a module for the FIELD statement to validate user entry on the input field. The entry on the input field associated with the FIELD statement is validated with the dialog module, and accordingly, you can send an error or warning message. The input field is ready for re-input if the dialog module sends an error or warning message for the user input on the screen field.

9. Correct answer: **A**

   If an ABAP dialog module called with the FIELD statement within CHAIN and ENDCHAIN sends an error or warning message, then all of the fields within the CHAIN and ENDCHAIN are ready for user input.

10. Correct answer: **A**

    The user interface for a screen consists of the GUI status and the GUI title.

11. Correct answer: **B**

    The menu bar can have up to eight menus including the system and help menu, which means six can be defined by the developer.

12. Correct answer: **D**

    The application toolbar can have up to 35 buttons per screen.

13. Correct answer: **A**

    A menu can have up to 15 entries including functions, separators, and submenus.

Take Away

You should be able to describe the steps required to write a dialog transaction. You need to create screens, design the screen layout, create screen flow logic, and write an ABAP program for dialog programming. You also need to create a GUI status and GUI title and assign them to each screen. This displays the menu bar, menu items, and optionally, the application toolbar if it has been defined in the GUI status. You should be able to code the PROCESS BEFORE OUTPUT, PROCESS AFTER INPUT, PROCESS ON HELP-REQUEST, and PROCESS ON VALUE-REQUEST event blocks and should be aware of the screen/dynpro keywords that can be used in screen flow logic.

Refresher

Table 12.5 shows the key concepts for dialog programming.

Key Concept	Definition
Dialog screen	A dialog screen is designed with the Screen Painter. You set the general screen attributes on the attribute screen, design the screen layout, set the field attributes in the element list, and write the flow logic in the flow logic editor. These steps are required for each screen.
Dialog screen events	For each dialog screen you can have up to four event blocks: PROCESS BEFORE OUTPUT, PROCESS AFTER INPUT, PROCESS ON HELP-REQUEST, and PROCESS ON VALUE-REQUEST. You can write code for these four events for a dialog screen. The PBO and PAI event blocks are required, whereas the other two, that is, POH and POV, are optional.
GUI status	A GUI status is created with the Menu Painter and is required for any screen. GUI status is assigned to the screen to define the menu bar, menu items, application toolbar, and so on.
PROCESS ON HELP-REQUEST	You can write your own F1 help for screen fields. F1 help for a screen field is coded in the PROCESS ON HELP-REQUEST event block.
PROCESS ON VALUE-REQUEST	You can write your own custom value help (F4 help) for screen fields in the PROCESS ON VALUE-REQUEST event block.

Table 12.5 Key Concepts Refresher

Summary

We have covered screen design, various attributes of the screen, and the screen elements. We have also covered in detail the screen events PBO, PAI, POH, and POV and discussed how the data is transferred from the screen area to the ABAP program and vice versa. We have covered in detail the use of the GUI status and GUI title for dialog programming and the Menu Painter tool to design the GUI status. Finally, we have discussed how to assign a GUI status and title to the screen. This knowledge will allow you to easily pass this topic on the certification examination.

Selection Screens

13

Techniques You'll Master:

- Explain the purpose of selection screens
- Design a selection screen
- Create input fields with `PARAMETERS` and `SELECT-OPTIONS`
- Define selection screens with tabstrip control
- Define the selection screen events and their processing
- Implement input checks on selection screens

Selection screens are used to provide the user an interface to supply starting value for a report. The selection screen can be defined using ABAP language declarative statements. You can define selection screens for executable reports and can control the program flow based on the user input.

In this chapter you will learn about selection screens and their use in ABAP programming. You will learn how to create selection screens using `PARAMETERS` and `SELECT-OPTIONS`. You will learn to design the screen layout using simple ABAP statements. You will also learn about the various selection screen events and selection screen processing within ABAP programs. Finally, you will learn to create tabstrip control selection screens.

Real-World Scenario

You have to write a user-friendly report with selection screen, which allows user to enter data on the screen to control program flow. The report should expect input from the user, and based on this input the data should be extracted from the database for processing. The program flow and the list display should be based on the user input on the selection screen. You need to coordinate with the business and gather business requirements for the report.

To write a user-friendly report you need to have a good understanding of the selection screen and the various program events for the selection screen. You also have to educate the development team about the concept of the selection screen, its features, and how to use it for program development.

Objectives of this Portion of the Test

The objective of this portion of the certification exam is to examine your understanding regarding the selection screen. The exam will verify your knowledge regarding the various options available to design the selection screen.

Key Concepts Refresher

Selection screens are required for your custom programs when you want the user to input data to control the flow of the program or to restrict data extraction from the database. Selection screens are often used with an executable ABAP program such as ABAP reports, conversion programs, and so on.

You can define a standard selection screen by using ABAP language declarative statements such as PARAMETERS and SELECT-OPTIONS. Simple statements allow you to create input fields, checkboxes, and radio buttons. The ABAP language also provides you with the declarative statement SELECTION-SCREEN to format the layout of the selection screen without using the Screen Painter or Menu Painter. You can also define a user-defined selection screen apart from the default standard selection screen for the program.

Selection Screens

Selection screens serve as an interface between the user and the program. You often use selection screens to provide the user with an interface to input data for the program. This input data is used to control the program flow or to restrict or filter the data selection from the database. Selection screens are typically used in an executable program. The user simply has to use ABAP statements to create input fields, checkboxes, and radio buttons, whereas the dynpros (dialog screens) are created using the Screen Painter, and each dynpro screen requires screen flow logic. For more information regarding dynpro screens, refer to Chapter 12, Classical Screens. You can design the selection screen to allow the user to enter a single value or complex selection criteria.

The ABAP language declarative statements are used to define a selection screen for an ABAP program. You can design the screen layout, input fields, checkboxes, and radio buttons using these simple ABAP language statements and do not require the Screen Painter to define the selection screen for ABAP programs.

Selection Screen Design

The selection screen for a program is defined using ABAP language declarative statements, unlike dialog screens, which are designed using the Screen Painter and Menu Painter. The two statements to define selection screens are PARAMETERS and SELECT-OPTIONS.

PARAMETERS

The PARAMETERS statement is used to define a single input field on the selection screen. PARAMETERS are used to control the program flow or restrict the database access, so typically we would use this in the WHERE clause of our SELECT statement to filter which records we retrieve.

The data object declared with the PARAMETERS statement appears as an input field on the selection screen. You declare parameters with the TYPE or LIKE statement. similar to a variable declaration with the DATA statement. You can use ABAP types, local data types, or global data types to define the parameters for your program. The parameter name can be up to eight characters long. Unless you maintain the selection text for the parameter, the parameter name is displayed as text to the left of the input field. The text label can be maintained as a SELECTION TEXT by following the menu path GOTO • TEXT ELEMENTS • SELECTION TEXTS.

The PARAMETERS statement adopts the attribute of the ABAP Dictionary field if it refers to the data type from the ABAP Dictionary. The selection text for the PARAMETERS statement can be derived from the Dictionary, if the DICTIONARY REFERENCE checkbox is selected on the selection text screen. Figure 13.1 displays the selection text box with the option to adopt the selection text from the ABAP Dictionary.

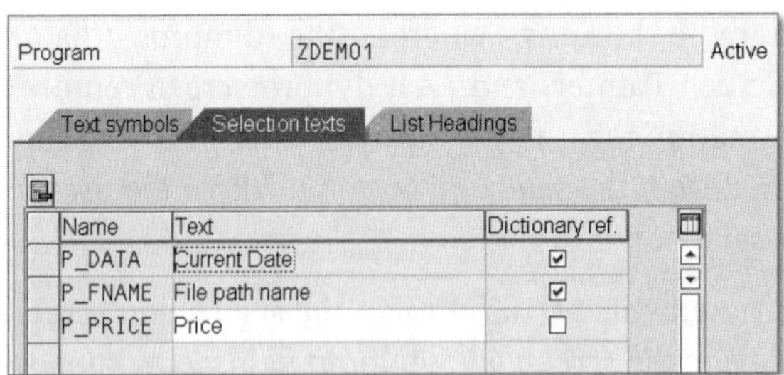

Figure 13.1 Selection Text for the Selection Screen Parameters

The following is an example to define for selection screen using the PARAMETERS statement:

```
REPORT ZDEMO1.
PARAMETERS:  p_fname TYPE rfpo-rfbifile OBLIGATORY,
             p_date  TYPE datum DEFAULT sy-datum,
             p_price TYPE P DECIMALS 2.
```

Figure 13.2 displays the selection screen for the above code.

Demo program for Selection Screen

File path name

Current Date 04/26/2009

Price

Figure 13.2 Selection Screen with Parameters Statement

With the DEFAULT addition you can set the default value for a parameter. The default value is displayed on the screen when the user executes the program, and he can change this default value on the selection screen if he wants. The addition OBLIGATORY is used to declare the input field as a required field on the selection screen. The addition MEMORY ID <PID> is used to specify the value of the input field from the SAP memory. <PID> is the PARAMETER ID for the data elements defined in the ABAP Dictionary. SAP memory is a user-specific memory area in which the value is stored for this PARAMATER ID for the duration of the user session. You use SET/GET PARAMETER ID to store or retrieve value from memory.

You can also use the PARAMETERS statement to declare checkboxes or radio buttons on the selection screen. The checkboxes are defined by using the addition AS CHECKBOX, and radio buttons are defined by using the addition RADIOBUTTON GROUP <GRP>, where <GRP> is the radio button group.

- Checkboxes can be used for data selection or program control. Technically, a checkbox is a one-character field of type C and can have a value of 'X' or blank (' '). You can provide a default value for the parameters object typed as a checkbox during the definition, or the user can check or uncheck the checkbox on the selection screen. The PARAMETER has the value 'X' if the checkbox is checked; otherwise, it has a blank value. Listing 13.1 is an example code to define and use a checkbox program.

```
REPORT ZDEMO_CHECKBOX.
PARAMETERS:   p_dispall AS CHECKBOX,
              P_archfl AS CHECKBOX DEFAULT 'X'.
              IF dispall IS INITIAL.
                WRITE: /'Display Error Records error only'.
              ELSE.
                WRITE: /'DISPLAY all records'.
              ENDIF.
              IF archfl IS NOT INITIAL.
                "Archive file
                WRITE: /'Archive File'.
              ENDIF.
```

Listing 13.1 Example Code to Define and Use a Checkbox in Program

- Radio buttons are always associated with a group in which you can select only buttons from the group. Technically, a radio button is a character field of type C and length 1. Radio buttons can have a value of 'X' or blank (' '). The radio button has a value of 'X' if it is selected on the screen; otherwise, it has a blank value. You can use radio buttons in your program to control the flow of the program. At any time only one radio button in the group can have a value of 'X', and the rest of the radio buttons in the group will have a blank value. Listing 13.2 is an example code to define and use of a radio button in program.

```
REPORT ZDEMO_RADIOBUTTON.
PARAMETERS:  p_pcfile AS RADIOBUTTON GROUP a,
             p_appfile AS RADIOBUTTON GROUP a.
             IF p_pcfile IS NOT INITIAL.
               WRITE: /'READ file from local PC'.
               "Read file from PC
             ENDIF.
             IF p_appfile IS NOT INITIAL.
               WRITE: /'READ file from application server'.
               "Read file from application server
             ENDIF.
```

Listing 13.2 Example Code to Define and Use a Radio Button in the Program

You can validate user entries against the check table or fixed values of the domain behind the ABAP Dictionary type. The input value entered on the selection screen will not be validated if the VALUE CHECK addition is not specified for the PARAMETERS. The check is performed even if the value for the parameter field is empty, so you should only use value check on a required (mandatory input) field. With the following parameter declaration, the user can only enter the value defined in the check table or the fixed value defined in the domain of the ABAP Dictionary data element s_carr_id.

```
PARAMETERS: p_carrid TYPE s_carr_id value check.
```

SELECT-OPTIONS

The SELECT-OPTIONS statement is used to define a complex selection that allows the user to enter value ranges and complex selection criteria instead of just a single input field. The variable name for the SELECT-OPTIONS input field can be up to eight characters. The SELECT-OPTIONS keyword generates a selection table. The selection table is an internal table with a standard structure and a header line. The internal table for the select option is populated automatically based on what the user enters in the SELECT-OPTIONS input fields, so you do not have to fill the field in the program.

The structure of the internal table consists of four components:

- SIGN
  The data type of SIGN is C, and it has a length of 1. The content of the SIGN determines whether the values are to be included or excluded. Possible values for this field are 'I' and 'E'. 'I' stands for inclusion criterion, and 'E' is for exclusion criterion.
- OPTION
  The data type for OPTION is C, and it has a length of 2. Table 13.1 shows the valid operators.

Value	Meaning
EQ	Equal
NE	Not equal
LE	Less or equal
LT	Less than
GE	Greater or equal
GT	Greater than
BT	Between
NB	Not between
CP	Contains pattern
NP	Does not contain pattern

Table 13.1 Valid Operators for Selection Table Field OPTION

- LOW and HIGH
  The data types for LOW and HIGH are the same as the type you give to the select-option. LOW is the lower limit HIGH is the higher limit for the selection criteria, and they correspond to the input fields on the screen. In combination with the operator in OPTION, the range specifies the selection criteria for the data selection.

  Use the addition FOR to specify the data object already defined in your program, which should be used to type, or define, the properties of the select option. Both the limit fields LOW and HIGH inherit the attributes of this reference field. Each line of the selection table formulates a condition for selection criteria.

The syntax for the SELECT-OPTIONS declaration is as follows:

```
TYPES: BEGIN OF ty_marc,
                  matnr TYPE marc-matnr,
                  werks TYPE marc-werks,
       END OF ty_marc.
DATA:  wa_marc TYPE ty_marc.
SELECT-OPTIONS:  s_matnr FOR wa_marc-matnr,
                 S_werks FOR wa_marc-werks.
```

MARC is a table, and matnr and werks are the fields of the table MARC. The above declaration creates two selection tables, s_matnr and s_werks, with corresponding input selection fields on the selection screen. Each SELECT-OPTIONS statement creates a selection table. Figure 13.3 displays the selection screen for the above declaration.

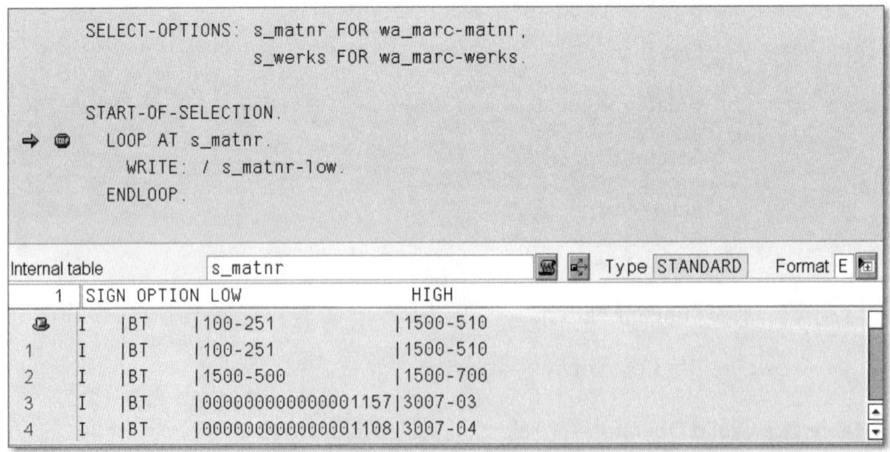

Figure 13.3 Selection Table for SELECT-OPTIONS Input Field

The user can specify multiple values for each of the SELECT-OPTIONS. Figure 13.4 displays the screen that specifies multiple values for the input field on the selection screen.

You can assign a default value for SELECT-OPTIONS. Use the following syntax to define the default value.

- To fill the default for the LOW field use:

  ```
  SELECT-OPTIONS:  s_matnr FOR marc-matnr DEFAULT 'A123'.
  ```

- To fill the default for the LOW and HIGH fields use:

```
SELECT-OPTIONS:  s_matnr FOR marc-matnr
                 DEFAULT 'A123' TO 'B123'.
```

- To fill the default for the OPTION field use:

```
SELECT-OPTIONS:  s_matnr FOR marc-matnr
                 DEFAULT 'A123' OPTION 'NE'.
```

- To fill the default for the SIGN field use:

```
SELECT-OPTIONS:  s_matnr FOR marc-matnr
                 DEFAULT 'A123' SIGN 'E'.
```

- To fill the default for all of the fields of the selection table use:

```
SELECT-OPTIONS:  s_matnr FOR marc-matnr
                 DEFAULT 'A123' TO 'B123'
                 OPTION 'NB' SIGN 'I'.
```

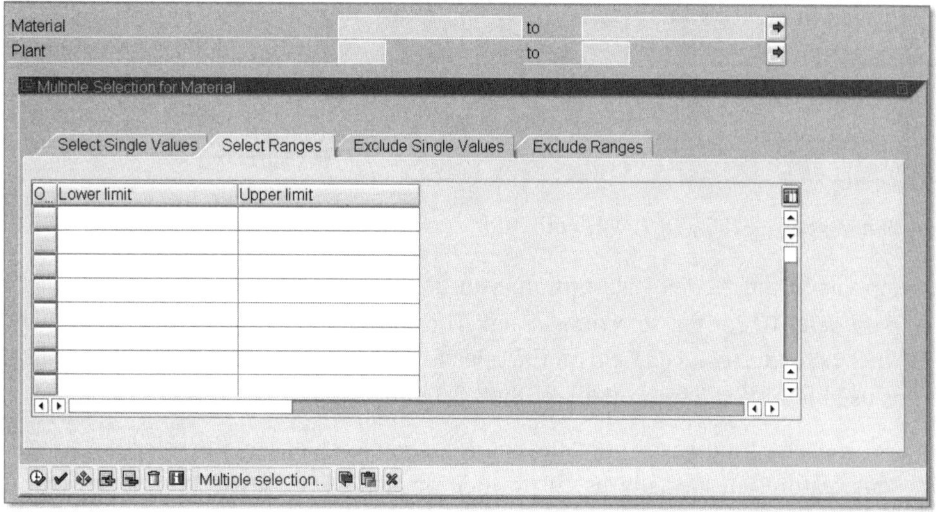

Figure 13.4 Value Range for Selection Table

You can populate default values dynamically in the selection table for the SELECT-OPTIONS fields in the program in the INITIALIZATION event block. For details regarding the INITIALIZATION event block refer to Chapter 9, Basic ABAP Programs and Interface Creation.

Use the addition NO-EXTENSION to restrict the user to adding only one range in the SELECT-OPTIONS input fields on the selection screen as follows:

```
SELECT-OPTIONS: s_matnr FOR marc-matnr NO-EXTENSION.
```

As a result, the push button for multiple selections will not appear on the selection screen as displayed in Figure 13.5.

Figure 13.5 SELECT-OPTIONS with Addition NO-EXTENSION

You can also use the addition NO INTERVALS to restrict the user to single field entry for the selection table. The syntax for single field entry is as follows:

```
SELECT-OPTIONS:   s_matnr FOR marc-matnr NO INTERVALS
                  S_werks FOR marc-werks.
```

As a result, the S_MATNR-HIGH is not displayed on the selection screen as displayed in Figure 13.6.

Figure 13.6 SELECT-OPTIONS with Addition NO INTERVALS

Similar to the PARAMETERS option, you use the addition MEMORY ID to GET/SET parameter ID for the selection screen. The addition OBLIGATORY is used to make the LOW field a required field on the selection screen. Also, the option NO-DISPLAY is used to hide the input field on the selection screen.

You can also modify the attributes of the screen element on the selection screen. This feature is especially useful to hide or change the attributes of the logical database selection screen within your custom program. You can modify the attribute of both the PARAMETERS and SELECT-OPTIONS fields on the selection screen. The event block AT SELECTION-SCREEN OUTPUT allows you to modify the selection screen directly before it is displayed. In a simplified form Listing 13.3 displays the code to modify selection screen attributes.

```
REPORT ZDEMO_MODIF_SCREEN.
NODES: SPFLI, SFLIGHT.
AT SELECTION-SCREEN OUTPUT.
LOOP AT SCREEN.
  IF SCREEN NAME = 'CARRID-HIGH'.
```

```
    SCREEN-ACTIVE = '0'.
    MODIFY SCREEN.
  ENDIF.
ENDLOOP.
```

Listing 13.3 Modify Selection Screen Attribute

Without the code within the `AT SELECTION-SCREEN OUTPUT` event block, the selection screen for the program with logical database appears as displayed in Figure 13.7, and with the code for the `AT SELECTION-SCREEN OUTPUT` the selection screen appears as displayed in Figure 13.8.

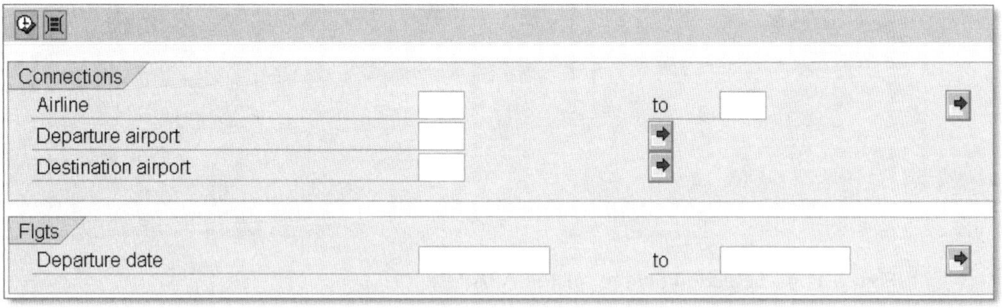

Connections
Airline to
Departure airport
Destination airport
Flgts
Departure date to

Figure 13.7 Selection Screen without Screen Modification

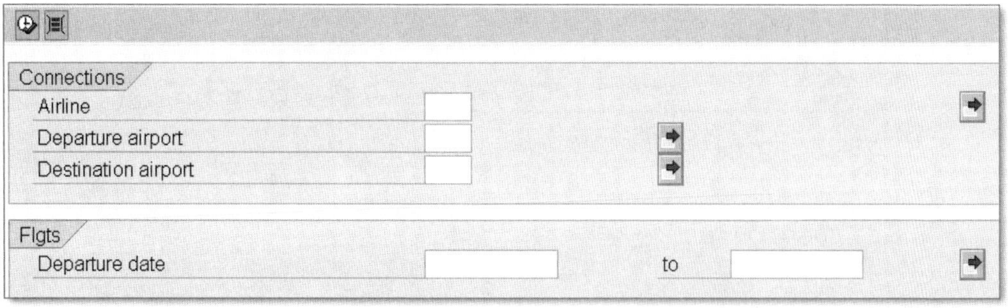

Connections
Airline
Departure airport
Destination airport
Flgts
Departure date to

Figure 13.8 Selection Screen with Screen Modification

Texts on the selection screen are stored as selection text in the program text elements. These selection screen texts can then be translated into other languages. The text elements for the program can be accessed from the program via the menu path GOTO • TEXT ELEMENTS • SELECTION TEXTS. Selection screen text can also be derived from the ABAP Dictionary if the selection screen elements refer to data types from the ABAP Dictionary as displayed in Figure 13.1. Figure 13.9

and Figure 13.10 show a selection screen and the selection texts for the selection screen in the ABAP program.

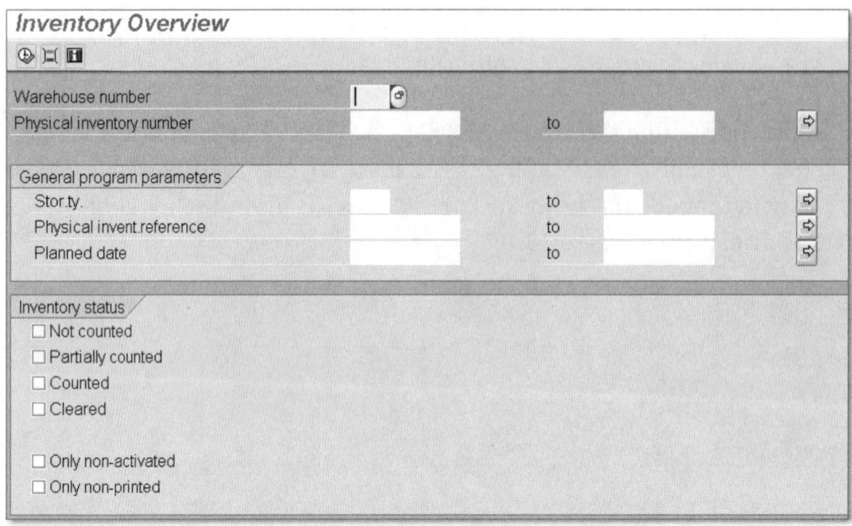

Figure 13.9 Selection Screen for the ABAP Report

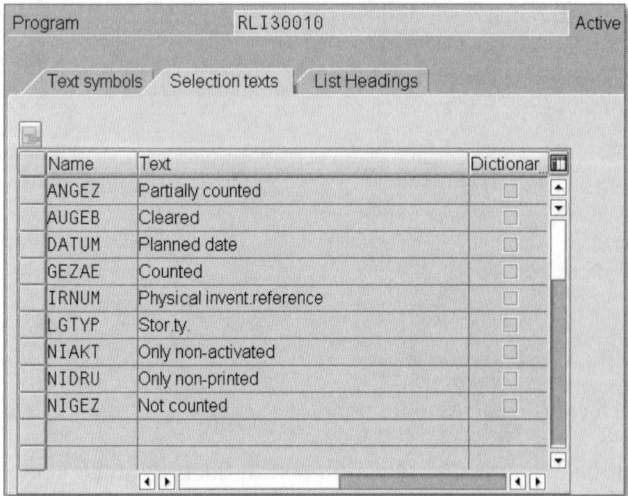

Figure 13.10 Selection Screen Texts

The user can create a program selection screen variant to store the input values for the selection screen. Selection screen variants are helpful if the user runs the program with the same sets of input value. It saves time and effort. The variant is also required if the program is scheduled to run in the background, so that the system knows which value is to be used to run the program.

The variant for the selection screen can be created in the ABAP Editor or from the selection screen itself by clicking on the SAVE icon (💾) on the screen or via the menu path GOTO • VARIANTS • SAVE AS VARIANT. Figure 13.11 displays the variant maintenance screen.

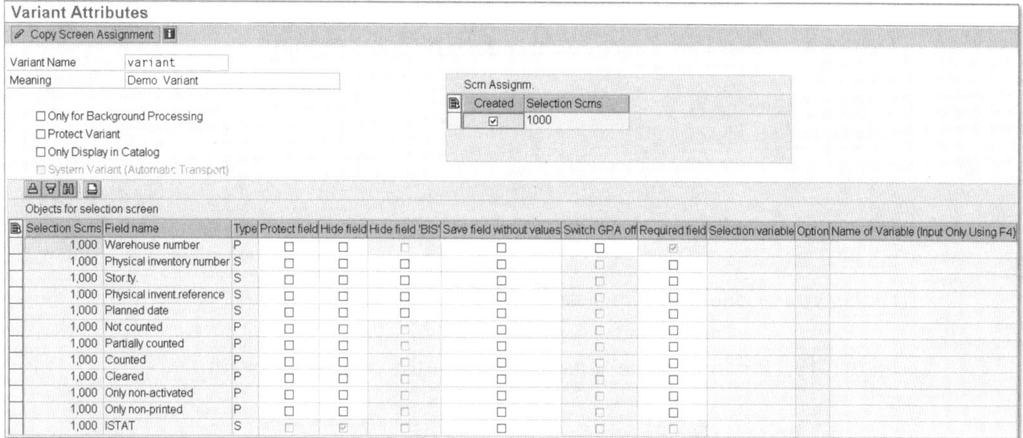

Figure 13.11 Variant Attribute Screen

You can define a standard selection screen and any number of user-defined selection screens. The standard selection screen is called automatically when you start the program, whereas the user-defined selection screen is called using the `CALL SELECTION-SCREEN` statement in the program. The standard selection screen has the default screen number `1000`, whereas the user-defined screen can have any screen number except `1000`.

Formatting the Selection Screen

The selection screen defined by the `PARAMETERS` and `SELECT-OPTIONS` statements has its own layout in which all of the `PARAMETERS` or `SELECT-OPTIONS` appear line by line. The `SELECTION-SCREEN` statement allows you to specify your own formatting options for the selection screen. You can define the layout of parameters and selection criteria and can display comments and underlines on the selection screen. In addition, you can place buttons on the selection screen or application toolbar. The formatting options can be used on the standard selection screen only if it has at least one input field.

Use the BEGIN OF BLOCK <block> addition to group together logically related screen elements and WITH FRAME to draw a frame around the logically related fields. You can nest frames to a depth of five levels. You should assign a heading to a block, using the TITLE addition; the block heading can be a text element or a field name up to eight characters long. Any block needs a SELECTION-SCREEN END OF BLOCK addition to indicate where it ends.

Listing 13.4 displays the code for a design screen layout:

```
SELECTION-SCREEN BEGIN OF BLOCK a WITH FRAME TITLE text-001.
PARAMETERS:  p_pc  RADIOBUTTON GROUP a,         "Local PC File
             p_app RADIOBUTTON GROUP a,         "Server File
             P_lgfile TYPE fileintern,          "Logical File
             P_phfile TYPE fileintern.          "Physical file
SELECTION-SCREEN END OF BLOCK a.
```

Listing 13.4 Code to Design Selection Screen Layout

Figure 13.12 displays the selection screen for the above example.

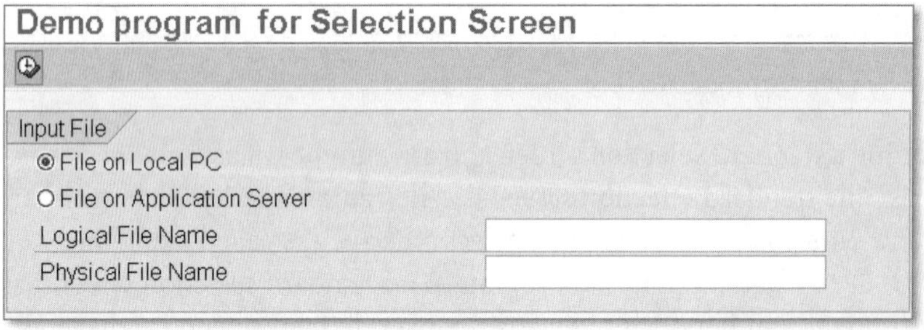

Figure 13.12 Selection Screen Formatting

You can also display multiple parameters and comments on the same output line. To do this you need to enclose them between SELECTION-SCREEN BEGIN OF LINE and SELECTION-SCREEN END OF LINE. The COMMENT addition allows you to include text in line. Comment text must always have a position and output length. You can define the position using POS_LOW and POS_HIGH. These are the positions of the upper and lower limits, respectively, of the field SELECT-OPTIONS on the selection screen. You can use POSITION <POS> to position the cursor on a line for the next output. This addition can only be used in between BEGIN OF LINE and END OF LINE.

Listing 13.5 displays the syntax to use the `BEGIN OF LINE` statement to design a selection screen layout:

```
SELECTION-SCREEN BEGIN OF BLOCK a WITH FRAME TITLE text-001.
PARAMETERS:  p_pc  RADIOBUTTON GROUP a,        "Local PC File
             p_app RADIOBUTTON GROUP a.        "Server File
SELECTION-SCREEN BEGIN OF LINE.
SELECTION-SCREEN POSITION 4.
PARAMETERS p_logi RADIOBUTTON GROUP 0002 DEFAULT 'X'.
SELECTION-SCREEN COMMENT  7(30) text-004 FOR FIELD p_logi.
PARAMETERS: p_lgfile      TYPE fileintern.
SELECTION-SCREEN END   OF LINE.
SELECTION-SCREEN BEGIN OF LINE.
SELECTION-SCREEN POSITION 4.
PARAMETERS p_phy RADIOBUTTON GROUP 0002.
SELECTION-SCREEN COMMENT  7(30) text-005 FOR FIELD p_phy.
PARAMETERS: p_phfile      LIKE  rfpdo-rfbifile.
SELECTION-SCREEN END OF LINE.
SELECTION-SCREEN END OF BLOCK a.
SELECTION-SCREEN BEGIN OF BLOCK b WITH FRAME TITLE text-003.
PARAMETERS: p_check RADIOBUTTON GROUP c DEFAULT 'X', "check fl
            p_procs RADIOBUTTON GROUP c.  "Process the file
SELECTION-SCREEN END OF BLOCK b.
```

Listing 13.5 Code for Selection Screen Layout

Figure 13.13 displays the selection screen with the formatted layout.

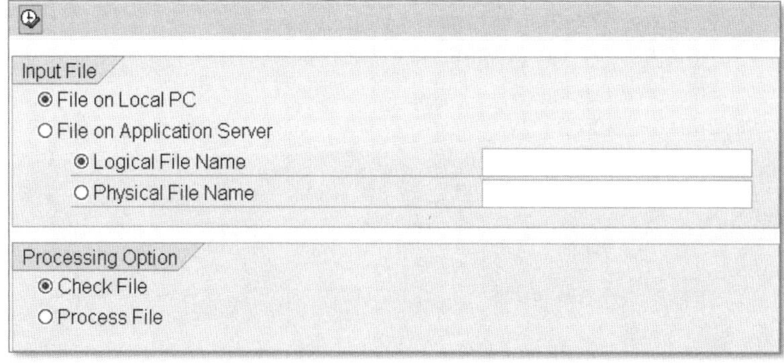

Figure 13.13 Formatted Selection Screen

You can also add a blank line to the selection screen by using `SELECTION-SCREEN SKIP <n>` or an underline by specifying `SELECTION-SCREEN ULINE`.

Selection Screen as Subscreen

It is also possible to define the selection screen as a subscreen in your ABAP program, and then this selection screen can be included as a subscreen on a screen or as part of a tabstrip control on a selection screen. The system processes the events `AT SELECTION-SCREEN OUTPUT` and `AT SELECTION-SCREEN` for each subscreen in addition to processing the surrounding selection screen. Refer to Chapter 9, Basic ABAP Programs and Interface Creation, for more information regarding program events. You work with the system variable `SYST-DYNNR` to determine which screen or subscreen is currently being processed. If you have many input fields on the selection screen, it may be a good idea to group together logically related screen elements in separate subscreens and display them as tabstrips.

Listing 13.6 defines the selection screen as a subscreen and includes it as part of a tabstrip control.

```
SELECTION-SCREEN BEGIN OF SCREEN 110 AS SUBSCREEN.
SELECTION-SCREEN BEGIN OF BLOCK a WITH FRAME TITLE text-010.
SELECT-OPTIONS: s_carrid FOR spfli-carrid,
                s_conn   FOR spfli-connid.
SELECTION-SCREEN END OF BLOCK a.
SELECTION-SCREEN END OF SCREEN 110.
SELECTION-SCREEN BEGIN OF SCREEN 120 AS SUBSCREEN.
SELECTION-SCREEN BEGIN OF BLOCK b WITH FRAME TITLE text-011.
SELECT-OPTIONS: s_cntrfr  FOR spfli-countryfr,
                s_cityfr  FOR spfli-cityfrom,
                s_airpfr  FOR spfli-airpfrom.
PARAMETERS:     s_depdt   LIKE sy-datum.
SELECTION-SCREEN END OF BLOCK b.
SELECTION-SCREEN END OF SCREEN 120.
SELECTION-SCREEN BEGIN OF SCREEN 130 AS SUBSCREEN.
SELECTION-SCREEN BEGIN OF BLOCK c WITH FRAME TITLE text-012.
SELECT-OPTIONS: s_cntrto  FOR spfli-countryto,
                s_cityto  FOR spfli-cityto,
                s_airpto  FOR spfli-airpto.
PARAMETERS:     s_retdt   LIKE sy-datum.
SELECTION-SCREEN END OF BLOCK c.
SELECTION-SCREEN END OF SCREEN 130.
SELECTION-SCREEN BEGIN OF TABBED BLOCK tab_block FOR 10 LINES.
SELECTION-SCREEN  TAB (20)  tab1  USER-COMMAND  comm1
 DEFAULT SCREEN 110.
SELECTION-SCREEN  TAB (20)  tab2  USER-COMMAND  comm2
```

```
 DEFAULT SCREEN 120.
SELECTION-SCREEN  TAB (20)  tab3  USER-COMMAND  comm3
 DEFAULT SCREEN 130.
SELECTION-SCREEN  END OF BLOCK tab_block.
INITIALIZATION.
  tab1 = 'Connection'(010).
  tab2 = 'Departure. City'(011).
  tab3 = 'Arrival City'(012).
  tab_block-activetab = 'COMM1'.
  tab_block-dynnr     = 110.
```

Listing 13.6 Example Code to Define Tabstrip Control for Selection Screen

Figure 13.14 displays the tabstrip on the selection screen for the above definition.

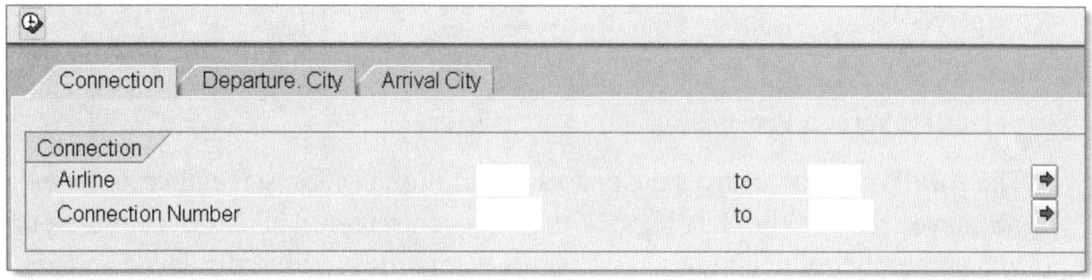

Figure 13.14 Tabstrips on the Selection Screen

You can use the optional addition `NESTING LEVEL` to further reduce the size of the subscreen. You can use it to prevent scrollbars from appearing when you use the subscreen in a tabstrip control on the selection screen and the tabstrip already has a frame. Use `NESTING LEVEL 0` if there is no frame around the tabstrip control; otherwise, for each frame around the tabstrip control, increase the `NESTING LEVEL` by one.

The tabstrip control is defined by the following syntax:

```
SELECTION-SCREEN BEGIN OF TABBED BLOCK tab_block FOR 10 LINES.
SELECTION-SCREEN  TAB (20)  tab1  USER-COMMAND  comm1
 DEFAULT SCREEN 110.
SELECTION-SCREEN  TAB (20)  tab2  USER-COMMAND  comm2
 DEFAULT SCREEN 120.
SELECTION-SCREEN  TAB (20)  tab3  USER-COMMAND  comm3
 DEFAULT SCREEN 130.
SELECTION-SCREEN  END OF BLOCK tab_block.
```

This defines a tabstrip control tab_block with a size of 10 lines. tab1, tab2, and tab3 are assigned to the tab area, and the length TAB (20) defines the width of the tab title. You must also assign a function code to each of the tab titles. For each tab title the system automatically creates a character field in the ABAP program with the same name. You can assign a text to this tab title variable before the selection screen is displayed. The field can be assigned a value during the INITIALIZATION event. The subscreen is assigned to each tab title, and is displayed when the user selects the tab.

For each tab area, the system automatically creates a structure in the ABAP program with the same name. This structure has three components: PROG, DYNNR, and ACTIVETAB. You can assign a value to this structure dynamically to control the display of the tabstrip. You can specify a value for ACTIVETAB and DYNNR to display a particular subscreen or tab by default when the selection screen is first displayed.

Selection Screen Processing

The ABAP runtime controls the processing of the selection screen because we do not have access to the flow logic of the selection screen. The ABAP runtime provides a number of selection screen events before the screen is displayed and after the user action on the selection screen. You can write your own code to control the display of the screen or to react to the user action on the selection screen.

Selection screen processing starts after the INITIALIZATION event. You can populate the default value for the input field on the selection screen in the INITIALIZATION event block. The INITIALIZATION event block is executed only once, even if the selection screen is processed several times.

The event AT SELECTION-SCREEN OUTPUT allows you to dynamically modify the screen before it is displayed or prepare the screen. Like PBO for a classical screen, this event block is executed every time the screen is displayed, unlike the INITIALIZATION event. The at SELECTION-SCREEN OUTPUT event is triggered when you click on the multiple selection button for the SELECT-OPTIONS input field, the dynamic selection button, or the tabstrip screens. You modify the screen attribute in this event block. This event is specifically useful to modify the logical database selection screen if you want to hide or change the attribute of the screen fields without modifying the code of logical database selection screen.

User action on the selection screen results in events that are either used to validate field input or possible entries or help request or trigger PAI processing of the selection screen.

The `AT SELECTION-SCREEN` event is triggered by the ABAP runtime after the user selects EXECUTE or presses [↵] on the selection screen. The programmer can validate the user input or action in the `AT SELECTION-SCREEN` event. You can trigger a warning message in the `AT SELECTION-SCREEN` event based on your validation for the screen field. A warning message is displayed, and after you press [↵], all of the fields will be ready for input. You can process this while the program is executing because it is just a warning message. Similarly, if the program has triggered an error message in this event block, all of the fields will be ready for input, and the program will expect you to enter a valid value on the input screen before it proceeds with the execution.

The `AT SELECTION-SCREEN ON <field_name>` event can be used to validate a specific input field `<field_name>`, and only that field will be ready for input if an error message is triggered in the block. You can have an `AT SELECTION-SCREEN ON` event for each of the input fields on the selection screen if you want to validate the user input on each of the screen.

The event `AT SELECTION-SCREEN ON BLOCK <block>` is triggered again when the user selects Execute, and this time the contents of all fields of the block are passed to the ABAP program. You should use this for validating user input. All of the fields in the block are ready for input again if an error message is triggered. You can control the program flow or validate the user input for the input field within this block. You have the following additional selection screen events:

- `AT SELECTION-SCREEN ON RADIOBUTTON GROUP <grp>`
  This event is triggered when the user clicks on the EXECUTE button on the screen, and then the content of the radio button group is passed to the ABAP program. You can validate the whole group and then, based on your validation, send an error message. The radio button group is ready for input if an error message is triggered as a result of validation within the event block.
- `AT SELACTION-SCREEN ON HELP-REQUEST FOR <FIELD>`
  This event is triggered when the user calls the F1 help on the selection screen. You can develop your own help routine for this event. The ABAP Dictionary help is displayed if no corresponding event block is defined for this event. We normally want to see the help from the ABAP Dictionary if the input field refers to the ABAP Dictionary data type.

- AT SELECTION-SCREEN ON VALUE-REQUEST FOR <Field>
  This event is triggered when the user calls value help (F4) on the screen field. The value help displays the possible values from the ABAP Dictionary if no corresponding event block for this event is developed; otherwise, it displays the possible value from the event block. We want to see ABAP Dictionary help if the input field refers to an ABAP Dictionary data type.

Important Terminology

You will need to understand ABAP statements to create selection screens. You should have a good understanding of ABAP statements to create selection screens and the statements for screen layout design.

You can use simple ABAP declarative statements such as PARAMETERS and SELECT-OPTIONS to create input fields for selection screens. You can also use SELECTION-SCREEN statements to design selection screen layout. The selection screen events allow you to control the display of a screen or react to user actions on screen. You can also program F1 help and possible F4 values for input fields on the selection screen by programming the F1 and value help in the event blocks AT SELECTION-SCREEN ON VALUE-REQUEST and AT SELECTION-SCREEN ON HELP-REQUEST.

Practice Questions

The practice questions below will help you evaluate your understanding of the topic. The questions shown are similar in nature to those found on the certification examination, but whereas none of these questions will be found on the exam itself, they allow you to review your knowledge of the subject. Select the correct answers and then check the completeness of your answers in the following solution section. Remember that you must select all correct answers and only correct answers to receive credit for the question.

1. The default selection screen number for the ABAP program is:

☐ **A.** 1000

☐ **B.** 100

☐ **C.** 1100

☐ **D.** None of the above

2. You can have only one selection screen for an ABAP program.

☐ **A.** True

☐ **B.** False

3. The declarative statements used to define the selection screen are:

☐ **A.** `PARAMETERS`

☐ **B.** `SELECT-OPTIONS`

☐ **C.** `SELECTION-SCREEN`

☐ **D.** None of the above

4. You use the addition `OBLIGATORY` to define the input field of a parameter as a required field.

☐ **A.** True

☐ **B.** False

5. Which of the following statements are correct:

☐ **A.** The `SELECT-OPTIONS` statement creates an internal table with a header line. The internal table is also known as the selection table.

☐ **B.** The structure of the selection table created with `SELECT-OPTIONS` has four components: `SIGN`, `OPTION`, `LOW`, and `HIGH`.

☐ **C.** You can use the addition `NO-DISPLAY` to hide the input field on the selection screen.

☐ **D.** You can only specify default values for the `LOW` and `HIGH` fields of the `SELECT-OPTIONS` input field.

6. Your selection screen can be modified at the event:

☐ **A.** `AT SELECTION-SCREEN OUTPUT`

☐ **B.** `AT SELECTION-SCREEN`

☐ **C.** `AT SELECTION-SCREEN on <field_name>`

☐ **D.** None of the above

7. Which of the following statements is correct regarding the event `AT SELECTION-SCREEN on HELP-REQUEST FOR <FIELD>`?

- ☐ **A.** Will display F1 help for the input field on the selection screen.
- ☑ **B.** This event will display self-defined F1 help for the input field programmed in the event block and will override any help possibly defined in the ABAP Dictionary for the field.
- ☐ **C.** None of the above

8. You can define multiple elements in a single line by defining the element within the block `SELECTION-SCREEN BEGIN OF LINE` and `SELECTION-SCREEN END OF LINE`.

- ☑ **A.** True
- ☐ **B.** False

9. The addition `NO-EXTENSION` for `SELECT-OPTIONS` will allow only one line in the selection table.

- ☑ **A.** True
- ☐ **B.** False

10. The addition `NO-INTERVALS` for `SELECT-OPTIONS` will allow only single fields on the selection screen.

- ☑ **A.** True
- ☐ **B.** False

11. You can define a selection screen as a subscreen or tabstrip control.

- ☐ **A.** True
- ☑ **B.** False

Practice Question Answers and Explanations

1. Correct answer: **A**

   The default selection screen number is 1000. You can define any number of user-defined screens with other numbers.

2. Correct answer: **B**

   You can have more than one selection screen within an ABAP program. You can have one default selection screen and any number of user-defined selection screens.

3. Correct answers: **A, B, C**

   You use PARAMETERS and SELECT-OPTIONS to define the input fields on the selection screen, and you use the SELECTION-SCREEN statement to format the layout of the selection screen.

4. Correct answer: **A**

   You use the addition OBLIGATORY to define the input field PARAMETERS and SELECT_OPTIONS as required fields.

5. Correct answers: **A, B, C**

   The SELECT-OPTIONS statement creates an internal table with a header line. The name of the internal table is the same as the SELECT-OPTIONS variable name. The row type of the internal table is a structure with the four components SIGN, OPTION, LOW, and HIGH. You can hide the input field with the addition NO-DISPLAY, and you can define default values for each of the structure components of the selection table.

6. Correct answer: **A**

   The selection screen can be modified in the event block AT SELECTION-SCREEN OUTPUT.

7. Correct answer: **A**

   The event AT SELECTION-SCREEN on HELP-REQUEST FOR <FIELD> displays the F1 help for the input field. It displays F1 help from the ABAP Dictionary if F1 help is not programmed in the event block.

8. Correct answer: **A**

   You can define multiple elements on the same line by defining the elements within the blocks SELECTION-SCREEN BEGIN OF LINE and SELECTION-SCREEN END OF LINE.

9. Correct answer: **A**

   The addition NO-EXTENSION for the SELECT-OPTIONS hide the button for multiple selection. As a result, the user cannot specify more than one line for the selection criteria.

10. Correct answer: **A**

    The addition `NO INTERVALS` hides the second input field (`HIGH`) for the `SELECT-OPTIONS` statement. As a result a user can only enter a value for a single input field (`LOW`) or range of value for the single input field. The user will see a single input field, but he will get the button for multiple selection. When you select the multiple selection dialog box, you can enter ranges, multiple ranges, multiple single values, and so on.

11. Correct answer: **A**

    You can define the selection screen with a subscreen or tabstrip control using the ABAP language declarative statement.

Take Away

You should be able to describe the use of selection screens in ABAP programming. You need to understand how to define the selection screen and should know the keywords and the syntax to define the selection screen. It is important to know the formatting options available to design the selection screen layout and to know the various events available for selection screens.

You should also be able to design standard selection screens, tabstrips on selection screens, and subscreens for use on these tabstrips within the ABAP program and be able to dynamically modify or validate the user input on the screen or provide the possible entries for the fields within the appropriate event blocks.

Refresher

Table 13.2 shows the key concepts for selection screen.

Key Concept	Definition
Selection screen	A selection screen is an interface between the user and the program. You can define a selection screen by using the ABAP language declarative statements such as `PARAMETERS` and `SELECT-OPTIONS`, and you can design the screen layout with the declarative statement `SELECTION-SCREEN` without using the Screen Painter or Menu Painter.

Table 13.2 Key Concepts Refresher

Key Concept	Definition
Selection screen events	You can dynamically modify the selection screen during the AT SELECTION-SCREEN OUTPUT event. You can validate the user input on the AT SELECTION-SCREEN ON <FIELD> event for each of the input fields on the screen, if required.
Tabstrip control	You can define subscreens for use on user-defined tabstrip controls on the selection screen with the ABAP language declarative statements for screen design.

Table 13.2 Key Concepts Refresher (cont.)

Summary

You should now be able to design and use selection screens in ABAP programming. You should know the syntax to define standard selection screens, subscreens, tabstrip controls on the selection screen, and the various events to validate user input or control the program flow. You should also know the ABAP statements and syntax for selection screen layout formatting. You should now be able to work with the selection screen design and use selection screens in the ABAP program. This knowledge will allow you to easily pass this topic on the certification examination.

ABAP Object-Oriented Programming

14

Techniques You'll Master:

- Understand the object-oriented programming concepts
- Describe the components of an ABAP class
- Explain the visibility sections of a class
- Understand the most important components of a class: attributes, methods, and events
- Create a local class definition and implementation, and a global class
- Describe the difference between instance and static components
- Define the instance constructor and the class constructor methods for a class

ABAP Objects is a complete set of object-oriented statements that has been introduced with the ABAP language. ABAP Objects supports complete object-oriented programming that includes definition of local and global classes, creation of objects from classes, and specialization of classes via inheritance. A class is the basis of an object-oriented programming language. A class is a template for an object. A class describes objects, and an object is the runtime instance of that class. You need to define a class to use objects in the program. You can create global and local classes in the ABAP language. Global classes are visible to every program in the system and can be used by every program, whereas local classes are visible to the program in which they are defined.

The main objective of this chapter is to provide you the concepts of ABAP object-oriented programming with ABAP Objects. We will discuss the concept of ABAP classes because it is the foundation of ABAP object-oriented programming. We will discuss the key components of ABAP classes such as attributes, methods, and events and the concept of visibility in a class. We will cover in detail the syntax to create local classes, attributes, methods, and events and the syntax to access and use them in ABAP programs. We will also cover global classes and the steps to create them. Finally, we will discuss class instantiation, various types of method and attributes, their visibility, and the syntax to create object access of individual class and object components in the ABAP program, as well as the syntax to trigger events and register handler methods.

Real-World Scenario

As a technical lead on a project you have to explain the basics of object-oriented programming to the developer in your team. Your development team has to develop a Web Dynpro application and reports using ALV grids and use GUI control using control framework and should be aware of ABAP Objects techniques.

To use the technique you should have a good understanding of object-oriented programming, ABAP class declaration, implementation, and the various components of an ABAP class. You should be aware of encapsulation, inheritance, polymorphism, and abstraction and should be able to use these concepts effectively in custom application development.

Objectives of this Portion of the Test

The objective of this portion of the exam is to judge your knowledge about object-oriented programming concepts. You are expected to be able to create ABAP classes for use in your programs, both the definition part and the implementation part, and to be able to use global classes for application development. You should be able to explain the various components of an ABAP class and the visibility sections such as public, private, and protected sections. You should be able to create ABAP Objects programs that contain all useful object-oriented programming techniques.

Key Concepts Refresher

It's important to understand the ABAP Object concepts because SAP is developing new applications using the object-oriented programming techniques. This chapter will introduce the basics of object-oriented programming concepts and the key components required to create an ABAP class. The key components discussed in this chapter are attributes, methods, and events. Advanced topics with regard to ABAP Objects programming are covered in Chapter 17, Class Identification Analysis and Design.

Object-Oriented Programming Concepts

Object-oriented programming involves programming using objects. Business objects such as customers, materials, and purchase orders are examples of real-world objects. The real-world objects have states and behaviors. For example, a purchase order has states such as purchase order number, vendor number, and purchasing organization and behaviors such as create purchase order, display purchase order, and change purchase order. The goal of object-oriented programming is to map the real-world object to a software object as accurately as possible. This helps the business user and the developer communicate more effectively with each other.

The state of the real-world object is represented by attributes, and the behavior of the real-world object is represented by methods. A method is a block of code, such as a function module or subroutine, associated with the object. Thus, a software object consists of attributes and methods.

Object-oriented programming encapsulates attributes and methods and provides a defined interface (Methods) to access the attributes of the object. The outside world can communicate with the object using the defined interface. If you want to access the attributes of the object, you call a method to do so, and this method has parameters that determine what data you must pass in and what data you get back from the method. The internal status of the object and its implementation is hidden from the outside world and cannot be modified or viewed. The attributes of the object can only be changed by calling public methods of the object and cannot be changed directly. You can change the attributes directly if they are public, but usually the attributes are private, so they are usually changed by calling public methods.

The object-oriented programming model supports following characteristics:

- **Abstraction process**
  The abstraction process refers to mapping the real-world processes in a class as accurately as possible. Abstraction is an essential element of object-oriented programming and is achieved through the use of hierarchical classification. A complex object can be broken into more manageable pieces. Each object describes its own unique behavior.
- **Encapsulation**
  The implementation of the class is hidden and can only be accessed by means of the class interface, that is, by calling the methods of the class. The purpose of a class is to hide complexity from the outside world. Each method and attribute can be private or public. A public method can be accessed by an external user, for example, an ABAP program. The private attribute or methods can be accessed directly only from within the class itself and can be accessed by an external application through public methods only.
- **Inheritance**
  Inheritance means deriving one class from another. The attributes and methods are inherited from the higher-level class, known as the superclass and can be extended; that is, the methods can be redefined, and new components can be added. A class inherits the attributes and methods from the parent class and can define new components that make it unique within its class hierarchy.
- **Polymorphism**
  Polymorphism is where objects of different classes react in different ways to the same method call. It can be achieved through inheritance or through the use of Interfaces.

ABAP Objects

ABAP Objects is an objected-oriented extension of the ABAP language, and it is now also the term used to refer to the entire ABAP language. ABAP Objects supports object-oriented programming techniques.

It basically consists of a set of ABAP statements that support object-oriented programming such as definition of classes, creation of objects from classes, specialization of classes via inheritance, independent interfaces that can be used in classes, and the event concept that is integrated into the language.

ABAP Class

Classes are the foundation of object-oriented programming. A class is a blueprint or template for objects. A class describes an object, and the object is a runtime instance of that class. You can create any number of objects based on a single class, and each instance (object) of the class has its own unique identity and its own set of values for its attributes.

Classes in ABAP Objects can be declared either locally within the application where they are to be used or globally as repository objects. The advantage of creating global classes is that they can be reused in many different applications. Global classes are defined in the Class Builder (Transaction SE24) in the ABAP Workbench. Global classes are stored centrally in the Repository. Global classes can be used by any program in the SAP system. Local classes are defined locally in the ABAP program and are visible in the program in which they are defined.

Local Classes

Local classes are defined within an ABAP program and can be used only in the program in which they are defined. Listing 14.1 displays the most important component of a local ABAP class in a code template. In the following section we will cover individual components of the class including the visibility concepts.

```
CLASS CL1 DEFINITION.
PUBLIC SECTION.
  DATA: d1, d2.
  METHODS: M1.
  EVENTS: EV1.
PROTECTED SECTION.
  DATA: d3, d4,
```

```
  METHODS: M2.
  EVENTS: EV2.
PRIVATE SECTION.
  DATA: d5, d6.
  METHODS: M3.
  EVENTS: EV3.
ENDCLASS.
CLASS CL1 IMPLEMENTATION.
  METHOD M1.
  ENDMETHOD.
  METHOD M2.
  ENDMETHOD.
  METHOD M3.
  ENDMETHOD.
ENDCLASS.
```

Listing 14.1 Template for ABAP Class

A class definition consists of a declaration part and an implementation part. The declaration part of the class is within the statement block `CLASS...ENDCLASS`.

Following is the syntax for the class declaration:

```
CLASS <class_name> DEFINITION.
ENDCLASS.
```

The declaration part of the program contains the definition of all of the components of the class. This includes attributes, methods, and events. Any methods defined in the `DEFINITION` part must be implemented in the implementation section of the class.

The methods of the class are implemented in the following statement block:

```
CLASS <class_name> IMPLEMENTATION.
  METHOD metha.
  ENDMETHOD.
  METHOD methb.
  ENDMETHOD.
ENDCLASS.
```

Each component of the class must be assigned to one of the following three visibility sections. All of the components are visible within the class. All components of the class are in the same namespace, which means that all components of the class must have a unique name.

The class components can be declared in three visibility areas: PUBLIC, PRIVATE, and PROTECTED. When defining local classes in ABAP Objects, you must follow the syntactical sequence of PUBLIC SECTION, PROTECTED SECTION, and PRIVATE SECTION.

Global Classes

Global classes and interfaces are stored in a class library and are visible system-wide. Global classes can be used by every program in the system. The Class Builder allows you to create and maintain global classes and interfaces. You can use the Class Browser to display global classes, interfaces, or business object types from the class library. The Class Browser is an integrated part of Class Builder and can be started via Transaction CLABAP.

To create a new global class, enter the name of the class on the initial screen of the Class Builder (Transaction SE24) and select CREATE. The name of the class should start with ZCL_<meaningful_name>. The CREATE CLASS dialog box appears with the name of the class. Figure 14.1 displays the Create Class dialog box.

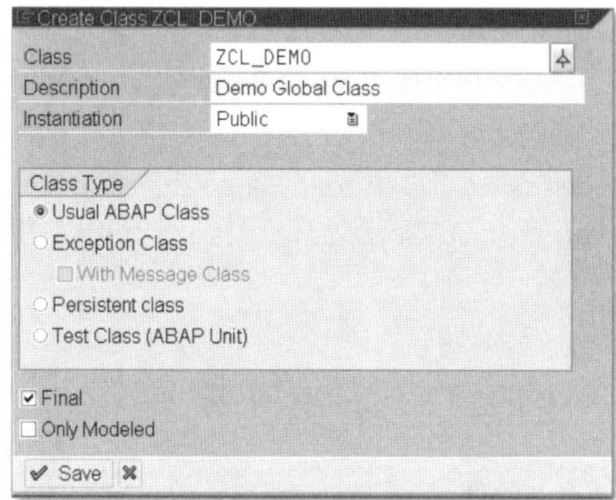

Figure 14.1 Create Global Class Dialog Screen

You need to populate the following detail on the create class dialog box.

- DESCRIPTION
  Enter a short text describing the class.
- INSTANTIATION
  Selects the instantiation option. You have the option to select PUBLIC, PROTECTED, PRIVATE, or ABSTRACT (see next section, Class Visibility and Instantiation, as well):

- Public
  Usually you select the public instantiation. This means the user can create an instance of this class with the CREATE OBJECT statement.
- Protected
  Protected instantiation specifies that only inherited classes or the relevant class itself can create the instances of this class.
- Private
  Private instantiation specifies that only the relevant class itself can create instances of the class using its own method.
- Abstract
  You select the abstract instantiation to define an abstract class. An abstract class is used as a template to create a subclass. You cannot create an instance of this class. You can access such a class with the static attribute or with its subclasses.

- Class Type
  You have the option to select Usual ABAP Class, Exception Class, Persistent Class, or Test Class:
  - Usual ABAP Class
    This is the standard ABAP class and is discussed in this chapter.
  - Persistent Class
    The mapping of ABAP Objects classes to relational database tables is referred to as object-relational mapping or O/R mapping. Classes with O/R mapping are referred to as persistent classes.
  - Exception Class
    These are special classes used for class-based exception handling.
  - Test Class
    This is a test call and cannot be instantiated.

  For our example we would select Usual ABAP Class radio button.
- Final
  You can define the final class by selecting the checkbox. This means you cannot create the subclass for this class.
- Only Modeled
  If you select this option, the class is not stored in class library and you cannot address it at runtime or test it.

Click on the SAVE button after you have entered the relevant detail on the create class dialog screen. You have to provide the package name after you click on the SAVE button on the dialog screen. Then the class editor appears with the method tab selected. From here on you can define individual components of the class. Figure 14.2 displays the class editor screen that is displayed after you click on SAVE on the CREATE CLASS dialog window.

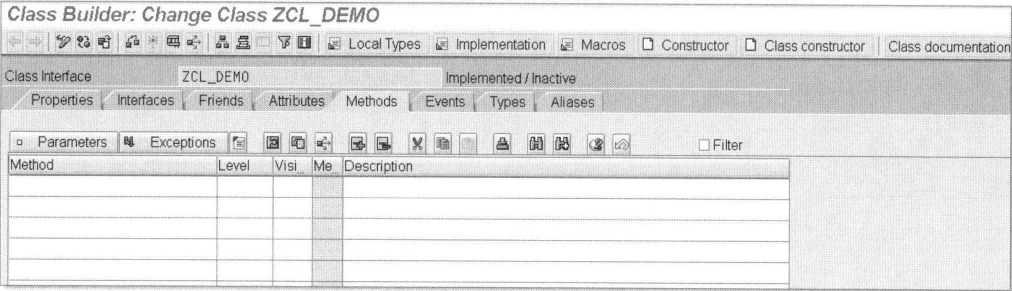

Figure 14.2 Class Editor Screen to Create a Global Class

You can define individual components of the class such as attributes, methods, events, friends, and so on in the class editor. We will discuss the definition of the individual components later in the relevant sections in this chapter.

Class Visibility and Instantiation

The visibility sections define the visibility of the components of the class and therefore the interface of the class to the application.

- **Public section**
  All components declared within the public section can be accessed by any users of the class. The methods of the class can also access the public components of the class and any classes that inherit from it. The public components of the class form the interface between the class and the user. The user can only access the public components of the class.
- **Private section**
  The components that are declared in the private section are only visible to the method of the class and are only accessible from inside the class itself. You can protect components against access from the outside by characterizing them as private attributes. The private components are not visible to the outside user. Using the private visibility section, you can hide or encapsulate the information from the outside user. Changing the private component does not

affect the outside user. As long as the classes interface (public components) remains the same, the outside user does not notice the changes in the class.

- **Protected section**
  All components declared in this section can be accessed by the method of the class and the subclasses. Protected components represent the interface between the class and its subclasses but are not the part of the interface between the class and the outside world.

Listing 14.2 displays the declaration of the public, private, and protected components of the class.

```
*---------------------------------------------------------------*
*       CLASS vessel DEFINITION                                 *
*---------------------------------------------------------------*
*       Superclass definition                                   *
*---------------------------------------------------------------*
CLASS vessel DEFINITION.
  PUBLIC SECTION.
    METHODS: constructor,
             drive IMPORTING speed_up TYPE i,
             get_id RETURNING value(id) TYPE i.
  PROTECTED SECTION.
    DATA: speed TYPE i,
          max_speed TYPE i VALUE 100.
  PRIVATE SECTION.
    CLASS-DATA object_count TYPE i.
    DATA id TYPE i.
ENDCLASS.

*---------------------------------------------------------------*
*       CLASS vessel IMPLEMENTATION                             *
*---------------------------------------------------------------*
*       Superclass implementation                               *
*---------------------------------------------------------------*
CLASS vessel IMPLEMENTATION.
  METHOD constructor.
    object_count = object_count + 1.
    id = object_count.
  ENDMETHOD.
  METHOS drive.
    speed = speed + speed_up.
    IF speed > max_speed.
      speed = max_speed.
```

```
    ENDIF.
  ENDMETHOD.
  METHOD get_id.
    id = me->id.
  ENDMETHOD.
ENDCLASS
*---------------------------------------------------------------*
```

Listing 14.2 Public, Private, and Protected Components in a Class

External users of the class (e.g., an executable ABAP program) can only access the public components. The private and protected components are invisible to the external user and are therefore internal to the class or the class and its subclasses in the case of protected components. This enables you to change the internal implementation of the class without affecting the external user. By assigning the components to the appropriate visibility section, you can determine which components should be part of the user interface and which components should be encapsulated.

For a global class the visibility of individual components is specified in the class editor. Figure 14.3 displays the visibility options in the class editor for methods. Similarly, you have the option to specify visibility for other components of the class.

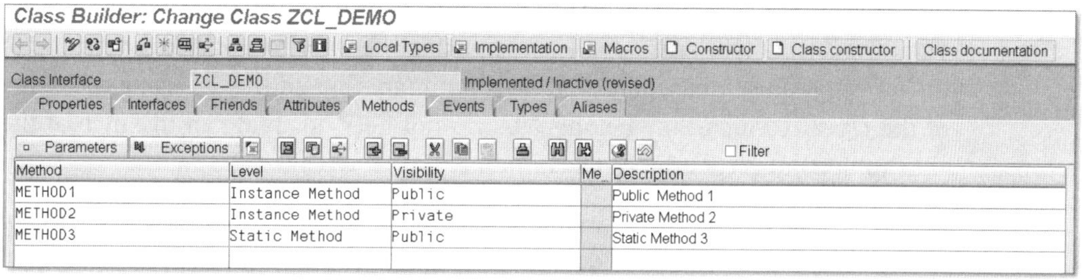

Class Builder: Change Class ZCL_DEMO

Method	Level	Visibility	Me	Description
METHOD1	Instance Method	Public		Public Method 1
METHOD2	Instance Method	Private		Private Method 2
METHOD3	Static Method	Public		Static Method 3

Figure 14.3 Method Definition for Global Class with Visibility

In addition to the specifying the visibility of the class components, you can also specify the instantiation type for the class. The instantiation type defines who can create the objects of the class. Following are the three types of instantiation for the class:

- Public instantiation
- Protected instantiation
- Private instantiation

The syntax to control the instantiation of a local class is as follows:

```
CLASS <class_names> DEFINITION
  CREATE PUBLIC | PROTECTED | PRIVATE
ENDCLASS.
```

If you do not specify the instantiation for the class, then the class is by default publicly instantiated. Only publicly instantiated classes can be used by the user to create objects for the class. Protected instantiated classes allow the creation of objects in methods of subsclasses. A class with private instantiation can create objects within the class itself, but nowhere else. Public instantiation classes normally provide a static component that can be accessed by the outside, which will provide the reference to the object that the class itself created.

For the global class you specify the instantiation type in the create class dialog window as shown in Listing 14.2 above.

Instance and Static Components

In addition to the visibility, you must define whether the component is an instance component or a static component. The instance components exist for each instance of the class (one copy for each object), and they are independent of each other. The static components exist once per class, no matter how many instances of this class there are, and all objects of the class share this one copy. The instance components are addressed using the reference variable pointing to the object in question, whereas static components are addressed using the name of the class to which they belong. You do not need to create an instance of the class (object) to access the static components.

The syntax to define static components and instance components is the same except that static component definitions begin with the `CLASS` keyword. For global class definitions in the Class Builder you must specify for each component whether it's a static component or an instance component. Figure 14.4 displays instance and static components for a local class.

For the global class the instance and the static components are defined in the class editor. Figure 14.3 displayed the instance and static method definition for the global class. Figure 14.5 displays the instance and static attributes definition for the global class in the class editor.

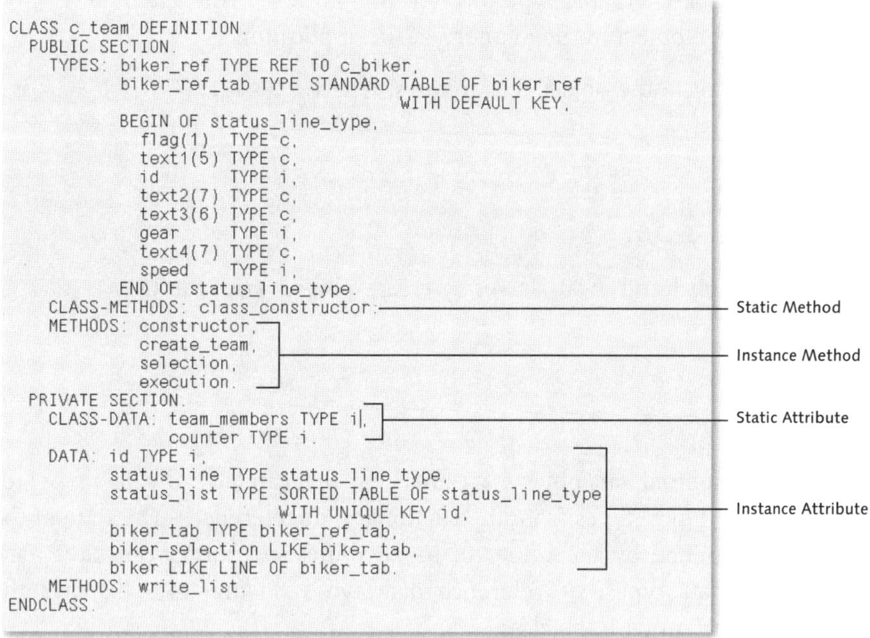

```
CLASS c_team DEFINITION.
  PUBLIC SECTION.
    TYPES: biker_ref TYPE REF TO c_biker,
           biker_ref_tab TYPE STANDARD TABLE OF biker_ref
                                      WITH DEFAULT KEY,
           BEGIN OF status_line_type,
             flag(1)  TYPE c,
             text1(5) TYPE c,
             id       TYPE i,
             text2(7) TYPE c,
             text3(6) TYPE c,
             gear     TYPE i,
             text4(7) TYPE c,
             speed    TYPE i,
           END OF status_line_type.
    CLASS-METHODS: class_constructor.
    METHODS: constructor,
             create_team,
             selection,
             execution.
  PRIVATE SECTION.
    CLASS-DATA: team_members TYPE i,
                counter TYPE i.
    DATA: id TYPE i,
          status_line TYPE status_line_type,
          status_list TYPE SORTED TABLE OF status_line_type
                          WITH UNIQUE KEY id,
          biker_tab TYPE biker_ref_tab,
          biker_selection LIKE biker_tab,
          biker LIKE LINE OF biker_tab.
    METHODS: write_list.
ENDCLASS.
```


Figure 14.4 Instance and Static Components Declaration

Class Builder: Change Class ZCL_DEMO

Local Types | Implementation | Macros | Constructor | Class constructor | Class documentation

Class Interface ZCL_DEMO Implemented / Inactive (revised)

Properties | Interfaces | Friends | Attributes | Methods | Events | Types | Aliases

Filter

Attribute	Level	Visibility	Read-Only	Typing	Associated Type		Description	Initial value
MATERIAL	Instance Attribute	Public	☐	Type	MATNR	➡	Material Number	
PLANT	Instance Attribute	Public	☐	Type	WERKS_D	➡	Plant	
MATERIALTYPE	Instance Attribute	Private	☐	Type	MTART	➡	Material Type	
INDUSTRYSECTOR	Static Attribute	Public	☐	Type	MBRSH	➡	Industry sector	
			☐	Type		➡		
			☐	Type		➡		

Figure 14.5 Instance and Static Attribute Definition for a Global Class

Objects

Objects are instances of a class. A class contains the description of the object and describes all characteristics that all objects of the class have in common. The process of creating a discrete object or instance of a class in memory is called instantiation. Objects are created using the syntax `CREATE OBJECT ref_name`, where `ref_name` must be a suitable type of reference variable. The statement `CREATE OBJECT` creates an object in the memory of the application.

The syntax to create the object is as follows, where `CL_ARTICLE_HIERARCHY` is a global class:

```
DATA: ref_var TYPE REF TO cl_article_hierarchy.
START-OF-SELECTION.
CREATE OBJECT ref_var.
```

You can use global and local classes to create objects with the `CREATE OBJECT` statement.

Attributes

Attributes are internal data objects within a class that can have any data type, for example, ABAP types, types from the Dictionary, or references. The state of the object is determined by the values of its attributes. Attributes can have local types, global data types, or reference data types. Figure 14.6 displays the attribute declaration with the class.

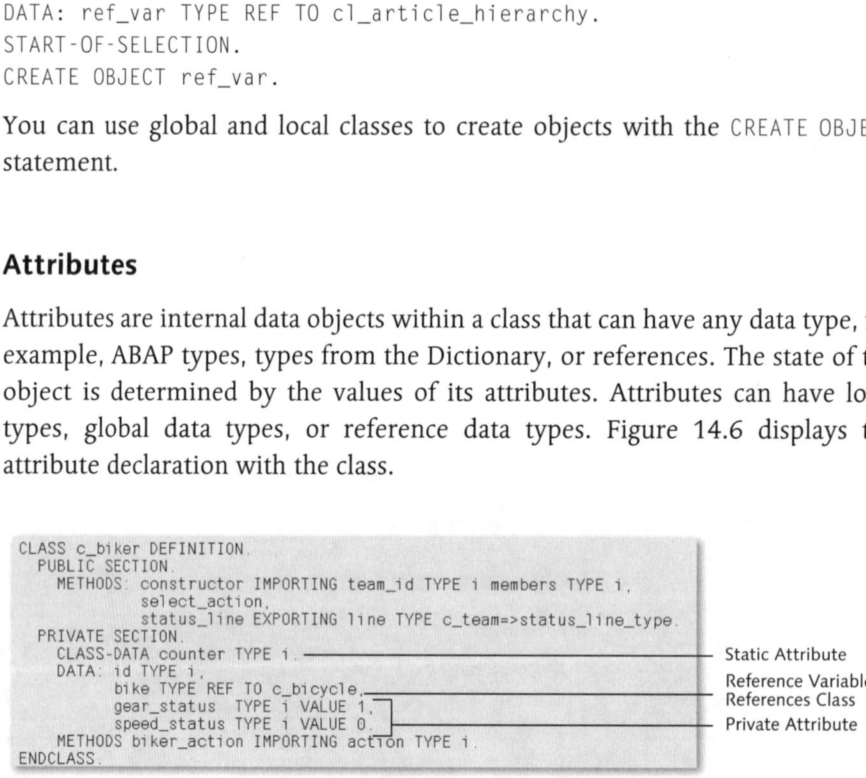

```
CLASS c_biker DEFINITION.
  PUBLIC SECTION.
    METHODS: constructor IMPORTING team_id TYPE i members TYPE i,
             select_action,
             status_line EXPORTING line TYPE c_team=>status_line_type.
  PRIVATE SECTION.
    CLASS-DATA counter TYPE i.
    DATA: id TYPE i,
          bike TYPE REF TO c_bicycle,
          gear_status  TYPE i VALUE 1,
          speed_status TYPE i VALUE 0.
    METHODS biker_action IMPORTING action TYPE i.
ENDCLASS.
```

Static Attribute
Reference Variable/
References Class
Private Attribute

Figure 14.6 Attribute Declaration in a Class

In classes, you can only use the `TYPE` addition when defining attributes. The `LIKE` reference is allowed only for local data types of system variables such as `SY-DATUM`, `SY-UNAME` and so on. With `TYPE REF TO`, the attribute can be typed as a reference variable. The reference type can be classes, interfaces, or types.

The `READ-ONLY` addition means that a public attribute that was declared with the `DATA` statement can be read from outside but can only be *changed* by methods of the same class. The `READ-ONLY` addition can only be specified in the public visibility section of a class declaration or in an interface definition. The `READ-ONLY` attribute for the global class can be specified in the class editor by selecting the READ-ONLY checkbox for the attribute, as displayed in Figure 14.5 above.

The syntax to declare a READ-ONLY attribute is as follows:

```
DATA:      variable1 TYPE I  READ-ONLY.
CLASS-DATA variable2 TYPE I READ-ONLY.
```

You can protect attributes against access from outside by declaring them as private attributes.

- **Private attributes**
  Private attributes cannot be addressed directly from outside the class and are not visible to the outside user. The friendship concept is an exception to this rule. You can find more information about the friendship concept in Chapter 17, Class Identification Analysis and Design.
- **Public attributes**
  Public attributes can be accessed directly by the outside user. The public components of the class are sometimes collectively known as the class's interface. This includes the public attributes and methods.
- **Instance attributes**
  Instance attributes are defined with the DATA keyword and exist once per object. The lifetime of an instance attribute is linked to the lifecycle of the object.
- **Static attributes**
  Static attributes are defined with the CLASS-DATA keyword, and they exist once per class, no matter how many instances there are for the class. They are visible to all of the runtime instances of the class and usually contain information, which applies to all instances of the class, for example, a counter for the total number of objects. Static attributes are also referred to as class attributes.

In the Class Builder, you can simply enter the attributes and their properties in the ATTRIBUTES tab as displayed in Figure 14.7, which displays the attributes definition for a global class.

In addition to instance and static attributes, you can declare constant attributes, whose values are defined during declaration and cannot be changed afterward.

The syntax to declare a constant attribute in a local class is:

```
CONSTANTS: const1 TYPE C VALUE 'A'.
```

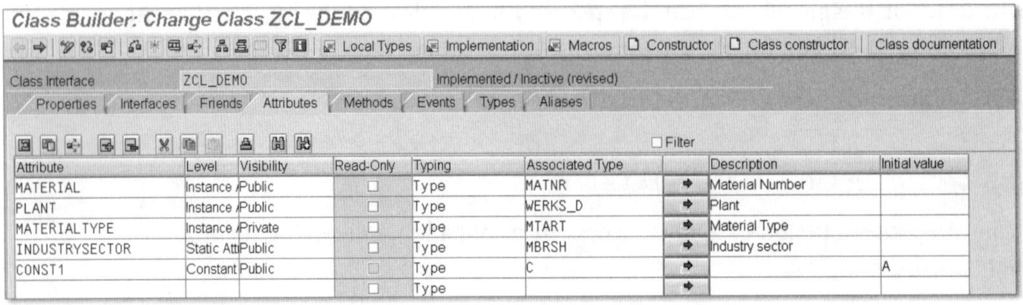

Class Builder: Change Class ZCL_DEMO

Local Types | Implementation | Macros | Constructor | Class constructor | Class documentation

Class Interface ZCL_DEMO Implemented / Inactive (revised)

Properties | Interfaces | Friends | Attributes | Methods | Events | Types | Aliases

Filter

Attribute	Level	Visibility	Read-Only	Typing	Associated Type		Description	Initial value
MATERIAL	Instance	Public	☐	Type	MATNR	➡	Material Number	
PLANT	Instance	Public	☐	Type	WERKS_D	➡	Plant	
MATERIALTYPE	Instance	Private	☐	Type	MTART	➡	Material Type	
INDUSTRYSECTOR	Static Att	Public	☐	Type	MBRSH	➡	Industry sector	
CONST1	Constant	Public	☐	Type	C	➡		A
			☐	Type		➡		

Figure 14.7 Attributes Definition for a Global Class

The constant attribute is accessed with the following syntax:

```
WRITE: / ZCL_DEMO=>const1.
WRITE: / class_name=>constant.
```

Methods

Methods are internal procedures in a class that define the behavior of an object. In other words, they are the blocks of code that contain the logic. Methods can access all attributes of the class and therefore can change the values of the attributes of the object. The private attributes of the class can be changed by the method of the same class.

Methods are declared in the `DEFINITION` section for the local class and in the class editor for the global class. Figure 14.3 displayed the method definition for the global class in the class editor. All methods declared in the declaration part must be implemented in the implementation part of the class. Methods must be assigned to a visibility section, just like attributes. Methods assigned to the `PUBLIC SECTION` can be called from outside the class, whereas the methods assigned to the `PRIVATE SECTION` can be called only within the same class.

Like the attributes of the class, you can declare instance methods or static methods. Instance methods are declared using the `METHODS` statement, whereas the static methods are declared using the `CLASS-METHODS` statement. Instance methods can access all of the attributes of the class (i.e., both instance and static) and can trigger all events of the class. Static methods can access only the static attributes of the class and can trigger only static events. Static methods can be called without instantiating the class, whereas instance methods are valid for the specific instance of the class. Hence, you need to instantiate the class (CREATE OBJECT) to access the instance method.

Static methods are defined at the class level. They can be directly accessed through the class and do not need an instance. Static methods can be accessed by all of the instances of the class, and from outside the class (as long as they are public). You have to create an object of the class to call an instance method. Both instance methods and static methods are implemented in the implementation part of the class.

The instance and static methods are implemented between the following statement block:

```
CLASS lcl_class IMPLEMENTATION.
  METHOD method_name.
  ENDMETHOD.
ENDCLASS.
```

The method statement does not require any additions because the properties and signature of the method are defined in the declaration part of the class. Listing 14.3 and Listing 14.4 display the declaration and the implementation of the methods.

```
CLASS c_team DEFINITION.
  PUBLIC SECTION.
    TYPES: biker_ref TYPE REF TO c_biker,
           biker_ref_tab TYPE STANDARD TABLE OF biker_ref
                                        WITH DEFAULT KEY,
           BEGIN OF status_line_type,
             flag(1)  TYPE c,
             text1(5) TYPE c,
             id       TYPE i,
             text2(7) TYPE c,
             text3(6) TYPE c,
             gear     TYPE i,
             text4(7) TYPE c,
             speed    TYPE i,
           END OF status_line_type.
    CLASS-METHODS: class_constructor.  "Static Attribute
    METHODS: constructor,
             create_team,
             selection,
             execution.
  PRIVATE SECTION.
```

```
    CLASS-DATA: team_members TYPE i,
                counter TYPE i.
    DATA: id TYPE i,
          status_line TYPE status_line_type,
          status_list TYPE SORTED TABLE OF status_line_type
                          WITH UNIQUE KEY id,
          biker_tab TYPE biker_ref_tab,
          biker_selection LIKE biker_tab,
          biker LIKE LINE OF biker_tab.
    METHODS: write_list.
ENDCLASS.                    "c_team DEFINITION
```

Listing 14.3 Declaration of Method in a Local Class

```
CLASS c_team IMPLEMENTATION.

  METHOD class_constructor.
    tit1 = 'Team members ?'.
    CALL SELECTION-SCREEN 100 STARTING AT 5 3.
    IF sy-subrc NE 0.
      LEAVE PROGRAM.
    ELSE.
      team_members = members.
    ENDIF.
  ENDMETHOD.                    "class_constructor

  METHOD constructor.
    counter = counter + 1.
    id = counter.
  ENDMETHOD.                    "constructor

  METHOD create_team.
    DO team_members TIMES.
      CREATE OBJECT biker
        EXPORTING
          team_id = id
          members = team_members.
      APPEND biker TO biker_tab.
      CALL METHOD biker->status_line
        IMPORTING
          line = status_line.
      APPEND status_line TO status_list.
    ENDDO.
  ENDMETHOD.                    "create_team
```

```
  METHOD selection.
    CLEAR biker_selection.
    DO.
      READ LINE sy-index.
      IF sy-subrc <> 0. EXIT. ENDIF.
      IF sy-lisel+0(1) = 'X'.
        READ TABLE biker_tab INTO biker INDEX sy-index.
        APPEND biker TO biker_selection.
      ENDIF.
    ENDDO.
    CALL METHOD write_list.
  ENDMETHOD.                    "selection

  METHOD execution.
    CHECK NOT biker_selection IS INITIAL.
    LOOP AT biker_selection INTO biker.
      CALL METHOD biker->select_action.
      CALL METHOD biker->status_line
        IMPORTING
          line = status_line.
      MODIFY TABLE status_list FROM status_line.
    ENDLOOP.
    CALL METHOD write_list.
  ENDMETHOD.                    "execution

  METHOD write_list.
    SET TITLEBAR 'TIT'.
    sy-lsind = 0.
    SKIP TO LINE 1.
    POSITION 1.
    LOOP AT status_list INTO status_line.
      WRITE: / status_line-flag AS CHECKBOX,
               status_line-text1,
               status_line-id,
               status_line-text2,
               status_line-text3,
               status_line-gear,
               status_line-text4,
               status_line-speed.
    ENDLOOP.
  ENDMETHOD.                    "write_list

ENDCLASS.                     "c_team IMPLEMENTATION
```

Listing 14.4 Implementation of Methods in a Local Class

Methods have interface parameters, sometimes referred to as the methods' signatures, that enable them to receive values when they are called and pass values back to the calling program. They can also have exceptions. Methods can have any number of EXPORTING, IMPORTING, and CHANGING parameters, which are mutually exclusive. All parameters of these categories can be passed by value or reference.

Listing 14.5 displays the method declaration and implementation with EXPORTING and IMPORTING parameters.

```
CLASS counter DEFINITION.
  PUBLIC SECTION.
    METHODS: set IMPORTING value(set_value) TYPE i,
             increment,
             get EXPORTING value(get_value) TYPE i.
  PRIVATE SECTION.
    DATA count TYPE i.
ENDCLASS.

CLASS counter IMPLEMENTATION.
  METHOD set.
    count = set_value.
  ENDMETHOD.
  METHOD increment.
    ADD 1 TO count.
  ENDMETHOD.
  METHOD get.
    get_value = count.
  ENDMETHOD.
ENDCLASS.
```

Listing 14.5 Class Definition and Implementation

Figure 14.8 displays the method definition in the Class Builder, and Figure 14.9 displays the EXPORTING and IMPORTING parameters for the method in the Class Builder.

A single return value for the method can be defined using a RETURNING parameter. Methods that have RETURNING parameter are called functional methods. If a method has a RETURNING parameter, there can be no EXPORTING or CHANGING parameters, and the method will pass back one thing and one thing only to the caller.

Class Builder: Display Class CL_GUI_FRONTEND_SERVICES

Local Types | Implementation | Macros | Class documentation

Class Interface CL_GUI_FRONTEND_SERVICES Implemented / Active

Properties | Interfaces | Friends | Attributes | Methods | Events | Types | Aliases

Parameters | Exceptions | Filter

Method	Level	Visibility	Method type	Description
IF_CACHED_PROP~GET_NEXT_F	Instance Method	Public		Read Next Property
IF_CACHED_PROP~SEEK_FIRST	Instance Method	Public		Set Cursor to 1st Property
IF_CACHED_PROP~SET_PROP	Instance Method	Public		Set a Property
IS_VALID	Instance Method	Public		Check If a GUI_OBJECT Represents a Valid Frontend Object
FREE	Instance Method	Public		Destructor
GET_PROPERTY	Instance Method	Protected		Get_Property
SET_PROPERTY	Instance Method	Protected		Set_Property
CALL_METHOD	Instance Method	Protected		Call_Method
ASSIGN_PROPERTY	Instance Method	Protected		Assign_Property
CALL_METHOD_RESULT_GUI_OE	Instance Method	Protected		Call Method rc=GUI_OBJECT, You can Check Obj. With IS_VALID
GET_PROPERTY_GUI_OBJECT	Instance Method	Protected		GetProperty rc=GUI_OBJECT, You Can Check obj With 'IS_VALID'
IS_CACHED_PROP	Instance Method	Protected		Property Managed in Cache?
ADD_CACHE_PROP	Instance Method	Protected		Add new Cached Property
REMOVE_CACHE_PROP	Instance Method	Protected		Remove Cached Property from Cache
GET_CACHE_PROP	Instance Method	Protected		Read Value of a Cache Property
SET_CACHE_PROP	Instance Method	Protected		Write Value of a Cache Property
IS_CACHE_VALID	Instance Method	Protected		Query: Is the Cache Valid for this Control?
INVALIDATE_CACHE	Instance Method	Protected		Invalidates the Cache
IS_VALID_HANDLE	Static Method	Private		
CHECK_GUI_SUPPORT	Static Method	Public		Checks GUI-Supported Features
CLASS_CONSTRUCTOR	Static Method	Public		Class Constructor
CLIPBOARD_EXPORT	Static Method	Public		Exports data to clipboard
CLIPBOARD_IMPORT	Static Method	Public		Imports data from clipboard
CONSTRUCTOR	Instance Method	Public		Create in Private Section
DIRECTORY_BROWSE	Static Method	Public		Shows a Directory Selection Window

Figure 14.8 Method Definition for a Global Class

Class Builder: Display Class CL_GUI_FRONTEND_SERVICES

Local Types | Implementation | Macros | Class documentation

Class Interface CL_GUI_FRONTEND_SERVICES Implemented / Active

Properties | Interfaces | Friends | Attributes | Methods | Events | Types | Aliases

Method parameters CALL_METHOD

Methods | Exceptions

Parameter	Type	Pa	Opt	Typing Me	Associated Type	Default value	Description
P1	Importing		X	Type	ANY		Parameters
P2	Importing		X	Type	ANY		Parameters
P3	Importing		X	Type	ANY		Parameters
P4	Importing		X	Type	ANY		Parameters
P5	Importing		X	Type	ANY		Parameters
P6	Importing		X	Type	ANY		Parameters
P7	Importing		X	Type	ANY		Parameters
P8	Importing		X	Type	ANY		Parameters
P9	Importing		X	Type	ANY		Parameters
P10	Importing		X	Type	ANY		Parameters
P11	Importing		X	Type	ANY		Parameters
P12	Importing		X	Type	ANY		Parameters
P13	Importing		X	Type	ANY		Parameters
P14	Importing		X	Type	ANY		Parameters
P15	Importing		X	Type	ANY		Parameters
P16	Importing		X	Type	ANY		Parameters
METHOD	Importing	X		Type	C		Name
P_COUNT	Importing	X	X	Type	I		Number of Valid Parameters
QUEUE_ONLY	Importing	X	X	Type	C	'X'	Queue_Only Use of RESULT
RESULT	Exporting			Type	ANY		Result of Call
KEEP_CACHE	Importing		X	Type	CHAR01		Is it Allowed to Continue Using the Ca
				Type			
				Type			
				Type			

Figure 14.9 Exporting and Importing Parameter for a Method of the Class

The `RETURNING` parameter must always be passed by value, and is passed with the addition `VALUE`. More information about functional methods can be found in Chapter 17, Class Identification Analysis and Design. All input parameters such as `IMPORTING` and `CHANGING` can be defined as optional using the `OPTIONAL` addition. You can also use the `DEFAULT` addition to assign a default value. These parameters do not necessarily have to be transferred when the method is called. The `DEFAULT` addition always allows you to specify a default value.

Methods can set the system return code `SY-SUBRC` if they raise an exception, but only if the exceptions raised by the method are classic exceptions, as opposed to class-based exceptions. You can identify the type of exception used by the method in the Class Builder by looking at the EXCEPTION tab in the Class Builder screen. For class-based exceptions the EXCEPTION CLASSES checkbox is selected; otherwise, the exception defined for the method is a classic one. Figure 14.10 displays the exception for the classic exception for the method.

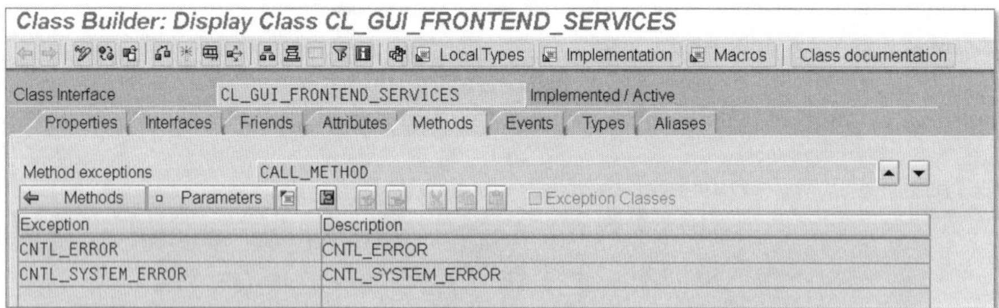

Figure 14.10 Classic Exception for the Method of the Global Class

Class-based exceptions are raised by either the `RAISE EXCEPTION` statement or the runtime environment. To propagate an exception from a method, you generally use the `RAISING` addition when you are defining the method interface. You can specify the `RAISING` addition directly when you define the methods of local classes.

The syntax to define a method with the `RAISING` addition is as follows:

```
METHODS m1 IMPORTING ... EXPORTING ... RAISING cx_excep ...
```

There are two special methods that you may find in a class: `CONSTRUCTOR` and `CLASS_CONSTRUCTOR`.

- The `CONSTRUCTOR` method (sometimes referred to as the *instance constructor*) is called automatically when you create an object to set a starting value for the new object. The instance constructor is called once per object, for every object. Each class can have no more than one CONSTRUCTOR method, and the constructor method must always be defined in the public visibility section. The constructor signature can only have importing parameters and exceptions. The instance is not created if an exception for the constructor is raised. Usually, you set the value of the attribute, validations, incrementing counter for the object, and so on in the CONSTRUCTOR.

The syntax to pass parameters to the constructor is as follows, where p1 and p2 are the parameters for the constructor:

```
DATA: ref_var TYPE REF TO zcl_demo.
START-OF-SELECTION.
CREATE OBJECT ref_var EXPORTING p1 = 10 p2 = 20.
```

- The static constructor (sometimes also referred to as the *class constructor*) is a special method in the class and is always named CLASS_CONSTRUCTOR. Each class can have only one static constructor, and it must be assigned to the public visibility section. The static constructor cannot have any importing parameters or exceptions, and it cannot be called explicitly. It is called when you access the class for the first time. It is executed no more than once per class. It can be triggered by creating an instance, accessing a static attribute, calling a static method of the class, or registering an event handler method for an event in the class.

Instance methods are called using CALL METHOD ref->method_name, or you can drop the CALL METHOD statement and call the method using the syntax ref->method_name( ), where ref is the name of the reference variable pointing to the object (instance of the class), and the method name is the object method separated by the instance component selector (->). The reference variable ref pointing to the object can be omitted when calling an instance method from within another instance method.

A shorter syntax to call a method is supported as of Release 6.10. In this case CALL METHOD is omitted, and the parameters are listed in parentheses; for example, you can call an instance method using the ref->method_name() statement if the method does not have any parameters. It is important to note that there must be no space before the parentheses.

Listing 14.6 displays the syntax to call an instance method within a program.

```
REPORT demo_class_counter .
*---------------------------------------------------------------*
*       CLASS counter DEFINITION
*---------------------------------------------------------------*

*---------------------------------------------------------------*
CLASS counter DEFINITION.
  PUBLIC SECTION.
    METHODS: set IMPORTING value(set_value) TYPE i,
             increment,
             get EXPORTING value(get_value) TYPE i.
  PRIVATE SECTION.
    DATA count TYPE i.
ENDCLASS.                       "counter DEFINITION

*---------------------------------------------------------------*
*       CLASS counter IMPLEMENTATION
*---------------------------------------------------------------*
*
*---------------------------------------------------------------*
CLASS counter IMPLEMENTATION.
  METHOD set.
    count = set_value.
  ENDMETHOD.                       "set
  METHOD increment.
    ADD 1 TO count.
  ENDMETHOD.                       "increment
  METHOD get.
    get_value = count.
  ENDMETHOD.                       "get
ENDCLASS.                       "counter IMPLEMENTATION

DATA number TYPE i VALUE 5.
DATA cnt TYPE REF TO counter.
START-OF-SELECTION.
  CREATE OBJECT cnt.
  CALL METHOD cnt->set
    EXPORTING
      set_value = number.
  DO 3 TIMES.
    CALL METHOD cnt->increment.
  ENDDO.
  CALL METHOD cnt->get
```

```
    IMPORTING
      get_value = number.
  WRITE number.
```

Listing 14.6 Calling Instance Methods

Similarly, static methods are called using the syntax `CALL METHOD class_name=>method_name`. The syntax consists of the class name and the name of the method separated by the static component selector (=>). Like static attributes, static methods are addressed with their class name because they do not need instances of the class. You can omit the class name when calling the static method from within the class, or you can use the shorter syntax to call the method, in which the `CALL METHOD` prefix is omitted and the parameters are placed in parentheses as mentioned above.

The syntax to call a method with `EXPORTING`, `IMPORTING`, and `CHANGING` parameters is as follows:

```
CALL METHOD oref->method_name
  EXPORTING im_par      = exp_val ...
  IMPORTING exp_par     = im_val ...
  CHANGING ch_par       = chg_val ...
  RECEIVING re_par      = res_val ...
  EXCEPTIONS exception  = re_val ...
```

The shorter syntax to call a method is as follows:

```
oref->method_name(
  EXPORTING im_par      = exp_val ...
  IMPORTING exp_par     = im_val ...
  CHANGING ch_par       = chg_val ...
  RECEIVING re_par      = res_val ...
  EXCEPTIONS exception  = re_val ... )
```

You can omit the `EXPORTING` parameter when you call the method that has only the import parameters.

Note

It is important to know that ABAP Objects does not provide a destructor method for the class, as in some other object-oriented programming languages.

Events

Events are another component of the class, along with attributes and methods. Objects or classes can trigger events, and other objects or classes can react to those events through special event handler methods. When an event is triggered, any number of handler methods can be called. These methods are not called explicitly; instead, the runtime system calls the handler methods, one by one, when the event is triggered. The definition of the handler method determines to which event it will react. You can declare handler methods in as many different classes as necessary.

To trigger an event the class must declare the event in the definition part and trigger the method in one of the methods of the same class. You can define a static event or an instance event. Instance events are defined using the `EVENTS` statement, whereas any static events are defined using the `CLASS-EVENTS` statement. Events are triggered by using the `RAISE EVENT` statement in a method of the class. The event can have exporting parameters that must be passed by value only. You use these if you want to pass the handler method some information that it may need. When an event is triggered, the reference to the triggering object is always available through the predefined importing parameter `SENDER`. By using this parameter you can place a reference to the event trigger object in the handler method. The `SENDER` parameter is not explicitly defined but can always be imported by the handler method.

Instance events can be triggered by an instance of the class (objects), whereas static events can be triggered by the class itself. You can trigger both static events and instance events from instance methods, whereas only static events can be triggered from static methods.

Events are also subject to the visibility concepts discussed above. You can assign events to a visibility section similar to other components of the classes. Events can be assigned to either the public, protected, or private sections. The visibility of the events determines where the event can be handled. An event defined in the public section can be handled in the public method; an event defined in the protected section can be handled by the class itself or its subclasses, whereas events defined in the private section can be handled only within the class itself.

Listing 14.7 displays the definition and the implementation of an event.

```
*---------------------------------------------------------------*
*       CLASS counter DEFINITION
*---------------------------------------------------------------

*---------------------------------------------------------------*
CLASS counter DEFINITION.
  PUBLIC SECTION.
    METHODS increment_counter.
    EVENTS  critical_value EXPORTING value(excess) TYPE i.
  PRIVATE SECTION.
    DATA: count     TYPE i,
          threshold TYPE i VALUE 10.
ENDCLASS.                    "counter DEFINITION
*---------------------------------------------------------------*
*       CLASS counter IMPLEMENTATION
*---------------------------------------------------------------*

*---------------------------------------------------------------*
CLASS counter IMPLEMENTATION.
  METHOD increment_counter.
    DATA diff TYPE i.
    ADD 1 TO count.
    IF count > threshold.
      diff = count - threshold.
      RAISE EVENT critical_value EXPORTING excess = diff.
    ENDIF.
  ENDMETHOD.                    "increment_counter
ENDCLASS.                    "counter IMPLEMENTATION
*---------------------------------------------------------------*
*       CLASS handler DEFINITION
*---------------------------------------------------------------*

*---------------------------------------------------------------*
CLASS handler DEFINITION.
  PUBLIC SECTION.
    METHODS handle_excess FOR EVENT critical_value OF counter
            IMPORTING excess.
ENDCLASS.                    "handler DEFINITION
*---------------------------------------------------------------*
*       CLASS handler IMPLEMENTATION
*---------------------------------------------------------------*
*
*---------------------------------------------------------------*
```

```
CLASS handler IMPLEMENTATION.
  METHOD handle_excess.
    WRITE: / 'Excess is', excess.
  ENDMETHOD                        "handle_excess
```

Listing 14.7 Event Declaration and Implementation

For the global class the event is defined on the EVENTS tab of the class editor, and the event handler method is defined in the METHODS tab, whereby you can specify additional attributes for the method by selecting the DETAIL VIEW icon ( ). Figure 14.11 displays the event definition in Class Builder, and Figure 14.12 displays the event handler method definition.

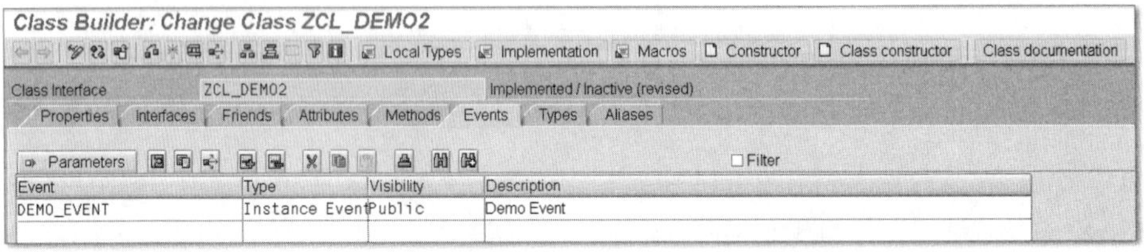

Figure 14.11 Event Definition in a Global Class

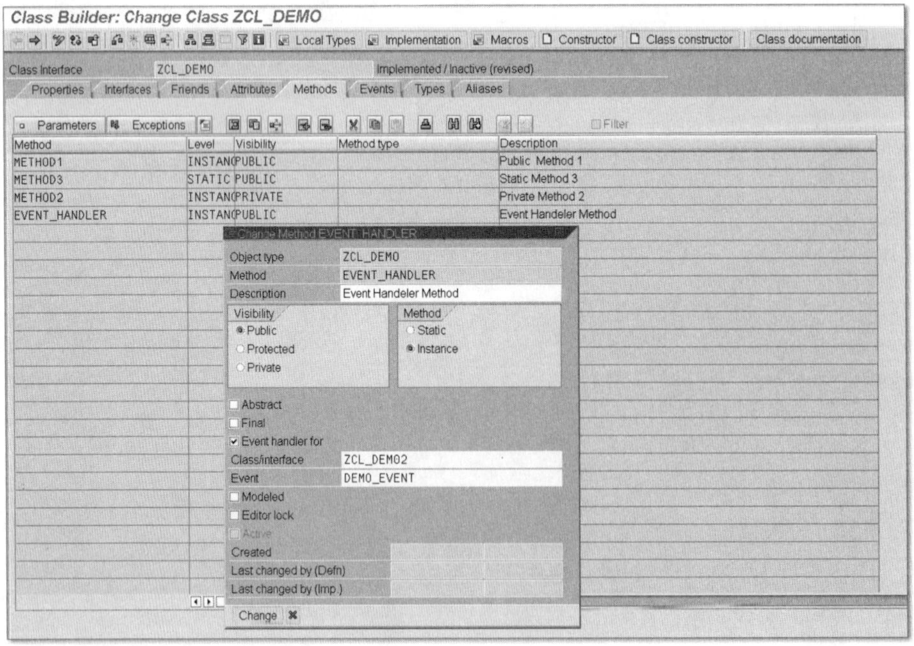

Figure 14.12 Event Handler Method Definition

When the event is triggered, the handler methods registered to this event are called in the sequence in which they were registered. Only the handler methods registered for the triggering event is started after the event is triggered. You can define any number of handler methods for an event. The handler methods can be defined in the same class or (usually) another class. The event handler methods are not called directly by the client; instead, the runtime system call the handler method automatically after the event has been triggered. The link between the event and the handler method is established dynamically in the program by using the SET HANDLER statement. Registration is only active at program runtime.

The syntax to register handler method is as follows:

```
SET HANDLER oref1->event_handler1.
```

Or you can register several handler methods with one statement as follows:

```
SET HANDLER evt_handler1 evt_handler2 FOR ALL INSTANCES.
```

Hence, to handle an event, a method must be defined as an event handler method and must be registered at runtime for the event. Listing 14.8 displays the handler method definition and implementation and event handler registration at runtime. If the event contains the exporting parameters, then the handler method signature should contain the IMPORTING parameters in the definition. The handler method signature should contain IMPORTING parameters equal to the EXPORTING parameters of the events.

```
*---------------------------------------------------------------*
*       CLASS counter DEFINITION
*---------------------------------------------------------------*

*---------------------------------------------------------------*
CLASS counter DEFINITION.
  PUBLIC SECTION.
    METHODS increment_counter.
    EVENTS  critical_value EXPORTING value(excess) TYPE i.
  PRIVATE SECTION.
    DATA: count     TYPE i,
          threshold TYPE i VALUE 10.
ENDCLASS.                    "counter DEFINITION
*---------------------------------------------------------------*
*       CLASS counter IMPLEMENTATION
*---------------------------------------------------------------*
```

```
*---------------------------------------------------------------*
CLASS counter IMPLEMENTATION.
  METHOD increment_counter.
    DATA diff TYPE i.
    ADD 1 TO count.
    IF count > threshold.
      diff = count - threshold.
      RAISE EVENT critical_value EXPORTING excess = diff.
    ENDIF.
  ENDMETHOD.                    "increment_counter
ENDCLASS.                    "counter IMPLEMENTATION
*---------------------------------------------------------------*
*       CLASS handler DEFINITION
*---------------------------------------------------------------*

*---------------------------------------------------------------*
CLASS handler DEFINITION.
  PUBLIC SECTION.
    METHODS handle_excess FOR EVENT critical_value OF counter
            IMPORTING excess.
ENDCLASS.                    "handler DEFINITION
*---------------------------------------------------------------*
*       CLASS handler IMPLEMENTATION
*---------------------------------------------------------------*

*---------------------------------------------------------------*
CLASS handler IMPLEMENTATION.
  METHOD handle_excess.
    WRITE: / 'Excess is', excess.
  ENDMETHOD.                    "handle_excess
  DATA: r1 TYPE REF TO counter,
        h1 TYPE REF TO handler.
START-OF-SELECTION.
  CREATE OBJECT: r1, h1.
  SET HANDLER h1->handle_excess FOR ALL INSTANCES.
  DO 20 TIMES.
    CALL METHOD r1->increment_counter.
  ENDDO.
```

Listing 14.8 Event Handler Declaration, Implementation, and Registration

If several methods are registered to one event, they are called in the sequence in which they were registered.

Practice Questions

The practice questions below will help you evaluate your understanding of the topic. The questions shown are similar in nature to those found on the certification examination, but whereas none of these questions will be found on the exam itself, they allow you to review your knowledge of the subject. Select the correct answers and then check the completeness of your answers in the following solution section. Remember that you must select all correct answers and only correct answers to receive credit for the question.

1. Which of the following is a true statement:

☐ **A.** Static attributes can be declared only in the private visibility section of the class.

☑ **B.** Static attributes are declared with the `CLASS-DATA` statement.

☑ **C.** A static attribute is the same across all instances of the class. There is only one static attribute across all instances of the class.

☐ **D.** Static attributes cannot be changed by an object.

2. Private components of the class cannot be addressed directly from outside the class except when the friendship concept applies.

☑ **A.** True

☐ **B.** False

3. Subclasses can access the private components of the parent class.

☐ **A.** True

☑ **B.** False

4. Subclasses inherent all the components of the parent class.

☑ **A.** True

☐ **B.** False

5. Public methods can access the private attributes of the same class.

☑ **A.** True

☐ **B.** False

6. Protected attributes can be accessed by methods of the class and its subclasses.

☐ **A.** True

☐ **B.** False

7. You cannot use the `LIKE` statement to define an attribute in a class.

☐ **A.** True

☐ **B.** False

8. The `READ-ONLY` addition for the attribute declaration can be used in the private and public visibility section.

☐ **A.** True

☐ **B.** False

9. The `READ-ONLY` attribute cannot be addressed outside the class.

☐ **A.** True

☐ **B.** False

10. Which of the following are correct statements?

☐ **A.** Class methods assigned to the public visibility section can be accessed outside the class using the static component selector and the class name.

☐ **B.** Static methods can be defined in both the public and private visibility section of the class.

☐ **C.** Only public methods can be addressed outside the class.

☐ **D.** You can call private methods within the public methods without reference to the object or class.

☐ **E.** None of the above

11. The constructor method is called automatically when you create an instance of the class.

☐ **A.** True

☐ **B.** False

12. The class constructor method is called automatically when you access the class for the first time.

- [x] **A.** True
- [ ] **B.** False

13. The constructor method is always defined in the private visibility section of the class.

- [ ] **A.** True
- [x] **B.** False

14. You can call the constructor method directly.

- [ ] **A.** True
- [x] **B.** False

15. Object or class events can trigger any number of handler methods.

- [x] **A.** True
- [ ] **B.** False

Practice Question Answers and Explanations

1. Correct answers: **B**, **C**

   Static attributes can be defined in the private and public visibility sections of the class. Static attributes are defined with the `CLASS-DATA` statement in the definition part of the class. Static attributes exist once per class and are the same for all of the runtime instances of the class. If you change the static attribute of the class, this change will apply for all of the instances of the class. Static attributes can be changed by an instance of the class. All of the objects of the class can access the static attribute of the class.

2. Correct answer: **A**

   Private attributes cannot be addressed outside the class, but a class that is a friend overrides this principle and can access the private attributes of the class.

3. Correct answer: **B**

   Subclasses inherit all components of the parent class but can only directly access public and protected components. However, the class also inherits the public methods from the superclass, which will indirectly allow access to the inherited private attributes. If a subclass inherits a private component, this private component cannot be accessed directly. Private means private; this is why we have protected sections — so that when we have a subclass, it can access inherited components.

4. Correct answer: **A**

   The subclass inherits all components from the superclass, but can then add additional components or can redefine inherited methods. Refer to Chapter 17, Class Identification Analysis and Design, for more information on this.

5. Correct answer: **A**

   Public methods can access all of the attributes of the class.

6. Correct answer: **A**

   Protected components can be accessed by the class and subclass. They cannot be addressed directly outside the inheritance tree.

7. Correct answer: **B**

   The `LIKE` statement is allowed only for local data objects (for example, within a method) or system variables.

8. Correct answer: **B**

   `READ-ONLY` attributes are defined in the public section and can be accessed outside the class. The value of the `READ-ONLY` attributes cannot be changed.

9. Correct answers: **A, B, C, D**

   These are correct for the following reasons:

   - Class methods or static methods assigned to the public visibility section of the class can be accessed outside the class with reference to the class because you do not need to instantiate the class to be able to work with them.
   - Static methods can be defined in both the public and the private visibility section of the class. You can access the static public methods outside the class, but not the static methods assigned to the private visibility section.
   - Only the methods assigned to the public visibility section can be addressed outside the class.
   - Private methods of the class can be called within the public methods of the same class without reference to the class or object.

10. Correct answer: **A**

    The constructor method is called automatically every time you instantiate the class, that is, every time a new object is created.

11. Correct answer: **A**

    The class constructor method is called automatically when you access the class for the first time, that is, when creating an object, calling a static method, and so on.

12. Correct answer: **B**

    The constructor method and the class constructor method are always defined in the public visibility section.

13. Correct answer: **B**

    You cannot call the constructor method directly; it is called automatically.

14. Correct answer: **A**

    When an instance or class event is triggered, any number of handler methods can be called. Only the handler methods registered for the triggering event are called when the event is triggered.

Take Away

You should be able to explain the basic object-oriented programming concepts. You should be able to explain the key components of an ABAP class such as attributes, methods, and events and be able to use them for object-oriented application development. You should be able to differentiate between instance components and static components. By now you should also have a good understanding about the visibility concepts in ABAP Objects and be able use them appropriately to create an ABAP class.

Refresher

Table 14.1 shows key concepts for ABAP Objects.

Key Concept	Definition
Class	A class is an abstract description of an object. A class is a template or a blueprint based on which all of the objects are created.
Attribute	Attributes are the global data of the class. The state of the object is determined by the content of its attributes. You can have attributes assigned to the public, protected, and private visibility sections of the class. You can also define static and instance attributes for the class.
Method	Methods are internal procedures that determine the internal behavior of the class. Methods can access all of the attributes of the class and hence can change the data content of the attributes. You can assign methods to the public, protected, and private visibility sections of the class. You can also define static or instance methods for the class.
Event	You can define events in the class to trigger event handler methods in other classes. Only handler methods registered for the triggering event are called when the event is triggered. Events can be assigned to the public, protected, or private visibility sections of the class. Similarly, you can define static or instance events in the class. Events are triggered using the `RAISE EVENT` statement, and the handler methods are registered using the `SET HANDLER` statement.
Object	An object is an instance of a class. The class describes all of the generic characteristics of the object. An object is created using the `CREATE OBJECT` statement.

Table 14.1 Key Concept Refresher

Summary

In this chapter you have learned basic object-oriented programming concepts. You have learned the concepts of the ABAP class because it is the foundation for ABAP object-oriented programming. You know the basic components of ABAP classes, both local and global, and have learned about the visibility concepts, instance and static components, and their syntax. You have also learned about events and how to trigger and how to register handler methods. You should now be a able to create local and global classes and use them to write programs using ABAP Objects. Your knowledge about ABAP Objects will enable you to answer ABAP Objects-related questions and successfully pass this topic.

15

ALV Grid Control

Techniques You'll Master:

- Identify the major functions of the ALV grid
- Understand how to produce a full-screen ALV
- Explore how to produce an ALV within a container
- Handle events triggered by the ALV

The ABAP List Viewer (ALV) has been available since Release 4.5a. With Release 4.6C it was renamed the SAP List Viewer, but the acronym remained ALV. The list viewer is rendered on the presentation server, which differentiates it from a report you produce using `WRITE` statements. You a use a container control on the presentation server to produce the ALV.

In this chapter you will be provided with a basic understanding of how ALV Grid Controls are produced. We will examine both versions of the class-based ALV and identify major differences between them. We will cover the techniques to produce a full-screen ALV and an ALV within a container. We will also cover how to handle events triggered by the ALV for processing within our program.

Real-World Scenario

You have been asked to explain to programmers just hired, who have never used ALV grids, the way to program a report using an ALV.

It is your responsibility to explain both the old and new class-based techniques to create an ALV Grid. You will need to provide an understanding of the basic methods to create a full-screen display used in your company's reporting and within dialog screens used in your company's programs to display multiple lists on a single screen. To do this, you will need to explain the two classes used to produce ALV grids and the process of placing an ALV into a container.

Because management often wants the data to be presented in the ALV in a specific way, because they want a different column heading or an order that does not correspond to the field structure found in the ABAP Dictionary, you must also explain how to change the display of an ALV programmatically.

Objectives of this Portion of the Test

The purpose of this portion of the certification examination is to verify that you have an understanding of the ALV. This portion of the examination will test your knowledge of a number of topics. The points you will need to understand from this section include:

- How to handle events triggered from the ALV; what steps are necessary to receive the events for processing
- The creation of a full-screen ALV because many customers prefer ALV reports because of their flexibility (sorting, filtering, or reordering columns) for the end user of the report
- The creation of an ALV within a container, which is useful for dynpro display of data
- How to modify the display of an ALV, in other words, changing the initial display to match customer requirements

The certification examination will give minimal weight to this chapter compared to all of the other topics in the examination. This means this chapter is among those where the percentage of questions related to the topic is smaller than most other chapters. An ALV can be produced simply. It is only when you modify the display of an ALV that it becomes more complicated. We believe that owing to its normally simple production, it does not require as much specialized knowledge as other areas and is therefore not given as much weight on the examination.

Note

The ALV Object Model has been available since SAP NetWeaver 6.40, but the certification examination could include questions on the older ALV that was implemented on the basis of the global class `CL_GUI_ALV_GRID`. In the future the exam may change to include questions on only the newer technique, but at present you will need to be prepared for questions on both, and therefore we will discuss both in this chapter.

Key Concepts Refresher

You need to understand and be able to perform the following types of tasks when developing ABAP programs:

- Producing reports that are flexible for the user
- Displaying data in a tabular format

Overview of ALV Programming

The graphical user interface (GUI) in the SAP system is based on SAP GUI windows (screens from the technical viewpoint of the programmer). Every dialog is implemented using dynpros of programs. Prior to Release 4.5 you could only use elements that were provided by the Screen Painter, for example, buttons. Starting with Release 4.5 it became possible to use controls that are stand-alone binary software components, one of these being the ALV Grid Control. These controls communicate differently than standard dynpro components. Rather than communication using the screen processor, these controls use the Control Framework (CFW).

You cannot create stand-alone instances of a control on the presentation server. You must provide a special control known as a *container control*. This container control is placed in a reserved area on the screen, and the ALV grid is within this container control. The steps to place a control on a screen are as follows:

1. You reserve an area in the screen for the container using a special screen element – the Custom Control Area. The process for this is similar to the way you reserve a subscreen area for a subscreen.
2. You create an instance of the container control class and link it to the area reserved on the screen. The container control is now visualized in the reserved area.
3. You create an ALV Grid Control instance then link it to the container control instance. The ALV Grid Control is now visualized in the container.

To reserve an area on the screen for the control, you use the Graphical Layout Editor of the Screen Painter, click on the CUSTOM CONTROL button, and "draw" the area for the container on the screen. You then need to provide a name for the created custom control area, so that you can link it to the container later.

ALV Grid Programming (CL_GUI_ALV_GRID)

You next need to generate an instance of a container. In your program, you need to do this before displaying the screen where the ALV Grid Control is to appear on the presentation server. The PBO (Process Before Output) of the screen that contains the reserved area is the usual place to create the container instance (the definition of the reserved area is shown in Figure 15.1). This event block is always called prior to displaying the screen.

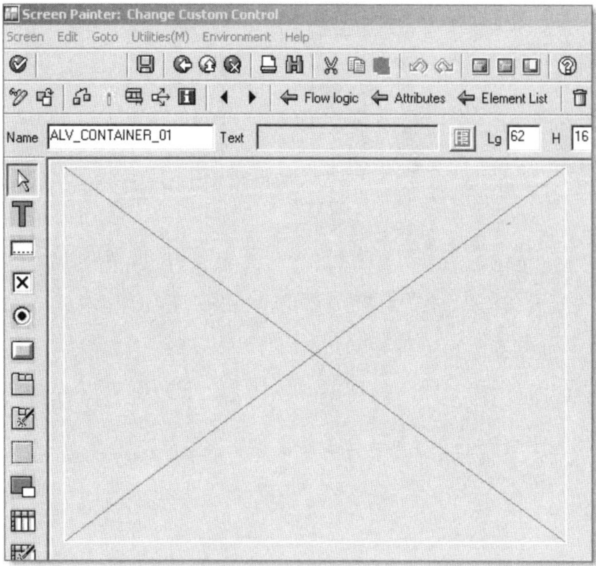

Figure 15.1 Screen Container Area

The process to create a custom container instance starts with a declaration of the reference variable. The reference variable needs to refer to the Container class, in this case `TYPE REF TO cl_gui_custom_container`. You generate a container control instance by using the statement `CREATE OBJECT` to generate an instance of the class `cl_gui_custom_container`. You link the container you are creating to the area you reserved for it on the screen by using the `IMPORTING` parameter `container_name` (see Listing 15.1 for an example). We recommend that you use either the ABAP Objects pattern (or dragging and dropping from the class name in the Object Navigator into your code to automatically produce the `CREATE OBJECT` call) to insert the `CREATE OBJECT` statement.

```
  DATA:
    gt_sflight            TYPE TABLE OF sflight,
    gs_layout             TYPE lvc_s_layo,
    gr_alv_grid           TYPE REF TO cl_gui_alv_grid,
    gr_custom_container TYPE REF TO cl_gui_custom_container.

  IF gr_custom_container IS NOT BOUND.
* Create an instance of a container
    CREATE OBJECT gr_custom_container
      EXPORTING
        container_name             = 'ALV_CONTAINER_01'
```

```
      EXCEPTIONS
        cntl_error                    = 1
        cntl_system_error             = 2
        create_error                  = 3
        lifetime_error                = 4
        lifetime_dynpro_dynpro_link = 5
        OTHERS                        = 6.
    IF sy-subrc NE 0.
      MESSAGE a001(z_message_class).
*   Container could not be created, program terminated
    ENDIF.
* Create an instance of alv control
    CREATE OBJECT gr_alv_grid
      EXPORTING
        i_parent = gr_custom_container.
  ENDIF.

  gs_layout-grid_title = 'Flights'(100).
  CALL METHOD gr_alv_grid->set_table_for_first_display
    EXPORTING
      i_structure_name = 'SFLIGHT'
      is_layout        = gs_layout
    CHANGING
      it_outtab        = gt_sflight.
```

Listing 15.1 Create ALV Grid

If you create this instance in a PBO module, which will be executed as many times as the screen is processed, you need to ensure that an instance is only generated the first time; you only want one container created, regardless of how many times the user processes the screen. Otherwise, you may generate a new object every time the dynpro is processed (or the code is reexecuted). You can stop unwanted instances from being generated by only creating one after checking if the reference variable is not valid with the condition IS NOT BOUND.

Tip

We prefer IS NOT BOUND over the more common IS INITIAL because IS NOT BOUND checks to see if the reference is invalid instead of just checking that the variable is empty. Resources the control occupies on the presentation server are typically released at the end of the program. However, these resources can also be released explicitly by calling the instance method FREE.

> An early release of the resource by this means invalidates the reference variable. If this code does not create a new object because a value still exists, the invalid reference is supplied to the ALV. However, by using IS BOUND the reference is determined to be invalid, and a new object is created.

You must create the instance of the ALV Grid Control after the container control instance because the container instance must exist before you can link the ALV grid to it. It also needs to be before the SAP GUI window is sent to the presentation server because the container and ALV grid must exist before its display. Therefore, we can again use the PBO of the screen (see Listing 15.1 for an example).

You declare a reference variable typed with reference to the class CL_GUI_ALV_GRID. You then provide the instance reference of the previously generated container control instance to the parameter i_parent during the instance constructor call that is triggered when you call CREATE OBJECT. Supplying the container during the creation of the ALV grid provides the link between these objects. If an error exception occurs when creating the instance, you should react with a termination message to abort the program.

If you want to display the ALV Grid Control in full-screen mode, which is most often used to display a report in the entire screen body, you do not reserve a control area on the screen and you do not create a container control. Instead, you assign a static value to the export parameter i_parent as shown in Listing 15.2.

```
CREATE OBJECT gr_alv_grid
  EXPORTING
    i_parent = cl_gui_custom_container=>screen0.
```

Listing 15.2 Create a Full-Screen ALV Grid

As a result of the above steps, you have created an ALV Grid Control as a screen element. However, you will only see a frame in the SAP GUI window because the controls do not yet display anything. You still need to supply the presentation server controls with data that they can display.

The calling program now needs to provide all of the data for display and the rules that define how this data is to be displayed (through the use of the field catalog). You must pass the data for display to the ALV grid as a standard internal table to the method SET_TABLE_FOR_FIRST_DISPLAY, which you call for the ALV grid instance. The ALV grid does not make a copy of the data, but instead manages a reference of the passed internal table. All actions of the ALV instance (for example, sorting and filtering) are performed by the instance on the internal table that resides in the calling program. This means you must ensure that the internal table has existed for at least as long as the ALV grid instance. Put another way, do not use a local table in a modularization unit that does not outlive the ALV Grid Control.

If the user sorts the data in the ALV grid, the contents of the internal table in the calling ABAP program are sorted. Therefore, the table supplied to the ALV grid must be a standard table. All other interactions by the user only read the data. You use the instance method `SET_TABLE_FOR_FIRST_DISPLAY` to pass the display data in the form of a standard internal table (parameter `it_outtab`), the field catalog, again in the form of a standard internal table (parameter `it_fieldcatalog`), and other additional information regarding the presentation or layout of the data to the ALV grid.

Table 15.1 shows the primary parameters for an ALV table display.

Parameter	Purpose
`it_outtab`	Display data in a standard internal table.
`it_fieldcatalog`	The field catalog is an internal table that contains information about the columns to be displayed
`i_structure_name`	If provided. it allows the ALV to automatically generate the field catalog for all fields contained in the structure, which must be an object from the ABAP Dictionary.
`is_variant`, `i_save`, and `i_default`	These parameters provide the user with the ability to change or save the display layout.
`is_layout`	This structure provides fields for setting graphical properties of the grid control, displaying exceptions, calculating totals, and enabling specific interaction options.
`is_print`	The print structure contains fields for settings when the list is printed.
`it_special_groups`	This table is used to pass texts for field groups defined in the field catalog.

Table 15.1 Primary Parameters for ALV Table Display

Parameter	Purpose
it_toolbar_excluding	The names of the standard functions you want to hide on the toolbar.
it_filter	Provides the initial settings for filtering.
it_sort	Provides the initial settings for sorting.

Table 15.1 Primary Parameters for ALV Table Display (cont.)

The data to appear in the ALV must be supplied to the parameter it_outtab; all other parameters are optional. If you supply the name of a global structure type (for example, a structure, table, or view from the ABAP Dictionary) to the parameter i_structure_name, the field catalog is automatically generated by the ALV grid for the fields in this structure, table, or view. However, each component in the structure must also exist in the data internal table as a column. This displays all columns from the data table with the same names as those in the provided structure in the ALV grid.

The minimum information you need to provide is the display data (it_outtab) from the internal table, which is mandatory, and field information for the display data. The simplest way to provide the field information about the display data is to provide an ABAP Dictionary structure, table, or view, in the parameter i_structure_name.

You can have the list data and the additional information sent to the presentation server again by using the method REFRESH_TABLE_DISPLAY. The parameter i_soft_refresh, if supplied with the value 'X', specifies that only the data contents are to be passed again, which keeps the current filter and sort criteria. If you assign the value 'X' to the ROW or COL fields of a structure using the global type LVC_S_STBL (for the parameter IS_STABLE), the scroll positions of the rows and columns will be retained during refreshing.

Tip

You cannot use the method REFRESH_TABLE_DISPLAY if you have changed the row structure of the display table. In this case you need to call the method SET_TABLE_FOR_FIRST_DISPLAY again to create the field catalog again.

Layout Variants

You use the parameters `is_variant` and `i_save` to determine what options are offered to the user for layout variant management. Using different combinations, you can produce one of three modes using these two parameters (see Table 15.2). Table 15.3 shows the permitted values for `i_save`.

Mode	Result	Values of Parameters
Changing the current layout only	Users can change the current layout (they can modify the selection and the order of the columns displayed).	▸ `is_variant` is initial ▸ `i_save` = space (default setting)
Loading delivered layouts only	The user can change the current layout variant and select existing variants.	▸ `is_variant` contains values supplied in structure ▸ `i_save` = space (or `is_variant` is initial and `i_save` is not equal to space)
Loading and saving layouts	The user can change the current layout variant and manage existing variants and save new variants.	▸ `is_variant` contains values supplied in structure ▸ `i_save` = either `X`, `U`, or `A`

Table 15.2 Layout Options

Value	Meaning
`space`	The user cannot save the variant.
`U`	The user can only save user-dependent variants.
`X`	The user can save cross-user layout variants.
`A`	The user can save both user-related and cross-user layout variants.

Table 15.3 i_save Values

User-dependent variants must start with a letter. A customer's cross-user variants (also known as standard variants) must start with a slash (/). SAP's cross-user variants start with a digit (0-9).

Note

Only standard layout variants can be transported. If the user has the required authorization, he can transport layouts in layout management by selecting LAYOUT • TRANSPORT... from the menu.

Display Settings

To change the ALV layout you provide a work area to the parameter `is_layout`. This structure allows you, for example, to supply a title, create a striped (zebra) pattern for the lines, or optimize the column width. You fill the structure's relevant fields such as `grid_title`, `zebra`, or `cwidth_opt`. This structure must be typed as `LVC_S_LAYO`.

To sort the data in a specific order in the ALV Grid Control when the grid is initially displayed, you must provide an internal table for the `IT_SORT` parameter. You use the table type `LVC_T_SORT` to declare this internal table. In this internal table, you create a record for each field that is part of the sort criterion. You specify the column name in the field `FIELDNAME`. If more than one field will be part of the sort criterion, you either enter the sequence for each field in the sort criterion in the field `SPOS`, or you provide the fields in the correct sequence for the sort order. To sort in ascending order, you place an `X` in the `UP` field.

Field Catalog

Because the display table does not have a fixed format, in order for the ALV grid to be able to display the data, a description of the columns of the ALV grid must be provided. The field catalog supplies this information, which is then used to display the data or when creating a print list.

As mentioned above, the simplest way to generate the field catalog is to supply the name of a structure from the ABAP Dictionary to the ALV grid in the parameter `i_structure_name`. If you cannot provide all details for all columns via the `i_structure_name` parameter, you provide this information to the ALV grid through the parameter `it_fieldcatalog`. The internal table you supply to the parameter `it_fieldcatalog` should be defined using the table type `LVC_T_FCAT`, which has the line type `LVC_S_FCAT`.

Common reasons for the inclusion of a field catalog are:

- You want to change the display of the output, for example, a different column position or heading.
- The internal table has columns that are not contained in the Dictionary structure that is supplied for the parameter `i_structure_name`.

If you supply the parameter `i_structure_name` with a Dictionary structure, table, or view, you need to provide a row in the field catalog for every column of the display data table that either differs from the underlying Dictionary structure or is not contained in the Dictionary object you supplied. This row must contain the technical properties and other formatting information for the column.

When you create a field catalog in the calling program, you must assign the name of the column from the display data internal table to the field `FIELDNAME`. This field assigns a row in the field catalog to a column of the display data table. Other fields of the field catalog can be divided into two groups based on their use when creating a field catalog:

- The field references a global type in the ABAP Dictionary. This applies to the fields `REF_FIELD` and `REF_TABLE`.
- All other fields of the field catalog provide values for the display properties of the column.

The field catalog row requires minimal information to be supplied; most of the information is optional. There are three basic ways of placing data into the catalog (each of these three global structures referenced below could also be either a global table or view):

- The field exists in a global structure with the same name.
- The field exists in a global structure with a different name.
- The field does not exist in a global structure.

If the field exists with the same name in a Dictionary structure, table, or view, it is sufficient to assign the name of the structure, table, or view to the field `REF_TABLE`. It is only necessary to add the field name from the structure to the `REF_FIELD` field if the column name of the display data table and Dictionary structure field name are different.

Assigning values to the fields `REF_TABLE` and, if necessary, `REF_FIELD` transfers all type definitions from the specified structure fields in the ABAP Dictionary. To override a definition from the ABAP Dictionary, you assign a value to one of the fields other than REF_FIELD and REF_TABLE. If the field does not exist in a global structure, you do not assign values to the fields REF_TABLE or REF_FIELD, and you instead assign values to the other fields in the field catalog.

Columns that require special handling based on either currency or unit of measure are defined in a similar fashion. The fields relevant for these definitions are shown in Table 15.4.

Value Applies to Entire Column	Column Name Containing Value for Row
CURRENCY	CFIELDNAME
QUANTITY	QFIELDNAME

Table 15.4 Special Handling for Columns

If the entire column is to be formatted using the same value, you specify this value in the field shown above. If this field for the column contains a value, the row-specific value is ignored if it exists.

So to format an entire column for a specific currency, you place the currency key in the field CURRENCY, and as a result, the contents of CFIELDNAME are ignored. The same is true for a quantity field. To format the entire column with the same unit of measure, you supply the unit of measure to the field QUANTITY. Doing so ignores any values in QFIELDNAME. If the entire column is not to be formatted the same, you specify the column name in the display table that contains the currency key in CFIELDNAME or the quantity's unit of measure in QFIELDNAME.

ALV Event Handling

An object can announce that its state has changed by triggering events. A common example with the ALV grid is a double-click: When the user double-clicks on a cell, the event DOUBLE_CLICK is triggered. You can program your own handler methods in your own class (normally a local class) that will react to this event when it is triggered.

To have the handler method "listen" for the triggered event, so that it is ready to react if the event occurs, you need to register this instance. If the event is triggered, the registered methods are executed in the order in which they were registered.

Your first task in handling events of a control is identifying what events can be triggered. Examining the associated class of the control (for our example, the class CL_GUI_ALV_GRID) and looking either at the EVENTS tab or in the hierarchal list in the Workbench expanding the node EVENTS provides you with all of the public events that can be triggered. The current version of CL_GUI_ALV_GRID has 32 public events. Some of the more commonly used events for this class are DOUBLE_CLICK, PRINT_TOP_OF_LIST, PRINT_TOP_OF_PAGE, PRINT_END_OF_PAGE, PRINT_END_OF_LIST, TOOLBAR, and USER_COMMAND.

To specify an event handler method in a local class, in the definition part you use the addition FOR EVENT <event_name> OF <class_name>. This addition specifies that this method can react to the event <event_name> of instances of the class <class_name>. You structure the names of event handler methods as follows: ON_<event_name>, where <event_name> is the name of the event. An example of this can be seen below in Listing 15.15.

Only formal parameters that were defined for the event can be used in an event handler method. The types of the parameters are taken from the event. Whereas you can only include parameters that are defined within the event, it is not necessary to IMPORT all parameters passed from the RAISE EVENT statement. Listing 15.3 shows the definition of a handler method, Listing 15.4 shows the implementation of the handler method, and Listing 15.5 shows how to register the handler method.

```
CLASS lcl_event_receiver DEFINITION.
  PUBLIC SECTION.
    METHODS:
      handle_double_click
        FOR EVENT double_click OF cl_gui_alv_grid
        IMPORTING e_row e_column.
ENDCLASS.                    "lcl_event_receiver DEFINITION
```

Listing 15.3 Definition of Handler Method

```
CLASS lcl_event_receiver IMPLEMENTATION.
  METHOD handle_double_click.
    READ TABLE gt_sflight INDEX e_row-index INTO gs_sflight.
  ENDMETHOD.                    "handle_double_click
ENDCLASS.                    "lcl_event_receiver IMPLEMENTATION
```

Listing 15.4 Handler Method

```
DATA:
  grid1               TYPE REF TO cl_gui_alv_grid,
  event_receiver      TYPE REF TO lcl_event_receiver.
CREATE OBJECT event_receiver.
SET HANDLER event_receiver->handle_double_click FOR grid1.
```

Listing 15.5 Registering the Handler

An example of the complete process for handling events with the ALV Object Model is shown at the end of the next section (see Listing 15.14 and Listing 15.15). The difference between them is that you need to get an event object before registering the handler.

To summarize the process:

1. Define the local class.
2. Define the handler method using the correct syntax and importing any parameters you want to use.
3. Implement the handler method.
4. Register the handler method using SET HANDLER, before the event can be triggered (normally before the ALV grid is displayed).

ALV Object Model

The ALV Object Model (ALV OM) is a new feature available from SAP NetWeaver 6.40 on. In earlier releases the ALV grid was based on the global class CL_GUI_ALV_GRID, which we have already discussed. ALV Object Method is simpler to use. We will discuss the three output formats of the ALV: the full-screen ALV, the classic ABAP list, and the output in a container control as a subarea of a screen.

You must call at least the following two methods in the ALV main class CL_SALV_TABLE to obtain the desired ALV output:

- The FACTORY static method to instantiate an object of the ALV main class. You pass into this method an internal table that will contain the data to be displayed (the display table) from which data is displayed. The display type (classic, full-screen, in container) is also defined. It is not necessary to actually supply the data in the display table at this point (in other words, the table can be empty). During the FACTORY method a reference to the actual table is created.

The data will need to be populated, however, prior to calling the next method.

- The DISPLAY method to place the ALV output on the screen.

Use the FACTORY method instead of the usual CREATE OBJECT. The FACTORY method is a class method and returns an ALV instance. (The CREATE OBJECT statement can be found in the FACTORY method itself; it generates the instance for you and passes back the reference so that you can then work with the ALV grid.) You use this instance during other method calls to individually adjust the ALV. If you have multiple ALV displays on a single screen, each will have its own instance or reference variable.

As with the older ALV, you need to define a reference variable typed with reference to the class CL_SALV_TABLE. Again you need a standard internal table for display. The definitions are shown in Listing 15.6 and Listing 15.7.

```
TYPES:
  BEGIN OF glt_outtab,
    carrid               TYPE s_carr_id,
    connid               TYPE s_conn_id,
    countryfr            TYPE land1,
    cityfrom             TYPE s_from_cit,
    airpfrom             TYPE s_fromairp,
    countryto            TYPE land1,
    cityto               TYPE s_to_city,
    airpto               TYPE s_toairp,
    fltime               TYPE s_fltime,
    deptime              TYPE s_dep_time,
    arrtime              TYPE s_arr_time,
    distance             TYPE s_distance,
    distid               TYPE s_distid,
    fltype               TYPE s_fltype,
    period               TYPE s_period,
    icon_flttype         TYPE icon_d,
    t_color              TYPE lvc_t_scol,
    t_celltype           TYPE salv_t_int4_column,
  END OF glt_outtab,
  gtt_outtab             TYPE STANDARD TABLE OF glt_outtab
                              WITH NON-UNIQUE DEFAULT KEY.
```

Listing 15.6 Definition of Internal Table to Pass to ALV

```
DATA:
  gt_outtab              TYPE gtt_outtab,
  gs_outtab              TYPE glt_outtab.
```

Listing 15.7 Declaration of Internal Table to Pass to ALV

You then create the ALV instance by calling the `FACTORY` method. Listing 15.8 shows the way to produce a classic list display, and Listing 15.9 shows the way to produce the standard table display. The other optional parameters are also shown in the first call. These commented parameters allow you to place the ALV in a container. Both of these calls produce a full-screen ALV because a container is not specified. The two necessary parameters are `r_salv_table`, which returns a reference to the created ALV, and `t_table`, which is the internal table that contains (or will contain) the display data for the ALV.

```
TRY.
    CALL METHOD cl_salv_table=>factory
      EXPORTING
        list_display = if_salv_c_bool_sap=>true
*         r_container    =
*         container_name =
      IMPORTING
        r_salv_table = gr_table
      CHANGING
        t_table      = gt_outtab.
  CATCH cx_salv_msg INTO gr_error.
    gv_str_text = gr_error->if_message~get_text( ).
    MESSAGE gv_str_text TYPE 'E'.
ENDTRY.
```

Listing 15.8 FACTORY Call for a List Display

```
TRY.
    cl_salv_table=>factory(
      IMPORTING
        r_salv_table = gr_table
      CHANGING
        t_table      = gt_outtab ).
  CATCH cx_salv_msg INTO gr_error.
    gv_str_text = gr_error->if_message~get_text( ).
    MESSAGE gv_str_text TYPE 'E'.
ENDTRY.
```

Listing 15.9 FACTORY Call for a Standard Table Display

To actually display the ALV, you call the appropriately named instance method `DISPLAY`. This is shown in at the end of Listing 15.10. The output of the classic list display is shown in Figure 15.2, and the standard ALV is shown in Figure 15.3.

Flight schedule

Flight schedule

Airline	Flight No.	Country	Depart. city	Depart	Country	Arrival city	Targe
AA	17	US	NEW YORK	JFK	US	SAN FRANCISCO	SFO
AA	64	US	SAN FRANCISCO	SFO	US	NEW YORK	JFK
AZ	555	IT	ROME	FCO	DE	FRANKFURT	FRA
AZ	788	IT	ROME	FCO	JP	TOKYO	TYO
AZ	789	JP	TOKYO	TYO	IT	ROME	FCO
AZ	790	IT	ROME	FCO	JP	OSAKA	KIX
DL	106	US	NEW YORK	JFK	DE	FRANKFURT	FRA
DL	1699	US	NEW YORK	JFK	US	SAN FRANCISCO	SFO
DL	1984	US	SAN FRANCISCO	SFO	US	NEW YORK	JFK
JL	407	JP	TOKYO	NRT	DE	FRANKFURT	FRA
JL	408	DE	FRANKFURT	FRA	JP	TOKYO	NRT
LH	400	DE	FRANKFURT	FRA	US	NEW YORK	JFK
LH	401	US	NEW YORK	JFK	DE	FRANKFURT	FRA
LH	402	DE	FRANKFURT	FRA	US	NEW YORK	JFK
LH	2402	DE	FRANKFURT	FRA	DE	BERLIN	SXF
LH	2407	DE	BERLIN	TXL	DE	FRANKFURT	FRA
QF	5	SG	SINGAPORE	SIN	DE	FRANKFURT	FRA
QF	6	DE	FRANKFURT	FRA	SG	SINGAPORE	SIN
SQ	2	SG	SINGAPORE	SIN	US	SAN FRANCISCO	SFO
SQ	15	US	SAN FRANCISCO	SFO	SG	SINGAPORE	SIN
SQ	158	SG	SINGAPORE	SIN	ID	JAKARTA	JKT
SQ	988	SG	SINGAPORE	SIN	JP	TOKYO	TYO
UA	941	DE	FRANKFURT	FRA	US	SAN FRANCISCO	SFO
UA	3504	US	SAN FRANCISCO	SFO	DE	FRANKFURT	FRA
UA	3516	US	NEW YORK	JFK	DE	FRANKFURT	FRA
UA	3517	DE	FRANKFURT	FRA	US	NEW YORK	JFK

Figure 15.2 List Display

Flight schedule

Flight schedule

Airline	Flight No.	Country	Depart. city	Depar	Country	Arrival city	Targe
AA	17	US	NEW YORK	JFK	US	SAN FRANCISCO	SFO
AA	64	US	SAN FRANCISCO	SFO	US	NEW YORK	JFK
AZ	555	IT	ROME	FCO	DE	FRANKFURT	FRA
AZ	788	IT	ROME	FCO	JP	TOKYO	TYO
AZ	789	JP	TOKYO	TYO	IT	ROME	FCO
AZ	790	IT	ROME	FCO	JP	OSAKA	KIX
DL	106	US	NEW YORK	JFK	DE	FRANKFURT	FRA
DL	1699	US	NEW YORK	JFK	US	SAN FRANCISCO	SFO
DL	1984	US	SAN FRANCISCO	SFO	US	NEW YORK	JFK
JL	407	JP	TOKYO	NRT	DE	FRANKFURT	FRA
JL	408	DE	FRANKFURT	FRA	JP	TOKYO	NRT
LH	400	DE	FRANKFURT	FRA	US	NEW YORK	JFK
LH	401	US	NEW YORK	JFK	DE	FRANKFURT	FRA
LH	402	DE	FRANKFURT	FRA	US	NEW YORK	JFK
LH	2402	DE	FRANKFURT	FRA	DE	BERLIN	SXF
LH	2407	DE	BERLIN	TXL	DE	FRANKFURT	FRA
QF	5	SG	SINGAPORE	SIN	DE	FRANKFURT	FRA
QF	6	DE	FRANKFURT	FRA	SG	SINGAPORE	SIN
SQ	2	SG	SINGAPORE	SIN	US	SAN FRANCISCO	SFO
SQ	15	US	SAN FRANCISCO	SFO	SG	SINGAPORE	SIN
SQ	158	SG	SINGAPORE	SIN	ID	JAKARTA	JKT
SQ	988	SG	SINGAPORE	SIN	JP	TOKYO	TYO
UA	941	DE	FRANKFURT	FRA	US	SAN FRANCISCO	SFO
UA	3504	US	SAN FRANCISCO	SFO	DE	FRANKFURT	FRA
UA	3516	US	NEW YORK	JFK	DE	FRANKFURT	FRA
UA	3517	DE	FRANKFURT	FRA	US	NEW YORK	JFK

Figure 15.3 Standard ALV

Note

The classic list display is still possible because it is the only way to display multiple rows for a record.

```
CLEAR: gt_outtab.
SELECT       * FROM  spfli
       INTO CORRESPONDING FIELDS OF TABLE gt_outtab
       WHERE  carrid  IN s_carrid.
TRY.
    cl_salv_table=>factory(
      IMPORTING
        r_salv_table = gr_table
      CHANGING
        t_table      = gt_outtab ).
  CATCH cx_salv_msg INTO gr_error.
    gv_str_text = gr_error->if_message~get_text( ).
    MESSAGE gv_str_text TYPE 'E'.
ENDTRY.
gr_table->display( ).
```

Listing 15.10 Select, Create the ALV and Display It

Notice that there is no field catalog and no structure name provided. If the fields referenced in the data table are defined with reference to data elements in the ABAP Dictionary, you need do nothing else. If you want, however, to change the display properties of the ALV, methods exist that allow you to change how the table is displayed.

You can, for example, display a column as an icon or change the heading of a column (short, medium, long, or tooltip). These methods allow you to reorder columns, specify the sort order, or hide columns, among other things. The biggest advantage of the new technique is the speed with which it is possible to write a program to produce an ALV. Because the field information is automatically produced or derived, you only need to program changes.

Caution

The classes discussed in the rest of this section are not superclasses and subclasses in the sense of object-oriented inheritance. This means that classes lower in the hierarchy do not inherit properties of classes higher in the hierarchy.

The terms *hierarchy*, *superobject*, and *subobject* are used to identify the parts of an ALV and show how all objects together represent the ALV as a whole.

To change an ALV using the ALV Object Model, you just need to have an object-oriented view of the ALV. Simply put, the ALV itself is an object, and its components, such as columns, functions, sorting, and so on are themselves objects, but are the subobjects of the ALV. If you want to change something about the ALV, you simply need to:

- Fetch the relevant subobject responsible for the property to be changed from the parent object (in this case the ALV instance), for example, columns.
- Call the method to change the status of the subobject.

Listing 15.11 shows the two steps by setting the zebra pattern. First, the ALV table reference is used to retrieve the display settings, and then the resulting object is used to call the appropriate method to change the attribute.

```
DATA:
  lr_display          TYPE REF TO cl_salv_display_settings.
lr_display = gr_table->get_display_settings( ).
lr_display->set_striped_pattern( value =
                                 if_salv_c_bool_sap=>true ).
```

Listing 15.11 Calling a Sub-Object

Nothing else is necessary; the change takes effect immediately. For some elements of the ALV, such as columns and functions, there are additional levels of subobjects. The plural named superobject "columns" contains properties that apply to all columns or that affect the interaction of all columns, such as column order. The singularly named subobject, for example the column AIRLINE, contains the properties that are only valid for that one column, such as the column title. The same two steps are repeated for as many levels as you need to process; retrieve the object reference from the parent object and use this object reference to call the method to make the change. Table 15.5 below contains the most-used subobjects, the method call to the ALV to retrieve the subobject, and the class of the subobject. Examples of this can be seen in Listing 15.12.

```
DATA:
  lv_short            TYPE scrtext_s,
  lv_medium           TYPE scrtext_m,
  lv_long             TYPE scrtext_l,
  lv_tooltip          TYPE lvc_tip,
```

```
  lr_column             TYPE REF TO cl_salv_column,
  ir_columns            TYPE REF TO cl_salv_columns_table.
ir_columns = gr_table->get_columns( ).

TRY.
    lr_column = ir_columns->get_column( 'FLTYPE' ).
    lr_column->set_visible( if_salv_c_bool_sap=>false ).
  CATCH cx_salv_not_found.                    "#EC NO_HANDLER
ENDTRY.

TRY.
    CALL METHOD ir_columns->get_column
      EXPORTING
        columnname = 'ICON_FLTTYPE'
      RECEIVING
        value      = lr_column.
    lv_short = 'Charter'(h37).
    lr_column->set_short_text( lv_short ).
    lv_medium = 'Charter flight'(h38).
    lr_column->set_medium_text( lv_medium ).
    lv_long = 'Charter flight'(h39).
    lr_column->set_long_text( lv_long ).
    lv_tooltip = 'Charter flight'(h40).
    lr_column->set_tooltip( lv_tooltip ).
  CATCH cx_salv_not_found .                   "#EC NO_HANDLER
ENDTRY.
```

Listing 15.12 Getting the Sub-Object from the ALV, Hiding a column, and Adding a Column Heading to a New Column

The uppermost class of the ALV Object Model class hierarchy is the class CL_SALV_TABLE. In ALV subordinate classes, naming conventions can help you identify the level of the object; if the name is plural (for example, CL_SALV_**COLUMNS**_TABLE), it refers to the properties of a group of ALV elements. If the name is singular (for example, CL_SALV_**COLUMN**_TABLE), you are dealing with the properties of a single element.

In Table 15.5, each of the GET methods (all are part of CL_SALV_TABLE) is shown with the object it delivers and a short description.

GET Method	Class of the Delivered Object	Description
GET_AGGREGATIONS	CL_SALV_AGGREGATIONS	Aggregated objects
GET_COLUMNS	CL_SAL_COLUMNS_TABLE	Columns superclass
GET_DISPLAY_SETTINGS	CL_SALV_DISPLAY_SETTINGS	Defining the display, i.e., title, stripe pattern, lines, etc.
GET_EVENT	CL_SALV_EVENTS_TABLE	Events
GET_FILTERS	CL_SALV_FILTERS	Filter criteria
GET_FUNCTIONAL_SETTINGS	CL_SALV_FUNCTIONAL_SETTINGS	Hyperlink and tooltip superclass
GET_FUNCTIONS	CL_SAL_FUNCTIONS_LIST	Functions such as sorting, aggregating, etc.
GET_LAYOUT	CL_SALV_LAYOUT	Layout variant storage, management, etc.
GET_PRINT	CL_SALV_PRINT	Printer settings
GET_SELECTIONS	CL_SALV_SELECTIONS	Selection mode and selections
GET_SORTS	CL_SALV_SORTS	Sorting criteria

Table 15.5 ALV Object Model Methods

There are also GET methods for subobjects of the second level (the subobject of the ALV object). These do not apply to the ALV object, but rather to the subobject's subobject, for example, the object containing all columns of the ALV (class CL_SAL_COLUMNS_TABLE). Table 15.6 shows the GET methods for these subclasses and the objects they deliver.

Class	Get Method	Returns Object of Type	Description
CL_SALV_AGGREGATIONS	GET_AGGREGATION	CL_SALV_AGGREGATION	An individual aggregation

Table 15.6 ALV Subobject Methods

Class	**Get Method**	**Returns Object of Type**	**Description**
CL_SAL_COLUMNS_ TABLE	GET_COLUMN	CL_SAL_COLUMN_ TABLE	One individual column
CL_SALV_FILTERS	GET_FILTER	CL_SALV_FILTER	One individual filter criterion
CL_SALV_ FUNCTIONAL_ SETTINGS	GET_HYPERLINKS	CL_SALV_ HYPERLINKS	Superclass for all hyperlinks
CL_SALV_ FUNCTIONAL_ SETTINGS	GET_TOOLTIPS	CL_SALV_TOOLTIPS	Superclass for all tooltips
CL_SALV_ FUNCTIONS_LIST	GET_FUNCTIONS	CL_SALV_FUNCTION	One individual function
CL_SALV_SORTS	GET_SORTS	CL_SALV_SORT	One individual sorting criterion

Table 15.6 ALV Subobject Methods (cont.)

The process used to place the ALV grid in a container on the screen follows the same initial steps as the older version of the ALV Grid Control, but then provides the container instance to the FACTORY. An example is shown in Listing 15.13.

```
IF gr_container_2100 IS NOT BOUND.
    CREATE OBJECT gr_container_2100
      EXPORTING
        container_name = 'CONTAINER_2100'.
  TRY.
      cl_salv_table=>factory(
        EXPORTING
          r_container    = gr_container_2100
          container_name = 'CONTAINER_2100'
        IMPORTING
          r_salv_table   = gr_table_2100
        CHANGING
          t_table        = gt_outtab_2100 ).
    CATCH cx_salv_msg.                          "#EC NO_HANDLER
  ENDTRY.
  PERFORM register_events_2100 USING gr_table_2100.
```

```
  gr_table_2100->display( ).
ENDIF.
```

Listing 15.13 Producing an ALV in a Container Using ALV Object Model

Because this routine is in code that is reexecuted, the code is placed in a check to see if the container already exists. If the container does not exist, a container is created. Once it creates the container, the FACTORY method is called, providing the container name and the reference to the created container (only the reference is actually necessary). Events are registered (the subroutine is shown in Listing 15.15) and the ALV is displayed. To provide a distinction between multiple containers, we have assigned a unique number to the various parts (in this case the screen number).

We have simplified this example slightly for space restrictions. Obviously, there should be error handling following the CATCH statement. Also, calls to subroutines to modify the technical attributes of the displayed table were omitted. We recommend placing these (sometimes lengthy) changes to the ALV in subroutines or other modularization units to provide clarity. Especially in the case of dynpro programming, where you may be providing many different containers, often you may be able to reuse some of these modularization units.

This leads us to the PERFORM that remains before the actual display. This process again is similar across both ALV classes (and any other type of event handling). Listing 15.14 shows the definition and implementation of a local class to handle the events raised (or at least the ones this program is interested in processing) from the ALV events class. The example concerns both double clicks and single clicks. When the event is triggered, our local class calls a subroutine to process the event.

```
CLASS lcl_handle_events_2100 DEFINITION.
  PUBLIC SECTION.
    METHODS:
      on_double_click FOR EVENT double_click
                      OF cl_salv_events_table
        IMPORTING row column,
      on_link_click FOR EVENT link_click
                    OF cl_salv_events_table
        IMPORTING row column.
ENDCLASS.                    " lcl_handle_events_2100 DEFINITION

CLASS lcl_handle_events_2100 IMPLEMENTATION.
```

```
  METHOD on_double_click.
    PERFORM double_click_2100 USING row column .
  ENDMETHOD.                      "on_double_click
  METHOD on_link_click.
    PERFORM link_click_2100 USING row column .
  ENDMETHOD.                      "on_link_click
ENDCLASS.              " lcl_handle_events_2100 IMPLEMENTATION
```

Listing 15.14 Definition of Local Event Handlers

After creating our ALV reference object and before displaying the table, we need to actually register the events. As with the older ALV (or any other type of event processing), you have the handler method of the instance "listen" for the triggered event. To do this you need to register this instance with the object that can trigger the event (producing effectively a list of listeners). An example of this is shown in Listing 15.15.

```
FORM register_events_2100  USING       p_gr_table
                           TYPE REF TO cl_salv_table.
  DATA: lr_events TYPE REF TO cl_salv_events_table.
  IF gr_events_2100 IS NOT BOUND.
    CREATE OBJECT gr_events_2100.
  ENDIF.
  lr_events = p_gr_table->get_event( ).
  SET HANDLER gr_events_2100->on_double_click FOR lr_events.
  SET HANDLER gr_events_2100->on_link_click FOR lr_events.
ENDFORM.                    " register_events_2100
```

Listing 15.15 Registering Events

Unlike the older version of ALV (where it is not necessary to create an object to the event class because the events belong to the ALV class), we create an object of the event class (CL_SALV_EVENTS_TABLE) if we do not have a valid reference and then set the handlers for the two events we are interested in processing.

Important Terminology

You should now know what a field catalog is and how to produce one for an ALV. You should also understand the process for producing an ALV in full-screen mode and in a container, in both versions of the ALV.

You should also have a thorough understanding of events related to an ALV. You need to understand how to write the handler method, how to register the event handler, and where to identify what events can be triggered. Figure 15.4 shows the events for the ALV Object Model and Table 15.7 shows the events for the grid control.

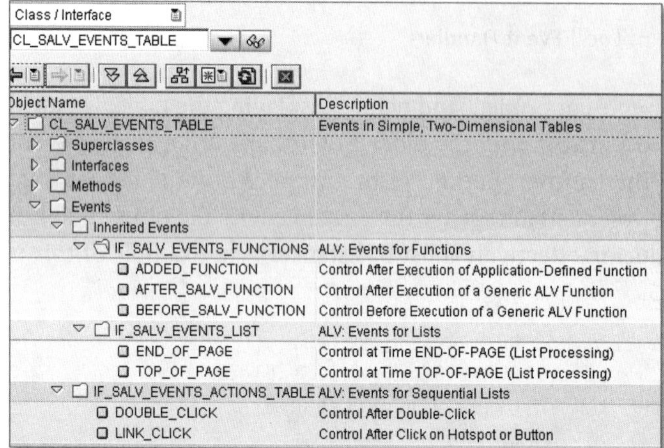

Figure 15.4 Events for CL_SALV_EVENTS_TABLE

Event	Description
AFTER_REFRESH	After list refresh
AFTER_USER_COMMAND	After user command
BEFORE_USER_COMMAND	Before user command
BUTTON_CLICK	Button click
CLICK_COL_HEADER	Click on column header
CLICK_ROW_COL	Click on cell
CONTEXT_MENU	Context menu
CONTEXT_MENU_REQUEST	Context menu
CONTEXT_MENU_SELECTED	Context menu entry selected
DATA_CHANGED	Data was changed

Table 15.7 Events for CL_GUI_ALV_GRID

Event	Description
DATA_CHANGED_FINISHED	Data in the output table was updated
DBLCLICK_ROW_COL	Double-click on cell
DELAYED_CALLBACK	Delayed callback
DELAYED_CHANGE_SELECTION	Selection has been modified
DELAYED_CHANGED_SEL_CALLBACK	The event is triggered if the user selects a row or column that has not yet been selected. The ALV Grid Control triggers this event with a short delay of 1.5 seconds.
DELAYED_MOVE_CURRENT_CELL	Focus cell has been moved
DOUBLE_CLICK	Double click
DOUBLE_CLICK_COL_SEPARATOR	Double-click on column separator
END_OF_LIST	End_of_list
F1	F1 chosen
HOTSPOT_CLICK	Hotspot was selected
LEFT_CLICK_DESIGN	Left mouse button pressed on control in design mode
LEFT_CLICK_RUN	Left mouse button pressed on control in run mode
MENU_BUTTON	Menu button
MOVE_CONTROL	Control moved
ONDRAG	For drag source
ONDROP	For drop target
ONDROPCOMPLETE	For drag source in case of success
ONDROPGETFLAVOR	Multiple flavors possible at a drop
ONF1	On help request
ONF4	On value request
PRINT_END_OF_LIST	Print mode: END_OF_LIST of classic ALV

Table 15.7 Events for CL_GUI_ALV_GRID (cont.)

Event	Description
PRINT_END_OF_PAGE	Print mode: END_OF_PAGE in list processing
PRINT_TOP_OF_LIST	Print mode: TOP_OF_LIST of classic ALV
PRINT_TOP_OF_PAGE	Print mode: TOP_OF_PAGE in list processing
RIGHT_CLICK	Right mouse button clicked on control
SIZE_CONTROL	Control resized
SUBTOTAL_TEXT	Edit subtotals text
TOOLBAR	Toolbar
TOOLBAR_BUTTON_CLICK	Toolbar button chosen
TOOLBAR_MENU_SELECTED	Toolbar menu entry selected
TOOLBAR_MENUBUTTON_CLICK	Toolbar menu button chosen
TOP_OF_PAGE	Top of page
TOTAL_CLICK_ROW_COL	Click on totals line
USER_COMMAND	User command

Table 15.7 Events for CL_GUI_ALV_GRID (cont.)

Practice Questions

The practice questions below will help you evaluate your understanding of the topic. The questions shown are similar in nature to those found on the certification examination, but whereas none of these questions will be found on the exam itself, they allow you to review your knowledge of the subject. Select the correct answers and then check the completeness of your answers in the following solution section. Remember that you must select all correct answers and only correct answers to receive credit for the question.

1. What is the best order to provide an event handler for an ALV:

☐ **A.** Create the ALV, write the handler, register for the event, display the ALV

☐ **B.** Register for the event, write the handler, create the ALV, display the ALV

☐ **C.** Write the handler, register for the event, create the ALV, display the ALV

☑ **D.** Write the handler, create the ALV, register for the event, display the ALV

☐ **E.** Write the handler, create the ALV, display the ALV, register for the event

2. The differences between displaying in a full screen and in a container are:

☐ **A.** The full screen requires dynpro programming.

☑ **B.** The container requires the use of an additional object (a container control).

☐ **C.** The only difference is that the container name must be specified when creating the ALV object.

☐ **D.** Only a full-screen ALV allows the use of event handling.

☐ **E.** Only an ALV in a container allows the use of event handling.

☑ **F.** Any type of ALV allows the use of event handling.

3. To reserve an area on the screen for an ALV Grid Control you must:

☐ **A.** Create an object (instantiate the object) of the class `CL_GUI_CUSTOM_CONTAINER`

☐ **B.** Create an object (instantiate the object) of the class `CL_GUI_ALV_GRID`

☐ **C.** Create an object (instantiate the object) of the class `CL_SALV_TABLE`

☑ **D.** Use the Screen Painter

4. You must call a method to actually display the contents of the display table after you create an ALV.

☑ **A.** True

☐ **B.** False

5. The field catalog allows you to:

☑ **A.** To add a field to the display

☑ **B.** To specify the sort order of the display table

☐ **C.** To produce a striped pattern for the display lines

☑ **D.** To change the title of a column

☑ **E.** To change the display order of a column

6. Which class is used to define a reference for an instance of the ALV Object Model:

☐ **A.** Class `CL_GUI_CUSTOM_CONTAINER`

☐ **B.** Class `CL_GUI_ALV_GRID`

☐ **C.** Class `CL_SALV_TABLE`

7. You use the `CREATE OBJECT` statement to create both types of ALV.

☐ **A.** True

☐ **B.** False

8. The ALV Object Model:

☐ **A.** Is a group of classes that describe the ALV grid as a whole and inherit from a single class

☐ **B.** Is a group of hierarchal classes that describe the ALV grid as a whole but do not inherit from a single class

Practice Question Answers and Explanations

1. Correct answer: **D**

   You should write the handlers, create the ALV, and then register the events of the ALV you just created before you actually display the ALV.

2. Correct answers: **B, F**

   The container requires the use of an additional object to link the control that exists on the presentation server to the program running on the application server. A container control provides this function and is produced from the class `CL_GUI_CUSTOM_CONTAINER`.

3. Correct answer: **D**

   To allocate an area on the screen you use the Screen Painter to "draw" the container on the screen and name it. Later when the program creates the object for the container, this name is used to assist in linking the control in the SAP GUI with the application program.

4. Correct answer: **A**

   This is true for both versions of ALV. In both cases you create the ALV and then call a display method for that object. The method for the ALV Grid Control is SET_TABLE_FOR_FIRST_DISPLAY of the class CL_GUI_ALV_GRID, and for the ALV Object Model the method is DISPLAY from the class CL_SALV_TABLE.

5. Correct answers: **A, D, E**

   The field catalog allows you to add a column to the display, hide a column from the display, change the title of a column, or place the columns in a different order. The ALV Grid Control expects different parameters to provide information for sorting, filtering, changing the layout, or providing variants.

6. Correct answer: **C**

   The ALV Grid Control uses the class CL_GUI_ALV_GRID, and the ALV Object Model uses the class CL_SALV_TABLE.

7. Correct answer: **B**

   The CREATE OBJECT statement is only used to instantiate the ALV Grid Control. The FACTORY method of the class CL_SALV_TABLE is used to instantiate an ALV Object Model ALV grid. The CREATE OBJECT is in fact inside the FACTORY method, so an object is created for you, and then the reference is passed back out of the method.

8. Correct answer: **B**

   The classes of the ALV Object Model are not superclasses and subclasses in the sense of object-oriented ABAP; that is, the classes lower in the hierarchy here do not inherit the properties of the classes higher in the hierarchy. The terms *hierarchy*, *superobject*, and *subobject* should rather illustrate how all objects together represent the ALV as a whole.

Take Away

You will need to understand the field catalog: how to produce one and how to modify it. You need to know the process for producing an ALV in a full screen and in a container, in both versions of the ALV. You also need to know about event handling for an ALV. You need to know the steps: write the handler, register the event, and where to identify what events can be triggered.

Refresher

You must understand the steps necessary to place an ALV grid in a container: from allocating space in the screen using Screen Painter to creating the container in your program and placing the ALV into the container. Effective use in a container requires an understanding of classic dynpro handling (see also Chapter 9, Basic ABAP Programs and Interface Creation, and Chapter 12, Classical Screens).

Table 15.8 shows the key concepts for ALV programming.

Key Concept	Definition
Container control	The container control is used to connect the dynpro to the control. This allows the ALV grid to "sit" inside the container, which itself sits inside the reserved area on the screen.
Control	Controls are stand-alone binary software components that are reusable.
Field catalog	The field catalog contains the rules that describe how the data table is to be displayed.
ALV Object Model	The ALV Object Model was a new feature in SAP NetWeaver 6.40. It is more modern and simpler to use than the original ALV Grid Control.

Table 15.8 Key Concepts Refresher

Tips

As with the majority of the subjects found in the certification examination, it is important to have as much practical experience with the subject as possible. We suggest that if you have not had much exposure to ALV programming, write a couple of quick programs to understand the concepts. You should use both versions of the ALV and both full screen and in a container. Simply select data from a database table and then produce the ALV.

Summary

You should now be able to produce ALV grids in a variety of ways and understand how to interact with the ALV and the user through events. This knowledge will allow you to easily pass this topic on the certification examination.

User Interfaces (Web Dynpro)

16

Techniques You'll Master:

- Understand the architecture of a Web Dynpro component
- Explore the navigation and data transfer in and between Web Dynpro components
- Identify the most important elements that are part of a Web Dynpro application
- Name the contents of a Web Dynpro controller
- Define the mapping between contexts of different controllers located in the same Web Dynpro component

Web Dynpro is a framework for SAP standard user interfaces and provides support for the development of the Web representation of business applications. Web Dynpro is available on both the ABAP and the Java development environments.

In this chapter you will be provided with a basic understanding of Web Dynpro ABAP. We will discuss the architecture of Web Dynpro components. We will discuss the Model View Controller design paradigm used in Web Dynpro ABAP and the differences between this and UI design models. We will cover the different types of controllers, identifying their differences and explaining how they are used. We will also explain data exchange between the components of a Web Dynpro application.

Real-World Scenario

You have been asked to identify what technology is best to develop ABAP-based web transactions. There are a number of encapsulated functions developed for use in your company's SAP system that management would like to make available in a web browser.

The thought is that a web-based application would be simpler to roll out to users and easier for them to learn. The fact that it is browser-based means that the SAP GUI does not need to be installed, so it would have minimal impact on both users and your IT department, and new functionality could be rolled out simply by providing links to this new functionality.

However, management also wants to have controls in place. They want to be able to control authorizations and job function access to some of the data. Of the available web-based user interfaces, you find that Web Dynpro meets the entire criterion for your company. Now you need to explain the technology to the other developers.

Objectives of this Portion of the Test

The purpose of this portion of the certification examination is to verify that you have an understanding of Web Dynpro ABAP and its capabilities. Therefore, this portion of the examination will test your knowledge of a Web Dynpro development. The points that you will need to understand from this section include:

- The architecture of a Web Dynpro component and how these components can be linked
- The use of a Web Dynpro component that is reusable and mandatory
- The contents of a Web Dynpro controller and how they work together

The certification examination will give medium weight to this chapter compared to the other topics in the examination. Because this is similar in concept to classical dynpro programming, it is given a similar weighting. This means there will be an average percentage of questions when comparing this chapter than any other chapter.

Key Concepts Refresher

You need to understand and be able to perform the following types of tasks when developing Web Dynpro ABAP applications:

- Navigation and data transfer within a Web Dynpro component and between Web Dynpro components
- Define the mapping between contexts of different controllers located in the same Web Dynpro component
- Declare the usage of a component in another component

Web Dynpro Design

Web Dynpro is one of the SAP NetWeaver standard programming models for user interfaces (UIs). The Web Dynpro framework is based on the Model View Controller paradigm to ensure a clear division between the definition of the user interface and the implementation of the application logic. It has the following features that build on the classic dynpro model:

- A clear separation between business logic and display logic.
- A uniform metamodel for all types of user interfaces. User interface patterns normally only contain generic functions of the user interface (for example, a search) and describe the general appearance of the interface.
- Execution on a number of client platforms. The metadata of Web Dynpro is independent of the platform where the application is executed. If the metadata is transferred to a different platform, new source code for that platform is generated.

Web Dynpro is available in both the ABAP and the Java development environments. It provides tools for developing a web-based business application. You use these tools to describe the properties and functions of Web Dynpro applications in the form of Web Dynpro metadata. The user interface source code necessary for Web Dynpro is automatically generated and executed at runtime.

Each user interface in Web Dynpro is always made up of the same basic elements, for example, UI elements. These elements of the metamodel are declared using Web Dynpro tools. This allows you to define the user interface you require for adding buttons, fields, and so on. The system automatically generates the necessary code for this metamodel.

Web Dynpro ABAP was released with SAP NetWeaver Application Server 7.0. To support this declarative concept of a Web Dynpro application, the ABAP Workbench (the central point of entry into the ABAP Workbench is Transaction SE80, the Object Navigator) now contains a range of Web Dynpro tools. You can generate a large proportion of a Web Dynpro application using the tools provided, without the need to create your own source code. This applies to the following parts of the application:

- Data flow between the frontend and backend
- Layout of the user interface
- Properties of user interface elements

Every Web Dynpro application is structured according to the Model View Controller paradigm:

- **Model**
  The model is the interface to the system and enables the Web Dynpro application access to the business data.
- **View**
  The view is responsible for the presentation of the data in the browser or other client.
- **Controller**
  The controller lies between the view and the model. It is responsible for formatting the model data for display in the view, processing the user entries made by the user, and returning them to the model; exactly as the name would suggest, it controls things.

A Web Dynpro component is a reusable entity. The creation of a Web Dynpro component is always mandatory, because the existence of the following is linked to the existence of the component itself:

- Web Dynpro window
- Views
- Controllers

The component interfaces are implemented to provide communication between the elements of two Web Dynpro components and their call by a user. Their close relationship with each other means it does not make sense to consider the individual parts of the component separately.

A Web Dynpro component can be thought of as the container for all of the things you need to create. It is similar to a module pool being the container for screens and code for a dialog transaction. Figure 16.1 shows an example of a Web Dynpro component.

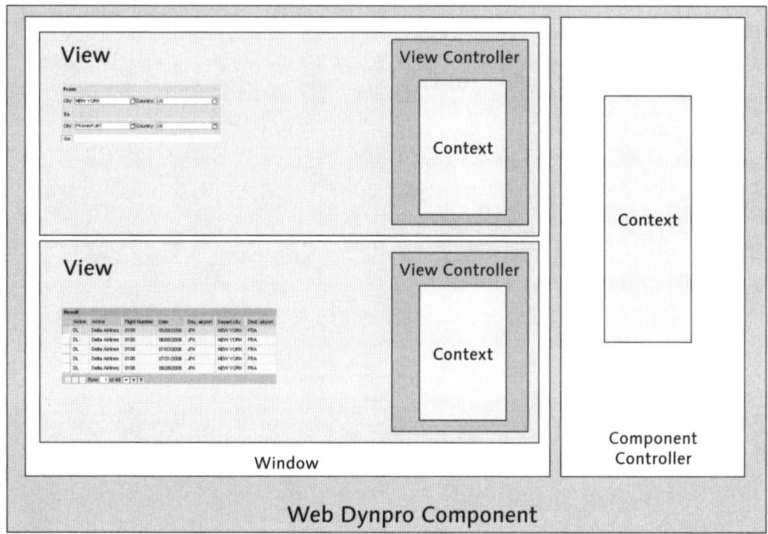

Figure 16.1 Web Dynpro Component

A view represents a rectangular portion of a page displayed by the client. Like a normal dynpro, it contains UI elements such as input fields and buttons (see Figure 16.2). The positioning of these elements is controlled by a property called the *layout* (see Figure 16.3). A single web page can be composed of a single view or multiple views. A window (see Figure 16.4) defines the combination of views and the navigation between these views. A window can contain an arbitrary number of views, and a view can be embedded in an arbitrary number of windows. A Web Dynpro application must have at least one view and at least one window.

Web Dynpro controllers contain the Web Dynpro source code. The hierarchical storage for the global data area of controllers is called the *context*.

A Web Dynpro component has a lifetime that begins the first time it is called at runtime and ends with the Web Dynpro application that called and instantiated the component ends.

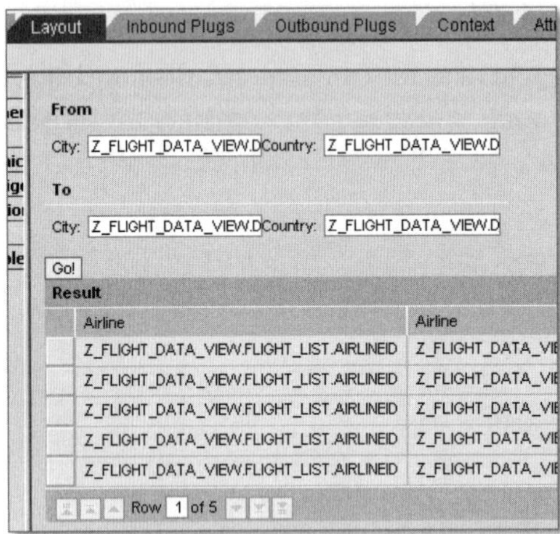

Figure 16.2 View Layout

Property	Value	Binding
Properties (TransparentContainer)		
ID	ROOTUIELEMENTCONTAINER	
Layout	FlowLayout	
accessibilityDescription		
defaultButtonId		
enabled	☑	
height		
isLayoutContainer	☑	
scrollingMode	none	
tooltip		
visible	Visible	
width		
Layout (FlowLayout)		
wrapping	☑	

Figure 16.3 RootUIElementContainer Properties

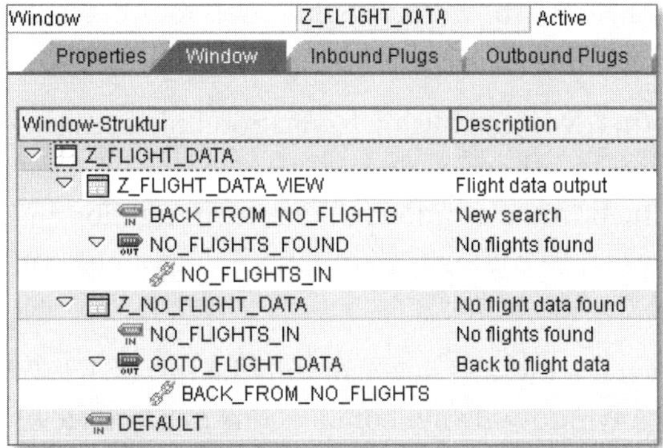

Figure 16.4 Window Structure

In addition to the visible part (the layout), a view also contains:

- A controller
- A context

The controller is the active part of the view and is where the code relating to the view is stored. It determines how the user interacts with the Web Dynpro. The data used in the view is found in the view context.

Navigation between different views is enabled by plugs. Plugs are your entry and exit points for views and are divided into:

- Inbound plugs (entry point)
- Outbound plugs (exit point)

The outbound plugs of a view can be used to navigate to a subsequent view. Plugs are part of a view's controller. They are assigned to exactly one view.

There are normally several views embedded in a Web Dynpro window. It is therefore necessary to specify one view as the view that is displayed first when a window is called. This view is assigned the Default property.

Note

The first view you create is assigned this property automatically, but you can change it if you later decide that the starting point should be a different view.

Entering a view using an inbound plug always causes an event to be triggered. As a result, an event handler method (whose use is optional) is automatically generated for every inbound plug. This allows the inbound plug itself to process the event to be handled.

To navigate from one view to another, you establish a navigation link from each outbound plug of the first view to an inbound plug of the subsequent view. These navigation links are maintained in the window. Only one navigation link can originate from one outbound plug. In contrast, an inbound plug can be controlled by several outbound plugs.

A window is used to combine several views. A view can only be displayed if it has been embedded in a window. A window always contains one or more views. These views are connected by navigation links as described above. One of these views is specified as the start view (default) and is displayed the first time the window is called. Each window has a uniquely assigned interface view (this is generated automatically by the system whe ever you create a window). This interface view represents the outward view of the window and is linked with a Web Dynpro application so that the window can be called using a URL. Each interface view is associated with one window, and each window is associated with one interface view.

A window has one or several inbound or outbound plugs. Through the use of these plugs, you can include a window in a navigation chain. Each window plug is visible within the entire window, and it can be used for navigating within this window.

Note

If you add an existing plug of a window to the component interface, it becomes part of the interface view belonging to this window. This also makes them visible beyond the limits of the component. These interface plugs are required whenever:

- You embed a component window in the window of another component
- You set a Web Dynpro application so that it can be called
- You exit a Web Dynpro application

Controllers

Controllers determine how the user can interact with the application. A Web Dynpro application can contain different.instances of controllers and contexts.

In addition to view controllers, which control the behavior of an individual view, there are also global controllers that provide more general services for all views of a component (see Figure 16.1 for the relationship of the controllers).

At least one global controller is contained in each Web Dynpro component that is visible from within the component for all other controllers: the component controller. The lifetime for this component controller extends from creating data within the controller to cover the whole period during which the component is in use. You can add additional global controllers in the form of custom controllers. Their lifetimes are as long as any view of the component exists.

Each view has exactly one view controller and exactly one view context. This view controller processes the actions performed by the user in the view. The view context contains the data required for the view. The life of a view controller and its corresponding context is at least as long as the view is visible in the browser. If you replace a view with a successive view, the local data (context) is also no longer available.

Each Web Dynpro component contains exactly one interface controller, which is a global controller that is also visible outside the component. This makes it part of the interface of a Web Dynpro component. Communication from one controller to another occurs by calling methods from a different controller or by triggering an event that other controllers have registered. You define these controller uses when you create a controller.

All controller contexts consist of a hierarchal list of nodes and attributes. A context always has a parent, known as a context root node. The context nodes are arranged in a hierarchy and can have attributes or other nodes as children. An attribute is not permitted to have children. All the child entries for a node are known as an element. You can think of a collection of elements in the same way that a table is a collection of rows.

There are five types of controllers in a Web Dynpro ABAP component. The different controller types differ in the entities of which they are composed:

- **Component controller**
  A Web Dynpro component has only one component controller. This is a global controller and is therefore visible to all other controllers. The functionality of the entire component is driven by the component controller. There is no visual interface for this controller.

- **Custom controller**
  Custom controllers are optional. They can be used to encapsulate subfunctions of the component controller.
- **Configuration controller**
  This is a special custom controller. You only need it if the corresponding component implements special configuration and personalization functionality.
- **View controller**
  There is exactly one view controller for each view (which consists of the layout part and the view controller). This controller processes view-specific flow logic, for example, checking user input and handling user actions.
- **Window controller**
  There is exactly one window controller for each window. This controller can be used to process the data passed via the inbound plugs when it is reused as a child controller. The inbound plug methods of the window can call methods of this controller.

All controller instances are singletons in respect to their parent component (each component has exactly one controller). Each controller has its own context with an existing context root node. You must define all other nodes and attributes.

For all controllers, methods exist that are called by the Web Dynpro framework in a predefined order. These are called *hook methods*. Different hook methods are available depending on the controller type. All controller types contain at least two hook methods. These methods are processed only once during the lifetime of a controller instance: when a controller instance is created (`wddoinit`) and when a controller instance is deleted (`wddoexit`). `wddoinit` can be used to create instances or triggering authorization checks, where `wddoexit` can be used to release record locks.

There are two predefined controller attributes; they are used to access the functionality of the controller (`wd_this`) and the context (`wd_context`). `wd_this` is a self-reference (it is not the same as `ME`, which is used in ABAP self-reference) to the current controller's interface (`IF_<controller_name>`). It represents all functionality implemented in the generated class. `wd_context` is a self-reference to the controller's context root node.

To share information between different controllers, one controller must declare the use of another controller. You do this on the PROPERTIES tab of the controller that needs to access another controller. You most frequently have a requirement for this kind of data sharing when you want to create a mapped context node or access another controller's user-defined methods.

Contexts

When a node is created in the context of a Web Dynpro component, you specify the cardinality of the node. The cardinality defines how often a node will be instantiated at runtime, in other words, how many elements of this node are available at runtime. Table 16.1 shows the possible cardinalities of a Web Dynpro component.

Cardinality	Description
`1...1`	Only one element can be instantiated.
`0...1`	No more than one element can be instantiated, but it is also possible that no element is instantiated.
`1...n`	At least one element must be instantiated.
`0...n`	Zero or more instances of the context node can be instantiated.

Table 16.1 Cardinality of a Web Dynpro Component

Within the Web Dynpro architecture, it is possible to link the contexts of the different controllers in different ways:

- You can link a UI element of the user interface of the view with an element of the view context. This is known as *data binding*.
- You can define a mapping between two global controller contexts or from a view context to a global controller context. This is known as *context mapping*, and only a reference to the data is made.

Events

The component controller allows you to create events that are used to provide communication between controllers. This communication allows one controller to trigger event handlers in different controllers. Interface controller's events allow cross-component communication to be implemented. Component controller events are only visible within the component.

Some UI elements, for example, the `Button` element, can react to a user's interaction. These events are predefined, and you have to link them with an action at design time (see Figure 16.5). If such an action is created, an event handler method is automatically created for this action. You can equip a UI element event (which may have been inserted several times into a view) with different actions. The event handler linked to that action will then process the event (see Listing 16.1).

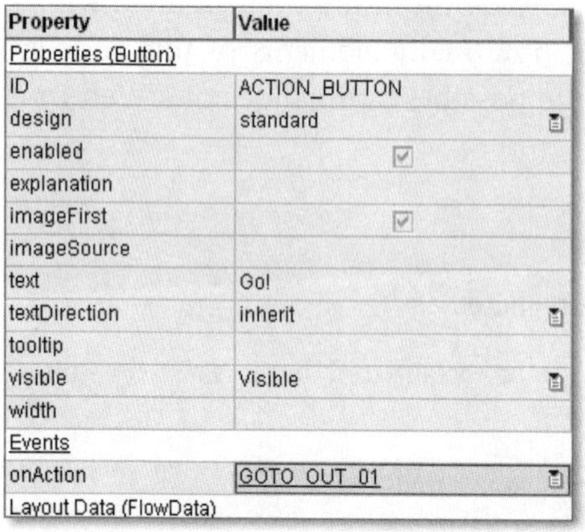

Property	Value
Properties (Button)	
ID	ACTION_BUTTON
design	standard
enabled	☑
explanation	
imageFirst	☑
imageSource	
text	Go!
textDirection	inherit
tooltip	
visible	Visible
width	
Events	
onAction	GOTO_OUT_01
Layout Data (FlowData)	

Figure 16.5 Button Properties and Event

```
METHOD onactiongoto_out_01 .
  wd_this->fire_out_01_plg(
  ).
ENDMETHOD.
```

Listing 16.1 Event Handler

Each component has an interface to enable communication between Web Dynpro components and to enable a component to be called by a user. The interface consists of two parts:

- Interface view
- Interface controller

Web Dynpro Application

A Web Dynpro application is an entry point into a Web Dynpro component and is the only Web Dynpro entity that can be addressed by a URL. A module pool again provides a good comparison. A module pool must be started with a transaction code, and the Web Dynpro application provides the same starting point for Web Dynpro. The Web Dynpro application is a link to an interface view of Web Dynpro through the use of an inbound plug declared as a startup plug that has a default starting view. It contains no information about the elements of the corresponding component or components behind the interface view. You must specify the following to define a Web Dynpro application:

- The component to be called; this component is known as the *root component*.
- The interface view of the root component will be initially used; the default view in this interface defines the default view assembly (the subset of visible views).
- The inbound plug acts as the entry point for the interface view (the type of this inbound plug must be `Startup`). If you create a Web Dynpro application for a component that has only one window (and therefore only one interface view), then the starting point will be determined automatically.

Graphical Elements

A UI element is any graphical entity (input field, button, textview, etc.) that occupies a position within a view layout. Each UI element is part of the hierarchal list (see Figure 16.6 for an example). This does not mean that all UI elements are visible on the screen. Some UI elements are never visible on the screen, such as the `TransparentContainer` or the `ViewUIElementContainer`. These elements structure the UI without being visible, but like the visible UI elements, they occupy a position in the UI element hierarchy. At runtime, all UI elements can be set to invisible without freeing the space they occupy as UI elements.

Numerous UI elements are available for designing the appearance of a Web Dynpro application. The UI elements are divided into categories (see the list below). These categories are displayed in the view designer when the layout preview is visible. You can drag and drop them into the layout, or alternatively, you can use the context menu of the `ROOTUIELEMENT` to create UI elements for your view layout. You should also be aware that the categories have changed through various support packages of SAP NetWeaver 7.0, but these changes will not be part of the examination. Also, placement of a UI element is only possible within the layout property. This means that unlike a classic dynpro, it is not possible to move a UI element to a specific point in the view, but it is automatically placed based on the layout property and the preceding UI elements.

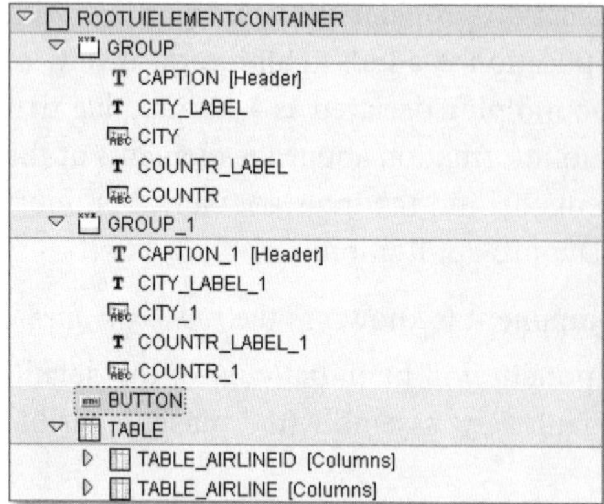

Figure 16.6 RootUIElementContainer Hierarchy

Some of the UI element categories are as follows:

- The standard simple category contains elements that are used frequently in Web Dynpro applications. Examples are `Button`, `Label`, and `InputField`.
- The standard complex category contains elements that need to have child elements to define a valid UI element that can be rendered. An example is a `Table`, which needs to have a child element of `TableColumn` for each column to be displayed.
- The standard container category contains elements that can have child elements. Container UI elements can structure the layout either visibly or invisibly.

Other categories contain elements to display ActiveX-based diagrams (Active Component), SAP Interactive Forms by Adobe (Adobe), or business graphics rendered by the Internet Graphics Server (BusinessGraphics) or to embed office documents such as Microsoft Word or Excel documents (OfficeIntegration) and some other special UI elements.

All view layouts are derived from a hierarchy of UI elements. The root node is always of type `TransparentContainer` (a non-visible container), and is always called `RootUIElementContainer`. You cannot change this. All UI elements added to a view layout are hierarchically subordinate to the root node `RootUIElementContainer`.

Container elements, as mentioned above, are UI elements that can have child elements. In the view's layout they occupy a rectangular area. All child UI elements of a container element are located within this rectangular area. All container elements also define how their children will be arranged using the Layout property that assigns a layout manager to the UI element. All of the child elements of a UI element container inherit a set of properties that relate to the value of the container's Layout property section Layout Data. The Layout property can have one of four values: FlowLayout, RowLayout, MatrixLayout, or GridLayout.

- FlowLayout
  The default layout manager is the FlowLayout layout manager. This layout displays all child attributes of this container in a row. If the container UI element is too narrow for all child elements to be displayed in one row, they will wrap automatically to the next lines. You cannot force the wrapping at design time. UI elements in different lines are not related to each other and are not aligned in columns. You use this kind of container to arrange subcontainers. An example of FlowLayout can be seen in Figure 16.7.

  Figure 16.7 FlowLayout

- RowLayout
  If the RowLayout layout manager is used with the container UI element. All children inherit the property LayoutData, which can have the values RowData and RowHeadData. If you set this property to RowHeadData, a break is forced, and this and subsequent elements appear in the next row. If you set the property to RowData, this child element will appear in the same line as the previous element, even if the right-hand margin is reached. UI elements located in different rows are not related to each other and are not aligned in columns. You can set the width of each cell by using the width attribute of each child element. An example of RowLayout can be seen in Figure 16.8.

  Figure 16.8 RowLayout (with RowHeadData set on Flight Number and Plane Type)

- `MatrixLayout`
  If the `MatrixLayout` layout manager is used with the container UI element, all children inherit the property `LayoutData`, which can have values `Maxtrix-Data` and `MatrixHeadData`. If you set this property to `MatrixHeadData`, a line break is forced. If you set the property to `MatrixData`, the child elements will appear in the same line as the previous element, even if the right-hand margin is reached. The child elements in this container are arranged in columns.

  When you use this layout manager, there is not a static number of columns, but the number of columns is defined by the maximum number of child elements in any row. You do not have to have the same number of elements in different rows. It is possible to span multiple cells with a UI element arranged in a `MatrixLayout` by using the `colSpan(property)`. An example of `Matrix-Layout` can be seen in Figure 16.9.

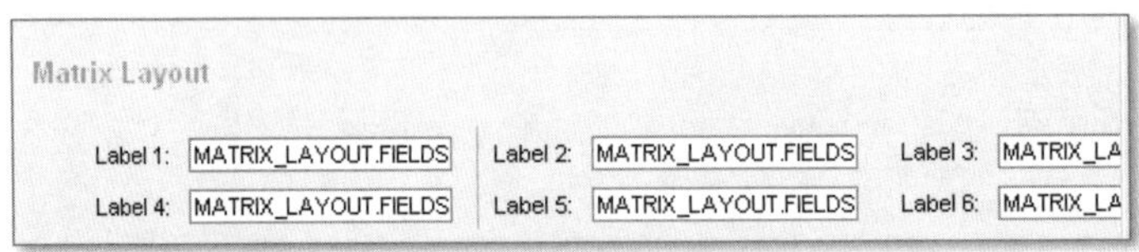

Figure 16.9 MatrixLayout

- `GridLayout`
  Like the `MatrixLayout`, the `GridLayout` layout manager can be used if you want a vertical alignment of the elements. Here the number of columns is static and is defined with the `colCount` property of the container element. A single child element does not therefore control whether it is the first element of a new row. A break will take place once all cells of a row are occupied. If an element or elements are removed, the arrangement following this point will shift "left" to fill the now empty cells.

  The best way to use the `GridLayout` layout manager is if all rows occupy the same number of columns and only complete rows are either inserted or deleted. Instead of removing UI elements completely, you can replace them with an `InvisibleElement` to retain the original element arrangement. An example of `GridLayout` can be seen in Figure 16.10.

You edit a view layout with the View Editor, which is a Web Dynpro-specific tool. The View Editor is only available for you to use when you are editing a view controller. A custom controller will not show the View Editor because these controllers have no visual interface.

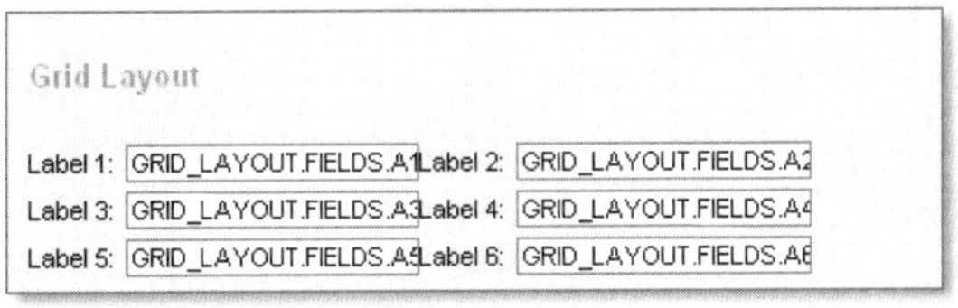

Grid Layout

Label 1:	GRID_LAYOUT.FIELDS.A1	Label 2:	GRID_LAYOUT.FIELDS.A2
Label 3:	GRID_LAYOUT.FIELDS.A3	Label 4:	GRID_LAYOUT.FIELDS.A4
Label 5:	GRID_LAYOUT.FIELDS.A5	Label 6:	GRID_LAYOUT.FIELDS.A6

Figure 16.10 GridLayout (with colCount of 4)

The PROPERTIES area displays all properties of a selected UI element (see Figure 16.5, above, for an example). The supported client-side events are listed in the EVENTS properties section if a UI element supports events. Properties related to client-side events begin with the prefix `on` (for example, `onFilter`, `onSort`, or `onAction`). You must associate actions with each of these events.

Once you have bound a UI element property to a context node or attribute, the UI element property is supplied with a value from the context data. If the user can update the UI element property, the context is automatically updated with the new value during the next round trip. An example of binding is shown in Figure 16.11.

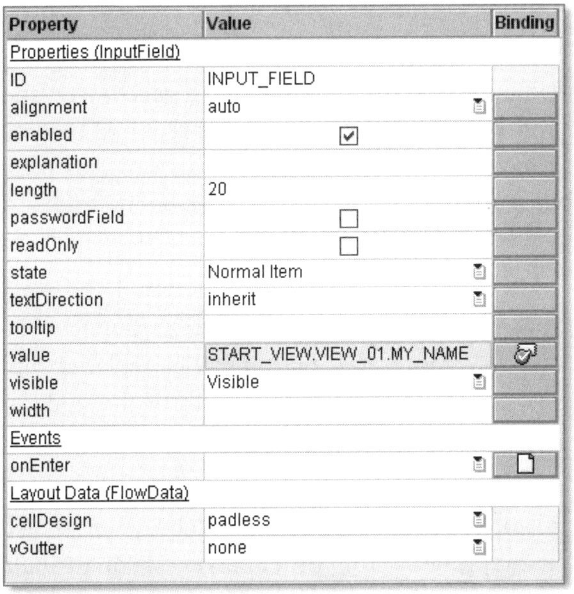

Property	Value	Binding
Properties (InputField)		
ID	INPUT_FIELD	
alignment	auto	
enabled	☑	
explanation		
length	20	
passwordField	☐	
readOnly	☐	
state	Normal Item	
textDirection	inherit	
tooltip		
value	START_VIEW.VIEW_01.MY_NAME	
visible	Visible	
width		
Events		
onEnter		
Layout Data (FlowData)		
cellDesign	padless	
vGutter	none	

Figure 16.11 Binding Example

Note

You can only have a binding relationship between the context and UI elements of the same view controller. For this reason, any data that you want to bind to the view UI elements must be stored in the context, as opposed to the attributes of the controller.

It is usually possible for you to have full control over the appearance of the screen layout through the use of the Web Dynpro view controller without ever needing direct access to the UI element objects. You bind any property over which you want to have programmatic control to an appropriate context node or attribute. Then you manipulate the context nodes or attributes to which the UI elements are bound to control the behavior of the UI elements.

To display data for a UI element, you must bind its value property to an appropriate context node or attribute. At a minimum you must do the following to display data in the view:

1. Create a node or attribute in the view controller's context to contain the data. It is not important whether this is a mapped context node or not.
2. Create the UI element in your view layout.
3. Properties requiring a context binding show a button with a yellow icon and an empty circle to the right of the property. You assign the required binding by clicking on this button. The view controller's context is displayed in a dialog box. All nodes or attributes of the appropriate type to be bound to the UI element property are displayed. You then select an appropriate node or attribute.

After you complete these steps, the context path to the node or attribute will be displayed as the property's value. The empty circle button will be replaced with a green check mark icon (see Figure 16.11). The context path of the node or attribute to which it is bound will also be displayed on the layout preview for the UI element.

When you establish a binding relationship, this instructs the Web Dynpro screen to obtain the value for a UI element property from the context node or attribute to which it is bound. You are not limited with context binding to just supplying an `InputField` with a value. The value property of a UI element is just one of the properties that can be supplied with data with a binding relationship. The binding between a UI element and a context attribute is a two-way relationship:

- Data is transported from a context to the client during screen rendering.
- Data entered by the user is transported back to the context when the HTTP return trip is processed. This is a similar concept to that used by a dynpro's input fields.

After you declare a binding relationship, the data in the bound nodes and attributes is transported automatically to the corresponding UI elements. After the user has interacted with the screen and initiated an HTTP round trip, the new or modified data in the UI elements is transported back to the same nodes and attributes in the view controller's context. Before the Web Dynpro framework turns control over to the action handler, the context already contains the updated information.

Note

There is nothing you need to do for this process. The two-way transport process is entirely automatic. You only need to declare a binding relationship.

Many UI elements (`TextViews`, `Labels`, `Captions`, and so on) display texts when rendered. You can obtain these texts from the ABAP Dictionary in two ways:

- You bind the property related to the text to a context attribute. This context attribute is typed with a data element defined in the ABAP Dictionary.
- The UI element is related to a second UI element, which is bound to a context element that is typed with a data element. In this case, the property related to the text must be left blank in order to use the dictionary text.

Note

A `Label` is related to an `InputField`, and the `Text` property of the `Label` is left blank. The label text then originates from the data element related to the `InputField`.

Important Terminology

You should be able to identify what makes up a Web Dynpro application. You should know the parts of a Web Dynpro component. In addition, you will need to understand the purpose of each part and how they exchange information or events with other parts of the same or another Web Dynpro component. You should know the types of controllers, the purpose of each, and the number possible.

Table 16.2 shows the terms used with Web Dynpros.

Term	Meaning
Web Dynpro components	Containers for other entities related to the UI and the Web Dynpro.
View	The layout of a view represents a rectangular part of a page displayed by the client. The view contains UI elements such as input fields and buttons.
Window	An entity related to the UI; it is the possible combination of views and flow between the views.
Web Dynpro controller	Where the Web Dynpro source code is located.
Context	The hierarchical storage area for the global data of controllers.
Plugs	Provide navigation. Outbound plugs connect to the inbound plug or starting point for a view. Plugs are part of the controller of a view. They are always assigned to one view.
Interface view	Each window has a uniquely assigned interface view. The interface view is linked with a Web Dynpro application so that the window can be called using a URL.
View controller	Processes the actions performed by the user in the view. Each view only has exactly one view controller.
Interface controller	A global controller that is also visible outside the component. It is thus part of the interface of a Web Dynpro component.
Component controller	Allows you to create events. Events are used to communicate between controllers and enable one controller to trigger event handlers in a different controller. Only one exists per component and has no visual interface. It drives the functionality of the component.

Table 16.2 Definitions for Web Dynpro

Term	Meaning
Custom controller	These are optional. Can be used to encapsulate subfunctions of the component controller.
Configuration controller	Only one configuration controller can exist in any component. It is only necessary if the corresponding component implements special configuration and personalization functionality.
Window controller	Only one per window. Can be used to process the data passed via the inbound plug when reused as a child controller.
Consumer component	A component that uses functionality (consumes) in another component (the used component).
Used component	A component that has functionality used by another component (the consumer component).

Table 16.2 Definitions for Web Dynpro (cont.)

Practice Questions

The practice questions below will help you evaluate your understanding of the topic. The questions shown are similar in nature to those found on the certification examination, but whereas none of these questions will be found on the exam itself, they allow you to review your knowledge of the subject. Select the correct answers and then check the completeness of your answers in the following solution section. Remember that you must select all correct answers and only correct answers to receive credit for the question.

1. Each component has an interface. This interface consists of:

☐ **A.** Interface view

☐ **B.** Interface context

☐ **C.** Interface controller

2. A plug:

☐ **A.** Can be defined as inbound, outbound, or both

☐ **B.** Forms the basis of navigation within a Web Dynpro

☐ **C.** Can be defined as default inbound

☐ **D.** Can be defined as a startup

☐ **E.** Can be defined as an exit

☐ **F.** Can be assigned to multiple views

☐ **G.** Can be defined as outbound controlling multiple inbound plugs

☐ **H.** Can be defined as inbound and be controlled by multiple outbound plugs

3. A Web Dynpro component contains:

☐ **A.** Multiple views within a window

☐ **B.** UI elements

☑ **C.** Component controller

☐ **D.** A context

☐ **E.** Exactly one interface controller

4. A view can:

☐ **A.** Contain other views

☐ **B.** Be contained in a window

☐ **C.** Contain windows

☐ **D.** If entered by an inbound plug cause an event handler method to be called

☐ **E.** Contain a view controller

5. Identify the types of controller:

☐ **A.** Component controller

☐ **B.** Custom controller

☐ **C.** Consumer controller

☐ **D.** Configuration controller

☐ **E.** View controller

☐ **F.** Window controller

6. Identify the types of layout managers:

☐ **A.** `FlowLayout`

☐ **B.** `RowLayout`

☐ **C.** `ColumnLayout`

☐ **D.** `MatrixLayout`

☐ **E.** `GridLayout`

☐ **F.** `TreeLayout`

7. The binding between a UI element and a context attribute is a two-way relationship.

☐ **A.** True

☐ **B.** False

8. Identify the ways to map context structures:

☐ **A.** Direct context mapping

☐ **B.** External context mapping

☐ **C.** Dynamic context mapping

9. The Web Dynpro programming model is based on:

☐ **A.** Classic Dynpro programming

☐ **B.** Business Server Pages (BSP)

☐ **C.** Model View Controller (MVC)

☐ **D.** Internet Transaction Server (ITS)

Practice Question Answers and Explanations

1. Correct answers: **A, C**

   Each interface component is composed of two parts: the interface view and interface controller.

2. Correct answers: **B, D, E, H**

   A plug is either inbound or outbound; it cannot be both. The view is defined as a default, but the plug is defined as a startup. Each plug can only be assigned to one view. Each outbound plug can only navigate to a single inbound plug. However, an inbound plug can be triggered by multiple outbound plugs.

3. Correct answers: **A, C, E**

   UI elements are placed within a view of the component. Although there is a context, it is actually part of either the component controller or a view controller. Therefore, the context is not directly part of the component, but of a subcomponent.

4. Correct answers: **B, C, D, E**

   A view can contain a window, which can contain another view, but a view can not be placed into another view.

5. Correct answers: **A, B, D, E, F**

   There is no consumer controller.

6. Correct answers: **A, B, D, E**

   `ColumnLayout` and `TreeLayout` are not valid layout managers.

7. Correct answer: **A**

   It is a two-way relationship, which is how data can be displayed in the browser and be retrieved from user input.

8. Correct answers: **A, B**

   Direct context mapping and external context mapping are the only ways to map context structures.

9. Correct answer: **C**

   The Web Dynpro programming model is based on the Model View Controller paradigm to ensure a clear division between the definition of the user interface and the implementation of the application logic.

Take Away

You will need to understand how Web Dynpro functions. Remember that it is a paradigm shift from existing types of dynpros. It is important to recognize the Model View Controller paradigm and what is available in each controller or view. It is important to understand how plugs allow navigation and the application to start or to exit. You will need an understanding of views and how they relate to windows and how the different Web Dynpro components are linked and exchange data. Finally, you will need to show your knowledge of the different types of controllers, their purposes, and their capabilities.

Refresher

You must understand the separation of duties in the Model View Controller paradigm. You must understand the purpose of each (see Table 16.3).

Key Concept	Definition
Model	This forms the interface to the backend system and thus enables the Web Dynpro application access to data.
View	This is responsible for the representation of the data in the client.
Controller	This lies between the view and the model. The controller formats the model data to be displayed in the view, processes the user entries made by the user, and returns them to the model.

Table 16.3 Key Concepts Refresher

Tips

It is important to have as much practical experience with this subject as possible. Unlike the majority of subjects found in the certification examination, this is an area where most will not have sufficient experience.

Whereas some of the topics may be familiar, for example, event handling, the majority of the concepts presented in this chapter require a mind shift. It is indeed a different paradigm and introduces a number of new terms and concepts. You must learn the terms and understand the concepts.

Summary

You should now understand the basics of Web Dynpro ABAP. You should have an understanding of the components and how these components relate with other components. This understanding of Web Dynpro ABAP will enable you to complete this portion of the certification examination successfully.

17 Class Identification Analysis and Design

Techniques You'll Master:

- Use functional methods
- Describe singletons
- Understand class friendship
- Identify inheritance
- Explore interfaces

This chapter expands on the material presented in Chapter 14, ABAP Object-Oriented Programming. The purpose of this chapter is to provide you with a basic understanding of how classes and objects can be organized, not to provide details regarding ABAP Objects. We will discuss the advantages of functional methods and the way to create a singleton class. We will cover the purpose of friendship between classes. We will also discuss inheritance including the up cast and down cast within the hierarchy of the inheritance tree. Finally, we will discuss interfaces and how they can be used to simulate multiple inheritance. Each of these topics will be covered separately and will be followed by the practice exercise and the solution to the exercise.

Real-World Scenario

You have been asked to take previously developed functionality and redesign it. The application provides data based on expected inventory movement and is currently developed as a large single program handling all types of purchase orders and sales orders. This program was changed by several different developers over the years, each only focusing on a single part of the program.

The objective is to produce a model and eventually a series of classes that can be used to implement the process using polymorphism.

The goal is to standardize the methods and their parameters. Although some of the classes involved are not closely related to each other, in other words they are not specializations or generalizations of each other, they all share methods and parameters. To simplify the inconsistent nature of these objects, you need to standardize the naming of these components; even though these objects are not related, they do need to share the same attributes and methods.

Objectives of this Portion of the Test

The purpose of this portion of the certification examination is to verify that you have sufficient knowledge to design different types of ABAP classes. This portion of the examination will test your knowledge of a narrow range of topics. The general topic is covered in Chapter 14, ABAP Object-Oriented Programming. The points that you will need to understand from this section include:

- The creation of a singleton (a class that can only be instantiated once)
- The use of functional methods and how they can simplify your programming
- Visibility of components and how different classes can interact
- Tools of the Class Builder, specifically the Refactoring Assistant
- Inheritance and polymorphism and how to use them correctly
- The use of interfaces to provide similar functionality to unrelated classes

The certification examination will give greater weight to this chapter compared to the other topics in the examination. This means there will be a higher percentage of questions covering this chapter than any other chapter. The reason for this is the direction of the ABAP language. The concepts described in this chapter are critical to knowing and using ABAP effectively.

Key Concepts Refresher

As development of ABAP programs leans toward object-oriented programming with ABAP Objects, you typically need to understand the advantages and restrictions of using object-oriented programming.

Functional Methods

As a refresher, we will cover a number of points that, although they may have been mentioned in other chapters, are important for a full understanding.

In Chapter 9, Basic ABAP Programs and Interface Creation, we discussed briefly the `RETURNING` parameter. Methods that have a `RETURNING` parameter are described as functional methods. This means they cannot also have either an `EXPORTING` or a `CHANGING` parameter. In this way, we guarantee that the method passes back one thing and one thing only to the caller. The `RETURNING` parameter must always be passed by value. Only one `RETURNING` parameter can be defined for a method. An example of a simple functional method can be seen in Figure 17.1, and the use of this method can be seen in Listing 17.1.

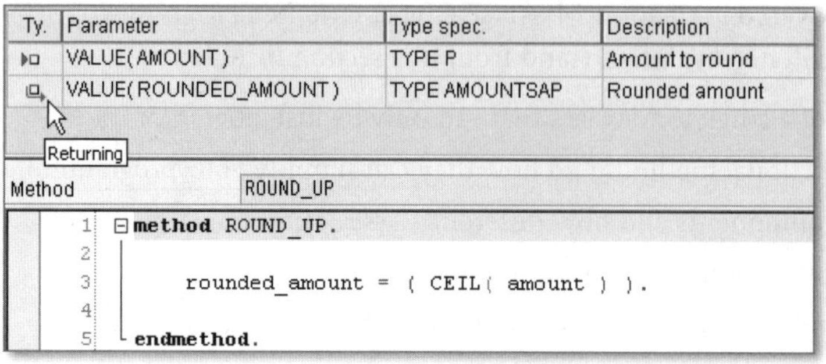

Ty.	Parameter	Type spec.	Description
	VALUE(AMOUNT)	TYPE P	Amount to round
	VALUE(ROUNDED_AMOUNT)	TYPE AMOUNTSAP	Rounded amount

Returning

Method ROUND_UP

```
method ROUND_UP.

    rounded_amount = ( CEIL( amount ) ).

endmethod.
```

Figure 17.1 Example of a Functional Method

```
lv_calc_amt = lv_source_amt / lv_factor.
IF lv_amt NE lr_util->round_up( lv_calc_amt ).
  lv_amt = lr_util->round_up( lv_calc_amt ).
ENDIF.
```

Listing 17.1 Functional Method Usage

The advantage of functional methods is that they do not require the use of temporary variables, because they can be used in conjunction with other statements. Prior to the introduction of functional methods, any call to any modularization unit (examples are a subroutine, a method, or a function module) always required the result to be stored in some data object. However, with functional methods they can be called directly from within various expressions, eliminating the need to temporarily store values. Functional methods can be used in:

- Logical expressions (`IF`, `ELSEIF`, `WHILE`, `CHECK`, `WAIT`)
- Case conditions (`CASE`, `WHEN`)
- Arithmetic expressions and bit expressions (`COMPUTE`)
- Sources of values as a local copy (`MOVE`)
- Search clauses for internal tables, assuming that the operand is not a component of the table row (`LOOP AT...WHERE`)

Static Methods

There are two kinds of attributes, instance attributes and static attributes, which are discussed in more detail in Chapter 14, ABAP Object-Oriented Programming. A static attribute exists once for each class and is visible for all runtime instances in that class. They typically relate to all objects, not just a single object. Examples include a counter or global constants. Likewise, static methods are defined at the class level. The restriction that only static components can be accessed in a static method applies to the implementation of the method. This makes sense because a static method can be called without creating any instance of the class. This means that static methods do not need instances; that is, they can be accessed directly through the class. An example would be to retrieve the current value of the static counter described above.

Static methods are called using the syntax `CALL METHOD classname=>method_name ...` or you can drop the `CALL METHOD` and put the parameters in parentheses at the end of the method call. Like static attributes, static methods are addressed with their class name, because they do not need instances (see Listing 17.2 for an example). As with instance methods, when you are calling a static method from within the class, you can omit the `classname`.

```
LOOP AT <table> ASSIGNING <wa>.
  MOVE-CORRESPONDING <wa> TO <structure>.
  zcl_utility=>create_csv_from_record(
    EXPORTING
      separator                    = gc_comma
      quote_all_fields             = 'F'
      output_initial_values        = 'X'
      source_contents              = <structure>
      rcd_ref_descr                = lr_struct_type
    IMPORTING
      csv_record                   = ls_output
    EXCEPTIONS
      invalid_structure_component = 1
      unable_to_preserve_space    = 2
      OTHERS                      = 3
         ).
  ASSERT sy-subrc = 0.
```

Listing 17.2 Example of a Static Method Call

Singletons

There are many cases in which you need to prevent a class from being instantiated more than once for each program context. You can do this using the singleton. A singleton is a class that is final (meaning it cannot have any subclasses), has a private instantiation level (meaning only the class itself can create an instance of itself), and is instantiated using its static constructor (which is executed only after the first time the class is accessed in an application). You can see this in Figure 17.2 and Figure 17.4. Figure 17.3 shows the static attribute used to store the singleton's reference. In this way, we ensure that only one instance of the class can be created in our application. A public static method could then make the reference to the class available to an external user as shown in Figure 17.5. The use of a singleton can be seen in Listing 17.3.

```
DATA:
  lv_singleton_ref       TYPE REF TO zcl_singleton.
lv_singleton_ref = zcl_singleton=>get_reference( ).
```

Listing 17.3 Instantiating and Using a Singleton

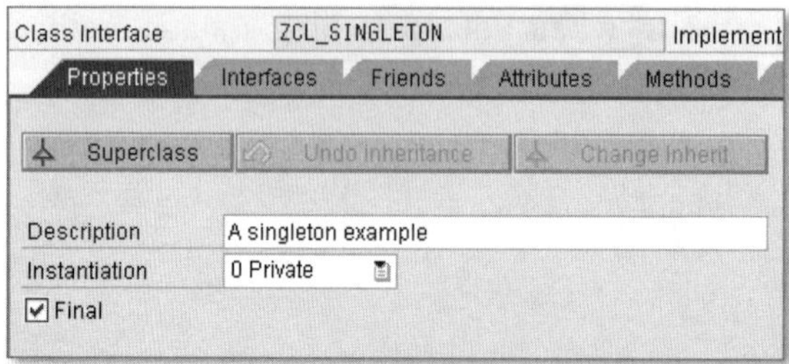

Figure 17.2 Singleton Class Properties

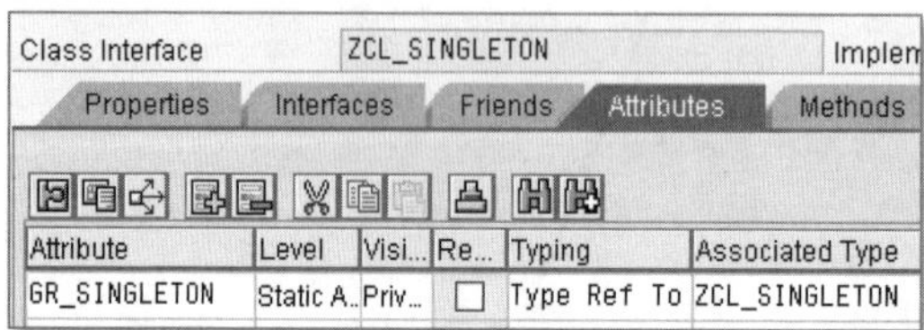

Figure 17.3 Singleton Attribute

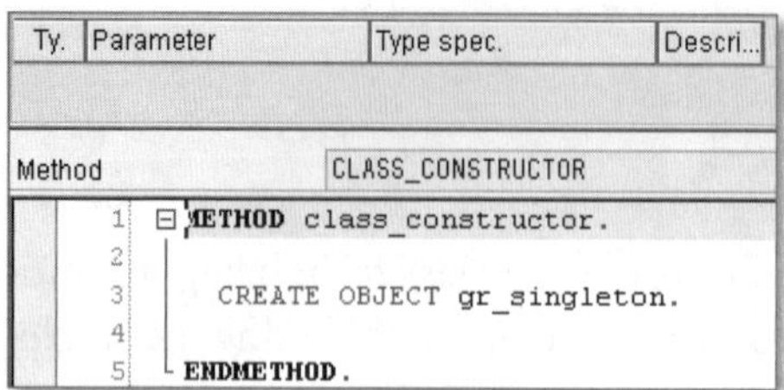

Figure 17.4 Singleton Class Constructor

Ty.	Parameter	Type spec.	Description
	VALUE(REFERENCE)	TYPE REF TO ZCL_SINGLETON	A singleton

Method GET_REFERENCE

```
METHOD get_reference.

  reference = gr_singleton.

ENDMETHOD.
```

Figure 17.5 Returning the Singleton Reference

Friendship

In classes, normally there is a strict division between what can be accessed outside the class itself (PUBLIC) and the inheritance tree (PROTECTED) or just the class itself (PRIVATE). From outside the class you can only access the public components of a class. In rare cases, classes have to work together so closely that they need access to each others' protected or private components. This can be achieved if one class grants friendship to another.

The concept of friendship between classes prevents these components from being made available to all applications, but the friend can access the protected and private components directly. A class can grant friendship to other classes and interfaces (and through the interface to all classes that implement the interface). The primary reason for friendship is performance; if a class can access the private attributes of another class directly, rather than having to call a public method to get hold of that data, then it will be faster because there is less overhead to obtain the data.

Note

You use the FRIENDS addition of the CLASS statement or the FRIENDS tab in the Class Builder to grant friendship.

Granting friendship is one-sided; a class that grants friendship is not automatically a friend of its friends. If the class that grants friendship wants to access non-public components of the friend, this friend must reciprocate and explicitly grant friendship back to the original class.

Typically, the friend relationship between classes occurs when methods that access the same data are distributed over several classes. The common data should not be accessed by classes that are not part of this relationship. In these cases you can make the class containing the data a singleton, which ensures that it can only be instantiated once in each program instance.

You should be aware that the friend attribute is *inherited*: Classes that inherit from friends and interfaces containing a friend (as a component interface) also become friends. You should therefore use extreme caution when granting friendship. The further up in the inheritance tree you make a friend, the more subclasses can access all components of a class that granted friendship. However, granting friendship is not inherited. A friend of a superclass is not automatically a friend of its subclasses.

Inheritance

Specialization is a relationship in which one class (the subclass) inherits all of the components of another class (the superclass). It is possible for the subclass to add new components (attributes, methods, etc.) and replace the implementations of inherited methods. This specialization emphasizes the similarities of the classes. The components they have in common are only defined and implemented in the superclass. They are inherited by all of the subclasses. You often will describe specialization as an "is a" relationship. For example, "A bus is a (specific type of) vehicle" or "A purchase order is a (specific type of) document." Reversing the point of view of specialization is referred to as generalization. Therefore:

- Common components are extracted and defined once in the superclass, allowing for central maintenance and eliminating redundant implementation.
- Subclasses contain extensions (in other words, new components that are unique to the subclass) and/or changes (implementing different versions of methods that were inherited).
- Subclasses are dependent on superclasses.

If you use inheritance properly, it provides a significantly better structure for your software because commonly used elements are only defined once in a central location (in the superclass) and then are automatically available to all subclasses. If you make changes later, they have an immediate effect on the subclasses. You therefore need to be careful if you make changes to the superclass, because they will directly affect the subclasses inheriting from it and when using the *Refactoring Assistant*.

Tip

A very common mistake made by those new to object-oriented design is an overuse of inheritance. This problem can be avoided by using the test:

X should inherit from Y only if you can say that X is a Y.

So whereas a checkbox is a type of button, you cannot say for example that a column is a table. This is why the object model of the ALV is not a group of inherited objects.

In object-oriented ABAP, you define an inheritance relationship for a subclass using the `INHERITING FROM` addition, followed by the superclass that is directly above the subclass. To do the same for a global class you click on the SUPERCLASS button on the class's PROPERTIES tab (shown in Figure 17.2). Because this superclass can inherit from another superclass above it, inheritance hierarchies of varying complexity can be produced, known as *inheritance trees*.

Unlike other languages, there is no multiple inheritance in ABAP Objects. You can only specify one superclass directly above a class. However, you can use interfaces in ABAP Objects to simulate multiple inheritance. Inheritance is a one-sided relationship. In other words, subclasses know their direct superclass, but a class does not know which class inherits from it.

Redefinition

Redefinition allows you to change the implementation of an inherited instance method in a subclass without changing the signature, in other words, without changing the parameters or adding new ones. The visibility section for the superclass must also remain the same. It is therefore not possible to use redefinition within the `PRIVATE SECTION`. When you use the `REDEFINITION` addition, you specify a new implementation for the inherited method. Because the signature cannot change, it is not necessary for you to define the method parameters and exceptions again. To do the same for a global class, you use the context menu of the inherited method and select REDEFINE. In this case a redefinition of the method is created (including a commented call to the superclass method). The superclass cannot be defined as `Final` (this attribute can be seen in Figure 17.2).

Within the redefined method's implementation, you can use the prefix `SUPER->...` to access components in the superclass directly above where you are working. This is often needed when you redefine a method to call the original method of the superclass.

A redefinition is not normally useful in the case of the constructor. Either the superclass's instance constructor can be used without any need to change it, or the subclass has been expanded (for example, new attributes have been added) and additional parameters are now required in the constructor's signature (perhaps to allow the values for the new attributes to be set when an instance is created). In ABAP Objects, the instance constructor can only be "overwritten" as part of inheritance. This overwriting allows both the signature and the implementation to be adjusted in the subclass, and it is the only case where extra parameters can be added.

- You must call the instance constructor of the superclass within the constructor of the subclass. This is due to the specialization relationship: If a constructor is defined in the superclass, it contains logic that must always be executed when an object is created for this superclass or its subclass. The runtime system, however, can only automatically ensure this if the subclass's constructor was not changed.
- Unlike the instance constructor, the static constructor in the superclass is always called automatically. The runtime system automatically ensures that the static constructors of all superclasses were executed before the static constructor in a particular class is executed.

Note

Overloading, which allows a method to have several definitions with different signatures and thus also different implementations, is not supported in ABAP Objects.

Visibility

When using inheritance, another visibility section can be useful, the `PROTECTED SECTION`. The protected component's visibility is between public and private and is visible to all subclasses and the class itself, but it still protected from outside the inheritance tree.

When you define local classes in ABAP, you must follow the syntactical sequence of `PUBLIC SECTION`, `PROTECTED SECTION`, and `PRIVATE SECTION`. The sequencing for a global class is handled automatically.

A subclass also inherits the private components of its superclass. You cannot, however, address them directly in the syntax of the subclass; private means private. The private components of superclasses can only be addressed indirectly by using public or protected methods from the superclass. These, in turn, can access the private attributes. The alternative is to change these private attributes to protected attributes, which allows direct access in subclasses.

Using the private visibility section, you can make changes to superclasses without the need to know details about the subclasses. If the changes you make do not affect the semantics, you do not need to adapt the subclasses. This is allowed because the private components of the superclass can only be indirectly accessed.

Because there is only one static component of a class exists per program context, it therefore follows that:

- All subclasses share a public or protected static attribute of the superclass.
- You cannot redefine static methods.

Casting

By assigning a subclass reference to a superclass reference, all components that can be accessed syntactically after the cast assignment are actually available in the instance. This is called either an *up cast* or a *widening cast* and can be seen in Listing 17.4. We know the subclass always contains at least the same components as the superclass and that the name and the signature of redefined methods are identical. This means you can only address those methods and attributes that were inherited from the superclass.

```
DATA:
  lv_name       TYPE c LENGTH 30,
  lr_person     TYPE REF TO lcl_person,
  lr_manager    TYPE REF TO lcl_manager,
  lr_employee   TYPE REF TO lcl_employee.
CREATE OBJECT lr_manager.
lr_person = lr_manager.       " Up cast
lv_name = lr_person->get_name( ).
```

Listing 17.4 Example of an Up Cast

You typically use an up cast assignment to prepare for generic access. When an instance receives a message to execute a particular method, the implementation of the method in the class of this instance is executed. If the class did not redefine the method, the implementation from the superclass is executed instead.

Objects from different classes reacting differently to the same method calls are known as *polymorphism*. Polymorphism is one of the main strengths of inheritance: A client can handle instances of different classes uniformly, regardless of their implementation. The runtime system searches for the right implementation of a method on behalf of the client.

Listing 17.5 and Listing 17.6 show the declaration and use of polymorphism. After creating a manager and employee, these subclass references are up cast and stored in a table of the superclass (in this case a table of persons). The loop retrieves each record and obtains the name and salary. Because a manager is a employee and an employee is a person, depending on the type of employee being processed, different calculations could be in place to determine the salary.

```
TYPES:
  llt_person     TYPE REF TO lcl_person,
  ltt_person     TYPE STANDARD TABLE OF llt_person.
DATA:
  lv_salary      TYPE betrg,
  lv_name        TYPE name1,
  lr_person      TYPE REF TO lcl_person,
  lt_person      TYPE ltt_person,
  lr_manager     TYPE REF TO lcl_manager,
  lr_employee    TYPE REF TO lcl_employee.
FIELD-SYMBOLS:
  <person>       TYPE REF TO lcl_person.
```

Listing 17.5 Declarations for Generic Handling

```
APPEND INITIAL LINE TO lt_person ASSIGNING <person>.
<person> = lr_manager.
APPEND INITIAL LINE TO lt_person ASSIGNING <person>.
<person> = lr_employee.
LOOP AT lt_person ASSIGNING <person>.
  lv_name = <person>->get_name( ).
  lv_salary = <person>->get_salary( ).
  WRITE: / lv_name, lv_bonus.
ENDLOOP.
```

Listing 17.6 Up Cast and Polymorphism Calls

Variables of the type "reference to superclass" can also refer to subclass instances at runtime. You may need to copy such a reference back to a suitable variable of the type "reference to subclass." (This is a key point in that the reference variable being cast must have originally started as a reference to the subclass; you are copying the reference back to reference the original class.) To assign a superclass reference to a subclass reference, you must use the down cast assignment operator MOVE ... ?TO ... or its short form ?= (see Listing 17.7). As a rule, the subclass class contains more components than the superclass.

```
lr_manager ?= lr_person.      "Down cast
```

Listing 17.7 Down Cast

After assigning this type of reference back to a subclass reference to the implementing class, clients are no longer limited to just inherited components. All methods and components of the subclass instance can now be accessed. A down cast can only be performed after first doing an up cast. Because the target variable can accept fewer dynamic types after the assignment, this assignment is also called *narrowing cast*.

You typically use down cast assignments when specific components of instances need to be addressed, and their references are kept in variables that are typed on the superclass, for example, a generic list of objects. You cannot use the superclass reference for access to subclass components because it only allows access to the shared or inherited components. Therefore, you need to do the down cast to be able to access the subclass components.

The runtime system checks before assignment if the current content of the source reference variable corresponds to the type requirements of the target variable. If not, an exception is triggered and the original value of the target reference variable remains unchanged.

Note

In our previous example, we up cast an employee and a manager into a person table. An attempt to down cast an employee reference into a manager reference will produce this error. However, because a manager is an employee, a down cast to an employee reference will always work, as long as the reference was up cast to start with.

You can catch this exception of the exception class CX_SY_MOVE_CAST_ERROR by using TRY ... ENDTRY and the CATCH statements. Another way you can prevent this runtime error is to use the runtime type identification (RTTI) classes. They can be used to determine the dynamic type at runtime and to set a condition for the cast.

Interfaces

From a technical point of view, an interface can be thought of as a little like a limited part of a superclass. However, they cannot be instantiated, do not have an implementation part, and only have public components. It is possible for you to simulate multiple inheritance using interfaces. Interfaces allow you to define uniform interfaces (protocols) for methods. Different classes that include the interface can therefore implement these methods in different ways but keep the same semantics. Interfaces therefore contain no implementations.

You can generally define the same components in interfaces and classes, in other words, attributes, methods, and events. To recognize the semantic differences from regular inheritance, you should focus on the following typical use case: to allow the option of having multiple classes implement a method in different ways, but using the same method names and with uniform signatures. With regular inheritance, you define this method in the shared superclass. It may not be possible for you to model a superclass suitably for inheritance (remember, there needed to be a strong relationship; we had to be able to say that our subclass "is a type of" our superclass). However, you want to treat instances of different classes in the same way. You need to define an interface and then define this method in these methods. The interface in this case can be compared with a generalization relationship with a superclass.

If you compare this use of an interface to regular inheritance, the distribution of roles is sometimes different: Interfaces are generally defined by the developer who wants to use them. It is then dependent on each class to decide whether it actually offers the methods defined there. This is similar to a specialization relationship with a subclass.

As occurs with regular inheritance, access to these methods is then usually generic; in other words you should use a reference that is typed to the interface. This means you can perform polymorphism with interfaces. This is the only time you will see reference variables typed with reference to an interface. Because the interface cannot be instantiated, these reference variables will only be used to point to instances of classes that include the interface.

Although the same components can be defined in an interface as in a class, interfaces do not know the visibility levels of components. All interface components are public.

Classes implement interfaces as follows:

- You list the interface name in the definition part of the class with the `INTERFACES` statement. This must be in the `PUBLIC SECTION` (interfaces can only be implemented publicly). Global classes define interfaces using the INTERFACES tab shown in Figure 17.6.
- You must implement the interface methods in the implementation part of the class.
- You can address components defined in the interface in the implementation part of the class.

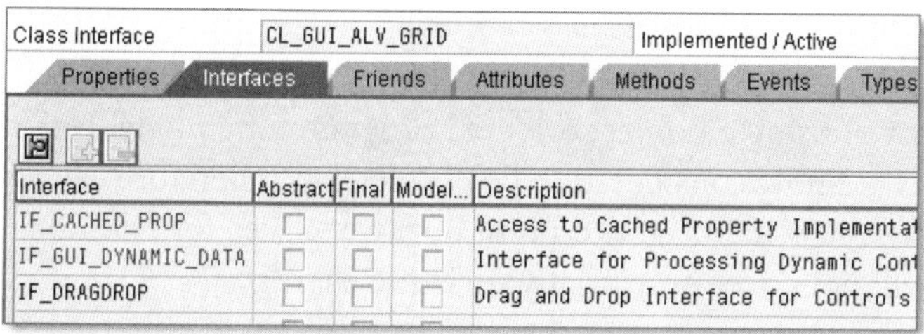

Figure 17.6 Interface Tab

You distinguish interface components from other components in the implementing class by prefixing the interface name followed by a tilde (~), which is the interface resolution operator. The use of the interface resolution operator enables you to access interface components using an object reference belonging to the class that implements the interface as you would the method defined in the implementation part of the class. You can see an example of the use of an interface in Listing 17.8.

```
l_r_bi_query_ad->if_rsroa_bi_query~set_fieldcatalog(
  l_ts_fieldcatalog ).
```

Listing 17.8 Object Reference to an Interface Component (set_fieldcatalog)

To simplify access to interface components (thereby providing you a shorter name to use), you can use alias names (see Listing 17.9). These can only appear in the definition part of a class or in the interface definition, and their use is subject to the visibility restriction of the defining class.

```
ALIASES true   FOR if_salv_c_bool_sap~true.
IF lv_state EQ true.
```

Listing 17.9 ALIAS for an Interface Component

You can only access interface components by using an object reference whose class implements the interface. Syntactically, this also takes place using the interface resolution operator (~).

Alternatively, you can use the alias names defined in the implementing class for the interface components. If this class is implemented in a subclass, you do not need to change the way you access these aliased components. However, the source code would then be less self-explanatory because the origin of the component is not clear. You could therefore conclude from the syntax that the components were defined in the class rather than as aliased interface components.

Class Identification

One of the implications of using an object-oriented programming model is that some ABAP statements are now considered to be obsolete and therefore cannot be used in ABAP classes. It is important to point out two places for additional information that we will not cover only briefly owing to their size.

- The first is a list of obsolete statements or forms of statements. The information can be found in the ABAP keyword documentation. Figure 17.7 shows the location (ABAP – KEYWORD DOCUMENTATION • ABAP – BY THEME • OBSOLETE STATEMENTS AND CONCEPTS) in the documentation, and Figure 17.8 shows some of the obsolete statements.

  Please note that in some of the cases only a particular variation or addition is obsolete. The statements you will find there are only available for reasons of compatibility with releases prior to 4.6 and 6.10. Most of the statements listed are syntactically forbidden in ABAP Objects (from Release 4.6) or Unicode (Release 6.10). Their restriction in ABAP Objects is why they are mentioned in this chapter.
- The second source is additional information on the Refactoring Assistant. It can be accessed by clicking on the APPLICATION HELP icon (shown in Figure 17.9) in either the Object Navigator (Transaction SE80) or the Class Builder (Transaction SE24) and then navigating to CLASS BUILDER • UTILITIES OF THE CLASS BUILDER to find information on the Refactoring Assistant. Figure 17.10 shows the initial screen.

  The Refactoring Assistant allows you to move components between superclasses and subclasses or between classes and interfaces, for example, if you have defined a component in a class and then realize that component should belong in the superclass instead.

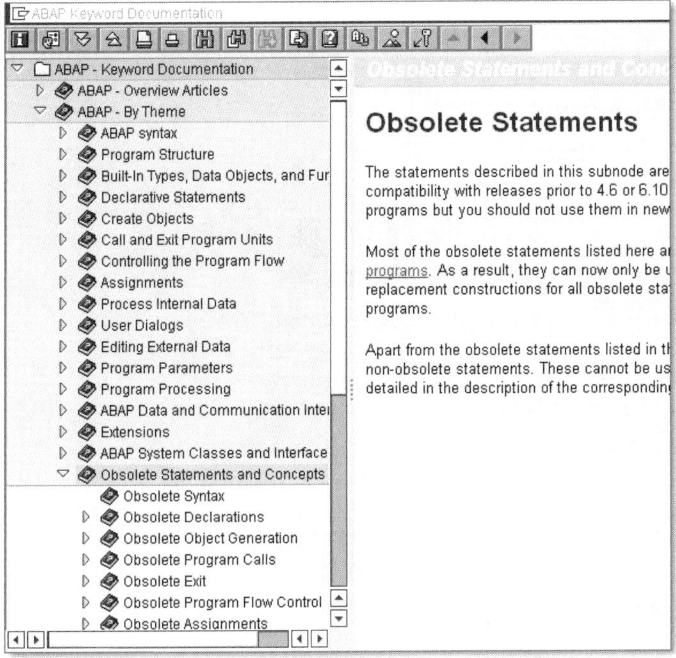

Figure 17.7 Obsolete Statement Location

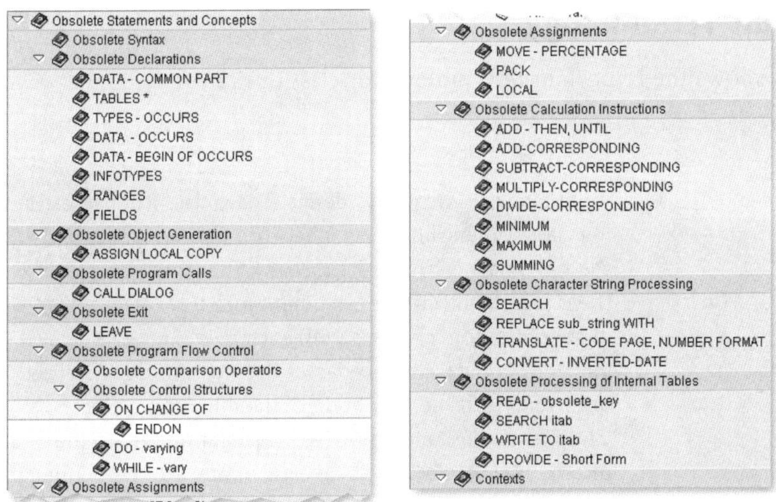

Figure 17.8 Some of the Obsolete Statements

Figure 17.9 Application Help Icon

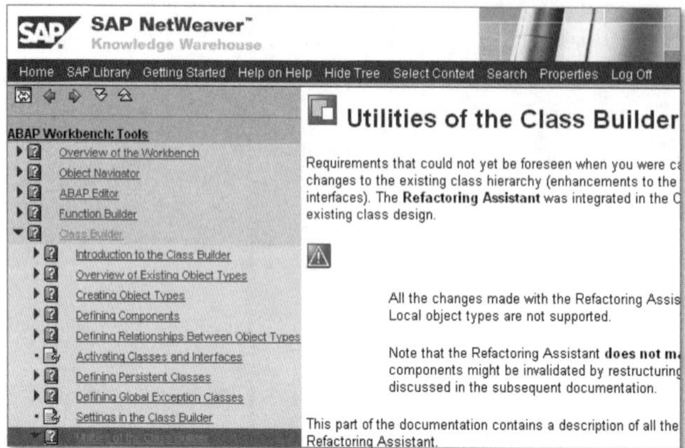

Figure 17.10 Utilities of the Class Builder

Important Terminology

Table 17.1 shows the important terminology for class design.

Term	Meaning
Inheritance	Inheritance allows you to derive a new class from an existing class. When subclasses inherit from superclasses and the superclass is itself the subclass of another class, all of the classes involved form an inheritance tree, whose degree of specialization increases with each new hierarchical level you add. Conversely, the classes become more generalized until you reach the root node of the inheritance tree. Within an inheritance tree, two adjacent nodes are the direct superclass or direct subclass of one another. Other related nodes are referred to as superclasses and subclasses.

Table 17.1 Definitions for Class Design

Term	Meaning
Single inheritance	A class can have more than one direct subclass, but it can only have one direct superclass.
Multiple inheritance	A class inheriting from more than one superclass.
Superclass	The class from which the specialization class inherits.
Subclass	The specialization class that inherits from the superclass.
Interface	Interfaces are extensions to class definitions and provide a uniform point of contact for objects. Instances cannot be created from interfaces. Instead, classes implement interfaces by implementing all of their methods. You can then address them using either class references or interface references. Different classes implement the same interface in different ways by implementing the methods differently. Interfaces therefore form the basis for polymorphism in ABAP Objects.
Up cast	An up cast assignment prepares for generic access. You are casting a reference up the inheritance tree to a more general object.
Down cast	A down cast assignment allows for more specialized access. You are casting a reference back down the inheritance tree to a more specific object. You cannot down cast any lower in the inheritance tree than where the object was created.
Polymorphism	Objects from different classes reacting differently to the same method calls are known as polymorphism.

Table 17.1 Definitions for Class Design (cont.)

Practice Questions

The practice questions below will help you evaluate your understanding of the topic. The questions shown are similar in nature to those found on the certification examination, but whereas none of these questions will be found on the exam itself, they allow you to review your knowledge of the subject. Select the correct answers and then check the completeness of your answers in the following solution section. Remember that you must select all correct answers and only correct answers to receive credit for the question.

1. Given the code in the exhibit (see Figure 17.11) and the knowledge that both `lcl_truck` and `lcl_car` inherit from `lcl_vehicle`, what statements are true?

```
TYPES:
  llt_vehicle     TYPE REF TO lcl_vehicle,
  ltt_vehicle     TYPE STANDARD TABLE OF llt_vehicle.

DATA:
  lr_vehicle      TYPE REF TO lcl_vehicle,
  lt_vehicle      TYPE ltt_vehicle,
  lr_truck        TYPE REF TO lcl_truck,
  lr_car          TYPE REF TO lcl_car.

FIELD-SYMBOLS:
  <vehicle>       TYPE REF TO lcl_vehicle.

CREATE OBJECT lr_vehicle.
CREATE OBJECT lr_truck.
CREATE OBJECT lr_car.
APPEND INITIAL LINE TO lt_vehicle ASSIGNING <vehicle>.
<vehicle> = lr_vehicle.
APPEND INITIAL LINE TO lt_vehicle ASSIGNING <vehicle>.
<vehicle> = lr_truck.
APPEND INITIAL LINE TO lt_vehicle ASSIGNING <vehicle>.
<vehicle> = lr_car.

lr_truck ?= lr_vehicle.
```

Figure 17.11 Question 1 Exhibit

☐ **A.** The code is not syntactically correct.

☐ **B.** The table `lt_vehicle` contains three vehicles.

☐ **C.** The code will produce a runtime error.

☐ **D.** The code shows three valid up casts.

☐ **E.** The code shows two valid up casts.

☐ **F.** The code shows no valid up casts.

2. What is unique about a singleton?

☐ **A.** It must be instantiated using a private instance constructor.

☐ **B.** It must be instantiated using a public instance constructor.

- ☐ **C.** It must be instantiated using a protected instance constructor.
- ☐ **D.** It must be instantiated using a static private constructor.
- ☐ **E.** It must be instantiated using a static public constructor.
- ☐ **F.** It must be instantiated using a static protected constructor.
- ☐ **G.** It must be defined as `FINAL`.
- ☐ **H.** It cannot be defined as `FINAL`.

3. What statements are true about a class that has granted friendship to another class:

- ☐ **A.** The friend has access to private attributes.
- ☐ **B.** The friend has access to protected attributes.
- ☐ **C.** The friend has access to public attributes.
- ☐ **D.** All of classes the friend has granted friendship access status to also have the same access.
- ☐ **E.** All classes that inherit from the friend (subclasses) also have the same access.

4. There can only be one level in the inheritance tree.

- ☐ **A.** True
- ☐ **B.** False

5. What statements are true regarding ABAP inheritance:

- ☐ **A.** You can access the superclass component with the prefix `SUPER->`.
- ☐ **B.** The instance constructor can be overwritten as part of inheritance.
- ☐ **C.** The static constructor can be overwritten as part of inheritance.
- ☐ **D.** Overloading allows a method to have several definitions with different signatures.
- ☐ **E.** Instance constructors must call the superclass's constructor.
- ☐ **F.** Static constructors do not need to call the superclass's constructor.
- ☐ **G.** Polymorphism requires the developer to specify which method to use with inheritance.

6. Which statements are considered obsolete and cannot be used in ABAP Objects:

- ☐ **A.** TABLES
- ☐ **B.** DATA...TYPE...OCCURS
- ☐ **C.** DATA...BEGIN OF...OCCURS
- ☐ **D.** INFOTYPES
- ☐ **E.** RANGES
- ☐ **F.** LEAVE
- ☐ **G.** ON CHANGE OF
- ☐ **H.** SEARCH
- ☐ **I.** LOOP AT dbtab

7. You can simulate multiple inheritance with:

- ☐ **A.** REDEFINITION
- ☐ **B.** INHERITING FROM
- ☐ **C.** INTERFACES

8. What is unique about a functional method?

- ☐ **A.** It must contain a returning parameter.
- ☐ **B.** It can contain an importing parameter.
- ☐ **C.** It can contain an exporting parameter.
- ☐ **D.** It can contain a changing parameter.
- ☐ **E.** It can be used in logical expressions.
- ☐ **F.** It can be used in SELECT statements.
- ☐ **G.** It must be a singleton.

Practice Question Answers and Explanations

1. Correct answers: **B, C, E**

   The table lt_vehicle does contain three vehicles: one vehicle, one truck up cast as a vehicle, and one car up cast as a vehicle. This also provides the correct number of up casts, which is two (the third is just an assignment of one vehicle to another vehicle). The code will produce a runtime error (`MOVE_CAST_ERROR`) on the down cast. The reason for the error is simple: `lr_vehicle` contains a vehicle, not a truck, and it cannot be down cast to either a truck or a car. If we took the second record in the table, we could down cast it because it started as a truck and was up cast to a vehicle. The other two records in the table would produce the same error as `lr_vehicle`.

The code is actually syntactically correct and can be executed (up to the down cast, which aborts the program). As we have already discussed, two is the correct number of up casts — not three and not zero.

2. Correct answers: **D, G**

   A singleton must be instantiated using a static private constructor. The reasons for this combination are: static so it is only called once and private so it cannot be called from anywhere else. It must be defined as `FINAL` so that it cannot be inherited.

3. Correct answers: **A, B, C, E**

   Friends have access to private, protected, and public attributes. The friend attribute is inherited: Classes that inherit from friends and interfaces containing a friend (as a component interface) also become friends.

4. Correct answer: **B**

   There can be many levels of specialization in the inheritance tree.

5. Correct answers: **A, B, E, F**

   You can access the superclass by using the prefix `SUPER->`. You can override the instance constructor, but not a static constructor, because it is shared between all inherited objects. Overloading is not possible in ABAP Objects. Instance constructors need to call the superclass's constructor to make sure that everything is created correctly. Static constructors do not need to explicitly call the superclass's constructor because it is called automatically by the runtime system. Polymorphism does not require the developer to do anything; the runtime system automatically determines which method to call.

6. Correct answers: **A, B, C, D, E, F, G, H, I**

   All of theses variations are obsolete.

7. Correct answer: **C**

   Multiple inheritance can be simulated with interfaces.

8. Correct answer: **A, B, E**

   A functional method must contain a returning parameter (it is what makes it a functional method), but cannot contain either changing or exporting parameters. It can contain an importing parameter. The functional method can be used in logical expressions, such as the source in an assignment, a computation, and case statements.

Take Away

You will need to understand the fundamentals of object-oriented programming. This includes the different types of classes and how the visibility of components affects use outside of the class or method. You will need to understand what makes a singleton or a returning method, when a class should inherit from a superclass, and how to specify the inheritance. You should know how interfaces can be used and how they can be addressed. Lastly, you will need an understanding of polymorphism and how both up casting and down casting are used.

Refresher

You must understand inheritance and polymorphism. Singletons, returning methods, friendship, and casting will all play a part in the certification examination. You must have an understanding of differences between instantiated objects and static objects. Also, you must have an understanding of obsolete statements.

Table 17.2 shows the key concepts of class design.

Key Concept	Definition
Inheritance	Inheritance allows you to derive a new class from an existing class so that one class (the subclass) adopts the structure and behavior of another class (superclass), possibly also adapting or extending it.
Polymorphism	This is when instances of different classes respond differently to the same method calls.

Table 17.2 Key Concepts Refresher

Tips

With this topic in particular, it is important to have as much practical experience with the Class Builder as possible. It is important that you understand the differences of inheritance and interfaces.

Summary

You should now be able to use the Class Builder effectively and produce functional methods and singletons. You should know the visibility of attributes and methods based on both inheritance and the visibility section in which they are defined. You should also know the reason for the use of interfaces in ABAP Objects. Your knowledge of class design will enable you to successfully pass this topic during the certification exam.

18

Enhancements and Modifications

Techniques You'll Master:

- Describe various enhancement techniques available in the SAP system
- Enhance ABAP Dictionary objects without modifying them
- Implement enhancements to the SAP standard using user exits, customer exits, Business Transaction Events, and Business Add-ins
- Modify standard SAP repository objects using the Modification Assistant
- Describe various enhancement techniques from the Enhancement Framework

If your development requirements cannot be fulfilled by customization or personalization, then you can either enhance the application, start a custom development project, or modify the standard SAP application. SAP provides various enhancement options to adjust standard SAP Repository objects without actually modifying them. Some of the techniques available for enhancements are user exits, customer exits, Business Transaction Events, BAdIs, and Enhancement Framework techniques such as enhancement points, enhancement sections, and so on, which can be implemented without even modifying the SAP system.

In this chapter we will discuss various enhancement techniques available to enhance the standard SAP system. We will discuss how to implement each of the enhancement techniques. We will also discuss how to locate the available enhancement options to adjust the standard SAP application.

Real-World Scenario

Your customer would like to know the various options available for modifying and enhancing the SAP system because the SAP standard application does not support the customer's business requirement. As an SAP developer on the project you should be aware of various enhancement techniques available in SAP so that you can explain about the enhancement technique, features, and benefits and so that you can use them.

Objectives of this Portion of the Test

The objective of this portion of the certification test is to judge your knowledge about the enhancement techniques available for enhancing the SAP system. It is expected that you are aware of user exits, customer exits, Business Transaction Events, and Business Add-Ins.

You should also be able to describe the new enhancement options available in SAP NetWeaver 7.0. You should be able to explain about the enhancement techniques available in the Enhancement Framework such as explicit and implicit enhancement points, explicit enhancement sections, and new Business Add-Ins (BAdI) technology.

Key Concepts Refresher

SAP provides various techniques to adjust the SAP system or application to meet a customer's business requirements. First, the application consultant on the project would try to fulfill the customer requirement by customization or personalization. If the requirement cannot be implemented by customization or personalization, then you have to see if the requirement can be met by enhancing the application.

SAP provides you with various techniques to enhance the SAP system. Some of the techniques available for enhancements are user exits, customer exits, Business Transaction Events, BAdIs, and Enhancement Framework techniques such as enhancement points, enhancement sections, and so on. These techniques can be implemented without modifying the SAP system (except for user exits, which is technically a modification but does not affect upgrade) and therefore do not require modification adjustment at upgrade or when you apply support packages. You should only modify SAP objects if the enhancement techniques mentioned above cannot fulfill the business requirement. In this chapter we will cover each of the enhancement techniques in detail.

Enhancing SAP Applications

You can enhance SAP applications to add your own functionality without modifying the standard SAP system. SAP provides a number of ways in which an application can be enhanced without modifying the original SAP application or program. SAP applications can be enhanced or adjusted using one of the following techniques:

- Customization
- Personalization
- User exits
- Customer exits
- Business Transaction Event (BTE)
- Business Add-Ins (BAdIs)
- Table and structure enhancements
- Enhancement techniques within the Enhancement Framework

Customization is used to configure the SAP application via the reference IMG (Implementation Guide). Customization is not your responsibility, but it allows you take the set of SAP templates for business processes and manipulate them to meet your business requirements. You can customize some applications to define the mandatory screen fields or even hide certain fields or screens from the application.

Personalization is used to simplify the SAP business transactions. The aim of personalization is to adjust the SAP transaction for a specific user or user group or for the company as a whole. Personalization includes things such as user menus, adding transactions to your FAVORITES menu, and shortcuts. Transaction variants are another way to personalize; using these, you can switch off screen elements and functions from the SAP transaction, thus simplifying the transaction for the user.

The functional consultants on a project should try to adjust the SAP standard transaction via customization or personalization before considering any development work. You enhance the SAP application or embark on custom development only if the customer requirement cannot be fulfilled through customization or personalization. Modifications can lead to complications during upgrade. When SAP delivers a new version of the object, you must decide whether you want to keep the new version of the object or continue with the old modified version. This process is known as *modification adjustment* and can slow down the upgrade process.

Enhancement Techniques

Enhancements are ways in which you can implement customer requirements that have not been provided as part of the standard SAP applications, without modifying the SAP standard objects directly. SAP provides user exits, customer exits, Business Add-Ins, and so on as preplanned exit points in repository objects that the customer can use to implement their own enhancement logic. Following are the details regarding all of the various enhancement techniques used in SAP applications.

User Exits

User exits are empty subroutines provided by SAP in which you can add your source code. This is the oldest enhancement technique to allow you to insert your programming logic into the SAP standard application without modifying it.

SAP will no longer provide new user exits, but you can still implement the existing ones.

User exits are implemented as subroutines and are sometimes called form exits. All user exits start with `USEREXIT_<name>` and are generally collected in an Include program that is attached to the standard application. SAP calls these subroutines from the standard program. If you implement them, your logic will be executed at these points. Most of the sales and distribution (SD) component still provides user exits for customer-specific enhancements. Figure 18.1 and Figure 18.2 display a standard SD component with the Include program and form subroutines inside them.

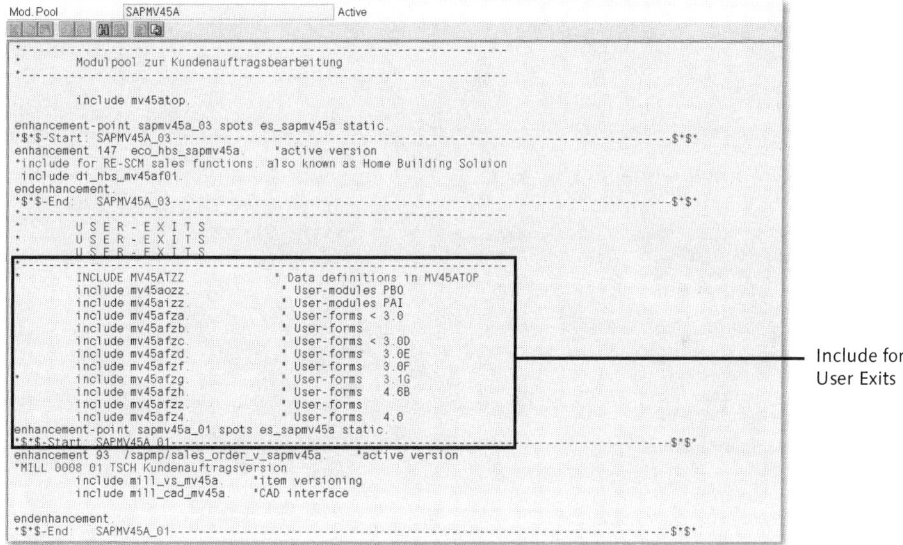

Figure 18.1 Program Includes for User Exits

You can locate user exits within a program by searching for the word `USEREXIT` in the main program of the application. You need to know where the user exit is called from within the program before you add your logic to the user exit to ensure that it's the right place for you to add additional logic.

You can double-click on the `FORM` routine of the user exit to locate the `PERFORM` statement, which calls the user exit, and then check if it is the right place to add additional logic (see Figure 18.1). You can also find the user exits for your application from the IMG in the SYSTEM MODIFICATIONS folder for the specific application (see Figure 18.3).

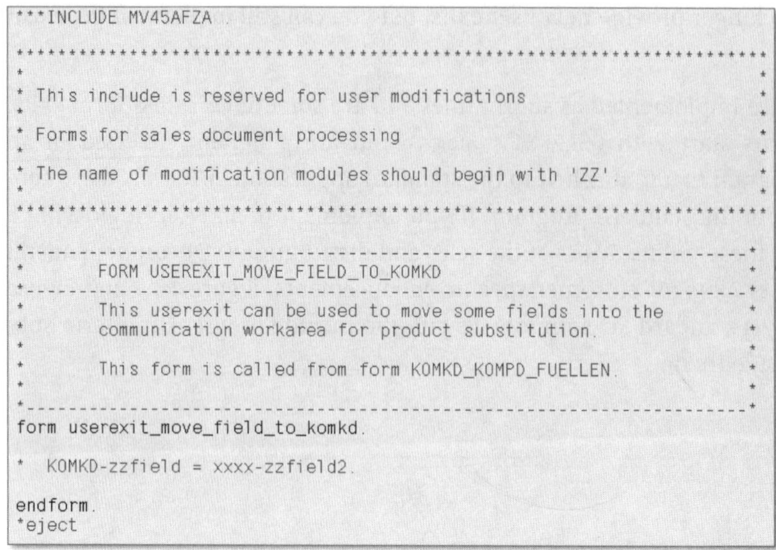

```
***INCLUDE MV45AFZA .
*********************************************************************
*                                                                   *
* This include is reserved for user modifications                  *
*                                                                   *
* Forms for sales document processing                              *
*                                                                   *
* The name of modification modules should begin with 'ZZ'.         *
*                                                                   *
*********************************************************************

*-------------------------------------------------------------------*
*       FORM USEREXIT_MOVE_FIELD_TO_KOMKD                           *
*-------------------------------------------------------------------*
*       This userexit can be used to move some fields into the      *
*       communication workarea for product substitution.            *
*                                                                   *
*       This form is called from form KOMKD_KOMPD_FUELLEN.          *
*                                                                   *
*-------------------------------------------------------------------*
form userexit_move_field_to_komkd.

*  KOMKD-zzfield = xxxx-zzfield2.

endform.
*eject
```

Figure 18.2 Form Routine for User Exits

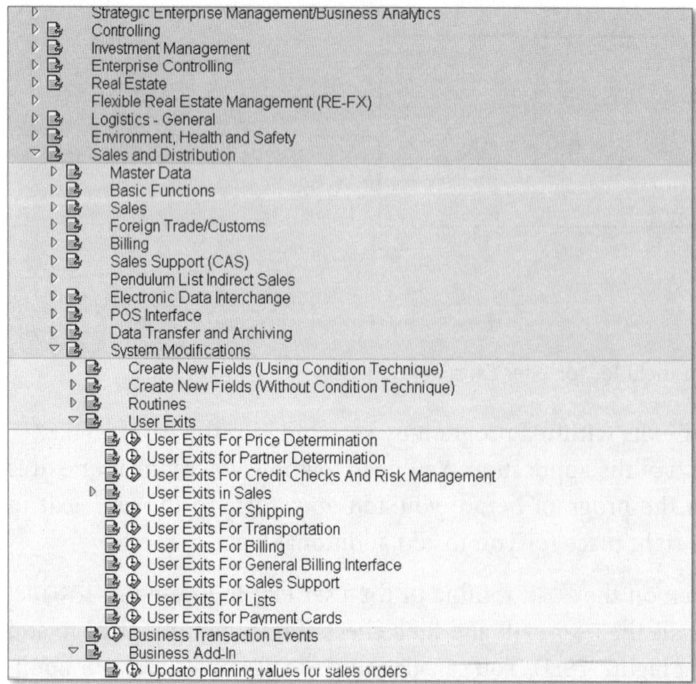

Figure 18.3 User Exits in the Reference IMG under System Modification

Most of the `USEREXITS` for the SD component are in the package VMOD and can be viewed via Transaction SE80 (see Figure 18.4).

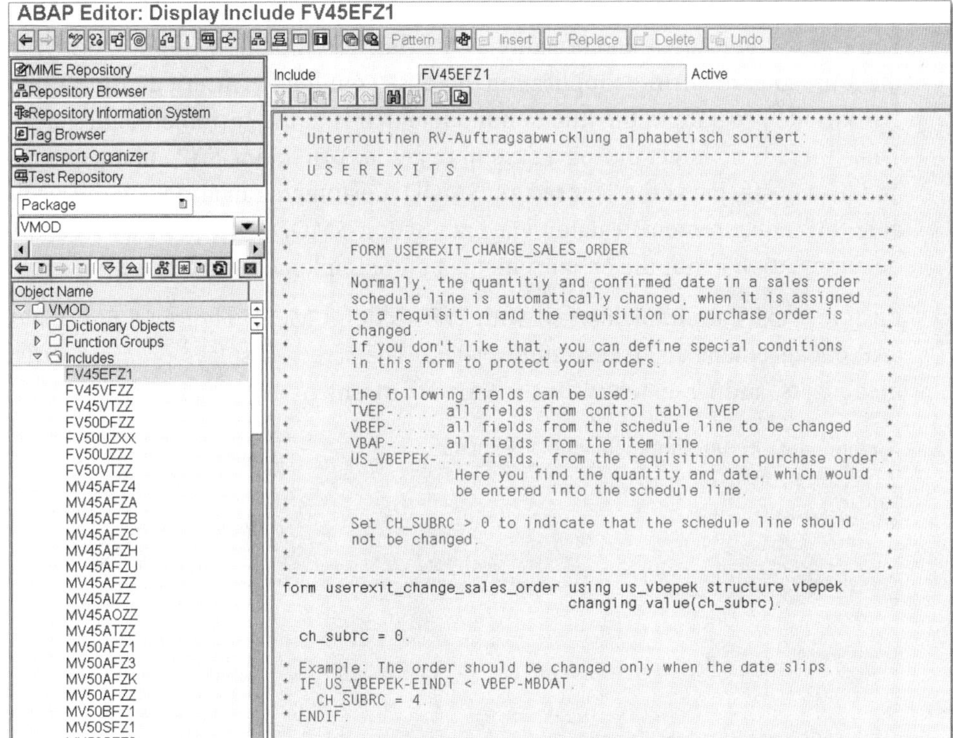

Figure 18.4 User Exits for the SD Component

User exits are called from the main program by the usual `PERFORM` statement within the application. Any customer enhancements made in the user exits are technically modifications because they require changes to SAP standard objects (i.e., the Include programs you have created). However, SAP never delivers a new version of a user exit Include program, and they will not change these programs, so the enhancements made using user exits will never impact an upgrade. If SAP has to deliver additional user exits for a new release, they will be placed in a new Include program.

Customer Exits

Customer exits were introduced after user exits to allow customers to enhance not only SAP standard code, but also screens and menus. The program exits are implemented as function modules within the SAP standard program. These function modules are delivered empty; that is, they do not contain any SAP standard code. Instead, they are provided so that the customer can insert their own logic.

You can add your own functionality to the function module without modifying the SAP standard business application (because your logic is inserted inside a special Include program in the function module that is in the customer namespace). Thus, there is no effect during a system upgrade. You define SAP enhancements and manage them via the Transaction SMOD. Customers can also view the available SAP enhancements catalog via Transaction SMOD, and perhaps read the documentation about the enhancements before implementing them.

Customer exits are implemented with Transaction CMOD. Figure 18.5 displays SAP enhancement via Transaction CMOD. The screen displays program exits, menu exits, and screen exits for the SAP enhancement `CNEX0003`.

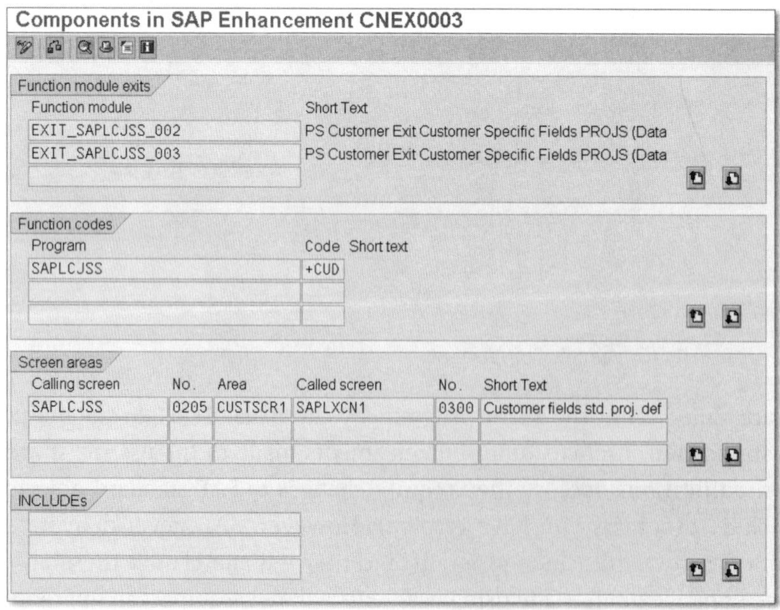

Figure 18.5 SAP Enhancement Project via Transaction SMOD

If the customer wants to implement a customer exit, they must create an enhancement project in Transaction CMOD. This is a way of grouping enhancements together so that they can be activated together. One project could contain several enhancements, each of which could consist of several components, which could be a mixture of program exits, screen exits, and menu exits. Customer enhancement projects consist of SAP enhancements. Each individual SAP enhancement can be used in only one customer enhancement project.

Following are the three types of customer exits.

Program Exits

The program exits are implemented as a function module within the SAP business application. The naming convention used for these function modules is `EXIT_<Main_Program>_NNN`, where `NNN` is a three-digit number. Program exits are also called function module exits and are called from the standard application by using the ABAP statement `CALL CUSTOMER-FUNCTION 'NNN'` where `NNN` is the three-digit number that is found at the end of the function module. Figure 18.6 displays the customer exit call within the program, and Figure 18.7 displays the actual function module corresponding to the `CUSTOMER-FUNCTION '004'`.

Include MV45AFFE_FELDAUSWAHL_LORD Active

```
  perform fieldmodification_rev_reg.

  call function 'GET_HANDLE_SD_SALES_BASIC'
    importing
      handle = l_sd_sales_basic_exit
      active = active.

  if active = charx.
    call method l_sd_sales_basic_exit->maintain_screen
      exporting
        ft180    = t180
        fvbak    = vbak
        fvbap    = vbap
        fxvbup   = xvbup[]
        fxvbuk   = xvbuk[]
        fxvbap   = xvbap[]
        fxvbpa   = xvbpa[]
      changing
        f_screen = screen.
  endif.

  call customer-function '004'
       exporting
            i_screen_name      = screen-name
            i_vbap             = vbap
            i_vbup             = xvbup
            i_screen_group4    = screen-group4
            i_t180_aktyp       = t180-aktyp
       changing
            c_screen_active    = screen-active
            c_screen_invisible = screen-invisible
            c_screen_input     = screen-input.

  perform userexit_field_modification.

  modify screen.

endform.                            "feldauswahl_lord
```

Figure 18.6 Customer Exit Call within the SAP Standard Program

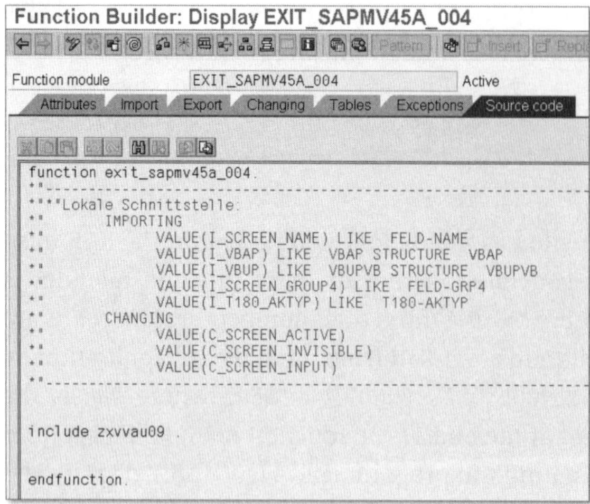

Figure 18.7 Customer Exit Implemented as a Function Module

You can search for SAP customer exit enhancements for an application via the Transaction SMOD by following the menu path UTILITIES • FIND to call the selection screen. In the selection screen you can specify the application component or package to search for the SAP enhancement (see Figure 18.8). You can also search for SAP enhancements from the Repository Information System browser within the Object Navigator.

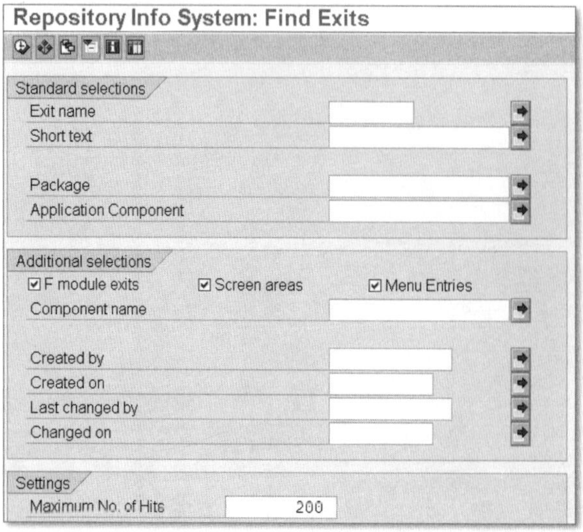

Repository Info System: Find Exits

Standard selections
Exit name
Short text
Package
Application Component

Additional selections
☑ F module exits ☑ Screen areas ☑ Menu Entries
Component name
Created by
Created on
Last changed by
Changed on

Settings
Maximum No. of Hits 200

Figure 18.8 Selection Screen to Search for SAP Enhancements

You can search in the program source code (which you want to enhance) for the statement `CALL CUSTOMER-FUNCTION`, and based on the search result decide if the customer exits within the program can be used to insert additional program logic.

To enhance a standard SAP application that contains a customer exit, you have to create a customer enhancement project to implement the customer exit. The customer enhancement project can be created from the ABAP Workbench by following the menu path UTILITIES • ENHANCEMENT • PROJECT MANAGEMENT or via the SAP Transaction CMOD. After you have created the customer enhancement project, you assign the SAP enhancement to the project.

You can find the SAP enhancement for the customer exits function module by entering the function module name on the SMOD selection screen (as displayed in Figure 18.8 above). The search result will provide you the SAP enhancement to which the customer exit function module is assigned, and it can be assigned to the customer enhancement project.

After the assignment you can access the enhancement component such as function module and insert code in the Include routine within the customer exit. You can use the data supplied in the function module parameters for the enhancement. You do not have access to the global program data. You can only access the function module interface parameter for enhancement. You decide which function module interface to use.

As a final step, you need to activate the project after implementing the functionality. Activating the project turns on the new functionality in the customer exits. Until you do this, your logic will not be executed as part of the standard application. You can also deactivate the customer project to turn off your functionality. This is useful because it doesn't require you to touch the code. Figure 18.9 and Figure 18.10 display the steps to create a customer project.

You can activate the project by clicking on the ACTIVATE PROJECT icon ( ) on the initial customer project screen or on the components screen. You can deactivate it by clicking on the DEACTIVATE PROJECT icon ( ) on the initial screen or on the components screen.

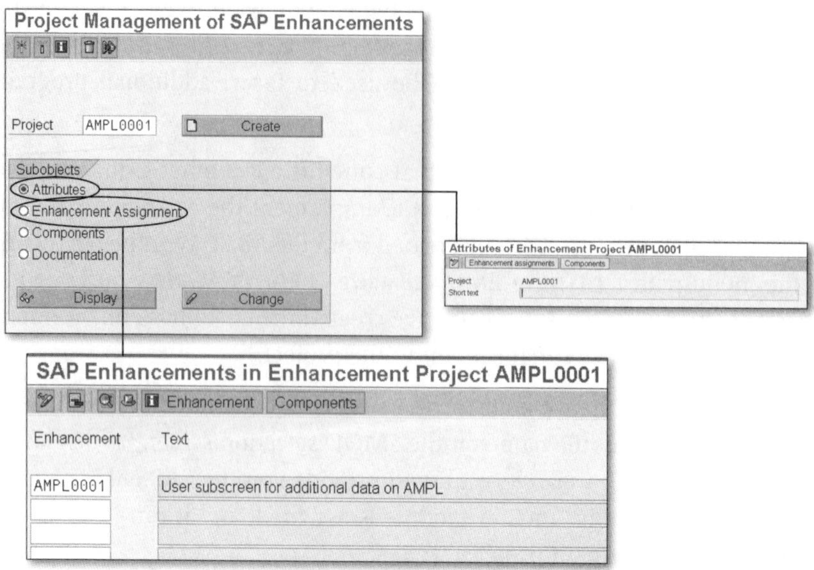

Figure 18.9 Create Customer Enhancement Project

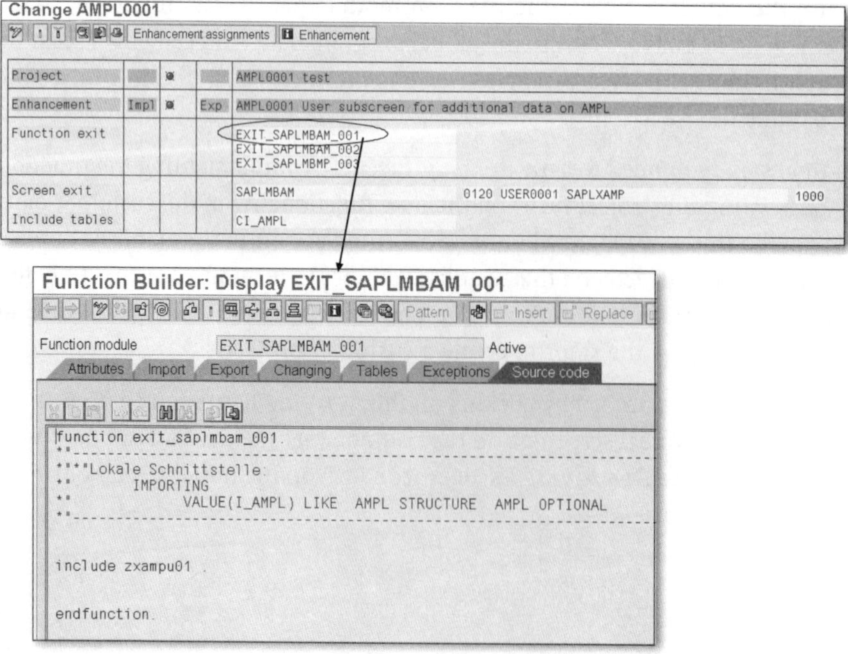

Figure 18.10 Edit Individual Enhancement Component

Screen Exits

With screen exits you can insert additional screen elements (for example, an input field, a table control, or a pushbutton) to a standard SAP screen. SAP provides screen exits by placing a special subscreen area on the standard SAP application screen. The customer screen is called from the standard screen flow logic and linked to the SAP standard subscreen area.

Figure 18.11 displays the FLOW LOGIC screen for the main screen of the subscreen that has a statement to call the subscreen in the PBO and a statement in the PAI to process the user's action on the subscreen. The statement `CALL CUSTOMER-SUBSCREEN` is called in the PBO and PAI for the screen exit instead of call subscreen. Also, looking at `CALL CUSTOMER-SUBSCREEN`, you can see that a screen exit is available for the application. The subscreen is called from the main screen, and the PBO and PAI of the subscreen are processed just like the normal screen. The PBO and PAI also have function exits inside the modules `DATA_TO_EXIT0100` and `DATA_FROM_EXIT0100` that can be used to transfer data from the main screen to the subscreen and vice versa.

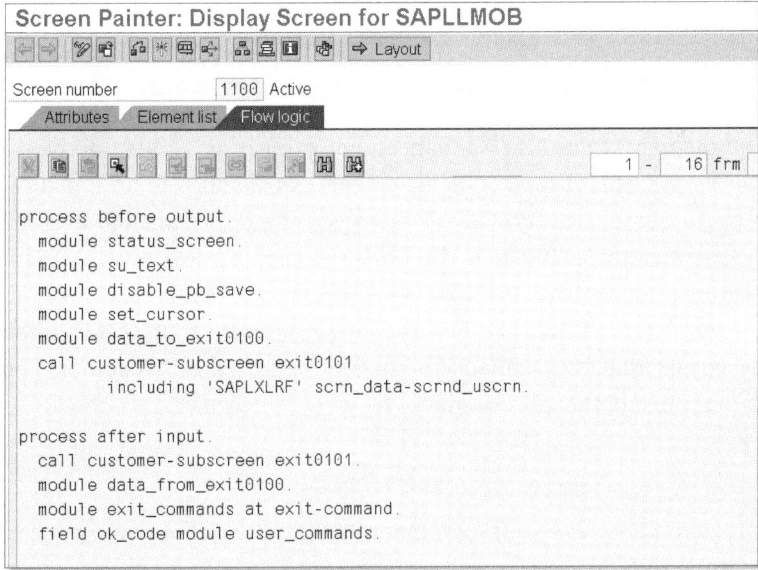

Figure 18.11 Subscreen Call with the PBO Event

For each screen exit, you also have a program exit, because of the need to transfer the data between the screen and the program. Figure 18.12 displays the program exits within the above-mentioned PBO and PAI modules.

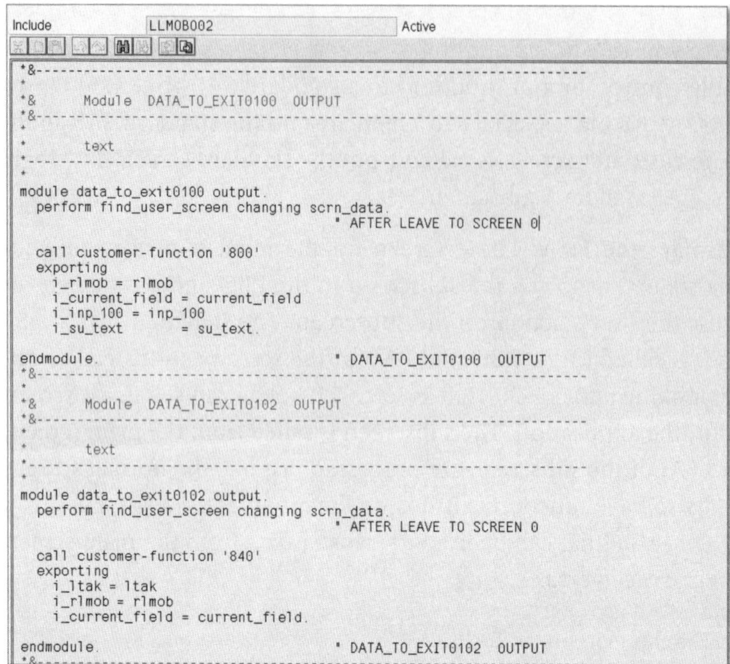

Include LLMOB002 Active
*&---
*& Module DATA_TO_EXIT0100 OUTPUT
*&---
* text
*--
module data_to_exit0100 output.
perform find_user_screen changing scrn_data.
* AFTER LEAVE TO SCREEN 0
call customer-function '800'
exporting
i_rlmob = rlmob
i_current_field = current_field
i_inp_100 = inp_100
i_su_text = su_text.
endmodule. " DATA_TO_EXIT0100 OUTPUT
*&---
*& Module DATA_TO_EXIT0102 OUTPUT
*&---
* text
*--
module data_to_exit0102 output.
perform find_user_screen changing scrn_data.
* AFTER LEAVE TO SCREEN 0
call customer-function '840'
exporting
i_ltak = ltak
i_rlmob = rlmob
i_current_field = current_field.
endmodule. " DATA_TO_EXIT0102 OUTPUT

Figure 18.12 Program Exits for Screen Exits with the PBO and PAI Modules

You have to implement a customer enhancement project as defined above to implement the screen exit. However, if the screen exit belongs to an enhancement for which you have already created a project, then you edit the existing project rather than creating a new one. You can also assign the SAP enhancement to another customer project that may contain other, related enhancements and can then work on the screen exit. Remember that you activate at project level, so if you want to ensure that your enhancements are "switched on" together, you should group them inside the same project.

Menu Exits

Menu exits allow you to attach your own menu item in the pull-down menus of the SAP standard application. SAP creates menu exits by defining special menu items in the Menu Painter. The function code for the menu exit item starts with a plus sign (+), and you have to specify the menu text when editing the menu exit component within the customer enhancement project. The menu exit item will not be displayed until the project is activated. A function module exit is provided for the specific function code of the menu exit.

You can add your own program logic for the menu item within the function module exit. Just like screen exits, menu exits go hand-in-hand with program exits. There is no point in being able to add a new entry to a menu unless you can program the logic that will be executed when the user selects this new entry (see Figure 18.13).

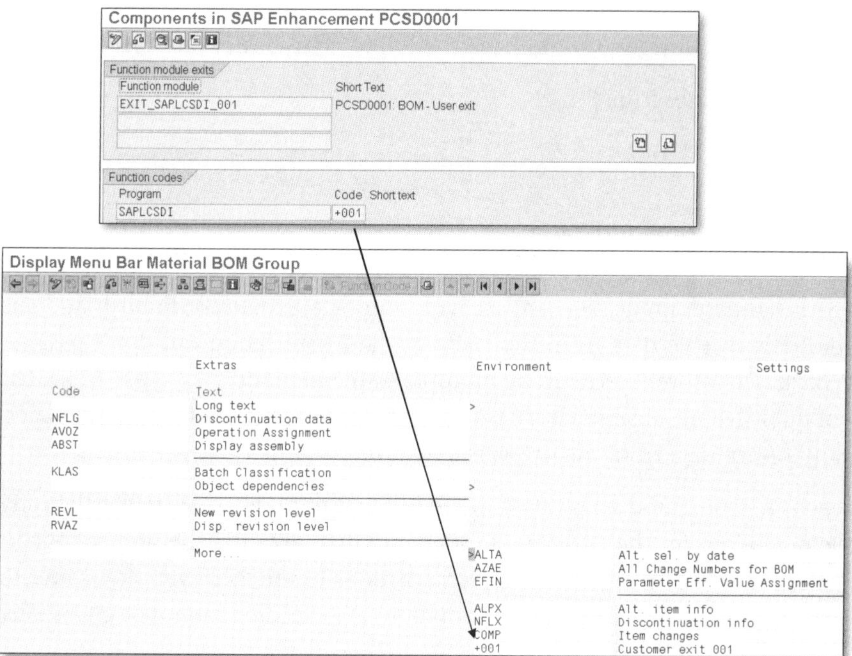

Figure 18.13 Menu Exit Enhancement

You have to create a customer enhancement project similar to the one created for program exits to implement menu exits. You can also add SAP enhancement for the menu exit to the existing customer enhancement project and then edit the menu exits component with the customer project.

Business Transaction Events

Business Transaction Events (BTEs) have been available as of Release 4.0 and are another technique for implementing program exits, and only program exits. Business Transaction Events are generally found in the general ledger accounting (FI-GL), accounts receivable and payable (FI-AR and FI-AP) and sales and distribution components.

A BTE has a predefined interface (once again, you decide what this will be) and allows you to attach additional functionality in the form of a service function module. Unlike customer exits, you create the function module yourself, but this function module must have the parameters you have dictated. By linking the function module to the Business Transaction Event, it will be called at the appropriate point in the SAP standard application.

Business Transaction Events can have the following types of interfaces:

- Publish and subscribe
- Process interfaces

Publish and Subscribe Interfaces

These interfaces inform external software that a certain event has taken place in the SAP standard application and provide the data produced. Publish and subscribe BTEs receive data from the SAP standard application but don't pass any data back. Therefore, there can be multiple implementations of these BTEs. One use of publish and subscribe BTEs is to pass data to external software, not expecting any return data from the external software.

An event function module is called in the SAP program that determines the active implementations for the event in question and then executes the service function modules for each of these active implementations of the BTE event, one after the other. The order in which the implementations are executed cannot be guaranteed.

The name of the event function module for publish and subscribe BTEs begins with `OPEN_FI_PERFORM_<NNNNNNNN>_E` or `OUTBOUND_CALL_<NNNNNNNN>_E`, where `<NNNNNNNN>` is the eight-digit event number. The service function modules for the event (i.e., the function modules that have been created and implemented) are executed as defined in the customization. Figure 18.14 displays the customization for the Business Transaction Event `00001025`, and Figure 18.15 displays the BTE call in the SAP program.

The customizing for BTE events is defined by calling the SAP Transaction FIBF. The customizing for publish and subscribe interfaces is defined by following the menu path SETTINGS • P/S MODULES and selecting the option for customer, partner, or SAP enhancements (see Figure 18.16).

Change View "Publish&Subscribe BTE: SAP Enhancement": Overview

New Entries

Event	Ctr	Appl.	Function Module
00001025		DI-DPC	/SAPPCE/DPC_INTERFACE_00001025
00001025		FI-CM	FDM_COLL_INTERFACE_00001025
00001025		FI-DM	FDM_AR_INTERFACE_00001025
00001025		FI-TAX	CREATE_DEFTAX_ITEM
00001025		IS-PS	FM_CHECK_FI
00001025		ISJP	ISJP_BTE_00001025
00001025		RE	REEX_CALLBACK_PAYMENT_00001025
00001025		UKM	UKM_INTERFACE_00001025
00001025	AR		AR_PROCESS_00001025_NUM_CHECK
00001025	GR		TURKEY_BOE_PERFORM_00001025
00001025	TH		TURKEY_BOE_PERFORM_00001025
00001025			TURKEY_BOE_PERFORM_00001025

Figure 18.14 BTE Customization for SAP Enhancement

Include MF05AFF0_FCODE_BEARBEITUNG Active

```
        perform simulate_ledger_view using 'C'.
      endif.
*----------------- Open FI --------------------------------------------
* DM                                                        note 0561898
      if postab ne space.
        refresh clrtab.
        loop at postab where xaktp = 'X'.
          move-corresponding postab to clrtab.
          append clrtab.
        endloop.
      endif.
      call function 'OPEN_FI_PERFORM_00001025_E'
        exporting
          i_bkdf            = bkdf
        tables
          t_ausz1           = xausz1
          t_ausz2           = xausz2
          t_ausz3           = xausz3
          t_bkp1            = xbkp1
          t_bkpf            = xbkpf
          t_bsec            = xbsec
          t_bsed            = xbsed
          t_bseg            = xbseg
          t_bset            = xbset
          t_bseu            = xbseu
          t_rsgtab          = rsgtab                       "note561898
          t_renum           = renum                        "note561898
          t_postab          = clrtab                       "note561898
        exceptions                                        "Note1097274
          error_message = 1.                               "Note1097274
```

Figure 18.15 BTE Function Call in SAP Program

Customers and partners have to define a product by following the menu path Settings • Products • Customer or Settings • Products • Partner before they can define the customizing of the event and the function module they want to be executed.

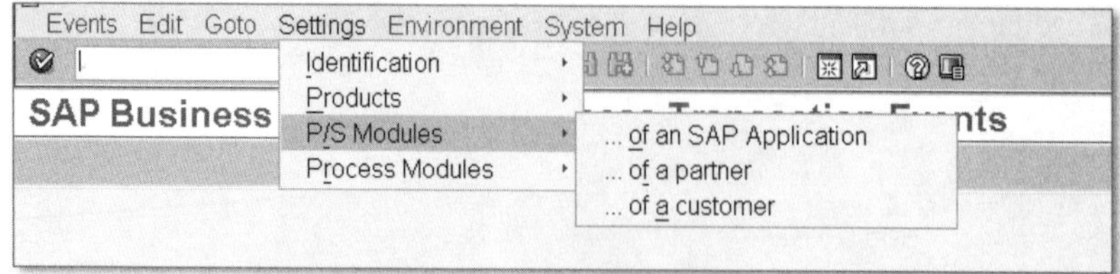

Figure 18.16 BTE Customization for SAP, Partner, or Customer

Publish and subscribe interfaces allow you to start one or more service function modules without interfering with each other. Customer, partner, or SAP enhancements can define their own service function module in the customization without interfering with each other by creating their own product. You can also switch on or off each product as a whole entity. This allows the user to control which enhancement should be processed and which should not be processed. In contrast to customer exits, Business Transaction Events allow you to use multiple interfaces for additional logic.

Process Interfaces

These interfaces are used to control the business process differently than the way it is handled in the standard SAP system. In contrast to publish and subscribe, data exchange takes place in both directions in process interfaces; that is, the SAP standard application passes data to the function module, and the function module can pass data back. A process BTE can therefore have only one active implementation.

SAP also provides you with sample function modules for the BTE, with a short text, interface (i.e., the parameters you need to use for your function module), and documentation that can all be used by the customer when creating their own function module. The name for the sample function module is SAMPLE_INTERFACE_<BTE-ID>, and the easiest way to proceed is to copy it as your starting point.

BTE Search

You can determine whether an SAP application offers a Business Transaction Event by searching for the character string OPEN_FI_PERFORM within the source code of the application transaction (because, as we've seen, the event function module name starts with this string).

You can also search for BTE events by calling the SAP Transaction FIBF and following the menu path ENVIRONMENT • INFO SYSTEM (P/S) or ENVIRONMENT • INFOSYSTEM (PROCESS).

Business Add-Ins

Business Add-Ins (BAdIs) are an SAP enhancement technique based on object-oriented ABAP. Business Add-Ins, like the previously discussed enhancement techniques, are predefined by SAP in the standard applications. The definition of Business Add-Ins can be viewed in the SAP Transaction SE18. You use this transaction to create BAdI definitions.

You create an interface for the Business Add-Ins, which contains the definition of the methods that will be provided for the customer. Then you create an adapter class that implements the interface and thus provides the interface for BAdI implementation. In the SAP standard application, you generate an instance of the adapter class and call the corresponding method within the application. This is where the customer can add their own logic, by creating their own implementation of this method of the BAdI.

The strength of Business Add-Ins lies in the fact that they can have multiple implementations if you intend that. You can have several active BAdI implementations if the MULTIPLE USE checkbox is selected (see Figure 18.17). When the BAdI is called in the SAP standard application, the instance of the BAdI adapter class is responsible for ensuring that all implementations are called. However because they can be called in any sequence, it is not possible to guarantee the order. If you have multiple-use BAdI definitions, the sequence must not play an important role. A typical example is the execution of checks before a document is saved.

Similarly, you can have several active BAdI implementations if the FILTER-DEPEND. checkbox is selected for the BAdI. The idea is that you can have different BAdI implementations for different filter values if the FILTER-DEPEND. checkbox is selected. An example of this is when the filter is based on the country code: The customer can create an implementation for different countries based on their differing legal requirements or practices. You can have only one active BAdI implementation at a time if the MULTIPLE USE and FILTER-DEPEND. checkboxes are not selected. Each Business Add-In can contain components for program enhancements, menu enhancements, and screen enhancements, similar to customer exits, described earlier.

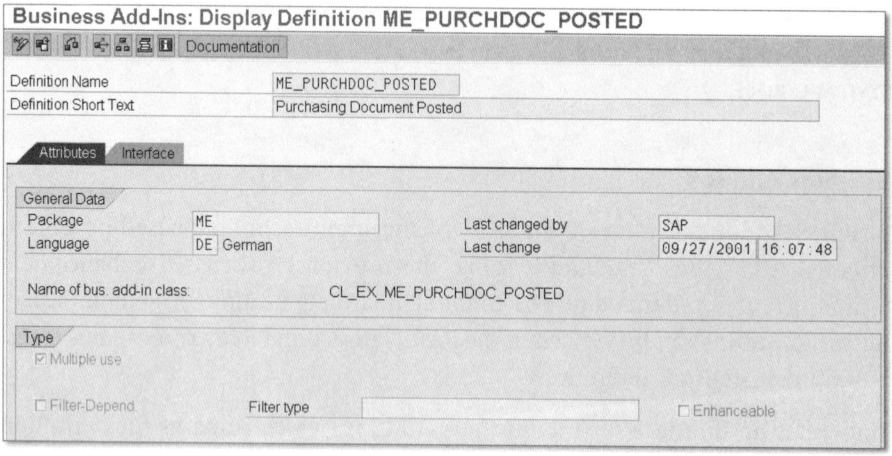

Figure 18.17 Business Add-In Attributes

Program enhancements are defined in the form of interface methods. You define the interface and the methods inside it, including their parameters. To implement the program enhancement, a BAdI implementation must be created, and a class is generated automatically for you to implement the method (see Figure 18.18).

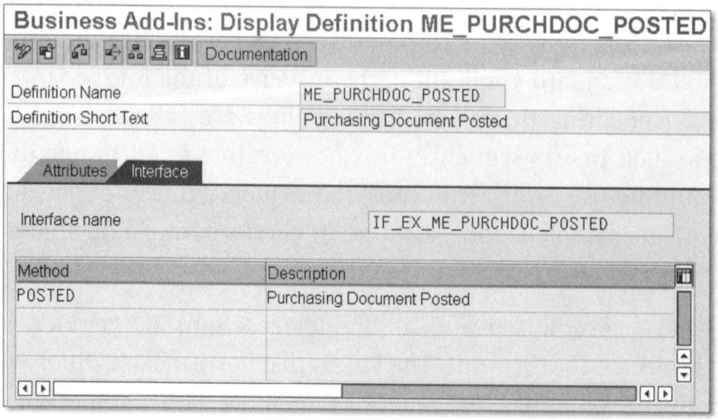

Figure 18.18 Business Add-In Interface and Methods

The Business Add-In definition can also have function codes for menu enhancements. The function codes for the menu entries are available in the GUI interface and are visible to the user only when the Business Add-In is implemented and activated. The function codes for BAdI menu enhancements start with a plus sign (+), similar to customer exits. Menu enhancements can have only one active implementation and are not found in multiple-use or filter-dependent Business Add-Ins.

In addition to program and menu enhancements, you can also find screen enhancements in Business Add-Ins. Screen enhancements, like menu enhancements, are not supported for multiple-use Business Add-Ins. Figure 18.19 and Figure 18.20 display the interface for menu enhancement and screen enhancement, respectively. Menu enhancements are defined under the FCodes tab, and screen enhancements are defined under the Subscreens tab.

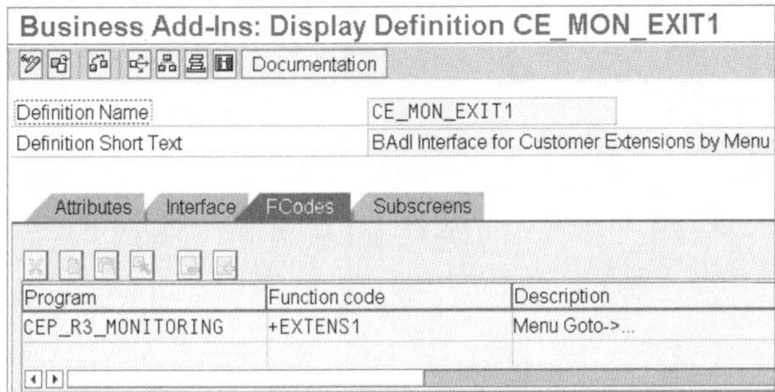

Figure 18.19 Business Add-Ins for Menu Enhancement

Business Add-Ins: Display Definition BADI_FDCB_SUBBAS01

Documentation

Definition Name: BADI_FDCB_SUBBAS01

Definition Short Text: Screen Enhancement 1 on FDCB Basic Data Screen (010, 510)

Attributes | Interface | FCodes | Subscreens

Call program	Scr.No	Subscreen area	Description
SAPLFDCB	10	SUBBAS01	Enhancement 1 Vendor Basic Data
SAPLFDCB	510	SUBBAS01	Enhancement 1 Customer Basic Data

Figure 18.20 Business Add-Ins for Screen Enhancement

Searching Business Add-Ins

There are various ways of searching for Business Add-Ins in SAP standard applications.

- You can search for a BAdI in the relevant application program by searching for the string `CL_EXITHANDLER`. If a Business Add-In is called in the program, then the `GET_INSTANCE` static method of this class is called in the program. This method returns an instance of the BAdI adapter class, and after that, you will see the BAdI method call that you can implement. Figure 18.21 displays the `GET_INSTANCE` method call in the program.

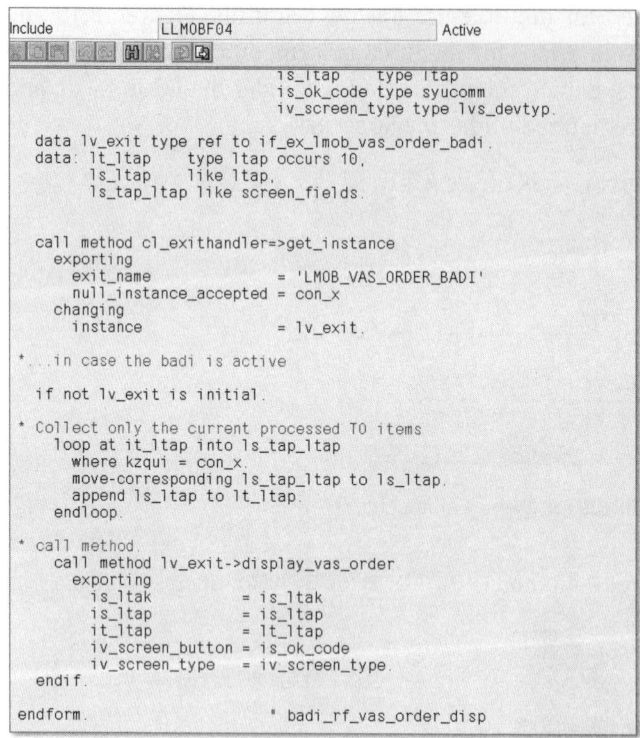

```
Include  LLMOBF04                                   Active

                   is_ltap     type ltap
                   is_ok_code type syucomm
                   iv_screen_type type lvs_devtyp.

  data lv_exit type ref to if_ex_lmob_vas_order_badi.
  data: lt_ltap     type ltap occurs 10,
        ls_ltap     like ltap,
        ls_tap_ltap like screen_fields.


  call method cl_exithandler=>get_instance
    exporting
      exit_name                = 'LMOB_VAS_ORDER_BADI'
      null_instance_accepted = con_x
    changing
      instance                 = lv_exit.

*...in case the badi is active

  if not lv_exit is initial.

* Collect only the current processed TO items
    loop at it_ltap into ls_tap_ltap
      where kzqui = con_x.
      move-corresponding ls_tap_ltap to ls_ltap.
      append ls_ltap to lt_ltap.
    endloop.

* call method.
    call method lv_exit->display_vas_order
      exporting
        is_ltak          = is_ltak
        is_ltap          = is_ltap
        it_ltap          = lt_ltap
        iv_screen_button = is_ok_code
        iv_screen_type   = iv_screen_type.
  endif.

endform.                    " badi_rf_vas_order_disp
```

Figure 18.21 GET_INSTANCE Method Call in SAP Standard Program

- You can use forward navigation to reach to the definition of the BAdI. In the above program you can double-click on the method `DISPLAY_VAS_ORDER` corresponding to reference variable `lv_exit`, which will display the interface used to define the BAdI. You can use the where-used functionality to determine which BAdI the interface is used in and then create the BAdI implementation.
- You can use the SAP Application Hierarchy to restrict the component in which you want to search for Business Add-Ins. The SAP Application Hierarchy displays all of the standard SAP application components and the packages that have been assigned to them. You can use the Application Hierarchy with the Repository Information System to locate BAdIs available for an application.

To locate the BAdIs available for purchasing proceed as follows:

- Place the cursor on the PURCHASING branch of the Application Hierarchy tree and click on SELECT SUBTREE (+/–; see Figure 18.22) or click on the SELECT SUBTREE +/– icon ( ). The PURCHASING node is under the SAP application MM.

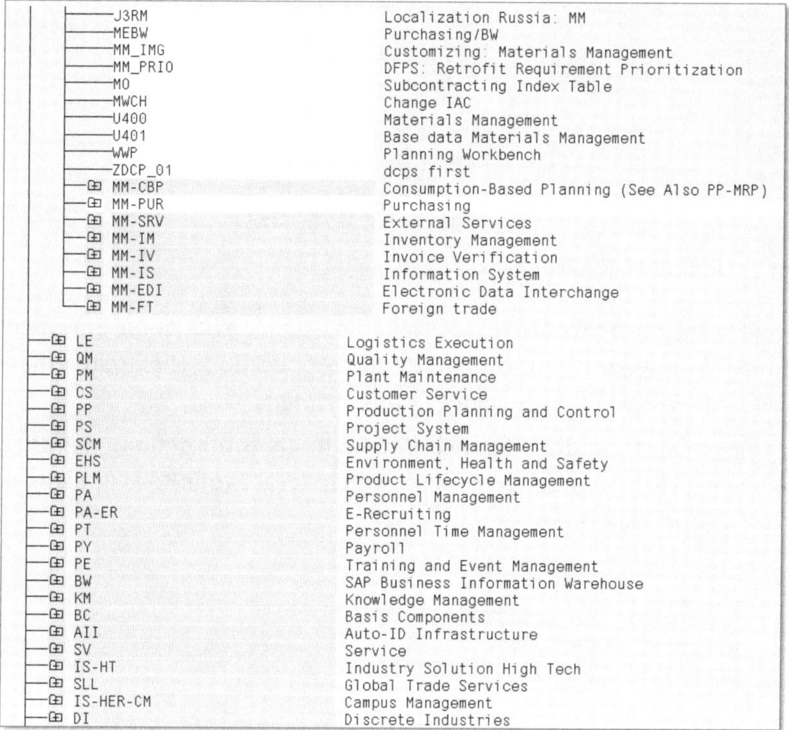

Figure 18.22 Application Hierarchy to Search for Exits in SAP Applications

- After selecting the APPLICATION HIERARCHY select REPOSITORY INFORMATION SYSTEM by clicking on the INFORMATION SYSTEM button on the screen. This starts the Repository Information System browser, and the application will let you search for any object within the selected application (see Figure 18.23). Expand the ENHANCEMENTS subtree, select BUSINESS ADD-INS, and then select DEFINITIONS or IMPLEMENTATIONS to search for the BADI definition or implementation, respectively, within an application. The system offers you a selection screen that allows you to narrow down your search, or you can leave the fields on this screen empty if you want to see all of the BAdIs within the component or package you have chosen.

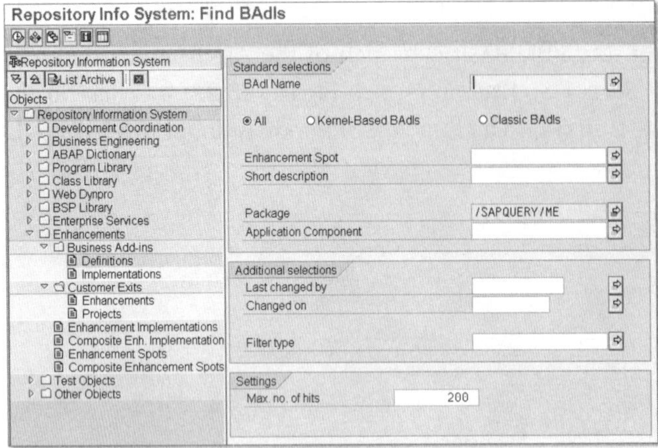

Figure 18.23 Repository Information System to Find BAdIs

You can also use the above technique to find customer exits or enhancement definitions or implementations within the Application Hierarchy (these enhancements will be discussed later in this chapter).

- Lastly, you can also use the reference IMG to locate BAdI definitions for an application and click on the Execute icon (⊕) to create your BAdI implementation (see Figure 18.24).

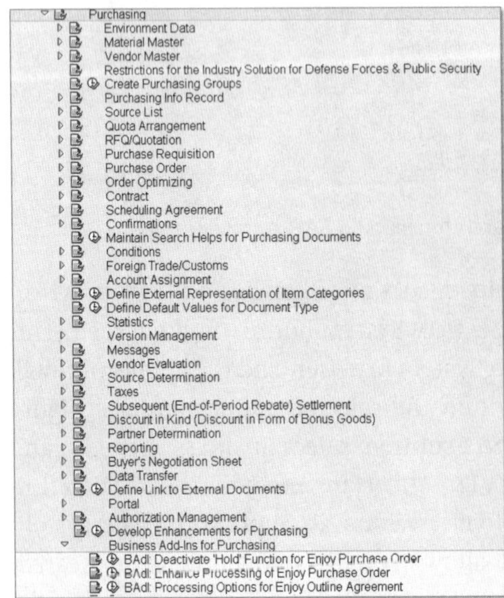

Figure 18.24 BADI Implementation from SAP Reference IMG

Implementing Business Add-Ins

To create BAdI implementations follow the menu path TOOLS • ABAP WORKBENCH • UTILITIES • BUSINESS ADD-INS • IMPLEMENTATION or use Transaction SE19. As of SAP NetWeaver 7.0, the user interface for Transaction SE19 has changed because there are new BAdIs in addition to the older classic BAdIs (those that we are discussing here; for details on new BAdIs, see the end of this chapter). Transaction SE19 allows you to create BAdI implementations for new and classic BAdIs (see Figure 18.25).

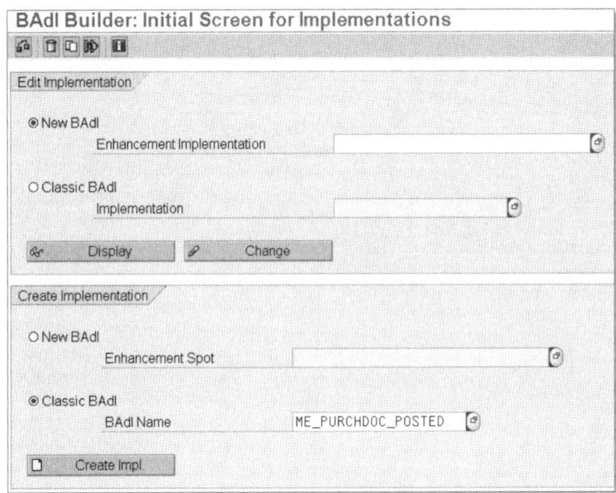

Figure 18.25 Implementing Business Add-Ins — Initial Screen

If the BAdI you want to implement is a classic BAdI, select the CLASSIC BADI radio button, enter the BAdI name, and click on the CREATE IMPL. button. In the subsequent dialog box enter the BAdI implementation name (which should be in the customer namespace), and enter the short implementation text on the next screen (see Figure 18.26).

Double-click on the interface method that you want to implement. This starts the Class Builder editor, where you can insert the desired source code. The system automatically creates a class inside which your method implementation will be created (you can see the class name in Figure 18.26). After you have inserted your code, you need to save the changes and activate the BAdI implementation.

You can activate the BAdI implementation by clicking on the ACTIVATE icon ( ) on the BAdI screen. Your source code in the method will be executed in the standard SAP application after the BADI is activated. You can only work with the data supplied by the method parameters for enhancement, which you define.

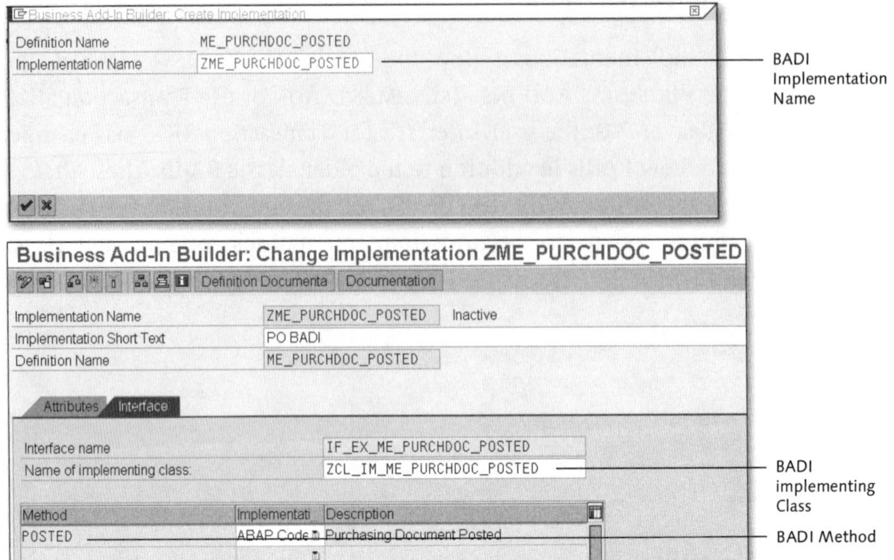

Figure 18.26 BAdI Implementation

Implementing Menu Enhancement

You create the BAdI implementation and select the FCodes tab to select the menu exits. You can double-click on the button on the BAdI implementation screen and enter the function text, icon name, icon text, and info text for the function code `+EXTENS1` as displayed in Figure 18.27.

Business Add-In Builder: Change Implementation ZCE_MON_EXIT1
Definition Documenta Documentation
Implementation Name ZCE_MON_EXIT1 Inactive
Implementation Short Text Menu Enhancement implementation
Definition Name CE_MON_EXIT1
Attributes Interface FCodes
Program Function code Description Function text
CEP_R3_MONITORING +EXTENS1 Menu Goto->... test
Business Add-Ins: Text Maintenance for Function Code +EXTENS1
Program CEP_R3_MONITORING
Function code +EXTENS1
Function text
Icon name
Icontext
Info. text
Texts

Figure 18.27 Menu Enhancement

You have to implement the appropriate interface method and program the action you want to system to perform when the menu item is selected. Finally, you have to activate the implementation. The menu enhancement only becomes visible after the BAdI implementation is activated.

Implementing Screen Enhancement

For BAdI screen enhancement you have to create your own screen and write the program for the screen by creating a module pool or function group. You use the BAdI interface method to transfer the data from the application program to the screen and vice versa.

You have to create the BAdI implementation for the screen enhancement and assign the customer screen in the SCR.NO column and the program name under PROGRAM CALLED column as shown in Figure 18.28. Next, it is important to implement the interface method to transfer the date between the application and the customer screen. Finally, you have to activate the BAdI to incorporate the customer screen in the SAP standard program.

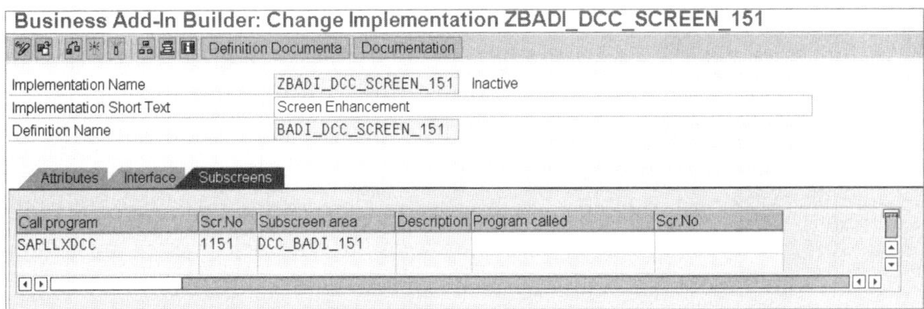

Figure 18.28 Screen Enhancement

Enhancing the ABAP Dictionary

There are two ways you can add extra fields to SAP standard tables without modifying that SAP table: SAP tables can be enhanced using either an append structure or a Customizing Include.

- Customers can create an append structure for almost any SAP table or structure (see restrictions below). Append structures allow you to enhance SAP tables by adding customer-specific fields that are not part of the standard application, without modifying the table. Append structures are table specific; that is, one append structure can only belong to one table. However, a table can have multiple append structures.

Whenever a table is activated, the system searches for the active append structures for that table and attaches them to the database table. Activating an append structure also activates the table to which it is assigned. You can use an append structure as a type in your ABAP programs in the same way that you can with any Dictionary table or structure. The append structure is always added as the last fields of the table.

The append structure is always created in the customer namespace. This protects it from being overwritten during upgrade. The field names in the append structure must also be in the customer namespace and must begin with `ZZ` or `YY`. This prevents any naming conflict with the new SAP field names that might be inserted in the future.

You cannot create append structures for pool or cluster tables. Also, you cannot create an append structure for a table that contains a long field such as the type `LCHR` or `LRAW` because the long field should always be the last field in that table.

- Some of the tables delivered by SAP contain a special Include structure. These Includes are called *Customizing Includes*, and you can add customer-specific fields to them. In contrast to append structures, Customizing Includes can be included in more than one table or structure, and if you add a field in the include structure, it will automatically appear in all of the tables or structures that have this Customizing Include. Customizing Include name begins with `CI`. Just like append structures, Customizing Include field names must lie in the customer namespace, and the names must begin with `ZZ` or `YY`.

Of course there is no point in having extra fields in your SAP tables unless you can do something with them. You have to enhance the standard SAP application to populate the fields attached to the append structure or Customizing Include. The customer-specific fields can be populated using one of the enhancement techniques discussed elsewhere in this chapter.

Enhancement Framework

As of SAP NetWeaver 7.0, the Enhancement Framework allows you to add functionality to the SAP standard application without actually changing the original repository objects. With this new technology it is possible enhance global classes, function modules, Web Dynpro ABAP components, and all source code units using explicit enhancement options and sections. You can also define additional implicit enhancement options for source code plug-ins.

The Enhancement Framework consists of:

- **Explicit enhancement points**
  These are points that are positioned in repository objects in which the customer can add functionality in the form of source code without making modifications. You define explicit enhancement options, whereas you do not preplan implicit enhancement options.

  Explicit enhancement points are explicitly flagged source code points or sections in ABAP programs and can be enhanced by the source code plug-ins. They are implemented using the syntax `ENHANCEMENT-POINTS`.
- **Explicit enhancement section**
  These allow you to replace source code in SAP programs, function modules, and methods without making modifications. The replaceable SAP source code is enclosed by the statements `ENHANCEMENT-SECTION` and `END-ENHANCEMENT-SECTION`.
- **Implicit enhancement points**
  These are always available to the customer, and they can be used to insert source code in programs, function modules, and methods without making modifications. They are also available for SAP objects developed before SAP NetWeaver 7.0.
- **Enhancement options**
  These allow you to enhance interface parameters for SAP function modules and class methods without modification. You can also add additional attributes and methods to SAP classes. Enhancement options are always available and can be used by customers to enhance SAP application. They are also available for SAP objects developed before SAP NetWeaver 7.0.
- **New BAdIs**
  For SAP NetWeaver 7.0 SAP implemented new BAdI technology and intends to use it for future enhancement. The new BAdI technology works in the same way as the classical BAdI, bit the adapter call is no longer required. Instead, the new BAdI technology uses the new language elements `GET BADI` and `CALL BADI`. Similar to classical BAdIs, new BAdIs provide you the enhancement for program, screen, and menu exits. To use the BAdIs you have to implement the enhancement implementation via Transaction SE19.

The system generates the BAdI handle in the kernel at the runtime of the application program. Listing 18.1 shows the new BAdI call in the standard SAP application.

```
DATA lf_badi_me_conf     TYPE REF to /spe/cd_me_confirmation.
TRY.
    GET BADI lf_badi_me_conf.
      CATCH cx_badi_not_implemented.
CATCH.
TRY
  CALL BADI lf_badi_me_conf->change_ibtyp
    EXPORTING
      it_likp          = xlikp[]
      it_lips          = xlips[]
      it_vbpa          = xvbpa[]
    CHANGING
      cv_ibtyp         = lfart_besttyp
      cv_no_po_update = lf_no_po_update.
    CATCH  cx_badi_initial_reference.
CATCH.
```

Listing 18.1 New BAdI Call in Standard SAP Application

The new BAdI handle is generated by the statement `GET BADI` by specifying the reference variable. The exception `CX_BADI_NOT_IMPLEMENTED` is triggered if no active implementation of the BAdI is found. The `CALL BADI` statement calls the method corresponding to the BAdI handle derived from the `GET BADI` statement. The system triggers `CX_BADI_INITIAL_REFERENCE` if the `CALL BADI` statement is called with an initial reference to the handle.

You can search the new BAdI definition by searching for the `GET BADI` string in the application program. You can also search for new BAdIs by using the Repository Information System or the Application Hierarchy with the Repository Information System.

- **Enhancement spots**
  These are containers for explicit enhancement options. Enhancement sections add new BAdIs and carry information about the positions at which enhancement points or BAdIs were created. Enhancement spots either contain new BAdIs or explicit enhancement sections and enhancement sections. One enhancement option can manage several enhancement options or BAdIs of a repository object, or alternatively, several enhancement spots can be

assigned to one enhancement option. Implicit enhancements do not need to be assigned to enhancement spots.

- **Composite enhancement spots**
  These contain one or some simple or composite enhancements. They are used to semantically bundle simple or composite enhancement spots.

Modification

An object can be original in one system only. For the SAP system the original system is SAP itself. In customer system SAP objects are available as copies. Your development system is the original system for the objects created on it. The objects created in your development system are assigned to development or correction requests if they are assigned to the package. The transport request is used to transport the development object from the development system to the subsequent systems. Changes to the original are assigned to the correction change request, and the change to the copy (an object that is not developed on the system where it is being changed) is assigned to the repair change request.

You should not change the SAP object unless the modification you want is absolutely necessary and cannot be implemented by the available enhancement techniques. When you upgrade your system or apply a support package, conflicts can occur with modified objects. These conflicts occur if you have modified an SAP object and SAP has delivered a new version of the object. The new object delivered by SAP becomes an active object in your system, and if you want to keep your changes, you have to carry out a modification adjustment for the object. The modification adjustment should always be carried out in the development system and then transported to the subsequent systems.

To change the SAP object you require an access key. You have to get the access key from the SAP Service Marketplace (*http://service.sap.com*) and register the object you are changing. The access key is also referred to as *SAP Software Change Registration* (SSCR). All objects that are being changed are logged by SAP. This helps SAP support quickly locate and fix the problem if it is as a result of modification of the SAP standard object. SAP recommends that you use the Modification Assistant to modify standard SAP objects, but you can switch Modification Assistant if required. Modification Assistant makes the modification easier and allows you to reset the modification.

Modification Browser

The Modification Browser provides you an overview of all of the changes made in the system. The Modification Browser differentiates between modifications made using the Modification Assistant and those made without it. Modification Browser can be started by calling Transaction SE95, and you can restrict object selection according to various selection criteria on the initial screen (see Figure 18.29).

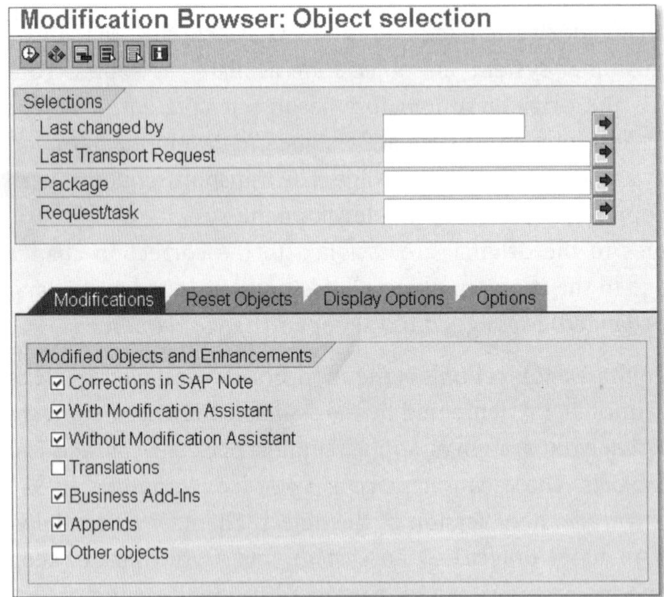

Figure 18.29 Modification Browser

Modification Browser can also be used to reset or undo the modification made in the system.

SAP Notes Assistant

The SAP Notes Assistant is used to implement SAP Notes, which are corrections to objects in the SAP system. Before the SAP Notes Assistant was introduced, system administrators had to apply the SAP Notes manually with the help of the developer. This increases the likelihood of errors. Without the SAP Notes Assistant, you would have to enter a registration key for the object before you can change it.

With SAP Notes Assistant, you no longer need to enter the registration key. SAP Notes Assistant automatically imports the correction without the Modification Assistant. You no longer have to maintain the source code manually, thereby saving time and reducing the likelihood of errors. Notes Assistant downloads the notes automatically from the SAP Service Marketplace directly using an RFC connection and reads the correction before applying the notes to the system. Notes Assistant also recognizes the dependencies between different notes. The system checks for the prerequisites and dependencies for other notes. It ascertains whether a note has a prerequisite note with it, and loads the prerequisite note if there is one. It displays the list of prerequisites in the dialog box, and you implement the note in the correct order as displayed in the list. You have the option to implement all of the selected notes at once, or you can implement each note individually. You also have the option to undo the note implementation if it has been implemented with Notes Assistant.

Practice Questions

The practice questions below will help you evaluate your understanding of the topic. The questions shown are similar in nature to those found on the certification examination, but whereas none of these questions will be found on the exam itself, they allow you to review your knowledge of the subject. Select the correct answers and then check the completeness of your answers in the following solution section. Remember that you must select all correct answers and only correct answers to receive credit for the question.

1. Which of the following is a true statement?

☐ **A.** An access key is required to implement Business Add-Ins.

☑ **B.** An access key is required to modify SAP repository objects.

☑ **C.** An access key is required to enhance an SAP application using a user exit.

☐ **D.** An access key is required to implement an implicit enhancement point.

2. SAP enhancement for customer exits are managed by transaction:

☐ **A.** Transaction SMOD

☑ **B.** Transaction CMOD

☐ **C.** None of the above

3. Customer exits provide program exit, screen exit, and menu exit enhancement.

- ☑ **A.** True
- ☐ **B.** False

4. The `CALL CUSTOMER-FUNCTION 'nnn'` statement, where `nnn` is a three-digit number is used in SAP programs for one of the following types enhancement.

- ☑ **A.** Customer exits
- ☐ **B.** Business Add-Ins
- ☐ **C.** User exits
- ☐ **D.** New BAdIs

5. How would you find out if an application program offers a program exit?

- ☑ **A.** Search for the character string `CUSTOMER-FUNCTION`.
- ☑ **B.** Use the Repository Information System.
- ☑ **C.** Use the Application Hierarchy.
- ☑ **D.** Look for a customer exit in the SAP reference IMG within an application area.

6. A Business Add-Ins can have multiple active implementations at a time.

- ☑ **A.** It can have multiple active implementations if the MULTIPLE USE checkbox is selected.
- ☐ **B.** It cannot have a multiple active implementation.
- ☑ **C.** It can have multiple implementations if the FILTER-DEPEND. checkbox is selected.

7. The statement `CALL BADI` and `GET BADI` is used for following type of Business Add-Ins:

- ☐ **A.** Classical BAdI
- ☑ **B.** New BAdI
- ☐ **C.** None of the above

8. Explicit enhancement points and sections are defined by the SAP application programmer.

☐ **A.** True

☐ **B.** False

9. Code within an explicit enhancement section can be replaced by the customer.

☐ **A.** True

☐ **B.** False

10. Code within an explicit enhancement point can be enhanced but cannot be replaced.

☐ **A.** True

☐ **B.** False

11. Which of the following are correct statements:

☐ **A.** An enhancement spot can contain explicit an enhancement point and an enhancement section.

☐ **B.** An enhancement spot can contain an explicit enhancement point, explicit enhancement section, and new BAdI.

☐ **C.** An enhancement spot can contain either an explicit enhancement point and enhancement section or a new BAdI only, but all three cannot be in the same enhancement spot.

☐ **D.** An enhancement spot can contain one or more simple or composite enhancements.

12. Which of the following is a true statement:

☐ **A.** An implicit enhancement point can be used to insert code in an SAP program and is always available to the customer.

☐ **B.** Implicit enhancement options allow you to enhance interface parameters for function modules and methods without modifying the repository object.

☐ **C.** Implicit enhancement can be used to enhance SAP objects developed prior to SAP NetWeaver 7.0.

☐ **D.** None of the above

Practice Question Answers and Explanations

1. Correct answers: **B, C**

   These answers are correct for the following reasons:

   - An access key is not required to implement Business Add-Ins because you provide the Business Add-In definition for the customer or partner to insert additional functionality for the application.
   - An access key is required to modify SAP repository objects. You need to register the repository object in the SAP Service Marketplace to generate the object key and have to enter it to modify the repository object.
   - An access key is required to enhance user exits because technically, user exit implementation is the system modification. User exits are included in the special Include program that is attached to the module pool program. SAP does not deliver any new version of Include, so user exit enhancement does not impact the upgrade even though it's a modification of the SAP repository object.
   - Implicit enhancement does not require an access key. It's an enhancement that does not modify the SAP repository object.

2. Correct answer: **A**

   SAP manages customer exist enhancement via Transaction SMOD. Transaction CMOD is used to manage customer enhancement projects.

3. Correct answer: **A**

   Customer exits provide program exit, screen exit, and menu exit enhancement.

4. Correct answer: **A**

   You use the `CALL CUSTOMER-FUNCTION 'nnn'` statement to define a customer exit with an SAP application. You also create function modules and groups in the system, but you would have to insert additional functionality within the function module as a part of customer exit implementation via SAP Transaction CMOD.

5. Correct answers: **A, B, C, D**

   You search for a customer exit by searching for the character string `CUSTOMER-FUNCTION` or via the Repository Information System, Application Hierarchy, or SAP Reference IMG.

6. Correct answers: **A, C**

   Business Add-Ins can have multiple implementations if the MULTIPLE USE checkbox is selected. A Business Add-In can have multiple implementations, one for each filter value, if the FILTER-DEPEND. checkbox is selected.

7. Correct answer: **B**

   The `CALL BADI` and `GET BADI` statements are used for new BAdI as of SAP NetWeaver 7.0.

8. Correct answer: **A**

   Explicit enhancement points and sections are defined by the SAP application programmer.

9. Correct answer: **A**

   Code with an explicit enhancement section can be replaced by customer.

10. Correct answer: **A**

    Code within an explicit enhancement point can be enhanced.

11. Correct answers: **A, C, D**

    These answers are correct for the following reasons:

    - Enhancement spots can contain one or more explicit enhancement points and explicit enhancement sections.
    - Enhancement spots cannot have explicit enhancement points, explicit sections, and new BAdIs together. They can have one or more explicit enhancement points and explicit sections or one or more new BAdIs.
    - Composite enhancement spots can have one or more enhancement spots or composite enhancement spots.

12. Correct answers: **A, B, C**

    These answers are correct for the following reasons:

    - Implicit enhancement points are used to insert additional code with the SAP program without modifying the application.
    - Implicit enhancement options are used to enhance the interface parameters for function modules and methods.
    - Implicit enhancement points and options are available for SAP objects developed prior to SAP NetWeaver 7.0. Implicit enhancement point and options are always available to the customer and can be used to enhance SAP applications without modification.

Take Away

You should be able to explain various enhancement techniques such as user exits, customer exits, Business Add-Ins, and enhancement techniques in SAP NetWeaver 7.0. You should be able to explain the features of each of the above enhancement techniques and be able to use them to enhance SAP applications.

You should know the tools used to implement customer exits such as program exits, menu exits, and screen exits to insert your own functionality. You should understand the difference between Transactions SMOD and CMOD. Similarly, you should be able to create BAdI enhancements, both the classical BAdIs and new BAdIs.

You should understand the tools and techniques to search various enhancements for SAP applications. You should be able to use the Application Hierarchy with the Repository Information System to search for customer exits, Business Add-Ins, composite enhancements, or enhancement spots for an application object.

Finally, you should be able to explain the difference between enhancement and modification. You should know the tools to list the system modification in your system and be able to use SAP Notes Assistant to apply notes to the SAP system.

Caution

You should try not to modify SAP objects unless it is absolutely required because modification can cause problems during upgrade. You should try to adjust the SAP objects by using one of the enhancement techniques and only modify the system if SAP has not provided you with one of the enhancement options to adjust the standard SAP objects.

Refresher

Table 18.1 shows the key concepts for enhancing SAP applications.

Key Concept	Definition
Enhancement concepts	Enhancement techniques are used to insert additional customer-specific functionality to SAP applications without modifying SAP repository objects.

Table 18.1 Key Concept Refresher

Key Concept	Definition
Enhancement search tool	The Application Hierarchy tool (Transaction SE81) along with the Repository Information System (Transaction SE85) can be used to search for SAP enhancement definitions with the application component.
Enhancement Information System	The Enhancement Information System is a tool to search for enhancement definitions and implementations in the SAP system.
SAP Notes Assistant	SAP Notes Assistant is the tool used to implement SAP notes in the system.
Modification Browser	Modification Browser is used to list the repository object that has been modified with the system. The tool can also be used to reset the modification for the repository objects.
Enhancement techniques	User exits, customer exits, classical Business Add-Ins, and BTEs are some of the enhancement techniques used prior to SAP NetWeaver 7.0 to enhance SAP applications without modifying SAP repository objects.
Enhancement Framework	As of SAP NetWeaver 7.0 new enhancement options such as explicit enhancement points, explicit enhancement sections, implicit enhancement points and options, and new BAdIs are available to enhance SAP applications.

Table 18.1 Key Concept Refresher (cont.)

Summary

You should know the various enhancement techniques and the steps to implement enhancements. You should know the techniques and tools used to search the SAP enhancement definition for a business application. You should also know the difference between enhancement and modification. You should be aware of the tools used to modify repository objects and the procedure to modify repository objects. You should be familiar with the tools used to list the modified object within the system such as the Modification Browser. Finally, you should know about SAP Notes Assistant, its use and benefits, and the ease with which it can be used to implement notes in the system. This knowledge will allow you to easily pass this topic on the certification examination.

19

Table Relationships

Techniques You'll Master:

- Reference data elements
- Explore search help design
- Check table enforcement
- Understand text tables

In this chapter you will be provided with a basic understanding of how tables relate to other objects in the ABAP Dictionary. We will discuss data elements and the capabilities they provide. We will cover the use of foreign keys for check tables and text tables. We will cover value help design and the mechanisms for attaching a search help to different Dictionary objects.

Each of these topics will be covered separately and will be followed by the practice exercise and the solution to the exercise.

Real-World Scenario

Your project has a number of issues with restricting the contents of screen fields to specific values. You need to identify why this is happening and how to correct the issues.

You know that part of the problem is that team members are not sure what data is actually available, but some of the problem is simply that some developers have not implemented value checks.

You will need to identify where help is needed in determining available values and where value checks need to be implemented. In both cases you will need to explain to other developers the options available and assist them in implementing either the value check or the search help.

Objectives of this Portion of the Test

The purpose of this portion of the certification examination is to verify that you have knowledge of the ABAP Dictionary and the relationships between different tables. This portion of the examination will test your knowledge of details related to data elements, including how they can be used and what capabilities exist with data elements. The points that you will need to understand from this section include:

- Enforcement of checks for screen field
- The difference between a value table and a check table
- Different uses of foreign keys
- The usc and design of search helps

The certification examination will give average weight to this chapter compared to the other topics in the examination. This means there will be an average percentage of questions related to this chapter. Understanding table relationships makes you a better developer. Although it is not necessary for all types of development (being strongly related to dynpros), it is nevertheless a necessary part of your understanding in order to become certified.

Key Concepts Refresher

You need to understand and be able to perform the following types of tasks when developing ABAP programs:

- Enforce field value checks during screen processing
- Link tables through foreign keys
- Implement search helps

Table Relationships

The ABAP Dictionary supports program development with a number of services:

- Value helps (F4 help) for screen fields can be defined with search helps or by assigning fixed values to domains.
- Screen fields can have field help (F1 help) assigned by creating documentation for the data element behind the screen field.
- An input check that ensures that the values entered are consistent is defined for screen fields through the use of foreign keys.
- The ABAP Dictionary provides support for you to set and release locks. To do this, you must create lock objects in the ABAP Dictionary. The function modules to set and release locks are automatically generated when the lock object is activated. These function modules can then be used in the application program (see Chapter 8, SQL Statements Including Update Strategies, for details).
- Buffering settings can improve performance when accessing data in database tables and views.
- You can enable the automatic recording of changes to table entries to a change log.

Data elements provide a complete description of a field in the ABAP Dictionary or an elementary data object in your ABAP applications. They provide the link between domains and the data objects and contain semantic and technical information about the data objects. The technical information typically comes from a domain, if one is defined. However, it is possible to define the technical attributes, such as type and length, directly within the data element. Defining the technical attributes within the data element directly, instead of using a domain, prevents the use of fixed values or value tables for the field that can only be defined at the domain level, and therefore it is recommended that a domain be used.

You can (and should) maintain the field labels for data elements you create. These field labels (short, medium, long, and heading) can be displayed later on screens or selection screens to explain or describe the field's purpose. On selection screens, only the long version of the field label can be drawn from the ABAP Dictionary, but when designing your own screens using the Screen Painter, you can choose. If you are creating your own data element, you can (and again should) also add documentation to the data element. This documentation is automatically displayed anytime a user presses the F1 key with the cursor in a field that references the data element. Standard fields also provide the ability to add supplemental documentation if the field is used uniquely for this customer's system.

If the field value is provided in a search help list, the entry from the field label is used for the title. These labels are also used in ALV displays (see Chapter 15, ALV Grid Control) as default headings for columns. You can specify a length for the respective field label, although if it is left empty, the dictionary calculates the length based on either predefined limits (10, 15, and 20) or the actual length if it is greater than the predefined limit. This length determines the maximum length for the field label. If you work for a global company, you can translate the field labels into other languages (GOTO • TRANSLATION or Transaction SE63). When specifying the length, remember that in another language, the same term in the field label might require more letters.

A search help (value or F4 help) can be appended or attached to a data element. In addition, search helps can be attached to other objects such as table fields, structure fields, or check tables (see Figure 19.7 below for details).

In different applications, you sometimes have to enter a particular value in several screens, for example, a company code or customer number. To save the user having to enter the same value over and over again, it is possible to assign a parameter ID to the data element behind those screen fields (see Figure 19.1). If a screen field is based on a data element with a parameter ID, the value the user enters in this field can be transferred to the parameter ID, that is, stored in memory, when the screen is exited. If an input field based on the same data element exists on a subsequent screen, this value can be read from the parameter and displayed in the screen field automatically and can be changed by the user. The SET/GET parameters hold the value per user session.

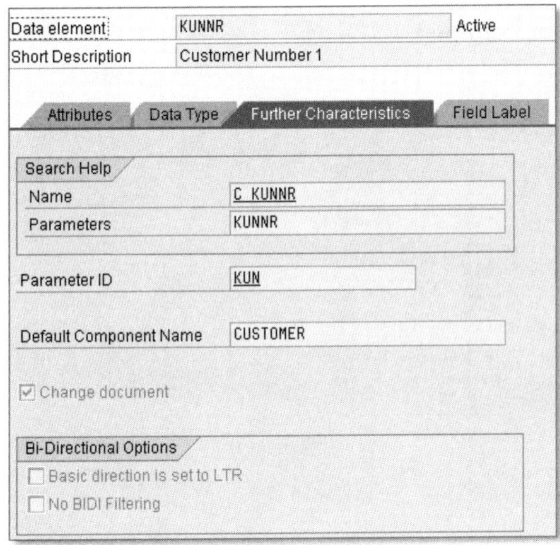

Figure 19.1 Parameter ID

After the user has logged off, these values are not retained. These parameters can also have permanent values assigned through the user profile, so if a user only deals with one company code, he would never need to actually type in the company code (in this case the value is retained between sessions). To use a SET/GET parameter for a field you created, you have to enter this in table TPARA; in other words, you have to create the parameter memory ID.

The technical properties for the data element are maintained on the DATA TYPE tab page. You should use mainly domains for technical typing, in other words, to give the data element its technical characteristics. However, you can also define the data element using the same integrated types that are used to define the domains. As a special case, you can also create a data element as a reference type. The referenced type is not restricted here to the type DATA ELEMENT. It can be any other reference type or even a generic reference to ANY, OBJECT, or DATA.

Note

A reference of the type `ANY` can point to both objects and data. The definition as a reference is the same as the type declaration in an ABAP program `TYPES tr_dt TYPE REF TO data.`

The domain describes the value range of a field by specifying its data type and field length. If only a limited set of values is allowed, these can be defined as fixed values (see Figure 19.2 for an example).

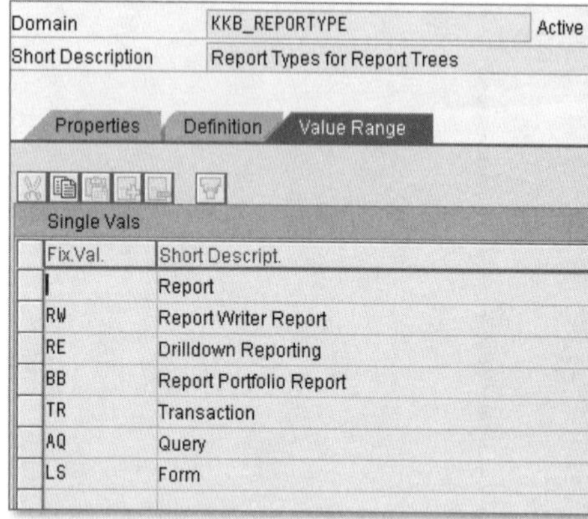

Figure 19.2 Fixed Values

Specifying fixed values causes the value range of the domain to be restricted by these values. Fixed values can be immediately used as check values in screen entries and for value help. Fixed values can either be listed individually or defined as an interval.

The value range of a field can also be defined by specifying a value table (see Figure 19.3) in the domain. Unlike fixed values, however, simply specifying a value table does not cause the input of a screen field with this domain behind it to be checked, and there is no value help.

Note

If you enter a value table for a domain, the system can make a proposal for the foreign key definition for any table fields with this domain behind them.

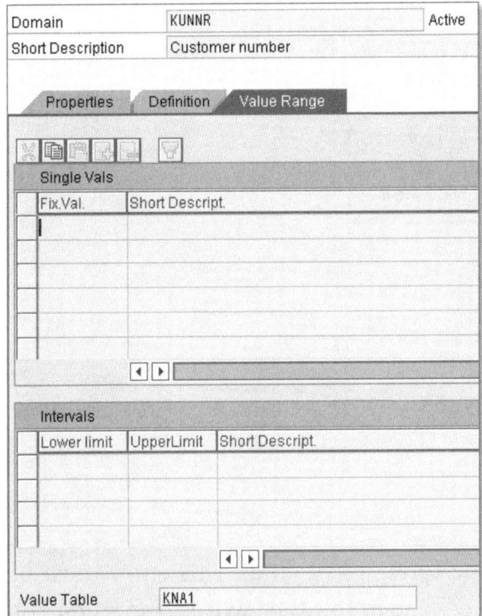

Figure 19.3 Value Table

In the ABAP Dictionary, this type of relationship between two tables is called a *foreign key* relationship, and the tables must be defined explicitly for the field. Foreign keys are used to ensure that the data is consistent. Data that has been entered on a screen is checked against existing data in the check table to ensure that it is consistent. This check does not prevent a program from directly updating the database table with an incorrect value. The check is part of the screen processing, not the database interface.

Note

A value table only becomes a check table when a foreign key is defined. If you have a field based on a domain with a value table, but no foreign key was defined at the field level, there is no check for the screen field.

A combination of fields in a table is called a foreign key if this field combination is the primary key of another table. A foreign key links two tables. The check table is the table whose key fields are checked. This table is also called the referenced table. The example in Figure 19.4 shows the table `VBRK` (in abbreviated form) with a foreign key relationship to `KNA1`.

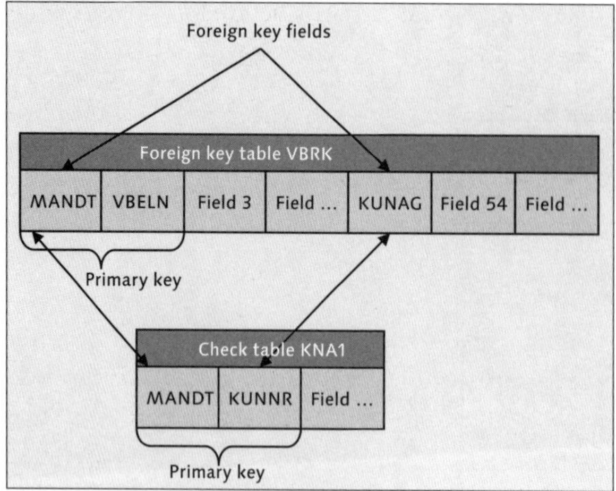

Figure 19.4 Check Table Example

Let's say an entry is to be written in the foreign key table. This entry must be consistent with the key fields of the check table. In other words, the value you want to insert must exist already in the check table. The field of the foreign key table to be checked is called the check field. Continuing our current example, the client and customer numbers are the check fields. Foreign keys can only be used in screens. You are able to either insert or change data records in the database table without this being checked using an ABAP program, in other words, if you do not go through screen validations. There is no way to automatically enforce this check in a program. A program must implement the check table validation within the program itself.

When you are maintaining foreign keys, domain equality is mandatory for check table enforcement. In other words, the same domain is required for the check field and referenced key field of the check table so that you do not compare fields with different data types or field lengths. Different data elements can be used, but they must refer to the same domain. The requirement for domain equality is only necessary for the check field. For all other foreign key fields, it is sufficient if the data type and the field length are equal. As a recommendation, you should always try for domain equality because it always simplifies making domain changes later, for all development not just for check tables. In this case, the foreign key will remain consistent if the field length is changed because the corresponding fields are both changed. If the domains are different, the foreign key would be inconsistent, for example, if the field lengths were changed. This domain equality also means that a check table can only be used for fields that use a domain to obtain their technical attributes.

Note

The system can automatically propose the check table for the check field if the domain has a value table. In this case, a proposal is created for the field assignment in the foreign key.

The *cardinality* describes the foreign key relationship with regard to the number of possible dependent records (records of the foreign key table) and the referenced records (records of the check table). The cardinality is always defined from the point of view of the check table. The cardinality is defined as `n:m`, the left side of the cardinality describes the number of records of the foreign key table, `VBRK` in our example above, and the right side of the cardinality describes the number of records of the check table or `KNA1`.

- There are two values for the left side: either `1` or `C`. The `1` indicates that there must be a match in the check table of one record, whereas the `C` indicates that the match does not need to exist in the check table.
- There are four values for the right side of the cardinality: `1`, `C`, `N`, or `CN`. The `1` indicates that there must be exactly one record in the foreign key table, `C` indicates there can be 0 or 1 records, `N` indicates 1 or more records, and `CN` indicates there can be any number of records.

The actual cardinality for our example is `1:CN`, which indicates that every value in `VBRK` must exist in `KNA1` once, and a value in `KNA1` can exist 0 or more times in `VBRK`.

The types of the foreign key fields describe what the foreign key fields in the foreign key table mean. The following types of foreign key field can be defined:

- **No key fields**
  The foreign key fields are not primary key fields of the foreign key table and they do not uniquely identify a record of the foreign key table. As a result, the foreign key fields do not identify the foreign key table.
- **Key fields**
  The foreign key fields are either primary key fields of the foreign key table or they already uniquely identify a record of the foreign key table. The foreign key fields therefore identify the foreign key table.

- **Key fields of a text table**
  The foreign key table is a text table for the check table. This means the key of the foreign key table differs from the key of the check table only in that it has an additional language key field. This is a special case of the type key fields.

Note

Only one text table can be linked with a table.

If you have two tables — we will use the flight tables SMEALT and SMEAL for our example — SMEALT is a text table of SMEAL if:

- The key of SMEALT comprises the entire key of SMEAL and
- SMEALT has an additional language key field (field of data type LANG)

SMEALT can then contain text in several languages for each key entry of SMEAL.

To link the key entries with the text, the text table (SMEALT) must be linked with SMEAL using a foreign key. An example of this foreign key can be seen in Figure 19.5. Key fields of a text table must be selected here for the type of foreign key fields.

Display Foreign Key SMEALT-MEALNUMBER

Short text: Check for correct meals
Check table: SMEAL

Foreign Key Fields

Check table	ChkTablFld	For.key table	Foreign Key Field	Generic	Constant
SMEAL	MANDANT	SMEALT	MANDANT	☐	
SMEAL	CARRID	SMEALT	CARRID	☐	
SMEAL	MEALNUMBER	SMEALT	MEALNUMBER	☐	

Screen check
☑ Check required Error message MsgNo AArea

Semantic attributes
Foreign key field type: ○ Not Specified ○ Non-key-fields/candidates ○ Key fields/candidates ◉ Key fields of a text table
Cardinality: 1 : CN

Figure 19.5 Linking a Text Table

If table SMEAL is the check table of a field, the existing key entries of table SMEALT will be displayed as possible input values when the value help (F4) is selected. The explanatory text (contents of the first character-like non-key field of text table SMEALT) is also displayed in the user's logon language for each key value in table SMEAL. Only one text table can be created for table SMEAL. The system checks this when you attempt to activate a table with text foreign keys for table SMEAL.

Value Help

Value help (input help or F4 help) is a standard function of an SAP system. It displays for a user the list of possible values for a screen field. The user can select a value from the list, which is then copied directly to the input field.

The value help button is shown to the right of fields that have value help (to see an example of this key, Figure 19.5 above contains one on the check table field). The key appears when the cursor is positioned within the screen field. The help can be started by either choosing this button for the screen element or using the function key F4.

It is often possible to further filter the list of possible entries shown through the use of further restrictions, depending on how the help was defined. The display of the possible entries is enhanced with further useful information about the displayed values such as the description. Given that the description of the value help for a field is usually defined by its use, the value help for a field is typically defined within the ABAP Dictionary. A search help definition contains the information the system needs to satisfy the described requirements.

To define the search help, you need to specify where to get the data (from the selection method), what is passed to and from the search help (the search help interface), and the behavior of the dialog. The search help interface dictates which values already entered by the user are passed to the search help and what values are copied back to screen when a value is selected. The internal behavior of the search help describes the selection method, determining which values are to be displayed and the dialog behavior with the user.

A user can only access a search help through a screen, in other words, for one of the input fields on that screen. Which search help is available is determined by the search help attachment; search helps can be attached to table fields, structure fields, data elements, or check tables. The editor for search helps enables you to test the behavior of a search help without assigning it to a screen field.

A selection from the database at runtime determines the field's possible values for display. When you define a search help, you must define the database object from which the data is selected. You do this by specifying a table or a view as the selection method.

- If the data to be displayed to the user in the search help is contained in just one table or in one table and its corresponding text table, you use the table as a selection method. If the data for the search help is located in multiple tables, it makes sense to use a view as the selection method. The system will automatically ensure that values are restricted to the user's logon client and language.
- If a view does not exist containing the information necessary for the value help, you must first create one in the ABAP Dictionary. It is not possible to use maintenance views as the selection method for search helps. Normally, a database view is used, but within an SAP system these are always created with an inner join. The value help therefore only offers those values with an entry in each of the tables. If you need to have the possible values determined with an outer join, you should choose a help view as the selection method.

The possible values are presented in list format in the dialog box from which the user can select the required entry. If the possible values are formal keys, you should provide further information in the display. For example, instead of a list of customer numbers, the customer name should also be included.

If you expect a very large hit list, you should allow the user to define additional restrictions for the attributes. By allowing these additional restrictions, the set of data displayed is more focused and reduces the system load, in other words, we reduce the amount of data that is fetched from the database by allowing the user to restrict which entries he wants to see in the hit list. Additional conditions can be entered in a dialog box for restricting values. You use the dialog type of a search help to define whether the dialog box for restricting values is displayed before determining the hit list.

- You define which fields are to appear on either (or both) of the dialog boxes as parameters in the search help. All fields of the selection method except the client field and non-key fields of your text table can be used as parameters.

- You define which parameter should appear in which dialog box and the order by assigning the parameters positions in the two dialog boxes. You can use different parameters or different orders in the two dialog boxes. The LPos column in Figure 19.6 identifies the order of the parameter in the hit list, and the SPos column identifies the position of the parameter in the dialog box for limiting the hit list.

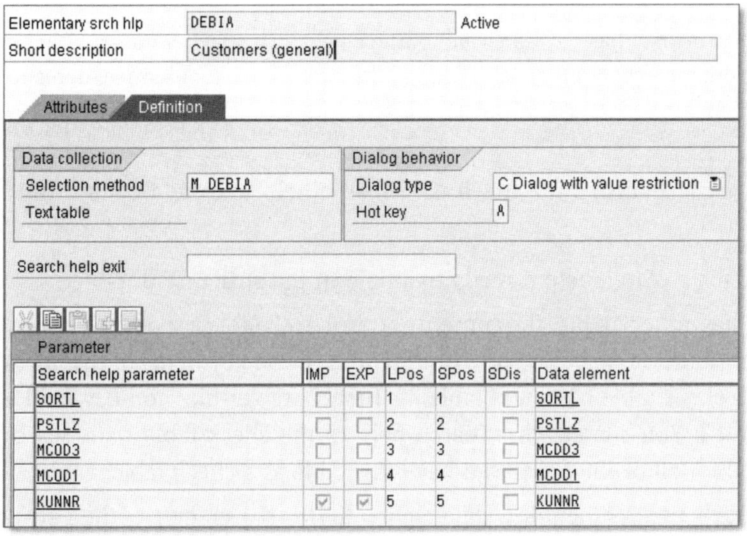

Elementary srch hlp: DEBIA — Active
Short description: Customers (general)

Attributes | Definition

Data collection
Selection method: M_DEBIA
Text table:

Dialog behavior
Dialog type: C Dialog with value restriction
Hot key: A

Search help exit:

Parameter

Search help parameter	IMP	EXP	LPos	SPos	SDis	Data element
SORTL	☐	☐	1	1	☐	SORTL
PSTLZ	☐	☐	2	2	☐	PSTLZ
MCOD3	☐	☐	3	3	☐	MCDD3
MCOD1	☐	☐	4	4	☐	MCDD1
KUNNR	☑	☑	5	5	☐	KUNNR

Figure 19.6 Elementary Search Help

You must use data elements to type the search help parameters. If you don't specify otherwise, the parameter uses the data element of the corresponding field of the selection method, and normally this would be what you would use.

When defining a parameter of a search help, you also specify whether it is to copy data from the screen to the value help (i.e., it acts as an `IMPORT` parameter) or if it returns data from the value help (i.e., it acts as an `EXPORT` parameter). These `IMPORT` and `EXPORT` parameters for a search help define the interface. After you have defined the search help, you need to attach it to the relevant object — either to a data element, a table or structure field, or a check table. The search help attachment defines where the `IMPORT` parameters of the search help get their values and which screen fields to return the contents of the `EXPORT` parameters.

You do not normally define the semantic and technical attributes of a screen field (type, length, F1 help, etc.) directly when you define the screen and create the input field. Instead, you reference an ABAP Dictionary field in the Screen Painter. The screen field then takes on the attributes of this Dictionary field. Likewise, you attach the search help to the ABAP Dictionary search field and not to the screen field. In this way we get consistency: Wherever an input field is based upon a Dictionary field, the same search help will be available for the user.

Note

Fields that do not have a search help attachment can still have a value help because other mechanisms are also used for the value help, for example, domain fixed values.

There are three mechanisms for attaching a search help to a field of the ABAP Dictionary:

- You can attach a search help directly to a field of the structure or table.
- If the field has a check table, the contents of the check table are offered as possible values in the value help. The display contains the key fields of the check table. If the check table has a text table, its first character-like non-key field is also displayed. You can attach a search help to the check table. This search help is used for all of the fields that have this table as a check table.
- You can attach a search help to a data element. This search help is then available for all of the fields that use this data element.

If you attach a search help to a check table or a data element, you will obtain a high degree of reusability.

The SAP system uses a number of mechanisms to provide value help to as many screen fields as possible, not just search helps. If more than one mechanism is available for a field, the system uses the hierarchy shown in Figure 19.7 to determine which to present.

It is also possible to define a value help for the screen field directly in the Screen Painter. This, however, does not provide automatic reuse and therefore is not encouraged. You can also program the value help yourself using the screen event *Process On Value Request* (POV), but this can require a lot of programming effort.

Performance of a search help, as with `SELECT` statements, should always be of concern. As a search help is selecting data from the database, it is sometimes necessary to search large amounts of data. This can result in a long wait time for the user and increase the load on the system. When defining a search help, as you do with a `SELECT`, you should take measures to optimize the selection method. If you expect a large number of entries, you should restrict the hit list with additional conditions. This increases the clarity of the hit list and reduces the load on the system. The additional conditions can be a result of the context or can be entered by the user in a dialog box. Options used for optimizing a database `SELECT` can also be used here. This includes buffering or secondary indexes.

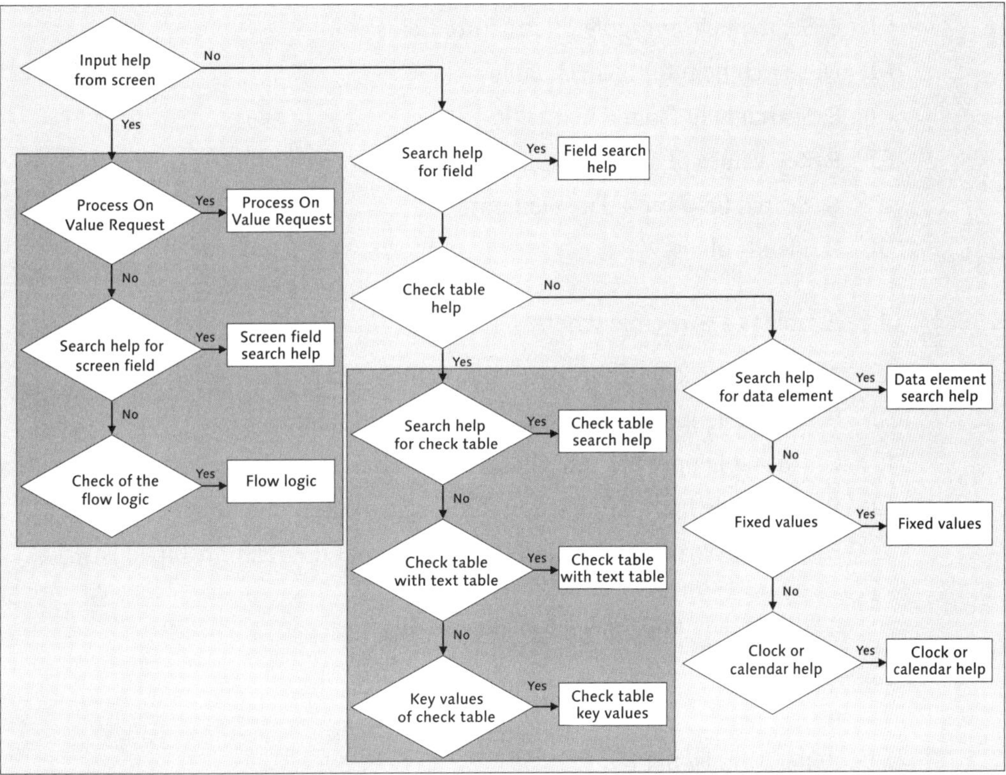

Figure 19.7 Value Help Mechanisms

Practice Questions

The practice questions below will help you evaluate your understanding of the topic. The questions shown are similar in nature to those found on the certification examination, but whereas none of these questions will be found on the exam itself, they allow you to review your knowledge of the subject. Select the correct answers and then check the completeness of your answers in the following solution section. Remember that you must select all correct answers and only correct answers to receive credit for the question.

1. Value help can be supplied from:

☐ **A.** Process On Value request

☐ **B.** Search help for a screen field

☐ **C.** Search help for table or structure fields

☐ **D.** Search help for a check table

☐ **E.** Search help from a text table

☐ **F.** Key values of a check table

☐ **G.** Search help for a data element

☐ **H.** Fixed values

2. A table is a text table when:

☐ **A.** The entire key of this data table is included as the key to this table.

☐ **B.** This table has an additional language key field.

☐ **C.** This table only has one character-based data field.

☐ **D.** This table has a foreign key to the data table as a text table.

☐ **E.** The ABAP runtime system determines that the relationship exists.

3. A foreign key must have domain equality:

☐ **A.** Always

☐ **B.** Not true

☐ **C.** For a check field

☐ **D.** For a text table

4. Where are fixed values for fields stored?

☐ **A.** Table

☐ **B.** Structure

☐ **C.** Field

☐ **D.** Data element

☐ **E.** Domain

5. Only one text table can be linked to a table.

☐ **A.** True

☐ **B.** False

6. What is the difference between a value table and a check table?

☐ **A.** No difference; they are the same thing.

☐ **B.** A value table is a check table after a foreign key is defined.

☐ **C.** A value table is defined in the domain, whereas a check table is defined in the data element.

☐ **D.** A check table is defined in the domain, whereas a value table is defined in the data element.

☐ **E.** A value table does not exist.

7. The order of fields for a transparent table in the database:

☐ **A.** Need to match the ABAP Dictionary

☐ **B.** Are created in the order of the ABAP Dictionary

☐ **C.** Are allowed to be different than the ABAP Dictionary

8. A search help must:

☐ **A.** Use a table or a view for data selection

☐ **B.** Determine the values for selection by the user

☐ **C.** Have a dialog with the user

☐ **D.** Allow the user to select a response

☐ **E.** Be used from a screen

9. Where should the labels for fields be stored?

☐ **A.** Table

☐ **B.** Structure

☐ **C.** Field

☐ **D.** Data element

☐ **E.** Domain

10. Which type of view cannot be used in a search help?

☐ **A.** Database view

☐ **B.** Maintenance view

☐ **C.** Help view

11. Which type of view uses an inner join in a search help?

☐ **A.** Database view

☐ **B.** Maintenance view

☐ **C.** Help view

Practice Question Answers and Explanations

1. Correct answers: **All options**

   All of the answers are correct. Value help can be obtained from any of these sources (and a couple more; see Figure 19.7 for the complete list).

2. Correct answers: **A, B, D**

   It is necessary for the entire key of the data table plus the language key for the table to be considered a text table. However, it is also necessary for the foreign key link to be specified; otherwise, they are just two similar tables. It is not necessary for there only to be one character-based field; there must be at least one. As mentioned above, only the first one (after the key) is used for the text,

3. Correct answer: **C**

   Domain equality can exist for other foreign keys, but it is only necessary for a check table. In other cases, a like type and length is sufficient.

4. Correct answer: **E**

   Fixed values are identified at the domain level in the ABAP Dictionary. You can specify individual values or intervals.

5. Correct answer: **A**

   You can only associate one text table to a data table. The system checks this when you attempt to activate a table with text foreign keys for a data table.

6. Correct answer: **B**

   Without the foreign key association, a value table, whereas it can provide help assistance, will not perform the check validation during screen processing.

7. Correct answer: **C**

   Since Release 3.0, SAP has allowed the fields to be a different order in the ABAP Dictionary and the database table.

8. Correct answers: **B, C, D, E**

   It is not necessary to use a table or a view (you can, but it is not the only way of selecting data).

9. Correct answer: **D**

   Labels and documentation are stored at the data element level.

10. Correct answer: **B**

    The maintenance view is not designed for data selection, but rather for maintenance of business oriented views of data.

11. Correct answer: **A**

    A database view uses an inner join for data selection. If you need an outer join, you should use a Help view.

Take Away

You will need to understand the relationship between database tables and both text tables and check table. You will need to understand the foreign key relationship between the tables. You also need to be able to distinguish between different mechanisms for value help and how they can be used on screens. As part of this, you will need to understand the types of checks that a field may have enforced from the ABAP Dictionary.

Refresher

You will need to understand how data checks can be enforced during screen processing and how value help can be provided. You will need to know the relationship between different areas of the ABAP Dictionary (domains and data elements) and relationships between tables with the use of foreign keys. You will need to understand how to specify a check table and a text table with foreign keys. You will need to know how to enforce checks for screen fields, the different uses of foreign keys, and the use and design of search helps.

Table 19.1 lists the key concepts for table relationships.

Key Concept	Definition
Validation checks	Either the use of a check table or fixed values to provide validation during screen processing.
Foreign keys	The use of foreign keys to link two tables together and provide additional information or validation.
Search helps	A means of providing value help to the user on a screen.

Table 19.1 Key Concepts Refresher

Tips

A number of the questions in this area will not be part of the normal class materials. These questions will require you to understand the underlying process to produce the correct answer. As with the majority of the subjects found in the certification examination, it is important to have as much practical experience with the subject as possible. Although the majority of the concepts presented in this chapter should be second nature, it is important that you understand the nuances of foreign keys and search helps.

Summary

You should now be able to create foreign keys to provide check tables or text tables. You should also be able to identify the different parts of a search help and understand where the search help can be used as well as how to design one. These skills will enable you to successfully pass this portion of the certification exam.

The Authors

Puneet Asthana is a recognized expert in ABAP development and has 14 years of development experience, and has been working for SAP for over seven years. Apart from ABAP development, he is also an expert in IDoc, ALE, EDI, workflow, and process integration. He has worked on a number of projects as a technical lead and is currently working as a technical architect for a global SAP Retail implementation for a major retailer. He has extensive experience in integrating SAP and non-SAP systems and leveraging SAP Integration Technologies including SAP NetWeaver PI to deliver innovative technical solutions.

Puneet has participated in solution reviews, customer project issue escalations, and presales activity and conducted workshops to help his colleagues. He also has good functional knowledge and has been involved in a broad range of SAP solution implementation including SAP SRM, IS-Mills, IS-Retail, SAP AFS, SAP NetWeaver Portal, and SAP NetWeaver PI.

David Haslam is a recognized expert in ABAP development, having worked for SAP for over 14 years. David has led or participated in over seven full lifecycle implementations of SAP, which include several multiple-phase projects and four large development projects. He was awarded the prestigious status of SAP Platinum Consultant more than eight years ago, and he enjoys helping others through workshops and white papers and sharing his knowledge and experience. In addition, David participates in development reviews, project estimates, and customer project issue escalations.

He has shared his experience and knowledge, providing guidance with the following SAP certification examinations: SAP Certified Development Associate – ABAP with SAP NetWeaver 7.0, SAP Certified Development Professional – ABAP System Integration – SAP NetWeaver 7.0, and SAP Certified Development Professional – ABAP User Interfaces – SAP NetWeaver 7.0.

Index

A

B

C

D

F

G

H

I

T

U

V

W

X